IGP

Blossom
of
Bone

Blossom

of

Bone

Reclaiming the Connections
Between Homoeroticism
and the Sacred

&

Randy P. Conner

HarperSanFrancisco
A Division of HarperCollinsPublishers

HarperSanFrancisco and the author, in association
with the the Rainforest Action Network, will facilitate
the planting of two trees for every one tree used
in the manufacture of this book.

Illustration and text credits begin on page 350 and are
considered a continuation of this copyright page.

BLOSSOM OF BONE:
*Reclaiming the Connections Between
Homoeroticism and the Sacred.*

Text design by George Brown

FIRST EDITION

Library of Congress Cataloging-in-Publication Data
Conner, Randy P.
Blossom of bone : reclaiming the connection between
homoeroticism and the sacred / Randy P. Conner. — 1st ed.
p.   cm.
Includes bibliographical references and index.
ISBN 0-06-250903-9 (cloth). — ISBN 0-06-250257-3 (pbk.)
   1. Homosexuality—Religious aspects.
   2. Androgyny (Psychology)—Religious aspects.
     3. Gay men—Religious life.   I. Title.
BL65.H64C66   1993   291.4'08'664—dc20   92-56126
                                          CIP

93 94 95 96 97 98 ❖ RRD(H) 10 9 8 7 6 5 4 3 2 1

*To David, Mariya, Gloria, Mother, and Dave,
and to the children of the rainbow*

The Mystical in Art, the Mystical in Life,
the Mystical in Nature—this is what I am looking for.
It is absolutely necessary for me to find it somewhere.

OSCAR WILDE, *De Profundis*

I live no longer in the usual world. I have forsaken the
familiar. And soon, by an extreme gesture, I shall cease
altogether to be human and become legend like Jesus,
Buddha, Cybele.

GORE VIDAL, *Myra Breckenridge*

Contents

List of Illustrations

Acknowledgments

This book could not have been written without the constant support of my companion, David Hatfield Sparks, his daughter Mariya, my mother and stepfather, and my feline master, Puck Shadowson. ¶ I would also like to acknowledge a number of individuals and groups who have aided in the creation of *Blossom of Bone:* for assistance in translation, Norma Aguirré, Christopher Ballantyne, James Chisholm, Thorfinn Einarsson, Michael Garcia, Saleta M. Gómez, Juan Isart, Nora Kelley, Ingrid Lansford, Peter Limnios, Mark Longley, Jeffrey McKillop, Ana Sisnett, and Charles Whitenberg; for technical assistance, Jo Bunny, Tom Gaines, Nikki O., Sherri Miles, and the staffs of the Humanities Research Centers and the Classics and Latin American Libraries of the Univeristy of Texas; for support and inspiration, Gloria Anzaldúa, A. Z., Richard

Bodien, Scott Casey, Ariban Chagoya, Miriam and Oswan Chamani of the Voodoo Spiritual Temple in New Orleans, Tamara Diaghilev, Wayne Dynes, Arthur Evans, Peter Fry, Judith Gleason, Guillermo González, Stephan Grundy, Harry Hay, Paolo Herzig, Candida Jacquez, William Karpen, Richard Labonte, Lily Litvak, Tom Manes, the Reverend Leo Louis Martello, Eduardo Mejía, Charles Nafus, Serena Nanda, Adrian Ravarou, Regla of Havana, Assotto Saint, Roy Teele, Luisah Teish, Michael Thorn, João Trevison, Chris Turner, the Faerie circles of Austin, Los Angeles, and San Francisco; for their invaluable help in the shaping of this manuscript, the staff at Harper San Francisco, especially Kandace Hawkinson, Steve Anderson, Andrea Lewis, Matthew Lore, Jeff Campbell, and Priscilla Stuckey; and finally, I would thank the gods, spirits, and ancestors, without whose aid this book could not have been written.

Blossom
of
Bone

Radical Faerie Gathering, near Los Angeles, 1985.

We Are an Old People, We Are a New People

It is late autumn, and the wind is howling. The moon is full, and the valley is lit with its light and that of many torches. A man wearing ankle bracelets, blossoms woven in his flowing hair, dances furiously with his comrades in a stone-bound circle. In the center of the circle is an altar to the ancient ones. The dancer seems possessed as he tramples dry leaves. His eyes are ponds in which the moon is drawn down, his howl the howling of the wind, of the wolves.

Many gay men (as well as some bisexual and gender-variant males and transsexuals) living at the end of the twentieth century have begun to reclaim the ancient association of homoeroticism, gender variance, and sacred experience or role. ❡ This task of reclamation is not an easy one. Indeed, due to the homophobic and anti–gender-variant communities in which many of us live, the journey toward self-realization can be an extremely arduous one. ❡ This process often begins with coming out as a gay or bisexual man, an experience that stresses not only self-acknowledgment but also public announcement of our same-sex desire. Coming out often includes acknowledging and coming to terms with behavior regarded by our communities as unmasculine or "sissyish." ❡ In recent years, the gay rights

1

movement has facilitated the coming-out process. Yet many of us continue to experience coming out as a harrowing journey bringing us face to face with a "shadow" or "other" that we have kept locked inside but that we, like Peter Pan, know must be retrieved if we are to survive.

Coming out may also be experienced as the shattering of a world we have known. We may face loss of a job or career, rejection by a religious, political, or social organization, or betrayal by those we have loved.

Unfortunately, the process of coming out is rarely experienced fully. This may be due in part to the fact that the coming-out process has not been ritualized, either by the communities in which we are reared or by the gay community. As with menstruation or nocturnal emission ("wet dreams"), the ecstasy associated with coming out has generally been covered by antierotic, shame-inducing puritanism. For this and other reasons, coming out is often experienced less powerfully than it might otherwise be.

Nevertheless, if we survive the journey—and many have not—we may find the shadow, or other, dwelling within us to be a strong and beautiful self yearning, like a child, to be acknowledged, respected, and loved.

Gradually, we begin to realize that to come out is not to become something or someone that we were not, but *to become what we already are, what we always have been.* Coming out is the armor falling, the butterfly emerging from the cocoon, the bud becoming the full-blown rose.

In this way, the process of coming out may be likened to the Native Alaskan creative process. "Eskimo carvers," writer on tribal religions Sam Gill explains, take "a piece of ivory in their hands, they contemplate it, and speak to it, in order to perceive the form that it contains. They do not approach the material as raw or neutral. . . . Rather, through their craftsmanship, they permit the material to reveal its underlying or inner form."[1] In this way, the act of coming out may be viewed as an act of creation by way of deciphering or excavating and then manifesting and personalizing an already embodied, perhaps archetypal, form.

We may also experience a transformation in relation to others. Once exiled, we now search for kindred spirits, for a community in which we may express ourselves more freely, in which our love for others of the same sex will be acknowledged and celebrated rather than shunned, in which we will be accepted as whole and "natural" human beings.

For many of us, coming to terms with our affection for and attraction to other men and engaging in gender variant behavior constitutes the beginning, and not the end, of the coming-out process. A second or later phase commences when we come out politically, as persons seeking human rights. In recent years, many of us have been profoundly influenced by the gay rights, feminist, and civil rights movements. Their influence has brought us to feel that if we are to come out fully, we must reject patriarchal ideology, the adherents of which have tried to rule our lives or else annihilate us.

In "Exorcism of the Straight/Man/Demon" (1971), the poet Aaron Shurin speaks of this need to reject a system that condemns same-sex desire and gender-variant behavior, an ideology that we have unconsciously or unwillingly internalized:

Man   Man   I call your name
in throwing you out.

. . . . . .

and reclaim my formlessness.
And re-interpret my desires.
And receive the world as made for me.[2]

Recent years have also witnessed the braiding together of the struggles for gay and civil rights by homoerotically inclined and gender-variant men of color. Describing two small flags that he has pinned to his knapsack, the Haitian American gay poet Assotto Saint writes in "Heart and Soul":

these flags are not chips on my shoulders
i carry them as beauty spots
markings of double brotherhood
they shine like mirror beads
to reflect prejudice

. . . .

one unfurls the future of queers
the other salutes african ancestors . . .

. . . .

   these flags are not crossbones on my life
       i carry them as amulets
   emblems of double brotherhood . . . [3]

For many of us, personal and political coming out have been followed by a spiritual reckoning. This encounter with the sacred has often been expressed as a desire to secure a place for ourselves within the spiritual traditions of the communities in which we have been reared, as, for example, within Judaism or Christianity. In the past two decades we have witnessed the emergence of gay-sensitive synagogues and churches, as well as the acceptance by certain congregations of same-sex unions and homoerotically inclined spiritual leaders.

Others among us have, however, come to believe that we will not find spiritual sustenance in Judaism, Christianity, or any other tradition that does not fully honor our way of life.

We have come to believe that if we are to survive our journey toward self-realization, we must either reject sacred experience altogether or we must discover, reclaim, or construct spiritual traditions in which persons engaging in homoerotic and gender-variant behavior play vital roles. This does not mean that we wish to displace other spiritual leaders, be they male or female, celibate or heterosexual, only that we wish to serve alongside them.

Blossom of Bone has emerged from the search for spiritual traditions that have historically embraced gender variance and same-sex desire, as well as from a growing movement known as Gay Spirituality, which seeks to construct a gay-sensitive spiritual path (or paths) by blending ancient beliefs, practices, and symbols with ones of our own creation. Gay Spiritual practices include but are not limited to mystical, transcendent, or transpersonal experience; reverence of divine beings or forces; healing, divinatory, and magical practices; and the creation of art (viewed in this context as a sublimated expression of the sacred).

In my own life, I first became aware of the interrelationship of homoeroticism, gender variance, and the sacred when, in 1971, I made a short film based on Walt Whitman's *Song of Myself* for a high school class in humanities. In the film I explored the poet's love for men as well as his imagined ability to transform himself not only into a woman but also into an animal, the cosmos, a blade of grass. This sensibility was strengthened through my experiences in the Yellow Rose Tribe, an Austin, Texas–based group comprised mainly of gay men, which met in the early to mid-seventies to celebrate the equinoxes, solstices, and the birthdays of gay luminaries including Whitman, Jack Spicer, and Jean Cocteau. It was in 1972 that I first learned from one of the members of the Tribe, Calvin Doucet, of the Native American *berdaches,* indigenous gender-variant males who served as sages, healers, and ritual artisans. Doucet led me to the works of Edward Carpenter, a nineteenth-century writer who spoke of the *berdaches* and related figures.

Several years later, I discovered works by Sybil Leek, the Reverend Leo Louis Martello, Arthur Evans, and others discussing the possible linkage of homosexuality and Witchcraft. I also began reading the journals *Gay Sunshine* and *RFD,* which frequently published articles relating to the growing Gay Spiritual movement. In 1977, in San Francisco, I met Arthur Evans, who told me of the fairy circle he had established. This was a group of gay men devoted to the study of the interrelationship described above. Unfortunately, by the time I met Evans, the group had largely disbanded. Shortly thereafter, however, I began to attend the circles and gatherings of another group of gay men involved in spiritual practice, many of them inspired by the writings of gay activist and sage Harry Hay. Like the members of Evans's circle, and also like a Bay Area neopagan group that included gay and bisexual members, these men referred to themselves as Faeries—now spelled with an "ae" and preceded by "Radical" to suggest a radical political stance.

In 1979, I met my present companion, David Hatfield Sparks, a gay father and musician deeply concerned with healing, divinatory, and magical practices. Together we began to investigate various manifestations of the emerging path(s) of Gay Spirituality per se, as well as other traditions that recognize the spiritual reasons-for-being of homoeroticism and gender variance. In the following year, I began publishing a series of articles on Gay Spirituality in the *San Francisco Sentinel;* these articles eventually led to the writing of *Blossom of Bone.* In 1981, I was fortunate to be able to participate in Jungian scholar Mitch Walker's "Gay Voices and Visions." This challenging workshop, focusing on the application of ancient beliefs and practices, served to deepen my commitment to the Gay Spiritual movement.

My experiences have led me to the realization that Gay Spirituality is rather like the Latin American magical realist writer Jorge Luis Borges's "garden of forking paths"; it is a multicultural, transhistorical path embracing a great number of beginnings, crossroads, and destinations, rather than a single road. In this sense, "Gay Spirituality" may ultimately prove to be a limiting and perhaps even inappropriate term, as it suggests a singular path and places emphasis on homosexuality at the expense of gender variance. Nevertheless, from time to time I have used this term, as it is the prevailing term being used in the early 1990s to describe the subject with which I am here concerned.

Angakok. Assinnu. Basir. Enaree. Fanatici. Gallus. Kelabim. Mahu. Manang bali. Megabyzos. Mexoga. Mwammi. Omasenge kimbanda. Qedeshim. Winkte. 'Yan Daudu.

Such are the names of men who, separated by vast stretches of time and space, have generally shared these vital traits: *they have behaved in ways regarded as gender variant (often termed "androgynous," "effeminate," or "transsexual" behavior) by their respective cultures; they have engaged in same-sex eroticism or have otherwise expressed homoerotic desire; and they have fulfilled a sacred role or carried out a spiritual task.*

Taken together, these three traits may be characterized as a "domain" or "web of associations."[4] In this book I focus on this domain or web of three traits and on various groups and individuals throughout human history who have embodied or expressed it. It is important to understand from the outset that a domain or web may express itself in more fluid, diverse, or fragmentary ways than one might think; thus, in terms of our domain or web, two of the traits might be expressed in an obvious manner, while the third might appear in a sublimated or somewhat imprecise form. Focusing on the definition of a domain, anthropologist Sandra T. Barnes explains, "no one feature gives definition to a domain. . . . [A domain is identified] through combinations of features. . . . No one thing need be present. . . . Rather, a sufficient number of features should be present to allow an identification to be made. . . . A useful way of dealing . . . [with this type of] classification is to think . . . of a chain of 'family resemblances.'"[5]

Thus, while in the case of a few of the men considered here, we are not absolutely certain whether or not they have engaged in sexual acts with other men, we may even so consider them, based on the presence of other traits (such as gender-variant behavior) and sub-traits (such as transvestism and the use of nonmasculine speech and gestures), as bearing a "family resemblance" to the primary figures of our domain and thereby participating to some degree in its embodiment.

Anthropologist Will Roscoe uses the example of cross-dressing to explain that the individual engaging in this practice need not necessarily engage in same-sex intercourse in order to be seen as bearing a strong resemblance to those who participate in what is an essentially "gay practice," or pattern of behavior, having a "strong empirical and historical association with homosexuality."[6]

Among those embodying this domain are the *berdaches* of Native America, to whom the domain's other members may also be compared. In *The Spirit and the Flesh*, anthropologist Walter Williams defines the *berdache* as

a morphological male who does not fill a society's standard man's role. . . . This type of person is often stereotyped as effeminate, but a more accurate characterization is androgyny. . . . Berdaches have special ceremonial roles. . . . They will do at least some women's work, and mix together much of the behavior, dress, and social roles of women and men. . . . Berdaches gain social prestige by their spiritual, intellectual, or craftwork/artistic contributions. . . . In their erotic behavior berdaches . . . [often become] the passive partner in anal sex with men.[7]

Williams stresses that these men do not reflect an "institutionalized homosexuality" or an "institutionalized transsexuality" as much as they do a "connection between homosexual behavior, gender variance, and spiritual power."[8]

These men, of course, being flesh and blood, have brought their individuality to bear upon the shape of the domain. They have shaped it through such factors as age, ethnicity, economic class, and the cultures and historical epochs to which they have belonged. For this reason, I examine the domain and its members in specific cultural and historical contexts, using culture-specific terms whenever possible. I have sought to bring forward the multicultural manifestations of our domain in part because I feel that works on pre–twentieth century homoeroticism focus too much on Greek pederasty—often going so far as to make no distinction between pederasty and homosexuality—at the expense of non-Greek and non-Western expressions of homoeroticism and gender variance.

In spite of many individual and cultural differences, the men we will encounter here share many features that seem to be both multicultural and multihistorical. These traits include transvestitism or the blending of feminine, masculine, and sacred garments; engaging in tasks traditionally assigned to women; special linguistic traits and gestures; creating or producing art (literature, music, dance, drama, and so forth); the practices of healing, divination, and magic; using various shamanic "techniques of ecstasy"—to borrow a term from historian of religion Mircea Eliade—including possession dance and mind-altering substances (or "entheogens" or "magical plants," as the ethnopharmacological writer Terence McKenna refers to hallucinogenic substances), in order to reach an altered state of consciousness in which the deity manifests; living an ascetic, itinerant, and/or mendicant lifestyle; participating in activities considered politically radical; forming special relationships with women, especially hierodules (sacred prostitutes), gender-variant, and lesbian women; and associating with various marginal, oppressed, or so-called deviant groups. Finally, these men have often reflected for others (who have accepted traditional sex and gender roles) the realm of the unknown, of mystery and chaos.

In this book, I also focus on the deities worshipped by these persons and groups and on the spiritual traditions to which they have belonged. The deities revered by these men, while representing a host of archetypes, most frequently have been Great or Mother Goddesses, amazonian female deities, the male consorts of goddesses, and deities of both sexes associated with metamorphosis, gender variance, and/or same-sex eroticism. Not surprisingly, the members of this domain have fared better in pantheistic systems than in monotheistic ones, as in the former they might well embody a god or goddess of beauty, spring, death, letters, homoeroticism, or gender variance rather than being limited to reflecting a father or his son.

This inquiry also reveals the ways in which hostile religious and political forces have conspired to destroy the domain and its members, as well as the ways in which certain men, in spite of oppression, have continued to enact or embody the domain, albeit in sublimated, fragmented, or metamorphosed forms.

In the earliest spiritual traditions known to humankind, gender-variant, homoerotically or bisexually inclined persons served as shamans and priests of goddesses, gods, spirits, and ancestors. With the so-called triumph of patriarchal, monotheistic religions, these men were slaughtered or driven underground along with female shamans and priestesses. In monotheistic cultures, they resurfaced in various guises—as fools, troubadours, and even as monotheistic or "bi-religious" mystics; some, however, remained staunchly nonmonotheistic, revering the older gods and practicing the arts of magic, divination, and healing.

In the West, from the Renaissance onward, and especially in the nineteenth and twentieth centuries, the sacred role of these men surfaced most often in sublimated form, as artistic impulse. This has been due in part to the increasing desacralization of Western culture, in part to the generally accepted transcendent function of art, and in part to the fact that men engaging in same-sex eroticism and gender-variant behavior were officially barred from the priesthood and were thus forced or at least encouraged to express their transpersonal feelings indirectly.

While the men we will learn to know here have often experienced cultural marginalization, frequently as exile or banishment, they have played not a marginal but rather an integral role in many shamanistic, pantheistic, and matrifocal spiritual traditions. Their experience of cultural marginalization, moreover, has encouraged them to form bonds with men and women of various ages, ethnicities, economic backgrounds, and professions. These alliances have resulted in the creation of resilient subcultures incorporating gender variance, same-sex eroticism, and often alternative forms of spiritual practice disapproved of by the dominant culture.

To a large extent, the collective history of men in whose lives sacred role, gender variance, and homoeroticism have interacted remains a "lost" history. A number of forces have conspired to bury these men and their experience of the sacred. These have included overtly hostile forces such as patriarchal religious and political ideologies as well as contemporary cultural theories like social constructionism, whose adherents tend to ignore or denigrate any writings concerned with the archetypal and transpersonal or spiritual dimensions of life.

Constructionists, for instance, maintain that terms or concepts such as *gay, gayness, woman, femininity,* and *Jewishness* are imaginary social constructs, *nothing more.* They question any belief in an entity or energy imagined to be, in the words of feminist theorist Diana Fuss, "transhistorical, eternal, [or] immutable."[9] They deny the possibility of a relatively stable, transhistorical, cross-cultural identity such as that of a gender-variant, homoerotically inclined spiritual functionary. They hold that while actions (such as same-sex intercourse or cross-dressing) may be performed, actors (such as gay people) having identities (gayness) do not as such exist. Some, however, are willing to concede the existence of subjects who *freely choose* subjectivities, such as *gay, feminist, African-American,* and *Chicana.* These subjectivities may apparently be discarded as easily as old shoes.

While constructionists are celebrating the "death of the subject" (not to mention the "death" of the God/dess), they are nevertheless indebted to the compartmentalization that grew out of Newtonian physics and Cartesian philosophy. They use it to argue that comparisons between twentieth-century "homosexuals" or "gay people" and the *cinaedi*, "sodomites," *berdaches*, and so forth, of other periods and cultures are "preposterous."[10]

This argument is buttressed by an extremely narrow definition of the term *gay*. Constructionists insist that *gay* basically refers to an individual (often male, traditionally masculine, and middle-class) who, living in the West in the late twentieth century, self-consciously *chooses* to identify himself as someone who engages in homosexual behavior and who participates in a related urban, subcultural lifestyle. In defining *gay* in this manner, constructionists are able to assert comfortably that gay people, or homosexuals, did not exist prior to the coinage of the word *homosexual* in the late nineteenth century or *gay* in the twentieth.

In order to stress cultural and historical differences among gender-variant and homoerotically inclined persons, constructionists must deny both cultural and historical interaction in the premodern world. They must pretend that gender-variant and homoerotically inclined persons of different cultures did not encounter each other in antiquity or in the premodern era. They must also pretend that such persons could not have not passed on knowledge from one generation to another; that is to say, an eighteenth-century "sodomite" could not have influenced a nineteenth-century "invert" or "homosexual," who, in turn, could not have influenced a twentieth-century "gay" man in any substantial way. In this text, we will encounter sub-Saharan African, gender-variant devotees of Isis who must have come into contact with Euro-Roman gender-variant worshipers of the same goddess. We will also encounter post-Renaissance associations linking Native American gender-variant shamans to the priests of the goddesses of antiquity. In my view, by ignoring such cross-cultural and cross-historical associations, constructionists do a disservice to the field of gay studies, for they short-circuit research concerning the influence of one group of gender-variant and/or homoerotically inclined persons upon another.

Of this opposition to comparative work among constructionists, anthropologist Walter Williams writes in *The Spirit and the Flesh:*

> Human behavior observed around the world does not exhibit limitless variety; there are patterns and similarities that repeat themselves beyond anything that can be explained by diffusion from one society to another . . .
>
> Because of the complexity of cross-cultural comparisons, the certitude of social constructionists in proclaiming that no other people before the "modern homosexual" had a similar identity seems foolhardy. Such a view ignores folk traditions about certain types of persons, called "fairies," "queers," and a myriad other terms, in Europe and elsewhere. And in emphasizing the discontinuities of a modern homosexual identity, social constructionists discount the implications from cross-cultural research. Their

view is quite ethnocentric, and in its focus on the modern West blithely dismisses anything we might learn from cross-cultural research.[11]

In his essay "The Thing of It Is," philosopher Richard D. Mohr suggests that if these theorists were to define *gay* differently, perhaps a bit more broadly, they might be better able to cite links between *gay* people of the twentieth century and homoerotically inclined persons of other times and places.

Mohr further challenges the basic belief of constructionists that concepts are dependent upon language, or, said another way, that terms precede ideas. In other words, these theorists maintain that a "hippie" could not have existed prior to the 1960s because this particular word had not been coined before that time. Of "hippies," Mohr argues, "If one tethers its [i.e., "hippie's"] definition to beat-up Volkswagens, one, by necessity, is not going to find hippies in the Roman Empire. . . . [But] if one . . . defined 'hippie' in culturally neutral terms such that hippies are communally living, socially detached spiritualists, then it is at least arguable that we should consider the early Christians as hippies."[12] Mohr further voices this concern: "It is my hope that, just because culture, gay and otherwise, currently has no term for the relation that my lover and I have, some future, benighted constructionist won't look back from a time in the next century when the term finally has been coined and claim that the relation, for want of a word, did not exist, ye verily, could not have existed, as indeed it has existed."[13]

Perhaps most significantly in terms of the relationship of homoerotically inclined and/or gender-variant men to sacred experience or role, constructionists, while priding themselves on stressing differences between groups and epochs, have often arrogantly assumed that a majority of the world's peoples, like themselves, have accepted the constructionist concept of identity or subjectivity. We will see in this text, to the contrary, that *a number of the world's peoples have believed homoerotic inclination and gender variance to have been traits bestowed prior to birth by a divine power or powers, a deity, or the stars.* While this view was not universally shared, it most certainly rivaled the view that homosexuality was freely chosen, a view that constructionists have emphasized in their revisionist accounts of Greco-Roman pederasty. In my estimation, it would behoove the constructionist or postmodernist to acknowledge that *many peoples have believed gender variance and homoerotic inclination to be essential qualities and not culturally-constructed behaviors*—whether we like it or not.

In spite of various forces of obscuration, however, awareness of the linking between male gender variance, homoeroticism, and sacred role or function has repeatedly surfaced across cultures and epochs. Those embodying the domain, while dwelling in the shadows, the wings, or the spaces between texts, have not been entirely erased.

While the interrelationship of gender variance, homoeroticism, and the sacred was first articulated in antiquity, frequently in texts relating to the art of divination, it resurfaced dramatically in the sixteenth through early nineteenth centuries with the exploration and colonization by Europeans of the Americas and elsewhere. One of its early eighteenth-century promulgators was the Jesuit missionary Joseph François Lafitau, who wrote of Native American and Mesoamerican *berdaches* as "adopt[ing] the garb of women," performing "all of women's occupations," "never marry[ing]," and participating "in all religious ceremonies." He compared such men to the priests of the goddesses of Western antiquity, writing, "Would these not be the same peoples as the Asiatic adorers of Cybele, or the Orientals of whom Julius Firmicus speaks, who consecrated priests dressed as women to the Goddess of Phrygia or to Venus Urania, who had an effeminate appearance, painted their faces, and hid their true sex under garments borrowed from the [other] sex?"[14]

The domain was again taken up in the late nineteenth and early twentieth centuries by the early homosexual rights activist, mystic, and utopian socialist Edward Carpenter, the German sexologist Karl Heinrich Ulrichs, and others, who described its members as belonging to an alternate gender category or "third sex," the spiritual offspring of Aphrodite Urania (hence the appellation Urnings). Carpenter wrote in *Intermediate Types Among Primitive Folk:* "A curious and interesting subject is the connection of the Uranian temperament with prophetic gifts and divination. . . . The fact is well known . . . that in the temples and cults of antiquity and of primitive races it has been a widespread practice to educate and cultivate certain youths in an effeminate manner, and that these youths in general become the priests or medicine-men of the tribe. . . . [There appears to be] a relation in general between homosexuality and psychic powers."[15]

Unfortunately, because Carpenter and other early homosexual rights theorists suggested that such traits as gender variance and same-sex eroticism might be of biological or sociobiological origin, a reaction against their theories ensued.

Archetypal psychologist Carl Jung also linked homoeroticism to gender-variant behavior and sacred experience: "Often he [i.e., the male displaying these traits] is endowed with a wealth of religious feelings, which help him bring the *ecclesia spiritualis* into reality, and a spiritual receptivity which makes him responsive to revelation."[16]

In recent years, a sophisticated version of this domain has been articulated by Will Roscoe, mentioned above. Referring to his model as one of "sociosexual specialization," Roscoe insists that gay scholars, or queer theorists, must look beyond confining Western definitions of *homosexual* and *gay* in order to formulate broader definitions of these terms. In his illuminating essay "Dreaming the Myth: An Introduction to Mythology for Gay Men," he suggests that we "imagine gayness as a multidimensional constellation of traits" in order to discover or reclaim myths and figures that embrace non-Western and non-contemporary models of homoeroticism, gender variance, and sacred roles.[17]

In the works of some feminist and lesbian postmodern theorists and writers, we find articulations, albeit subtle ones, of our domain. In *The Newly Born Woman,* for instance, Hélène Cixous and Catherine Clément write, "There have always been those uncertain, poetic persons who have not let themselves be reduced to dummies programmed by pitiless repression of the homosexual element. Men or women: beings who are complex, mobile, open. Accepting the other sex as a component makes them much richer, more various, stronger, and—to the extent that they are mobile—very fragile. It is only in this condition that we invent."[18]

And in their introduction to *Angry Women: Re/Search #13*, editors and feminist thinkers Andrea Juno and V. Vale write, "The gay and lesbian community are pioneers in . . . playing with the fixed biological gender identities of 'man' and 'woman' which our society has deemed sacred and untouchable. . . . The very act of subverting something so primal and fixed in society as one's gender role can unleash a creativity that is truly needed by society—like a shamanistic act."[19]

In her queer-theoretical essay "Tracking the Vampire," postmodernist theorist Sue-Ellen Case describes a "queer compound" that bears remarkable likeness to our domain. It includes the features of "same-sex desire," "gender inversion" (gender variance), and "ontological shift," which may be related, through her description of the Christian mysticism of San Juan de la Cruz (St. John of the Cross) and the anti-Christian mysticism of the homoerotically inclined Symbolist poet Rimbaud, to our domain's sacred role or function. In the poems of San Juan, for example, the "queer compound" appears in the following manner:

> The flame of this desire . . . sears into a world where being is reconfigured.
> John, the mystic lover, desires a being of a different order. . . . In order to
> "know" this being, the senses . . . must be reconfigured. . . . [In] "The Spir-
> itual Canticle," where his love finds full expression in the trope of marriage,
> John inverts his gender, writing his desire as if he were the bride with the
> other being [Christ] as the bridegroom. John, the bride, languishes for her
> lover, seeks him everywhere. . . . The wound of love liberates the lover from
> the boundaries of being. . . . Ontology [metaphysical significance] shifts
> through gender inversion and is expressed as same-sex desire. This is queer,
> indeed.[20]

Since the 1970s, literary texts focusing on our domain have proliferated. Indeed, a canon of such works is emerging. It includes Arthur Evans's *Witchcraft and the Gay Counterculture*, Mitch Walker's *Visionary Love*, Larry Mitchell's *The Faggots and Their Friends Between Revolutions*, Judy Grahn's *Another Mother Tongue*, Mark Thompson's *Gay Spirit*, Walter Williams's *The Spirit and the Flesh*, Will Roscoe's *Living the Spirit* (with Gay American Indians) and *The Zuni Man-Woman*, Bradley Rose's *Of Intermediate Concern*, the essays of Harry Hay and John Burnside, and the journals *RFD, Ganymede, The Crucible, White Crane, Marilyn Medusa, New Uranian, Coming Out Pagan,* and *Lavender Pagan*.

Also since the 1970s, fueled in part by the emergence of the neopagan, gay, and feminist-spiritual movements, groups and gatherings embracing the interrelationship of homoeroticism, gender variance, and sacred experience have proliferated. These have included Gay Voices and Visions, the Yellow Rose Tribe, the Radical Faeries, the Congregation of Hermes, Tayu Center for Gay Spirituality, Body Electric School of Massage, the Gay Metaphysical Spiritual Association, COGS (Conference of Gay Spirituality), EroSpirit, Treeroots, Shaman's Circle, Gay Spirit Journeys, Heart and Fire Gay Men's Gatherings, Light Touch Retreats,

Wicca for Gay Men, the Queer (or Lavender) Pagans, and Faggot Witch Camp. Gatherings of these groups, often held outdoors, frequently include self- and group-empowering rituals blending ancient wisdom with contemporary psychological and political perspectives.

While this book examines many figures living in various cultures and epochs, the book is *not* an encyclopedic work; I have dealt primarily with cultures and periods with which I am somewhat familiar, and have avoided, generally speaking, focusing in depth on figures such as Christian priests, Native American *berdaches*, and the *hijras* of India, which I feel have been adequately covered elsewhere by experts in the field. I have also limited my discussion of the role that gender-variant, lesbian women have played in sacred histories, feeling that such a project needs to be undertaken by a lesbian-feminist scholar or scholars; indeed, Paula Gunn Allen, Judy Grahn, Monique Wittig, Gloria Anzaldúa, and others have already discussed certain manifestations of this domain. I have also limited my discussion of the role that HIV/AIDS has played in relation to our domain and its agents, feeling that this subject deserves to be treated by writers more versed than myself in matters related to HIV/AIDS. I should also point out that I have frequently focused on what have been termed "microhistorical" elements—such as the color purple—which have often outlived the spiritual traditions to which they have been linked.[21]

Beyond the introduction and conclusion, I have divided this book into four sections of three chapters each. In each of the four sections I focus on a related complex of ideas, figures, and experiences. The first section, "Bone," focuses on the relationship between our domain and the often non-Western phenomenon of shamanism. The second section, "Earth and Moon," relates our domain to Goddess reverence in West Asian (or Near Eastern) and Greco-Roman antiquity. The third section, "Cauldron," looks at the metamorphoses of our domain in Western late antiquity, the Middle Ages, the Renaissance, and the seventeenth through early twentieth centuries. The fourth section, "Crossroads," examines expressions of our domain in the New World, spanning the period from the conquest of Mesoamerica and the arrival of the slave ships to the late twentieth century, ending with an exploration of the contemporary Gay Spiritual movement. Each section is preceded by a "Meditation"; these, I hope, will serve to guide you, the reader, along the serpentine path of our domain.

In doing research for and in writing this text, I have encountered many persons, both living and dead, with whom I have felt a deep sense of kinship, and I have journeyed to worlds in which I have felt strangely at home. It is my hope that in reading this text, you will also experience these resonances, these homecomings.

TWO HUNDRED MEN are linking hands around the pond, its rim marked by artemisia. One wears the robes of Isis, and one the horns of Pan. One plays the harp of Orpheus, another Shangó's drum. Their canticles echo in the mountains near Los Angeles, among the cliffs at Bolinas, in the swamps of Linden, Texas. Lifting their hands to the full moon, they chant:

Cauldron of changes
Blossom of bone
Arc of infinity
Holding the stone
We are an old people
We are a new people
We are the same people
Different from before[22]

PART ONE

Bone

❧

BONE

I AM SITTING under a mesquite tree in the burning Texas noon, posing for a photograph at the ruins of Mission San Francisco de la Espada in San Antonio. From where I sit, I can see the descendants of those who once lived here. They are working in their gardens, washing their cars, playing with their children. While the church has been rebuilt, and a new statue of St. Francis holding a sword has replaced the old one, little remains of the village that once occupied this site.

A few mountain laurel trees with their fragrant purple flowers, reminiscent of wisteria, and red beans whisper of ritual dances that once took place here, long before the Christmas carnivals, before the blankets dipped in smallpox, before the rains stopped and the earth cracked.

Samîn, THE PEOPLE called the red beans. The Spanish named them *frijolillos.* The deer had known their magic, had danced beneath their spell. The People had found the beans in their bellies. They honored the deer's spirit, Tamóx, whom the Huichols called Kauyumai, with great dances, *txé,* which mimed the movements of the deer. The *txé* were held outside on late summer evenings and in the tiopas, the sacred dwellings, when the winter rains fell.

The shaman, the *kutatzé,* who wore antlers, led them. Among the dancers were those dressed in the garments of women, those who loved the other men of the village. Perhaps the *kutatzé* himself was such a man.

Those who dared drank of the brew of peyote, herbs, and roasted, powdered red beans. They painted their faces red like the beans, wore necklaces made of them. The beans had eyes, they said. The beans would allow them to see into the future.

Some played instruments—drums, rattles, bone flutes—while others danced. The dancers carried spears and stalks adorned with feathers. They whipped themselves with the vertebrae of snakes. They vomited as they danced, cleansing themselves of transgressions.

The rose of dawn found them sleeping beside the smoldering fire, slowly returning from the meadow of the deer.

The PRIEST of La Espada entered the small, dark room in which a single candle flickered. Anua Aptjam, Moon Dweller, sat trembling in silence as the pale, wrinkled man opened the book of death, the *Manual para Administrar los Santos Sacramentos de Penitencia,* composed by Father Bartolomé Garcia especially for his people, the Coahuiltecas, the People of the Serpent, of the place now called San Antonio. So wise was Father Garcia that he had learned the language of the people, learned of Tamóx and the deer and the little red beans, learned so that he might save the people's souls, watch their spirits rising from the flames.

"*Pajé chem mamâiham am é? Samîn chem mamâihám am é? Tje' mam'ija yam e?*"

Yes, I say. I have taken *paxé*, peyote, have eaten the *samîn*, the little red beans, have danced the dance of the deer. You know I have done these things. You have watched me. Have you not done them yourself, I want to ask him. But I do not.

"*Jagû pîl't'an jac'áu mám é?*"

Yes, I would say, if I were to answer you honestly. I have always been drawn to men. But I do not, cannot, trust you.

"*Jat âjacó apchîca, jagû pitapôyô sajpâm pin apsac' auj mahôi salaté?*"

Xuyopamaux axté axakó, I think, ten years I have been with my lover, but I do not answer you.

"*Jagû tapô japatjâm tucuêt pitapámoyó mitjám am é?*"

Where else would he live, I wonder. Of course he lives with me. But I will not tell you.

"*Jagû p'îl t'án atîl' tucuêm mami pî yam é?*"

I cannot believe you are asking me these questions. These things are between my *japatjti* and myself. And yet I know I must answer. No, I lie, I have never made love to him by entering him while lying on top of him. It is not hard to guess what your next question will be.

"*Jagû pî' t'án jatîl' tucuét mamîc pî yam é?*"

What does it matter what I say? I have been brought before you. Tamóx has deserted me. My hands and feet are bound, I wear a crown of iron thorns. I know I am to die. I know that whatever I say, you have used me to bring him to the fire.

ANUA APTJAM and his People of the Serpent are gone, as the grim father is gone.

Their spirits live on, however, in the priest who says mass here each Sunday, in the mountain laurels growing in this place, as they grow on Mount Bonnell in Austin. In the children living in the vicinity of Espada, who play games with the little red beans. In the botanicas and *hierberias* where the beans, now called *colorines,* are sold for good luck. In the spiritual practices of Rafael, a gay Mexicano/Native American student of mine whose family has decided to return to the old ways. In the necklace my friend Hyperion wears when he dances on Enchanted Rock. In the bones beneath the ruins.[1]

Gender-variant male Yukaghir shaman's costume, 19th century.

Wearing Our Long Wing Feathers

> He wanders throughout the long nights across plains
> filled with the chilly whiteness of the moon; he listens to
> the wind. . . . Many a time he has felt himself in the pres-
> ence of Sedna, the Eskimo Demeter, he has divined it by
> the shiver which ran through his veins, by the tingling of
> his flesh and the bristling of his hair. . . . He sees stars
> unknown to the profane. . . . The soul of the *angakok*
> flies upon the wings of the wind. . . .[1]
>
> Elie Reclus, *Primitive Folk*

Where, among the many cultures and epochs of human history, do we find *the interrelationship of male gender variance, homo- eroticism, and sacred experience, function, or role?* Our search begins with a brief exploration of the earliest spiritual tradi- tions of humanity and the surviving primal or tribal traditions that preserve the basic beliefs and practices of those earliest peoples. ¶ What primal traditions seem to share in common is a belief that the divine, expressed in spiritual practices and the arts, is inseparable from the body and nature. They also tend to share a belief that gender-variant behavior and same-sex eroti- cism, together with traditional gender roles and heterosexual- ity, are both natural and sacred. Indeed, they often look upon gender-variant persons as especially capable of performing spiritual functions, as these are believed to hold the knowledge of gender transformation and other forms of metamorphosis. Unfortunately, primal traditions also tend to share the experience of being demonized and dismantled by European, Anglo-American, and other colonial forces.

My use of the terms *primal* and *tribal* to speak of cultural groups whose traditions in some ways reflect those of the Paleolithic and Neolithic eras (2,500,000–10,000 B.C.E. and 10,000–4,000 B.C.E. respectively) has been inspired by Jamake Highwater's *The Primal Mind,* an illuminating study of Native American and other "tribal" peoples.[2] I wish to stress that while I am speaking of traditions that are deeply rooted both in the earth and in the heart, soul, breath, and loins of humanity, I do not in any way wish to convey the idea that primal peoples are "primitive" or "savage." Nor do I wish to suggest that primal spiritual traditions are less complex than other religions. To the contrary, primal, like Paleolithic and Neolithic, traditions often embrace complex theological concepts, pantheons, and rituals. To become a spiritual functionary, typically a shaman, in such traditions often requires many years of study.

EARLY SPIRITUAL TRADITIONS

During the Paleolithic era, men and women lived primarily by hunting, fishing, and gathering wild plants. Chief among their material concerns was survival, both individual and collective. They looked toward the female to perpetuate the tribe. They may or may not have recognized the role of the male in reproduction. Their spiritual beliefs and practices reflected their way of life.

Above all, they worshiped female deities and spirits as the sources of life. To a lesser extent, they revered male deities and spirits as guardians and hunters. Males also appear to have been perceived as human reflections of "rising and dying vegetation . . . ephemeral and mortal." As such, they, like animals and plants, were seen as embodiments of the principle of sacrifice, and they represented the eternal return of animal and plant life in the springtime. The central themes of both Paleolithic and Neolithic religions appear to have been birth, death, rebirth, and metamorphosis. Two of the key themes of this text, the belief in the power of animal transformation—that is, becoming an animal or hybrid human-animal—and the belief in the power of gender transformation—becoming a person of the opposite sex, a hermaphrodite, or a person of an alternate or "third" gender role—may have emerged during these early epochs of humankind. With its reverence of the feminine and also of the male principle and of animals and plants—not to mention the elements of earth, air, fire, and water—the spiritual beliefs of the first peoples appear to have been matrifocal (or gynocentric) and pantheistic (or animistic) in character. These beliefs were often manifested in the practice of shamanism.[3]

Shamanism is narrowly defined as the spiritual practices of the early peoples of Siberia, but it may be more broadly defined as a cross- or multicultural phenomenon. It focuses on the practices and character of the shaman and the beliefs, often matrifocal and/or pantheistic, that the shaman shares with his or her people. The shaman is a spiritual functionary who, in a state of trance—an "altered" or "shamanic state of consciousness" often triggered by the use of chant, drumming, ecstatic dance, and mind-altering substances—travels mentally or spiritually to other worlds or realms of consciousness. Otherworld journeys may be undertaken for several reasons: in order to retrieve a wandering soul (often believed to be a cause of illness); to escort the soul of the deceased to the afterlife; or to communicate with a deity or spirit. The shamanic trance is closely linked to the state of possession, also referred to as "embodiment," "enthusiasm (from *en-* + *-theos,* "taking the god within")," or "channeling." The primary difference is that the shaman visits a deity or spirit, while the possessed person is instead visited or "ridden" by that divine being.

The shaman functions as a healer, psychopomp (guide of souls), intercessor, diviner, worker of magic, and teacher of the mysteries. Persons traditionally become shamans because other family members have been shamans or because they are called by deities or spirits while dreaming or experiencing an altered state of consciousness. Prior to becoming shamans, they often experience illness and deathlike states. They frequently work with animal and spirit helpers, and they are believed to hold the power to transform themselves into animals and other entities.[4]

THE VISION OF THE PHALLUS IN ARCHAIC TIMES

While the matrifocal, pantheistic, and shamanic traditions of the Paleolithic and Neolithic eras appear to have emphasized the feminine principle—often characterized as a Great or Mother Goddess—the masculine principle was not neglected. There is little evidence that in these early epochs of our history reverence of the masculine conflicted with reverence of the feminine. To the contrary, evidence suggests that men honored both the masculine and feminine, as did women. It does appear, however, that rituals were often sexually segregated occasions. It is helpful to bear this in mind as we discuss the roles of the phallus and semen in Paleolithic, Neolithic, and primal rituals.

Philip Rawson, historian of art and religions, suggests that our ancestors may have been profoundly moved by the "visual shape of the phallus," that the sight of an erect penis may have triggered "a range of powerful, inner experiences, including the feelings of sexual arousal, active penetration, and seminal ejaculation."[5] Alexander Marshack, a scholar of Paleolithic history and art, suggests that certain rites may have centered on the image of, and processes associated with, the phallus, including "the ejaculation of semen and urine," and that such rites may have included the initiations of hunters, shamans, and boys into manhood.[6]

Early males may have been even more deeply inspired by the sight of two or more erect phalli in close proximity to one another. This is suggested by a baton found at Gorge d'Enfer in France, which not only depicts a fish, believed by archaeologist Marija Gimbutas and others to be a manifestation of the Great Goddess, but also twin erect phalli. Says Marshack, "Fish, [double] phallus and water seem aspects of a larger myth which [while here focusing on the male principle] also includes the 'goddess.'"[7]

That early males were inspired by the sight of erect phalli other than their own is also indicated by the myriad depictions of groups of nude men with erect phalli occurring in Paleolithic and Neolithic art. Such a representation is found in the cave of Les Trois Frères in France. Here three men, shamanlike figures, appear to be dancing. One wears antlers and two wear bison masks. In Marshack's view, "The Trois Frères sorcerers seem to be involved in a rite that is 'sexual' . . . because they are naked and their sexual organs are exposed." He stresses, however, that by "sexual rite" he does not necessarily refer to a reproductive rite. Rather, such a rite might focus on "virility without fertility connotation."[8]

Marshack also suggests that ceremonies that took place in the cave of Tuc d'Audobert in France may have included phallic initiation rites. Phallus-shaped clay forms and fifty footprints of young males indicate that a ritual involving a group of men and youths who became sexually aroused during its course may have occurred there 11,500 years ago.[9]

Neolithic engravings found on rocks on the eastern shore of Lake Onega near the White Sea (in the vicinity of Russia) depict a number of naked males with erect phalli hunting and skiing. Art historian Anne Ross believes that the phalli indicate that the skiers were "probably engaged in some sacred activity," thus linking group male sexual arousal with both sacred activity and sport, hunting, or transportation.

Ross also draws our attention to a group of rock carvings from Bohuslen, Sweden, which were probably executed during the first millennium B.C.E. One of these carvings "shows men with erect genitalia engaged in a ballgame with sticks." Ross indicates that this scene, like that of the Lake Onega skiers, points toward a linkage of group male eroticism, ritual, and sport.[10]

We must be cautious when making comparisons between Paleolithic or Neolithic archaeological remains and the beliefs and practices of primal or tribal peoples. Nevertheless, such comparisons may help us understand how homoeroticism and male gender variance intersected with the sacred in the earliest periods of our history. As scholar of religion Karl Narr asserts, "[With] certain reservations . . . it is possible to show continuity between the Paleolithic period and present-day 'primitive' societies that follow a similar way of life."[11]

Two examples of present-day practices including groups of symbolically erect males can be found in Curt Sachs's book, *World History of the Dance*. In one, Christian Theodor Köch-Grünberg (1872–1924), an ethnologist who spent two years among the Cobeua of northwestern Brazil, describes a ritual in which the dancers, sporting enormous red, artificial phalli, mimic anal intercourse as they chant, "*Ai (ye)-ai (ye)-ai (ye).*" The same book includes a photograph of a piece of pottery depicting a similar ritual dance undertaken by the Hopi. This depiction of the "phallic rain dance of the Hopi" portrays a circle of a dozen dancers, one behind the other, moving in a clockwise direction. Each holds an artificial erect phallus attached to his waist with one hand while placing his other hand near the buttocks of the dancer in front of him. All of the men are bending forward in a thrusting movement and appear to be simulating masturbation or anal intercourse.[12]

AN ENGRAVED DRAWING appears on a wall of the Addaura cave near Palermo, Sicily. Executed around 10,000 B.C.E., the drawing is undoubtedly one of the most provocative works of Upper Paleolithic art. Discovered in 1952 by Iole Bovio-Marconi, it depicts, in the words of Marija Gimbutas, a group of "superbly drawn bird-masked male figures engaged in a ritual drama." Gimbutas suggests that these figures "were probably . . . participants in rituals [dedicated to the] Goddess." From the bird masks, it appears that the men may have been honoring that aspect of the Great Goddess now referred to as the Bird Goddess.[13]

The bird-masked men are dancing in a circle. They are nude except for the masks, thick with plumage, that they wear. Their genitals are visible. At least two of the men have erections.

In the center of the circle of dancers are two men, one lying above or beside the other. They face opposite directions. The legs of the figure above are bent at the knees. His penis is erect, or he wears an artificial phallus or penis sheath. He wears a bird mask, though his is without plumage. Parallel lines connect his neck to his buttocks or ankles. His arms cover the legs of the male below him. The man beneath, larger in size, wears a plumed mask. He faces downward. His arms appear to be outstretched before him. He, like the other man, has an erection. Parallel lines link the penis of the male above to the buttocks of the male beneath.[14]

While some art historians have described the Addaura ritual as a sacrificial rite and the two central figures as victims, with the parallel lines representing cords, it occurred to me, as I examined the work, that the parallel lines might instead represent lines of energy—specifically, male erotic energy—and that the ritual might be one of initiation, including same-sex eroticism, rather than one of sacrifice.

That the lines might represent male energy rather than nooses was suggested to me by a seven thousand-year-old figurine from the Dimini culture of northern Greece, described by Gimbutas in *The Language of the Goddess*. Just above the genitals of this male figure, whom Gimbutas believes to be a "Year God symbolizing [the] revival of nature," is an arc with a series of parallel lines, perhaps representing male energy or even ejaculated semen. This possibility is strengthened by the fact that the man is holding his phallus.[15]

Without sharing my thoughts with them, I showed several others, including a scholar of religion and an art historian, the image of the Addaura rite and asked them to describe it to me. To my surprise, all noticed the possible homoerotic content. I soon learned that while later observers have tended to emphasize the sacrificial interpretation of the Addaura ritual, the discoverer of Addaura, Bovio-Marconi, referring to the pioneering work of Magnus Hirschfeld in gay studies, first noted its potential initiatory, homoerotic connotation.[16]

Thus, it is conceivable that the Addaura ritual combined two elements of our domain: homoeroticism and sacred experience, perhaps in the form of shamanic reverence of a Bird Goddess.

It is also possible that the third element of our domain, gender variance, was given expression at Addaura. This is suggested by the bird costumes worn by the dancers. First, these costumes, by way of creating the image of a hybrid human-bird, suggest animal transformation, which is often linked in shamanic traditions to gender metamorphosis. Second, if the men are indeed honoring the Bird Goddess, then they may also be celebrating a gynandrous ("woman-man") aspect of the divine and trying to embody that aspect. The Bird Goddess's gender-mixing quality is indicated by a host of figurines showing her as having an avian torso, female breasts, and a phallic neck. Gimbutas explains that these figurines appear to have been associated by early peoples with other depictions of androgyny, or what we have here termed gender variance.[17]

In this way, the three elements of our domain—homoeroticism, gender variance, and sacred experience—may have been expressed at Addaura over ten thousand years ago.

It is noteworthy that while art historians and others have been quick to point out any possible expressions of heterosexual activity in early art, few have considered the auto- and homoerotic implications of the Addaura, Trois Frères, Lake Onega, and other depictions of groups of sexually aroused males. When the subject is broached, we are treated to coy statements like, "A ceremony can generally be sufficiently excitable to cause erection," and then we are left to figure it out for ourselves.[18] While Rawson, Marshack, and others have been willing to admit that from time immemorial penile erection has been linked to erotic pleasure (and not always to reproductive urges), they have not been willing to admit that the experiencing of erection and ejaculation by men in group rituals may indicate cultic homoeroticism.

SEMEN AS DIVINE LIQUOR

As hunters, the men and women of early history experienced a constant and intimate awareness of death. They may well have come to view themselves as eaters of life, their strength or vitality restored by the essences of wild animals and plants. Watching the flesh of their beloved dead, or the remaining pieces of flesh on the bones of animals, being consumed by vultures, they may have come to look upon life as a relationship between that which eats and that which is eaten, and perhaps to imagine that the spirit or soul of that which is eaten ultimately returns to a common source, from which it one day emerges as new life.

Philosopher Richard Onians, anthropologist Weston La Barre, art historian Rawson and other scholars have speculated that early peoples may have imagined certain bodily fluids, including bone marrow, saliva, sweat, cerebrospinal fluid, the synovial fluid of the knee, and, most importantly, semen, to constitute the essence of the *élan vital* in males, just as they may have held menstrual blood to be the essence of female energy. Whether or not the peoples of the Paleolithic were conscious of the male's role in reproduction, it is evident that they recognized semen as a magical substance.

Paleolithic males may have felt a need to consume semen and other "white" liquids due to a belief that while women stored in their bodies an immeasurable supply of blood, men's bodies carried only a small supply of vital energy. Thus, men needed to consume white liquids in order to replenish their strength. If indeed they imagined semen as having its source in the brain and to be virtually identical to cerebrospinal fluid, and to have further imagined that the semen and cerebrospinal fluid of the bear were roughly equivalent to those of human males, the Paleolithic consumption of semen may have been linked to practices including bear hunting, head hunting, cannibalism, and the preservation of human skulls.[19]

A carved bone discovered at La Madeleine in France seems to speak of this web of associations. It depicts an emanation flowing from a human phallus to the head of a bear. The emanation apparently signifies the divine liquor that is at once cerebrospinal fluid and semen.[20]

Having acknowledged the problems in comparing early human and present-day primal or tribal beliefs and practices, we may note that among the Big Nambas of Vanuatu and among many peoples of New Guinea, including the Kaluli, Sambia, Etoro, Asmat, Keraki, and Kiwai, the consumption of semen plays a key role in initiatory rites. In these cultures the consumption of semen is believed to replenish male energy, and consuming it may lead to prowess in hunting and a deeper awareness of nature's mysteries. While it is believed to replenish masculinity, semen may also be related, in certain instances, to gender variance or metamorphosis. The Sambia, for instance, believe that the ancestors of their people were the creation of a deity who experienced gender transformation, pregnancy, and birthgiving after having fellated his male companion. Understanding the beliefs and practices of the Sambia and other primal peoples may lead us to a greater understanding of similar practices among the peoples of the Paleolithic.[21]

SAME-SEX RELATIONSHIPS AMONG PRIMAL PEOPLES

The evidence concerning sexual *acts*, both heterosexual or homosexual, among early humans is fragmentary, and the evidence concerning sexual *relationships* is even scantier. If we are to make an educated guess about such relations, we are forced to rely on ethnographic accounts of primal peoples.

Several general types of male homoerotic relationships have been documented in tribal groups. Many are *transgenerational* (often referred to as "pederastic"), which refers to one partner being younger than the other. Some are *transgenderal*, in which at least one of the partners is perceived as gender variant, androgynous, or effeminate. A few are *egalitarian,* in which the partners, often childhood friends becoming warriors, are perceived as socially similar. Erotic relationships between cross-cousins of the same community and between blood brothers of different communities, which tend to be roughly egalitarian, are often formalized by means of rituals.

Transgenerational relationships are typically formed between a young male, often an adolescent, and an older male who acts as the younger's lover, mentor, and initiator into the mysteries of the community. The older partner is occasionally viewed as a representative of the male ancestors of the community or as a representative of a deity or spirit.[22]

Among the Big Nambas of Malekula Island in the new Hebrides, the older partner was in the past called the *dubut*. *Dubut* probably means "shark" and referred to the hybrid man-shark creator god Qat. Because the elder partner almost always assumed the role of spiritual guide and channel for the divine, the relationship was perceived as being both sacred and erotic in character and as being divinely sanctioned.[23]

Transgenderal relationships often occur between a traditionally masculine male and a male who is perceived as gender variant, androgynous, effeminate, or of a mixed, third, or alternate gender—a "not-man" or "man-woman"—although occasionally both partners may express gender-variant behavior. These relationships have historically tended to be more stable than transgenerational relationships, which often end when the younger partner marries a woman. Transgenderal relationships have been documented among Paleosiberians, Tahitians, and many other cultural groups. We will encounter transgenderal relationships in our discussion of the "transformed" or "soft" shaman and, indeed, throughout this text.

In researching early and primal peoples, I have often wondered whether or not the presence of gender-variant male shamans may have had a negative impact on the institution of the female shaman, in particular, whether these men may have displaced shamanesses as part of a patriarchal takeover, as some feminists have suggested. While this question continues to be a subject of great controversy, evidence gathered among such primal peoples as the Siberians, Dayaks, and Tahitians suggests that gender-variant homoeroticism has been associated with a reverence of the feminine and a "generally high social status of women." Based on such evidence, sociologist David Greenberg argues that "men and women [probably] both shamanized" or served as spiritual functionaries "throughout the Old Stone Age and have continued to do so up to the present in many groups."[24]

TRANSFORMED SHAMANS

At some point during the Paleolithic, certain shamans came to be looked upon as individuals belonging to a third or alternate gender. This gender category represented a blending of traits assumed by the cultures concerned to be masculine, feminine, and godlike or supernatural. According to Joseph Campbell, such shamans represented a "sphere of spiritual power transcending the male-female polarity."[25] These shamans are variously known as "soft" or "transformed" shamans; the first of these terms suggests fluidity of gender role, while the second indicates gender metamorphosis.

Gender-variant shamans have found a place in many cultures. In Korea, where shamanism was greatly influenced by Tungusic tribes journeying from Siberia between 1000 and 600 B.C.E., a majority of shamans have been female. However, there have been male shamans also. One class of these has been comprised of traditionally masculine males who are visually impaired. The other class of male shamans, the *paksu mudang*, have been described as gender-variant males who wear female garments during rituals. They have been linked to the *hwarang*, the so-called flower boys, who from around the first century B.C.E. until 1895 C.E., formed a military elite in Buddhist Korea, who were believed to engage in same-sex relationships, and who "seem to have been involved in shamanic practices."[26]

In Vietnamese villages, so-called hermaphrodite witches were still practicing shamanism in the mid-1970s. Typically beginning their shamanic training during childhood, these men, believed to be possessed by female deities or spirits, dressed in feminine attire and functioned as healers and intercessors.[27]

Among Polynesians, gender-variant males dressing in women's garments, engaging in homoeroticism, and sometimes practicing shamanism have been named *mahus*. Anthropologist Walter Williams explains that while among twentieth-century Hawaiians, "the status of the *mahu* has declined considerably," in previous eras, *mahus* often played key roles in the *tahiku*, an ancient, sacred form of the hula involving both dance and chant.[28]

In Japan, evidence suggests that gender-variant shamans may have served in Shinto rites as *miko*, that is, as spiritual functionaries becoming embodied by deities and spirits—in this case, female ones—during possession or trance. Evidence for this practice was discovered in the 1950s on Tanegashima Island, where the skeleton of a youth was found dressed in feminine and sacred garments and jewelry, including an "extraordinary profusion of shell ornaments—necklaces, abundant bracelets, square brooches decorated with an endless knot pattern at the waist and loins."[29]

In Okinawa, where shamanism has been practiced primarily by females, there was in the past a ceremony known as *winagu nati*, "becoming a woman," in which males were dressed in feminine attire and by which they were allowed to enter sacred groves and to become shamans. According to anthropologist William P. Lebra, "Male shamans [in Okinawa] tend to be regarded as more deviant than their female counterparts," and their "assumption of a role identified with females . . . may suffice to categorize them as effeminate." He also notes that one informant told him, "There are not many male *yuta* [shamans], and some of them seem like *wikiga-winagu*," that is to say, gender-variant males engaging in same-sex eroticism.[30]

Gender-variant shamans have often been symbolically or physically isolated from others in their communities. Anthropologist Erik Jensen explains that among the Iban Dayak of Borneo, the gender-variant male shaman, the *manang bali*, a figure surviving from the remote past into the early twentieth century, was "set apart from normal people. . . . He does not fully belong to the world in which Iban men and women live." As a marginalized individual, the *manang bali* was both ridiculed for his alleged weakness—"To be like a *manang* . . . implies that a man grows insufficient rice" for his family—and admired for his skill as a shaman. Likewise, the Ngaju Dayak both revered and ridiculed the gender-variant *basir*. Anthropologist Hans Schärer explains that while *basir* were generally respected from the ancient past until the twentieth century, it was nevertheless "regarded as . . . shameful if a son or relative [became] a *basir*." Walter Williams reports that Native Americans generally tended "to fear and respect" gender-variant shamans; this fear "made for a nervousness that was sometimes alleviated by joking" about them.[31]

As mentioned above, another trait besides gender-variant behavior associated with male shamans is visual impairment. While in Korea, the gender variant and the visually impaired belong to two different classes of male shamans, in other cultures, such as among the Iban Dayak of Borneo, these traits are joined. Both visual impairment and gender variance, along with mobility impairment, are believed to foster prophetic talent.[32]

DEITIES ASSOCIATED WITH TRANSFORMED SHAMANS

Gender-variant shamans have often revered or otherwise been associated with certain deities and spirits. Joseph Campbell maintained that these deities and spirits have generally pointed toward a "Primal Bisexual Divinity."[33]

One such deity is Sedna, a Native Alaskan Mother Goddess. She is the mother of wild animals—especially seals, walruses, and whales—who gives her children to the hunter or fisher if he or she conforms to the hunting or fishing ritual but who withdraws the game if the hunter or fisher fails to observe her rites. Sedna is not only the patroness of animals, hunters, and fishers, however; she is also a goddess of destiny, death, and the afterlife. As ruler of the afterlife, she reigns over three heavens of the Native Alaskans, including Omiktu, where the souls of deceased humans and whales live in harmony.

Once a young woman who refused to marry, Sedna lives with her female companion Qailertetang at the bottom of the sea in the company of seals, whales, and other sea creatures. Her rejection of marriage and her wild appearance—her matted hair is thick with the blood of her "children" whom hunters and fishers have killed—have contributed to her identity as a gynandrous goddess. Her companion Qailertetang may have also encouraged this perception. Qailertetang is amazonian—a "large woman of very heavy limbs." In rituals, she is "represented by a man dressed in a woman's costume and wearing a mask made of seal-skin." Qailertetang is a weather goddess; like Sedna, she is also a guardian of animals and a patron of hunters, fishers, and gender-variant shamans.[34]

The Inuit deity most often associated with female gender-variant shamans is White Whale Woman. She is believed to have transformed herself into a man or a woman-man and to then have married a woman of the Fly Agaric clan. Her marriage to this woman suggests that her worship may have been associated with the use of fly agaric, the *amanita muscaria* mushroom.[35] This association with the mushroom is important, as many figures associated with our domain have employed mind-altering substances in ritual contexts.

Several Siberian Koryak deities are also associated with gender-variant or transformed shamans; these include the creator deity Big Raven, his wife Miti, their son Eme'mqut, and the son's wives. In one tale, father and son turn into ravens after putting on cloaks of raven feathers. In another, Eme'mqut and his wives turn into fly agaric mushrooms after putting on wide-brimmed, spotted hats. Such tales have spawned others involving transformation of sex or gender. In one of these, Big Raven transforms himself into a woman by castrating himself. From his penis, he fashions a needle-case; his testicles become bells. In another tale, Miti transforms herself into a man by creating a phallus from a stone hammer.[36]

From ancient times until the twentieth century, the *basir* of the Ngaju Dayak of Borneo revered an androgynous deity named Mahatala-Jata. The male aspect of this deity, Mahatala, represented as a hornbill, lives on a mountaintop high above the clouds and rules the Upperworld. The female aspect of the deity, Jata, is a watersnake who dwells in the sea with her were-crocodile companions and rules the Underworld. The two aspects of the deity are joined by a jeweled bridge that is the rainbow. The *basir*, along with the *balian*, hierodulic shamanesses, were seen as reflections of this androgynous deity; they were both referred to as *tambon haruei bungai*, "watersnakes which are at the same time hornbills." Scholar of Indonesian and related cultures Justus van der Kroef writes of the *basir:* "The transvestism of the *basir* and his homosexual practices are symbolic . . . of the total Ngaju godhead."[37]

The Iban Dayak *manang bali* worshiped Menjaya Raja Manang. It is said that Menjaya was a male being until he decided to become the world's first healer when his brother's wife became ill. Upon curing the wife of Sengalang Burong, Menjaya transformed into a female or androgynous being.[38]

Native American gender-variant shamans of the Hidatsa tribe worshiped a triune goddess or trinity of goddesses: Village Old Woman, the creator of women, who lives in the south and who instituted goddess reverence; Holy Woman of the Four Directions; and Holy Woman Above. This triune goddess often manifests as a magpie. Gender-variant shamans often became possessed by Village Old Woman during the course of dance rituals; when this occurred, they would chant, "You can't kill me, for I am holy. I am holy, I can do anything."[39]

BECOMING A TRANSFORMED SHAMAN

Becoming a transformed shaman is often viewed as a process that includes several relatively distinct phases. Metamorphosis might begin as early as infancy. An eighteenth-century Russian explorer explained that among the Koniag Inuit, "When father or mother regard their son as feminine in his bearing, they will often dedicate him in earliest childhood to the vocation of Achnutschik [*angakok*, gender-variant shaman]." Such children were "highly prized" by the Koniag Inuit. They were dressed and reared as girls by their mothers until they were fifteen, when they were given to an older man, a tribal leader or *angakok*, to focus on the process of becoming a shaman.[40]

Metamorphosis might also begin when a deity or spirit visited the young male in a dream or otherwise altered state. Among the Koniag, this sometimes occurred when a *ke'let* spirit visited a young man in his dream and told him he was destined to become an *angakok*. Similarly, among the Iban Dayak, a young man who was destined to become a *manang bali* might be "summoned in a dream" by Menjaya Raja Manang or by the Great Goddess Ini. In this dream, the young man would experience himself "in a new way, commonly in the dress of the opposite sex." He would see himself wearing a chignon braid (*besanggol*) and a woman's skirt (*bekain*) and performing feminine and shamanic tasks.[41]

Among Native American Hidatsa, young men destined to become gender-variant shamans dreamed that the triune goddess instructed them to leave behind traditionally masculine attire, speech, behavior, and pursuits and to adopt those of women or individuals of alternate gender. Following such dreams, the young men came to be viewed as "mystic possessors of unique ritual instructions secured directly from the mysterious Holy Woman [Above]" and were "treated as a special class of religious leaders."[42]

Among the Plains Indians, especially among the Omaha and Lakota, young men destined to become gender-variant shamans also dreamed of a feminine or gynandrous being. The Omaha youth would dream of the deity of the moon. The moon would ask the young man to choose between a warrior's bow and a woman's burden strap, both of which she held in her hands. If he chose the burden strap, he would become a gender-variant shaman. Following this dream, the young man would be stopped on the road by a "matronly woman" who would address him as "daughter" and would begin to instruct him in the mysteries. He was then called *mexoga*, "instructed by the moon." Soon he would become a member of a brotherhood of men who had had similar visions, men considered different from the other men of the tribe.[43]

Among the Oglala Sioux, gender-variant shamans-to-be dreamed of the female divinity Double Woman. Double Woman had many faces: she could appear as twins, as a beautiful maiden, a woman warrior, a hermaphroditic buffalo calf, a vampiric deer. The young man who dreamed of her would become a shaman and a member of the society of "they [who] dream of face-on-both-sides," *Anukite Ihanblapi*.[44] Many of these practices, it seems, emerged in remote antiquity, and most survived into the late nineteenth and early twentieth centuries.

Of course, some young men refused to accept the role. One young Native American who was determined to escape the deity's call began to see loops of sweetgrass, emblematic of gender-variant shamanhood, everywhere he looked. Should the young Iban Dayak refuse the deity's call, he would bring ruin not only upon himself but upon his entire family and, further, upon his entire community.[45]

The young man who accepted the call, whether he be Iban, Hidatsa, or of another people, would usually begin to grow his hair long and to wear it like a woman's. If Iban, he would wear a chignon; if Ngaju, he would part his hair in the middle; if Paleosiberian, he would braid his hair in the feminine style. He would also begin to wear feminine attire, along with sacerdotal clothes and sometimes masculine clothes as well.

Hidatsa gender-variant shamans wore magpie feathers in their hair and white dresses made of sheepskin, white being the symbolic color of ash and oak, sacred trees in which the magpies lived. The men also carried staffs made of ash and decorated with white sage, sacred to the Goddess. Beyond this, they painted red ovals on their cheeks and foreheads, wore braids of sweetgrass looped around their left shoulders, and carried red blankets. The Yakut gender-variant shaman of Siberia wore a "woman's jacket of foal-skins and a woman's white ermine cap." The Siberian shaman often tattooed his face, tattooing being a sign of feminine beauty.[46]

With the onset of the next stage, the young man would leave behind "all pursuits and manners of his sex." The Russian ethnographer Vladimir Bogoras (1865–1936) wrote of the Chukchi shaman in the early twentieth century:

He throws away the . . . lance, the lasso of the reindeer-herdsmen, and the harpoon of the seal-hunter, and takes to the needle and the skin-scraper. . . . Even his pronunciation changes from the male to the female mode. At the same time his body alters . . . his psychical character changes. The transformed person . . . becomes . . . fond of small-talk and of nurturing small children.[47]

During this stage of transformation, the young man might even change the way in which he entered a dwelling. Among the Koryak, he would now enter the opening reserved for females and gender-variant males. He might also change the place where he slept. The young Koryak who had once slept on the right side of the animal hide would now sleep on the left.[48]

Also during this stage, or at the beginning of the next stage, his training as a shaman would intensify. While some, like the Iban *manang*, were instructed primarily by deities in dreams, others, like the Ngaju *basir*, were taught primarily by elder shamans or shamanesses.[49]

During the next stage, same-sex eroticism and homoerotic relationships were often emphasized. At this time, the Iban *manang* was said to move from being "unripe," *mata*, to being "completely transformed," *bali*. This stage was marked by the Iban with an "elaborate and costly initiation" ceremony.[50]

As mentioned above, gender-variant male shamans of Polynesia, and probably also those of Korea, Vietnam, and Japan, engaged in homoeroticism. Native American gender-variant shamans, including those of the Hidatsa and Oglala Sioux tribes, often married traditionally masculine males.[51]

Of the Ngaju, historian of Indonesia Justus van der Kroef explains that the *basir* were expected to "act as women sexually." He stresses that failure to perform homosexually might place the *basir* in an "inferior position." Hans Schärer indicates that the *basir*, like the female *balian*, functioned as sacred prostitutes or hierodules. He also indicates that prior to or even during major ceremonies, *basir* might engage in public, cultic homoeroticism. Through the experience of sexual union with a *basir* or a *balian*, a traditional Ngaju male might be brought into the presence of the androgynous deity. Both the Ngaju *basir* and the Iban *manang bali* established marriagelike relationships with traditional males.[52]

Among the Chukchi, the young shaman, according to Bogoras,

seeks to win the good graces of men, and succeeds easily with the aid of "spirits." Thus he has all the young men he could wish for striving to obtain his favor. From these he chooses his lover.[53]

While writers on shamanism have tended to avoid explicit descriptions of same-sex eroticism, Bogoras infers that sex between the gender-variant Siberian shaman and his male lover may have consisted largely of anal eroticism, with the shaman typically taking the receptive role. Certain myths, such as that of Big Raven castrating himself and that of an Inuit man exposing his genitals to the sun in order to cause them to shrivel, suggest that at one time castration may have been practiced by transformed shamans. This hypothesis is strengthened by a statement made to Bogoras by Ya'tirgin, the male companion of the gender-variant Chukchi shaman Tilu'wgi. Describing the shaman as "wholly masculine, and well developed," Ya'tirgin "confessed that . . . he hoped that in time, with the aid of the *ke'let* [spirit], Tilu'wgi would be able to equal the real 'soft men' of old, and to change the organs of his sex altogether." If castration had at one time been practiced by Siberian shamans, it is not difficult to see why anal eroticism may have become the primary erotic activity among shamans and their companions.[54] Among Polynesian *mahu*, fellatio seems to have been practiced, with the *mahu* taking the role of fellator.[55]

The Chukchi are said to have celebrated marriages between gender-variant shamans and their lovers "with the usual rites." Such relationships usually formed, in Bogoras's words, "a quite solid union, which often last[ed] till the death of one of the parties." Among the Chukchi, this earthly marriage was seen as a reflection of the divine marriage existing between the shaman and a deity or spirit.[56]

While scholars have tended to downplay the importance of transgenderal homosexuality in soft shamanism, the eighteenth-century Russian explorer Stepan Krasheninikoff (1713–1755) and the Lithuanian ethnologist Vladimir Jochelson (1855–1937) believed that, at least among the Siberian Kamchadal (or Itelmensy), its role was crucial: "[It] may be inferred that the most important feature of the institution of the *koe'kcuc* [gender-variant male shaman] lay, not in their shamanistic power, but in their position with regard to the satisfaction of the unnatural inclinations of the Kamchadal. The *koe'kcuc* . . . were in the position of concubines."[57]

The relationship of the shaman and his male companion cannot, however, be reduced to a typical husband-wife relationship. Their spiritual function, combined with their special relationship to a deity or *ke'let* spirit, caused shamans to be regarded as the true heads of their households. If mortal companions failed to treat shamans with respect, the shamans' supernatural companions would punish them. That the Chukchi shaman was head of his household is also evidenced by the fact that the mortal companion often took the shaman's name "as an addition to his own name; for instance, Tilu'wgi-Ya'tirgin ("Ya'tirgin, husband of Tilu'wgi").[58]

Relationships between shamans and their companions did not generally emphasize age differences. Bogoras, for example, mentions a sixty-year-old male Chukchi shaman named Kee'ulin who, upon the death of his companion of twenty years, now "was said . . . to have a new lover,—another old man who lived in the same house with him."[59]

FUNCTIONS OF TRANSFORMED SHAMANS

While gender-variant shamans apparently comprised a special class of shamans in many cultures, this categorization does not seem to have greatly limited their functions. Among the Chukchi, for example, soft or gender-variant shamans were said to "excel in all branches of shamanism."[60]

Ngaju *basir,* along with the female *balian,* officiated during new year's ceremonies. They were especially gifted as ritual chanters and singers. Koniag *angakok* not only practiced the arts of divination, magic, and healing, but also instructed young women in etiquette and dance. Navajo *nadles* and Lakota *winktes* were thought to be able to heal mental and physical illness and to aid in childbirth through the employment of magical songs.[61]

Among the Iban Dayak, the *manang bali* was believed to be able to heal the sick by way of prayers (*pelian*), the employment of crystals (the *bata ilau* or "stones of light"), and journeying to the realms of the gods and spirits in order to retrieve the wandering soul, which was at least partly responsible for the patient's illness. Similarly, gender-variant shamans—like other shamans—often served as psychopomps, guiding the souls of the dying to the afterlife.[62]

Like other shamans, gender-variant shamans were also thought to be capable of raising storms and of transforming into animals, plants, stones, and other entities.

The ethnologist V. F. Trostchansky has suggested that among the Yakut of Siberia, the soft shaman may have mastered the art of destructive magic, a branch of magic thought to have originated among female shamans in response to hostile invaders. Soft shamans may have undertaken spells not only of a destructive but also of an amatory nature. In a scene depicted by a Chukchi artist, a naked shaman wearing only a shaman's cap "crawls on all-fours to invoke the moon." The shaman cries out,

> O moon! I show you my private parts.
> Take compassion on my angry thoughts.
> I have no secrets from you.
> Help me on such and such a man![63]

Gender-variant Hidatsa shamans were thought to be especially gifted in hunting and agricultural magic. Anthropologist Alfred W. Bowers reports, "Inasmuch as the organization of Holy Woman was considered to be a benevolent group, doing much to assist the people in time of starvation, berdaches [here, gender-variant shamans] were well thought of."[64]

Like other shamans, gender-variant shamans are perceived as intermediaries or intercessors between the mortal and other realms. They typically visit other realms when in an altered state of consciousness such as possession or trance, often triggered by chant, dance, simulated or actual erotic activity, or the use of hallucinogenic or intoxicating substances.

Among the Inuit, the *angakok* would often begin his journey while naked, being bound, and having artificial wings tied to his back. In this manner he would embark on the treacherous journey to Adlivun, abode of the goddess Sedna. Passing through the regions of the dead and places of terrible iciness and boiling water and cauldrons of ferocious seals, he would finally arrive at the dwelling of the goddess. He would find her sitting inside, covered with dirt, her hair matted with the blood of slain and sacrificed animals. He would comb her hair and speak softly to her, and she would forgive his people for slaughtering too many seals, would tell him of things to come, and would grant his people's wishes. He would then return to his village to share the goddess's words with the people.[65]

Among the Ngaju *basir* and *balian,* communication and ultimately union with the deity occurs during a state of possession, when the deity (*sangiang*) enters the stomach—rather than the head, as is customary in African traditions—and begins to speak to and then through the shaman or shamaness. Among the Ngaju, as in some African traditions, the possessed individual, whether male or female, is perceived as feminine, while the deity, whether male or female, is perceived as masculine, during the time of possession; the *basir* or *balian* is a boat (*bandong*) in which the deity sails. In Ngaju, both *bandong* and *mangumpang,* another term referring to possession, also connote sexual intercourse.[66]

Gender-variant shamans, like other shamans, frequently used mind-altering substances in rituals. The Siberian shaman often used the fly agaric mushroom in this manner. Other participants in these rites, by way of drinking the shaman's urine, were able to share in his ecstasy.[67]

DEATH AND THE TRANSFORMED SHAMAN

When a gender-variant shaman dies, he is sometimes buried "on the man's side of the cemetery," as were the Zuni *Ihamana.* The Lakota shaman Lame Deer reported that in "the old days *winktes* . . . had a special hill where they were buried." Even when such shamans, or *berdaches,* were buried alongside other males, their funeral dress, which they would wear into the next life, often reflected their alternate gender status; they would apparently remain persons of alternate gender in the afterlife. Lame Deer remembered asking a *winkte* "what he would be in the spirit land, a man or a woman." "Both," the *winkte* replied.[68]

The Ngaju Dayak not only believed that the gender-variant *basir* would retain his identity after death but also that he would share a special "village of the dead in the Upperworld" with the *balian* shamanesses.[69]

WHILE WE MUST be careful to acknowledge the differences between early (as in Paleolithic) and primal or tribal societies, the study of the latter, when viewed in the light of archaeological evidence, can perhaps help us to better understand the spiritual and erotic traditions of the world's first peoples. From the evidence gathered by anthropologists, archaeologists, and others, we can speculate with some certainty that the interrelationship of homoeroticism, male gender variance, and the sacred was embodied by the earliest shamans, as it has continued to be embodied by the sacred workers of many primal peoples.

Zulu *isangoma* initiate wearing mixed-gender and sacred garments, 20th century.

Ancestors

Blessed are the Ancestors because They are why I AM.

Michael S. Smith,
"African Roots, American Fruits:
the Queerness of Afrocentricity"[1]

*P*rofessor Griff of the rap group Public Enemy stated in a 1990 interview, "There's not a word in any African language which describes homosexual." Challenging any who disagreed with him, he continued, "If you want to take me up on that, then you find me, in the original languages of Africa, a word for homosexual, lesbian, or prostitute. There are no such words. They didn't exist."[2] ¶ It seems, however, that homoerotically inclined and gender-variant individuals may have a long history in Africa. Still, Professor Griff may have a point. It may be that in terms of African traditions, as in shamanic traditions (including Native American), words like *homosexual* and *lesbian* do not adequately describe the individuals and groups we are encountering, as they indicate isolated traits or behaviors. I am reminded of Alice Walker's term *womanist*, which embraces spiritual function and same-sex love among women while not isolating these practices from others.[3] ¶ In African cultures, same-sex eroticism and androgyny were often linked to other traits, including military prowess. These traits combined to form a domain or web of associations that manifested as a behavioral complex—a complex which often took the form of a gender-variant, homoerotically inclined spiritual functionary. Africans spoke not of "gays" or "transsexuals" but of the *isangoma,* the *jo apele,* the *mwammi,* the *omasenge kimbanda,* the *'yan Daudu,* and others.

In order to better appreciate how our domain has been embodied in African cultures, it might be helpful to briefly examine African spirituality as well as various African manifestations of gender variance and homoeroticism.

AFRICAN SPIRITUAL TRADITIONS: A SKETCH

Rock paintings executed by the San people of southern Africa in the remote past, perhaps before 2000 B.C.E.—although, as with much of African history and archaeology, it is difficult to determine a precise date—indicate that the earliest spiritual traditions of Africa may have been shamanic in character. These paintings appear to document rituals still practiced in the twentieth century, such as individuals dancing ecstatically to attain an altered or shamanic state of consciousness. In this altered state, they acquire powers such as luring "large game animals to hunters," curing illnesses, and bringing rain.[4]

Unfortunately, as is typical of much contemporary anthropology, so much stress has been placed upon the differences between the shamanic state of consciousness and the state of spirit possession common to many African religions practiced in the twentieth century that the great similarity between these states has been obscured. In a sense, shamanic rituals emphasize a shaman's control over his or her experience, while possession rites emphasize the yielding of the worshiper to a divine being. Both states, however, are typically reached by ritual combinations including chant, drumming or other music, and dance. In both states, communication between divine beings and mortals occurs. And both states ultimately function to help the processes of healing, divination, and magical transformation.

What is more, shamanism and religions incorporating possession often revere a central divine being capable of manifesting in many forms, including male, female, and androgynous ones; and in both systems, intermediaries, be they female or male, are thought to be able to embody these manifestations. In a number of African religions, as in shamanic traditions, a man may embody (or become possessed by) a female or gynandrous being as well as a male one.

The German ethnologist Hermann Baumann (born 1902), tracking two key elements of shamanism—belief in an androgynous/gynandrous godhead and the process of gender transformation among practitioners—has documented the occurrence of one or both in a number of African spiritual traditions, including those of the Akan, Ambo-Kwanyama, Bobo, Chokwe, Dahomeans (of Benin)́, Dogon-Bambara, Etik, Handa, Humbe, Hunde, Iba, Jukun, Kimbundu, Konso,

Kunama, Lamba, Lango, Luba, Lulua, Musho, Nuba, Ovimbundu, Rundi, Shona-Karonga, Venda, Vili-Kongo, and Yoruba.[5]

Other elements of African religions, most if not all of which may be found in shamanic traditions, include ancestor worship, herbal medicine, animal sacrifice, complex systems of divination, initiation rites, and secret societies.

In chapter 11 we will explore in greater depth one African-diasporic religious tradition, that of the Yoruba (primarily as practiced in the Americas), and its associations with gender variance and same-sex eroticism.

HOMOEROTICISM AND MALE GENDER VARIANCE IN AFRICAN CULTURES

Contrary to the current Afrocentric view, both same-sex eroticism and gender-variant behavior apparently were known to Africans long before Africa, except perhaps for Egypt and Libya, was subjected to non-African influences.

Among the Azande, living in what today is southwestern Sudan, northern Zaire, and the southeastern corner of the Central African Republic, a form of intergenerational homoeroticism was practiced from remote antiquity until the beginning of the twentieth century—a form strikingly similar to Greek pederasty. Anthropologist Edward E. Evans-Pritchard has insisted that this and other forms of same-sex eroticism were indigenous and not the result of foreign influence.[6]

The typical intergenerational relationship was that between a ruler or warrior and a younger male. Younger males who were the intimate companions of rulers were sometimes referred to as the "king's old barkcloth" and as the *amoyembu*, "those who could be summoned."[7] The most common form of sexual intercourse practiced between warriors and youths was interfemoral, a practice also popular among the Greeks.

Relationships were formalized by way of marriage ceremonies. The ritual of betrothal included the older partner giving spears to the younger's parents, building a hut for his mother-in-law, his *negbiore,* and giving the younger partner "pretty ornaments," this last gift suggesting that the relationship may have included a transgenderal (gender-variant) element. The older partner now addressed the younger's father as *gbiore* (father-in-law), while the partners addressed each other as *badiare* ("my love [r]"). The relationship stressed the training of the younger partner as a warrior.[8]

Azande women also practiced same-sex eroticism from the remote past until the present century, although this activity was apparently feared by most men. That same-sex eroticism was thought by men to double a woman's power indicates an earlier period in Azande history in which women held greater power. Lesbianism appears to have been especially common among women living in the courts of princes. The preferred form of sexual intercourse appears to have involved the use of a dildo fashioned from a root. Evidence suggests that Azande women engaging in same-sex eroticism may have also engaged in magical practices or served as spiritual functionaries. In folkloric belief, they were associated with witchcraft and were linked to the *adandara,* a supernatural wild cat with gleaming ebony skin and luminescent eyes. Indeed, lesbian lovemaking was referred to as *adandara,* and it was imagined that such lovemaking practices led to the birth of cat people.[9]

The Nama(n), a tribe of Khoisan people, practiced from time immemorial a form of egalitarian homoeroticism. This relationship was formalized by means of a ceremony of communion at which a beverage, in earlier times water and in later times coffee, was shared by the lovers. This relationship was referred to as a *sore//gamsa,* a "water bond." The relationship was thought to be rooted in "deep friendship" and aimed at "mutual assistance." The preferred form of sexual intercourse appears to have been *oa/huru* (mutual masturbation).[10]

Transgenderal or gender-variant homosexuality has been documented among the Nuba peoples of the Nilotic Sudan. The Nuba tribes have various names for gender-variant males engaging in same-sex eroticism, including *domere* (Tira), *korre* (Nyima), *londo* (Korongo), *tomere* (Heiban, Otoro), and *tubele* (Mesakin).[11]

Among the Nuba, according to anthropologist S. F. Nadel, "homosexuals . . . wear women's clothing, do women's work, and adopt women's ways." Transgenderal same-sex marriage is practiced by the Korongo and Mesakin; writes Nadel, "[Transvestite] 'wife' and husband live together and keep a common household."[12]

GENDER-VARIANT AND HOMOEROTICALLY INCLINED SPIRITUAL FUNCTIONARIES

Gender-variant males and those engaging in homoeroticism have traditionally served as spiritual functionaries in a number of African cultures.

Among the Lango, a Nilotic people of the Uganda, gender-variant males engaging in same-sex eroticism were still being called *jo apele* or *jo aboich* in the early twentieth century. *Jo apele* saw themselves as the children of the gynandrous deity Jok. According to anthropologist J. H. Driberg, Jok is said to be "*bala yamo muweto,* like moving air. . . . Jok is an indivisible entity penetrating the whole universe." The most ancient manifestation of the polymorphous Jok is as Atida, also known as Min Jok, the "Mother of God." Atida is a woman warrior, a hunter, and rainmaker.[13]

Jo apele believed that this deity had been present "at their fertilization (*jok manywala,* it was god who begat me)." They were said to have been "transformed into women." It is not clear from Driberg's description whether they were treated differently from birth or whether they underwent a kind of shamanic transformation as adolescents. He suggests, however, that their special status became known to them gradually, in stages. As persons of transformed gender, the *jo apele* were known as *dano mulokere* or *mudoko dako.*[14]

Jo apele dressed in women's garments, decorated their faces like Lango women, and wore their hair long. They took women's names and did the work of women, which may have included serving as spiritual intermediaries, delivering oracles while sitting beneath Atida-Jok's sacred banyan tree. According to Driberg, they "even simulate[d] menstruation." They were formally wedded to men "without offending against Lango law."[15]

While such people have not survived into the late twentieth century in the Konkomba culture of Togo and Ghana, evidence indicates they may have existed in earlier times. This is inferred from a folkloric belief that both homoerotically inclined males and sorcerers (shamans, priests) are believed to "creep into the rooms of sleeping youths at night."[16]

Among the Lugbara, spiritual functionaries are regarded as marginal persons and more specifically as gender-variant; these qualities promote their serving as messengers between the human and spirit worlds.[17] Gender-variant male mediums are named *okule* ("like women"), while female gender-variant mediums are called *agule* ("like men").[18]

Among the Kenyan Meru, the *mugawe*, a "powerful religious leader" who is "considered a complement to . . . male political leaders," wears women's clothing and often women's hairstyles as well. According to sociologist David F. Greenberg, the *mugawe* is "often homosexual, and sometimes marries a man."[19]

Gender-variant male spiritual functionaries have also been documented among the Ila people of what is now southern Zambia. In the early twentieth century, such men were called *mwammi*, "prophets." They "dressed always as women, did women's work such as plaiting baskets, and lived and slept among, but not with, the women."[20]

THE KWANYAMA ARE a tribe of the Ambo people who live in southern Angola. They believe in a supreme being named Kalunga, who may manifest in various forms, and in a host of lesser spirits. Those who serve Kalunga and other spirits are called *kimbanda*.

In the twentieth century, a majority of *kimbanda* have been women. Apparently, however, some gender-variant males have continued to serve alongside female *kimbanda*.

In order to become a *kimbanda*, one has to be chosen by a spirit, following which one undergoes a kind of shamanic transformation. Frequently, divine choosing of a *kimbanda*-to-be first manifests as an illness that cannot be healed by way of herbs or sacrifices alone. The sick person becomes well again only when he or she recognizes and accepts the destiny of spiritual service.[21]

Gender-variant male *kimbanda*, who engage in same-sex eroticism, are referred to as *omasenge*. "An [oma-]*esenge*," ethnologist Carlos Estermann explains, is "essentially a man who has been possessed since childhood by a spirit of female sex." *Omasenge kimbanda* dress like women, do women's work, and "contract marriage" with other men.[22]

Omasenge and female *kimbanda* typically dress in a garment made of genet, a kind of civet cat, decorated with cowrie shells. Their spiritual tasks include performing sacrifices, healing with herbs, divining by way of palmistry and other methods, and working magic.[23]

Omasenge and female *kimbanda* are apparently the only spiritual functionaries among the Kwanyama who are allowed to possess or play the *omakola,* a musical instrument played at initiation rites and other ceremonies to aid in summoning divine beings. The *omakola,* a stringed instrument, is presented to the *kimbanda* at the time of his or her initiation. This link of music and the gender-variant male worshiper is noteworthy, since in certain African and African-diasporic traditions, such men are forbidden to play sacralized musical instruments, especially drums.[24]

As we shall see in a later chapter on the Yoruba religion, African spiritual traditions, and with them certain associations with homoeroticism and gender variance, were carried to the Americas by slaves and others. The gender-variant *kimbanda* also arrived in the New World. The religion of the *kimbanda* blended with other traditions including that of the Yoruba of Nigeria, with the deity Kalunga becoming syncretized with the Yoruba sea goddess Yemayá (or Iemanjá).

In Brazil, the term *calunga,* directly derived from Kalunga, came, as *calungagem,* to be linked to male gender-variant or effeminate behavior, specifically to a swaying gait or a "languid inflection or gesture," while *kimbanda,* by the late sixteenth century, had come to refer to a "passive sodomite," and by the mid-twentieth century, to an African-diasporic tradition associated with destructive magic: Quimbanda.[25]

Among the Zulu, the gender-variant male spiritual guide is also said to undergo a kind of shamanic transformation. This process is referred to as *ukuthwasa,* which suggests a "'coming out' or 'emergence,' as of the appearance of the new moon." The process begins when a certain spirit decides to take possession of, or become the spiritual guardian of, an individual. That individual will then proceed to become an *isangoma,* a "diviner."[26]

The spirits that take possession of new *izangoma* (plural) are those that, unlike spirits of the newly deceased, have "reached the desired complete state of spiritual being," rather like avatars or *bodhisattvas.* They tend to "return to this world through their daughters." Occasionally, however, an ancestral spirit of this type takes possession of a male. In *Body and Mind in Zulu Medicine,* contemporary Zulu anthropologist Harriet Ngubane writes, "Divination is a woman's thing, and if a man gets possessed he becomes a transvestite, as he is playing the role of a daughter rather than that of a son."[27]

As with female *izangoma,* the man experiencing transformation often falls ill. He begins to eat less and less and frequently experiences nausea. He may also experience nervousness, insomnia, and intense itching in the area of the shoulders. Eventually, he has a dream or series of dreams in which a spirit or spirits speak to him, telling him that he is destined to become a diviner. *"We are your ancestors. . . . We have long tried to make your people understand that we want you to be our house—to speak for us."* The individual may also experience a kind of shamanic dismemberment. Some report being "carried away by a river" to a strange place where a group of men dismembers them and then begins, but does not finish, putting them back together again.[28]

The individual often retreats to the wilderness, where he continues to have visionary experiences. Indeed, he is said to become a "house of dreams." He runs wild in the river and may be commanded to catch a snake from the water. This snake is commonly a python or mamba. He then places the snake around his neck. S. G. Lee thinks that this event may be linked to the "*inkata*, the central . . . sacred object of the Zulu," which is covered with a python. Lee also states that in most accounts "the power-giving snake is . . . female." After placing the serpent around his neck, the individual often pulls some plants from the riverbank, some of which he eats and others of which he wraps, alongside the snake, around his neck.[29]

In the next phase of the process, the individual, still experiencing illness, is taken by members of the community to an elder *isangoma*. By this time, the individual is "but skin and bones," his skin parched, his hair falling out. He may also have acquired a soft spot on his head, a sign of *ukuthwasa* suggesting rebirth. The diviner will then begin to heal him. The healing process is also a transformative process, for, in being healed, the individual will metamorphose into an *isangoma*, "possessed of diagnostic and thaumaturgic [magical] power, and a figure of some consequence in the society."[30]

The individual is then taken by one or more *izangoma* to be further healed and initiated. This process may last several months. During this time he is isolated from the community and associates only with *izangoma*. Here he will learn about healing, divination, magic, and other beliefs and practices. It is usually during this time that the male diviner-to-be undergoes gender transformation and may begin to engage in same-sex eroticism. At this time, he "adopt[s] female dress" and begins to "speak in high-pitched tones."[31]

The male *isangoma* finds his complement in the female *isangoma*, described as "active" and "masculine." Unlike other Zulu women, she is allowed to "carry a shield and a spear, those badges of manhood," and she enjoys "meat and beer."[32]

At the time of formal initiation, the initiate is adorned with "crossed strips of magical goatskin over the shoulders," his hair is plaited, he is given beads, and his face and body are painted. He may also carry a serpent. A celebration called the *ukuhunga* takes place at which goats and oxen are sacrificed. The initiate is now believed to have completed the process of *ukuthwasa* and will be allowed to become a full-fledged *isangoma*, called upon by his community to heal, divine, work magic, and perform sacrifices.[33]

Among the Maguzawa, the non-Muslim Hausa of Nigeria, gender-variant, homoerotically inclined men comprise much of the male membership of the *bori* cult.[34] This spiritual tradition, much like others we have encountered, involves a divine being or spirit called a *bori* or *iska*, nicknamed a "divine horseman," deciding to take possession or to "ride" a practitioner, a "horse" or "mare." Practitioners of *bori* tend to be regarded as marginal persons by Muslims. *Bori* faithful include the physically and mentally challenged, prostitutes, and gender-variant and homoerotically inclined persons. Not finding a place in ordinary society, they are accepted and even exalted in *bori*.

Gender-variant, homoerotically inclined male practitioners wear a mixture of men's and women's clothes. While they wear somewhat masculine shirts and trousers, these garments are made from fabrics considered feminine. They speak in soft, high-pitched voices and mimic traditionally feminine gestures. Their functions include cooking for ceremonies and acting as intermediaries between female practitioners who are prostitutes and their male clients.

While these men are sometimes parodied by traditionally masculine practitioners of *bori* and by Muslims, they are generally treated with respect in this primarily pre-Islamic spiritual tradition. They are revered as the children of the *bori* spirit Dan Galadima, the Prince. Galadima is a playboy who wears fancy clothes, reeks of perfume, and loves to gamble. Special songs are sung to him, and sacrifices of rams and cocks are made to him. When he "descends," gender-variant practitioners dance for him "in an effeminate manner." As the children of Dan Galadima, gender-variant, homoerotically inclined practitioners are called *'Yan Daudu* or *'yan hamsin.*[35]

MANY GAY, BISEXUAL, and gender-variant individuals of African heritage with whom I have spoken have told me that they look forward to a time when others will acknowledge the cultural contributions that they and their spiritual ancestors have made. Envisioning themselves as the descendants of the *omasenge kimbanda,* the *izangoma,* the *'Yan Daudu,* and others, they see the love they share in the late twentieth century as imbued, like the lives of their ancestors, with sacred energy. Ron Simmons, an assistant professor of Radio, Television, and Film at Howard University, writes:

> We should acknowledge the "sensitivities" and "talents" within us, the root of which is black gay genius. . . . As we balance and synthesize the male and female energy within our souls, we come closer to the Supreme Being. The inner Voice tells us that our feelings of love are righteous. Black men loving black men is indeed a sacred act.[36]

Lan Zai He, one of the Eight Immortals of the Chinese pantheon, artist and date unknown.

Chapter

3

The Fragrance of Orchids

Roving glances gave rise to beautiful seductions;
Speech and laughter expelled fragrance.
Hand in hand they shared love's rapture,
Sharing coverlets and bedclothes.

Couples of birds in flight,
Paired wings soaring.
Cinnabar and green pigments record a vow:
"I'll never forget you for all eternity."

Ruan Ji[1]

The words of Ruan Ji's poem, composed in the third century C.E., celebrate two young men, Anling (fifth century B.C.E.) and Long Yang (third century B.C.E.), who were loved by kings. The words also subtly evoke the intermingling of same-sex love, gender variance, and sacred experience in ancient China. References to fragrant flowers, perfumes, and incense suggest the possibility of gender variance, while the vow of love in sacred elements of cinnabar and jade bring the experience of love into the domain of the sacred. In this chapter we examine the interplay of same-sex love, gender variance, and sacred experience in premodern China. We will begin with brief examinations of early spiritual traditions and of homoeroticism and gender variance in ancient times.

47

EARLY SPIRITUAL TRADITIONS OF CHINA

The pre-Confucian and pre-Buddhist spiritual traditions of China were shamanic, pantheistic, and matrifocal in character. Goddess reverence was especially strong in southern and central China. Water deities dominated the pantheon, perhaps due to the importance of the rice-growing and fishing industries. While males were included in spiritual service, the chief functionaries were female shamans. Responsibilities of Chinese shamans, like those of other cultures, included communicating with deities and spirits, divining the future, diagnosing and healing illnesses, working magic (especially bringing rain), and guiding the souls of the deceased to the next life. As in other shamanic traditions, ancestor reverence, sacrifice, and reaching altered states of consciousness via drumming, dancing, and other techniques played key roles in early Chinese traditions.

Shamanism may have been partly responsible for the emergence of Taoism (or Daoism) in the sixth century B.C.E. The Tao is the source of all that is, a divine energy pervading all life. In the Tao are contained all dualities, all oppositions. It is from the Tao that both *yin* (traditionally feminine, receptive) and *yang* (traditionally masculine, active) energies spring; thus the Tao reflects gender totality or wholeness. In China, as in many other places, this gender wholeness tends to be perceived as gender variance when it manifests in a mortal male or female. In Taoism, feminine, androgynous/gynandrous, and receptive energies are more highly valued than traditionally masculine energy. Taoists revere Nature as the earthly manifestation of the Tao and believe that people should imitate its fluid patterns rather than accepting constricting patterns of thought and behavior promoted by political leaders and many spiritual and philosophical teachers. While Westerners are familiar with Taoism primarily as a philosophical movement, it is also a spiritual tradition, a matrifocal religion in which the one Tao may divide itself into many deities and spirits. As in shamanic traditions, divination—especially with the aid of the *Yi Jing* (or *I Ching*)—healing, and magic are practiced. Alchemy also holds a special place in Taoism, one of its primary forms being erotic alchemy, similar to the Tantric tradition of India.[2]

Shamanism, goddess reverence, and Taoism were all negatively affected by Confucianism, which stressed, among other things, respect for hierarchies and emotional restraint. Women were perhaps most seriously harmed by Confucianism, since, with its widespread acceptance, women lost not only spiritual but also political and economic power. Male shamans and gender-variant males, however, also suffered. David Hawkes, historian of Chinese culture and translator, writes of the advent of Confucianism: "Shamanism was the Old Religion of China, dethroned when Confucianism became a state orthodoxy and driven into the countryside, where it fared much as paganism did in Christian Europe. . ."[3]

ANDROGYNOUS MALE DEITIES

Among the vast number of deities and spirits, or Immortals, worshiped by the ancient Chinese were those associated with gender variance and possibly with homoeroticism. One of these was the Taoist Immortal Lan Zai He. This deity is described as a pauper who once traversed the earth playing a flute and singing of the transitoriness of life. Whenever he was given money, it is said, he would scatter it on the ground for the poor to retrieve. One day, he became intoxicated while singing and playing at an inn in Feng Yang Fu. The Immortals, then seven in number, noticed him and, admiring him for his wisdom and generosity and amused by his tipsiness, lifted him into the heavens to join them as the eighth Immortal. As he was ascending, one of his shoes dropped. For this reason, he is sometimes depicted as wearing only one shoe. Over the centuries, he has come to be regarded as a patron of musicians—especially flute players—vagabonds, and the poor.

Although "variously stated to have been a woman and a hermaphrodite," Lan Zai He is generally perceived as a man who "could not understand how to be a man (which is perhaps the reason why he has been supposed to be a woman)." Indeed, only one of the Eight Immortals of Taoism is female: the goddess Ho Hsien Ku. As a gender-variant male, Lan Zai He is depicted as a sixteen-year-old wearing feminine attire.[4]

Another Taoist deity (although not one of the Eight Immortals) sometimes regarded as a gender-variant male is Shan Gui, the mountain spirit. While some scholars and spiritual practitioners consider Shan Gui to be a goddess, others, including Arthur Waley and Peng-leung Chan, have described the deity as male. As such, Shan Gui bears likeness to the Hindu deity Kama, the lord of erotic love. Shan Gui is described as wearing a garment made of vines with a belt of mistletoe and as reeking of galingale perfume. He drives a chariot decorated with magnolias and pulled by red leopards. In an ancient poem, Shan Gui asks a worshiper if he (or, possibly, she) is attracted to him. The worshiper explains that while he (or she) had originally come to Shan Gui's grove to be consoled after being treated cruelly by a lover, he (or she) now realizes that the true object of affection is indeed Shan Gui. This experience, the poem suggests, culminates in erotic union between the worshiper and the deity, Shan Gui perhaps being represented by a spiritual functionary. Ritual sexual intercourse often occurred in the bamboo grove over which Shan Gui presided.[5] While the ambiguity of Chinese pronouns does not allow us to confirm absolutely the gender of the worshiper, Peng-leung Chan is among those who believes that "the love in this poem is homosexual." Ritual homosexual intercourse, nicknamed "upside down clouds," perhaps to indicate both secrecy or mystery and the inversion or reversal of sex or gender roles, appears to have been associated with certain places, including mountains and bamboo groves.[6]

SAME-SEX LOVE AND GENDER VARIANCE IN ANCIENT CHINA

Same-sex eroticism was widely accepted in ancient China, especially in pre-Confucianist China, where eroticism in general seems to have been much more exalted than in later epochs. In pre-Confucianist China, few distinctions were drawn between opposite-sex and same-sex bonds or between erotic and so-called platonic relationships. Sociologist Marcel Granet (1884–1946) explains that the same term was used to signify "comrade," "friend," "husband," and "lover," its written character suggesting two hands.[7]

In *The Construction of Homosexuality,* David F. Greenberg asserts that homo-erotic relationships appear to have been "entirely secular; if there had ever been . . . ritualized homosexual . . . rites, no evidence of them has survived." Similarly, in *Passions of the Cut Sleeve: The Male Homosexual Tradition in China,* Bret Hinsch states, "Homosexuality in historic China was not usually ritualized or made a component of religion."[8]

Perhaps Hinsch and Greenberg define ritual experience too narrowly. In ancient China, as in many cultures, ritual or sacred experience may be expressed in veiled forms that have the appearance of being ordinary or mundane, without spiritual import. This is especially true of cultures in which all experience is thought to be imbued with divine energy.

A ceremony celebrating male-male union may have included these words:

For death, or life, or toil,
To thee myself I join
I take thy hand in mine,
With thee I would grow old.[9]

We have already mentioned the same-sex unions that Peng-leung Chan suggests may have taken place in the grove of the androgynous deity Shan Gui.

The interplay of sacred and profane in ancient Chinese experience may be seen even in nicknames given to same-sex eroticism.

For instance, homoeroticism is even in the twentieth century occasionally referred to as *dong xian,* "torn sleeve." This nickname is derived from a tale concerning the Han emperor Ai (reigned 6 B.C.E.–1 C.E.) and his lover, nicknamed Dong Xian. Legend has it that one morning, the emperor wished to get out of bed without disturbing his still-sleeping beloved. In order to do so, he tore or cut the sleeve of the garment he was wearing. In naming the love of one man for another *dong xian,* it would seem that the Chinese paid homage to these lovers. It is evident from literary texts that men-loving men of later epochs looked upon Emperor Ai and Dong Xian as nonbiological ancestors. It is conceivable that when certain men, especially poets, expressed their love for one another, they viewed themselves as ritualistically remembering these lovers of long ago.[10]

Likewise, men naming their love for each other "eating peaches," *yu tao,* may have quietly paid homage to two other like-minded ancestors, Duke Ling of Wei (reigned 534–493 B.C.E.) and Mizi Xia. The duke, it seems, was strolling through an orchard one day when Mizi Xia offered to share his peach with him. This simple action caused the duke to fall instantly in love with the young man. Unfortunately, the expression "eating peaches" or "sharing the peach" is also a cautionary one, as the relationship of these two men was marred by betrayal. Still, it is primarily their joy that is recalled in this expression. While such nicknames as "eating peaches" and "torn sleeve" might seem rather ordinary, even quaint, they take on greater significance when we remember the important role ancestor reverence plays in Chinese spiritual traditions.[11]

In like manner, lovers naming their feelings for each other *long yang jun* may have been subtly acknowledging the love of two other nonbiological forebears, the King of Wei and his beloved Long Yang. Their tale from the Zhou Dynasty tells of how the king became enamored of Long Yang when the young man decided to let a fish he had caught return to the sea. The name Long Yang is, like Dong Xian, probably a nickname. Translated as "dragon-yang-emperor," it suggests that their relationship may, in terms of Taoist erotic alchemy, have been characterized by the equal exchange of *yang* energy.[12]

A fourth nickname for homoeroticism or same-sex love, one that we have already encountered, is "upside-down clouds." This nickname appears to have been linked to the deity Shan Gui, the sacred places of mountain peak and bamboo grove, and Taoist erotic alchemy, clearly indicating ritual or spiritual associations. A fifth nickname, "golden orchid bond," will be discussed below.

In the lives of various other rulers, same-sex eroticism and gender variance appear to have played key roles. Occasionally, these became interwoven with ritual or sacred experience.

The emperor Xiao Wendi (reigned 179–157 B.C.E.) was a religious eclectic who sought to syncretize shamanistic practices with both Taoism and Confucianism. His chief interest, however, was in Taoist alchemy, which emphasizes the balancing of *yin* and *yang* energies. Probably inspired by his alchemical studies, the emperor one night had a homoerotic dream. In this dream, a handsome young boatman ferried him across a celestial river to the abode of the Immortals. Several days after the dream occurred, the emperor encountered a boatman whom he recognized as the young man of his dream. Without hesitating, he asked the young man, nicknamed Deng Tong, to be his lover. The two lived together in the palace until the emperor's death.[13]

Xiao Wudi (reigned 140–87 B.C.E.) was also a religious eclectic. He is credited with founding China's first universities and instituting certain rites honoring the spirits of the earth, rites known as *feng shan*. Like Wendi, Xiao Wudi spent a great amount of time studying Taoist alchemy. Through this study, Wudi hoped to discover an elixir of immortality. Among Wudi's male lovers was the eunuch Li Yannian. Eunuchs, however masculine they might behave, were, due to the loss of genitalia, considered gender-variant persons. (We shall discuss eunuchs at greater length below.) Bestowed with the official title of "Harmonizer of Tunes," Li Yannian was a musician who composed and performed hymns for use in the *feng shan* rites.[14]

Same-sex relationships, like heterosexual ones, were often believed to arise from the cycle of reincarnation. For each individual soul, there exists another with whom it is destined to unite lifetime after lifetime—its "soul mate." While in some lifetimes these souls may come together as opposite-sex partners, in others, they may be joined as partners of the same sex. Some Chinese also believed that both gender variance and homosexuality resulted from an "overly powerful *yin* constellation."[15]

GENDER-VARIANT SHAMANS IN ANCIENT CHINA

While Bret Hinsch states that "the Chinese lacked the basic impetus for institutionalized trans-gendered homosexuality," there is evidence to suggest that
gender-variant persons played significant roles as spiritual leaders in early traditions and, further, that some of these individuals may have engaged in same-sex
eroticism and relationships.[16]

In ancient China, shamans were generally known as *wu*. Gender-variant
shamans, however, were specifically referred to as *shih-niang*, a term meaning
"master girl," which indicates gender transformation. *Shih-niang* dressed in a fusion of feminine, masculine, and priestly clothes. They were described as "not
male and not female," as well as "not dreaming and not awake," the latter phrase
suggesting that they operated in an altered or shamanic state of consciousness.
They were employed in various cults, including that of the canine warrior deity
Pan Hu and the serpent king Ta Wang Shen.[17]

THE TALE OF QU YUAN

As with Moses, Jesus, the Buddha, and Muhammad, it is difficult when speaking of Qu Yuan to separate historical fact from spiritual "truth" and aesthetic em-
bellishment. Bearing this in mind, let us try to reconstruct the life of this partly
historical, partly legendary figure whose experience and works have been commemorated in China for over two millennia.

Qu Yuan is considered China's first major poet, author of the epic *Li Sao (Encountering Sorrow)*, the *Tian Wen (Heavenly Questions)*, and various other works.
He was born around 340 B.C.E. in the kingdom of Chu, on what was said to be the
most auspicious day of the first month of the lunar calendar. From the time of his
birth, astrologers realized that he was destined to become a poet and a shaman.
He was bestowed with two sacred names, True Exemplar and Divine Balance, the
latter a nickname of a mountain goddess.[18] The people of Chu were of Mongolian
heritage and had long practiced shamanism and Goddess reverence, and their
chief deity was the Goddess of Wushan Mountain. By the time of Qu Yuan's birth,
however, shamanism and Goddess reverence were being displaced even in the
kingdom of Chu by Confucianism.[19] Nevertheless, when Qu Yuan was still a
youth, he began to study with an elder shamaness. As a shaman, he would learn
how to divine the future by reading bones and to exorcise demons with bundles of
reeds and peach branches. He would learn how to heal the sick by retrieving their
wandering souls while in a shamanic state of consciousness. He would learn to
make objects fly through the air, to make spirits appear, and to bring rain.[20]

Qu Yuan's gender-variant status is partly suggested by his clothing, which
blended feminine, masculine, and sacred articles. Referring in a poem to his primary garment as a "skirt," he infers that its design was floral. In ancient China,
floral garments were worn primarily by women and shamans, flowers generally

evoking femininity and spirituality. The garment may have included designs of selinea, angelica, water chestnuts, orchids, and lotus blossoms.

Of these, the lotus symbolizes love, the red lotus, erotic love. While the flowers are perceived as feminine, the stem is seen as masculine; thus, the lotus becomes a sign of androgyny or gender variance. The orchid, in Chinese symbolism, is a spring flower. While the flowers of summer and winter, including the peony and the plum, tend to represent traditional gender roles and heterosexuality, the flowers of spring and autumn, including the orchid, iris, lily, magnolia, and chrysanthemum, represent the "intermediate stages between man and woman." Worn by a male shaman, the orchid may thus signify an alternate gender role.[21]

The Chinese shaman, like shamans of other cultures, often dressed in the garments of a divinity he served. If devoted primarily to a goddess, he might dress in feminine garments. However, he might also dress in feminine clothes if, in revering a male deity, he considered himself that deity's spiritual bride. The wearing of feminine garments sometimes suggested homoerotic inclination; Qu Yuan is referred to by women jealous of his beauty as a "wanton," a word typically used to describe prostitutes and gender-variant, homoerotically inclined catamites.[22]

If the wearing of such garments indicated gender variance and perhaps also sexual variance, this desire to integrate *yin* and *yang* within the male self was also reflected by the ingesting of certain foods and beverages. Qu Yuan's diet, like that of Taoist sages, or *hsien*, probably included herbs and flowers as well as mushrooms and gem elixirs. Such substances were considered essential because they provided a rich supply of *ch'i* or vital energy, because they satiated the body so that one did not crave mundane foods, and because ingesting them was said to prolong life. Moreover, eating such substances tended to lighten the physical body, allowing shamans and sages, freed from gravity, to fly. Among the herbs and other flora that Qu Yuan may have included in his diet are angelica, sedge, orchids, melilotus, lichens, asarum, valerian, castor, cinnamon, and chrysanthemums.

In addition to prolonging life, gem elixirs were thought to prevent decomposition of the body after death. Thus drinking them conferred not only spiritual but also physical immortality. Qu Yuan may have drunk elixirs made of finely ground jasper and jade. Like other shamans, he was probably aware that if he indulged in ordinary foods, he would lose his supernatural powers.

Such a diet, however, demanded much determination on the part of the shaman. In the *Li Sao*, Qu Yuan reminds himself that although he frequently feels like fainting from hunger, this is the price he must pay in order to attain enlightenment.

The healing properties of herbs and gems ingested by the shamans are widely known. Chrysanthemum flowers, for instance, are said to reduce stress and to lengthen life, while magnolias and orchids detoxify or purify. These substances, however, also carry erotic energy. As mentioned above, chrysanthemums, magnolias, and orchids all are associated with the "intermediate stage between man and woman." Jade "nectar" or elixir also carries erotic associations. Widely used for decorating belts, girdles, or sashes—articles often sacrificed to deities—jade is a symbol in Chinese alchemy of sexual intercourse and of the coming together of masculine and feminine elements within the psyche; the "jade gate" refers to the vagina and perhaps also to the anus, the "jade stem" to the phallus, and "jade fluid" to semen.[23]

While Qu Yuan undoubtedly served both male and female deities, it is evident that in his life goddess reverence predominated. The theme of goddess reverence is dominant in his poem *Li Sao* and in other works attributed to him. Indeed, it is from his *Li Sao* that we learn a great deal about goddess worship in ancient China. The worship of goddesses remained strongest in Qu Yuan's homeland, southern China, since the northern Chinese had adopted more patriarchal traditions at a much earlier date. While there were goddesses of the sun and other celestial bodies, of music, silk spinning, and other professions, female deities were most often linked to water and to entities and objects associated with water: the moon, the rainbow, water dragons, serpents, carp, and crabs. These goddesses were thought to dwell primarily in seas, lakes, rivers, springs, and pools. They were considered the source of *yin* energy.[24]

Among the goddesses mentioned in works by, attributed to, or about Qu Yuan are Fu Fei, Nu Wa, Xi Ho, Nu Qi, the Lady of Tu Shan Mountain, Xian E, Xi Wang Mu, and the goddess(es) of the Xiang River.

In the *Li Sao*, Qu Yuan searches for the home of Fu Fei. Goddess of the Luo River, Fu Fei is usually depicted as a hybrid being, half female and half serpent, dragon, whale, or swan. A goddess of the air, sun, moon, and waters, she is associated with shamanism and with the invention of the drum.[25]

Qu Yuan implores the goddess Nu Wa to aid him in his search for the abode of Fu Fei. Nicknamed "Lame Beauty" because she has the lower body of a serpent, dragon, or snail, Nu Wa is believed by many to have created the universe.[26] Of Nu Wa, translator Stephen Field notes, "Modern scholars speculate that remnants of her myth are evidence of an ancient matrilineal culture."[27]

Xi Ho is the mother of the ten suns of Chinese cosmology. It is she who drives the suns across the heavens. Nu Qi (Mother Star) is a virgin goddess of the Tail constellation. The Lady of Tu Shan Mountain is a bear goddess associated with shamanism. She is believed to have invented the "southern style of singing . . . used by Chu shamans [like Qu Yuan] in their invocations." Xian E, also known as Wang Shu, is the goddess of the moon.[28]

Xi Wang Mu is referred to indirectly by Qu Yuan in the *Li Sao*, primarily in association with the Xiang goddess(es) and the magical paradise of Kun Lun. Known as the "Queen Mother of the West," she may appear in various forms. In one of these, she is a death-wielding sorceress with disheveled hair, the teeth and voice of a tiger, and a leopard's tail. In another, she is a beautiful fairy who grants immortality to her devotees. In this latter aspect, she dwells in a palace of precious jewels, surrounded by fairy maidens and male fairy courtiers who "wave the feathers of their marvellous fans" to cool their mistress.[29]

The goddess of the Xiang River was in the earliest times depicted as a single deity and in later times as a solitary being as well as a divine female couple, Nu Ying and O Huang. She and they are believed to inhabit not only the Xiang but also the Yangtze River and Lake Dong Ting. She and they are associated with torrential rains, spring and autumn—the "intermediate"—seasons, wind instruments, the special concerns of women, and shamanic flight.[30]

Qu Yuan, like other shamans and shamanesses, offered sacrifices to the goddesses he revered. Sacrifices to aquatic goddesses were often dropped into the water. The shaman would use a boat, often one painted with floral designs or decorated with fresh or dried flowers and embellished with figures of phoenixes and dragons. He would sail to the middle of a body of water or to an island or shoreline shrine, where he would shower the water with offerings. He may have been accompanied by a flotilla of boats crowded with worshipers and spectators.

To aquatic goddesses like Fu Fei and the Xiang goddess(es) he would sacrifice pieces of jade, often a thumb ring or sash with dangling ornaments (an erotic symbol). For the Xiang goddess(es), he may have constructed a floating shrine in a lake. Such a shrine is described in a poem sometimes attributed to Qu Yuan that is addressed to the Xiang goddesses. The shrine is shaped like a temple and constructed with lotuses, irises, orchids, lilies, and cinnamon.[31]

Preparing to meet the Goddess was an important rite undertaken by shamans. They would first bathe in purified water scented with iris and orchid and then dress in the garments of the deity they intended to visit or summon. Holding a bouquet of herbs and flowers, they would then dance until they fell into a shamanic state of consciousness. In this state they would journey to the submarine, subterranean, or celestial abode of the deity.[32]

Perhaps reflecting the rapid patriarchalization of the world in which Qu Yuan lived, the shaman's ability to communicate with the Goddess had become impaired. The Goddess had come to be seen as somewhat distant, evasive, unapproachable. Because the Goddess frequently chose not to appear, the relationship between the shaman and the Goddess came to be marked by an element of disappointment or sorrow, a relationship that David Hawkes describes as "larmoyant" or "lachrymose," that is, "tearful."[33]

The "larmoyant" relationship with the Goddess experienced by Qu Yuan and other Chinese shamans was mirrored in his relationship with the King of Huai. As a young man the shaman-poet came to live at the palace, where he became intimate with the king. Such a relationship would not have surprised anyone, since same-sex unions, as we have seen, were common in ancient China. Moreover, shamans rarely joined in traditional marriages, as they were already considered married to deities.[34] In a rather apologetic tone, Peng-leung Chan writes, "If Ch'u Yuan happened to be a homosexual, it is by no means a disgrace . . . [His] originality and creativity may also be the result of homosexuality."[35]

In the *Li Sao*, the shaman-poet Qu Yuan describes both his quest for the Goddess and his love for the king with metaphors of flowers. As we have seen, flowers in ancient China were linked to femininity, androgyny or gender variance, and spirituality and perhaps also were a sign of homosexuality.[36] In Qu Yuan's poem he refers to the king as the "Fragrant One" and the "Fairest One." The term used for "fragrant" is *quan*, which literally means an iris. The term used for "fairest one" is *ling xiu*, which suggests not only a shaman but also a beautiful person. In Hawkes's view, Qu Yuan's use of *ling xiu* indicates that he may see the king as an embodiment of a deity, perhaps Fu Fei, crowned with "feathers, flowers, and jewels."[37]

While stressing that the use of floral images is a poetic convention in Chinese literature, Hawkes nevertheless suggests that these terms may infer a homoerotic relationship: "Is the poet imagining himself as a handsome, flower-decked youth and his king as a beautiful maiden whom he seeks to woo? . . . One possibility . . . is that the relationship here imagined is a homosexual one: flower-decked male in pursuit of a beautiful male lover."[38]

Floral-inspired references to the king and the shaman-poet himself seem especially significant when examined in the light of references to orchids in the *Li Sao* and related works. Wolfram Eberhard points out that in the *I Ching*, the thirteenth hexagram reads:

> But when two people are at one in their inmost hearts,
> They shatter even the strength of iron or bronze.
> And when two people understand each other in their
>   inmost hearts,
> Their words are sweet and strong, like the fragrance
>   of orchids.[39]

Orchids, in Chinese symbology, bear a special relationship to same-sex love, for yet another nickname for a homoerotic or lesbian relationship is golden orchid bond, *jin lan qi*.[40]

What is especially interesting is that both the shaman-poet and the king are described in feminine terms, implying a sophisticated form of a transgenderal homoerotic relationship. What is more, if Qu Yuan did indeed look upon the king as a mortal embodiment of the Goddess, then it becomes clear why he chose to interweave the tale of his search for the Goddess with that of his love for the king. He apparently viewed both the Goddess and the king as forms of the Divine Beloved.

The shaman-poet realized, however, that unlike the Goddess, the king of Huai was not immortal; he, like the flower, was destined to bloom and fade. Qu Yuan also realized that the majority of men were unworthy of such devotion; he referred to these others, especially those whose lives were ruled by jealousy, ambition, and greed, as "rank weeds."[41]

Qu Yuan uses other images as well to describe his relationships with the Goddess and the king. He compares himself to a horse and the Goddess and king to riders, a metaphor found also in possession-trance traditions. The horse itself is a symbol of androgyny, since in Chinese symbology it is perceived as feminine or *yin*, while its eyes are symbols of the male urethral opening. Qu Yuan also links horse and rider with his shamanic chariot, of phoenix design and pulled by dragons. Again, this hybrid symbol suggests androgyny, with the dragons representing *yang* and the phoenixes *yin*. Other symbols of androgyny used by the shaman-poet to describe his relationships with the Goddess and the king are bridges, gates, and rainbows, all serving to connect *yin* to *yang*. In Chinese alchemy, bridges may represent the area between the genitalia and the anus, while gates may represent either the vagina or the anus. According to Peng-leung Chan, the rainbow is an "ambisexual" symbol associated with the serpent (as in certain African and African-diasporic traditions) and representing the "copulation of the two ethers [*yin* and *yang*]," often but not always embodied by females and males, respectively. Images of clouds and dew also serve as metaphors for the shaman-poet's relationships. In Chinese alchemy, the expression "clouds and rain" refers to heterosexual lovemaking, while "upside-down clouds," as noted above, refers to homosexual lovemaking. Dew often symbolizes "the grace and beauty which flow downwards from the Emperor" to his subjects—here, to the shaman-poet as the king's beloved—but it may also signify a "fleeting love affair which passes like morning dew."[42]

Beyond his use of floral and other imagery, the shaman-poet employs a term that indicates the attraction Qu Yuan felt for the king as well as the latter's gender variance. This is the term *mei-ren*, "beautiful person," usually used of women. In early times, however, it also referred to "sexually ambiguous" individuals.[43]

QU YUAN'S RELATIONSHIP with the king apparently began on a joyous note and was a source of nourishment and inspiration to both partners. "There was a time," the shaman-poet recalls, "when he spoke with me in frankness." This period of joy was, however, brief. From the outset, the king's love of flattery and his apparent inability to distinguish trustworthy from untrustworthy persons marred his relationship with Qu Yuan. Although Qu Yuan warned the king that both the males and females of the court were jealous of their relationship and would stop at nothing to destroy their love for each other, the king ultimately placed his trust in those who claimed Qu Yuan was seeking only wealth and political power. "The Fragrant One refused to examine my true feelings," the poet tells us. "He lent ear instead to slander, and raged against me." After declining to appear at a farewell rendezvous, the king banished the shaman-poet, who wandered in exile, emotionally devastated, until his death. Meanwhile, the king's trust in the untrustworthy led to his downfall and imprisonment. Some say that he died in captivity.[44]

On the fifth day of the fifth lunar month, probably during the final decade of the fourth century B.C.E., Qu Yuan drowned himself in the Miluo River, a small river in the vicinity of Lake Dong Ting, sacred to the Xiang goddesses and near the city of Changsha. It is believed that Qu Yuan committed suicide for two reasons: first, because of the king's betrayal, and second, because this was a day on which shamans traditionally sacrificed themselves so that the gods might be pleased and humanity prosper. It is further conceivable that his suicide was linked to the alienation he must have felt in the face of antishamanic, antimatrifocal forces that were then impinging upon the cultures of southern and central China.[45]

THE SEVEN SAGES OF THE BAMBOO GROVE

In the third century C.E., homoeroticism, male gender variance, and sacred experience became intertwined in a Taoist circle known as the Zhulin Qi Xian, the "Seven Sages of the Bamboo Grove."

The founding members of the circle were Ruan Ji, Xi Kang, Shan Tao, Ruan Xian, Liu Ling, Xiang Xiu, and Wang Rong. At their meetings, they wandered about in a bamboo grove (the place of perfection) drinking, dancing, playing music, and discussing aspects of Taoist philosophy and alchemy.[46]

At least two of the circle's founders, Ruan Ji and Xi Kang, are "generally regarded as homosexuals."[47]

Xi Kang, born in 223 C.E., spent his youth "sitting under a willow tree . . . practicing the art of breathing with a view to securing immortality" and "experimenting in the transmutation of metals." In later years, he became an accomplished lutenist, poet, and essayist, the author of a number of Taoist treatises including *Poetical Essay on the Lute* and *Dissertation on the Nourishment of the Vital Principle*.[48]

Although Xi Kang married into the royal family and received a government appointment, neither marriage nor political power seemed to interest him. Indeed, it was lack of interest in these matters that cost him his life. The emperor, who admired Xi Kang, announced under great pressure that Xi Kang was a traitor and that he should be put to death. Although "three thousand disciples offered to take the place of their beloved master," the execution was carried out, Xi Kang meeting his fate with "fortitude, calmly . . . playing upon his lute."[49]

Hinsch points out that Xi Kang was described in Taoist (or Neo-Taoist) terms, as having the "grace of a dragon and the beauty of a phoenix." What Hinsch does not say, however, is that this expression, in describing Xi Kang as exhibiting both dragon-*yang* and phoenix-*yin* qualities, is depicting him in androgynous terms.[50]

Although in his youth Xi Kang was deeply attached to a man named Lu Ngan, Ruan Ji was to become his most intimate companion. Born in 210 C.E., Ruan Ji was a wild, rebellious young man who spent much of his time wandering in the hills and shutting himself up in his room reading. Extremely close to his mother, it is said that he wept tears of blood when she died. As a musician, he was known especially for his whistling and for a treatise on the wind instrument called the *cheng*. Although he married, the great love of his life was Xi Kang. Ruan Ji spent the final years of his life wandering about naked, drinking excessively, and performing erotic dances. All these were elements of his own path, which had been inspired by Taoism and the Seven Sages circle and which came to be called "free wandering." By the time of his death, he had gathered many disciples who became known as the "unimpeded ones."[51]

Ruan Ji celebrated same-sex love in his poetry, and one of his most celebrated poems is quoted in part at the beginning of this chapter. As noted above, references to fragrance in this poem may connote—as we have just seen in the work of Qu Yuan—male gender variance, homoeroticism, and reverence of the feminine principle (as a goddess or *yin*). Also as noted above, the cinnabar and jade pigments used by the lovers to inscribe their vow of union evoke the practice of Taoist alchemy. While the expression "cinnabar and jade (or green)" is occasionally used to mean simply paint, here these substances carry greater significance. We have already seen, in our discussion of Qu Yuan, that jade refers in Chinese alchemy to both female and male genitalia, to sexual intercourse, and to androgyny. Jade is also believed to confer longevity and even physical immortality; folklorist Wolfram Eberhard notes that it was "an ancient custom to place a piece of jade in the mouth of a dead person in the belief that this prevented decomposition." Cinnabar, a reddish mineral containing mercury and sulfur, the "basic substance of Taoist alchemy," not only signified the vagina (the "cinnabar cave"), which in a homoerotic context may become symbolic of the anus, but also was used in elixirs to confer, like jade, longevity and immortality. These images suggest that male lovers may not only have ritualized their unions but also practiced Taoist alchemy in an attempt to heighten their lovemaking and to ensure the immortality of their souls and their relationships.[52]

Xi Kang and Ruan Ji may also have shared a brief erotic interlude with a third member of the circle, Shan Tao, a Taoist alchemist. Like Xi Kang and Ruan Ji, he was married and held political office, but also like them, he enjoyed being with male companions.

One day, after talking with a friend whose husband had been having an affair with another man, Shan Tao's wife asked her husband if he might also be so inclined. He replied yes. Wishing to understand this type of relationship better, she then asked her husband to invite Xi Kang and Ruan Ji to spend the night at their house and then allow her to secretly observe them making love. She did so and was quite impressed. Incidentally, Shan Tao was nicknamed "Uncut Jade," which in Taoist erotic alchemy signifies an uncircumcised penis. It is conceivable that all three men, and probably Shan Tao's wife as well, were familiar with and perhaps even practiced Taoist erotic alchemy. The relationship of the three men was described as one having both "the power to break metal" and "the fragrance of orchids."[53]

EUNUCHS

Eunuchs occupy a prominent position in Chinese history from remote antiquity to the twentieth century, and throughout that history they have linked themes of gender variance, homoeroticism, and sacred work.

While a eunuch is typically described as a male whose penis and testicles have been removed, Chinese texts indicate that many eunuchs were deprived only of their testicles. Still others retained both penis and testicles and merely pretended to be eunuchs. Young men usually became eunuchs for one of several reasons: because they had been taken captive; because they had committed a crime punishable by castration; because they had been born to poor parents who had sold them to wealthy individuals; or because they desired to become eunuchs.

Poverty, however, produced the greatest number of eunuchs, and, as Asian studies scholar Ulrike Jugel explains, the institutionalizing of eunuchs allowed many Chinese of low economic status to achieve both wealth and power. In 135 C.E., eunuchs were first allowed to adopt children, thus not only permitting them to parent but also increasing their power substantially. Incidentally, the Chinese eunuch parent may be one of the earliest examples in history of the gender-variant and (often) homoerotically inclined father. Although later epochs witnessed antieunuch hostility, it is evident that a great number of eunuchs were still living in China at the end of the nineteenth century.[54]

Homoerotic relationships involving eunuchs often began in adolescence, when a eunuch was chosen to be the companion of a royal or noble youth. Eunuchs were chosen "according to criteria of beauty and willingness." Their relationships with royalty often lasted into and throughout adulthood, with the eunuchs enjoying "honors, wealth, favors, and political power." The preferred form of sexual intercourse in these relationships was anal intercourse, with the eunuchs taking the receptive role. Many noneunuch males apparently preferred eunuch to either female or noneunuch male lovers; some, like the ruler Yuan-ti, "preferred eunuchs exclusively."[55]

Eunuchs have traditionally been associated with sacred experience. Indeed, it was believed that the eunuch carried magical power with him wherever he went, in the form of an urn in which his genitalia were preserved. These urns were often exhibited publicly during rituals that celebrated a eunuch's attaining a new degree of political or spiritual power or wealth. When a eunuch died, the urn was buried alongside him.[56]

A number of myths link eunuchs with the supernatural. In one such myth, a man named Jen Ku is penetrated anally by a shaman wearing a feathered costume. As a result, Jen Ku becomes pregnant. When the time comes for him to give birth, the shaman reappears. He slices off Jen Ku's penis and proceeds to deliver the "child," a serpent. In ancient Chinese sacred traditions, the serpent is a *yin* symbol. In this particular context, it is linked to gender-variant homoeroticism. Jen Ku, now a eunuch and a shaman himself, goes to live at the palace, where he becomes intimate companion to the emperor.[57]

During the Han dynasty (202 B.C.E.–8 C.E.), shamanism, which had experienced a decline with the emergence of Confucianism, enjoyed a vogue among those who felt Confucianism to be too constricting when practiced by itself. This led to the development of a syncretic spiritual tradition blending elements of Confucianism with shamanism and Taoism. Women and gender-variant males—in the form of eunuchs—once more became, for a time, the chief spiritual functionaries.

As shamans, eunuchs took part in various significant rituals. Among these were sacrifices to the deities, ceremonies installing new rulers, hunting rites, funerals, and seasonal celebrations. At funerals, eunuchs acted as ritual musicians, playing flutes and drums to aid in transporting the soul from this life to the next.

At the winter solstice, eunuch shamans, wearing black robes and red headdresses, exorcised demons and invoked the spirits of the twelve beneficent animals of Chinese astrology.

Eunuchs were also believed to be highly skilled in the magical, divinatory, and healing arts. They divined by observing the movements of the four winds and by interpreting the oracles of the *I Ching* and were said to be expert acupuncturists.[58]

❧

BY THE MIDTWENTIETH century, only traces of the ancient association of gender variance, same-sex eroticism, and sacred experience might be found. In the few existing cases, moreover, the association was found primarily in parodied or burlesque form.

In the 1930s, for instance, anthropologist Cornelius Osgood described a shamanic ritual in which a traditionally masculine shaman was assisted by a man
wearing makeup and feminine attire—"elaborate shoes, a green skirt, and a red
jacket with a black vest on top of it," all these articles "covered with rich embroidery." He also wore the headdress of a shamaness. During the ceremony, this assistant helped the shaman to enter an altered state of consciousness by playing a
gong and a shaman's drum. Following the ritual sacrifice of a chicken and other
events, the transvestite assistant and a second assistant engaged in simulated
erotic activity. At the climax of the rite, the deities and spirits being invoked descended. At this time, the transvestite assistant began prophesying. From the observer's description of this event, it would seem that the ritual alternated between
the sublime and the carnivalesque.[59]

In Taiwan and Hong Kong, homoerotically inclined and gender-variant persons currently face great discrimination and are typically prevented, especially in
Christianity, from becoming spiritual leaders. In the People's Republic of China,
spiritual experience is generally discouraged, and individuals not conforming to
rigid gender roles and prescribed heterosexual behavior face arrest, torture, and
execution. In the United States, however, and presumably elsewhere, gay, lesbian,
and gender-variant individuals are gradually becoming aware of the significant
roles played by their erotic and spiritual forebears in ancient China. In 1992, the
ancient, legendary name *Cut Sleeve* (*dong xian*), applied to the beloved of the Han
emperor Ai, was given to a documentary concerning the lives of contemporary
Asian-American lesbians and gay men. At this time I also learned that some gay
male Chinese-Americans were beginning to adopt Lan Zai He as a patron of gay
and bisexual men.

In the late twentieth century, the Chinese, Chinese-Americans, and others continue to honor the shaman-poet Qu Yuan annually on the fifth day of the fifth
month of the lunar calendar with such things as dragon boat races and offerings
of *zongzi* dumplings, which are often cast into bodies of water. Most, however, except for certain scholars and gay people, know Qu Yuan only as a poet, patriot, or
hero of the working class. The tales of his search for the Goddess and his love for
the king have been erased; they lie buried in the depths of the sea.

PART TWO

Earth and Moon

❧

EARTH AND MOON

*I*T IS 1981, and a chill, clear evening in San Francisco. We have gathered at the Women's Building to celebrate the Feast of Flames, the renewing of light at winter's end. The darkness of the room is transformed as each white candle is lit on the altar. On pieces of paper, we write our wishes. We burn them so that they, like incense, will be accepted by the Goddess.

Sweet incense, they say, soothes the spirit of Inanna. In the great temple, there are those who can tell the future by observing incense flow. The worshipers grow silent as the priestesses and priests enter the room. "Great Inanna," the priestess chants, lifting her eyes and palms to the heavens, "accept our offerings. Hear our prayers." The *assinnu* priest, his long, ebony hair almost touching the ground, seats himself, takes his harp, and sings a hymn to the Goddess.

"This is the tale of Asushunamir, created by Enki to rescue Inanna from the Land of No Return."

Inanna, the Queen of the Heavens, was given great gifts by Enki the Wise. Wisdom, justice, love, the sacred women, and the fruit of the vine. That gift which saved her from death Enki fashioned from the dirt beneath his fingernails. A being of light, renewing of light, *Asushunamir*.

He-she whose face is brilliant. Beautiful in countenance. *Asushunamir*.

Clothed in stars. Both male and female. Companion to Inanna. *Asushunamir*.

The spell of Ereshkigal, the Queen of the Dead, could not possess this luminescent being.

Yet she was charmed by Asushunamir's beauty, moved by his-her voice, amused by the creature's dance. She demanded a great feast be held in his-her honor, the best wine brought to the table. She dreamed of taking this beautiful being to bed, of keeping it with her in the Land of the Dead.

But Asushunamir was careful to pour the wine upon the floor and to eat no food prepared by ghosts. When she had fallen into a stupor, the man-woman asked her if he-she might taste the water of life, which Ereshkigal kept locked in a cellar. The water of which Enki had spoken when Asushunamir came into the world. The water with which one must be sprinkled to pass through the seven gates of Irkalla, to renew one's life on the earth. Ereshkigal cried out, "Namtar, bring the jug containing the water of life! I shall grant the wish of this charming creature!"

When Ereshkigal fell asleep, Asushunamir made his way to the lampless cell where Inanna, held captive, lay dying. He-she sprinkled Inanna with the water of life. As the drops fell upon her, weakness left her body. Her eyes opened, and she breathed as a child might.

Beautiful and flowing with the energy of life, she quickly made her way through the seven gates of Irkalla, ascending to earth and bidding the flowers grow. The people returned to their planting, their weaving, their making of wine. They held a great feast in her honor.

Asushunamir was not as fortunate. Ereshkigal awakened as he-she approached the seventh gate, and neither dance nor song nor praises of her beauty could extinguish the fires of passion turned to hate.

"The food of the gutter shall be your food!" great Ereshkigal cried. "The drink of the sewer shall be your drink. In the shadows shall you abide." Having pronounced her curse upon the creature, she banished Asushunamir.

When Inanna learned of the curse placed upon the man-woman, she wept and spoke so that no one might hear. "The power of Ereshkigal is great. No one dares defy her. But I may soften her curse upon you, as spring arrives to banish winter. For many ages you will suffer. Those who are like you, my *assinnu* and *kalum* and *kurgarru* and *kalaturru*, lovers of men, kin to my sacred women, shall be strangers in their homes. Their families will keep them in the shadows and will leave them nothing. The drunken shall smite their faces, and the mighty shall imprison them.

"But if you will remember me, how you were born from the light of the stars to save me from an early death, to rid the earth of winter, then I shall harbor you and your kind. You shall be my children, and I shall make you my priests. I shall give you the gift of prophecy, the wisdom of the earth and moon. You shall banish illness from my children, as you have stolen me from the clutches of Ereshkigal.

"And when you robe yourselves in my robes, I shall dance in your feet and sing in your throats. And no man shall be able to resist your enchantments.

"When the earthen jug is brought from Irkalla, lions shall leap in the deserts, and you shall be freed from the spell of Ereshkigal. Once more you shall be called Asushunamir. Being clothed in light. Your kind shall be called Those Whose Faces Are Brilliant. Those Who Have Come to Renew the Light. The blessed ones of Inanna."

THREE THOUSAND YEARS have passed since the *assinnu* sang this song and the priestess of Inanna raised her palms to the heavens. And yet their spirits haunt this room. Once more, a man invokes the Queen of Heaven with his harp, a priestess leads us in a spiral dance.

When my lover's daughter was five, we took her to see Judy Chicago's *Dinner Party*. "Papa," she asked, "when are the goddesses coming?" They are here tonight, Mariya, they are with us in this room. "*Isis Astarte Diana Hecate Demeter Kali Inanna. Isis Astarte Diana Hecate Demeter Kali Inanna.*"[1]

Mesopotamian singer Ur-Nanshe, Mari, ca. 2600–2300 B.C.E.

Lands of Milk and Honey

It was a good land.
Figs were in it and grapes. It had
more wine than water.
Plentiful was its honey, abundant its olives.
Every kind of fruit was on its trees.
Barley was there, and emmer wheat.

the Egyptian traveler Sinuhe,
describing the land of Canaan[1]

T wo religions of the ancient Near East fostered the expression of male gender variance, homoeroticism, and sacred experience. In the religions of both Mesopotamian goddess Inanna/Ishtar and the Canaanite goddess Athirat (or Asherah), these elements intermingled freely.

THE EMERGENCE OF PATRIARCHY, THE NEAR EAST, AND OUR DOMAIN

During the transition from the Paleolithic to the Neolithic that occurred between fourteen to seven thousand years ago, hunters and gatherers in many cultures were gradually displaced by farmers. Likewise, shamans and shamanesses were becoming displaced by, or were metamorphosing into, priests

and priestesses. The revering of nature deities appears to have continued throughout the Neolithic, despite the development of the priesthood, with the Great Goddess in her myriad aspects remaining dominant.

In the view of archaeologist Marija Gimbutas and others, Neolithic cultures
were relatively matrifocal, peaceful, and nonhierarchical in their social arrangement. It should be noted that proponents of this theory do not necessarily believe
that matriarchy preceded patriarchy; as writer Riane Eisler suggests, it is more
likely that roughly egalitarian societies, in which women and men shared responsibilities and power, preceded patriarchal forms of cultural organization.

Several millennia ago, many Neolithic agrarian cultures were transformed into
patriarchal, militaristic, and class-oriented cultures. Some scholars suggest that
the earlier cultures were violently disrupted and ultimately subjugated by intrud-
ing bands of herders migrating from the region of present-day Russia. Others believe that patriarchy was not thrust upon other cultures from the outside but
rather that it developed from within, at least partly brought about by the living
conditions at the time. Rapidly increasing populations were crowded together in
villages, towns, and cities that lay in relatively fertile areas. Such living conditions
fostered the development of caste systems and at the same time inspired militarism, imperialism, and colonialism. Both theories indicate that militarism was
encouraged by the growing use of metal weapons and of horses and horse-drawn
chariots as vehicles of war. Whether from without or within, however, patriarchal
systems of government and religion continued to gain in strength from the fourth
millennium B.C.E. onward, in South Asia, the Near East, Europe, and elsewhere. I
do not wish to condemn patriarchal civilizations out of hand; we must admit that
Euripides, Lao Tze, Joan of Arc, Leonardo da Vinci, Sei Shonagon, Clara Schu-
mann, Mahatma Gandhi, Golda Meir, Anwar Sadat, Wole Soyinka, and countless
others have made valuable contributions while being reared in patriarchies. Yet I
do wish to stress that the transition from Neolithic to patriarchal civilization appears to have been marked especially by women's loss of economic, political, and
priestly powers and by an increasing victimization of persons performing gender-
variant behavior and engaging in certain forms of same-sex eroticism.

While patriarchal rulers, warriors, and priests established the worship of militaristic male deities of sun and sky, they did not entirely succeed in eradicating
the reverence of female, androgynous, and nonmilitaristic male deities, nor
could they completely rid society of their worshipers. Female and gender-variant
male spiritual intermediaries continued to serve, for a time, in temples and in
sacred groves, as they had once served as shamanesses and shamans. Now, however, they did so under the watchful eyes of the fathers. Eventually, patriarchally
oriented, traditionally masculine, heterosexual males would replace their female
and gender-variant male predecessors.

With the emergence of patriarchal cultures came growing distinctions between
"masculinity" and "femininity," with so-called feminine traits being devalued, *especially when expressed by males.* This apparently led to a fairly self-conscious,
flamboyant, and even rebellious expression of gender variance, gender wholeness,

or androgyny by certain groups of males, with the nude bird-men of Addaura and the mixed-dressing shamans of Siberia becoming the transvestite priests of Near Eastern, West Asian, and European antiquity.

Although several forms of homoerotic expression had emerged during the Paleolithic, only the intergenerational form was now tolerated, while egalitarian and transgenderal forms suffered condemnation. Indeed, in patriarchal Greece, intergenerational, or pederastic, homoeroticism would become institutionalized, celebrating as it did the rule of the powerful over the less powerful. In other patriarchal cultures, however, any expression of homoeroticism might result in the death of one, both, or all of the partners. This was especially true of cultures that perceived homosexuality as a "feminizing" of the men involved.[2]

WE KNOW LITTLE of the indigenous and pre-Sumerian populations of Mesopotamia. From archaeological remains, we can tell, however, that they were not only prosperous farmers but also highly skilled artisans. Sometime during the fourth millennium B.C.E., one of these cultures, the Ubaid, was disrupted and colonized by Semitic-speaking intruders. The military power of these intruders, whom we know as the Sumerians, increased substantially with their inventions of bronze weapons and wheeled chariots in the third millennium. Sumerians, however, were not only warriors. Indeed, their skills in art and literature led to great accomplishments in these fields. The Sumerians were conquered by the Akkadians in the middle of the third millennium B.C.E. During the following two millennia, Mesopotamia would be ruled in succession by the Amorites, Kassites, Hittites, Assyrians, Medes, Chaldeans, and Persians. Needless to say, warfare was ever present.

While attitudes toward women differed from one epoch to another, we may say that, in general, nonelite women, like nonelite men, were without power, while the power of elite women depended largely upon their ability to satisfy their husbands, fathers, and other men. Even celebrated women, such as the poet and priestess Enkheduanna, daughter of King Sargon of Akkad, had little security. When Enkeduanna's father died, the new ruler of Ur removed her from the office of high priestess of the goddess Inanna.

Both homoerotic and gender-variant traits were apparently considered *mes*, qualities distributed by the gods; in late twentieth-century terminology, we might say that the Mesopotamians were *essentialists* in this regard. Thus, it does not appear that males expressing gender-variant behavior or engaging in same-sex eroticism were universally condemned by Mesopotamians, as they were by a majority of Egyptians and Israelites, although certain texts suggest that they frequently suffered disrespect and ridicule. What is clear is that, in spite of the case of Enkheduanna, both women and gender-variant, homoerotically inclined males found themselves most protected and most respected in the realm of the sacred. If a campaign like those undertaken by the rulers of Israel and Judah against the Canaanites was ever conducted by Mesopotamians against female and gender-variant male spiritual functionaries, history has left us no record of this event.[3]

THE GODDESS INANNA/ISHTAR

While empires rose and fell in the Fertile Crescent, the worship of the goddess Inanna/Ishtar remained a constant in the lives of Mesopotamians. Ancient texts say that Inanna/Ishtar controls the seasonal cycles as well as those of human life. She bestows bounty in crops, and is a patron of artists and craftspersons. She is also associated with eroticism, especially as linked to spiritual enlightenment. As such, she is a patron of *hierodules* or "sacred prostitutes" as well as of noncultic prostitutes. Indeed, she is often depicted as a hierodule or prostitute, "visiting 'taverns' and converting her own temples into such establishments." As a patron of prostitutes, she is sometimes depicted as an owl, or hybrid woman/owl, "which, like the harlot, comes out at dusk." In this aspect, she is called Ninnina, "Mistress Owl." She is also a patron of gender-variant women; as such, she was served by gender-variant, perhaps lesbian, priestesses titled *sinnisat zikrum*.[4]

THE "WOMEN-MEN" PRIESTS OF THE GODDESS

Inanna/Ishtar, who will hereafter be referred to as Inanna, is also a patron of gender-variant men. She was served by gender-variant male priests who were divided into several groups, including the *assinnu, kurgarru, kulu'u,* and *kalu[m]* (who may have been identified with the *kulu'u*). In later times, they all may have been generally referred to as *kalbu,* a Babylonian term for a servant of the Goddess. The term *kalbu* is related to the Semitic *kalebh,* which may signify either a dog or a gender-variant person who serves the Goddess. As a faithful companion, the dog was a common symbol for the male worshiper of the Goddess, and the Sumerian goddess Gula was pictured accompanied by a dog. Male priests of the Goddess were also generally referred to as *sal-zikrum,* "women-men." As such, they were considered as being *essentially different* from other men, their collective identity a gift of the gods, a *me*.[5]

Evidence suggests that the gender-variant priests of Inanna dressed in a combination of feminine, masculine, and sacred garments. They also let their hair grow long and wore colorful necklaces. A hymn to Inanna indicates that they may have worn a bifurcated costume, with masculine articles making up the left side of the costume and feminine articles the right. The priestesses of Inanna apparently wore a complementary costume, with the masculine and feminine articles reversed. What a spectacle of androgyny this must have seemed to the Mesopotamian audience of the third millennium B.C.E.! In terms of gender variance, certain texts indicate that at least some of the priests may have been eunuchs.[6]

Their gender-variant status was also expressed in the language they used. During a certain period of their history, they spoke in the Sumerian dialect of Emesal. This dialect, distinct from Eme-ku, the dialect used by traditionally masculine males, was spoken only by women and gender-variant men and was believed to be an invention of the Goddess. Gender-variant priests also ate a diet of delicate and exotic foods. Most importantly, however, their status was confirmed in the belief that the physical bodies of the priests differed from those of other men in that they carried magical power. For instance, simply touching the head of an *assinnu* would allow a warrior to conquer his enemy. Indeed, even looking upon a gender-variant priest, in this case, a *kurgarru*, could bring good fortune.[7]

Gender-variant priests, like priestesses, were considered the mortal representatives of the Goddess. The priests were also seen as human reflections of certain spirit-companions of Inanna. In a myth concerning the Goddess's descent to the Underworld, an androgynous being named Asushunamir, or "He Whose Face Is Light," is created to rescue Inanna from the grip of her sister Ereshkigal, the Queen of the Underworld.[8] In another myth of Inanna's descent, two such beings, the *kalaturru* (or *galatur*) and the *kurgarra*, are created to rescue Inanna. In an ancient text we read of the god Enki's creation of these beings:

> He fashioned the dirt into a *kurgarra*,
> a creature neither male nor female.
>
> . . . .
>
> He fashioned the dirt into a *galatur*,
> a creature neither male nor female.
> He gave the food of life to the *kurgarra*,
> He gave the food of life to the *galatur*.[9]

While these beings are referred to as "neither male nor female," Samuel Kramer and other Sumeriologists agree that they are meant to represent gender-variant males rather than hermaphrodites or gender-variant women. Not surprisingly, they were blessed by Inanna, while they were cursed by her sister Ereshkigal, who wished to see Inanna remain in the Underworld. "The shadow of the wall shall be thy station," she told them, "the threshold shall be thy habitation. The besotted and thirsty shall smite thy cheek."[10] Ereshkigal's dislike of the gender-variant beings was appropriated in later epochs by patriarchal religious leaders who insisted that Inanna herself had created them in order to show men what they might become if they failed to make sacrifices to her or insulted her in some other way. Indeed, Mesopotamian warriors even begged Inanna to curse their enemies by transforming them into eunuchs. Clearly, some considered being an androgynous priest of the Goddess a curse.[11]

Although the priests of Inanna occasionally suffered ridicule, they nevertheless held respected positions in the worship of the Goddess, being employed as magicians, ritual artists, and hierodules (or sacred prostitutes). As magicians, they were said to excel in making talismans and amulets to protect the wearer from destructive magic and other dangers.[12]

As ritual artists, they functioned as singers, musicians, composers, dancers, and actors. The *kurgarru* played various instruments, including the lyre, the two-stringed lute (*zinnutu* or *sinnatu*), the flute, and metal clappers. The *kalum* priests were known as composers of hymns, lamentations, and incantations, which they chanted in the Emesal dialect. Among the types of compositions composed by the *assinnu* was the *inhu*, a lament concerning the life of Ishtar. The term *inhu* refers to the sorrowful, melancholy song of the *ursanu* bird. "You seat the *assinnu*," an ancient text reads, "and he will sing his *inhus*." Of such laments, another text reads, "*In-hi-ia sunuhuti Istar ismema*, Ishtar (Inanna) heard my sorrowful *inhu* songs."[13]

It is possible that a well-known gypsum statuette discovered at Mari represents a "man-woman" priest. While some scholars maintain that the figure is female, it is my opinion that the celebrated singer *Ur-Nanshe* is rather a gender-variant male priest. Although the figure's wide buttocks and long hair suggest a female, it is wise to bear in mind not only that gender-variant priests grew their hair long but also that males often have fleshy buttocks. Indeed, Ur-Nanshe may have been a eunuch; the plumpness of eunuchs is proverbial. Moreover, while certain Mesopotamian statuettes depict women with one breast uncovered, the exposure of Ur-Nanshe's entire chest suggests that the figure is male. Not only this, but in terms of Mesopotamian art, the breasts of the figure are clearly those of a fleshy male and not a female. Further, the figure wears the *kanaukes*, a garment resembling a sheep's fleece, in the masculine rather than the feminine fashion, with breasts uncovered. Accepting that Ur-Nanshe was a gender-variant male priest, we know not only that he was a celebrated singer but also that he was the favorite harpist of King Iblulil, who reigned during the third millennium B.C.E. Many other long-haired, often more obviously male, figures of musicians depicted on plaques may also represent gender-variant priests; of these, some, like Ur-Nanshe, play harps, while others play flutes and tambourines.[14]

As ritual actors, the *kurgarru*, led by the *rabi kurgarri*, performed in dramas depicting epic struggles. The *kurgarru* and the *assinnu* also took part in a ritual drama honoring both Inanna and the goddess Narudu, in which the priests dressed in the garments of the goddesses. Gender-variant priests also played a role in the ritual of the *hieros gamos*, or "sacred marriage," of Inanna and her consort Dumuzi, embodied by the high priestess and the king. This rite was celebrated each year in order to promote fertility. In a hymn dating from the third millennium B.C.E., composed during the reign of Iddin-Dagan (ca. 2255 B.C.E.), we read that in this ritual, gender-variant priests and priestesses wearing bifurcated costumes, the men carrying mirrors and combing their hair, joined in a procession, chanting, "Hail, Inanna!"[15]

Foremost among their tasks, however, was that of making love with, in most cases, traditionally masculine worshipers in order to bring the latter into intimate contact with the Goddess. In this respect, the gender-variant priests dedicated their bodies, including their anuses, to the Goddess. Like the priestesses of Inanna, they engaged in anal intercourse with male worshipers, usually taking the receptive role.[16]

The Epic of Gilgamesh

The *Epic of Gilgamesh*, written down near 2100 B.C.E., concerns the life and adventures of the hero Gilgamesh, ruler of the city of Uruk. Gilgamesh may have actually lived some seven hundred years prior to the epic's composition.

In the epic, Gilgamesh has an insatiable appetite for intimacy, which is finally relieved when a deity creates not a female but rather another male, Enkidu, to become his intimate companion.

Together, Gilgamesh and Enkidu journey into the wilderness, where they conquer the giant Humbaba. During the course of their exploits, Inanna—here as Ishtar—tries to seduce Gilgamesh. When he spurns her advances, she becomes infuriated. Her rage explodes, however, when Enkidu slays her sacred bull. She curses Enkidu, and he dies shortly thereafter. Gilgamesh then sets out on a journey in search of the secret of immortality.[17]

In recent years, several writers have attacked both the characters of the epic and the text itself as promoting patriarchal values, including militarism and misogyny.[18] Others have asserted that Gilgamesh should not be considered a hero because of his relationship with Enkidu, which they perceive as infantile. The otherwise brilliant historian and archaeologist Thorkild Jacobsen, in a homophobic statement using neo-Freudian rhetoric, describes Gilgamesh as a Peter Pan who, because he rejects heterosexual marriage for a relationship with another male, will never grow up.[19]

That the epic fosters patriarchal values, however, is a plausible theory. It is my own opinion, however, that matrifocal elements permeate the text and struggle against patriarchal elements in the psyches of the male characters. Further, it would seem that in the epic patriarchal values are ultimately condemned. As in Euripides' *Iphigenia* and *The Trojan Women,* such values here bring not joy but rather sacrilege, death, and separation of loved ones. Values that remain positive in the text and in its characters are those considered feminine and linked to Goddess reverence; these encompass nurturance, compassion, and faithfulness.

Near the beginning of the epic, Gilgamesh dreams of a shooting star, which he at first embraces "like a wife" and then presents to his mother. He then dreams of a supernatural ax, which he likewise embraces. It is his mother Ninsun, the goddess of wisdom, who interprets his dreams. She explains that the shooting star and the ax both symbolize a man whom Gilgamesh will encounter shortly and whom he will love "as a woman." This lover will "never forsake" him.[20]

Another goddess, Aruru, then takes clay and creates the soon-to-be companion of Gilgamesh. In the Mesopotamian pantheon, Aruru is the creatrix and nurturer of all life. Enkidu, the creature she creates to be Gilgamesh's companion, is an archetypal "wild man" who dwells in the wilderness and lives on honey and wild foods. However, Enkidu is also described in androgynous or gender-variant terms: "His whole body was covered thickly with hair,/his head covered with hair like a woman's."[21]

A hierodule or prostitute-priestess of the Goddess civilizes the wild Enkidu by first making love to him and then dressing him in her own garments; we are told that "she took off a part of her clothing and covered him." It is she who makes Enkidu aware that he will soon become Gilgamesh's companion, and it is she who leads him to the city to meet Gilgamesh.[22]

To return to Ninsun, she not only sanctions the relationship of Gilgamesh and Enkidu but also adopts Enkidu as her own son:

"Enkidu, strong one, you are not the child of my womb—you.
Now I adopt you,
along with the cultic lovers of Gilgamesh,
the high-priestesses, wives of Uruk's gods,
the holy women,
those who throw away the seed."[23]

Finally, when Gilgamesh sets out on a journey to unravel the mystery of death and rebirth following the death of his beloved friend, he is aided by Siduri, the Celestial Barmaid (*sabitu*), a manifestation of Inanna. She directs him toward the abode of Utnapishtim, the Noah of Mesopotamian myth and the only human being to have escaped death, and she cautions that this journey will involve a difficult shamanic descent.[24]

Thus, apparently due to his erotic orientation, Gilgamesh spurns the advances of one manifestation of Inanna/Ishtar, but he remains, nevertheless, the loving son of a goddess who seeks counsel from goddesses, including another manifestation of Inanna. In other myths, moreover, Gilgamesh is the friend and helper of Inanna/Ishtar.[25] As for Enkidu, he makes the tragic mistake—under the influence of patriarchal-heroic passion—of slaying the Bull of Heaven, yet he remains the handiwork of a goddess, is civilized by a priestess of the Goddess, and is adopted by a goddess as the loving companion of her son.

Scholar of Near-Eastern studies Anne Kilmer has suggested that Enkidu may have become a gender-variant priest, an *assinnu,* of the Goddess. That Enkidu enters the city of Uruk wearing the garment of a priestess and that his adoption by Ninsun is linked to that of the hierodulic priestesses corroborates this interpretation.

Kilmer observes that wordplay is used in the epic to inform the reader not only of Enkidu's possible role as an *assinnu* but also of the erotic nature of the relationship he shares with Gilgamesh. She suggests that the ax of Gilgamesh's dream is not only meant to convey the action of chopping—an action possibly linked to ritual castration—but also to indicate an association between this ax, called a *hassinu,* and a gender-variant priest, an *assinnu.* She further suggests that the other object of which Gilgamesh dreams, the shooting star, or *kisru,* is used in the story to remind the Mesopotamian reader of the term *kezru,* which signifies a male wearing a feminine hairdo, or in other words a male hierodulic priest (or male prostitute). "The implication of the double pun is, of course," writes Kilmer, "that the often suspected . . . sexual relationship between Gilgamesh and Enkidu is, after all, the correct interpretation."[26]

If Enkidu is a wild man who "ranges over the hills with wild beasts and eats grass," he is also a mortal embodiment of the Goddess. His hair is specifically compared to that of the goddess Nisaba, patron of agriculture, divination, and the arts. The epic, then, is not only the tale of a wild man become ruler; it is the tale of a ruler's love for a gender-variant priest of the Goddess, a love that becomes tragic when patriarchal heroism, in the form of slaying the sacred bull of Ishtar, rears its head.[27]

Within the psyche of Gilgamesh, matrifocal and patrifocal elements also do battle. When Enkidu dies, Gilgamesh himself metamorphoses into an *assinnu*-like figure. Referring to himself as Enkidu's mother and widow, he weeps "like a wailing woman" and paces back and forth like a "lioness whose whelps are lost." What is more, both Gilgamesh and Enkidu experience gender transformation in this scene, with the former becoming a widow and mother and the latter having his face covered "like a bride's." That both lovers are compared to women indicates a transgenderal, homoerotic relationship of much greater complexity than scholars have imagined.[28]

ATHIRAT, GODDESS OF THE LAND OF CANAAN

Canaan, named for the rich purple dye produced from the murex shellfish, *kinahu*, was settled by the Natufians twelve thousand years ago, nine thousand years before anyone had heard the names of Noah, Abraham, and Moses.

By 8000 B.C.E., the Natufians had begun building great cities, the most renowned of which was Jericho, a major trading center, with markets as far away as Anatolia and Nubia. Thriving stone-cutting and basket-making industries emerged. A pottery industry also formed, with elegant pots displaying impressed patterns of murex shells.

Primarily fishers, the Natufians worshiped a goddess of the waters who would one day be named Athirat. Religious artifacts from the eighth and seventh millennia B.C.E. include figurines of the Goddess and human skulls decorated with cowrie eyes. Natufian artwork reveals a celebratory attitude toward eroticism, as evidenced by a statuette of an embracing couple found at Ain Sakhri and by necklaces with beads fusing the shape of female breasts with that of phallus and testicles.

In the sixth and fifth millennia B.C.E., the Yarmukians of Canaan, who displaced the Natufians, continued to worship the Goddess, her eyes resembling cowries, her tiara shaped like a glans penis.

While Yarmukian-Canaanites adopted a relatively patriarchal form of government in the fourth millennium B.C.E., they continued to revere the Goddess, and matrifocal elements continued to influence their legal system. Canaanites of the third millennium became known for their "social conscience," especially in their emphasis on "justice, and . . . charity, to the underprivileged" and their concern for women's rights.[29]

The primary goddess of the Canaanites, Athirat (or Asherah), is traditionally depicted as a nude woman with upraised arms, sometimes holding a lily in one hand and a serpent in the other—symbols of birth, death, and new life. As a goddess of fertility, she is sometimes shown standing beneath a tree or holding branches of palm or papyrus. In this aspect, she is accompanied by young male goats. She is a goddess of the heavens as well, winged and wearing a lunar tiara.

Athirat is above all a goddess of the waters, fish and waterfowl being her sacred animals. In this aspect, she is known as Rabbatu Athirat Yammi, the "Lady Who

Traverses the Sea." As an aquatic goddess, she is linked not only to the fishing industry but also to eroticism, marriage, and childbirth. In this aspect, she is also called Qudshu or Qadesh, the "Holy One." As such, she is the goddess of erotic pleasure and is depicted as a hierodule. As Qudshu, Athirat was worshiped not only by the Canaanites but also by the Egyptians.

Finally, Athirat is known as the "Mother of Kings." In this aspect, she is, along with her sister Anat—who is more frequently portrayed as an Amazon—depicted as a horned female nursing male twins.[30]

ATHIRAT'S CONSORT AND HIS "SWEET-VOICED YOUTH"

In biblical times, Athirat was seen as the consort of a male deity, El, who became syncretized with the Hebrew Yahweh (or Jehovah), but in earlier times she was depicted as a Great Goddess having a younger male consort named Baal. Although Baal himself was later patriarchalized, becoming a god of war, he began as a god of agriculture. Between his first and final appearances, he was, as a patron of the cattle industry, depicted as a golden calf. He is linked to Dumuzi, the consort of Inanna, as well as to Adonis, whom we shall encounter later.[31]

Ugaritic (basically, Canaanite) literature indicates that Baal may have also been a lover of men. Baal lived on the holy mountain Sapanu; here he was served by a "gracious lad" who sang to him in a sweet voice while playing cymbals or the lyre. This young man may have been the god Kinar, the Orpheus of Canaanite myth. The relationship of Baal and the youth, or Kinar, has been compared to that of Zeus and Ganymede, suggesting a homoerotic aspect. Scholar of Near-Eastern studies Johannes De Moor also maintains that a gender-variant priest may have taken the role of the "sweet-voiced youth" in ritual dramas.[32]

The "sweet-voiced youth" or "gracious lad" has survived in both Jewish and Islamic literature. In the Old Testament, David assumes this role, while in Islamic literature, the figure survives as one of the *wildan,* "boys of perpetual youth," who serve divine liquor to the deceased in Paradise.[33]

THE *QEDESHIM* OF ATHIRAT

The gender-variant priests of Athirat were known as the *qedeshim,* or "holy ones," as well as the *kelabim,* or "dogs," the faithful companions of the Goddess and her consort. In most respects, they resembled the priests of Inanna. They served in Canaanite temples stretching from Ugarit to Jerusalem from 1400 B.C.E. onward, if not much earlier. They typically dressed in long-sleeved, multicolored caftans. These garments were meant to evoke the Goddess and the vision of the earth in springtime, described in the *Epic of Gilgamesh* as a "couch of many colours." The *qedeshim,* or *kelabim,* may have also veiled their faces.[34]

The *qedeshim* maintained temple grounds and sacred groves and created ritual objects, especially pots and weavings. They were also credited with the power to bring rain.[35]

They participated in sacred dances using self-wounding and flagellation to reach altered states. They may have also played a role in the *hieros gamos* of Athirat and Baal or El, embodied, as in Mesopotamia, by the priestess and the king. During this rite, a gender-variant priest or *qadesh,* taking the role of the "gracious lad" or "sweet-voiced youth," chanted as he performed a ritual involving the mixing of milk, butter, mint, and coriander in a cauldron and lighting seven cakes of incense over this brew. His chant or song celebrated Athirat and her sister Anat as the nurturers of kings. He, or perhaps another *qadesh,* also sang of the Goddess's seductive powers and of the strength of Canaanite warriors.[36]

The *qedeshim* were primarily known, however, as hierodules. While some scholars, including Raphael Patai, do not believe that the *qedeshim* engaged in cultic homoeroticism, others, including Michael Grant, Samuel Terrien, and W. L. Moran, have asserted that the *qedeshim* did indeed participate in same-sex eroticism, primarily with traditionally masculine worshipers of the Goddess. If they were eunuchs, as the texts suggest, it seems plausible that they engaged in anal intercourse, taking the receptive role. Like their female counterparts, the *qedeshtu,* they may also have employed dildoes in erotic situations. Union with a *qadesh* priest, like union with a priestess of Athirat or with an *assinnu* of Inanna, was believed to bring the worshiper into intimate contact with the deity. It also made possible the total embodiment of the deity in the body of the priest or priestess. Terrien and Moran have further suggested that the *qedeshim* may have used sexual intercourse as a means of triggering an altered or shamanic state of consciousness. This practice will be familiar to students of Indian tantra. Gay male practitioners of tantra employ anal intercourse to stimulate the Kundalini, the serpentine Goddess of Wisdom, in the body of the receptive partner. As Terrien writes, "The function of the male prostitutes . . . was related to an ecstatic . . . divination technique," while Moran asserts that the *qadesh* priest "may well have obtained his oracular function through sophisticated techniques of sexual trance."[37]

THE FATE OF THE *QEDESHIM*

Most of what we know of the *qedeshim,* unfortunately, concerns the campaigns conducted against them by Israelite zealots. These campaigns, beginning in the tenth century B.C.E., lasted more than four hundred years.

The *qedeshim* were condemned by the Israelites on four accounts. First, they were mostly Canaanites, although biblical passages suggest that a number of Jewish men and women may have forsaken Judaism to become *qedeshim* and *qedeshtu.* Second, they worshiped the Goddess and her male consort rather than Yahweh, or Jehovah. Third, they were effeminate, dressing in feminine attire and behaving in a gender-variant manner. Fourth, they engaged in cultic eroticism and, more specifically, in same-sex eroticism.

The destruction of the institution of the *qedeshim* apparently began shortly after King Solomon's death, when the conquerors of Canaan divided the land into Israel and Judah. Some Hebrew rulers, to be sure, not only allowed the worship of

Athirat and Baal to continue but also adopted the religion themselves or blended it with Judaism, allowing *qedeshim* to perform their services in the Hebrew temple. Jeroboam, Rehoboam, and Abijam, all rulers of Judah, revered the Goddess in the face of Hebrew opposition. Indeed, Rehoboam's mother was a priestess of Athirat. During her lifetime, the religion of the Goddess prospered, and, as 1 Kings 14 (RSV) tells us, "there were also male cult prostitutes in the land."

Asa, a son of Abijam, became a Yahwist, despite the fact that his mother was a priestess of Athirat. Ruling Judah from 908 until 867 B.C.E., he exiled many *qedeshim* and destroyed many temples of the Goddess. He also removed his mother, Maacah, from the throne because she was a priestess of Athirat.

The infamous Jezebel, Queen of Judah, and her husband Ahab, both devotees of Athirat and Baal, were slain by Yahwists, among whom may have been *qedeshim* converts to Judaism. Jehoshaphat, who ruled Judah from 870 until 846 B.C.E., like Asa, carried out a campaign against the *qedeshim* and other worshipers of Athirat. We read in 1 Kings 22:46 (RSV): "And the remnant of the male cult prostitutes who remained . . . he exterminated." Well, not all.

Shortly thereafter, Queen Athalia of Judah launched an attack on Judaism, which ended with her assassination. King Jehu, in an attempt to destroy the worship of Athirat and Baal once and for all, issued a proclamation inviting the faithful of the Goddess and her consort to the Jerusalem temple for a celebration. When all the worshipers had arrived, including the *qedeshtu* and *qedeshim,* Jehu signaled to his guards, who locked the doors of the temple and murdered every person therein. Jehu then had their bodies thrown into the city's garbage dump.

An eight-year-old boy named Josiah, son of the Goddess-revering monarch Amon, came to reign over Judah in 639 B.C.E. Ten years later, he initiated a campaign against worshipers of the Goddess. First, the young Josiah ordered all images of the Goddess and her consort to be collected and burned in the Valley of Kidron. He then removed the bones of those who had worshiped the Goddess from their tombs—a sacrilege—and, after burning them on the altars of Athirat and Baal, scattered the remains. He then proceeded to round up all the worshipers of the Goddess and Baal from the tribal areas of Naphtali, Manasseh, Ephraim, and Simeon. These persons were slaughtered by his troops.

Among the chief victims of this campaign were the *qedeshtu* and the *qedeshim,* who lived, worked, and served the Goddess together, and who suffered the same fate at the hands of patriarchal zealots. We read in 2 Kings 23:14 (RSV): "And he broke down the houses of the male cult prostitutes . . . where the women wove hangings for . . . Asherah. . . . And he broke in pieces the pillars, and cut down the *Asherim* [representations of the Goddess], and filled their [sacred] places with the bones of men."[38]

A comment made by historian and classicist Michael Grant stresses the importance of this campaign in the religious history of humankind. He writes, "Yahwism had been severely eroded in recent years, and without Josiah's strong actions it might never have survived."[39]

SURVIVALS AND TRANSFORMATIONS

Canaanite beliefs and practices, including the figure of the *qadesh* priest, survived and were transformed in fragmentary, often complex, ways.

For example, in the biblical story of Noah's drunkenness, the wine-making industry of the Canaanites is condemned, and Ham, one of Noah's sons, is also condemned for "discovering his father's nakedness." Wine, a product of the Goddess's domain of agriculture, has caused Noah to lose control of his senses. Ham takes advantage of this loss of control by anally penetrating Noah. In this manner, Noah is transformed into a *qadesh*-like figure. This tale succeeds in condemning at once the Goddess, the wine industry associated with her worship, and homoeroticism, suggesting that the latter not only destroys men by feminizing them but is also linked to incest.[40] In the words of biblical scholar and mythologist Walter Beltz,

> The text [of Noah's drunkenness] disavows [the land of] Canaan. . . .
> To the pious Jew, Canaan . . . was a source of horror. . . . Men would
> castrate themselves and put on women's clothing, in order to be like the
> great mother goddess. The myth [of Noah's drunkenness] attacks these
> customs.[41]

What is more, Ham is depicted in biblical and apocryphal literature and in early biblical commentary not only as a carrier of Canaanite beliefs and practices and as a practitioner of homoeroticism but also as the ancestor of the Africans. The first-century C.E. Jewish theologian Philo Judaeus explains that as the descendants of Ham and his son Cush, the Africans are cursed; in his words, "Pure evil has no participation in light, but follows night and darkness."[42] In this way, xenophobic, antimatrifocal, antilibertine, misogynistic, homophobic, effemiphobic, and racist attitudes intermingled in Judeo-Christian antiquity.

Another biblical tale evoking a *qadesh*-like figure concerns Joseph and his "coat of many colors," echoing the description in the *Epic of Gilgamesh* of the earth at springtime as a "couch of many colors." Various scholars, including Beatrice Brooks, W. F. Albright, Joseph L. Henderson, and Maud Oakes, have suggested that Joseph's coat may have marked him as a gender-variant priest of the Goddess. The garment has been linked more specifically to Joseph's mother, Rachel, who is believed to have been a devotee or priestess of the Goddess; it may even have functioned as her wedding dress.[43] "For Joseph to possess this [garment]," Henderson and Oakes write, would have "enraged his brothers as much as a group of college students today [1963] would be enraged if one of their number appeared in women's clothes and expected to have his transvestitism accepted." Further, the gift of this garment to Joseph may have signified his father Jacob's desire to return to the worship of the Goddess.[44]

In *Joseph and His Brothers,* Thomas Mann breathes new life into this ancient tale of a father, his dearest son, the memory of a loving wife and mother and priestess of the Goddess, and a sacred garment:

The lad [Joseph] stared in amaze. . . . The metal embroideries glittered in the lamplight. The flashing silver and gold . . . the purple, white, olive-green, rose-colour, and black of the emblems and images, the stars, doves, trees, gods, angels, men, and beasts, lustrous against the bluish mist of the background.

. . . . "How beautiful! [said Joseph]. . . . I see the paramours of the goddess. . . ."

. . . . It covered his head and wrapped his shoulders. . . . [The] festal garment became his face to such an extent that nobody who saw him could have disputed the popular verdict upon his charms. It made him so lovely and so well-favoured that the phenomenon was actually no longer quite earthly; in fact, it bordered on the supernatural. . . .

It was the mother-goddess who stood there before him [Jacob] smiling, in the boy's lovely guise.[45]

We are told in the Midrash, a collection of biblical exegesis gathered between the fifth century B.C.E. and the second century C.E., that Potiphar purchased Joseph for the pharaoh of Egypt because of the young man's beauty. Potiphar is described in the Midrash as a eunuch priest of a pagan deity, probably a goddess. It is apparent that he and his wife, who also desired Joseph, did not have a monogamous marriage. While the Midrash tells us that Joseph, being a biblical hero, did not yield to either Potiphar or his wife, various scholars have questioned this aspect of the story. Indeed, it seems that Joseph and Potiphar, or the persons upon whom these characters were based, may have enjoyed a complex transgenderal relationship.[46] Indeed, even when depicted as a prophet of Yahweh, an interpreter of dreams, Joseph seems more like a *qadesh* priest, guided "by a secret knowledge of the feminine principle." Henderson and Oakes, following psychologist Erich Neumann, point out that both Joseph's experience in the pit at the hands of his brothers and his interpretation of the dream of seven lean cattle and seven fat cattle may be linked to the shamanic, underworld journey undertaken by the Goddess and her consort.[47]

The figure of the *qadesh* priest may have survived also in the androgynous cherubs of Judaism and Christianity. Biblical scholar Samuel Terrien states that the cherubim "may have been . . . related both to the . . . Magna Mater [the Great Mother] and to the ritual of cultic male prostitution."[48]

Finally, the figure of the gender-variant, homoerotically inclined *qadesh* may have survived also in the story of Sodom. While both Jewish and Christian apologists have argued that the tale of Sodom concerns *not* homosexuality but rather inhospitality, with the men of Sodom expressing rudeness toward Abraham and the angels, I am in accord with those who believe that the tale focuses on divine vengeance visited upon practitioners of homoeroticism, gender-variant behavior, and Goddess reverence. As Michael Grant so wisely states, "Sodom and Gomorrah [were] representatives of Canaanite religion. The shrines of Canaan harboured male prostitutes, [thus] the cities of the plain became emblems of the homosexuality that Yahweh so strongly condemned."[49]

Archaeologists believe they have located the site of the city of Sodom. Located in the vicinity of the Dead Sea, its contemporary name is Bab edh-Dhra. Beginning as a sacred site and necropolis, Sodom, or Bab edh-Dhra, later became a prosperous agricultural community producing grapes, pistachios, and chickpeas. It was apparently destroyed by fire, perhaps linked to an earthquake, near 2300 B.C.E.

While remains have not yet revealed evidence of the institution of the *qedeshim*, they have verified the worship of the Goddess at the site, burial chambers yielding "clay figurines of the mother goddess." One such figure, however, resembling the gynandrous Bird Goddess, indicates reverence of androgyny and points toward the recognition of an alternate gender role, thus perhaps evoking the figure of the *qadesh*.[50]

Many think of Sodom as a place of evil. I envision it as a place where male gender variance and homoeroticism were celebrated, as they had been once in all of Canaan and in Mesopotamia, as aspects of Goddess worship. I share the view of the gay American poet Robert Duncan, who wrote:

This place rumord to have been Sodom is blessed
in the Lord's eyes.[51]

Effeminate Eros, Column Krater, ancient Apulia.

Isis Astarte Diana Hecate

Nor had they any War-god, or Battle-din, nor was
Zeus their king, nor Cronus, nor Poseidon, but Cypris
only was their queen. Her folk appeased her with pious
offerings—painted animals and richly-scented salves,
with sacrifices of pure myrrh and fragrant frankincense,
while they poured upon the ground libations from the
yellow honeycomb.[1]

Empedocles

Perhaps best known for his theory of the elements, Empedocles believed that everything in the universe is produced by the intermingling of various degrees of love and hate with earth, air, fire, and water. Philosopher, mystic, and magician of the fifth century B.C.E., Empedocles was a vegetarian, believed in reincarnation, and healed people of grave illnesses. He was also a lover of males, his most intimate companion being a younger man named Pausanias. According to legend, Empedocles ended his life by throwing himself into the crater of Mount Aetna in order to become one with the gods.[2] ¶ Empedocles dreamed of an age when people had worshiped the Goddess, had dwelt in peace rather than in a constant state of war, and had sacrificed honey, incense, and breads shaped like animals rather than either animals or humans. The dream of such an age haunted not only Empedocles but many persons in the fifth century. In the centuries that followed, it would spark a spiritual revolution. The dream would fade only with the triumph of Christianity over paganism, and, even then, it would never die.

In this chapter, we will explore the renaissance of male gender variance, same-sex eroticism, and sacred experience in the Goddess-centered religions that flourished in the latter days of the Greco-Roman Empire.

THE RENAISSANCE OF GODDESS REVERENCE

It was the glorious twilight of Greco-Roman paganism, its last mecca Alexandria with its soon-to-be-burned monument, the fabled library. It was an era of internationalism, cosmopolitanism, and eclecticism. Many Greeks were abandoning Zeus and the Olympian pantheon. Some became skeptics, cynics, agnostics, or atheists. Others became humanists. Still others were discovering solace in a burgeoning spiritual movement that focused on a desire for peace, respect for nature, an intimate relationship with the deity, and personal salvation. This spiritual movement also embraced the healing, divinatory, and magical arts and rediscovered the shamanic state of consciousness. Shamanic trance was now referred to as "ecstasy," letting go of the ego in order to experience the divine. It was also called "enthusiasm," literally meaning, "the god (-*theos*) within (*en-*)," acting as a channel for the deity, that is, possession trance.[3] While the Hellenistic religious system, as historian of religions Luther Martin describes it, was eclectic, syncretic, and polytheistic, it was above all Goddess centered. Martin writes,

> The goddess became sole sovereign of the cosmos and all therein, and only
> through her sacred rites could humans come to their at-homeness. . . .
> For Hellenistic existence the story of the wanderings, sufferings, and final
> homecoming of the universal goddess offered the possibility that one's
> own wandering and suffering might . . . end in a . . . homecoming. . . .
> Her story became the paradigm of salvation for the individual initiate and
> offered a transformed life to those willing to follow the spiritual path of
> her Mystery.[4]

While people from all walks of life took up the Goddess-centered mysteries, a high percentage were women and gender-variant men, some of whom appear to have been homoerotically inclined. This may have been due in part to their exclusion from positions in the state priesthood. It may have also been due to an apparent desire on the part of some women and gender-variant men for a more intimate relationship with the deity than was promoted in patriarchal religions. Among the goddesses whose followers included such men were Isis, Hera, Hecate, Demeter, Ma, Kotys, Astarte/Aphrodite, Atargatis, Artemis/Diana, and Cybele (whose worship will be examined in the next chapter).[5]

ISIS AND HER RETINUE

While the worship of the goddess Isis immediately brings ancient Egypt to mind, it is her worship in the Greco-Roman world that chiefly concerns us here, as it was among Greeks and Romans that Isis's relationship to our domain most vividly expressed itself. Nevertheless, it is of some importance to know of her beginnings in Egypt.

While the worship of the Great Goddess in Egypt apparently began during the Paleolithic, her manifestation as Isis dates from the period between 3600 and 3000 B.C.E. A goddess of nature, the arts, healing, and magic, she was called the Mother of the Pharaohs. Although her worship was eventually displaced by a state religion focusing on Osiris, Horus, and other male deities, a renaissance of Isis reverence began in the seventh century B.C.E. and reached its apex in the Greco-Roman world of the fourth century B.C.E., coming to an end only with the triumph of Christianity over paganism. The revived religion of Isis gathered followers of both sexes, various ethnicities, and all economic classes; included among the faithful were gender-variant, homoerotically inclined men.[6]

Isis was associated with gender variance and homoeroticism from an early date by way of her association with her brother or son Set and his relationship with her son Horus. Set is a god of sexuality, sacrifice, and the mystery of death. He is frequently depicted as a gender-variant male. Two of his attributes, the lettuce plant and the flint knife, are associated with eunuchs and ritual castration. The lettuce plant, however, is also an aphrodisiac, suggesting Set's paradoxical erotic-ascetic character. Set's gender and erotic variance are also revealed in his relationship to his wife, the amazonian Anat, whose favorite sexual activity is anal intercourse.

Set's gender variance and homoerotic desires become clear in his relationship with Horus. While Osirian religion tended to demonize Set on a superficial level, portraying him as the enemy of Horus—an Apollonian god of harmony, order, and light—it inferred that, on a more mystical plane, Set and Horus merged to form an indivisible union, rather like the Tao. This mystery, known as the "Secret of the Two Partners," was envisioned, as Egyptologist H. te Velde tells us, as "a union consisting of a homosexual embrace."[7]

In Egyptian myth (as in Hindu myth), reproduction is not an activity limited to a heterosexual couple, at least not in the realm of the gods. Thus Set gives birth to Horus's child. While it is the case that in the Osirian, or patriarchalized, version of the myth, Set is ridiculed as a *hmty*, a word meaning "vagina" and here connoting an effeminate, homoerotically inclined male, it is also true that even in this version, Set's offspring is coveted by the gods. The "child" first appears as a golden disk on Set's forehead, suggesting his "third eye" and hence a mystical rather than a physical birth. In one version, the god Thoth, the Egyptian judge, takes the child from Set. Upon his doing so, the disk transforms into the youthful lunar deity Khonsu. In another version, the child produced is Thoth himself. Thus Thoth is sometimes referred to as the "son of the two lords." Due to the manner of his conception, as well as his association with the anus, symbolized by the self-douching ibis, Thoth is also referred to as the "Shepherd of the Anus." Sometimes the pharaoh also was considered the product of this homoerotic union, containing within himself or herself (as in the case of Hatshepsut) "the dual power in which the two gods are at peace." In general, we may say that even if Set experienced a certain amount of ridicule by allowing Horus to assume the traditionally masculine role in their relationship, the product of their union was nevertheless perceived as a divine or semidivine being worthy of reverence.[8]

THE GENDER-VARIANT priests of Isis comprised one of several groups of priests. They dressed in the linen garments of the Goddess. In the second-century C.E. Latin romance *The Golden Ass*, the writer Lucius Apuleius describes his strange transformation into an ass and his eventual return to his original state, the latter brought about by the priests of Isis, who initiate Lucius into her cult. One of her priests is described as wearing "gilt sandals, [a] silken gown, and costly ornaments."[9] While some of Isis's priests shaved their heads, ancient sources indicate that her gender-variant priests may have grown their hair long or worn indigo wigs made of horsetail plumes. According to classical scholar Ramsay Macmullen, "their long hair was thought to be a sign of inspiration, the longer the better."[10] Some priests also grew their nails long; a horrified Christian observer referred to these as "claws."[11] Some shaved their faces daily and smeared them with milk-soaked bread to make them seem smoother. Some depilated their bodies, wore exotic perfumes, and walked "with a woman's mincing gait."[12] At least some may have undergone ritual castration.[13]

Where same-sex eroticism is concerned, classical scholar Peter Green assures us that the Temple of Isis in the Campus Martius in Rome was "used as a rendezvous by male homosexuals." We also know the names of several homoerotically inclined worshippers of Isis, one of the most well known being the Roman emperor Otho, a lover of Nero.[14]

One of the most important functions of the gender-variant priests of Isis was to join her priestesses in magically causing the Nile to rise so that the land might be made fertile. A company of priests and priestesses would sail the Nile singing antiphonal hymns to encourage its rising. This ceremony appears to have been an ecstatic dance-drama that included the ritual raising of skirts by both the priestesses and the gender-variant priests. While the priestesses' exhibition of genitalia was believed to represent fertility, the priests' exhibition represented rather their forfeit of virility—via ritual castration, gender-variant homoeroticism, or both—to the Goddess, and hence the earth, so that the crops might prosper.[15]

A similar dance-drama is depicted on a marble relief found in a tomb on the Appian Way at Ariccia, near Rome. Several, if not all, of the participants are of black African descent. Some are dancing ecstatically, shaking their buttocks, bending their knees, tossing their heads, and raising their arms toward the heavens. Others are clapping. Still others are playing cymbals and clappers.

According to Frank Snowden, who is well known for his works exploring the early interpenetration of Greco-Roman and African cultures, a number of those who carried the worship of Isis from Egypt to Rome were black Africans. However, nonblack worshipers also may have carried African elements of her worship to Rome, returning home from pilgrimages to her temple at Meroe. We know, for instance, of a Roman noblewoman who journeyed to Meroe to obtain holy water for the temple of Isis in Rome.

While Snowden is to be commended for his observation that the rite depicted on the Ariccian relief is an African-based dance performed by black Africans or Afro-Romans, he is incorrect in supposing all the dancers to be female. Indeed, some are clearly male, while others may be men dressed as women. According to Ramsay Macmullen, the male dancers are *cinaedi,* that is, gender-variant and homoerotically inclined males, shown in the characteristic pose of shaking the buttocks (in Greek, *kinein*). Thus the Ariccian relief depicts female and gender-variant, homoerotically inclined African or Afro-Roman worshipers engaging in an ecstatic, African-based dance-drama in honor of the goddess Isis.[16]

Gender-variant male priests continued to serve Isis until the fourth century C.E., when the Christianized Roman emperor Constantine, as part of his campaign against paganism, forbade them to participate in the rite of raising the Nile and other ceremonies. When they refused, they were murdered. Not long after, the priestesses of Isis fell at his hands, and the temples of the Goddess were desecrated and destroyed.[17]

THE PRIESTS OF HERA

Hera, ruler of the heavens, overseer of animals, and patron of women, was served on the island of Samos not only by priestesses but also by gender-variant priests. At the time of Athenaeus, that is, during the third century C.E., Hera's male priests continued to dress as they had done for centuries, in feminine garments, "snowy tunics that swept the floor of wide earth." They also wore arm bracelets "wrought with cunning" and golden headpieces that "surmounted them, like cicadas." They grew their hair long, braided it, and decorated it with yellow or gold ribbons, hence the poetic fragment "marching to the Heraeum with braided hair." That sherds of Samian pottery were traditionally employed by the priests of another goddess, Cybele, to perform ritual castration suggests that the priests of Hera may have also been eunuchs. While it is not clear whether or not the priests of Hera engaged in same-sex eroticism, it is highly probable that they did so. The island of Samos was a place of luxury, known for its exotic foods and perfumes and its prostitutes of both sexes. The prostitutes, nicknamed the "flowers" of Samos, lived in a sort of French quarter designed by the tyrant Polycrates, an effeminate man "passionately devoted to liaisons with males."[18]

THE *SEMNOTATOI* OF HECATE

Hecate is a goddess of witchcraft as well as a dispenser of justice, bestower of wealth, overseer of horses and dogs, and patron of sailors and fishers. She is especially associated with crossroads, places where three roads meet. As such, she is a goddess of the threshold or edge and a patron of marginal and marginalized persons.

Her gender-variant priests, of whom little is known, were called *semnotatoi*. Undergoing ritual castration, it was said of them, "The revered ones of the Goddess are eunuchs." They were also known as the *demosioi*, a name suggesting "belonging to a tribe." It is probable, although not certain, that they engaged in homoerotic relationships. Their work included casting horoscopes, performing spells, and maintaining the temples and sacred groves. Their chief function, however, appears to have been directing choruses of flower-garlanded children in singing hymns to Hecate.[19]

SONS OF THE MOTHER

Demeter, Goddess of Grain, presided over bountiful harvests and was worshiped as the mother of Persephone. The Eleusinian mysteries were founded to commemorate Demeter's grief-stricken search for Persephone after the latter had been abducted by Hades, lord of the underworld.[20]

During that period of grief, Demeter encountered two eccentric female figures, Baubo and Iambe. Baubo's name signifies "belly"; she is the goddess of "belly laughter." She is sometimes associated with Heqt, the Egyptian frog goddess of birth, as well as with Hecate. Beyond her amphibian aspect, Baubo has been depicted as having a "headless and limbless body, with her genitals forming a bearded mouth, and her breasts staring like eyes." Iambe, whose mobility is impaired, is considered a twin or double of Baubo. She is the goddess of obscene speech and iambic pentameter. Legend has it that Baubo and Iambe conspired to shake Demeter out of her depression, Iambe by telling her bawdy rhymes and Baubo by lifting her skirts. While most scholars have accepted the version of the myth that says Demeter laughed when she looked upon the odd positioning of Baubo's body parts, a lesser-known version of the myth recounts that Demeter smiled when Baubo lifted her skirts because she was delighted by the beautiful body of a young woman who had depilated herself. This lesbian variant of the myth, incidentally, was linked by Arnobius to a homoerotic myth concerning Dionysus and a mortal named Polymnus who once fell in love with him.[21]

Perhaps it was the tale of Demeter and Baubo that led to the participation of gender-variant and homoerotically inclined people as well as hierodules or prostitutes in her rites. Priestesses and gender-variant priests took turns playing the role of a fused Baubo-Iambe figure at Eleusis.

The appearance of Baubo-Iambe in the mysteries occurred after the procession of worshipers left the temple of Zeus and crossed the bridge over the River Cephisus. This was the scene of the *Gephyrismos*, a word meaning "to joke at the bridge." At this time, the gender-variant priest, dressed in women's clothes, lifted his skirts. Certainly if he were a eunuch, the sight of his genitalia might provoke surprise or laughter. First mocking the worshipers, the priest playing Baubo-Iambe would then lead them in a chorus of obscene chants or songs composed in iambic pentameter. Following this, he led the others in chanting, "Iakchos! Iak-chos!" referring to an aspect of Dionysus appearing in the mysteries. He then of-fered the participants a beverage akin to mead.[22]

Beyond the participation of gender-variant priests in the *Gephyrismos,* the Eleusinian mysteries attracted a number of men whose homoerotic inclinations were well known. These included the Roman emperor Hadrian and his lover An-tinous.

In 125 C.E., Hadrian was initiated into the lower order of the mysteries, becom-ing a *mystes.* Three years later, Antinous became a *mystes,* while Hadrian gradu-ated to *epoptes,* "one who has seen." Antinous, whose life would soon end in suicide, an act of self-sacrifice performed in Egypt in order to save Hadrian's life, must have been deeply moved by experiencing Persephone's descent to the under-world and triumph over death.

Following Antinous's death, Hadrian compared his young lover to Persephone as well as to Dionysus and Osiris. He established a cult honoring him at Eleusis and elsewhere, and he commissioned an altar frieze depicting Antinous ap-proaching the throne of Dionysus, presented to the god by Demeter and Perse-phone. For the remainder of his life, Hadrian remained a faithful devotee of Demeter and a generous patron of the Eleusinian rites.[23]

MA'S FANATICS

Ma, or Enyo, is primarily envisioned as a death-wielding goddess. Her worship was centered at Comana in Cappadoccia. By the first century C.E., more than six thousand people, including hierodulic priests and priestesses, were serving in her temple at Comana. They and her worshipers were referred to as the *fanatici,* her "fanatics."

Gender-variant male *fanatici* wore heavy black robes with necklaces and tiaras resembling flower garlands. They dyed their hair blond and braided it, or they wore blond wigs. In processions, they carried double axes and branches of leaves. Some appear to have been eunuchs.

The rites of Ma were wild and rather bloody. The *fanatici* would let their hair down and begin to dance faster and faster in a circle until they reached an altered state of consciousness. In this state, they would wound themselves with the axes, splattering the statue of the Goddess, which stood in the center of their circle, with blood. They would then begin to utter the words of the Goddess. Their prac-tices are similar to other cultures that open the flesh and release blood in order to fully embody the deity; in many places cutting and flagellation of the body are linked to possession and trance.

At Rome, Ma became fused with Bellona, the goddess of war, to whom Lady Macbeth would be compared centuries later. The *fanatici* came to be called the *bellonarii.* Their beliefs and practices, however, remained virtually unchanged. Comana, as the seat of Ma's worship, came to be seen by more reactionary Greeks as a mecca of effeminacy and decadence, being nicknamed "Little Corinth."[24]

THE BAPTISTS OF KOTYS

Kotys, originally a Thracian or Phrygian goddess, was worshiped in Greece by the seventh century B.C.E. In the Hellenistic Age, however, her worship experienced a great revival after lying dormant for several centuries.

Her name probably derives from either *kued-* or *kuod-*, "energy" or "avenger." Associated with Ma as well as Artemis, she is a goddess of the hunt and the waning moon. She is also a patron of musicians and, along with the goddess Cybele, is sometimes considered the inventor of cymbals and the aulos, or double flute.

She is sometimes accompanied by a male consort, Sabazius, who is linked to the mysteries of sex, death, and regeneration. A god of healing, magic, and mystical wisdom or *gnosis,* Sabazius has been associated with Aesclepios, a Greek god of healing, and with the Gnostic, wisdom-giving Serpent of the Garden of Eden. He is represented by, and offered sacrifices of, magical hands fashioned of metal.[25]

The faithful of Kotys and Sabazius were called *baptai,* that is, "baptists," because they underwent a ritual cleansing, being smeared with a mixture of bran and clay and then bathed. After this baptism, they would celebrate communion— theirs included beer and rare or raw meat—and would chant in unison, "I have fled the evil, I have found a better way."[26]

From the seventh century B.C.E. onward, male worshipers of Kotys were linked to homoeroticism and gender variance. They often dressed in feminine attire, which included wigs—probably blond—and head garlands of poplar and fennel. The philosopher Synesius, equating the male *baptai* with homoerotically inclined, gender-variant men, wrote, "One who participates in the orgies of Kotys is identical with a *cinaedus,*" a homoerotically inclined, gender-variant male. In the Roman Empire, the term *baptai* came to mean "effeminate and licentious." Further, *baptai* became associated with another term, *impudicus,* which refers generally to lustfulness but "more particularly [to] sodomy."[27]

The *baptai* served primarily as workers of magic and ritual musicians, and they were especially celebrated as flute players and as drummers, their drums made of bronze cauldrons covered with hides.

Leading a somewhat itinerant lifestyle, they often sojourned briefly in towns and cities, dancing wildly while waving serpents—sometimes real and sometimes made of gold—above their heads and shouting, "*Evoe Saboi,* Hail Sabazius!" Their major rites, however, took place in the mountains by torchlight. Here, at the *kotyttia* or *sabazia,* they would again handle serpents, guiding them over their bodies, especially the genital region, and would dance furiously in a circle until they fell into an altered state. In this condition, as we have observed with other priests of goddesses, the *baptai* would become possessed by the deity and utter her words.[28]

THOSE WHO SERVED THE QUEEN OF HEAVEN

Astarte, goddess of love and later also of war, is also known as Ashtoreth, the Lady of Byblos, and the Queen of Heaven. She is frequently identified with Aphrodite and Venus (identifications I have accepted for the purposes of this

work). She was worshiped at various times from around the third millenium
B.C.E. through the first few centuries of the Common Era by the Egyptians,
Canaanites, Phoenicians, Greeks, Romans, and even heretical Hebrews. As a
manifestation of the life-bestowing aspect of the Great Goddess, she is often depicted as a nude woman holding her breasts or raising her arms above her head.
She sometimes wears a bird mask and is occasionally flanked by male goats. She
may also appear as a gender-variant goddess, both as a woman warrior crowned
with horns and driving a chariot and as a hermaphrodite with female breasts and
an erect phallus. In this aspect, she is known as Aphroditos or Bearded
Aphrodite and is associated not only with the planet Venus but also with the
moon.[29]

Above all a goddess of love, Astarte/Aphrodite was nicknamed Philommedes,
"genital loving." According to classical scholar K. J. Dover, the Greek term *aphro-
disia,* meaning the "things of Aphrodite," refers to sexual intercourse.[30] She is the
patron of both hierodulic priestesses and secular prostitutes. In Sappho's poetry,
she becomes a patron of lesbian women, and as Aphrodite Anosia, she may have
presided over rites of lesbian sadomasochism.[31] She was also called Androphonos,
"Man-Slayer." In this aspect, she may have presided over rites of castration. This
manifestation may be traced to her birth, brought about by the coming together
of the maternal sea and the severed genitals of her father, Cronus.[32]

Through her association with the castrated Cronus as well as her own gender-
variant aspects, Astarte/Aphrodite becomes linked to gender-variant males. She
also gives birth to Hermaphroditus, the very emblem of gender variance. What is
more, Cinyras, a lover of Apollo, is a legendary ruler of Cyprus and a transvestite
priest of the Goddess. Paris, another of Aphrodite's favorites, despite his role in
the Trojan War is said to be "unwarlike and effeminate." He is blessed by the Goddess with a retinue of eunuchs.[33]

Astarte/Aphrodite, especially as Aphrodite Urania, is a patron of men-loving
men. K. J. Dover notes that in the poetry of Theognis, celebrated for his homoerotic verse, the beloved is considered a "gift of Aphrodite."[34] One of the Goddess's loyal servants is Eros, a patron of homoerotic love.

Astarte/Aphrodite's consort is the beautiful youth Adonis, sometimes identified with Tammuz, the consort of the goddess Inanna/Ishtar. Adonis is the son of
Myrrha, who is changed into a myrrh plant after becoming pregnant with her father's child. As a youth, Adonis is loved by Astarte as well as Persephone and
Dionysus. One day, while hunting in the forest, Adonis is slain by a wild boar. Although the young man tries to hide from the animal in a lettuce bed, the boar discovers him and fatally wounds him in the groin. From his mutilated genitals,
scarlet anemones grow.

In the myth of Adonis, according to French classical scholar Marcel Detienne,
myrrh (from Adonis's mother) and lettuce (his useless refuge) signify conflicting
traits. While myrrh suggests sensuality, lettuce was associated in the Greek psyche
(as in the Egyptian) with eunuchs and also with death. Paradoxically, Adonis is
also linked, along with Dionysus and Sabazius, to fennel, believed to produce an
abundance of sperm. Taken together, says Detienne, these vegetal signs relay that
"Adonis is not a husband." Rather, he is a "lover, and an effeminate one." Classicist

and feminist theorist Eva Keuls goes so far as to describe Adonis as a "counter-cultural male sex symbol," perhaps the Prince of his day.[35]

Each summer in Athens and elsewhere, at the time of the rising of Sirius, women and gender-variant males celebrated the festival of Adonia in honor of the youth. They did so by planting seeds in small pots. These "gardens of Adonis" were allowed to thrive for a few days only before they were uprooted. Detienne suggests that the gardens symbolized the youth's fragility, sexual precocity, and early death. Both the gardens that grow quickly and then die and the sensuous youth are manifestations of *aklosia,* or early and unnatural ripening. *Aklosia* was linked by the Greeks to nonreproductive ("unfruitful") sexual behavior, including homosexuality. While patriarchal Greeks disapproved of such activity, except in the case of institutionalized pederasty, the devotees of Adonis did not.

Both Detienne and Keuls stress the sociopolitical, radical aspect of the Adonia. Detienne describes the festival as a "fleeting moment" when a "social order noted for its . . . masculine character" was rejected, while Keuls echoes, "Everything in the cult of Adonis spelled protest against the existing order."[36]

THE GENDER-VARIANT priests of Astarte were generally known as the *ke-labim,* the "dogs" of the Goddess, a term we have already encountered in reference to the priests of Athirat. Some of them also were called *gerim,* a name that suggests either a mask wearer or a eunuch. The *kelabim* and *gerim* served the Goddess at Kition on the island of Cyprus and in many other places. At Kition, where she manifested as Aphroditos, her worship was linked to moon worship as well as gender variance and same-sex eroticism.[37] Here, according to Philochorus, she was served by men "dressed as women, and women dressed as men, because the moon is thought to be both male and female."[38] According to classical scholars Olivier Masson and Maurice Sznycer, the *kelabim* at Kition functioned as "sacred prostitutes employed for sodomitic purposes."[39]

Kelabim also served the Goddess at Afqa (in ancient times, Aphaca, near the river Nahr Ibrahim, once the Adonis River, in present-day Lebanon). Here they also dressed in feminine attire and worked alongside the priestesses as hierodules. They maintained and protected the temple grounds and divined the future from the kidneys of sacrificed animals. They also participated in a variant—and perhaps the original—form of the Adonia.

Each April, together with the priestesses, they formed a procession, walking from the temple at Afqa to the river. As they walked, they sang praises and laments recounting the life and early death of Adonis. At the river, which seemed red with the blood of Adonis, they gathered and cast into the water pieces of gold and silver, exquisite fabrics, and anemones.

They then returned to the temple, where they gathered around a pool. By some feat of magic, a ball of fire would appear floating above the water. The ball of fire was associated in the minds of the *kelabim* and the priestesses with both the planet Venus and Sirius, the Dog Star. This was a sign of Adonis's rebirth or resurrection and of his reunion with the Goddess.

A massive attack on the worshipers at Afqa was launched in the fourth century C.E. by the Christianized Roman emperor Constantine. Eusebius states that Constantine, on discovering a "hidden snare of souls . . . at Aphaca . . . dedicated to Venus," gave orders to raze the temple and to slaughter its priests and priestesses. "Here men undeserving of the name forgot the dignity of their sex," writes Eusebius, "and propitiated the *demon* [italics mine] by their effeminate conduct." He continues, "The hand of military force was made instrumental in purging the impurities of the place."[40]

"This violence," twentieth-century travel writer Colin Thubron laments in *The Hills of Adonis*, "is remembered in the humped wreck of the sanctuary and in the stones which slide beneath it to the river. . . . Here it seemed the goddess died, where Adonis was buried."[41]

THE *GALLI* OF ATARGATIS

Atargatis, also known as Dea Syria and Derceto, is generally depicted as a young woman wearing an Egyptian dress or as a mermaid wearing a fortress-shaped tiara. Mother of the legendary Queen Semiramis, she has a male consort named Hadad or Attah. According to Lucian, Hadad castrated himself after offending the Goddess by taking up with a mortal woman. While divine or semidivine himself, Hadad thereafter became a *gallus* (a name also used by the priests of the goddess Cybele), dressing in feminine attire, leading an itinerant life, and singing praises to the Goddess wherever he went. Indeed, Hadad is described as a messiah who descended to earth in order to teach mortals how, by following the path of the Goddess, they might achieve salvation and everlasting life.[42]

Atargatis's seat of worship was at Hierapolis in Syria. Here she was served by a multitude of priests and priestesses. Her *galli* dressed as she and Hadad did, in Egyptian feminine attire. It is probable, although not certain, that they engaged in same-sex eroticism. Their duties included caring for the sacred fish kept in the pool on the temple grounds and participating in the Feast of Fire in early spring. At this rite, clothes, jewelry, figurines, and other objects were cast upon a great bonfire in sacrifice to the Goddess. When *galli* died, they were not buried like other men but rather carried on biers to a place beyond the city walls (suggesting their marginal status in society), where their bodies were covered with mounds of stones.[43]

Many of Atargatis's male worshipers apparently were slaves, freedmen, and peasant laborers. These men may have included black Africans. Some were married, but many others were gender-variant men whose erotic partners were other men.

The worshipers of Atargatis participated in a great slave rebellion occurring in the Greco-Roman Empire between 135 and 131 B.C.E. According to historian Michael Grant, the revolt was inspired by an "unusual degree of ill treatment, including the withdrawal of food and clothing allowances" as well as physical torture. The *galli* and other devotees were led in this revolt by Eunus, a married, possibly bisexual and probably eunuch, priest of Atargatis. Eunus managed to raise an army of seventy thousand men before the revolt was crushed. This rebellion led by worshipers of the Goddess did, however, succeed in encouraging many ancient writers to adopt antislavery positions.[44]

The faithful of Atargatis were the victims not only of Greeks and Romans but also of Hebrew zealots. Perhaps as many as twenty-five thousand, both men and women, died at Carnaim in 164 B.C.E. at the hands of Judas Maccabeus. This massacre, when combined with the slaughter of Eunus's comrades, must have devastated the congregation of Atargatis. We last hear of her gender-variant *galli* in the fourth century C.E.[45]

THE *MEGABYZOI* OF DIANA

Diana. Artemis. These names evoke the crescent moon, a lone deer running through the forest, bands of Amazons. A manifestation of the Great Goddess of Old Europe, Diana came to be worshiped in Crete, England, France, Italy, Spain, and elsewhere. Her worship continued several—if not many—centuries after the birth of Christ.[46]

Her priestesses were called *melissae,* "bees," her high priestess their queen. Although the existence of Amazons remains controversial, Diana may have been served also by amazonian or *antineirian* priestesses. The term *antineira* refers to a collection of traits including rejection of marriage, love of hunting, skill as a warrior, hatred of traditionally masculine men, a sense of comradeship with gender-variant males, and a desire to remain in the company of women. These priestesses are said to have used their shields and swords in a circular dance around a sacred oak or beech at Ephesus.[47]

WHILE THE GENDER-VARIANT priests of Diana may have been divided into various groups, perhaps including the *essenes* (referring to male bees), those about whom we know most are the *megabyzoi.* Gender-variant males probably served Diana for several millennia, but the particular institution of the *megabyzos*—a Persian term—dates from the seventh century B.C.E.

The *megabyzoi* arrived in Ephesus from all parts of the known world and were celebrated both for their wisdom and their beauty. Ancient artists painted portraits of *megabyzoi* to hang in Diana's temples and tombs, bypassing the wishes of Quintillian, a Roman rhetorician of the first century C.E., who insisted that painters and sculptors refrain from depicting a *megabyzos* on both aesthetic and moral grounds.[48] Unfortunately, temple portraits have apparently been lost. Most of the representations of *megabyzoi* that remain are in the forms of statuettes, columns, and literary descriptions.[49]

The *megabyzoi* shaved and powdered their faces or painted them with an ointment containing flecks of gold. They wore their hair in a feminine style, looping one lock in front of each ear. They wore a mixture of feminine, masculine, and priestly articles. In early times, they may have worn panther skins in emulation of the Goddess, as evidenced by columns at Ephesus and a large vase housed in the Madrid museum.

In later times, they wore long-sleeved garments, *chitons* or *calasires,* decorated with golden circles, meanders, diamond shapes, swastikas, flowers, and animals sacred to the Goddess. These garments were of different colors, including vermilion, saffron, and sea green. But the garments most frequently worn by the *megabyzoi* were purple, the dye made from the murex shell, which had been used earlier in Canaan (as *kinahu*). In the Greco-Roman Empire, this dye became associated with both royalty and effeminacy. The most exquisite purple garments were the *actaea,* sewn with purple and gold threads and ornamented with golden sheaves of millet. The *megabyzoi* also wore turbans or tiaras, often of gold, necklaces resembling rosaries, and delicate slippers.[50]

WHILE SCORNED BY many Greeks and Romans, the *megabyzoi* apparently were respected by the Ephesians. Ephesian men are described as being "effeminate and voluptuous, and clothed very delicately." Certain Ephesians, among them harpists, flute players, and dancers, were considered extremely effeminate and yet were greatly admired. Such behavior extended to Magnesia, a neighboring city where another magnificent Artemision, the temple of Diana, stood. Magnesian men known to have been gender variant and homoerotically inclined were the orator Hegesias, inventor of the so-called "florid" or "Asiatic" prose style, and Cleomachus, a boxer and poet credited with inventing a style based on the speech of *cinaedi,* gender-variant, homoerotically inclined men.[51]

The most famous lovers of men who revered Diana were, however, Alexander the Great and the poet Callimachus. Alexander was a close friend of a *megabyzos* at Ephesus. On one occasion, Alexander wrote to the latter asking if a runaway slave finding sanctuary in the temple might be allowed to join him as a companion. Alexander also loved to dress as Diana in parades honoring the Goddess.[52]

Callimachus, born in Alexandria, as a young man became an intimate companion of Pharaoh Ptolemy Philadelphus and was invited by him to live in the palace as a royal poet. Callimachus may also have served as a librarian at the famed library of Alexandria. In his poems, Callimachus frequently celebrates homoerotic love. His hymn to Diana is perhaps his finest work. Callimachus depicts the goddess primarily as an Amazon and lover of women, her amours including Britomartis, Cyrene, and Anticleia. "These were the first," he writes, "who wore the gallant bow and arrow-holding quivers on their shoulders."[53]

THE *MEGABYZOI* were often eunuchs. In the latter days of the worship of Diana, however, it appears that ritual castration was replaced by sacrifices of phallus-shaped breads. Texts dating from the fourth century B.C.E. suggest that the rite of castration was partly undertaken to sever family ties and that, upon becoming a eunuch, the initiate was adopted by an elder member of the *megabyzos*

community. A similar event, incidentally, is described by anthropologist Serena Nanda in *Neither Man Nor Woman,* a study of the *hijras* of India, eunuch priests living in the twentieth century who serve the goddess Bahucharamata.[54]

The work of the *megabyzoi* included composing and performing hymns, casting horoscopes, overseeing temple finances, and organizing public festivals. The great festival of Diana took place each year on May 25, the birthday of the Goddess. Gold, silver, and other images of the Goddess were carried by the *megabyzoi* and priestesses to all parts of the city for public viewing. At least one of the statues was dressed in an ornate purple and gold *actaea. Megabyzoi* and priestesses dressed as Diana also rode through the city in stag-drawn chariots.[55]

The *megabyzoi* were best known, however, for their ability to divine the future by way of the Ephesian letters. The poet Anaxilas refers to their "carrying in sewn leather bags / The Ephesian letters of gold omen." Roughly equivalent to Scandinavian runes, the letters, made of wood and painted gold, were carried in pouches that hung from the waist. The letters were six in number and referred to such things as the elements, the seasons, and various traits associated with the Goddess. They were used not only as a divinatory tool but also as an amulet or talisman, protecting the wearer from harm.[56]

As noted above, Diana was honored not only by the *megabyzoi* and *melissae* but by other gender-variant people and activities. For instance, in the *kordax,* a dance-drama in which women and men dressed in the garments of the opposite sex, the women, wearing *lombai,* "enormous artificial phalli," pretended to penetrate the male dancers. At one of Diana's festivals, young Lakedaimonian men, preparing for combat, flagellated themselves and engaged in same-sex eroticism. The Goddess was also revered at the initiation rites of young men joining the order of the *Kouretes,* a band of warriors whose functions may have included serving as guards at birthing rituals. From rock inscriptions on the island of Thera, we know that the rites of the *Kouretes* included homoeroticism. The couples, usually initiator and initiate, dedicated their lives to Diana and other deities.[57]

DURING THE REIGN of Emperor Tiberius, the *megabyzoi* began to diminish in number as a result of the emperor's homophobic and effemiphobic policies. Later, invading Goths apparently killed many priests and priestesses of the Goddess. The Christian church, however, played the greatest role in destroying the religion of Diana and killing her followers. The apostle Paul said to early Christian converts, "The temple of the great goddess Artemis may count for nothing, and . . . she may . . . be deposed from her magnificence, she whom Asia and the world worship."[58] Responding to Paul's invitation, Christians destroyed the temple at Ephesus in the third century C.E. It was rebuilt but was again burned by the Christians in 405 C.E. At this time, the patriarch of Constantinople proudly proclaimed that Christians succeeded in stripping "away the treasury of Artemis."[59] As classicist and historian of religions John Holland Smith explains, the destruction of the temple provided the funds and materials to build the Church of Sts.

Mary and John at Ephesus and Hagia Sophia at Constantinople. This did not prevent Christians from worrying, however, that the stones used to build these churches might still be "infected" with the "evil" energy of the Goddess.[60]

A poet nearer our own time, perhaps imagining how the few remaining *megabyzoi, melissae,* and other faithful of Diana must have felt as they looked upon the ruins of the temple at Ephesus, wrote, "We now seek the Temple in vain: the city is / prostrate, and the goddess gone."[61]

Gallus-priest of the goddess Cybele, Appian Way, mid-2nd century C.E.

Sons of Earth

They are sons of earth. [The] earth is their mother.

Augustine, describing the priests of Cybele[1]

hile the Roman goddess Cybele's retinue included many priest-esses as well as traditionally masculine functionaries such as the *dendrophori* and *cannophori*, the "tree-" and "reed-bearers," our focus in this chapter will be upon the *galli*, her gender-variant priests. Before we turn to the *galli*, however, I want to speak briefly of Cybele and her worship.

CYBELE

Cybele was probably first worshipped at Çatal Hüyük, one of the most ancient cities in the world and one of the earliest sites of Goddess reverence, located near present-day Konya in Turkey. The inhabitants of Çatal Hüyük depicted Cybele as a powerful, heavy-set woman seated on a throne and flanked by leopards. The leopards, which became lions in later times, are thought to represent the Goddess's male sons, consorts, or priests.[2] Classical scholar Walter Burkert describes the leopards as the Goddess's "satellites." He suggests that the male worshipers at Çatal Hüyük may have formed a secret men's society of "leopard men" under "the guidance of [the] Great Goddess." It is possible that these "leopard men" were the spiritual ancestors of the *galli*.[3]

Cybele was known by many names, including Kubaba, Dindymene, Rhea, and the Mother of the Gods.

Seated on her throne between the leopards or lions, Cybele wears a fortress-shaped tiara and holds a pair of cymbals.

While perceived as omniscient and omnipotent, Cybele came to be primarily associated with the concerns of women, protection against one's enemies, the healing of grave illnesses, guardianship of the dead, and the gift of prophecy. In the latter days of her worship, during the first centuries of the Common Era, she was recognized as a savior who was accessible to prayer, granting boons and promising her worshipers a joyous afterlife.

While the center of her worship was at Pessinus, near Sivrihisar in Turkey, Cybele came to be worshiped in many places, including Macedonia, Thrace, Carthage, Spain, Gaul, Italy, Britain, and northern Africa. Her worship was carried to Greece during the eighth century B.C.E., where it became syncretized with the worship of Rhea, Gaia, and Meter. The majority of Greek male citizens, however, did not welcome her arrival; they only accepted her worship because a priestess of Apollo had warned that if they did not do so, the wrath of the goddess would surely follow.

The male citizens of Rome, like the Greeks before them, felt compelled to accept the worship of Cybele in order to fend off ill fortune. In 204 B.C.E., when the Sibylline Books were consulted, the Romans were advised to import the worship of Cybele to Rome in order to ensure success in their struggle with the Carthaginians. Roman emissaries to Phrygia persuaded the rulers of Pergamon, the Attalids, to allow them to transport the statue of Cybele and the obsidian stone, which may have formed part or all of her face, to Rome. They constructed a ship, painted in brilliant colors, in which to carry the statue. On arriving in Rome, the statue, emissaries, and a group of Phyrgian *galli* were received by a great throng led by Claudia Quinta, a noblewoman who was already a devotee of the Goddess.

A temple to Cybele was dedicated in 191 B.C.E. After being destroyed by fire, it was rebuilt by Caesar Augustus, who acknowledged Cybele as the chief divinity of the Roman Empire.[4] Walter Burkert writes, "It was from the new center in the *ager Vaticanus* [that] the cult of Magna Mater pervaded the whole Roman Empire."[5]

THE *GALLI*

The *galli* were variously known as *bakaloi, bakèles, bakides, kybèbes, metragyrtes,* and *metrizantes.* They were considered gender variant in both appearance and behavior, and they appear to have engaged in same-sex eroticism.

While the term *gallos* is said to be derived from the Gallos River, a tributary of the River Sangarios in Phrygia, *gallos* became associated with the Latin term *gallus,* "rooster," in the Roman empire. This bird thus became a sacred attribute of Cybele and her male consort Attis and a symbol of the *galli*. At the same time, the erotic association of "rooster-cock-phallus," already in currency, served as an inside joke among the *galli* and was later used by Roman citizens to ridicule them.

The high priests of Cybele were called *Archgalli, Battakes,* or *Attises.* At Rome, the high priest was called Attis Populi Romani, "Attis of the People of Rome."

Unlike many of the anonymous worshipers of goddesses, some of the *galli* are known to us by name: Publius Sulpicius Gallus, Genucius, Eutychès, Soterides, M. Modius Maximus, Baeticus of Andalusia, Moschos of Egypt, Dindymus, and many others.

At least three of these men were slaves who found freedom from their masters in the worship of Cybele. The name Dindymus, incidentally, fuses one of Cybele's appellations, Dindymene, with the masculine ending *us.* Such a name clearly suggests a gender-variant male. Their gender variance also caused the *galli* to be labeled *gallae,* with the feminine ending *-ae.*[6]

The institution of the *galli* may date back to the religion of the Goddess of Çatal Hüyük. It is almost certain that the *galli* were functioning as priests of Cybele in Phrygia by the third millennium B.C.E. As an institution, the *galli* remained most firmly established in Phrygia. According to one account, the *galli* actually ruled Pessinus until 164 B.C.E., when the city was ravaged by invaders.[7]

Outside Phrygia, however, the *galli,* until the latter days of the Roman Empire, led mendicant, itinerant lives. They were prevented from establishing stationary quarters by male citizens opposed to the worship of Cybele, to male gender variance, and, more specifically, to ritual castration. It also seems that when a Greek or Roman male citizen chose to become a *gallus,* he came to be looked upon as a foreigner. Like other *galli,* he became the victim of various prejudices including homophobia (because his same-sex expression was not of the accepted intergenerational, or pederastic, type), effemiphobia, and xenophobia.

While groups of *galli* may have journeyed to Greece or emerged from the Greek population prior to the fifth century B.C.E., their presence in Greece remained largely undocumented until 415 B.C.E. As eunuchs and transvestites, the *galli* were abhorred by the Greeks. Indeed, only one eunuch priest was allowed to serve officially in Greece; this was the *labys* or *neocorate* priest of Apollo at Delphi.[8] Even after temples of Cybele were established in Greece, the *galli* were usually forbidden to enter them. Thus in Greece the *galli* became known as the *metragyrtes,* "the wandering, begging priests of the Mother."[9] If the Greeks were repulsed by the *galli,* they also feared them. The Athenian general Nicias, for instance, considered it an omen presaging defeat for the Greek fleet in the Sicilian expedition when, just before the fleet embarked, "a young man," a *gallus* of Cybele, "ran up to Nicias . . . and emasculated himself."[10]

When Cybele's worship was officially introduced to the Romans in the third century B.C.E., *galli* had to be imported, as Roman citizens could not undergo ritual castration. In spite of this, a number of citizens formed fraternities to demonstrate their reverence for the Goddess. In 101 B.C.E., the law was amended so that certain citizens might become *galli* if they so desired, and between 41 and 54 C.E., the emperor Claudius removed all restrictions preventing citizens from becoming *galli*. This period of tolerance ended with the accession of Domitian to the throne. Between 81 and 91 C.E., Domitian forbade citizens to become *galli*. By 239 C.E., however, this policy had been reversed. This second period of tolerance ended with the triumph of Christianity.[11]

ATTIS

One of the chief deities besides Cybele worshipped by the *galli* was the goddess' youthful male consort, Attis. Attis's name suggests "goat" or "goatherd." He is commonly depicted as a handsome goatherd or shepherd playing the pipes or dancing, and sometimes he wears wings. He is also depicted as leaning on his staff in a melancholy pose. Linked to the seasonal cycle, he might wear a wreath of pine cones and pomegranates on his head or carry corn and fruit. In the last years of his worship, he was portrayed as a celestial deity, wearing a crown of stars and associated with the moon, the sun, and the Milky Way.[12] The Christian theologian Arnobius wrote, "When we name Attis . . . we mean and speak of the sun."[13]

In the earliest times, Attis was compared to Adonis, Pan, and other vegetation deities. In later times he, like Cybele and also like Ganymede, with whom he came to be linked, was envisioned as a savior deity. A famous hymn to Attis considers him the invisible cause behind embodied forms and praises him for descending to earth from the stars, sacrificing himself so that mortals can prepare themselves for the spiritual journey that leads back to the heavenly throne of the Mother.[14]

Both male gender variance and homoeroticism play a role in the myth of Cybele and Attis. Zeus desires intercourse with Cybele. She resists him, however. He masturbates, and his semen falls onto a rock. From the rock springs an androgynous being. Because of this creature's enormous physical strength, the gods decide to castrate the being; from that moment he is perceived as a eunuch named Agdistis (sometimes mistakenly identified with Cybele).

Agdistis goes to live in the forest and becomes a hunter. From the blood that spills when he is castrated, a pomegranate tree grows.

Nana, daughter of the river-god Sangarios, eats a pomegranate from the tree and becomes pregnant. She gives birth to Attis. Sangarios, refusing to accept the miracle of virgin birth, forces Nana to surrender the infant to goatherds.

One day, when the youthful Attis is hunting, he meets the older eunuch Agdistis, who immediately falls in love with him. The two become intimate companions, Agdistis presenting Attis "with the spoils of wild beasts." Attis, under the influence of wine, confesses to others that he and Agdistis have become lovers, and that Agdistis has honored him with many gifts.[15]

Attis satisfies the lust of Agdistis "in the only way now possible," that is, either by allowing Agdistis to fellate him or by having Agdistis take the receptive role in anal intercourse. The topsy-turvy nature of this version of the Greek pederastic model is underscored by the fact that both partners are intermittently portrayed as hunters and transvestites.[16]

Agdistis, however, is not alone in loving Attis; the young man is also loved by Cybele. Together, they form a kind of trinity, not unlike that of Isis, Set, and Horus or Ninsun, Gilgamesh, and Enkidu. Attis, however, is pledged to marry the daughter of King Midas. Opposing the event, Cybele and Agdistis bring chaos to the wedding. The young bride, Ia, chops off one of her breasts, while Attis castrates himself beneath a pine tree. It is difficult, incidentally, not to see in these actions a mythic depiction of the relationship between the gender-variant priests of the Goddess and the Amazons, whose existence, as mentioned above, remains controversial.

Before succumbing to death from the botched castration, Attis utters these words: "Take these [my testicles or genitals], Agdistis, for which you have stirred up so great and terribly perilous emotions."[17]

From Attis's blood spring violets, and they become his sacred flowers. The Goddess weeps and from her tears an almond tree emerges, signifying "the bitterness of death." Cybele then bathes Attis's testicles or genitals, anoints them with fragrant oils, wraps them in the youth's garments, and buries them in the earth or conceals them in a jar to be housed in a secret chamber. She then chops down the pine tree, emblematic of self-sacrifice, and transports it to the sacred cave in the vicinity of Pessinus. While this tale might be read as one of jealousy and intrigue, on a deeper level it speaks to a spiritual crisis leading to enlightenment and reunion with the Goddess.[18]

By the third century B.C.E., salvation had become an important theme in religious thought, especially among those participating in Goddess-centered and other mysteries. Perhaps influenced by Hinduism or Buddhism, salvation had become linked—as is evident in Orphism—to escape from the cycles of reincarnation that bound mortals to the earth. The Goddess now dwelled in the heavens, and spiritually inclined mortals, often by rejecting procreation (referred to as the "superabundance of generative life"), could strive "upwards to the goddess of our forefathers, to her who is the principle of all life."[19]

The figure of Attis demonstrates that "in all things the conversion to what is higher [spiritual development] produces more power . . . than the inclination to what is lower [reproduction]." Following his act of self-sacrifice, Attis is "led upwards as though from our earth" to resume again "his ancient sceptre." The fourth-century C.E. Roman emperor Julian, who abandoned Christianity to become a pagan, writes, "Immediately after the castration, the trumpet sounds the recall for Attis and for all of us who flew down from heaven and fell to earth." Once more, and forever, Attis becomes the "servant and charioteer of the Mother." Moreover, he is made "the leader of all the tribes of divine beings" as well as the leader of the *galli,* "who are assigned to him by the mother" and who are represented by her lions. Attis, now crowned with stars, is identified with the Milky Way.

In one version of the myth of Cybele and Attis, Agdistis and Cybele plead with Zeus to restore Attis to life. Zeus refuses. He grants, however, "that the body should not decay, that his hairs should always grow, [and] that [one] of his fingers should live, and should be kept ever in motion."[20] In this variant, Attis is neither reborn nor resurrected but lives on eternally in a kind of vampiric state, referred to as "survival in death."[21]

The finger has an erotic connotation in this context. In Greco-Roman iconography, the finger and the penis are often interchangeable symbols. Moreover, the finger in perpetual motion is a Greek sign signifying digital or penile stimulation of the anus, referred to as "siphnianizing," as the inhabitants of Siphnos were thought to be especially fond of anal eroticism.[22]

Arnobius links the moving finger of Attis with another legendary finger, namely, that of Zeus on a statue created by Phidias. On this finger, the artist inscribed the name of Pantarces, a young man he loved. To inscribe the name on a finger suggested that the youth willingly yielded to anal eroticism.[23]

MARSYAS

Another deity who played a prominent role in the story of Cybele and Attis was Marsyas, generally depicted as a herdsman or satyr. Music teacher and lover of the youth Olympus, Marsyas was also a *gallus* of Cybele who "roamed the country[side] with the disconsolate goddess to soothe her grief for the death of Attis." According to the Celaeneans of Phrygia, Marsyas was the legendary composer of "the Mother's Air, a tune played on the flute in honour of the Great Mother Goddess." Marsyas was crucified on a pine tree and then flayed by Apollo after having lost in a musical competition to the latter. It is quite possible that this competition reflected a larger struggle between the worshipers of the Goddess and those of the Olympian pantheon.[24]

As a worshiper of Cybele, Marsyas, although vanquished, was revered by the Calaeneans and others as semidivine musician. It was believed that his flayed skin, which hung in a cave at Calaenae, would dance when Phrygian melodies were played, while remaining motionless when hymns to Apollo were played.[25]

If Attis may be seen as a prefiguration of Christ in descending to earth, proclaiming the word of the deity, performing self-sacrifice, and ascending to the heavens (in some variants), then both Marsyas and Agdistis might be compared to John the Baptist, the herald of Jesus.[26]

THE APPEARANCE OF THE *GALLI*

While the poorest, wandering *galli* may have been forced to wear whatever rags they possessed, most *galli* showed their reverence for the Goddess through their clothes. They dressed in a combination of feminine and sacred clothes, only infrequently donning men's garments, and these chiefly of foreign design.

They dressed in *stolae,* robes worn by Greek and Roman women, and *chiridotae,* tunics covering the arms and legs, almost exclusively worn by women and gender-variant men. Such garments were usually made of silk or linen. They were typically of colors associated with effeminacy and with the receptive role in homoeroticism: grass green or chartreuse, purple, and saffron. They may also have worn white *chiridotae* or *stolae* having designs of arrows, checks, and purple stripes. On their feet they wore gold, red, or pink sandals or slippers, sarcastically referred to as "cymbals," due perhaps to the musical instruments they played.[27]

On their heads they wore golden hairnets or wreaths of golden leaves. On more solemn occasions, the highest in rank among them would wear miters (or *mitras*), turbans or tiaras with ribbons falling to the shoulders. The miter was considered a "mark of effeminacy" by Greeks and Romans who did not revere the Goddess. Its association with effeminacy seems to have sprung from its being of Phrygian, and hence "barbarian," rather than of Greco-Roman origin. Among male gods, it was worn only by gender-variant deities like Dionysus, Adonis, and Attis. Given its association with effeminacy, "It is curious," writes archaeologist George W. Elderkin (1879–1965), "that the western church should have made use of it as a name for a bishop's liturgical cap."[28]

The *galli* sometimes wore exquisite jewelry—necklaces, brooches, rings, earrings, and ankle bracelets. Pierced ears, incidentally, signified bondage—chosen, destined, or enforced. While this custom was eventually borrowed by the Hebrews to identify their slaves, it was originally a sign of devoted service to the Goddess. Necklaces, quite often elaborate, displayed portraits of Cybele, Attis, and other deities. The *galli* also carried mirrors and scourges made of wool, leather, and sheep knucklebones as they processed.

Galli also wore makeup. They rubbed their faces with pumice stones and smoothed their skin with salves of balsam and fenugreek. Faces were then painted with a white ointment containing flecks of gold. The *galli* also wore rouge, plucked their eyebrows, and outlined their eyes with kohl. Some also appear to have tattooed themselves with ivy patterns, perhaps a sign of affiliation with the mysteries of Dionysus as well as with those of Cybele.

They let their hair grow long, frequently to their waists; indeed, they were nicknamed the "longhaired ones." They rarely let their hair down in public, however, except during ecstatic dance rituals. The rest of the time they wore elaborate hairstyles, having their hair curled or corkscrewed. Those who were balding wore wigs.[29]

The Roman rhetorician Quintillian and the Christian bishop Clement of Alexandria were especially irritated by this excessive attention to hair grooming, a fashion that seemed to be rapidly spreading to the male population at large. Quintillian attacked the *galli* and other males for dressing "their locks by scorching them with the curling iron," while Clement complained of those who carried mirrors with them in order, so he thought, to comb their hair and clip stray hairs. "Oh, these preoccupations of immoral androgynes," Clement wailed, "and their coifing sessions!" The *galli,* moreover, dyed their hair blond, "from the religious belief that the Goddess would only accept offerings of blonde hair."[30] The hair of the *galli* could be cut only on three occasions: when they wished to sacrifice a lock to the Goddess by hanging it from the branch of a sacred tree; when, due to grave illness or advanced age, they felt they could no longer actively serve the Goddess; and at the time of death.

The *galli* also employed rich oils, perfumes, and unguents to enhance their attractiveness and to serve as a sign of reverence for the Goddess. These fragrances, containing rose, iris, and myrrh, included the famous Lydian perfume *Bakkaris.* It has been recently stated that "the use of perfume . . . played its role in the corruption and effeminization of Greek cities."[31] Despite the condemnation and eventual banning of male scents, however, they continued to be worn by men in defiance of ethics and laws. Alexander the Great was among those condemned as effeminate because of his use of perfume. Indeed, in both Greece and Rome, the perfume industry became an extremely lucrative one. The typical perfumer was depicted as shading himself from the sun with a parasol, "talking about fashions, and playing the sodomite." In the view of some Greeks and Romans, to rub scented unguents on another man's feet was tantamount to being anally penetrated by him.[32]

The *galli* also practiced depilation, using depilatories of "resin, pitch, white vine or ivy gum extracts, ass's fat, she-goat's gall, bat's blood, and powdered viper" or a less Macbethian compound of arsenic and bryonia. The *galli* practiced depilation in order to more closely resemble women and the Goddess as well as to appear younger and to attract certain males. This custom, like that of wearing perfume, quickly spread to the general male populace. In *The Art of Love,* Ovid warned young men not to curl their hair or depilate their legs, telling them, "Leave such matters as those to the members of Cybele's chorus, / Howling their bacchanal strains under the dark of the moon."[33]

In spite of such warnings, the popularity of depilation only increased. Indeed, during the first centuries of the Common Era, salons for depilation may have outnumbered traditional barbershops. And opponents of the practice raged against them. Dio Chrysostom, a first-century C.E. Greek rhetorician, especially condemned the depilation of the genital area as an action growing out of men's desire to become women, complaining that the men of his day saw masculine males as "defective" and thus desired to become "whole beings and natural—epicenes!"[34] Attacking depilation in particular and the "perversity of modern tastes" in general, the rhetorician Quintillian bemoaned the fact that men's admiration of the artificial over the natural had led them to "glow with a complexion that is not their own."[35] The early Christian theologian Arnobius railed in a similar vein against depilation and related practices, insisting that god had not created men to wear jewelry, curl their hair, wear makeup, or engage in gender-variant or homoerotic behavior.[36] Still another writer posed this question: "Does anyone doubt that the man who wears perfume, who practices depilation, and who reclines in a full-length tunic on the inner side of a divan at symposium is a *cinaedus*?"[37]

The writers quoted above would almost certainly have agreed with the playwright Aristophanes, who once wrote that males, including the *galli*, who depilated themselves and who engaged in related practices should be burned alive "upon a heap of sixteen wooden phalluses."[38]

THE BEHAVIOR OF *GALLI*

Certain gestures were also attributed to the *galli*. One such gesture involved rolling the eyes and raising them toward the heavens, a gesture also attributed to hierodules and courtesans. Another consisted of holding the neck in a lilting or tilted manner. Augustine was especially perturbed by the "gliding," "languorous" stride of the *galli;* the *galli* were known especially for swaying the hips as they walked. While reclining the *galli* usually pulled the legs up to the chest, with the buttocks on the floor and the lower legs resting on a pile of cushions or on a small platform.

Galli and other gender-variant men spoke in distinctive ways. Like hierodules and courtesans, *galli* were said to converse with the palms of their hands turned upward, a gesture depicted on figurines portraying female deities. They were also said to speak in shrill tones, to lisp, to giggle and whisper, to use obscene language, to employ women's oaths, and to address each other in the feminine gender.[39]

Finally, the *galli* and other gender-variant males used a special verbal signal to communicate with each other. Unfortunately, we are familiar with this signal only from hostile sources; still, from these sources, we can guess at what this signal may have sounded like. Dio Chrysostom, in a speech to the men of Tarsus, names this signal the *regkeis,* commonly translated as "snort." From Clement of Alexandria, who also suggests that the *regkeis* signal was nasal in character, we learn that the men using this signal "make a sound in their nose like a frog." The *regkeis* signal may actually have sounded more like heavy breathing or hissing.

Dio Chrysostom describes the *regkeis* as "belonging to neither man nor woman." In another place he asks, "But who are they who make that sort of sound? Are they not creatures of mixed sex? Are they not men who have had their testicles lopped off?" He answers himself, "It [the *regkeis* signal] is reserved for themselves, a sort of password of their own."

The *regkeis,* which apparently made hostile men laugh, was clearly used to announce an erotic desire; Clement refers to it as a signal of "lewdness and fornication to provoke lust," continuing to say that it sounds as if its users have "concentrated their bad behavior in their nostrils."

Dio Chrysostom insists that, even more than appearance, the *regkeis* may reveal a man to be a *cinaedus,* a gender-variant man engaging in same-sex eroticism. He relates the story of an elderly man who is brought before a certain sage so that the sage might determine what sort of man he is. Even though the elderly man is a "person of rugged frame and knitted brows . . . with calluses on his hands, [and] wrapped in a sort of coarse, gray mantle," the sage recognizes him to be a *cinaedus* and perhaps also an elderly *gallus,* because he utters the *regkeis* during their brief encounter.[40]

WANDERING AND WILD FOODS

While some *galli,* particularly those living in Phrygia, led settled lives, dwelling in communal apartments in or near the temple grounds, a majority were apparently itinerant and mendicant; hence their Greek appellation *metragyrtes,* the ascetic or begging priests of the Mother. The related term *metriazein* referred both to begging for the Goddess and being initiated into her worship.

Many *galli* apparently viewed sedentary life and the owning of property as obstacles to spiritual development. Their views were fortunate in light of Greek and Roman laws, which for centuries forbade them to own or inherit property. Many of the *galli,* moreover, were freedmen, fugitive slaves, and men from the poorest economic classes.

Galli generally traveled in caravans. In a wagon or on the back of a donkey they carried a small shrine containing a statue of Cybele. When they reached a town or a city, they would set the shrine on a rock or beneath a tree or on an improvised stage, and this would become the temporary temple of the Goddess. They would proceed to dance around the shrine, chanting, singing, and telling fortunes in exchange for alms—coins, cheese, and wine.[41] If the *galli* could be said to have a true home, it would undoubtedly have been the mountain forests considered sacred to Cybele.[42]

The *galli* ate meat, as opposed to many others leading spiritual lives who were vegetarians. Their diet consisted chiefly of wild game and birds. Considering such a diet "savage," they held that it was essential to follow because it reminded people of that time when only Cybele, the Mother of the Beasts, ruled the earth, long before the arrival of Demeter and other deities associated with agriculture. The *galli,* for this reason, abstained from grain as well as apples, pomegranates, dates, and pigs. They sometimes ate meat raw, tearing it apart with their teeth.

On feast days, they prepared a sacrificial meal for Cybele (eating of it communally), which included the Goddess's favorite dish, *moretum. Moretum* was prepared by blending garlic, celery, rue, coriander, vinegar, and olive oil into feta cheese. Ovid explains in the *Fasti* that the *galli* prepared *moretum* so "that the ancient goddess may know [be reminded of] the ancient foods."[43]

During the period of initiation, the *galli,* like initiates of other mysteries, were fed only milk; according to the Roman historian Sallust, this was because they were thought of as *hosper anagennomenon,* that is, "those who are being born again."[44]

RITUAL CASTRATION

Ritual castration was generally required of *galli.* It is difficult to say whether only the testicles or both the penis and the testicles were removed, as different texts suggest both possibilities. The ritual of castration took place on March 24, the Day of Blood. While this ritual undoubtedly originated in Phrygia, probably during the Neolithic, it came to be performed at the Metroon in Athens, the

Campus Matris Deum in Rome, in London near the Thames, and in many other places.

Elder *galli* and initiates would begin to chant, sing, play their instruments, and dance in a circle. Soon they would attain a state of *mania* or *enthousiasmos,* in which they would begin to tear their clothes and to bite, cut, and flagellate themselves and each other. Their "womanish" blood, as Apuleius called it, would splatter on the statue of the Goddess in the center of the circle. At the climax of this rite, ritual castration of certain initiates was performed.

In the earliest times, the instrument employed in castration was a sharp, chipped stone of flint, an instrument that classical scholar Günther Zuntz indicates may be traced to Çatal Hüyük. In later times, knives, double axes, and potsherds were used.[45] According to Pliny, "The priests of the Mother of the Gods called *galli,* castrate themselves . . . with a piece of Samian pottery, the only way of avoiding dangerous results."[46] In later times elaborate bronze instruments, clamps resembling those used to geld horses, came into use. One such tool was discovered in the Thames near London Bridge. This was an elaborate clamp with ornamental busts of Cybele, Attis, and other figures. It suggests that, at least in later times, only the testicles were removed. Found in London, it indicates the widespread diffusion of the institution of the *galli.*[47]

Following the ritual of castration, the organs were bathed in holy water and then wrapped in the old, masculine attire of the initiate, clothes he would not wear again. Occasionally the testicles were embalmed, allegedly even gilded. They were then buried in the earth or placed in an earthenware jar and stored in an underground chamber. "Here they became a cult object, and played a role in the mysteries."[48]

Throughout this ritual, devotees of Cybele and Attis showered the *galli* with coins and white roses. Slowly the chaotic atmosphere dissolved into joyous solemnity. Sometime thereafter, the initiates processed to the houses of priestesses or female devotees, where they were dressed in feminine garments, which they would wear from that time on.

Several theories concerning this ritual among the *galli* have been advanced. One suggests that the *galli* underwent castration in order to more closely resemble the Goddess and women. Another, espoused by Porphyry, suggests that it "is in memory of . . . Attis that the *galli* mutilate themselves" because they, like Attis (and perhaps also like Adonis, not to mention Narcissus and Hyacinthus, other beloved youths of Greco-Roman myth), represent "the earth in spring . . . the flower [that] falls before the fruit."[49] Others hold that the *galli* sacrificed their organs to the Goddess because it was thought that their seed would fructify the earth. Still others argue that castration symbolized leaving behind an ordinary for an extraordinary existence.[50] Walter Burkert insists that above all, ritual castration carries the message that these men are "totally different, both superior and inferior to average men, inferior in sexual status," in terms of their ability to reproduce, but "superior as to blood and death," in other words, superior in embodying the principle of sacrificial death and spiritual regeneration; "thus awe spreads from the holy beggars."[51]

It seems that in the latter days of Cybele's worship, that is, in the first few centuries of the Common Era, castration was no longer required of the *galli*. The rite was displaced by the *taurobolium,* a bull sacrifice, and by offerings of phallus-shaped breads. The emperor Julian tells us in his "Hymn to the Mother of the Gods" that he is grateful to the Goddess for not requiring his castration in order to be initiated into her mysteries. In some places and among some groups, however, castration continued to be practiced. In the town of Autun, France, for instance, young men were still castrating themselves in honor of Cybele (as Berecynthia) in the fifth century C.E.[52]

THE *GALLI* AS GENDER-VARIANT PERSONS

It should be clear by now that the *galli* were not considered masculine by Greco-Roman standards; indeed, in the eyes of traditional males, they were, at best, *semiviri,* "half men." But if the *galli* were only "half men" or *anandreies,* "not men," they were not women either. Indeed, in spite of certain feminine traits, they were rarely if ever mistaken for women. Obscene speech, for instance, was not a marker of femininity; besides working-class traditional males, only prostitutes and devotees of Baubo-Iambe might be expected to "talk dirty." Physical size also prohibited many from being perceived as women. In his *Sixth Satire,* Juvenal mentions a "giant eunuch" who leads a troop of other *galli.* It is also doubtful that the *castrati* voices of the *galli* were mistaken for those of women. There is also the suggestion that lisping and the *regkeis* signal were specifically associated with the *galli* and other "not men." In Greek, the word *batalos* means both a lisper and a *kinaidos* (*cinaedus*) or gender-variant, homoerotically inclined male.

Nor did their ascetic character conform to standards of femininity or masculinity. An itinerant, mendicant lifestyle that included rejecting procreation definitely represented an alternative to Greco-Roman concepts of masculinity and femininity.

Sources differ, however, as to how a man came to be a *gallus.* A number of texts suggest that individuals became *galli* as a result of a psychological or spiritual crisis. Such a crisis might occur as the result of a dawning awareness of having behaved in a brutally partriarchal manner and a desire to atone for that behavior. This appears to have been the case with Dionysius the Younger, a tyrant of Sicily who, after a lifetime of abusing women, was banished to Corinth where, during the final years of his life, he became a *gallus.*

Others appear to have become *galli* after dreaming of the Goddess, from drinking or bathing in the rivers Gallos or Sangarios, after eating an herb growing along the banks of the Maeander River, or on seeing a reflection of the Goddess—perhaps merging with one's own image—in a piece of obsidian.

Other sources suggest that certain individuals may have freely chosen to become *galli* after witnessing a ritual performance, while others may have done so in order to find sanctuary from slavery. There is also the possibility that individuals who were already eunuchs or otherwise gender variant may have found companionship among the *galli*.[53]

Still other sources indicate that *galli* were born, not made. These sources include astrological treatises like the *Matheseos* of Firmicus Maternus. In the view of astrologers, to become initiated into the worship of the Goddess and to undergo a process of gender transformation was to fulfill a destiny ordained before birth, a fate controlled by the Goddess and revealed by the stars.

In the treatise of Firmicus Maternus, several forms of homosexual behavior are mentioned. Many of these references concern mundane as opposed to cultic behavior.[54] Several, however, refer directly to the *galli*, emphasizing sacred function while also speaking of gender variance and same-sex eroticism. We find, for example: "In general if the Moon, sun, and ascendant are in the face or back of Capricorn, Aries, Taurus, or Leo, they indicate *all kinds of sexual impurities together with extreme effeminization of the body*. In all charts, if the Moon is found in the Tail of Leo, *it will produce homosexuals who serve as tympany players to the mother of the gods*" (italics mine).[55]

The writings of Firmicus Maternus and other astrologers clearly demonstrate that many individuals, especially those living in late antiquity, reckoned that to become a *gallus* was to live out a preordained destiny that, like the shaman's, could be ignored or rejected only if one were willing to accept divine retribution. These writings also indicate that links were made between *galli* and other gender-variant males and men engaging in same-sex eroticism, as well as between *galli* and hierodules and women engaging in lesbian eroticism. The belief that *galli* were born as such clearly stood in opposition to the belief that one freely chose to become a *gallus* or that one became a *gallus* as a result of certain life experiences. It is possible to see the visionary dream or the drinking or eating of special substances as a fated occurrence that triggered the awareness of one's destiny. Such experiences were said to cause an individual to experience *sophrene,* to "recover one's senses."[56]

Whether one sees the *gallus* as a product of destiny (genetics?) or social circumstance, it is evident that the ancients regarded him as "totally different" from other men—and women. This becomes remarkably clear in the case of Genucius, a freed slave who became a *gallus* in (or near) 101 B.C.E. When another freed slave, Naevius Anius, died, he left his possessions to Genucius. It is unclear but certainly conceivable that the two were intimate companions. Genucius was allowed to inherit the property, apparently in spite of the regulation against eunuchs inheriting goods, by way of a decision handed down by the praetor Aufidius Orestes. This decision was appealed, however, by Sordinus Naevius, the previous owner of both parties. He apparently felt that he still had a right to their belongings. Thus in 77 B.C.E. the case was reopened. The consul Mamereus Aemilius Lepidus reversed the decision, insisting that Genucius had no right to inherit the property of Naevius Anius. In Rome, only men and women could inherit property, and Genucius, having "voluntarily mutilated himself" in order to become a "*gallus* of the Great Mother," had forfeited his claim to any inheritance because he could now be counted "neither male or female, *neque virorum neque mulierum*."[57]

THE *GALLI* AS DISSIDENTS

Due to their gender-variant appearance and behavior, their rejection of reproduction, their lives as holy beggars, and other factors, the *galli* may well have been
considered social or political radicals, perhaps even enemies of the state. We must
recall that Roman religion, during the time when Goddess reverence experienced
a renaissance, was more concerned with imperialism than anything else. Real belief in a deity or deities often inspired mockery, while magical texts were being
gathered up and burned by the authorities. The beliefs and practices of the "old
religion" were being increasingly discarded by urban elites, leaving their survival
to the urban poor and to rural peasants, the "pagans." Classical scholar Richard
Gordon explains that Goddess-centered religions like that of Cybele, as well as
other mystery religions, "should . . . be understood as implicitly opposed to elite
culture" and "seen as forms of resistance to dominant elite goals."[58] As adherents
of Goddess worship, the *galli* might thus have been seen as rebels, especially considering that their numbers included fugitive slaves, freedmen, and men of the
lowest economic classes.

Classical scholar and historian Cristiano Grottanelli further points out that in
the ancient world, forms of "archaic" social and political rebellion included exodus, suicide, and tyrannicide as opposed to complex forms of rebellion such as
armed revolution. The *galli*, as wandering individuals frequently living in the
wilderness, might thus be seen as participating in the first form of archaic rebellion. In Grottanelli's view, however, the *galli* engaged in other forms of rebellion
as well, most important of which was their "refusal not only of production, but
also of the sexual roles that guarantee reproduction," a refusal that potentially
brings about "the end of any social order based on marriage and reproduction," in
other words, patriarchy.

Grottanelli seems convinced that the Romans were acutely aware of the threat
posed by the *galli*. He also links the *galli* with other radical groups, including male
laborers of the fifteenth through nineteenth centuries, who stole game from
forests of the manors (1451), sacked a ship full of grain that was to be exported, in
spite of a grain crisis (1629), destroyed field boundaries (1760–1779) and demol-
ished weaving machines (1812). Grottanelli explains that these men, like the *galli*,
"dressed in women's clothes," some even "pretending to be . . . fairies."[59]

THE *GALLI* AND GENDER-VARIANT WOMEN

From an early (although unspecified) date, the *galli* were associated with gender-variant women, including amazons or female warrior-priestesses (whose existence remains controversial).

In a lengthy treatise on the Amazons, the ancient historian Diodorus Siculus
describes these women as worshipers of Cybele. After relating how Myrina,
queen of the Amazons, founded the city of Mitylene on the island of Lesbos,
Diodorus tells how Myrina then sailed to Samothrace, which "she made sacred to
this goddess, and set up altars there and offered magnificent sacrifices." While

Myrina and the Amazons did not choose to remain on the island, Diodorus explains that "the Mother of the Gods [was] well pleased with the island, [and] settled in it her own sons," the *galli*.[60] Swedish archaeologist Axel Persson (1888–1951) agrees with this view, stating that the Amazons were functionaries "of the same kind as the *galli* . . . consecrated to the goddess."[61] Classicist Walter Tyrrell also makes this connection: "Amazons worship . . . the Phrygian Mother, Cybele. . . . Their rites were orgiastic, attended by frenzied dancing and music; their votaries were women and eunuchs."[62]

One of the most intriguing comments on the subject was made by the philosopher Sextus Empiricus in the third century C.E. Empiricus claimed that when Amazons gave birth to male children, they castrated them both in honor of Cybele and so they would be unable to make war, which they considered their own prerogative.[63] *Galli* were also associated with *tribades* and *fricatrices*, gendervariant women engaging in lesbian eroticism. Clement of Alexandria wailed that just as men of his day enjoyed playing the "passive role of women," so women enjoyed acting "like men, letting themselves be possessed in a way that is contrary to nature." Similarly, the third-century Christian theologian Tertullian stated bitterly: "I do not call a cup poisoned which has received the last of a dying man; I give that name to one that has been infected by the breath of a *frictrix*, [or] of [the breath] a high priest of Cybele . . . and I ask if you will not refuse it [the cup] as you would such persons' actual kisses."[64]

The *Galli*, Hierodules, and Heterosexuality

Both *galli/cinaedi* and Amazons/*tribades* were associated with sacred and profane "prostitutes," hierodulic priestesses and courtesans or *hetaerae*. Amy Richlin, a classicist interested in sex and gender studies, suggests that these groups were linked because both were considered abnormal. Pederastic homoeroticism and certain forms of heterosexual lovemaking were viewed as "obscene," a term used to describe types of intercourse that, while perhaps inappropriate, were still considered "masculine" activities and thus somewhat condoned by patriarchy. Forms of eroticism primarily attributed to *galli/cinaedi*, Amazons/*tribades*, and hierodules, on the other hand, were deemed "filthy," a term used to designate deviant or perverse forms of eroticism that were also considered "feminine" and in some sense antipatriarchal.

Rather than always focusing on phallic pleasure, these "filthy" (and "feminine") forms of eroticism recognized and celebrated oral, anal, and clitoral pleasure. Richlin states, "The sexuality of women and of adult male pathic homosexuals is by definition abnormal. . . . Any sexual desire felt by women or male homosexuals was thus out of place."[65]

As eunuchs, the *galli* were grouped legally with the courtesans or *hetaerae*. While neither group was supposed to inherit property, both were bound to pay poll tax. Prostitutes, like *galli*, were considered gender variant. Perhaps their alleged participation in lesbian eroticism, coupled with the myth of an enlarged clitoris (attributed to both *tribades* and *hetaerae*) encouraged this perception.[66]

According to Clement of Alexandria, the *galli* and other gender-variant men spent a great deal of time in the company of hierodules and *hetaerae*. "But these women delight in intercourse [conversation] with the effeminate [also translated as "androgynous males"]; among them may be found bands of infamous debauched males [*kinaides*]."[67]

It is possible that some *galli* may have temporarily shared quarters with hierodules or *hetaerae*. It is conceivable that Clement has them in mind when he speaks of *hetaerae* and gender-variant males raising birds, including peacocks and parrots, as well as Maltese or Melitane puppies. These dogs, incidentally, are known for their lack of physical force and for their shrill voices, traits reflecting those attributed to *galli*. Moreover, Maltese or Melitane puppies were said to be "bred only for delight."[68]

Little is known concerning the erotic lives of the *galli*, and what we do know comes primarily from hostile sources. In any event, an epigram of the satiric Roman poet Martial suggests that some *galli* may have occasionally, albeit rarely, engaged in cunnilingus with female companions; in one of his satirical poems, he reprimands the *gallus* Baeticus for engaging in oral sex with a woman.[69]

Such relationships, if they existed, must have outraged traditional Greco-Roman males. Indeed, such relationships were outlawed in early Christian times. At the Synod of Elvira in Spain in 305 C.E., it was declared that marriages between women and eunuchs were henceforth forbidden. In this and similar documents, these men are referred to as *comatos, cinerarios,* and *spadones*. In Charles Hefele's *History of the Christian Councils,* we find:

> Many pagan women had foreign slaves, and especially hairdressers, in
> their service, who ministered not only to the needs of luxury, but to the
> secret satisfaction of their passions. Perhaps these effeminate slaves—these
> *spadones*—encouraging the licentiousness of their mistresses, wore long
> hair. . . . These eunuchs wore long hair like women in order that they
> might be called *comati*.[70]

Hefele notes that this type of relationship, and the law proscribing it, confused medieval copyists, who "could not understand why a Christian woman was not to marry a man having long hair, or even a hairdresser." While the edict of the Synod of Elvira does not apply directly to the *galli*, it does reveal the extreme hostility that must have surfaced when a Greco-Roman male learned of a relationship between a generally homosexual, gender-variant male and a female companion. For the typical male of late antiquity and the Middle Ages, things couldn't get much more topsy-turvy than this.

THE *GALLI* AND HOMOEROTICISM

While the *galli* were believed to engage occasionally in variant, or "filthy," forms of heterosexual lovemaking, they were much more frequently alleged to practice same-sex eroticism. As Graillot explains, the terms "*galli* and *cinaedi* ended up being synonyms."[71] Several other terms first used to describe *galli* also came to be used interchangeably with *cinaedus*. This included: *umbraticola,* "one who carries a parasol or who stays in the shade"; *cymbala pulsans,* "pulsating cymbals," referring to the cymbals employed by the *galli* and connoting anal eroticism; and *tympan-otriba,* "a drummer . . . an effeminate companion like one of Cybele's drumming priests."[72] In twentieth-century terms, Burkert states that the *galli,* following initiation, "would present themselves as passive homosexuals."[73]

Apuleius indicates that the *galli*'s erotic partners were traditionally masculine males who may also have been followers of the Goddess. He mentions, for instance, a "certain stout young man with a mighty body, well skilled in playing the flute," who led a procession of *galli* and who (in this satire, unwillingly) played an "active" role in same-sex erotic activities with them.[74]

Juvenal suggests that some *galli* or other gender-variant priests may have even married other men. In "Satire II," he describes such a wedding. "The contract was signed," he writes,

> . . . . the blessing
> Pronounced and the blushing bride
>   hung round
>   "her" husband's neck
> At a lavish wedding-breakfast.[75]

Extremely dismayed by such celebrations—or at least appearing to be so—Juvenal envisions a time when same-sex marriages will become commonplace. "We have only to wait now," he rails,

> Such things will be done,
> And done in public: male brides will yearn
>   for a mention
> In the daily gazette.[76]

Juvenal may be referring to an actual marriage ceremony that took place in Rome during the first century C.E. between a gladiator named Gracchus and an unnamed horn player. While a majority of scholars describe Gracchus as a *sallus* or priest of Mars, it is clear that, although "once / [he] Was a priest of Mars," he has now become a priest of the Goddess, as is evident from his apparel.[77] The *galerus* he wears is clearly not the "tall bonnet of a Salian priest," as one scholar thought thirty years ago, but rather, as a more recent translation of Juvenal indicates, the miter of a *gallus;* "Who," we might ask with Juvenal, "could mistake that . . . / . . . mitre with dangling ribbons?"[78] Once a priest of Mars who joined in Cybele's celebrations, Gracchus has now become a *gallus* and a male bride.

Cultic or ritual homoeroticism also appears to have played a role in the worship of Cybele and Attis. Firmicus Maternus writes, "In their very temples one may see scandalous performances . . . men letting themselves be handled as women, and flaunting with boastful ostentatiousness this ignominy of their impure and unchaste bodies."[79]

Augustine, not surprisingly, also deplores the cultic homoeroticism "openly professed in . . . religious ceremonies" dedicated to Cybele.[80]

Cultic homoeroticism was not, as we have already seen, limited to the worship of Attis and Cybele; indeed, it apparently experienced a kind of renaissance between the fourth century B.C.E. and the third century C.E. It played a role in many spiritual traditions. In all of these, "Religious initiation [included a] union with [the representative of the] God [or Goddess] a sexual union whereby the man [the worshiper] receives the inner-most essence and power of a god."[81]

Although shrouded in mystery, it is conceivable that cultic homoeroticism as manifested in the worship of Cybele and Attis played a role in the Pannychis or Mesonyctium, an induction ceremony that usually occurred on the evening of March 24, which, amazingly, took place after initiates had experienced ritual castration earlier in the day. On that night, the elder *galli* and the initiates processed to "a subterranean or hidden space in or near the temple" of Cybele. The ritual began with a series of laments sung over the effigy of Attis, which lay on a bier. A symbolic *katabasis*, or descent, followed; this represented Attis's death and "survival in death." At this time, the initiates may have repeated, "I have crept below to the bosom of the Mistress, I have entered the house of Hades." This shamanistic descent was followed by a rite of communion, in which a substance, perhaps *moretum*, was eaten from a tambourine, while a beverage, perhaps milk, was drunk from a cymbal.[82]

The ritual of induction climaxed with a *hieros gamos*, a sacred marriage ceremony, with the elder *galli* and initiates playing complementary roles. According to Philostratus, the initiates assumed the role of yielding worshipers whose intimate interaction with the elders, playing the role of or embodying Attis, allowed the former to enter into an altered state of consciousness in which they, too, could come to embody Attis. Philostratus writes,

> The initiate no longer beholds what the deity has experienced, but he himself experiences it and thereby becomes the deity. . . . When the high priest himself is called *Attis*, he must be understood to be the embodiment of the deity already in his own lifetime.
>
> The tie between god and man cannot be thought of in closer or stronger terms, and they are joined by a feeling not only of lifelong gratitude but of personal love, which in its expression passes over into sensual terms.[83]

While writers agree as to the feeling of union with the deity during this ceremony, they do not always agree as to the roles assumed by participants. In *Pagan Regeneration*, historian of religions Harold Willoughby (1890–1962) writes:

> As a new *Attis* the votary [initiate] assumed the role of a bridegroom to the goddess. . . . From another standpoint [however,] the newly consecrated priest was thought of as a male counterpart of the goddess. Hence, he was called a *kubebos*.[84]

The *archgallus* concluded the induction ceremony with these words: "Be of good heart, you novices, because the god [Attis] is saved. / Deliverance from distress will come for us, as well."[85]

The *Megalensia*

While the *galli* paid homage to Cybele and Attis throughout the year, the Goddess and her consort were especially honored in the spring, during the period between March 15 and April 10. This period was known as the Megalensia, *Megale* referring to the Great Mother.

The first day of the festival celebrated the birth and infancy of Attis. On March 16, nine days of fasting began. Six days later, the passion of Attis was commemorated. An effigy of Attis tied to a pine trunk and decorated with bunches of violets and woolen bands, or perhaps purple ribbons, was carried in procession. This was the day of the *arbor intrat,* "the entry of the pine," and commemorated Attis's sacrifice and death. The effigy was mourned by Cybele's priestesses and the *galli* with "ululations . . . [and] the rhythmic beating of . . . tambourines."[86]

March 24, as we have seen, was known as the *dies sanguines,* "the day of blood." On this day, the *galli* participated in ritual dances involving flagellation and castration. In the evening of that day, they took part in the *hieros gamos* described above.

On March 25, Attis's triumph over physical death was celebrated. In later times, this occasion commemorated Attis's ascension to the heavens (unlike the earlier view that he survives in death). Attis was carried by Ganymede to the heavens.[87]

The coupling of Ganymede and Attis links two important elements in the worship of Cybele: that of spiritual transformation, symbolized by ascension to the heavens, and that of cultic homoeroticism, as both Attis and Ganymede are loved by other divine male beings—the former by Agdistis and the latter by Zeus.

On March 27, a statue of Cybele and other sacred objects were ritually bathed. Between April 4 and April 9, games and other entertainments were held. On April 10, Cybele's birthday was celebrated with banquets and sacrifices. It was customary on this day for Roman citizens to be especially generous with their gifts of food and money to the *galli.*[88]

The *Galli* as Artists

The *galli,* like the priests of other deities, fulfilled an artistic function as ritual poets, musicians, dancers, and actors. It is ironic, and tragic, that while the priests of Cybele were especially well known as poets and composers of hymns, little work of *galli* has survived.

The *galli* are credited with inventing the *galliambic,* a poetic meter also known as the *metroaic* or the "Mother Goddess's meter." It was appropriated by several ancient poets including Catullus and Callimachus, and many centuries later, Tennyson used it in his poem *Boadicea.* Many, however, like Quintillian, were repulsed by the "wanton measures that suggest the accompaniment of castanets." Quintillian, criticizing the "effeminate modulations now in vogue," linked the *galliambic,* despite its ancient origin, with the "modern music" of his day, which he described as "emasculated by the lascivious melodies of our effeminate stage."[89]

Although most writers agree that little if any work by *galli* survives, it seems possible that two poems may have been composed by *galli* or at least in imitation of their work. The second stanza of an anonymous poem includes these lines:

Thou art powerful, of the Gods Thou art
The queen and also the goddess.
Thee, Goddess and Thy power I now invoke,
Thou canst easily grant me all that I ask,
And in exchange I will give Thee, Goddess,
    sincere thanks.[90]

The second poem was composed by the poet Erucius between 50 and 25 B.C.E. If Erucius was not a *gallus,* as an inhabitant of Cyzicus, he would surely have been familiar with the Goddess's worship and priesthood. This poem reads:

I, the priest of Rhea, long-haired
castrato, Tmolian dancer, whose
high shriek is famed for carrying power,
now, at last, rest from my throes
and give the Great Dark Mother on
the banks of the Sangarius all:
my tambourines, my bone-linked scourge,
my brazen cymbals, and a curl
of my long heavy perfumed hair
in dedication, Holy Rhea.[91]

THE *GALLI* USED distinctive sounds while singing and chanting. From comments made about their shrill voices, it seems likely that they sang in a *castrati* voice and also exaggerated this voice. It is possible that they also employed the *regkeis* signal in chanting.

High-pitched chants by holy men are known also in other parts of the world. Mongolian shamans perform a chant in which they open and close their mouths while humming or singing nasally, causing a "very high pitch" or "shrill melody" to be produced. A similar technique developed among Islamic *muezzins,* who intone the Koran from the minaret by placing both hands on their temples and singing in an unnaturally high tone. In Sufi chanting, the singer, using the head voice or falsetto, produces a kind of hiccup that "as with an overblown flute, switches the voice to a higher harmonic pitch."[92]

The *galli,* it is conceivable, used such forms of chanting in their rituals. We also know that they employed ululation like that performed today by women in the Middle East. The Greeks referred to this type of ululation as *rigelos ulagmos,* which roughly translates as "shuddering yelp."[93]

The nasal, high-pitched voice used in a sacred context can induce altered states and effect spiritual transformation. As one scholar of music and religion notes, some vocal forms, "though outwardly 'unnatural,' [can] release mystic powers of insight and enlightenment not only in the singer, but also in those listening to the ritual office." It is not hard to imagine that the *galli*, who have been compared to the Sufis, chanted, as they danced, the names of the Goddess and her consort in shrill tones, "faster and faster and ever more loudly," in an attempt to reach a "summit of ecstasy" in which they would participate in a "deep communal experience."[94]

THE FAVORITE MUSICAL instruments of the *galli* were the flute, cymbals, tympanum, panpipe, and krotala. The flute played by the *galli* was believed to produce music that invoked the Goddess and also drove hostile forces away. The flute was associated with effeminacy because of its high, piercing tones. Its rasping quality may have also reminded hearers of the *regkeis* signal. What is more, the flute may have been associated with fellatio, since one played it by holding the flute's pipes in one's mouth and hands. There is a myth in which Athena, playing the flute, sees her image reflected in a spring. She suddenly throws the flute to the ground, exclaiming, "Far from me, shame and taint of my body, I do not indulge in such indecency!" Flutes and flute players, we may recall, had also been associated with both gender and sexual variance since the seventh century B.C.E., when these traits were first attributed to a flute-playing "baptist" of Kotys.[95]

The altered state of consciousness or *enthousiasmos*, entered by the hearer of sacred music, makes the worshiper receptive to embodying the deity. In pre-Christian religions this state was also referred to as *pathein*, or being passive and yielding. As such, it was often associated with the traditional female role in sexual intercourse. Thus, in a sense, becoming "possessed" was linked by Greeks and Romans to femininity and in males to both gender variance and the taking of the receptive or *pathic* role in same-sex eroticism. Needless to say, this association led many Greeks and Romans to view the enthusiastic or ecstatic state, and the mysteries requiring it—such as those of Dionysus and Cybele—in negative terms. This is one of the reasons why, even after the patriarchal takeover of Delphi by Apollo's worshipers, the oracle there, the Pythian priestess, remained female.

In terms of musical tonality, it was the Phrygian mode that was thought to convey the worshiper most successfully into another state of consciousness. Indeed, its success in doing so caused it to be nicknamed the *entheos* mode. A seven-note scale with semitones, the Phrygian mode was particularly linked to the worship of Cybele. Aristotle is quoted as saying, "Among the modes, the Phrygian has the same power as the flute among instruments, for both are orgiastic and both heighten consciousness." The Phrygian mode was often opposed to the Dorian mode, a five-note scale with semitones. While the Dorian mode was thought to be "calm," "aristocratic," and "virile," the Phrygian was considered "agitated," "plebeian," and "effeminate."[96]

The *galli* also used the tympanum, famed in ancient Egypt for its power to drive away demons, to help trigger the state of *enthousiasmos*. The cymbals may have served a similar function. We may recall that both the tympanum and the cymbals also became associated in the popular psyche with gender-variant homo-eroticism, as shown in such expressions as *tympanotriba* and *cymbala pulsans*. Once the *gallus* had entered into the state of *enthousiasmos*, he would begin to utter the words of Cybele, prophesying the future to the worshipers present.[97]

IN THE WORSHIP of the Goddess, music was frequently combined with dance. Like music, dance helped to trigger an altered state. From various fragmentary sources, we can speculate that the dances of the *galli* may have been inspired by Greek, Egyptian, and black African dances. The relief discovered at Ariccia (discussed in the preceding chapter) reveals that Romans were familiar with both Egypto-African and sub-Saharan African dance styles. The fact that the male dancers of Ariccia may have been *cinaedi*, coupled with the fact that a number of males were followers of both Isis and Cybele, suggests that the *galli*, like the Roman worshipers of Isis, may have also drawn upon African dance, specifically on dance styles associated with ecstatic states.[98]

The erotic movements described by ancient writers to condemn the dances of the *galli* may have been derived from the Egyptian *danse du ventre* or belly dance, performed in Egypt as early as the Eighteenth Dynasty (1567–1320 B.C.E.). Dance historians Leona Wood and Anthony Shay have suggested that belly dancing may well have originated in the worship of the Goddess; they point to a similar dance performed in the twentieth century in Malabar celebrating the "Goddess' invincibility when doing battle with her foes." Wood and Shay also point out that belly dancing "is essentially female dancing, whether done by a male or female," and that its male performers, including the *batcha* of Persia, the *kocek* of Turkey, and the *qawwal* of Arab countries, traditionally wear feminine clothes and employ finger cymbals in their performances.

What is more, belly dancing often includes a homoerotic element. Wood and Shay mention that in one particular dance performed in Egypt and Uzbekistan until very recently, "at a certain point in the dance between two performers of the same sex, one kisses the other."

This and other data suggest that the sub-Saharan "possession" dances and the Egyptian belly dance may lie behind the dance most frequently associated with the *galli*, the *sikinnis*, also performed by other Greco-Roman worshipers of the Goddess and Dionysus.[99] *Sikinnis* means "to shake." The dance is said to have originated in Phrygia, the seat of Cybele's worship, or in Crete, another center of Goddess reverence. It was believed by some to have been invented by a priestess of Cybele named Sikinnis. Lucian tells us that in the beginning Cybele, "charmed with the art [of dance], ordered dances to be performed not only in Phrygia . . . but [also] in Crete."[100]

The *sikinnis* was apparently "lively, rapid, vigorous, and lewd," using "expressive gestures, many of them obscene." The shaking or undulation of the belly, buttocks, and genital area was all-important. It emphasized eroticism, which, in males, usually indicated the receptive role in anal intercourse, since *kinein* meant to shake (the buttocks) and *kinaidos/cinaedus* referred to a gender-variant male engaging in homoeroticism. But at the same time the dance emphasized the state of *enthousiasmos*. Movements employed in the *sikinnis* included leaping, stamping, crouching, slapping or kicking the buttocks, and spinning furiously. The dancer also used a movement known as the "*saulomenos,* an affected, mincing [effeminate] walk with exaggerated movements of the hips." The term *saulomenos* also implies walking like a lizard.[101]

The *sikinnis* appears to have been performed primarily by three groups: female hierodules or courtesans; men playing satyrs in satyr plays; and worshipers, both male and female, of the Goddess in her various manifestations. When performed by males—even by satyrs—both gender variance (here, including ultramasculine as well as effeminate behavior) and homoeroticism are inferred. This won the *sikinnis* the title of "most offensive dance" in the eyes of early Christian polemicists. Arnobius, for instance, wrote, "Was it for this He [the God of the Christians] sent souls, that . . . souls should be led in their wantonness . . . to . . . form rings of dancers, and . . . raising their haunches and hips, float along with a tremulous motion of the loins?" Those who perform the *sikinnis,* he said, "abandon themselves to the lust of all . . . prepared to do violence to their mouths," in other words, to engage in oral sex.

Flagellation and self-wounding, as we have seen, were also part of the dances of the *galli*. But if horrified Christians reported "blood streaming from their self-inflicted wounds" as they danced, they were also profoundly inspired by the *galli*.[102] The sadomasochistic element in Catholicism is proverbial in terms of its own harsh rituals of penitence and, some would say, even in the image of the scarred and bleeding Christ.

The *sikinnis* and other dances performed by *galli* appear to have had an impact on secular dance forms. By the second century B.C.E., a variant of the *sikinnis* had become extremely popular among Romans, especially males. Reactionary writers were horrified by the emergence of same-sex dance clubs in which so-called *drauci*—a derogatory term signifying the active partner in anal intercourse—danced with gender-variant males. The latter often wore feminine attire and were variously referred to as *cinaedi, androgyni, malti,* and *exoleti.*[103]

The *galli,* together with professional dancers, founded companies called the *ballatores Cybele,* which presented performances recounting the myths of Cybele, Attis, Marsyas, and others. These companies seem to have drawn great crowds, especially at Alexandria in the late third century B.C.E. An epigram by Dioscorides contrasts the cool reception given to a military procession with the glorious reception given to a performance by the *ballatores.* One of the chief sponsors of the *ballatores* at Alexandria was Pharaoh Ptolomaeus IV Philopator (reigned 221–205 B.C.E.), who "espoused the cause of Cybele . . . and called himself *gallos.*"[104]

While the dances of the *galli* clearly played a role in the development of secular dance traditions in Greco-Roman antiquity, however, it is important to bear in mind that for the *galli* themselves, dance remained primarily a technique of ecstasy by which to attain union with the Goddess.

THE *GALLI* AS DIVINERS, HEALERS, AND MAGICIANS

The *galli* were believed by many to be adept in the divinatory, healing, and magical arts. They used a number of divinatory techniques, chiefly astrology, since Cybele, as the planet Venus, was a patron of astrologers, and geomancy, since Cybele, as Mother Earth or Mountain Mother, was a patron of geomancers. Other techniques included ornithomancy, the observation of the songs and flight patterns of birds; astragalomancy, divination by hucklebones or knucklebones made to resemble dice; and oneiromancy, the interpretation of dreams, since as Oniropompus or Onirophantus, Cybele was a patron of dream interpreters. In sacred caves and dream temples, the *galli* would interpret the dreams of clients or would be asked to dream prophetic dreams themselves in order to determine a client's destiny.[105]

The *galli* were most celebrated, however, for their divinatory techniques requiring an altered state. Iamblichus writes, "Many, through enthusiasm and divine inspiration, predict future events. . . . Some also . . . energize enthusiastically on hearing cymbals or drums, or a certain modulated sound, such as those who are corybantically inspired [by Dionysus] [or] those who are inspired by the Mother of the Gods."[106]

Enthousiasmos could also be triggered by descent into caverns called *plutonia*, a name suggesting descent into the underworld, governed by Proserpina (or Persephone) and Pluto (or Hades). These caverns allegedly emitted toxic vapors. Cattle approaching them were said to succumb to the vapors and die. Among humans, the *galli* and certain other priests and priestesses were the only ones thought to be able to withstand the experience. Surrounded by the vapors, they would become possessed by the Goddess. Emerging from the caverns, as if from a shamanic death/rebirth experience, they would begin to prophesy by speaking in verses, typically in *galliambic*, or in foreign or nonsensical tongues. When they prophesied, the *galli* were said to *vaticinate*, a term later appropriated by Christians not only to signify the same action but also to refer to a center of religious activity, the Vatican.[107]

THE *GALLI* ALSO SERVED as healers. Many of the pilgrims who journeyed to dream clinics and to the vicinity of vaporous caverns were ill, physically disabled, or experiencing psychological crises. The *galli* were thought to be especially gifted in healing childhood illnesses, problems occurring during pregnancy, illness caused by the sirocco, and epilepsy. Such illnesses as epilepsy and schizophrenia were sometimes thought to be inflicted upon individuals because they had seriously offended the Goddess or, conversely, because their suffering and subsequent healing would lead them, like shamans, toward divine service. In Athenaeus, we find a description of an illness bestowed by Cybele: "If a sick person imitates the bleating of a goat, if he grinds his teeth, if he has convulsions from his right side, it is the Mother of the Gods who [has] caused him to be in this state."[108]

The *galli* also prescribed healing baths for clients, as well as prayers and sacrifices.[109]

AS PRACTITIONERS of magic, the *galli* composed spells, created philters, and fashioned amulets and talismans for persons seeking lovers, travelers making long journeys, and farmers desiring abundant crops. The classicist Graillot quotes from a spell that is believed to have been composed by a *gallus* and that may have been used in later centuries by Christians. The spell, to be read by a farmer wishing to banish rats from his land, reads, "I exorcise the rats which I have spied in this place. . . . I'm going to give you this field over here . . . but if I should come upon you again, I will, with the help of the Mother of the Gods, separate each of you into seven parts."[110]

The *galli* were thought to be highly skilled in fashioning talismans and amulets. Their specialty may have been designing amulets to be used in amatory magic. One such object was phallus shaped, carved from a pomegranate root. Another, which may have been fashioned by *galli* and which must have been extremely rare, was prepared from the hairs encircling the anus of a hyena. These hairs, explains Pliny, were "reduced to ashes, mixed with oil, and used as an ointment on men of shocking effeminacy" in order to protect them from violence while at the same time attracting lovers. The hairs of the hyena, as opposed to those of some other animal, were probably used because the hyena was "popularly believed to be bisexual and to become male and female in alternate years." Moreover, the hyena is "fond of a great deal of sexual indulgence," "has certain magic arts by which it causes every animal at which it gazes three times to be rooted on the spot," and because it "geld[s] [its] male offspring." Incidentally, a potion made of honey and the genitals of a hyena was believed to cause men to become sexually attracted to other men.[111]

Galli were believed to hold the power to tame wild animals. Legend has it that Cybele granted this power to the *galli* in order to commemorate an event in the life of Attis. Once, when he was journeying from Pessinus to Sardis, Attis wandered into a cave, where he was confronted by a lion. He managed to tame the lion, however, by beating rhythmically on this tympanum. On the death of Attis, this power was transferred to the *galli*.[112]

The *galli* were also believed to be able to make rain, a power attributed to shamans and other gender-variant holy people such as the *hijras,* devotees of the Hindu goddess Bahucharamata.[113] It was also thought that, like certain shamans, the *galli* could exorcise evil spirits by circling rapidly around the possessed person while beating on their tympana or tambourines. This technique became known as *tympanism;* some believe it to be related to the tarantella of later centuries.[114] The *galli* also appear to have used eggs in rituals of purification resembling those undertaken by Latin American *curanderas,* healers.[115]

Finally, the *galli*, like the Hindu goddess Kali, the Huastec goddess Tlazolteotl, and Jesus Christ, among others, may have acted as "sin eaters," taking the transgressions of others upon themselves in order to purify the others and in order to transform negative into positive energy. The *galli* did so by receiving the garments of devotees, primarily women, who felt they had in some way offended the Goddess. The *galli* either sacrificed the garments, perhaps by burning them, or, more probably, wore them in order to accomplish the purpose of transforming energy. Garments typically received were magenta in color, suggesting that these garments may have been worn in a ritual by women wishing to atone for transgressions prior to their being offered to the *galli*.[116]

DEATH AND BURIAL

When a *gallus* died, his hair was cut for a final time and sacrificed to the Goddess. Cult objects in his possession may have been sacrificed, given to others, or buried with him. It is not clear whether his severed testicles or genitals were buried with him.

Although some *galli* may have been buried above the ground under piles of stones, others were buried in tombs, some even in elaborate sarcophagi bearing images of Cybele, Attis, lions, roosters, doors leading to Hades, and even the figures of *galli* themselves.

When a *gallus* died, it was believed that Cybele, as Mother Earth, received him "into her bosom." The classical scholar Franz Cumont wrote at the end of the nineteenth century, "The belief seems to have been that the deceased were absorbed in the Great Mother who had given them birth, and that they thus participated in her divinity."[117]

HOSTILE FORCES

Cybele's worship spanned several millennia, and it has been suggested that the institution of the *galli* may be traced to the Neolithic. Still, it was a cult or religion that was continually being attacked by hostile forces.

In his *Interpretation of Dreams*, Artemidorus expresses the opinion of many Greeks and Romans concerning the Goddess and her male devotees, saying that in dreams *galli* represent untrustworthy persons. The Roman emperor Julian condemned the Greeks for rejecting the worship of Cybele and the institution of the *galli*; they had not only exiled priests of Cybele but also had occasionally tortured and murdered them.[118]

Graillot relates, however, that for the most part, the Romans, like the Greeks,

did not spare the *galli* either injury or accusation. . . . They were [considered] vile beings, impure ones, men who brought unhappiness, evil, and sickness. They were drunkards and frequented dens of iniquity, in the company of sailors. . . . Along with their virility they had lost all shame. They gave a bad reputation to the environs of the temple. They had the traits of courtesans.[119]

Clement of Alexandria invoked both Moses and the apostle Paul in his diatribes against gender-variant men like the *galli,* who acted in sacred roles and who engaged in same-sex eroticism. "Do you not see Moses," he asked rhetorically, "ordering that no eunuch or mutilated man shall enter the assembly, nor the son of a harlot?" He suggested that the apostle Paul had such men in mind when he demanded that such persons cease leading lives of "debauchery and licentiousness" and insisted that "no immoral or impure man" would be accepted in to the Kingdom of Heaven.[120]

Augustine's condemnation of the Goddess and her priests is even more specific and vituperous. Referring to Cybele as a "demon" and a "monster," he concludes, "The Great Mother surpassed all the gods . . . not by reason of the greatness of her divine power but in the enormity of her wickedness." For Augustine, the priests of the Goddess are "mountebanks," "madmen," "castrated perverts," those "foully unmanned and corrupted."[121]

The faithful of Cybele did not, however, surrender without a struggle. When a Christian fanatic "made a demonstrative protest against a procession in honour of Cybele," her followers demanded he be punished, and he was put to death.[122]

From the first century C.E. onward, however, conflicts between pagans and Christians increased at an exponential rate. In 362 C.E., Julian condemned the inhabitants of Pessinus for abandoning their patron goddess. Two or three decades later, the patriarch of Constantinople praised John Chrysostom for decimating the worshipers of Cybele, for leaving, in Phrygia, "without sons her whom they called the Mother of Gods." A decade later, Valentinian II officially banned the worship of Cybele, forbidding citizens to visit her temples or to make sacrifices to her. Immediately following Valentinian's death, Eugenius, in 392 C.E., removed the ban. This period of tolerance was, however, short-lived. Christian emperors—Theodosius, Justinian, and others—would stop at nothing to destroy the worship of the Goddess and to rid the earth of her priests and priestesses.[123]

Theodosius, on August 6, 390, issued an edict that unquestionably applied to the *galli* as well as other gender-variant men and men engaging in same-sex eroticism: "All those who shamefully debase their bodies by submitting them, like women, to the desire of another man, and in giving themselves to strange sexual relations, shall be made to expiate such crimes in the avenging flames, in view of all the people."[124]

Of the Christian emperors, however, Justinian was by far the most intolerant of worshipers of the Goddess, gender-variant persons, and those engaging in same-sex eroticism. Such persons had their property confiscated; they were tortured, forced to commit suicide, or burned alive. Their sacred texts were burned; their temples were razed. Inspired by the tale of Sodom and Gomorrah, Justinian imagined men who engaged in same-sex eroticism as responsible for "famines, plagues, and earthquakes." While critics of Justinian "alleged that the trials [of such men] were a farce, that men were [being] condemned on the single testimony of one man or boy," the emperor paid no attention. According to classical scholar J. B. Bury (1861–1927), men found guilty of such acts were "shamefully mutilated, or exquisitely tortured, and paraded through the streets of the capital before their execution."[125]

SURVIVALS AND TRANSFORMATIONS: GNOSTICS AND OTHERS

Despite centuries of persecution, the *galli* and the priestesses of Cybele continued to worship their Goddess. "The old religion was not dead," writes Graillot,
"in the countryside, on the wild plains, on solitary mountains, sources of rivers,
trees, grottoes, and rocks guarded their divine prestige." The *galli*, for a long time,
lived in the mountains in Asia Minor. They and others continued to make pilgrimages to a rock sacred to Cybele at Latmos, in order to thank the goddess for
sending rain. And while the *plutonia* at Hierapolis where the *galli* had once
prophesied were destroyed in the fourth century C.E., pilgrims were still journeying to Hierapolis in the sixth century to pay homage to the Goddess and to have
their dreams interpreted. At Autun, in France, Cybele's statue was still being carried in procession through the fields in hope that the Goddess would bring the
farmers abundant crops. Burkert indicates that the *galli* may have played a key
role in preserving the worship of the Goddess and her consort because, as eunuchs, they were often spared by conquerors, who typically killed the men and
raped the women.[126]

The philosopher Damaskios wrote several centuries after the birth of Christ, "I
dreamed that I had become one with Attis, and that the Mother of the Gods was
celebrating, in my honor, the festival of the Hilaria."[127]

During the intensely syncretic period immediately preceding the emergence of
Christianity and continuing for several centuries thereafter, the Gnostic religion
or spiritual tradition was born. This was a tradition constructed from Egyptian,
Indian, Greek, Roman, Jewish, Christian, and other elements. It was divided into
many branches or sects, some of which were deeply influenced by the worship of
Cybele and Attis. These included the Montanists, Euchites (or Messalians),
Naassenes, Collyridians, Nicolaitans, and Phibionites.

The Montanists followed Montanus, a Phrygian *gallus* who tried to synthesize
Christianity with the worship of Cybele and Attis and who was himself likened to
Attis and Christ. Like the *galli*, the Montanists practiced ritual castration, citing
Matthew 19:12 as support for this practice: "For there are eunuchs who have been
so from birth, and there are eunuchs who have been made eunuchs by men, and
there are eunuchs who have made themselves eunuchs for the sake of the kingdom of heaven. He who is able to receive this, let him receive it" (NRSV). Mon-
tanist priestesses incidentally, were identified with Cybele, just as Montanus was
identified with Attis.

Believing that spiritual revelation was forever unfolding, Montanists prophesied in the manner of the *galli*. Their teachings became known as the "New
Prophecy" and were gathered into a "third testament." Like some early Christians,
Montanists believed in "the imminent arrival of the Heavenly City"; naturally,
this city would be one sacred to the Goddess, Pepuza in Phrygia. Founded in 157
C.E., Montanism by the sixth century had spread throughout the Roman Empire
and counted devotees as far apart as Africa and Spain.[128]

THE EUCHITES, another branch of Gnostic religion, strongly resembled the *galli* in several respects. They "subsisted solely by begging . . . slept in the open air . . . practiced communal ownership," and "rejected all obedience and submission to authority." They were nicknamed the "Dancers" because they adopted the prophesying techniques of the *galli*. Writer on the Gnostics Jacques Lacarrière notes, "The Euchites used analogous instruments and musical modes which, in addition to the drinks consumed before the prayers, provoked trances and collective possession."[129]

THE NAASSENE SECT or branch of Gnosticism has been described as "an altogether Hellenized Phrygian mystery-community that worships the Mother of the Gods and Attis, but at the same time appeals to the Jewish prophets and writers"; moreover, the Naassenes are said to have taken part in the rites of Cybele and Attis as well as in their own mysteries.

The Naassenes believed in a gynandrous or androgynous deity, which they envisioned as a boundless ocean named Bythos or The Deep or as an ouroboros, a serpent biting its tail, named Naas or Ophis (hence their appellation as Ophites). They identified the feminine aspect of the godhead with Cybele, Isis, and Demeter, while the masculine aspect was identified with an androgynous figure named Adam Aeon. They also spoke of a son-consort of the deity whom they identified with Attis, Christ, Adonis, Osiris, Endymion, and Brimo. The destiny of this being was to stop himself or be stopped from reproducing so that he might pass "from the material condition . . . to the eternal essence" without participating in the cycle of reincarnation. The Naassenes also believed in the God of the Old Testament. Naming him Ialdabaoth, they saw him as a cruel tyrant who created Adam and Eve to be his slaves. Naas, taking the role of the serpent in the garden, granted both Adam and Eve *gnosis,* mystical wisdom, by sexually penetrating them. In their communion rite, Naassenes honored Naas by having a live serpent slither over the consecrated bread and by then passing the serpent to each other as they, in a circle, joined in the "kiss of peace."[130]

The Naassenes insisted that if a person wished to become enlightened and to return to the godhead at the end of his or her life (rather than be reincarnated), he or she must undergo a process by which he or she might become "neither male nor female, but a new creature . . . who reunites the two sexes." In defense of this belief, the Naassenes quoted the words of the apostle Paul: "Therefore, if any one is in Christ, he is a new creation; the old has passed away, behold, the new has come" (2 Corinthians 5:17, RSV), and "there is neither male nor female; for you are all one in Christ Jesus" (Galatians 3:28, RSV).

For the Naassenes, however, becoming "neither male nor female" did not require ritual castration. Linking castration with circumcision, they again quoted Paul: "For neither circumcision counts for anything, nor uncircumcision, but a new creation" (Galatians 6:15, RSV), inferring that just as Jesus' sacrifice had rendered circumcision unnecessary, so Attis's sacrifice had rendered castration unnecessary. Still, while the Naassenes did not ritually castrate themselves, male adherents were required to "abstain, as if they were emasculated, from intercourse with a woman." Similarly, female adherents were also to abstain from coitus with males. Again, the Naassenes believed that abstaining from phallic-vaginal intercourse might prevent one from becoming attached to the cycle of generation and mundane existence. In the case of male adherents, such as abstention would allow Naas-Cybele-Adam Aeon to recall "the male power of the soul to itself." According to the Naassenes, "the intercourse of woman with man is demonstrated to be exceedingly wicked." With typical idiosyncrasy, they understood Jesus' words "Do not give dogs what is holy . . . do not throw your pearls before swine" to mean that one should abstain from phallic-vaginal intercourse (Matthew 7:6, RSV).

On the other hand, the Naassenes appear to have approved of masturbation to celebrate the phallus. From the Egyptians they borrowed the image of the phallic Osiris, while from the Greeks they appropriated the phallic image of Hermes as depicted on herms. The Naassenes linked these phallic figures with the reborn Attis and Christ, whose phalli had not been employed for procreative purposes but were considered instruments of erotico-spiritual transformations.

Like other Gnostics, the Naassenes held that certain biblical passages were meant to be interpreted in one way by nonmystics and in another, often a reversed or inverted way, by mystics like themselves. Thus, when the apostle Paul spoke in condemnatory terms of women exchanging "natural relations for unnatural" and men giving up "natural relations with women" for "passion for one another . . . committing shameless acts with men" (Romans 1:26–27, RSV), the Naassenes heard something like this: "While same-sex eroticism is to be considered inappropriate behavior when undertaken by nonmystics, for mystics such behavior represents a path to spiritual enlightenment." As Hippolytus relates, "In these words which Paul has spoken they say the entire secret of theirs, and a hidden mystery of blessed pleasure, are comprised."[131]

What is more, a certain group of mystical images suggests that Naassene rituals may have included the use of semen, in the form of the "ineffable *alale* ointment" rubbed on the forehead and used as an ingredient in the sacred beverage. Semen was referred to by the Naassenes as the "beauteous seeds of Benjamin," "the water in those fair nuptials which Jesus changing made into wine," and as "the great and ineffable mystery of the Samothracians."

The Naassenes allegedly borrowed an image from the Samothracians to express the mystery of fellatio (and perhaps other forms of homoerotic activity), that of two "naked men . . . their pudenda turned upwards as [is the case with] the statue [or herm] of Mercury on Mount Cyllene." In their peculiar, syncretic way, they associated this image of two sexually aroused males, presumably side by side and perhaps facing each other, with the gospel of Jesus. Hippolytus explains, "the aforesaid images are figures of the primal man, and of that spiritual one that is born again, in every respect of the same substance with that man. This is what is spoken by the Savior: 'If ye do not drink my blood, and eat my flesh, ye will not enter into the kingdom of heaven.'"[132]

Of the possible function of cultic homoeroticism among the Naassenes, Lacarrière writes,

> For the Gnostics, this act [of anal intercourse, as performed by Naas in the garden] evidently had the force of example and no doubt certain of them did *also* practice sodomy in the name of the serpent, as a ritual repetition of his first act, a way of opening up the "passages" of knowledge and thereby unsealing the blind eyes of the flesh . . . No doubt fellatio (a strict enactment of the image of the snake biting its tail) [was also practiced]. The term *inversions,* so oddly used by sexologists to designate these . . . erotic practices, would certainly have delighted the Gnostics.[133]

Whether or not male Naassenes dressed in women's garments is unclear. It is more likely that they attended rituals wearing simple tunics or nothing at all. According to Hippolytus, they believed that "those who come thither ought to cast off their garments, emasculated through the virginal spirit."[134]

Like the *galli,* the Naassenes were renowned musicians. Indeed, they described the cosmos in musical terms. As Amygdalus, Naas-Cybele-Adam Aeon was the source of music and hence of all creation. As Syrictas the Piper, Attis was the "harmonious spirit" given birth by the God/dess. A Naassene hymn praising Attis reads:

> Whether [Thou art of] the race of Saturn or happy Jupiter, or mighty Rhea [Cybele], Hail Attis, gloomy mutilation of Rhea. Assyrians style thee thrice-longed-for Adonis, and the whole of Egypt [calls thee] Osiris, celestial horn of the Moon; Greeks denominate [thee] wisdom; Samothracians, venerable Adam; Haemonians, Corybas; and the Phrygians [name thee] at one time Papa, at another time Corpse, or God, or Fruitless, or Aipolos, or green Ear of Corn that has been reaped, or whom the very fertile Amygdalus produced—a man, a musician.[135]

THE COLLYRIDIANS and Nicolaitans sought to secure a place for the Goddess by identifying her with the Holy Ghost of Christianity. The Nicolaitans, like the *galli* of Cybele, practiced ritual castration and engaged in nonprocreative forms of eroticism.[136]

The Nicolaitans and the Phibionites, among other Gnostic sects or branches, renamed Cybele Barbelo. As Barbelo, Cybele was associated with other Gnostic goddesses including Sophia, Prunikos (the Lewd One), and Norea. It was the desire of the Goddess, said the Nicolaitans and Phibionites, to gather to herself and to replace in her womb the "light" that had been scattered upon the earth when she gave birth to human beings, as well as to gather the "light" that had divided itself from her when Attis or Christ had descended to earth.

This ingathering was to be accomplished in part by her worshipers, both men and women, who engaged in an *agape* rite or "love feast" involving the "extraction, collection, and solemn, sacramental consecration of bodily fluids," namely, semen and menstrual blood, in an effort to recover the lost light. Only in this way might men and women avoid "the further propagation of the human race, and . . . the continued entrapment of divine substance" in matter, linked in Gnosticism to evil.[137] By way of the *agape* rite, religious historian James Goehring explains, the lost light was "gathered and offered to the divine." This belief in the necessity of gathering bodily fluids and sacrificing them was referred to as *syllexis.*[138]

Male worshipers apparently often used ritual masturbation, both of self and other males, and fellatio in order to gather semen. It is possible that interrupted forms of anal and phallic-vaginal intercourse were also undertaken. With ritual masturbation, the male devotees would recite passages from the New Testament: "These hands ministered to my necessities, and to those who were with me" (Acts 20:34, RSV); and, "Let him labor, doing honest work with his hands, so that he may be able to give to those in need" (Ephesians 4:28, RSV).[139]

A male worshiper would take his own semen or that of another, would offer it in prayer to the godhead, and would consume it, invoking Attis-Christ: "This is the body of Christ; and this is the Pascha, because of which our bodies suffer and are made to acknowledge the passion of Christ."[140]

Of the centrality of homoeroticism among the Phibionites, Epiphanius writes, "since they are not satiated with their promiscuous intercourse with women, [they] are inflamed towards one another, men with men, as it is written. . . . For these, who are utterly abandoned, congratulate each other, as if they had received the choicest distinction."[141]

Within the Phibionite sect or branch, moreover, was the Levite subsect, whose members appear to have been "exclusively homosexual" and "regarded as the elite of the [Phibionite] sect."[142] According to Epiphanius, "Those among them who are called Levites . . . do not have intercourse with women, but with each other. And it is these who are actually distinguished and honoured among them."[143]

As a sacred text defending their autoerotic and homoerotic practices, the Levites quoted from the apocryphal Gospel of Philip, which speaks of "knowing oneself," which they interpreted as masturbation, of "collecting all that has been scattered of oneself into oneself again," which they interpreted as saving or eating one's own semen, and of "sowing no children" for the evil God of the Old Testament, which they interpreted as sanctioning auto- and homoeroticism.[144]

GNOSTICISM, not surprisingly, was attacked viciously by antilibertine Christians, and much of what it had retained of the worship of the Goddess and her consort was lost. Still, mainstream Christianity as well as folk Catholicism preserved certain elements of the ancient faith, although, as Graillot stresses, the process of syncretism was not a balanced one: "Christianity alone was to profit from this exchange of influences."[145]

One of the Virgin Mary's titles, *Theotokos,* "the Mother of God," was stolen from Cybele. Further, when Mary officially assumed Cybele's seat at Cyzicus, she was nicknamed "Our Lady of Dindymus," an obvious reference to the Goddess. Cybele also survived into the sixteenth century in France as the folk Catholic saint/goddess Copia or Abundance. In France, on Christmas night, Ean Begg relates, "women presented candles and offerings of fruit or animals to the goddess, and departed walking backwards."[146]

In France, Cybele also survived as Our Lady of Victories and Our Lady of Perpetual Succor. In both Europe and the Americas, she may have further survived as St. Barbara, who wears a fortress-shaped tiara, and as St. Jerome, who is accompanied by a lion. Cybele's memory has also persisted in the works of many artists and writers. She is even depicted as a woman accompanied by a lion in the Strength or Lust card of the Tarot deck.[147]

It is beyond doubt that many symbols and rites associated with Cybele and Attis were appropriated by Christians. Christmas, with its male child born of a virgin and its decorated pine, provides one example. The Easter celebration provides another, with spring and flowers and a holy, young, and innocent divine male who experiences sacrifice, death, and possibly rebirth.

The influence of the *galli* revealed itself in a subtler fashion. The eunuch priest of the Goddess, stripped of obvious homoerotic and gender-variant behavior and also of his close alliance with female hierodulic and gender-variant priestesses, became the celibate priest or monk of Christianity.[148] The flagellatory rites were appropriated as well, as seen in the ritual of the Penitent Kings during Passion Week in Italy.[149]

In the sixth century C.E., Christian priests continued to employ the magical formulas of the *galli,* as when St. Theodore used one of their spells to rid a farmer's field of grasshoppers. Graillot has also speculated that a relationship exists between the *galli* and the Mawlawiyah (or Mevleviyah) Sufi, the brotherhood of whirling dervishes founded in the thirteenth century by the poet Rumi of Konya (or Iconium), in the vicinity of Çatal Hüyük and an ancient center of Cybele's worship. In their dances, Graillot observes, "Bounding and turning to the sound of flutes and cymbals," the Sufis "are the last descendants of the *galli.*"[150]

PART THREE

Cauldron

CAULDRON

A HARSH WIND reminds us that this is Mother's Night, when the day is dark and the Wild Hunt thunders in the clouds.

Inside the temple, we warm ourselves near the Yule log and dip our horns in the cauldron of dark mead that the women of the village have made. We have gathered here to honor the gods and the dead, to ask their blessing in the year to come.

Here are boar-helmeted and boar-masked warriors. Once the goddess Freyja and the god Freyr ruled our lands in peace, and weapons were banned from our temples. But these are cruel times, and we must protect ourselves.

The warriors have come from the outlands where the giants and elves dwell. They carry exquisite swords engraved with runes.

Tonight we shall taste of the sacrificial boar. We will place our hands on his head, crowned with laurel and bay, as we swear to do the gods' bidding.

Here, too, are the bearshirt and wolfshirt warriors. Outlanders, they howl like the beasts whose skins they wear when they enter battle. They partake of the mystery of becoming the beast, and know as well the mystery of becoming woman, *argr*. Thus are they called the *vargr*.

And here are the Valkyries, the helmeted women who will share mead and tales of valor with the warriors in Valhalla. Some say they are the daughters of Skaði, warrior goddess of the wintertime.

Here are the priests of Oðinn and Thor, and the priestesses of Freyja.

And here are the men called *ergi.* Like the *vargr,* they possess the secret of metamorphosis. As men lie dreaming, they work their magic. In the falcon cloak of Freyja, they fly forth between the worlds, gathering herbs and wisdom, cavorting with the dead and with the elves. They are the children of Freyja and Freyr, and even Loki smiles upon them. Like Oðinn and the priestesses of Freyr, they have learned the secrets of the powerful magic of *seiðr.*

Once, on a winter's night, a man of the village ridiculed a *seiðrman,* saying someone should tell him he was not a woman.

The *seiðrman,* cloaked in purple and wearing the ship of Freyr, the *Skiðblaðnir,* about his neck, stood in the shadows in silence. The joy he had felt had left him.

An elder priestess approached the man and asked him, "Have you forgotten that the gods you worship have rested in each other's arms? The great steed Sleipnir was born from such a union."

A warrior then approached him, brandishing a sword and carrying a drinking horn of an animal the man had never seen. "Drink with me," he told the man, and drink the man did and thanked him for his warmth.

The warrior then whispered in the *seiðrman's* ear, "Little does he know the brotherhood we share." Together they toasted the gods and the dead, shared meat and mead, and shared the bed. And at life's end, they shared the ship of fire.

Enaree-priest (on the left) serving a high priestess of the Scythian goddess Argimpasa, gold plaque of the tiara from the Karagodeuaskh Tumulus on the Kuban River, late 4th century B.C.E.

Womanish and Beastly Ways

But thou, say they, on Sám's isle once wovest spells like a
witch: in warlock's shape through the world didst fare:
were these womanish ways, I ween.

from the *Lokasenna*[1]

*In this chapter, we will examine the expression of male gender
variance, homoeroticism, and sacred experience among three
Indo-European groups: the Scythians, the Celts, and the Germanic peoples.*

THE INDO-EUROPEANS: A BRIEF SKETCH

Beginning in the fifth millennium B.C.E. (or thereabouts),
patriarchal forms of social organization—and here we return to
a familiar theme—began to overpower less patriarchal, perhaps
even matrifocal, societies existing in Europe and elsewhere. This
dramatic shift in cultural organization is usually attributed to
the military prowess of the Indo-European peoples, represented
by the Germanic peoples, the Celts, the Scythians, the Greeks,
and others. ¶ According to archaeologist Marija Gimbutas, the
movements of these peoples westward beyond their homeland,

generally speaking, ancient Russia and Manchuria, resulted in the destruction of the Old European culture, characterized as "matrifocal, sedentary, peaceful, art-loving, earth- and sea-bound." Indo-European culture, as opposed to Old European culture, has been generally characterized as "patrifocal, mobile, warlike and ideologically sky oriented."[2]

While this theory has been the subject of great controversy, the histories of the Scythians, Celts, and Germanic peoples tend to corroborate Gimbutas's view.

I would reiterate, however, that I believe it is wise to acknowledge the significant contributions of Indo-European groups even as we remember the violent manner in which they have subjugated those with whom they have come into contact. I do not agree with Gimbutas's statement that Indo-Europeans "were . . . indifferent to art."[3]

I think it also wise to bear in mind that while the destruction wielded by the early Indo-Europeans cannot and should not be denied, these peoples, as practitioners of polytheistic (even if patriarchal) religions, were much more likely to tolerate such things as Goddess reverence and same-sex eroticism (albeit in restricted forms) than their Jewish, Christian, and Islamic counterparts of later centuries. It is noteworthy that a number of feminist scholars, especially—and not surprisingly—practitioners of Judaism and Christianity, have ignored this difference; indeed, some have even suggested that women have experienced greater religious power in patriarchal, monotheistic religions than in Greco-Roman and other forms of "paganism" that allowed for Goddess reverence. This view is fortunately not universally held, even among feminists; as the narrator of *The Burning Times,* a brilliant film documentary on the Inquisition, relates of a sacred site of the Celts:

> The Romans didn't destroy the religions of the peoples they conquered.
> They, too, took the healing waters, and dreamed by the hot pools. They,
> too believed that nature was sacred, and that the spirit of the Earth Goddess was alive in all things.[4]

THE *ENAREES* OF ANCIENT RUSSIA AND NEIGHBORING COUNTRIES

Long before the patriarchal Scythians assumed power in ancient Russia and neighboring countries, gender-variant priests served the goddess Artimpasa (or Argimpasa). Although little information concerning this deity has survived, she appears to have been viewed as a Great Goddess. She was often accompanied by a lion and sometimes by a male consort. She appears to have been especially associated with plant life, and even more specifically with cannabis (or marijuana). The use of this "magical plant"[5] indicates, as does other fragmentary data, that her religion or cult included elements of shamanism. As a Great Goddess accompanied by a lion, Artimpasa would one day be compared by Greeks and Romans to Meter ("the Mother") and Cybele. That this earth goddess was also a goddess of the heavens, however, is evidenced by the fact that Artimpasa would also be likened to Aphrodite Urania. As this aspect of Aphrodite, she would become further linked to male gender variance and homoeroticism.[6]

THE SHAMAN-PRIESTS OF ARTIMPASA

We do not know the name by which the indignous, pre-Scythian, gender-variant priests of Artimpasa called themselves; the Greeks and Romans, many of whom strongly disapproved of them, called them the *enarees* or the *anandreies*, the "unmanly" or "effeminate ones."[7]

Many writers have suggested that the *enarees* may have been the spiritual descendants of Paleolithic shamans and may even have been directly influenced by Siberian shamans. Indeed, we might say that the figure of the *enaree* lies midway between the "transformed" or "soft" shaman and the gender-variant priest of the Goddess, such as the *kelabim* of Astarte, the *megabyzoi* of Artemis, and the *galli* of Cybele.[8] Classical scholar Marie Delcourt writes, "It is in the bisexuality of the shamans that the explanation of the mysterious *Enarëes* must lie. . . . Hippocrates . . . describes the *Enarëes* precisely enough for us to recognise in them shamans similar to those of Eastern Asia."[9]

Archaeological evidence supports this theory. From the Paleolithic onward, peoples living in the vicinity of present-day Russia and the Ukraine practiced both shamanism and Goddess reverence, worshiping a "cave mother and mistress of the animals." Goddess worship is especially evidenced by a "profusion of female figurines from the Paleolithic and Neolithic eras." In terms of shamanism the use of cannabis and other hallucinogens, employed to reach an altered, shamanic, or ecstatic state, has been documented at various sites.[10]

The ancient Maeotae, a people living in the vicinity of the Sea of Azov, bordering Southwestern Russia and the Weraini, are believed to have worshiped a goddess and to have developed a matrifocal and possibly matrilineal culture resembling the Tripolye or Cucuteni culture of Old Europe. A group of proto-Adygeians dwelling in the northern Caucasus are also thought to have revered the Goddess, embodied in the moon, and to have practiced shamanism. The pre- or non-Scythian Sauromatians, Sindians, and Sarmatians probably also worshiped the Goddess.[11]

GENDER, EROTICISM, AND THE *ENAREES*

The *enarees* may have practiced ritual castration or may have simply abstained from heterosexual sex; apparently they did not, however, practice celibacy. Hippocratic writings and other texts indicate that they engaged in same-sex eroticism. Writers report that the *enarees* not only "live like women" but also "play the woman" in all things, suggesting their assumption of the receptive role in same-sex erotic encounters. The term *malakia* is employed by Aristotle to describe the *enarees*. This term refers not only to "softness," as some scholars (especially gay Christian apologists) would have us believe, but also to effeminacy or gender variance. It is further related to *malakos,* which signifies not only a gender-variant male but also one who takes the receptive role in anal eroticism. Herodotus, moreover, uses the term *androgynous* to refer to the *enarees.* It is important to understand that in Greece, as is pointed out in Plato's *Symposium,* this term not only carried the meaning of one in whom masculine and feminine traits are combined but also that of a male who engages in anal eroticism, a "catamite."[12]

APPEARANCE, BEHAVIOR, AND ORIGIN OF THE *ENAREES*

The *enarees* wore a fusion of feminine and priestly clothes. In speaking they used the vocabulary and register of the women of the region, and they performed tasks traditionally assigned to women.[13]

The *enarees* apparently were accepted by the pre-Scythian peoples. While in later times, Greek and Roman writers became convinced that the *enarees* were products of either divine punishment or illness (the ancient equivalents of fundamentalist and medical approaches), becoming so after offending a god or riding horses too much, the indigenous persons of the region appear to have "respect[ed] and worship[ped] these creatures." They held that the *enarees* were essentially different from other males, their condition being a divine dispensation. They further held that *enarees* were repeatedly born into certain families, suggesting either a belief in reincarnation or a protogenetic theory.[14]

FUNCTIONS OF THE *ENAREES*

While ancient documents provide little information concerning the specific work performed by *enarees,* it seems safe to assume, with the Russian historian Michael Ivanovich Rostovstev (1870–1952), that the "Enareans fulfilled the same function[s] . . . in the worship of the Great Goddess . . . as the eunuchs elsewhere." From a plaque that forms the frontal part of a queen's tiara, dating from the fourth or third century B.C.E., we learn that *enarees* officiated in a ceremony of holy communion. This plaque, discovered in a burial chamber at Karagodeuashkh, in the vicinity of the Kuban River (in what is today southwestern Russia, near the Georgian border, in the region of the Caucasus Mountains), portrays a chief priestess of the Goddess, probably the queen herself, surrounded by spiritual leaders and a traditionally masculine worshiper. Two priestesses stand behind the chief priestess or queen. To her left stands an *enaree,* "beardless . . . clad in a woman's garment." He holds a vessel containing the communion beverage in his right hand. It appears that he has filled a rhyton with the beverage and is handing it to the chief priestess, who will administer it to the traditional male devotee. According to Rostovstev, this beverage was believed to confer power upon the individual drinking it. The beverage may have been made of grain, or perhaps of a concoction of herbs or hallucinogenic plants.[15]

From Herodotus, we learn that *enarees* acted as diviners by taking "a piece of the inner bark of the lime-tree [linden]" and cutting it "into three pieces," "twisting and untwisting" the pieces around their fingers in order to arrive at information concerning the future or the truth of hidden matters. While Herodotus does not specifically describe the contents of oracles delivered by *enarees*, it is likely that they were called upon to determine, among other things, what might have led to the ill health of a ruler. This usually involved discovering the identity of a rebellious subject who had placed a curse upon a ruler.[16]

The *enarees* may have also taken part in shamanic, funerary rituals described by Herodotus and confirmed by archaeological evidence. According to Herodotus, upon the death of a ruler, his or her body, rather like the Egyptian corpse, was cleaned out and filled with "aromatic substances, crushed galingale, parsley-seed, and anise," after which it was covered with wax. After the corpse had been exhibited to the subjects and had been buried, the *enarees* took a ritual vapor bath, a "sweat." Herodotus, noting that "hemp grows in Scythia . . . wild as well as under cultivation," describes the bath as follows:

> On a framework of three sticks, meeting at the top, they stretch pieces
> of woolen cloth . . . and inside this little tent they put a dish with red-hot
> stones in it. Then they take some hemp seed, creep into the tent, and
> throw the seed on the hot stones. At once it begins to smoke. . . . The
> Scythians . . . howl with pleasure.[17]

Archaeological evidence confirms Herodotus's description. In *Plants of the Gods*, Richard Evans Schultes and Albert Hofmann report that

> archaeologists have excavated frozen Siberian tombs . . . and have found
> tripods and pelts, braziers and charcoal with remains of *Cannabis* leaves
> and fruit. . . . The use of *Cannabis* by the Scythians is evidenced by various
> objects excavated from a chief's burial in mound no. 2 at Pazyryk in the
> western Altai. The pot contained *Cannabis* fruits, and the copper censer . . .
> was used to burn the sacred plant.[18]

A rug found at Pazyryk (near the Altai mountains and bordering Siberia and Mongolia), which has been uncritically accepted as depicting the Goddess or a priestess may in fact portray an *enaree* holding a cannabis plant in the presence of an approaching horseman. Ceremonies involving the use of cannabis may have included both communal celebrations and funerals or ceremonies for the dead. If *enarees* did participate in these rites, then they may have been among the first religious leaders to use cannabis in order to trigger an altered state of consciousness. This would in turn suggest that the association of the gender-variant religious leaders with mind-altering substances is an ancient one indeed.[19]

SCYTHIANS, GODS, AMAZONS, PRIESTS

The Scythians, who alternately respected and ridiculed the *enarees*, were an extremely patriarchal people. They loved to drink liquor, delighted in battle, and flaunted "the scalps of their foes as trophies."

The Scythians worshipped a male deity whom they envisaged as a young man on horseback or driving a chariot, his horse or chariot trampling upon the bodies of his enemies. His attributes included weapons, cattle, horses, and the sun. The

Greeks compared him to Ares, the Romans to Mars, Mithra, and Sol Invictus. His worshipers paid homage to him by sacrificing horses, cattle, and humans to him annually.

It was probably their use of the horse as a military vehicle, coupled with their superior weapons, that allowed the Scythians to conquer the indigenous peoples of the area. By the sixth century B.C.E., they ruled the greater part of the present-day Russia and various neighboring lands.[20]

A tale told by Herodotus suggests that armed struggle may have occurred between the Scythians and the indigenous peoples. According to this tale, female warriors who lived in the vicinity of the Sea of Azov bordering southwestern Russia and the Ukraine, engaged in battle with the Scythians. Conflict ceased when the two groups decided to intermarry. For a time, Herodotus reports, the "two camps were . . . united." He points out that while the "men could not learn the women's language . . . the women succeeded in picking up the men's." Ultimately, however, the female warriors decided to separate from the Scythian males. "We are riders," they said. "Our business is with the bow and the spear, and we know nothing of women's work. . . . let us go off and live by ourselves."

Strabo tells a similar tale. A tribe of female warriors once lived in the Caucasus between the Kuban and Terek rivers. Indeed, these tales may refer to the same groups, as the southeastern corner of the Sea of Azov is within sixty miles of the Kuban River in southwestern Russia near the Georgian border. These women hunted, farmed, and raised cattle and horses. They removed their right breasts to facilitate throwing the javelin, and they wore animal skins. In the spring, they journeyed to a sacred mountain, where they participated in ritual sexual intercourse with the men of a neighboring tribe, the Gargarenses. "The female children that are born," Strabo tells us, "are retained by the Amazons," while "the males are taken to the Gargarenses," presumably an all-male community, "to be brought up." Like the men and women of Herodotus's tale, they decide that "there should be companionship only with respect to offspring, and that they should each live independent of the other."[21]

The strict separation of the sexes in these tales may be legendary rather than actual. Such tales suggest, however, that battles may have occurred between matrifocal indigenous peoples, represented by the female warriors or Amazons, and patriarchal invaders. If such battles did in fact occur, they probably involved both the men and women of the indigenous groups struggling against the invaders. Such tales may also point toward earlier male-female arrangements, suggesting that sexual separation may have once been the norm, interrupted intermittently by periods emphasizing reproduction. As in certain present-day tribal cultures, such arrangements may have encouraged same-sex eroticism. While many writers have vociferously argued against the existence of female warriors or Amazons, archaeological evidence may ultimately settle this dispute. For example, "Excavations have uncovered the burials of wealthy [Sauromatian] women containing weapons, equestrian gear, and objects suggesting a priestly status." Archaeological evidence appears to confirm, moreover, that even among the Scythians, female warriors may have been esteemed. In a Scythian tumulus near the village of Balaban, for instance, "archaeologists have found a woman-warrior, buried . . . with weapons. Beautiful ear-rings, shaped into animal headlets, lay at her head."[22]

Although the Goddess-revering peoples of the area were coerced into paying homage to the god of the Scythians, they continued to worship the Goddess. "The cult of [the] Great Goddess," moreover, "appears to have been assimilated by Greek and Scythian intruders." According to historian of Russian culture and feminist scholar Joanna Hubbs, "Despite the marked growth in the representation of male power, the worship of a Great goddess was . . . central to the initiation of Scythian warriors."[23]

THERE IS REASON to believe that as Scythian domination increased, men who continued to revere the Goddess came to be looked upon as being different from other men. The Scythians appear to have been especially disturbed by those who imported foreign Goddess-revering traditions into Scythia.

Such an importation may have occurred during the final decades of the seventh century B.C.E. following a Scythian expedition to the Near East. According to Herodotus, the Scythians, in pursuit of the Cimmerians, had decided to invade Egypt. They were halted, however, by Pharaoh Psamtik of the Twenty-sixth Dynasty, who is said to have given them riches in exchange for their not invading Egypt. Herodotus tells us that the Scythians then "withdrew by way of Ascalon in Syria."

At Ascalon, he reports, "a small number of men . . . robbed the temple of Aphrodite Urania." Herodotus compares the temple at Ascalon to Aphrodite's temple on the island of Cyprus, thus suggesting its architectural magnificence and spiritual importance. According to Herodotus, "The Scythians who robbed the temple at Ascalon were punished by the goddess with the infliction of what is called the 'female disease.'" It is conceivable, although improbable, that the Scythian robbers were ritually castrated by the priests or priestesses of the Goddess. It is more likely the case that Herodotus meant to describe parabolically how certain Scythians, drawn to the worship of Aphrodite—perhaps because it reminded them of the worship of the indigenous Goddess of ancient Eastern Europe—decided to carry the worship of Aphrodite from Ascalon to Scythia during the final years of the seventh century B.C.E. The Scythians might have also told such a tale in order to suggest that the institution of the *enaree* priesthood was linked to a foreign cult rather than to an ancient, indigenous religion.[24]

Another tale of Herodotus speaks of the importation of the worship of foreign goddesses, Cybele and Aphrodite and perhaps also Demeter, to Scythia. Anacharsis, a Scythian noble who traveled west in search of wisdom around 600 B.C.E., became friends with the Athenian poet Solon and perhaps also with Aesop. After being initiated into the Eleusinian mysteries, he visited Cyzicus, where he found "the people of this town engaged in celebrating a magnificent festival in honor of the Mother of the Gods [Cybele]." Herodotus writes, "Anarcharsis made a vow that, if he got home safe and sound, he would himself celebrate a night-festival and offer sacrifice to this goddess in exactly the same way as he had seen it done at Cyzicus."

True to his promise, Anarcharsis, on returning to Scythia, donned the apparel worn by the *galli*, with "the images [of Cybele and Attis] fastened to his dress," and "went through the ceremony with all the proper rites and observances," which presumably included dancing, flagellation, and prophesying. As Michael Grant explains, Anacharsis was "attempting to introduce Hellenic rites . . . into the Scythian cult of the Great Goddess." Scythian men disturbed by Goddess-revering practices were deeply threatened by the belief that the transformation of certain men might be the work of an all-powerful Goddess. While this belief may have originated within the worship of the Goddess, where it was thought that the Goddess transformed men in order to teach them piety, patriarchal Scythians may have recounted the tale in order to encourage fear and hatred of the Goddess and her worshippers.

Indeed, some Scythian men were so disturbed by Goddess-revering men that they occasionally resorted to murder. One evening as Anacharsis was performing his "night-festival" in honor of the Goddess, he was murdered by his own brother, Saulius, King of the Scythians.[25]

Centuries later, Clement of Alexandria praised this fratricide. "Blessings be upon the Scythian king," he wrote. "When a countryman of his own [his brother] was imitating among the Scythians the rite of the Mother of the Gods as practiced at Cyzicus, by beating a drum and clanging a cymbal, and by having images of the goddess suspended from his neck after the manner of a priest of Cybele, this king [Saulius] slew him [Anacharsis] with an arrow, on the ground that the man, having been deprived of his own virility in Greece, was now communicating the effeminate disease to his fellow Scythians."[26]

SURVIVALS AND TRANSFORMATIONS: SHAMANS, KHLYSTY, SKOPTSY, AND POETS

Artimpasa was still being worshiped in Scythia during the first centuries of the Common Era; by this time, however, she was known to many as Venus Apatura. The center of her worship was at Phanagoria, in the vicinity of the Kuban, not far from Karagodeuashkh (in the region already spoken of, bordering the Sea of Azov and the Caucasus Mountains in Southwestern Russia, near Georgia).[27] During this period, her worship was greatly influenced by the Greeks. In turn, the *enarees* and other worshipers of the Scythian goddess appear to have wielded influence upon Greek religion. Michael Grant writes:

> Another contribution made by the Scythians to the Greeks, and transmitted, no doubt, through their Black Sea colonies, was the range of beliefs and emotions covered by the term shamanism. . . . Ideas of this kind were widespread, finding their completest expression in Siberia but also deeply rooted in Scythia. . . . The result was the appearance of the Greek *iatromanteis*—shamanistic seers, magical healers and religious teachers—some of whom are specifically associated with northern lands.[28]

A controversial theory states that Scythian religion may have influenced Paleosiberian shamanism and that it may have aided thereby in creating the institution of the gender-variant *berdache* of Native American tribes. Mythologist Joseph Campbell, a proponent of this theory, writes, "It is not unlikely that some of the practices of the Scythian *anandreies* [*enarees*] crossed the Bering Strait."[29]

Not so controversial is a theory suggesting that beliefs and practices of the *enarees* survived in the Russian pagan-Christian cults of the Khlysty (Flagellants) and Skoptsy (Castrators, Eunuchs). These groups emerged in the seventeenth century as part of a radical spiritual rebellion associated with the rise of the so-called Old Believers.

In general, the Khlysty and Skoptsy worshiped Mother Earth, sometimes in the guise of the Virgin Mary, and Christ, the latter envisioned as the consort of the Mother. These groups tended to revere women and to reject the institutions of marriage and the patriarchal family, opting instead for more egalitarian relationships.

Believing that every man and woman was potentially capable of embodying the Mother or Christ, these groups used ecstatic dance (called *radeniia,* or "joyful whirling"), flagellation,[30] and "a kind of *lucerna extincta* [lights-out] rite, in which men and women . . . had intercourse [including] homosexual intercourse," in order to attain an altered state of consciousness, in which they would deliver prophecies.[31] In *Mother Russia* Joanna Hubbs has wisely compared both the Khylsty and the Skoptsy to the Sufi dervishes; she has further compared the Skoptsy, who practiced ritual castration in order to promote spiritual development, to the *galli* of Cybele. Religious scholar Ioan Couliano writes of the Skoptsy practice of ritual castration:

> For men, emasculation took place in five stages, called "seals": in the
> first, the testes were removed; in the second, the penis; in the third,
> a part of the pectoral muscles. Cross-shaped brandmarks followed on
> the shoulders, the abdomen, and the legs. One could thus become an
> "angel with five wings."[32]

It is my understanding, based on conversations with various Russian scholars, that homoerotic relationships often occurred between Skoptsy elders and initiates. It is possible that, echoing the ancient trinities of Ninsun-Gilgamesh-Enkidu, Isis-Set-Horus, Cybele-Attis-Agdistis, and others, the two were joined in a trinitarian relationship with a prophetess or "Mother." The Skoptsy were still in existence and continuing to practice ritual castration in prerevolutionary, twentieth-century Russia.

Both of these cults inspired the work of the Russian poet Nikolai Klyuev (1887–1937), a member of the Khlysty and a lover of men, including the poet Sergei Esenin (who was also the lover of Isadora Duncan). Images of the Goddess abound in Klyuev's work, as when he writes,

Udilyona, mother of the rye,
Comb out your golden hair from the straw
And plunge each ear into mead and molasses.

He describes himself as "A priest visiting Baba-Yaga," who is, in Gimbutas's words, "the ancient Goddess of Death and Regeneration in Slavic mythology." His love for Nikolai Ilich Arkhipov was wedded to his reverence of Mother Russia; "My love," he writes,

> . . . is a thousand-faceted stone
> In whose pools splashes Satan, the pike.
> In a snake mask, on a gray boar
> Carnality guards the dwelling of dream.
> My lover is a harvest on a northern field. . . .[33]

Another Russian who may have been inspired by the ancient beliefs and practices of his homeland was the bisexual writer Vyacheslav Ivanov (1866–1945). In his poem "Incantation," Ivanov, describing the trinity of two male lovers and the Goddess (or possibly a female representative), writes:

> Come, my son, my brother! Our wife awaits us:
> Night, our Magical Mother. . . .[34]

GODS, HEROES, AND BARDS OF THE CELTS

The Celts were a group of related Indo-European nomadic tribes whose superbly crafted iron weapons, well-trained horses, and expertise in raiding villages fueled their rise to power in the fifth century B.C.E. While never truly becoming an empire, they eventually came to occupy the British Isles as well as France, Spain, northern Italy, southwestern Germany, Austria, much of eastern Europe, and parts of Asia Minor. If the Celts were a warlike people, they were also expert artisans, producing masterful works of decorative art and lyrical poetry. Because they transmitted their spiritual ideas and myths orally, however, much of what we know about these subjects derives from non-Celtic sources, such as Greco-Roman or Christian-influenced writings. We do know that the Celts worshiped a number of gods and goddesses; these deities may have been viewed as various aspects of a primal female-male couple. These deities were primarily responsible for providing sustenance, protection, and foreknowledge. We also know that the Celts sacralized springs, wells, and other natural sites and that they practiced a number of forms of divination and magic.[35]

In terms of gender variance, little has yet been uncovered regarding men, although the presence of amazonian, often death-wielding, goddesses like Macha and accounts of the *gwiðonot,* a group of warrior women, suggest that gender-variant women may have been not only tolerated but also respected and depended upon in ancient Celtic society.[36]

Where homoeroticism is concerned, the Celts appear not only to have tolerated same-sex relationships but actually to have preferred them. Diodorus Siculus, writing in the first century B.C.E., described Celtic warriors as sleeping on animal skins flanked by male lovers. His testimony indicates that among the Celts, homoerotic relationships embraced elements of all three models we have discussed—the intergenerational or pederastic (often military in character), the gender variant (our chief focus), and the egalitarian. Diodorus's statement that "they abandon without a qualm the bloom of their bodies to others [and] don't think this is shameful" indicates that the Celts, in marked difference to most other Indo-European groups—particularly the Greeks—did not look with disdain upon the male taking the receptive role. Diodorus's report further suggests that the couple was not the only numerical model for a homoerotic relationship.[37]

GODS, HEROES, AND OUR DOMAIN

In terms of deities linking male gender variance and homoeroticism, little has yet been uncovered, although I think major breakthroughs may shortly be expected, thanks to the work of historian Jean Markale, art historian Anne Ross, archaeologist Timothy Taylor, neopagan writer Caradoc ap Cador, and others.[38]

In spite of the relative dearth of information, however, we can say with some certainty that one of the earliest divine beings worshiped by the Celts, or the indigenous people who would later be assimilated to Celtic culture, was an androgynous or gynandrous deity. A statuette depicting this deity, carved from ash wood, was discovered beneath the Bell Track in Somerset, England, in the 1960s. The statuette appears to have been buried beneath the earth sometime during the Neolithic as part of a dedication ceremony celebrating the opening of a new road.[39]

A second deity who may conceivably be linked to homoeroticism, gender variance, and Goddess reverence is Cernunnos. Although he is commonly known as the "horned god of the Celts," his worship almost certainly predates the arrival of the Celts. He is a god of the forest and its creatures, abundance, self-sacrifice, the underworld, and eroticism. Often seated in lotus position, either naked or clothed in a short tunic, he is bald or has long, curly hair and wears a torque (choker) around his neck and antlers on his head. His attributes include the cornucopia, a bag of coins, a ram-headed serpent, the stag, the bull, and the rat. His worship appears to have included shamanic elements.

Certain artworks also indicate that his cult was linked to Goddess reverence, such as a votive relief discovered at Nuits-Saints-Georges in France, which portrays him seated beside a goddess holding a cornucopia. This goddess shares much in common with Cybele; it is significant in this respect that one of Cernunnos's centers of worship was Autun, also one of Cybele's cult centers.

A third deity depicted on the relief just described, seated between the goddess and Cernunnos, is an androgynous figure. Jean Markale suggests that this figure may represent Cernunnos's androgyny, a reflection of totality (as in the Taoist yin/yang symbol) and a deity in his-her own right, and his linkage to the matrifocal religion of the indigenous peoples of the region. In another syncretic Celtic-Roman depiction, Cernunnos is shown flanked by Apollo and Hermes. This votive stela emphasizes the androgynous aspects of both of these deities. Indeed, Apollo is portrayed almost as a hermaphrodite, with plump breasts and belly and a feminine hairdo. Both deities are nude except for caps and shoulder wraps that do not cover their genitals, and both are standing in relaxed, sensuous poses. Taken together, these works indicate that Cernunnos's worship was associated with both Goddess reverence and androgyny or gender variance.[40]

It is an earlier portrait of Cernunnos, however, that has caused some writers to entertain the possibility homoeroticism and perhaps also gender variance played a role in the god's worship. This portrait, discovered at Val Camonica in northern Italy, dates from 400 B.C.E. It depicts Cernunnos standing "chastely in a full-length chiton" while "his worshipper, smaller in size and having his hands raised in the same . . . posture as the god," is naked and has an erection.[41] This representation indicates, in the view of some writers, that cultic auto- or homoeroticism may have figured in the god's worship and, further, that the worshiper may have seen himself as the lover of the "chaste" and seated—hence receptive more than active—god.[42]

Three of the most important Celtic myths concerning our domain have survived in literary texts. The first, a Welsh tale, focuses on the warrior Gilfaethwy and the magician Gwydion; the second and third are Irish tales, with the second centering on the heroes Cú Chulainn and Ferdia, and the third on the men of Ulster and the goddess Macha.

In the first, Math, the lord of the Welsh province of Gwynedd and an ancestor of the Great Goddess of Wales and Ireland, is in love with the maiden Goewin. This young woman, however, is also desired by the warrior Gilfaethwy. The young warrior would also like to take Math's place as lord of Gwynedd. To aid him in his efforts, Gilfaethwy employs his brother, the magician Gwydion. Because Math is also a very powerful magician, Gwydion and Gilfaethwy fail in achieving the latter's ends. Math decides to punish the foe by transforming them into animals of opposite gender and having them mate. Together, they give birth to a deer, a pig, and a wolf. Their "children" are then transformed by Math into human males, becoming the heroes Hyddwn, Hychtwn, and Bleiden. The shamanic elements of gender and animal transformation are clearly present here. In veiled form, homoeroticism is also present, for even if on one level Gilfaethwy and Gwydion become female and male animals, on another they remain themselves. In the case of Gilfaethwy, he is made to take the receptive role in intercourse each time, probably because it was he who desired to take Goewin away from Math. In French historian Bernard Sergent's view, based on the work of mythologist Georges Dumezil (1898–1986), this tale may refer to cultic homoeroticism occurring among Indo-European, here Celtic, warrior bands; the name Bleiden, "Wolf," is especially suggestive of this, as we will see in our discussion of the *vargr*, warrior-outlaws of the Germanic peoples. Echoing the story of Set and Horus, while the sexual relationship of Gilfaethwy and Gwydion begins as a punishment, it culminates with the creation of great warriors, one known for his swiftness, the second for his strength, and the last for his cunning.[43]

The second tale describes how the foster brothers Cú Chulainn and Ferdia are trained in the martial arts by the gender-variant female warrior (and perhaps goddess) Scáthach ("Shade"), only later to find themselves on opposite sides of a battle, due to the desire of Queen Medb of Connacht to obtain the Brown Bull of Cuailnge. Ferdia, not wishing to fight against Cú Chulainn, says of their relationship, which is reminiscent of that of Gilgamesh and Enkidu:

Fast friend, forest-companions
We made one bed and slept one sleep
In foreign lands after the fray.
Scáthach's pupils, two together,
We'd set forth to comb the forest.

They were forced, however, to battle one another. At the end of the first day, we are told, they found and kissed each other, traded food and herbal medicines, and placed their horses in the same stable. While they could not sleep together, "their charioteers slept by the same fire." These events repeated themselves on the second and third days. In the fourth day, however, Cú Chulainn slew Ferdia, perhaps mistakenly. Holding his dying companion in his arms Cú Chulainn cried out, "Oh, Ferdia! your death will hang over me like a cloud forever."[44]

The folklorist and poet Hamish Henderson has pointed out the similarity between this episode and certain tales of Greek warrior-lovers; he writes, "The combat of Ferdia and Cuchulain has been compared . . . to the duel between Hector and Achilles, and Cuchulain's lament over the body of his lover recalls Achilles' lament for his beloved."[45]

While the tale of Cú Chulainn and Ferdia does not specifically involve gender or animal transformation, it does include them in sublimated form, by way of the warriors' tutelage under the gender-variant Amazon Scáthach and by way of the central role a bull plays in their story.

The third tale, "The Sickness of the Men of Ulster," tells how the Ulaidh (excepting Cú Chulainn) are cursed to experience gender transformation by the goddess Macha.

Macha, as mentioned above, is conceived of as a gender-variant goddess. Beyond being gynandrous, she is also envisioned as a hybrid woman-horse and thus is also associated with animal transformation. In legends, however, both her gynandrous and animal identities are secrets, the discovery of which commands a great price.

In this tale, Macha first appears as a beautiful fairy maiden who pays a visit to the house of a peasant named Crunniuc. She lies down on his bed, and the two become lovers. Soon he is no longer a peasant. He must never, however, reveal the identity of his lover. If he does so, all will be lost.

One day, at a great assembly, Crunniuc becomes angry when the king brags about the swiftness of his horses. "My wife," he says unthinkingly, "can run faster than all your horses put together." "We'll see," says the king; "if you're lying, you'll find yourself headless."

Macha, now pregnant, is dragged out of bed and forced to run with the horses. While she is a goddess, her involvement with a mortal results in her human feelings of great pain as she is forced to race against the horses. In a moment of great suffering, she gives birth to children on the track. Having experienced enough agony and humiliation among the mortals, Macha reveals her true identity, a fierce, horselike, gynandrous goddess.

For their cruel treatment of her, Macha places a curse upon the "men of Ulster." Periodically, and especially during moments of great crisis, they will experience feminization and the pangs of childbirth. This will continue for nine generations.

This tale, reminiscent of those portraying the Scythians as cursed by Aphrodite to become *enarees* (as well as of Ereshkigal's curse upon gender-variant males), reflects the struggle between patrifocal and matrifocal traditions. While the power of the Goddess is acknowledged, the fear and humiliation experienced by patriarchal males on realizing themselves to be her subjects is emphasized.

Jean Markale, whose work on the Celts is profoundly illuminating, suggests that the men of Ulster *must* experience gender transformation because they have discovered the secret of the Goddess. Markale writes, "They had seen Macha in her androgynous reality; thus, they must [also] become androgynous."[46]

In this and other myths of struggle between matrifocal and patriarchal traditions, males must pay the price of their masculinity (or imagined superiority) either for having offended the Goddess or for desiring to share her love or knowledge.

With this in mind, Markale links the tale of Macha and the warriors not only to that of the Scythian *enarees* but also to those of gender-transformed shamans. In this respect, they also bear likeness to the *assinnu, qadeshim, megabyzoi, galli,* and others whom we have encountered.

What we see in many such stories is that while on one level—generally the social level—gender-variant, often homoerotically inclined, males are "cursed" in being forced to live in a patriarchal society that devalues effeminate behavior in men, on another level, such males are "blessed" in that, through experiencing gender (and often animal) transformation, they attain great wisdom.

Unfortunately, the tale of Macha and the men of Ulster lacks the blessing aspect, suggesting that the values of the matrifocal tradition are being overpowered by those of the patriarchy. Indeed, some would say that while the gynandrous Goddess is an image of great antiquity, the emphasis on Macha's military prowess indicates a patriarchal revisioning of an older myth.[47]

We shall see, however, in the figure of the Irish *filidh*, that the blessing aspect was not entirely forgotten by the Celts and their descendants.

THE *FILIDH*, THE ANCIENT IRISH BARD

Little is known of the Druid priesthood, even less of pre-Druidic spiritual figures. Still, it appears that the Celts may have embraced a gender-variant, perhaps homoerotically inclined spiritual figure who came in Ireland to be called the *filidh*.

The *filidh* was, at once, a poet, a storyteller, a composer, a singer, a historian, and a practitioner of the divinatory arts.[48] In the earliest times, the *filidh* performed various shamanic-like rituals. One such rite included sacrificing a bull, eating its uncooked flesh, drinking its blood, and sleeping in its hide. Another involved sleeping on a grave. Both of these rites were thought to inspire prophetic dreams. The *filidh* also may have dressed in a cloak of bird feathers during certain rites.[49] While it is not clear whether or not the *filidh* ever dressed in feminine attire, it does seem that, along with the priestess and the queen, he was considered a representative of the Goddess. In this association, he and the king or ruler might enter into a formal relationship, perhaps even a kind of *hieros gamos,* in which the king or ruler would become the representative of the male consort of the Goddess. Although it is not clear whether their relationship was openly erotic or expressed in sublimated form, it is evident that a kind of "romantic attachment" existed "between the ruler and the poet [*filidh*], in which the poet play[ed] the role of the woman," or rather, the gender-variant representative of the Goddess. Literary historian Maire Cruise O'Brien claims that this ancient relationship resonates in the poems of the fourteenth-century writer Gearóid Iarla and the sixteenth-century writer Eochaidh O'hEoghusa.[50]

MYTH AND MAGIC AMONG THE GERMANIC PEOPLES

Among the peoples of northern and central Europe, as elsewhere, the interrelationship of male gender variance, homoeroticism, and the sacred was profoundly affected by the arrival of Indo-European groups in the region. Although in the case of the ancient Germanic peoples it is difficult to clearly demarcate indigenous from Indo-European groups, a struggle does seem to have occurred between the indigenous or an early Indo-European group on the one hand and a later Indo-European group on the other. The first group is generally known as the Vanir, while the second is known as the Aesir. Each of these groups had its own family of gods.[51]

THE PRIMAL GODS AND THE VANIR

The earliest inhabitants of northern and central Europe apparently worshiped, in the words of H. R. Ellis Davidson, a respected scholar of Scandinavian cultures and religion, an "all-powerful goddess . . . of death and fruitfulness."[52] At some point, this goddess was joined by a male deity or, having been gynandrous, may have split into female and male halves, often depicted as sister-brother twins. Eventually, the image of a male consort, possibly named Yngvi or Ing, developed; this consort was a dying god who experienced ritual castration or sacrificial death followed by periodic renewal.[53] (It is noteworthy that in the fifteenth century, and perhaps earlier, the term *ingle* was used by the English to refer to a young man who accepted the receptive role in a same-sex relationship.) The Great Goddess of these peoples over time split and multiplied.

The memory of the Great Goddess has been preserved in myths of the Vanir that speak of a gynandrous or androgynous deity named Nerthus-Njord who ultimately split into male and female halves, with Nerthus becoming Mother Earth and Njord becoming the god of the sea. The memory of the Goddess has also been preserved in the persona of Freyja, just as that of the consort Yngvi has been preserved in Freyja's brother, Freyr. Not surprisingly, Freyja and Freyr were held to be the children of Nerthus-Njord.

As writer and rune master Kveldulf Gundarsson asserts in *Teutonic Magic*, Freyja "was probably the most widely worshipped of the Norse goddesses."[54] Although perceived as a Great Goddess, her primary concerns appear to have been agriculture, eroticism, and magic. That her worship was linked to or preserved elements of shamanism is inferred by her garment of falcon or hawk feathers, which she used to travel to other worlds, and by the type of magic she practiced and taught to others, which incorporated the shamanic state of consciousness. That her worship was matrifocal in character is indicated by the fact that this type of magic, *seiðr*, was practiced primarily by women and gender-variant men and was in later times branded "feminine magic." It was contrasted with *galdr*, or runic magic, the runes being a sacred and divinatory alphabet; *galdr* was "masculine magic." While *seiðr* was thought to be of Vanic origin, *galdr* was the magic of the Aesir.

As a goddess of eroticism, Freyja is believed to have enjoyed pleasure with many divine and semidivine beings, including her brother Freyr and the dwarfs who fashioned Brisingamen, her magic necklace or torque. A foremother of the fairy tale witch, Freyja rides upon a cat.[55]

In later centuries, Freyja, like other originally peaceful deities, became a goddess of battle, having the responsibility of overseeing the spirits of fallen warriors. In remote areas of the north, Freyja was still being worshiped in the twelfth century C.E. In recent decades, as a combined result of the emergence of the feminist and neopagan movements, Freyja's worship has experienced a revival. As Gundarsson explains, "Freyja is particularly called upon today by women who wish to regain the strength which Christian culture has denied them for so long."[56]

Freyja's brother Freyr, linked to the male consort Yngvi, is nicknamed "the Fruitful."[57] He is a god of earth, water, eroticism, love, magic, self-sacrifice, and peace. That his worship, like Freyja's, employed shamanic elements is suggested by two vehicles attributed to him, a ship that is not confined to sailing on the water, and a golden boar that has the ability to fly through the air. A link to shamanism is also indicated by Freyr's association with the horse and the stag, animals playing a key role in shamanic traditions. Freyr is also a patron of elves. He was especially honored at Yule, when boars were sacrificed to him and boars' heads and boar-shaped cakes were baked and sacrificed.

As a god of eroticism and love, Freyr is often depicted with an erect penis. Small images of this sort appear to have been carried or worn by his worshipers, while larger images were found at holy sites. As such a god, Freyr is also remembered for his passionate love of a young woman named Gerðr. His love for her becomes linked to self-sacrifice when he renders his magic sword or horse to her in exchange for her yielding to his desires. Because he does so, he is later left without a weapon at the cosmic battle of Ragnarok, which occurs at the end of the present world; this results in his death. This myth links Freyr to male gender variance, as the surrender of his sword or horse is perceived as a "symbolic gelding" or ritual castration.[58]

On a subtle level, the myth of Freyr and Gerðr may remind us of the tales of Attis and Cybele, Astarte and Adonis, and other similar stories, all of which suggest that in order to truly know the feminine, a man must—temporarily or permanently—sacrifice the masculine. He may do so, as we have learned, by serving a goddess, yielding to a woman's will, experiencing metaphoric or actual castration, or emulating a woman in terms of dress, behavior, speech, tasks, and other attributes. As we have also learned, offending the Goddess may also teach him these things.

As a seasonal or dying god, Freyr was thought to experience birth and death periodically. "We know that Freyr was said to have been laid in a mound," Davidson relates, "and to have rested there while offerings were made to him." When the old gods were being driven underground by Christian forces in the tenth century, Freyr was believed by some—who had apparently forgotten his demise at Ragnarok—to have died a final time; according to Davidson, his "death was kept secret from the Swedes for three years." Even so, among others Freyr was still being worshiped in the eleventh and later centuries. Today, as with Freyja, his worship is experiencing a revival, chiefly among men who do not feel comfortable emulating a patriarchal, war-oriented deity.[59]

Together, Freyja and Freyr, as Nerthus-Njord and the Goddess and Ing before them, represented the "peace and fertility of the inhabited earth."[60] Archaeologist P. V. Glob (1901–1985) of Denmark has suggested that their worship may have been influenced by the Goddess religion of Malta and Gozo. Their worship also appears to have been intimately linked to the Passage Grave culture of ancient Scandinavia.[61]

THE COMING OF THE AESIR

This matrifocal culture was disturbed during the second millennium B.C.E. by warriors belonging to the Battle-Axe culture, almost certainly an Indo-European group. The gods of the Battle-Axe people became known as the Aesir, while those, including Freyja and Freyr, of the earlier inhabitants became known as the Vanir. The Aesir gods, unlike the Vanir, tended to represent the "powers of destruction."[62] Chief among the Aesir were Oðinn and Thorr. As opposed to the worship of the Vanir deities, which centered on a peaceful, "settled community"— weapons had once been banned in Freyr's temples—worship of the Aesir focused on "battlefields far from home," "warriors . . . full of the ecstasy of battle," and a "band of men living a bachelor life in a bachelor community." Well, not only men. Valhalla was also the celestial abode of the Valkyrjur (or Valkyries), gender-variant female warriors.[63]

Oðinn, whose name signifies "fury," "wildness," and "inspiration," was primarily a god of "battle, death, and spiritual wisdom."[64] As a battle god, he was the leader of a band comprised of the souls of fallen warriors. The approach of this band, nicknamed "the Wild Hunt," often signaled death. Oðinn was also the master of Valhalla, the paradise of warriors.

As a diviner whose cult, like those of Freyja and Freyr, was apparently inspired by shamanism, Oðinn is master of the runes and a necromancer who divines the future by way of communicating with a skull. That his worship was linked to shamanism is indicated by the manner in which he acquires the knowledge of the runes: by hanging himself on a sacred ash tree, by his possession of the eight-legged horse Sleipnir (the horse being an archetypal shamanic vehicle), and by his avian companions, the ravens Huginn and Muninn, who function as all-seeing eyes. Like many shamanic figures, Oðinn is often depicted as one-eyed, another sacrifice to gnosis. In this respect, he resembles the blind Greek prophet Tiresias as well as the Yoruba god of medicine, Osanyin. As a magician, Oðinn is owner of a ring and a spear possessing supernatural powers.[65]

In terms of gender variance, Oðinn is said to have assumed female clothing on various occasions. Moreover, one of his aspects or nicknames is Jalkr, which means "gelding."[66] Gundarsson suggests that this appellation may refer to "Oðinn's initiation into the art of *seiðr*-magic. [To] assume the feminine powers of vision and understanding or to give himself up totally to the feminine principle, a man had to be capable of giving up his masculine identity, even to the point of dressing and living as a woman for a time—a practice common to many forms of shamanism, and something which Oðinn is implied to have done in his practice of *seiðr*-magic."[67]

In a broader context, this description of Oðinn indicates, incidentally, that while the traditions of the Vanir and the Aesir have many differences—the former matrifocal and generally nonviolent, the latter patrifocal and aggressive—both appear to have emerged from shamanic traditions.

Thorr, whose name means "Thunderer," is, in a nutshell, a storm god and the Germanic Hercules. A burly, wild-eyed, red-haired man wearing iron gloves, Thorr rides in a chariot drawn by goats. In Gundarsson's words, he is the "common man writ large: a tireless eater, drinker, and fighter." Thorr's most well known attribute is his hammer, Mjollnir. Gundarsson also suggests that Thorr is a god of eroticism, his hammer being a phallic symbol.[68]

Loki is another deity important to our domain. While an Aesir, he often seems to express qualities associated with the Vanir and, indeed, in many situations acts as an emissary between the groups. In other situations, however, he seems to dwell outside both the Vanic and Aesic realms. Loki is above all a trickster, a prankster, a sinister and rather delightful brew of Puck, Marlowe's Mephistopheles, and Disney's Chernabog from the movie *Fantasia*. He delights in mockery, gossip, scandal, and social chaos. Like the Greek Hermes, he is also a thief, stealing, among other things, Freyja's magic necklace. In his more sinister manifestation, he is the slayer of Balder (the Aesic Apollo) and a catalyst of universal destruction.

A protean being, Loki experiences both gender and animal transformation. Although scholars generally agree that he was not the subject of an independent cult, his reverence may have been linked to the cults of Oðinn, Thorr, or Freyja. Loki, for instance, often assumes Freyja's falcon- or hawk-feathered cloak, which suggests at once an association with her cult, with shamanism, and with both gender and animal transformation.[69]

The stories of Oðinn, Thorr, Freyja, and Loki are woven together in various ways, including ways that suggest the intermingling of gender variance, homoeroticism, and the sacred. One of the most well known myths concerning Thorr involves the theft of his hammer by giants. Thrymm, the Giant King, lets it be known that he will return the hammer only if Freyja is brought to him as a bride. It is decided that rather than risk sending Freyja to Jotunheim, the land of the giants, Thorr will journey there dressed in the goddess's garments, with Loki at his side, dressed as the "bride's" handmaiden. At the bridal feast, where Thorr, forgetting his manners, consumes an ox, many fish, and much mead, Loki is able to convince the Giant King that the bride has not eaten since their journey began. Finally, when the hammer is customarily placed in the "bride's" lap to bless the union, Thorr reveals his true identity and slays the giants.

On the surface, this tale is reminiscent of many others in depicting transvestism as a disguise by which one male surreptitiously comes to overpower another. Cross-culturally, this use of transvestism is often linked to negative rather than positive attitudes toward gender-variant persons. Viewed esoterically, however, this tale again speaks, echoing those of Oðinn's tutelage under Freyja and Freyr's love of Gerðr, the necessity of becoming feminized, of undergoing gender metamorphosis, in order to attain what one desires, be it a possession, a person's love, power, or spiritual enlightenment. This would perhaps be an unjustified interpretation were it not that Thorr, Loki, and Oðinn are all said to have assumed the garb and behavior of women on various occasions. In this instance, it is only when two powerful Aesic gods, Thorr and Loki, submit to feminization, however superficial, that they are able to conquer the giants and thus ensure the safety of Asgarðr, the Olympus of the Germanic gods.[70]

Homoeroticism—specifically, anal eroticism—and gender variance play a key role in the tales of Loki and Oðinn. During one of the many times when Loki experiences both gender and animal metamorphosis, as he does when he dons Freyja's feathered cloak, he becomes a pregnant mare, giving birth to the eight-footed Sleipnir, which becomes Oðinn's mount.

This tale, incidentally, links both Oðinn and Loki to the sacred mushroom Fly Agaric. Once, as Oðinn is being chased by hostile forces, he races Sleipnir so hard that drops of blood begin falling from the horse's mouth. Upon touching the ground, the drops become toadstools. Thus the plant so essential to shamanism is a gift of the gods.[71]

In the *Lokasenna*, a Norse tale in which Loki and Oðinn engage in a "flyting" or verbal duel, Oðinn attacks Loki for allowing himself to become feminized and impregnated. He accuses him of spending eight years as a female being, alternately a human female and a cow. "In that," says Oðinn, "I find the mark of one who is *argr*."[72]

According to Norse philologist Martin Larsen, *argr* is the "crudest term of abuse in old Norse. Applied to a man it indicated not only that he was effeminate but also that he submitted himself to being used sexually as a woman."[73] In our terms, to be *argr* is to participate in both gender-variant and homoerotic behaviors, taking the receptive role in anal intercourse. The noun *ergi* suggests that persons repeatedly and willingly engaging in such behavior may have been perceived as essentially different from other males.[74]

Loki counters Oðinn's remark by announcing that Oðinn practices *seiðr*, mentioned above, having managed to convince Freyja to teach him this magical art. He has served as a *volva* or *seiðkona*, practicing *seiðr* on Sám's island in Denmark.[75]

Historian of Germanic religions Folke Ström, in "*Nið, Ergi*, and Old Norse Moral Attitudes," explains *ergi* refers not only to a gender-variant male who takes the receptive role in anal eroticism but also to a practitioner of *seiðr*. In other words, the "true" *ergi* individual is one in whom the elements of homoerotic behavior, gender variance, and spiritual function merge. Ström insists that it was the acceptance of the receptive role in anal intercourse, coupled with a yielding attitude toward the gods (as allowing oneself to be embodied by them), and not homosexuality *per se*, that caused a man to be looked upon, or to look upon himself, as *ergi*.[76] In Ström's words, "The factor which . . . gave *ergi* its altogether special connotation . . . was the female nature of the *argr* man."[77] *Ergi* may also refer to a "cowardly" male. It is my feeling, however, that this use of the term may have emerged from a Germanic perspective that equated nonviolence (or pacifism), which characterized the early Vanir (no weapons in Freyr's temples), with cowardice.[78]

Linguist and historian of religions Edgar Polomé feels that the *Lokasenna* is "very instructive because it tells us explicitly about his [Loki's] blood-brotherhood with Oðinn," because it states that "Loki was Oðinn's adopted son," and because it emphasizes Loki's "sexual inversion."[79] I would add that the *Lokasenna* attributes *argr* behavior or *ergi* identity, which includes both gender variance and homoeroticism, to both Loki and Oðinn, further suggesting that their own relationship may have included an alternation of sex roles. Moreover, the relationship of Loki and Oðinn is one partaking of both gender metamorphosis and animal transformation.

In a wider context, the *Lokasenna* episode suggests how homoeroticism may have played a role in bridging the spiritual and, more generally, the cultural systems of the followers of the Vanir and those of the Aesir, with the former contributing the gender-variant model and the latter the intergenerational, military model. The relationships of blood brotherhood and adoptive father-son existing between Oðinn and Loki further indicate that same-sex relationships may have been cemented with formal rites. What is more, Sleipnir, the child of Loki who becomes the horse of Oðinn, may in some veiled way symbolize the magical power engendered by such relations. Indeed, the "gift" of the horse (often symbolic of the phallus) may even speak of a transference of masculinity from one male to another.[80]

GENDER-VARIANT PRIESTS AND PRACTITIONERS OF MAGIC

From Saxo Grammaticus, a twelfth-century Christian historian, we learn that the god Freyr was served by gender-variant male priests who dressed in feminine attire, employed effeminate gestures, behaved generally in a "lascivious," "wanton" manner, and used bells, considered unmanly, in their rites. Moreover, they apparently participated in a symbolic *hieros gamos* that may have involved cultic homoeroticism, in order to "ensure the divine fruitfulness of the season."[81] This rite appears to have been linked to the Fröblod, a sacrificial rite that took place at Freyr's temple at Uppsala, where the god was revered in his manifestation as erect phallus. At this rite, which was celebrated every nine years, on nine consecutive nights, nine "males of every living species—dogs, horses, men" were sacrificed to Freyr and then "hung from the trees near the shrine," grim ornaments that, rather surprisingly, shocked Christian zealots.[82] The priests of Freyr also may have experienced animal transformation during rites in which they donned boar masks. Unfortunately, little else is known of the *ergi* priests of the god. However, they have been compared to other gender-variant priests of Germanic antiquity, including the priests of the Alcis, twin warrior deities revered by the Naharvali during the third century C.E.[83]

APPEARANCE AND BEHAVIOR OF *ERGI* PRIESTS AND MAGICIANS

While it is as yet unclear, it seems plausible that the *ergi* priests of Freyr may have been associated with, and perhaps even identified with, the gender-variant, *seiðr*-practicing priests of Freyja.[84]

It is fairly certain that the *ergi* priests of both Freyr and Freyja wore a mixture of feminine and priestly articles of clothing. If this is true, we may speculate—chiefly based on data concerning priestesses and female *seiðkonur*—that, when they did not go skyclad (without clothes), they dressed in either feathered cloaks or blue, hooded cloaks, wore glass bead necklaces, bearskin belts, calfskin shoes, and catskin gloves. *Seiðr* practitioners also carried magical staffs inset with jewels.[85]

Ergi priests of Freyja who practiced *seiðr,* like other gender-variant spiritual figures we have encountered, apparently performed tasks traditionally assigned to women. These may have included planting, weaving, and childrearing.[86]

It is not clear whether or not the *ergi* priests-*seiðrmen* were eunuchs, although Oðinn's nickname or aspect Jalkr, or "gelding" as well as other data, indicate that ritual castration was not unknown.[87] If the *ergi* priests-*seiðrmen* were in fact eunuchs, this may have accounted for the strange quality of their voices referred to as *skratta* or *seið-laeti* and possibly suggesting falsetto or castrati voice.[88]

HOMOEROTICISM, METAMORPHOSIS, AND *ERGI*

While among Germanic peoples homosexual behavior does not appear to have been restricted to *ergi* individuals, it does seem that *ergi* priests-*seiðrmen* were viewed as essentially different from other men. They were clearly differentiated from men who occasionally had sex with other men and who took the active role when they did. Truly bisexual men, however, seem also to have been viewed as essentially different, sharing close ties with *ergi* individuals. These men, usually "passive" in terms of their male partners, were often imagined to undergo gender metamorphosis every ninth night, when, like werewolves or vampires seeking victims, they would go out hunting other men.[89]

Ergi priests-*seiðrmen,* in this respect, were associated not only with gender metamorphosis but also with animal transformation, much like Loki and Oðinn. This is suggested by the term *seiðberender,* with *berendi* referring to a female animal.[90] While Ström stresses the derogatory nature of this term, it occurs to me that beyond its derisive use, *seidberender* might refer to becoming both the Goddess and the falcon by donning the feathered cloak of Freyja, or to alternately embody the Goddess and another of her sacred animals—also linked to Freyr—by wearing the mask of the boar, these costumes used in journeying shamanically into other worlds.

Such metamorphoses may have been deemed necessary because, in order to explore and survive in the Germanic wild, the *utangards,* one would do well to understand profoundly both the "feminine" and the "animal," as both, according to Kirsten Hastrup in *Culture and History in Medieval Iceland,* belonged to "the 'other' world of man" and were "associated with uncontrollable nature."[91]

FUNCTIONS OF *ERGI* PRIESTS AND *SEIĐRMEN*

One of the services that may have been performed by the *ergi* priests-*seidrmen* involved journeying about the countryside, stopping for festivals and on other occasions when people felt the need to communicate with the Goddess and other divine beings. The *seidrman* (or -*woman*) would be offered a sacrificial meal, sometimes comprised of the hearts of various animals. He would then mount a high platform called the *seidjaller,* where he would begin to chant, as others below accompanied him. The *vardlokkur* songs they sang (from which the English *warlock* may come) were used to summon spirits, protect participants from harm, and facilitate a shamanic or an altered state of consciousness in the *seidrman.* The *seidrman* would then journey, often in the form of a falcon or cat, to the world of the gods. Upon his return, he would share the words of the divinity or spirit with the other participants. He would answer questions concerning the destinies of persons in the year to come, the probable abundance or failure of crops, and other matters.[92]

This rite of shamanic journey was only one of the rites undertaken by *seidrmen.* Other types of divination, perhaps even including runic divination—normally considered Odinnic and "masculine"—were also practiced by *seidrmen.*

Indeed, two of the runes, Berkano and Ingwaz, seem especially linked to the worship of Freyja, the other Vanir, and practitioners of *seidr.* The Berkano liturgy speaks of the Goddess as the giver and taker of life and of the need for her "powers of fertility . . . [to be] renewed by the sacrifice of her consort each year," either by death, castration, or some other means. Ingwaz echoes this theme of sacrifice but focuses on the male consort, functionary, or devotee rather than on the Goddess. The central meaning of Ingwaz is a familiar one: in order to "assume the feminine powers of vision and understanding," a man must be willing to give up "his masculine identity, even to the point of dressing and living as a woman for a time." Gundarsson, who specifically links this rune to the gender transformations of Odinn and Loki, and to their child-producing relationship, describes Ingwaz as hieratically expressing either semen or a castrated male.[93]

Working magic, however, appears to have been the chief function of the *ergi* functionaries. While their rituals have generally been lost, we know that they held the power to bestow wealth and fame and to take these away. They could bring plenty during a time of famine or cause the land to be blighted. They could cause persons to fall ill, just as they could heal them with herbs and charms. They could bring lovers together and sever relationships. In later times, they aided warriors by magically dulling enemies' swords, halting enemy arrows in flight, raising storms at sea, and unbinding the chains of imprisoned comrades. Indeed, they were believed capable of bringing an end to war. They were also thought to be able to transform persons into animals and to transfer speech, knowledge, and power from one person to another and from human beings to animals.[94]

In terms of our specific context, it appears that *ergi* priests-*seiðrmen* may have engaged in rites of sexual magic by which the body of a male, via anal intercourse or other means, became feminized, transformed into a vessel or channel of the divine.

This state of being *ergjask* (or *sorðinn, stroðinn, sannsorðin, rassragr*), of being "fucked," becomes the erotic-sacred expression of surrender or yielding of the masculine to the feminine, the mortal to the divine.[95]

Seiðr practitioners were even thought to be able, after having passed away, to pay visits to the living. Practitioners of *seiðr* may have sometimes been associated with the *draugr*, or "undead." Once the bones of a *seiðkona* were unearthed. Described as "blue and ill-looking," they conjured images of the corpses of the undead, depicted as showing signs of "swelling or changing color."[96]

DEATH AND THE *ERGI*

This brings us to a controversial subject regarding the deaths of *ergi* priests-*seiðrmen*. According to Tacitus, *ergi* males were drowned in mudholes and marshes. While he suggests that it was due to their being *ergi*, it is not clear that he was certain of this. A number of writers have suggested that these men may be among those whose corpses have been discovered in peat bogs. Folke Ström has argued, however, that the male corpses discovered in peat bogs appear to have been hanged first before being lowered into the bogs, which he believes represents a more honorable punishment than that allotted to *ergi* males. He insists that the "last resting-place[s] of the 'unmanly'" were not peat bogs but rather "morasses, quagmires, and swamps," which have "not attracted archaeologists."[97]

Nevertheless, a theory voiced by P. V. Glob suggests that while in later, increasingly patriarchal (or Aesic) epochs, such men probably did suffer the fate described by Ström, in earlier times, *ergi* priests-*seiðrmen* may well have ended up in the bogs. According to Glob, where bog corpses are concerned, "the circumstances of the bog people's deposition . . . have many of the characteristics of . . . sacrificial deposits." Glob writes, "At the beginning of the era of the bog people it was not a male but a female god that was dominant; and her servant . . . had to be sacrificed . . . so that the cycle of nature might be supported and helped forward. . . . [Through] their sacrificial deaths, they were themselves consecrated for all time to . . . Mother Earth, who in return so often gave their faces her blessing and preserved them through the millennia."[98]

As evidence in support of Glob's theory, one may point to the nooses encircling the necks of a number of male corpses, nooses that Ström sees merely as evidence of hanging but that Glob sees as 'replicas of the twisted neck-rings which are the mark of honour of the goddess, and a sign of consecration to her." Glob writes of the celebrated "Tollund man": "Thus we can speak of the skillfully plaited noose as the designating sign of the Tollund man, marking him out as consecrated to the goddess."[99]

Perhaps Glob is correct as concerns earlier epochs, while Ström is correct as concerns later times. The chief problem that I observe with Ström's theory is that, within the worship of Freyja, Freyr, Nerthus-Njord, Yngvi, and the Great Goddess as opposed to outside of it, *ergi* priests-*seiðrmen* appear to have been respected and not looked upon as degenerates or criminals. Further, we are fairly certain that human sacrifice was practiced in the worship of the Germanic Goddess(es), and, as male representatives of the Goddess and her consort, *ergi* functionaries may have been considered especially appropriate sacrifices.[100] If *ergi* males were *not* placed in bogs, then I would guess that the peat bog may have been the final resting place of traditionally masculine devotees of the Goddess who were sacrificed during the Fröblod. It should be noted that whether Ström or Glob is correct, or whether the truth lies somewhere in the middle, *ergi* males were being drowned, burned, and otherwise tortured and slain at the time of Christianity's "triumph" in the tenth and eleventh centuries. It is also rather eerie to consider that as late as the midtwentieth century, the Nazi leader Himmler, in an attempt to demonstrate his admiration for the ancient practice of drowning *ergi* men, suggested that homosexuals should be disposed of in this manner. "That was no punishment," said he, "merely the extinction of an abnormal life."[101]

SEIÐRMEN

We know of several legendary men who were said to have been *seiðrmen*. One of these was Haddingr, son of Gram of Denmark. Haddingr was raised by a priestess of Freyja named Harðgrep(a). As a young man, Haddingr was said to have been a favorite of Oðinn. Later he established an annual sacrifice to Freyr. He is said to have ended his life in suicide, "in Oðinnic fashion," after his companion Hundingr drowned. Mythologist Jaan Puhvel points out that the life of Haddingr reveals an intermingling of both "Odinic and Vanic features." The name Haddingr is associated with the Haddingjar, twin warrior deities who are in turn linked to the Alcis, who, as we have seen, were served by gender-variant priests. The name Haddingr is also related to the word *haðr*, "denoting a feminine hairdo."[102]

Two other men who practiced *seiðr* were Ragnvaldr Rettilbeini and Eyvindr Kelda. Rettilbeini lived during the ninth century C.E. and was a son of King Harald Fairhair. As a young man, Rettilbeini became well known as a practitioner of *seiðr*. When his father, who despised *seiðrmen*, sent a threatening letter to Vitgeir, another *seiðrman*, the latter responded:

> It is little strange
> If we do wizardry,
> Who are the sons of carls
> And of low-born mothers,

When Ragnvald Rettlebone,
Harald's noble son,
Can be a wizard
In Hadeland [Haðalandia].[103]

Not long after, King Harald sent another of his sons, Erik Bloodaxe, to
Haðalandia, where Ragnvaldr lived. There Erik carried out the royal father's orders, burning his brother and eighty other *seiðrmen* alive.[104]

Eyvindr Kelda, related to Rettilbeini and King Harald, practiced *seiðr* during
the tenth century. For this, he was brought before King Olaf Tryggvason, a Christian fanatic, in 998 C.E. Tryggvason, who found pleasure in threatening to sacrifice pagans to their own gods, prepared a feast for Kelda and other *seiðrmen*
whom he was holding captive, causing them to think he had experienced a change
of heart. When he was certain that all the men were drunk, Tryggvason ordered
the doors locked and the house set on fire. Kelda and a few other *seiðrmen* managed to escape. They were eventually caught, however, and in chains were taken in
a boat to a rock in the water, where they were left to drown. (If not fire, then
water.) For this reason, the rock at Karmoy, near Haugesund, is called Skrattasker
or Skrattaskerry, the "place where the *seiðrmen* perished."[105]

The term *Skrattasker* deserves further mention here. It is derived from the old
Norse *skratta,* which appears in old Icelandic, Old High German, Old English,
Middle English, and other tongues in such variants as *scarte, schrat, scraette,
scritta, strac,* and *strat,* and signifies at once a monster, a sorcerer, a hermaphrodite, a eunuch, and a promiscuous person. *Skratta* and *seið-skratti* were also used
interchangeably to refer to a practitioner of *seiðr. Skratta* was also synonymous
with *seið-laeti,* the term describing the strange noises made by *seiðrmen* during
rituals.[106]

WOLFISH OUTLAWS AND OTHER HEATHENS

The persecution of *seiðrmen* and gender-variant priests (as also in the case of
priestesses and *seiðkonur*) by Christians resulted in the former being labeled "hea-
thens," just as those Romans who had once refused to adopt Christianity were labeled "pagans," country dwellers ("hicks"). This is a fascinating word choice, for
although meant as an insult, the word *heathen* served to preserve the memory of
the *seiðrmen* and *seiðkonur,* their beliefs and practices. As the instructress of *seiðr,*
Freyja assumed one of her many manifestations, that of Heiðr ("Heidi") the
Witch. The name Heiðr is linked to the Germanic *heide* or "heath," hence "heathen." Fantasy writer, Germanic scholar, and priestess Diana L. Paxson, in "The
Holy Hag," relates that the "heath is the wilderness outside the *garth* [the community or society] to which the *seiðmaðr* or *seiðkona,* and later anyone who wished
to worship in the old way, retired to work their magic."[107]

Which brings us to speak of the "outdweller" and the outlaw.

The contemporary anthropologist Kirsten Hastrup explains that in Germanic
countries, the world of earthly existence was divided into the "social" and the
"wild," with the former being the "controlled space of social relations" and the

latter being the "uncontrolled, unknown environment."[108] While the former is called *innangarðs,* the latter is called *utangarðs.* Gundarsson describes the *utangarðs* or the "wild" as follows:

> The *utangarðs* is the realm of disorder, the . . . uncanny, and the unknown.
> It is the wild world of the forest and the outlaw. It is also the realm into
> which you fare to gain wisdom and magical power. . . . Magic is, indeed,
> by nature characteristic of the *utangarðs.*[109]

The *utangarðs* is populated not only by outlaws such as criminals but also by giants, ghosts, trolls, and elves. As Gundarsson suggests, practitioners of *seiðr* journey to the *utangarðs* when they journey shamanically to perform magic or to communicate with the gods.

Hastrup explains that outlaws, who were relatively permanent residents of the *utangarðs,* were generally referred to as *vargr,* "wolves."[113] *Vargr* is related to the English words *vagrant* and *vagabond.* According to Gundarsson,

> The outlaw, being outside of the *garðr,* had ceased to be human; he is
> "*wod-freka werewulf* "—the fury-greedy werewolf—in the laws of Canute,
> *wulf-heafod* (wolf's head) among the Anglo-Saxons.
>   It is obvious that the *vargr* (outlaw) is closely related to and frequently
> the same as the *vargr* (ravening wolf). He is, in fact, often a skin-changer,
> or a berserker.[111]

Gundarsson is here linking the outlaw or *vargr* to a group, or perhaps two groups, of warrior-priests of Oðinn who lived on the edges of the "social" or in the wild, as outlaws. These men dressed in animal skins and entered battle in shamanic or altered states of consciousness, perhaps partly triggered by the ingestion of mind-altering substances, possibly the fly agaric or ergot, another substance we will discuss shortly.[112] Those *vargr* warriors who donned bearskins were called *berserkers,* while those who donned wolfskins were called *ulfserkers* or *ulfhednar.*[113] While the "bearskins" and the "wolfskins" may have formed separate fraternities, they appear to have been virtually identical.[114]

The *vargr* or wolf warrior may be traced to the earliest Indo-Europeans. In Greece, both Zeus and Apollo had wolfish aspects and were followed by wolf warrior bands. Followers of these and other wolf deities were known to undergo a long and powerful initiation that included murdering another human being (sacrificially) and, while wearing only a wolfskin, living as a beast for up to nine years. During this period, the initiate was treated as an outcast. While he retained this outlaw status on completion of his initiation, he was at the same time revered as a powerful warrior. It is highly probable that initiation into the wolf warrior band included cultic homoeroticism. Long after such practices declined, the link between homoeroticism and lycanthropy remained. Indeed, in intergenerational relationships, the lover or *erastes* became known as the "wolf," with the beloved or *eromenos* taking the role of the "lamb." In Rome, *lupus,* "wolf," came to connote lascivious behavior (*lupanaris*), sexual intercourse (*lupari*), and prostitution (*lupatria*). Also at Rome, the wolf warriors were transformed into the *luperci*, the wolf-priest celebrants of the Lupercalia.

As in Greece, the Germanic wolf warrior, the *vargr*, was considered an outlaw and was often identified with the werewolf.

The term *vargr* is related to the terms *argr* and *ergi*, forming an etymological link between the wolf warrior and the *ergi* priest-*seiðrman*. The wolf warrior was linked not only to cultic homoeroticism but also to gender variance; indeed, he was at once variant in terms of being supermasculine or "beastly" and in terms of embracing the concept of *ergi*. In late twentieth-century terms, he might be envisioned as a leather queen who is also familiar with the experience of the drag queen. While at first this linkage may seem strange, it seems more plausible when we remember Loki's union with Oðinn, blending elements of shamanism as well as the intergenerational, gender-variant, and egalitarian models of homoeroticism.[115] The relationship between *argr* and *vargr* is expressed in a "wolf charm" that reads:

Call me *varg*
and I'll be *arg*.
Call me golden,
I'll be beholden.[116]

It appears that the association of wolfishness and homoeroticism may be traced to the Hittites. The Hittite word **Hwergh-* signifies strangulation and seems to refer to both a punishment meted out to individuals engaging in anal intercourse (*hurkel*, also applied to incest) and to a tribe of demonic beings who hold power over serpents and wolves. The term *hurkel*, moreover, may refer to individuals capable of shapeshifting.[117]

These ideas resonate in the tale of the warriors Sinfjotli and Gundmundr. If we look beyond the sarcastic tone of the flyting in which their story is told, it seems that we have here yet another tale blending gender variance, homoeroticism, and animal, here wolfish, transformation. Sinfjotli has spent time, we know from another text, as a wolf warrior or werewolf. He is thus linked to the Oðinnic *ulfhednar* tradition. Gundmundr, on the other hand, is associated with both the Oðinnic and the Vanic traditions being depicted as both a female or an effeminate practitioner of *seiðr* and as an Oðinnic Valkyrie, desired by "all Valholl's warriors." What is more, Gundmundr is also portrayed as a female wolf or werewolf who has given birth to nine wolves. Not surprisingly, Sinfjotli claims to be the father. It is conceivable that this myth tries to describe metaphorically, as does the tale of Oðinn and Loki's union the process of conflict and syncretization experienced by the Indo-European Germanic tribes and the earlier inhabitants of northern Europe.[118]

A controversial theory suggests that *vargr* may be related not only to *argr* and *ergi* but also to *ergot*. Ergot is a fungal disease that certain grasses, especially rye, can develop, and LSD is a synthetic derivative of it. Ergot appears to have been used in the Eleusinian mysteries of Demeter and Persephone and has also been blamed for the European dance "crazes" of the Middle Ages. Germanic literary scholar Mary R. Gerstein writes, "Thus, *ergot* would be an umlauted form based on Germanic *arg[r]* an accusation of shape and sex change . . . made . . . against the werwolf shapechangers (and sexchangers), Odin and Loki. Like *warg* [*vargr*] and the word *wolf* itself, it has . . . associations [with the] 'disease of rye.'"[119]

The relationship of *argr, ergi, vargr,* and ergot suggests that the link between the *ergi* priests-*seiđrmen* and the wolf warriors not only may have consisted of variant forms of gendered and erotic behavior but that it may have also embraced the use of ergot as a sacred hallucinogen by which to enter a shamanic or altered state of consciousness, either to journey to other worlds or to become embodied by a beastly (wolfish, and so forth) and/or feminine being.

The possible link between *vargr* and *seiđr* may also be strengthened by the presence of the term *morđvarg* or "murder-warg." This term signifies murdering someone by "unmanly" means, such as by *seiđr* or poison (feminine means), or killing during a lycanthropic episode (beastly means). Gerstein also points out that the word *vargr* may in fact be semantically linked to the word *seiđr*. One of the meanings of *var-/wer-* is "to bind," and *seiđr* is defined as "that which binds magically." In the following quotation, Gerstein weaves together many of the threads which run throughout this chapter and this text:

> The *binder god* of the Old Norse pantheon is, of course, Odin, lord of the hanged and gallows burden, *patron of outcasts and leader of the berserkir [and* ulfhednar*], frenzied, shape-changing* warriors, Odin, who binds his foes with battle fetters and with *seiđr*. Odin differs ideologically from other binder gods in his *essential amorality:* he delights in strife. . . . The strangled warg [here, outlaw] belongs to him more from a sense of "*like seeking like*" than in punishment. . . . Odin is the embodiment of every form of frenzy . . . , from the insane bloodlust that characterized the werwolf warriors who dedicated themselves to him, to *erotic* and *poetic madness* [italics mine].[120]

Rites of initiatory homoeroticism possibly linked to the condition or institution of *vargr* may have survived into later times in the sublimated form of (or may be otherwise connected to) the *jarđarmen* ceremony, a rite of blood brotherhood in which young male initiates passed under three strips of turf, referred to as "earth-torques." The *jarđarmen* rite reveals an intermingling of matrifocal, Vanic and patrifocal, Aesic or Ođinnic traditions. While one is being initiated into a warrior society, the primary symbol of the initiatory rite is the Brisingamen, the magical necklace or torque of Freyja. It was a symbol of the Goddess's fertility (in the Germanic psyche, the necklace was a vaginal symbol) as well as of her death-wielding aspect (as a "choker"). It has been suggested that torques may have been used to strangle males being sacrificed to the Goddess.

The torque was also associated with gender-variant women known as *fordoeđa* who not only assumed masculine roles but who were believed capable of rendering men *ergi. Fordoeđa* was one of Freyja's appellations. The torque also came to signify the anus, anal intercourse, and *argr* behavior. By extension, to form the hands into a ring was to suggest that one held the power to cause another to submit to anal intercourse. Germanic scholar Margaret C. Ross reminds us of an incident when Oðinn directed this gesture at Thorr, boasting that he could render him *rassragr*—that is, penetrate him anally—whenever he liked. In the context of the *jarðarmen* rite, the multivalent significance of Freyja's necklace or torque became linked to simulated or actual anal intercourse.

Ross explains that in the rite, the three strips of turf under which the youths passed represented not only Freyja's necklace, her vagina, and the womb-tomb from which all life emerged and to which all life returned, but also the anus, anal intercourse, and yielding to a spiritual male elder. Ross concludes that since the *jarðarmen* is "connected with ceremonies of *fóstbrœðralag* [foster brotherhood], one might suspect that its significance in the . . . initiation ceremony . . . was anal rather than vaginal in that the boys might have participated in a rite of communal sodomy to mark their entry into adult male society."[121]

With the triumph of Christianity in the tenth and eleventh centuries, *vargr* outlaws and warriors, practitioners of *seiðr*, elves, trolls, and other beings to whom otherworldly powers were attributed were joined in the wild by many others who refused to convert to the new religion or who refused to accept Christianity's dictates concerning eroticism and gender.[122]

HOMOEROTICISM, GENDER VARIANCE, AND GERMANIC REVIVAL

Since the emergence of Romanticism and German nationalism in the nineteenth century, groups revering the deities of the ancient North have proliferated. Unfortunately, some of these groups have been linked to right-wing political movements. However, to equate devotees of the Germanic gods with the Nazis is to grossly misinterpret or misrepresent a spiritual movement seeking primarily to honor Germanic or Scandinavian heritage. Indeed, a number of Germanic practitioners I have encountered embrace liberal, feminist, and gay-positive attitudes. It is true that general societal homophobia and effemiphobia have prevented some prominent members of the tradition from being candid about gender role or sexual orientation. Fortunately, this is not the case with my friend William Karpen, a priest of Freyr, who in the 1990s edits a California Bay Area Gay Spiritual journal, *Lavender Pagan.*

Karpen was originally put off by the Germanic tradition because of its alleged association with rightist politics. At the same time, he was drawn to the tradition because it spoke to his own ethnicity. He became more deeply involved when he learned of the homoerotic and gender-variant elements present in the cult of Freyr. In Karpen's view, "Freyr signifies desire." Moreover, this deity signifies the "process" of desire, or lovemaking, rather than focusing on a goal such as reproduction of offspring. For this reason, gay men involved in the Germanic tradition frequently relate deeply to Freyr. Karpen also feels a deep connection to a number of goddesses, including Freyja, Holda, and Helle. In particular, he links Helle, goddess of the underworld, to the shamanic journey that gay persons take when confronting their same-sex desires and internalized homophobia.

Karpen now belongs to a circle named Hrafnar, "Raven." This circle includes several feminist-identified women and gay people, including Karpen's friend Gandor, who is especially drawn to Freyja and the giants. Members of Hrafnar are reclaiming the practice of *seiðr*. During rituals, Karpen often cross-dresses, wearing earrings and long, traditionally feminine robes. He tells me that Gandor and he have made the circle aware of the role of the gender-variant fool, with Gandor ritually mocking the other participants as they perform solemn actions. Gandor has also made sure that the figure of the gender-variant, homoerotically inclined "walker between" is blessed during the circle's rites. In terms of solitary practice, Karpen pays homage to Freyr at an altar dressed with attributes of the god, including leeks, linen, images of horses and stags, and phallic icons. Karpen sees himself as helping to create a gay priesthood that exists within, rather than separate from, the broader Germanic tradition.[123]

THE GUNDESTRUP CAULDRON

Finally, one of the finest artistic expressions of the Indo-European peoples—and one possibly linked to our domain—is the Gundestrup Cauldron. A large silver bowl covered with figures of deities, humans, animals, and objects, it was discovered in a peat bog in Denmark in 1891. Fashioned near the second century B.C.E., its creation has been variously attributed to Celts, Germanic peoples, and Thracians. Among the figures depicted on the bowl are several female divinities who are generally acknowledged to be aspects of a Great Goddess, and a male deity believed to be Cernunnos. He is shown here seated in the characteristic yogalike pose, wearing a torque and antlers. In his left hand, he holds a ram-headed serpent; in his right, another torque. He is surrounded by a twining plant, perhaps ivy, and by various animals, including a stag, a boar, and a lion.

In a recent article in *Scientific American,* Timothy Taylor, a lecturer in archaeology at the University of Bradford, brings our attention to a beardless male figure wearing a horned helmet and holding a wheel, kneeling beside the figure of a god variously identified as Cernunnos and Taranis, the Celtic god of thunder. Taylor suggests that this figure may represent a "ritual specialist" and silversmith who may have helped four or five other artisans create the cauldron. Taylor further suggests that the creators of the cauldron may not have viewed themselves in ethnic terms—that is, as Celts or Germans—but rather as individuals belonging to a special class consisting of gender-variant (and possibly homoerotically inclined) religious specialists. He compares the hypothetical Gundestrup silversmiths not only to the Scythian *enarees* but also to the Irish *filidh.* "They might . . . have resembled the Enarees of Scythia," he writes, or the bards of Ireland. In Ireland the biologically male bard who praised the king was described as female, in opposition to the ruler's maleness.[124]

In order to more ably decipher enigmatic works of art like the Gundestrup Cauldron, Taylor stresses that we must first recognize that "ethnicity, gender and mythology may have all been more complex than previously supposed. Firm cultural boundaries may not have existed, humanity and its gods may have been viewed as having more than simple male and female genders, and religious beliefs may have been flexible and multifaceted."[125]

Altar (alleged) of King Henri III of France, late 16th century C.E.

Cauldron of Changes

> BENVOLIO: . . . I'll be Actaeon and turn myself into
> a stag.
> FAUSTUS: And I'll play Diana, and send you the
> horns presently.
>
> Christopher Marlowe,
> *The Tragical History of Doctor Faustus*[1]

As Christianity spread throughout Europe (and eventually to other parts of the world), and especially with the emergence of the Inquisition in the early thirteenth century, the figure of the gender-variant, often homoerotically inclined priest, alongside that of the priestess, gradually began to fade, suffering dispersion, fragmentation, and in some places eradication. Likewise, as more and more temples were burned and their stones were used to build cathedrals, the goddesses and gods of antiquity retreated to the wild. Many, including peasants, or *pagani*, continued, however, to revere the elder gods, albeit as folk figures or in the costumes of saints, with pre-Christian rites often taking the form of folk festivals, carnivals, and saints' days' celebrations. In like manner, gender-variant priests frequently appeared in the guises of carnival celebrants, troubadours, fools, and even Christian mystics. Those who continued to practice the divinatory and magical arts more or less openly or who engaged in other practices associated with paganism, from midwifery to transvestism and same-sex eroticism, were branded as witches or heretics.

With the emergence of the Renaissance, the elder gods discovered a refuge in the world of art, and the gender-variant priest reappeared as the homoerotically inclined artist who depicted the interrelationship of androgyny, homoeroticism, and the sacred (often a blend of Christianity and paganism) in his works, often in sublimated form.

With the arrival of the eighteenth century, it became evident that, in spite of having undertaken the most horrific holocaust the world had thus far known, the Church had lost its battle against pre-Christian beliefs and practices as well as against persons engaging in gender-variant and homoerotic behaviors.

FROM GODS TO FOLK FIGURES

As Pamela Berger explains in *The Goddess Obscured,* the Great Goddess and her myriad manifestations survived the onslaught of Christianity primarily by assuming the guises of folk figures and saints; yet in rare instances, people continued to worship feminine deities as such, including Diana and the Germanic Holda.[2]

Among the gods who survived was the male guardian of the forest and its creatures, known to the ancients as Pan and Cernunnos and by other names as well. In the Middle Ages, he often appeared as a fusion of the androgyne and a beastly or vegetal "Wild" or "Green" man.[3]

Crokesos was a French manifestation of this figure. A blend of fairy, elf, wild man, androgyne, and fool, Crokesos was a companion of Hellekin (another name of Oberon), the Fairy King. He was further linked to two other groups of fairies, the *follets* and the *lutins.* Like these, Crokesos was immune to holy water. He was a merry, independent creature who knew no master, not even Hellekin. A shapeshifting trickster reminiscent of Puck, Crokesos appeared at various times as a goat, a stallion, a spider, a monk, and a fool wearing a multicolored coat ornamented with bells.

Certain terms used in connection with him also indicate a link to homoeroticism. For instance, he is mentioned in association with the *canebustin,* a drinking vessel that, in medieval France, apparently connoted not only the belly but also the anus as a receptacle for the penis in same-sex eroticism. His name may also be divided into *croquer,* "to beat" or, connotatively, "to anally penetrate, the *sot,*" a type of fool who—as we shall see—was thought to engage in gender-variant behavior and in homoeroticism.[4]

Another such figure is Scrat, or "the scrat," who was revered in the seventh century by some Germanic and Anglo-Saxon groups. As mentioned in the previous chapter, the term *scrat* is related to the Germanic practitioner of *seidr* magic while also carrying the meanings of monster, hermaphrodite, eunuch, and prostitute. Apparently Scrat was, like Crokesos, an archetypal "hairy androgyne" (far from the Greek conception of androgyny). Like Crokesos, Scrat was a shape shifter; he might also appear as an infant, a giant, a bear, a horse, a butterfly, or a red-capped dwarf resembling Rumplestiltskin. His nickname Katzaus (also Katzenveit) may suggest a link to the cult of Freyja. This appellation may also indicate an association with *katzenmusik,* a "deliberately distorted and noisy" musical performance elsewhere known as *charivari* or "rough music."

Scrat was honored with gifts of food, often placed in houses or at forest shrines. If remembered, he, like the fairy tale elf, would perform tasks for the faithful. His cult may have survived into the sixteenth century. Places sacred to him include Scrathawe, Strathawe, Scrachawe, and other sites in England and elsewhere. Eventually, he became identified with the devil, taking the nickname of Old Scrat or Mr. Scratch.[5]

Beyond Scrat and Crokesos, other medieval figures, half folkloric and half literary, reflected the elements of our domain. These include the Idiot of Adam de la Halle's burlesque medieval drama *Le Jeu de la Feuillée* (*The Play,* or *Game, of Falling Leaves*), Gargantua, immortalized in Rabelais's Renaissance classic *Gargantua and Pantagruel,* Renart (also, Reynard) the Fox, and the werewolf Bisclavaret.

The Idiot of *Le Jeu,* a play that includes three transvestite fairies, experiences both animal and gender transformation. Metamorphosing into a toad, he becomes associated with magical brews. As a bull, he yearns to mount his own father, whom he perceives as a heifer. Later, however, he turns into a female calf, thus becoming associated with a French proverb used to castigate promiscuous women and gender-variant, homoerotically inclined men: "*Tu n'as plus d'arrest qu'un jeune veau,* Thou art as wanton . . . as a milch calfe." To *faire* (or *trousser*) *le pied de veau,* "to make the calf's leg," a gesture depicted in medieval illustrations, is to lift the leg in order to urinate, defecate, or ready oneself for anal penetration. The play *Le Jeu* culminates with the Idiot becoming a bride. "Look," he says to his father, "I am your wife."[6]

Gargantua is an equally burlesque creator-giant of European myth, primarily associated with the French. He is responsible for creating hills and valleys, which often come into being accidentally when he stops to "shit and piss." In Rabelais's depiction, which overflows with autoerotic, heterosexual, and homosexual references (including "peas and bacon," a dish connoting same-sex eroticism), Gargantua is a symbol of the maxim "Do What Thou Wilt," which the would-be monks of Medmenham Abbey and the ritual magician Aleister Crowley would appropriate centuries later. His attitude is reflected in his codpiece, which is encrusted with diamonds, rubies, emeralds, and pearls and which is always "sappy and moist, always . . . full of every delight," and in his hat-medallion, which portrays the "two-rumped" double male "androgyne" of Plato's *Symposium.*[7]

Renart the Fox was a medieval trickster and rake. Although he was not worshiped, he apparently played a central role in the Feast of Fools. While rape, murder, and robbery were all credited to him, he somehow remained an amiable character and was admired as an outlaw. Literary theorist and translator Patricia Terry explains that tales of Renart functioned to attack, "with gusto and subterranean idealism, the government . . . [and the] Church." A great sinner, Renart delighted in confession. As literary historian Gerald Herman notes, "Renart . . . recites his past sins in the same manner that a warrior might display old battle scars." Not surprisingly, one of these "sins" is homoerotic activity. In the *Roman de Fauvel,* a propagandistic Christian text of the early fourteenth century, Renart appears not as a fox but as Fauvel, a "fawn-coloured stallion" who, in being linked to the Knights Templar, a heretical group we shall mention a bit later, is credited with introducing humankind to homosexuality.[8]

Bisclavaret, the central character of Marie de France's medieval tale "The Lay of the Werewolf," has pre-Christian roots that lie in the *vargr-argr* mythos described in our previous chapter.

Once, we are told, there was a respected and handsome baron of Brittany who, due to a spell that had been placed upon him, turned into a werewolf for three days each week. One day the baron fell in love with a beautiful young woman. They married, but soon the wife became suspicious of her husband's frequent disappearances. After promising she would accept the truth, the baron explained his plight. The wife immediately called upon a knight who had once loved her. The knight was to steal the baron's clothes from the cave in which he left them so that the baron would remain a wolf and the wife, being thought a widow, might marry the knight. The knight obeyed the lady's wishes, and the two married.

Not long after, the king, hunting in the forest, came upon an amiable, handsome wolf. He took the wolf home to the palace, and the two soon became inseparable companions. One day, the king held a banquet. The lady and the knight were among the guests. Not surprisingly, the wolf became enraged. The king, knowing something must be the matter, asked his wise counselor, who assured him some magic was at work here. The king, realizing what had happened, demanded that the couple return the wolf-baron's clothes. The king placed the garments and the wolf inside his own bedchamber and left them alone for a time. When he returned, a handsome man lay in his bed. We are told that the king "ran swiftly to the bed and taking his friend in his arms, embraced and kissed him fondly, above a hundred times." As in all fairy tales, the king and Bisclavaret lived happily ever after.[9]

In medieval and Renaissance texts authored by Christians, homoeroticism was described as "unnatural." Gilles de Corbeil went so far as to claim that the "most ferocious beasts surpass man in that they couple and reproduce according to what is their natural sexual function," as opposed to many men, who have taken up homosexuality. De Corbeil and others placed heterosexuality under the category of nature, while they placed homosexuality under that of culture. (This may have been partly inspired by the writings of Plato). Indeed, the homoerotically inclined were even placed in a subcategory of culture: grammar. Those who "connect to each other [in] terms of the same gender" are "grammarians." Homoerotically inclined men become "adjectives," while lesbian women become "nouns." (I cannot help but think of Proust and Gertrude Stein.) Nevertheless, the ancient shamanic associations of gender and animal transformation endured, as did their links to same-sex eroticism. We even find this association in Chaucer's *Canterbury Tales,* where the effeminate, homosexual Pardoner, who dispenses papal pardons, is referred to as a mare.[10]

A JOYOUS SUBCULTURE

The Middle Ages and the Renaissance witnessed the growth of a subculture that, like earlier shamanic, Goddess-revering, and other traditions, embraced gender-variant and homoerotic persons who also expressed the sacred. Was this, then, a "gay" subculture? That depends on one's definition of *gay.* If by *gay* we mean a subculture of persons defined *solely* in terms of homoerotic object choice or inclination, then no, it was not. If, however, we refer to a subculture that values homoerotic expression and at the same time sees it not as a trait unrelated to other behaviors but rather as linked to other expressions such as gender variance and spiritual seeking, then possibly it was a gay subculture. This subculture, however, also allowed for heterosexual behavior and other behaviors as well. Perhaps it could best be defined as a *proto-bohemian* subculture. Later on we will see, however, that the medieval to Renaissance French use of the terms *gai,* or *gay,* and its cognate *joyeux* may well have been appropriate terms by which to label this subculture. It should be pointed out that not all males who engaged in homoeroticism perceived themselves as belonging to this subculture, especially those men who were married, who did not veer from traditional masculine roles, and/or who held positions of power.

This subculture included vagabonds, wandering minstrels, fugitive criminals, pilgrims, prostitutes, sorcerers, gamblers, and "sodomites."

The tavern was the mecca of this subculture. In the Christian psyche, not surprisingly, the tavern (including the inn often adjacent to it) was the temple of Satan. If gambling was the sixth branch of the sin of avarice, the "sin against nature" was the sixth branch of the sin of luxury; and luxury meant the tavern and the inn. In 1192, Richard of Devizes warned good Christians not to "mingle with the throngs in eating-houses," for here were "actors, jesters, smooth-skinned lads [*glabariones*], Moors, flatterers, pretty boys [*pusiones*], effeminates [*molles*], pederasts [*mascularii*], singing and dancing girls, quacks [persons describing themselves as healers or diviners], belly-dancers, sorceresses, extortioners, nightwanderers, magicians, mimes, beggars, buffoons: all this tribe fill all the houses."[11]

Incidentally, this subculture may have been responsible for the growth of Polari, a branch of the so-called lingua franca, which was a hybrid language first used by sailors, Crusaders, and vagabonds (including migratory theater troupes) in the Middle Ages. Many of its users appear to have been gender-variant and/or homoerotically inclined persons. We may assume this because most of the Polari terms—unfortunately only one hundred or so—that have survived into the twentieth century have been documented among these groups, especially among drag queens, sailors, circus workers or "carnies," and actors. Polari terms, some of which may be recognizable to readers, include: *aesprow* ("male prostitute"); *baet* ("to dance" or "to shuffle"); *batts* ("shoes"); *bonar* ("attractive"); *cartso* ("penis"); *charva* ("to fuck"); *feelie homies* ("young men"); *homi-polone* ("man-woman," a homosexual or gender-variant male); *ogle riahs* ("eyelashes"); *scarper* ("to escape"); *troll over/off* ("to wander"); and *varda* ("to look at"). By far the most well known Polari terms, however, are *kaemp* or "camp," ("to be excessive or showy," "to affect feminine mannerisms") and *punk* (male homosexual). Romany-American linguist Ian Hancock mentions in passing that as late as the nineteenth century, Polari was also being employed by "peddlers of crucifixes." This suggests that a centuries-old association of the gender variant, the sexually variant, and spiritually "variant" may have persisted for almost a thousand years.[12]

CELEBRANTS

In the Middle Ages, the gender-variant and sexually variant domain was often expressed in folkish, festive, and carnivalesque forms, since the carnival was a fairly acceptable vehicle of pagan expression in a Christianized world. In the words of literary theorist Mikhail Bakhtin, "The carnival processions . . . were interpreted as the march of the [officially] rejected pagan gods." The members of our domain appeared as celebrants, *jongleurs* or troubadours, and fools. Among the figures featured in celebrations, those of the "beastly" (or vegetal) and "womanish" male predominate, among them the Wild Man, the Green Man, Bessie, Judy, Mollie, and Our Old Lass.[13]

One festival that incorporated elements of gender and animal transformation and, by implication, cultic—however comic—homoeroticism was the *hieros gamos* of Maia, the goddess of spring (sometimes depicted as having pointed ears, like an ass, as well as being a grandmother and a relative of Scrat and the fairies), and Orcus, god of the harvest and the Underworld (apparently linked to Hades, Cernunnos, and Freyr). A penitential of the ninth century condemned those males who "wear feminine garb in their dances and carry on the monstrous fiction of being Maia and Orcus."[14]

Mock weddings like that between Orcus and Maia were common in medieval and Renaissance Europe (sometimes even surviving into the twentieth century). In the Eastern Balkans, a comic *hieros gamos* was celebrated between the Wild Man Kuker and his "pregnant," male transvestite "bride" Kukeritza or Baba. In France, similar ceremonies took place between Monsieur Henri and Dame Douce and between Caramantran and his "bride." In these rites, the "brides" were depicted as elderly prostitutes who, miraculously becoming pregnant, gave birth to "sons" at Mardi Gras, while the "grooms," representing the old year, were symbolically slain. A similar rite was recorded by the Flemish painter Bruegel. Here, the bride, a male transvestite wearing a white mask, tempts a Wild Man with a ring. In London, the *hieros gamos* of the Lord and Lady was celebrated on May 1, or Beltane, an ancient Celtic festival, with the part of the Lady often being assumed by a transvestite male. On the Isle of Man on this day, a mock battle took place between the Queen of May and the Queen of Winter. While the May Queen might be represented by either a young woman or a young man, the Queen of Winter was usually portrayed by an older male.[15]

Other festive rites emphasized the link between gender and animal transformation. According to Janet and Colin Bord, the "most frequent animal disguise recorded in Britain is the horse" (as we have already noted, an archetypal shamanic animal). As recently as the nineteenth century, the central figures of the Samhain (Halloween) rite of the Hooden Horse included "Mollie," a male transvestite carrying a broom, and a man dressed as a horse. A similar ceremony was the Horn Dance, which took place at Abbots Bromley in England, originally at the winter solstice and more recently in September. In this dance, the central figures included six "stags" wearing reindeer antlers, a hobby horse, and Maid Marian, played by a man dressed in women's clothes. In some places, mock weddings took place between womanly and beastly figures. In the French Pyrenees, for instance, a man dressed in women's clothes was joined in marriage to a man costumed as a bear.[16]

Male gender variance, expressed as transvestism, was also associated in the Middle Ages and the Renaissance, as it had been in the past, with Goddess reverence, as well as with the cult of fairies and other spirits of the wild.

In Germany, the goddess Holda (also Hulda, Berchta, Herke), depicted as a beautiful woman wearing white who caused it to snow when she shook the feathers out of her mattress, was still being revered in the Middle Ages and the Renaissance. Linking backward to Freyja and forward to Hans Christian Andersen's Snow Queen, she would fly over the earth in a wagon at the winter solstice, stopping at the windows of her devotees to give them presents. At this time, women and men dressed in feminine attire, all carrying brooms, would travel in Holda's name from house to house, blessing families and distributing gifts.[17]

In Italy, a woman or transvestite male customarily took the role of La Befana, a kindly crone who, like Holda, blessed families and bestowed them with presents during the winter solstice.[18]

In England, male peasants dressed as fairies would enter a house and begin chanting, "Take one and give back a hundred," and dancing wildly before stealing everything they wanted, promising to "return what they had stolen a hundredfold." Males dressed as fairies also performed at wedding ceremonies, as did the *Feien* in Prussian and Bavarian marriages.[19]

Needless to say, the church condemned such rites. "Whosoever, at the beginning of January, ventures forth disguised as a young stag . . . or a calf," one document read, shall endure a "three-year penance, for such things are devilish." Another posed the question, "Have you done as the peasants do, who on the first day of the year, disguise themselves in masks representing deer or old women?"[20]

Nevertheless, these rites took place within the church as well as outside of it. During the Feast of Fools, monks dressed in women's clothes and bearded nuns sang hymns to asses in churches perfumed with the incense of burning shoes.[21] In the midfifteenth century, despite the efforts of the church, Ludovicus, the archbishop of Sens, was still complaining about individuals who during the Feast of

Fools wore "masks with hideous features," in other words, those of beasts, and "dressed like women." They danced inside the church, running, leaping, and singing "indecent songs." Not only this, but the crowd included "naked men with even their private parts uncovered" who indulged in "infamous shows" too "shameful to remember."[22]

While the figure of the transvestite male celebrant has often been downplayed or discussed as merely a comic element of certain festive gatherings, it is my opinion that we must begin to look behind and beyond the carnivalesque layer of these figures and rites in order to more fully appreciate the deities, celebrants, and traditions that inspired them or from which they have emerged. As Janet and Colin Bord suggest, the "she-male" is not a piece of "tomfoolery," but rather "an attempt to encompass [the] Godhead . . . every polarity, including male and female . . . totality."[23]

We approach the ancient priest of the Goddess or the "soft" shaman when we consider the *caluşari* of Eastern Europe. According to the contemporary micro-historian Carlo Ginzburg and others, the *caluşari* would dress in feminine garments, including white veils placed over their faces, and would speak or sing in falsetto. As evidence of belonging to a third or alternate gender (at least for the duration of a ritual), they would brandish swords while wearing feminine attire and behaving in an otherwise feminine manner. Joining together in groups of seven, nine, or eleven, they revered a goddess variously named Irodeasa (Herodias), Arada (Aradia), or Doamna Zinelor. The last name is associated with the goddess Diana and refers to the Mistress of the Fairies (*zinê*).[24]

The *caluşari,* like "soft" shamans and the priests of goddesses, were ecstatics who entered an altered state of consciousness as they danced faster and faster in a ring, "so fast that their feet seemed to 'fly.'" Their dances, performed at the houses of the village during spring, were thought to bring health, fortune, rain, and abundant crops; they were also thought to exorcise evil spirits.[25]

The *caluşari* were especially adept as healers. When someone became seriously ill and spirits were believed responsible, the *caluşari* would be summoned. They would take the sick person to a crossroads, where he or she would lie down. Then they would begin to leap over the patient's body and dance in a circle. Eventually, one of the *caluşari* would fall into an altered state, a *doborire,* in which he would do such things as smash a pot and sacrifice a chicken. As the evil spirits left the body of the patient, the patient would rise up to his or her feet, while the possessed *caluşar* would return to ordinary consciousness.[26]

In recent centuries, the role of the *caluşari,* who have survived into twentieth-century Eastern Europe, as gender-variant spiritual figures has diminished. Moreover, the emphasis on transvestism has been partly assumed by a comic figure called "the mute." Still, references to both gender variance and homoeroticism (largely sublimated) abound in their rites. For instance, flirtation and simulated erotic activity sometimes occurs between the mute and the other *caluşari.* In another instance in which the androgynous mute's masculinity is emphasized, a possessed *caluşar,* imagined as a woman dying in childbirth, must suck the mute's wooden phallus as part of his returning to ordinary consciousness. What is more, the *vataf,* the leader of the *caluṣari*, often warns them of punishments and loss of special powers they will suffer if they lose their virginity to women. These ritual situations serve to encourage temporary, if not permanent, homoerotic object choice.[27]

WITCHES AND FAGGOTS

A number of gay, lesbian, and feminist writers whose works have focused on spirituality, including Arthur Evans, Z. Budapest, and Starhawk, have been heavily influenced by Margaret Murray's theory of witchcraft. Murray, in her day a respected anthropologist, folklorist and Egyptologist, has suggested that witchcraft was an organized medieval cult whose adherents worshiped a divine male-female couple, gathered in covens, and met periodically at sabbats to celebrate and work magic.

Of these, Arthur Evans has specifically linked homoerotically inclined males, and with them the term *faggot*, to the cult or religion of witchcraft, also called Wicca and nicknamed the Old Religion. According to Evans, the association of witches, homoerotically inclined men, and faggots emerged during the Inquisition, when bundles of sticks were used to ignite the accused.

While I cannot wholeheartedly accept this theory, I am inclined to agree with Carlo Ginzburg that while Murray's theory of witchcraft seems to have been "formulated in [an] uncritical manner," it nevertheless contains a "core of truth." This core refers to a complex web of associations linking, among other things, shamanism, Goddess reverence, and gender variance. My own research suggests that medieval and later Christians may have collapsed many cults, including Dianic cults and those devoted to fairies, cults of St. Cuthbert, the pagan-Christian dog saint (whose cult has been depicted in the film *La Sorcière et le Moine*), and even cults paying homage to Lucifer as the Prince of Light, into a single phenomenon variously named witchcraft or Satanism.[28]

Unfortunately, Murray's theory of a single cult not only reflects to some degree this reductionist error, but it also has allowed academics, who use it as a tool, to deny the existence of pagan cults altogether. Neopagans compound this problem by accepting uncritically the notion of a solitary cult that somehow managed to protect itself from the influence of Christianity and from the passing of time in general. Rather than explaining that the Diana-Pan (Green Man)-fairy cult resembling contemporary Wicca, described in the works of King James, Reginald Scot, John Aubrey, and others, was *even during the Renaissance* differentiated from more sinister cults, contemporary neopagans find it easier to collapse positive-magic, primarily matrifocal, rural cults into a single religion and to categorically deny the existence of Luciferan, Satanic, and other cults. In my opinion, this sort of reductionism, practiced by Christians, academics, and neopagans alike, must be shelved if we are ever to come to grips with the spiritual cornucopia that overflowed in Europe and elsewhere from late antiquity until the Inquisition.

While Evans's theory linking homoerotic men with witchcraft is rooted in Murray's, it may also contain a core of truth, although the linkage between the gender-variant, homoerotically inclined male, the witch, and the bundle of sticks may be much more complex than originally imagined. While I have not found any direct connection between these meanings of *faggot*, I have discovered a rather intriguing word chain.

By the sixteenth century, the French word *fagot* ("faggot") had come to enjoy many meanings. It signified not only a bundle of sticks but also a symbol of the same, which, as Evans and others point out, heretics were required to wear. Moreover, to *fagoter* someone was to "fuck" them. Further, *fagot* was used interchangeably with *bourre* (related to *bourée, bourelé, bourrer,* and *bourreur*). *Bourre,* however, referred not only to a bundle of sticks but also to an individual who stuffs something or tortures or fucks someone. What is more, *bourre* referred to the "backe-part, of a man." There is also this proverb: "*Fagot cherche boureé,* Like will to like." Further still, the *bourée* was a lively round or spiral dance that, as seen in medieval illuminated manuscripts, clearly had pre-Christian roots in ecstatic dance and was frequently condemned by Renaissance Christians as "lewd and lascivious."

While this word chain proves nothing, it may indicate an association of the bundle of sticks, the heretic, one who sexually penetrates, the buttocks, attraction to likeness, and pre-Christian music and dance. Thus, in the absence of a direct association of *faggot* and *witch*, an indirect association may perhaps be discovered in the linkage of *fagot* and *bourre*.[29]

Certainly if one moves beyond the boundaries of England and France, one discovers, as we have seen, terms like the Germanic *ergi, argr,* and *scratta,* which weave together the concepts of gender variance, homoeroticism, and the practice of magic. Furthermore, it seems quite plausible that those rejected by Christianity, and perhaps other patriarchal religions as well, may have sought sustenance in spiritual traditions more likely to tolerate gender variance and homoeroticism, as historian of religions Jeffrey Burton Russell, Wiccan priest Leo Martello, and others have suggested.[30]

MINSTRELS

Wandering minstrels of several kinds, including *jongleurs* and troubadours, like transvestite male celebrants and the *calușari,* reflected, often in sublimated form, the elements of our domain.

While some people respected minstrels as the descendants of the Roman mimes and the Celtic bards, like the Irish *filidh* described in the previous chapter, others treated them as outcasts. The church, not surprisingly, generally refused to administer communion to them. The church's hostility toward them combined with their itinerant lifestyle to place them in a subculture comprised of dancers, jugglers, prostitutes, card players, thieves, homeless persons, persons with physical and mental impairments, practitioners of magic, and the gender variant and homoerotically inclined.[31]

Minstrels typically dressed in garments of red, yellow, and green, resembling those worn by fools. During carnivals, they would disguise themselves as women or beasts; some even went about naked.[32]

They were frequently condemned as effeminate or foolish or both. Their behavior seems to have been perceived as belonging to a third or alternate gender category. While their graceful body movements and alleged delight in gossip were categorized as feminine, their love of belly laughter, yelling, obscene gestures, and equally obscene language was perceived as crudely masculine.[33]

In terms of erotic behavior, minstrels were generally depicted as ribalds, as erotic rebels having multiple partners. They were often grouped with female prostitutes, and they appear to have been associated with both male prostitution and homoeroticism. As the spiritual descendants of Orpheus, they were often thought to have forsaken the love of women for that of men.[34]

These associations are reflected by word chains. For instance, the term *jongleur* is related to *jogleor,* which in turn is linked to *burdoun* (*bourdon, bordon, burdon,* etc.). *B[o]urd-* refers to a young woman or to a jest, while *bourdon* refers to a scepter or staff, with all its phallic import. A *burdon* is a ninny or a mule, a sterile animal, while *burdoun* refers to a strong bass voice or a ground melody. While these words may seem to contradict each other, most evoke sexuality. What is more, literary historians Paull F. Baum and D. Biggins have demonstrated that all of these related terms may have inspired Chaucer to use the term *bourdon* to describe the voice of the Summoner. He may have done so, they suggest, in order to depict the Summoner as the androgynous, homoerotically inclined lover of the Pardoner.

Following this association, it appears that the *bourd[on]/jo[n]gleor* chain may be linked to the *fagot/bourre* chain described above and thus also to other musical/dance terms, including *fauxbourdon* (four-part harmony), *faggottino* (the tenor oboe), and *faggottone* (the contrabassoon).

Jongleur, via *jogleor,* was also linked to *galiard* and its cognates, referring to a "gaily dressed" male, a description that may have indicated gender variance and perhaps even homoeroticism. *Jogleor* was further linked to *pauton(n)ier* and *poltron,* words describing a "saucy," "base," and "knavish" male. *Pauton(n)ier* and *poltron* were in turn linked to *femmelette,* an effeminate male.[35]

While some writers described minstrels as mercenaries and male prostitutes, others reported that it was their *savoir gai* ("gay wisdom") that attracted noblemen to them, and that many intimate relationships were thus formed between nobles and minstrels. Of individual minstrels, two are widely believed to have engaged in same-sex relationships: Arnaud Daniel and Blondel.[36]

As for Daniel, several lyrics suggest that he may have been a lover of men, beyond the fact that in *The Inferno* Dante placed him among the homoerotically inclined. An exemplary lyric reads, "I am Arnaut who gathers the wind / and hunts the hare with an ox / and swims against the tide." In medieval iconography, as historian John Boswell points out, the image of the hare and the pursuit of hunting were both associated with homoeroticism. Boswell also suggests that the term *hare* or *rabbit* may have been adopted by homoerotically inclined males to refer to one another. He notes the twelfth-century assumption that hares, like hyenas, were thought to be both androgynous and sexually excessive and that "effeminate men who violate the law of nature are thus said to imitate hares." Beyond the hare, the ox has also been associated in medieval literature with the receptive role in anal eroticism. Yet again, the association of androgyny, same-sex intimacy, and animal transformation is inferred. "Swimming against the tide," by indicating a reversal of the natural, may also speak to gender variance and homoeroticism.[37]

The minstrel Blondel, a chevalier of Artois, was, according to some historians, the handsome, golden-haired lover of Richard the Lionheart. Legend has it that when Richard was imprisoned in Austria, Blondel stood beneath the fortress tower, playing on the lute and singing to his beloved. The song was one they had composed together in happier times.[38]

In terms of our domain, minstrels were believed to practice sorcery and were often referred to as the "Devil's Disciples." (I am reminded of references to blues as "the Devil's music.") Through the use of ecstatic music and dance, it was believed that they led many women and men away from the church. Perhaps they were using music (along with ergot?) as the shamans and priests of the Goddess once had, to facilitate an altered state of consciousness. The thirteenth-century theologian, historian, and scientist Thomas de Cantimpre told a story of one *jongleur* who "caused young men and women to dance in circles whenever he played. One evening, when he began playing . . . the Devil himself appeared, dancing before him."[39]

Before leaving this subject, I would note that one of the most celebrated female troubadours, Bieris de Romans, is widely believed to have been a lover of women.[40]

SOTS

Of the various types of fools wandering the earth or living at court during the Middle Ages and the Renaissance, the *sot,* most frequently associated with France and the Netherlands, was among those associated with gender variance, same-sex intimacy, and spirituality, albeit a carnivalesque one.

In the view of Mikhail Bakhtin, the *sots,* while they performed in dramas called *sotties,* were not actors as such but "remained fools and clowns always. . . . They stood on the borderline between life and art." Literary historian A. Struebel describes them as the "children" of pre-Christian worshipers, "banished from the sanctuaries."[41]

The history of the *sots* is a complex one, as clerics and others who joined them in performing *sotties* and who further joined fraternities organized by the *sots* also claimed or pretended to be "true" *sots.* The *sots* per se were often vagabonds who performed plays and other feats in exchange for food and lodging. Eventually some of them became more established, even renting a building in the Rue Darnetal in Paris, which they named La Maison des Sotz Attendans.

Cutting a figure that might remind us of Harlequin or Pierrot, the *sot* often dressed in a costume of green, yellow, and red, sometimes wearing artificial asses' ears attached to his cap, as well as articles of feminine clothing such as aprons and headscarves, suggesting both animal and gender transformation. He sometimes also dressed in more somber tones, as a peasant woman or a nun. He might paint his face white or cover it with flour, conveying a mimelike presence and perhaps, as one scholar has suggested, indicating his desire to be "whitened" with another man's semen. He frequently carried a *marotte,* a scepter topped by a bladder or a doll head depicting a *sot.*

His costume apparently inspired a fashion craze among bisexually and homoerotically inclined, gender-variant courtiers: French literary theorist Ida Nelson explains in *La Sottie Sans Souci* that the "gallants of the court, in order to attract male minions, would wear tights with one leg of one color and the second of another." If the courtier's tights opposed green and yellow, he might wear a red cap.[42]

The *sots* were, as noted above, the originators of the *sottie,* a type of burlesque performance meant to celebrate sex, food, games, and other pastimes, and to ridicule church and state. Bawdy and outrageous, the *sotties,* say Nelson, "were founded on gay (*gai*), homosexual desire." Indeed, the use of the word *gai* to refer to persons engaging in same-sex eroticism may have originated in the *sottie,* through its relationship to the word *joyeux.*

The *sotties,* through their characters, reveal a complex medieval French categorization of homoerotic activities and relationships. The *sot* himself signifies the receptive partner, while the *galant* represents the active partner. The *fol,* or "fool," signifies a bisexual male. While all three characters display gender-variant traits, the *sot* is considered the most effeminate, while the *galant* is considered the most masculine.

Even the structure of the *sottie,* developing from the *rondeau,* an Old French poetic form in which the opening lines also serve as a refrain, seems to underscore its relationship to homoeroticism. As Nelson explains, the circle functioned in medieval France as a multivalent sign. Spiritual, divinatory, and magical meanings linked the circle to the cycle of birth, death, and regeneration and to the related Wheel of Fortune. The circle also carried erotic connotations. One of these linked the circle to the "roundness of the anus, that part of the body which is indispensable to anal intercourse." Another erotic meaning linked the circle to the loop or cycle believed to be generated by the practice of simultaneous fellatio by both parties in a homoerotic relationship.[43]

The *sots* not only were homoerotically inclined, gender-variant males but also, as noted above, pagans. As such, they honored, albeit in their own carnivalesque style, a goddesslike figure and her male consort. Those who speak of retentions and survivals believe that this figure, known variously as Mère (Mother) Sotte, Mère Folle, and Folle Bobance, may have at one time been linked to Cybele, since, like the Celtic Cernunnos, both were revered at Autun, a citadel of paganism. If she has Greco-Roman roots, however, I would guess that Baubo and Iambe may be other figures that played a role in the creation of the Mother of the *sots.*

Mère Sotte was typically portrayed as an elderly woman wearing a multicolored skirt and a cap with asses' ears. While the contemporary art historian Pamela Berger views her as a "figure of ridicule only," Nelson, perhaps more sensitive to "camp," sees Mère Sotte as a creative force, a figure bringing joy, and, above all, celebrating the "joy of receptive homosexuality." "As soon as I'd cease being perverse," Mère Sotte tells us, "I'd die."[44]

Each February, from the Middle Ages until at least the midseventeenth century, the *sots* would parade through the streets of Autun pulling a cart in which Mère Sotte, represented by the local leader of the *sots,* would be seated. This figure may be the seated transvestite, nunlike figure being pulled by two similarly dressed figures in Bruegel's *Fight Between Carnival and Lent.*

The male consort of Mère Sotte was the Seigneur de Joye (the "Lord of Joy"), also known as the Seigneur de Gayècté (the "Lord of Gaiety"); he is traditionally depicted as a *galant.*[45]

As his name suggests, a link may indeed exist between *gai* or *gay* in medieval and Renaissance French and the concepts of homoeroticism and gender variance, although this link, rather than being a direct one, may refer to a complex web of associations embracing not only homoeroticism and gender variance but also foolishness, or sottishness, and sacred experience (however carnivalized).

In French and English dictionaries of the Middle Ages through the seventeenth century, the synonyms *gai/gay* and *joyeux* were linked to joyous and sensuous behavior—"loose, immoral, wanton, lewd, lascivious." Terms such as *wanton* and *lascivious* more often than not signified gender-variant, homoerotic behavior when applied to males. John Palsgrave, in *Lésclarissement de langue française,* suggests that *joyeux* may also connote a "blythfull glad *co[u]e*," in other words, a "joyful ass or anus." Both *joyeux* and *gai/gay* also frequently referred to the behavior of horses and fools.[46]

We know that in the fourteenth, and perhaps as early as the thirteenth, century, homoeroticism was linked in the popular psyche to the world of fools, including the *sots.*

In an unfortunately homophobic and effemiphobic, dystopian novel of this period, *Berinús,* we read of a "sodomite" king, Agriano, who rules the inhabitants of the isle of Gamel. Here, homoeroticism and gender-variant behavior are mandatory. The author of *Berinús* refers to the practice of same-sex eroticism as "foolish," not only because it is performed in defiance of God but also, and more importantly, because it "goes against reason."[47]

Thus, while we may not be able to posit a direct connection between *gai/gay* and *homosexual,* an indirect connection may apply, one linking *gai/gay* behavior not only to homoeroticism and gender variance but also to the realm of the carnivalesque and its transformation of pre-Christian rites.

With the *sots,* in this regard, another element is also added to the web of associations linked to our domain, a web that already includes gender and animal transformation and the use of chant, dance, flagellation, sacred hallucinogens and other substances to trigger an altered state of consciousness in which the mortal and divine realms merge. This is the element of foolishness, the carnivalesque, the

burlesque, "camp." While we have not really focused on this element, except perhaps in our discussion of Baubo and Iambe, it is an extremely important one in
terms of shamanic, matrifocal, and henotheistic (in which many deities emerge
from a primal source) traditions. Stephen Larsen notes in *The Mythic Imagination,* for example, that among "the Hopi and Zuni . . . clowns are priests" whose
performances not only link spirituality to "sexuality . . . and perversity" but also
mock traditional ceremonies, often at the very moment the latter are being
undertaken.[48]

In the midtwentieth century, Harry Hay, a founder of the contemporary gay
movement, as well as an elder of the Radical Faeries (whom we shall encounter
later), named one of the first American homosexual rights organizations the Mat-
tachine Society. In doing so, he and his comrades sought to evoke the image of the
sot—the *matachin* is the Hispano-Arabic *sot*—and the ancient association of homoeroticism, gender variance, and the carnivalesque.[49]

TWO KINGS

While a number of monarchs might be examined in the light of our domain,
including Richard the Lionheart, Edward II, Richard II, and Richard III, as well as
the homoerotically inclined, virulently antipagan James I, I have chosen to focus
here on King William Rufus of England and King Henri III of France.

William Rufus ruled England for a very brief period, from 1087 until 1100 C.E.
He was in many ways a wise ruler, and it is not surprising that more conservative
scholars wish to whitewash his image in order to restore to him the respect he deserves. Unfortunately, these scholars are too often guided by homophobic, pro-
Christian, and chauvinistic agendas, which encourage them to ignore or deny
certain aspects of Rufus's character.

Rufus has been described as a "powerfully built, thick-set" man, "red-haired
and ruddy in complexion," who dressed in the "latest foppish fashions, his long
locks framing a clean-shaven face."[50]

According to Jack Lindsay in *The Normans and Their World,* "Rufus seems certainly to have been homosexual." Lindsay reminds us that "sodomy was . . . a
common practice" among Norman nobles.[51]

Rufus apparently was attracted to other men who, like himself, displayed a
mixture of feminine and masculine traits. Like Rufus, they wore their hair long
and wore colorful, form-fitting clothes, and, also like the king, they were expert
soldiers as well. One of Rufus's lovers may have been his nephew, Prince William,
who died in 1120 C.E. in the famous wreck of the White Ship, a catastrophe believed by Christian zealots to have been a divine punishment for homoerotic orgies occurring on board.[52]

Rufus was despised by Christian authorities not only for his homoerotic and
gender-variant behavior but also for his respectful treatment of Jews and his alleged worship of pre-Christian deities, including Loki, by whose face he was said
to swear. While Margaret Murray's theory that Rufus was one of a long line of

kings who were ritually sacrificed strikes me as farfetched, certain instances sur-rounding his death do appear peculiar. Not only did his final words suggest that he may have known he was to die, but, if we may trust the Abbot of Clugny, the latter had a prophetic dream of the king's death the night before he died. Furthermore, Rufus died on Lammas morning, the date of an important Celtic festival concern-ing sacrifice and the harvest. Still further, the Earl of Cornwall claimed to have seen, shortly after Rufus's death, a goat carrying the corpse of the king on its back.

One of those Christian authorities who viciously attacked the court of Rufus was Anselm, who participated in a reactionary movement against the homo-erotic, gender-variant, and possibly pagan expressions of Rufus's court. Christian attacks on the court culminated in the midtwelfth century, with the Council of Nablus declaring burning alive as the penalty for sodomy. An old homophobic belief of Roman converts to Christianity, that sodomy causes earthquakes, was also resuscitated at this time.[53]

Gender variance, homoeroticism, and spiritual experience also merge in the figure and court of Henri III, a ruler of France during the final, turbulent years of the sixteenth century.

The son of Catherine de Médicis and Henri II, he often wore makeup and a mixture of men's and women's garments. In a celebrated etching, he wears ear-rings, has a thin beard and a feminine hairstyle, and wears a feminine cap deco-rated with a brooch and feathers. He also wore the infamous tights called *garguesques,* which were nicknamed *chausses à la bougrine,* "hose fit for buggery." These *garguesques,* incidentally, were extremely tight-fitting and were worn with-out codpieces beneath "excessively short tunics which . . . revealed the buttocks." The term *garguesque* is related to the French terms for throat, gargle, and gar-goyle. The gargoyle was not only a mythic figure but also a conduit, a channel for conveying fluids, thus signifying, in erotic terms, fellatio. *Garguesque* may have also been related to a word chain clustered around *gouge,* the cognates of which referred not only to Gentiles (*goy*) but also to prostitutes and lesbian women. In this context, we might note that Henri occasionally appeared at parties dressed as an Amazon. We might also note that the chief fool at court during this time was a gender-variant, quite possibly lesbian, woman named Mathurin.[54]

By 1574, Henri's court was overflowing with androgynous, homoerotically in-clined minions who shared his taste in fashion. There was, however, another side to Henri, equally eccentric, which his minions also shared. This was his interest in spiritual matters, which surfaced in both superficial and rather profound ways.

To begin with the superficial. Christian proponents of sumptuary laws branded *garguesques* and *poulaines,* the elfish, pointed shoes often worn with *gar-guesques,* as demonic fashions. Henri also delighted in wearing a fusion of femi-nine and monastic attire. He was especially enchanted with the "fashionable Capuchin girdle of ivory skulls," which he wore around his waist.[55] In Henri's cos-mos, hell and heaven, like male and female, merged.

On a less superficial yet equally baroque plane, Henri founded the Order of the Holy Spirit, a monastic order comprised of himself and his minions. Besides spending long hours in devotions and taking pilgrimages, Henri and his companions engaged in essentially Catholic rites including flagellation. The historian l'Éstoile describes in his *Journal* a procession that took place on Holy Thursday, April 7, 1583: "On Holy Thursday . . . at nine o'clock in the evening, the procession of the Penitents, in which the King appeared with all his *mignons,* journeyed for the remainder of the night through the streets and to the churches, in a great magnificence of illumination and excellent music. . . . And there were among them . . . several who flogged themselves during the course of the procession, whose backs, one could see, were totally red from the blows they had inflicted on themselves."[56]

It would seem, however, that Henri's Order was not altogether Christian in terms of its beliefs and practices. Many believed that Henri, like his mother, also practiced the divinatory and magical arts and worshiped, alongside Christ and the Virgin, the elder goddesses and gods. Catherine's interest in the occult was widely known. She was especially fascinated with astrology and scrying. Among her most prized possessions were a magic mirror in which the entire history of France might supposedly be observed and a talisman depicting Jupiter (in his link to Ganymede), Venus, and an androgynous Anubis. On both sides of the talisman were engraved the names of angelic and demonic beings.

Of Henri's minions, at least two, Nogaret, the duke of Epernon, and Saint-Megrin, were believed to practice sorcery. It was thought that Nogaret, along with Catherine, instructed Henri in the magical arts. Nogaret supposedly also instructed Henri in the particular art of sex magic. A legendary account described Henri as waking up in Nogaret's arms only to realize, somewhat like Rosemary, that he had made love to, and at the same time sold his soul to, the devil. Some suggested that paintings depicting Henri engaging in intercourse with the demonic Nogaret were housed in a secret gallery. If such paintings ever existed, they have been lost, destroyed, or remained a secret.

Nogaret and Saint-Megrin, like Catherine, apparently made little attempt to conceal their participation in the magical arts. Indeed, legend has it that they introduced Henri to sorcerers from all parts of the world. When the house of Nogaret was ransacked by enemies of the king, the men reported finding a "chest full of papers on sorcery" written in "Hebrew, Chaldean, Latin, and several unknown scripts." In the chest they also claimed to have found a magic mirror and various unguents and elixirs.

Henri, Nogaret, and other minions of the order were believed to engage in magical rites primarily in a tower room at his castle at Vincennes. The altar they employed displayed both Christian and pre-Christian elements, including an alleged relic of the cross on which Jesus was crucified and two crystal goblets held by silver Pans.

While some might attribute the linking of Henri's court with paganism and the divinatory and magical arts to the overactive imagination of a Christian zealot, it seems to me that the abundance of data, derived from various sources, suggests that there may be, at the very least, a kernel of truth in the tales of Henri, Catherine, and the minions. Not surprisingly, the minions were frequently compared to the *galli* of Cybele, while Henri took the role of Attis and Catherine, that of the Goddess herself.[57]

The alleged beliefs and practices of Henri and his companions were satirized by Thomas Artus in *L'Isle des Hermaphrodites*, published in 1605. In *L'Isle*, a traveler is carried to an exotic island ruled by an androgynous king/queen. The text opens with these "sottish" lines: "The world is a fool, and man a comedy; one carries a *marotte*, and the other is folly." Thus, from the outset, the island and ultimately Henri's court are associated not only with gender variance and homoeroticism but also with the world of fools or *sots* and the carnivalesque.

When the narrator first steps onto the island, he sees a palace that more closely resembles a Greek temple, its columns topped with the heads of goddesses. Sensing a mystery, he follows a glittering path, which leads him to the royal bedchamber, where the king, at first a sleeping statue—perhaps a reference to the Greco-Roman sculpture of the *Sleeping Hermaphrodite*—is magically brought to life by his minions. The moment the statue comes to life, it begins speaking in an effeminate, sarcastic manner (*une parole toute effeminée, avec desdain*).

The narrator leaves this scene only to witness a transsexual operation. Following this, he discovers a gallery filled with artworks depicting Pan, Ganymede, Dionysus, Hermaphroditus, and other gods, as well as homoerotically inclined, gender-variant rulers of antiquity, including Sardanapalus and Heliogabalus. The reigning female figure is Semiramis, a legendary amazonian queen who serves here as another manifestation of Catherine de Médicis.

He then discovers the sacred texts of the religion of the hermaphrodites; these include the works of Ovid, Catullus, and Anacreon. Rites include celebrations of Eros, Dionysus, and Aphrodite, as well as the Roman-Celtic rites of May.

All religious observances that do not promote "voluptuousness" are forbidden. Articles of faith include the rejection of the concepts of damnation and of paradise as a realm other than the island itself.[58]

Some readers might interpret Artus's satire as little more than an attack on Henri's court and upon gender-variant and homoerotically inclined males. In my opinion, this reading ignores the important contribution that the text makes to our understanding of the development of our domain. For example, this text links Henri III and his court, a Renaissance phenomenon, not only to the gods, rulers, and spiritual figures of Greco-Roman antiquity, but also to the *berdaches* of the Native Americans, gender-variant shamans, often assumed to be hermaphrodites, who were then being encountered on the "islands" that formed the New World.

The term *berdache* is known from late antiquity; it appears in the fifth century C.E. dictionary of Hesychius of Alexandria as *badás*, meaning *kinaidos*, a gender-variant male engaging in same-sex eroticism. *Badás* may be, by way of Alexandria, linked to the Arabic *bardaj*, meaning "slave." Renaissance Europeans used *berdache* to describe the receptive partner in a homoerotic relationship, as opposed to *bougeron* ("bugger"), the active partner. Innocent, a youth loved by Pope Julius III and bestowed with a cardinal's hat, was called the Pope's *bardasseau*, while a French mythologist spoke of the *galli* of Cybele as *berdaches*, describing Kotys as the "tutelary goddess of *berdaches* and whores." Finally, conquerors, explorers, and missionaries to the Americas often used the terms *berdaches* and *cinaedus* (Latin for gender-variant, homoerotically inclined males, from the Greek *kinaidos*) interchangeably to describe the Native American spiritual figures. Not surprisingly, they came to associate the *galli* of Cybele and the *baptai* of Kotys with the *berdaches* of the Americas. In this way, Henri III and his minions became linked to spiritual figures of the Americas as well as to those of antiquity.

Becoming aware of associations like these can only further our understanding of the ways in which the figure of the gender-variant, homoerotically inclined person, especially the spiritual functionary, was perceived, shaped, and transformed by various epochs and cultures, and perhaps also how the concepts of the "gay" male and the "gay subculture" emerged.[59]

EXQUISITE TORTURE

While Christian forces were carrying out genocidal campaigns in northern Europe during the tenth through twelfth centuries, primarily against women and those men who engaged in gender variance, homoeroticism, and spirituality, in other parts of Europe, including England and France, the church was not always assured of the upper hand. This period of vigorous struggle would decline in the thirteenth century with the emergence of the Inquisition.[60]

Several episodes of tolerance and rebellion focusing on gender variance and homoeroticism may be cited as evidence of this unstable—yet far safer—climate.

In the late tenth century, King Hugh Capet discovered two men making love in a corner of an otherwise empty church. He merely covered them with his cape and moved on. A century later, King Philip I of France fell in love with a young, effeminate man named Jean, nicknamed Flora (the goddess of spring). Apparently, the archbishop of Tours also fell in love with him. Despite a harsh letter written to Pope Urban II by the canonist-bishop Yves of Chartres, Flora was elected bishop of Orlèans.[61]

During the same period, the sort of fashions described above in association with Henri III experienced a vogue at the court of William Rufus: elaborately coifed hair, revealing tights, pointed and curled shoes. In Norman England, the *poulaine* shoes were called *cornadus,* were thought to resemble ram's horns, and were said to have been invented by a *nebulo,* the Norman equivalent of a *sot.* Along with these fashions, the courtiers of Rufus wore goatees. Christian authorities, needless to say, were deeply disturbed by this fusion of androgyne, lusty goat, and fool, and in 1094 C.E. they demanded that all males entering church avoid these fashions. To refuse to obey would mean to sacrifice communion and proper Christian burial. The church reiterated its edict in 1096 and again in 1102 and 1103 because so many, including members of the clergy, refused to submit.[62]

A third incident concerns the French Cistercian abbot Bernard of Clairvaux (1090–1153 C.E.). According to the English chronicler Walter Mapes in *Courtiers' Trifles,* a group of monks was praising Bernard's powers when one chimed in to say that he recalled a time when the abbot's power to heal had failed him. A father had come to Bernard, begging him to heal his dying son. By the time Bernard reached the house, the young man was dead. Even so, Bernard lay on top of the youth, thus hoping to resuscitate him. "He was surely the most unlucky of monks," said the one telling the story, relating the action to same-sex eroticism, "for never have I heard of a monk lying down upon a boy without the boy arising immediately after the monk."[63]

Penitentials of the early Middle Ages, as John Boswell has noted, demonstrated relative tolerance for transvestism and same-sex eroticism, with penances often confined to fasting for a period of time. Of course, this was not always the case. Sometimes, as in Norman England, a man might face excommunication for engaging in such acts.

The church's hostility toward those expressing elements of our domain grew steadily. By the thirteenth century, the terms *heretic* and *bugger (bougre)* had come to be used interchangeably for religious heretics and persons engaging in anal intercourse. Maurice Lever, a contemporary French literary theorist and historian, points out that in the Middle Ages, the homoerotically inclined were envisioned as "heretics in love." This expression, Lever notes, was still being used in seventeenth-century France to describe males engaging in homoeroticism.[64]

It appears that the state played a crucial role in transforming the attitude of the church from one of relative to absolute intolerance. This trend was especially encouraged by the Spanish government. The much-admired Queen Isabella and King Ferdinand were largely responsible for insisting that sodomites be stoned or burned rather than simply excommunicated or imprisoned.[65]

The rise of two heretical sects, the Cathars and the Knights Templar, may have also contributed to the dramatic rise of religious and political intolerance of such persons. The Cathars were associated with the Bogomils, a dualistic sect acknowledging the power of both good and evil, also known in France as *bougres,* hence "buggers." The Cathars, like the Gnostics before them, believed that their spiritual task was to detach themselves from earthly existence. Hence they abstained from eating meat and from bearing children, which they saw as further tying them to the earth. In this light, they appear to have condoned homoerotic behavior among all practitioners besides the chief male and female priests, who dared not engage in any form of erotic behavior.[66]

The association of homoeroticism and Catharism is found in a poem or song composed by the minstrel Gautier le Leu in the midthirteenth century. In "The Widow," an angry wife complains that her second husband pays less attention to her than to the local garbage dump. She is not surprised, however, because he does not really love women. He is like "those on Mount Wimer." The wife is referring to an event that took place on Mt. Wimer (also known as Mt. Aime) in Champagne in 1239. On this occasion, at Pentecost, Robert the Dominican, who had once been a Cathar himself, rounded up 183 Cathars living on the mountain and executed them. Other groups of Cathars met their deaths at the hands of Christian fanatics at Montségur and elsewhere. From "The Widow" and other texts, it appears that the association of homoeroticism and Catharism was commonplace. It has been argued, of course, that the Cathars, being heretics, were unfairly or conveniently linked to homoeroticism by an ill-informed church. Although this early form of "fag-baiting" must have at times been used to destroy the lives of individuals and groups, the doctrines of the Cathars would seem to promote same-sex eroticism as a form of erotic activity that would not bind them to a karmic cycle of birth, death, and rebirth.[67]

Less certain is the case of the Order of the Knights Templar. The order, founded in 1188 by Hugh de Payens, began as a Christian military organization with the purpose of ridding the earth of Arabs. It seems that over the years, however, the order became influenced by spiritual beliefs and erotic practices of the Arabs and other peoples as well. They may have developed a syncretic cult centered around a deity of the "hairy androgyne" type, whose name has come down to us as Baphomet. They may also have engaged in cultic homoeroticism, in rites that included the *osculum obscoenum,* the kiss on the anus and phallus. For these and other alleged beliefs and practices, as well as for the enormous wealth they managed to collect quite rapidly, they were tortured and burned at the stake. Oddly, the homoerotically inclined, pagan-leaning Edward II was among those rulers who made certain they were caught and tried. This suggests that their treasury, and not their spiritual beliefs or erotic practices, may have been the primary reason they were persecuted, at least by the state, if not by the church.[68]

It is hard to imagine that Christian authorities actually came to look upon burning alive those accused of homoeroticism, gender-variant behavior, and paganism as a merciful action, and yet, we know that they did so. The contemporary historian of Italian culture Guido Ruggiero stresses, however, that some authorities were "troubled by the brutality of burning sodomites" and "sought to make the execution less painful" while still ensuring the "salvation of the convict's soul." Their solution was to strangle first, burn later. They were voted down, their solution considered too merciful. Of course, burning alive was not the only method of ensuring a sodomite's salvation; some, like Paduano d'Oltranto and Marino Alegreti, were decapitated instead.[69]

In spite of its so-called exquisite tortures, however, the church was not entirely successful in its drive to eradicate same-sex desire, gender variance, or pre- (or non-) Christian spiritual traditions. Indeed, one of the most beautiful expressions of this domain may be seen in the poetry of San Juan de la Cruz (St. John of the Cross), who lived during the sixteenth century and suffered imprisonment and torture in the dungeon of a monastery in Toledo. In his poem "Dark Night," he describes a secret journey to a grove of cedars where Jesus awaits him. There, Christ lays his head on the mystic's "flowering" breast—he is experiencing gender metamorphosis—while the priest plays with Christ's hair. When Jesus serenely "wounds" his neck, the priest yields to him, now in a state of bliss, which he describes in terms of the "lilies of oblivion."[70]

REFUGE IN THE ARTS

In describing the painting *Pan* by the Renaissance artist Luca Signorelli, the contemporary art historian Michael Levey describes the god and his companions as the "banished creatures of mythology who had always existed and who . . . now crept back in the welcoming Renaissance air."[71]

In a similar vein, literary critic James Robinson Howe, following historian Frances Yates, asserts that both scientific discoveries and the philosophy of humanism contributed to a Renaissance fascination with the magician or magus, as a figure in whom the elements of Christian faith and classical despair mingled with scientific wonder, personal power, and pre-Christian wisdom. The humanist tradition, Howe tells us, "opened up the study of classical belles lettres and religious writing" and demonstrated "parallels among [the] Egyptian, Roman, Greek, Christian and Hebraic religions." Hermetic, or ritual magic, texts, like other texts of the period, promoted a "high view of man's spiritual potential . . . asserting the possibilities of natural magic as a form of worshipping God." Not only God, but also *the gods,* and a host of spirits, *within the context of art.*[72]

In this sense, that is, in an *aesthetic* sense, the Renaissance indeed signaled a rebirth of paganism. Botticelli was painting the three Graces and Shakespeare was writing of witches in *Macbeth* and fairies in *A Midsummer Night's Dream* during that same period when those who danced in circles round oak, ash, and thorn were being carted off, tortured, and burned at the stake. As Shakespeare's Prospero worked his magic in *The Tempest,* Neoplatonist philosophers and magicians like Giordano Bruno, were, like the witches, burning. Generally speaking, aristocratic male magicians who claimed their powers came from God fared far better than poor men or women who spoke of Diana. Still, the magician who lived in the pages of a text slept better than all the others, unless, of course, the text, like the witch, tasted the flames.

Renaissance artists, contemporary art historian James Saslow explains, recognized androgyny as "the type of male beauty appropriate in a homoerotic context." Shakespeare sang of the "master mistress of [his] passion," and paintings depicting Ganymede and a paganized St. Sebastian proliferated. All the while, sodomites, like witches, were being ignited like fireworks in the public square.[73]

In this period of cosmic struggle between the old gods and the new, beginning in late antiquity and reaching an apex in the Renaissance and the Baroque, that is, in the Burning Times, a magical transformation occurred. While the Maypole was not neglected, the androgynous priest of antiquity more often than not appeared as an artist who served the goddesses and gods of old by remembering them in his works or performances. *If he were to escape the flames, he must sublimate his own androgyny, his own homoerotic desires, his own true feelings for the elder gods, in the creation of art.* If he expressed affection toward others, he might, like the fortunate Leonardo, survive the accusations. He might, however, like Richard Renvoisy, who set the poems of Anacreon to music, find fire his last embrace.[74]

The death of Christopher Marlowe, the playwright, remains a mystery. Some said he and another drunken man fought over a youth, and that Marlowe lost. Others claimed that Marlowe knew too much of a government grown corrupt. Still others suggested that Marlowe had been slain by a conspirator who disapproved of his erotic interests and irreligion.

What an iconoclast, a veritable Doctor Faustus, Marlowe must have seemed. Beyond his own wide reading of hermetic texts, his dabbling in the magical arts, and his association with Sir Walter Raleigh's mysterious salon, the School of Night, Marlowe espoused views Mark Twain would share three hundred years thereafter. "Moses was but a Juggler," and "all protestantes are Hypocritical asses," Marlowe was heard to say. "Christ was a bastard and his mother dishonest. . . .

St. John the Evangelist was bedfellow to Christ and leaned alwaies in his bosome, that he used him as the sinners of Sodoma." And this Wildeian epigram: "All they that love not Tobacco & Boies were fooles." (Foolish, we have learned, to love men, and foolish not.)[75]

In Marlowe's works, the elements of our domain are woven into an exquisite tapestry. Neptune desires the androgynous hero Leander. "Some swore he was a maid in man's attire, / For in his looks were all that men desire."[76] Jove fondles an equally androgynous, though far more mischievous, Ganymede in *Dido, Queen of Carthage;* and in *Edward II,* brilliantly restored to life by the filmmaker Derek Jarman, Gaveston, the beloved of the king, dreams of the court he and Edward will not live to share:

> Like sylvan nymphs my pages shall be clad,
> My men like satyrs grazing on the lawns
> Shall with their goat feet dance in antic hay;
> Sometime a lovely boy in Dian's shape,
> With hair that gilds the water as it glides,
> Crownets of pearl about his naked arms,
> And in his sportful hands an olive-tree
> To hide those parts which men delight to see. . . .[77]

In the paintings of Leonardo and Caravaggio, the sculpture of Cellini, the poems of Barnefield, Beccadelli, Poliziano, and Sidney (especially his "Ode to Pan"), the music of Orlando di Lasso, the voices (now ghostly) of *castrati*, our domain survived and was transformed.

The seventeenth-century composer, dancer, and actor Jean-Baptiste Lully, like many twentieth-century gay men, scorned his modest beginnings, seeking to live out a dream. Like Marlowe, Caravaggio, Renvoisy, and other homoerotically inclined artists, Lully was an iconoclast. He quickened the steps of dancers, delighting ballet audiences with the *bourée* and introducing the ballerina. For a time, he acted in and wrote incidental music for the company of the bisexual playwright Molière. The "father" of French opera, he served as a latter-day priest of the Goddess and her consort, giving new voice to the tales of Isis, Persephone, and Attis and Cybele. Despite his accomplishments, he was severely warned by Louis XIV to cease loving men—he did not comply—and at a musical fireworks display he arranged in 1674, it was remarked that Lully himself might soon become a work of fire in la Place de Grève, where burning sodomites lit the night.[78]

THE DELIGHTS OF HELL

This Town abounds too plentifully with a Sect of brutish Creatures called SODOMITES. . . . It is a melancholy Sight to see Men in full Strength and Vigour go to publick Executions unpitied and unlamented. . . . It would be a pretty scene to behold them in their Clubs and Cabals, how they assume the Air and affect the Name of *Madam or Miss, Betty or Molly,* with

a chuck under the Chin, and *O you bold Pullet I'll break your Eggs,* and
then frisk and walk away to make room for another, who thus accosts the
affected Lady, with *Where have you been you saucy Queen?. . .* It is remarkable that these effeminate Villains are much fonder of a new *Convert* than
a Bully would be of a new *Mistress.* (*Hell Upon Earth: or The Town in an
Uproar,* 1729)[79]

And so we come to the eighteenth century.

The ashes of the Inquisition are smouldering, and Europe is witnessing the
birth of the Enlightenment, the Age of Reason. There is a renewed interest in
Greco-Roman culture and in the occult, an explosion of anti-Christian sentiment,
and the subculture embracing gender-variant and homoerotically inclined males
is exploding.

The spirit of the age is as irrational as it is rational, as sinister as it is carnivalesque—and everyone is obsessed with sexuality.

The philosopher Diderot powerfully evokes this sensibility as he ponders, reminiscent of Marlowe:

What if the Virgin Mary had been the mother of pleasure . . . ? What if
the angel Gabriel had been extolled for his handsome shoulders? . . . What
if, at the marriage, at Cana, Christ between two wives, a bit of a noncon-
formist, had caressed the breast of one of the bridesmaids and the buttocks
of St. John. . . ?[80]

One of the many cults that proliferated during the eighteenth century was centered at Rome at the villa of Cardinal Albani. Here, according to G. S. Rousseau, "a
cult of Antinous . . . flourished among homoerotic men bonding together in exile."
Among those believed to participate in the rites of Antinous were Johann Winckel-
mann, Raphael Mengs, Richard Payne Knight, and le Comte de Caylus. Rousseau
suggests that Pan also may have been revered by the group, relating that "each
night before retiring to bed, the Comte de Caylus kissed the statue of a faun."[81]

Among the more sinister occult groups emerging in eighteenth-century Europe were the erotic-satanic clubs. It is probably fair to say that if the church, via
the Inquisition, had not created Satanism—if it in fact did not exist previously—
the eighteenth century would have done so. These clubs quickly became notorious for their black masses in honor of Satan, their parodies of Christianity, and
their sexual rites.

Many of the members of these erotic-satanic clubs were rakes. While rakes
were of various ages, classes, genders, and perhaps even races, they were typically
young white males who had been born into wealthy families but who had chosen
to reject an aristocratic destiny in favor of an anarchistic street life. Spiritual radicals, they have been described as "bantering heaven, burlesquing the Trinity, and
jesting with every sacred thing."

Certain groups of rakes were associated with gender variance and homoeroticism. These included the Brights, the Flashes, the Jessamies, the Macaronis, the
Mollies, and the Sharps. Such young men were queried by the intolerant or the ignorant: "Tell me, gentle hobdehoy! Art thou Girl, or art thou Boy?"

While the most infamous of the erotic-satanic clubs were undoubtedly the Hell-Fire Club and the Medmenham Abbey, where "Do what thou wilt" was the motto of the "monks," there were many others. In some of these, like the Tuesday Club, the Dublin Blasters, and the Somerset House Club, men would meet to hold "Corybantic orgies" and to reenact "the rites of Priapus," often engaging in "group masturbation."

The leader of these rites was typically a "merry Gentleman" who took the role of Satan. This man, a spiritual functionary of sorts, would sometimes wear a bearskin, suggesting animal transformation and evoking the image of the *berserker.* On other occasions, he would appear naked at the rites.

Rites that parodied religious rituals also took place at a hunting lodge near Dublin, Ireland. Gender-variant, transvestite participants with names like Lady Gomorrah would drink a brew of whiskey, butter, and brimstone, would kiss a cat on its backside, and would perform mock crucifixions.[82]

Even those gender-variant and homosexually inclined males not belonging to such clubs often participated in rituals incorporating same-sex intimacy. For instance, the sodomites described at the beginning of this chapter may have been among those who participated in "mock marriage ceremonies" in "chapels" at the White Swan and other establishments and who also "developed elaborate pregnancy rituals," which culminated in birthing rites, when "the 'pregnant' person was delivered of a doll or other appropriately sized object, such as a Cheshire Cheese or a pair of bellows."[83]

Also in the eighteenth century, the myth of Sodom resurfaced. Indeed, to many travelers, the city of Sodom appeared to have risen phoenixlike from the ashes, its latest manifestation being one of the three Italian meccas—Rome, Florence, or Venice. (The association of Sodom and Venice would culminate in the early twentieth century with Thomas Mann's *Death in Venice.*) Indeed, the "condition of Sodom" for these homosexual elites of the eighteenth century was as geographical as it was spiritual. The heavenly City of Sodom for them was eternally Italian, however impermanent a "Sodom of the Soul" it may have been.[84]

WITH THE RISE of Christianity, as we have seen, the goddesses and gods of antiquity were reduced to folk figures and saints. The spirit of paganism was preserved primarily in the worlds of art and carnival, in sublimated form; and those embodying our domain frequently took the form of minstrels, artists, festival celebrants, and fools. There were those, however, who appear to have clung tenaciously to the ways of their ancestors. Revering the elder gods and keeping their feast-days, practicing the arts of healing, divination, and magic, they also kept alive, through cross-dressing and other practices, the memory of the gender-variant, homoerotically inclined priest or shaman. Many, unfortunately, branded heretics and sodomites, perished in the flames of the Inquisition. Nevertheless, our domain continued to resurface throughout the Middle Ages and the Renaissance and into the seventeenth and eighteenth centuries. In the nineteenth and twentieth centuries, our domain would experience a renaissance no iron mask and no burning stake would be able to eradicate.

Simeon Solomon, *Then I Knew My Soul Stood by Me,* ca. 1871.

Splendours of an Exiled Court

And he hath kissed the lips of Proserpine,
  And sung the Galilæn's requiem,
That wounded forehead dashed with blood and wine
  He hath discrowned, the Ancient Gods in him
Have found their last, most ardent worshipper. . . .

Oscar Wilde, *The Garden of Eros*[1]

*I*n the nineteenth century, many Europeans and Americans, finding themselves rushing into modernity, struggled intensely with their attitudes toward nature and art, capitalism and socialism, antiquity and "the new," puritanism and hedonism, humanism and nihilism, feminism and antifeminism, intolerance or acceptance of gender variance and homoeroticism, racism and antiracism, and other such issues. They tackled these controversial subjects as frequently in diaries and works of art as in sermons and manifestoes. While many individuals remained adherents of Judaism, Christianity, and other "traditional" faiths, others took up Western occult and Eastern paths. In general, the sacred took on a more personal appearance. In *The Varieties of Religious Experience*, philosopher William James gave voice to the new conception of religion:

Religion . . . shall mean for us the feelings, acts, and experiences of individual men [and women] in their solitude, so far as they apprehend themselves to stand in relation to whatever they may consider the divine. . . .
Like love, like wrath, like hope, ambition, jealousy, and every other instinc-
tive eagerness and impulse, it [religious feeling] adds to life an enchantment which is not rationally or logically deducible from anything else. This
enchantment . . . is either there for us or not there. . . . If religion is to
mean anything definite for us, it [should refer to] this added dimension of
emotion, this enthusiastic temper. . . . It ought to mean nothing short of
this new reach of freedom for us . . . the keynote of the universe sounding
in our ears.[2]

For many, the experience of the sacred was now to be found in art. This was especially true for those disillusioned with the Judeo-Christian tradition. While in
"The Aesthetics of Silence," essayist Susan Sontag focuses on twentieth-century
art, a statement she makes concerning the spiritual and art may be applied to the
Romantic, Transcendentalist, Aesthetic, Symbolist, and Decadent movements of
the nineteenth century. She writes,

Every era has to reinvent the project of "spirituality" for itself. (Spirituality
= plans, terminologies, ideas of deportment aimed at resolving the painful
structural contradictions inherent in the human situation, at the completion of human consciousness, at transcendence.)
   In the modern era, one of the most active metaphors for the spiritual
project is "art."[3]

For others, the sacred was to be (re-) discovered in nature, which was rapidly
disappearing. For still others, the sacred was to be found in eroticism, in simple
delight in the body and in complex rites of sex magic.

THE ADAMANTINE VEIL: PERCY BYSSHE SHELLEY

In the early nineteenth century, "religious feeling" surfaced in the poetry of the
romantics. In terms of our domain, linkages tend to be subtle and difficult to decipher. In the life and work of the poet Shelley, however, we may find traces of the
intermingling of homoeroticism, gender variance, and the sacred. As to whether
or not Shelley was a lover of men as well as women, we possess no definitive
proof. Certainly, he experienced passionate friendships with other men, but such
relationships did not always include an erotic element. It is clear that Shelley
cared deeply for other men, was attracted to the male body, and was friend to
more than one lover of men, including Byron. His attraction to the male body
was linked to Greco-Roman religious art. He spoke of the joy he discovered in the
"womanish vivacity" and "passive happiness" of Apollo and of the "flowing ful-
ness and roundness" of Dionysus's "breast[s] and belly," the latter reminding him
of "the pleasure of love with one whom we most love."[4] In the early twentieth century, psychologist George Barnefield said of Shelley:

Shelley, in fact, belonged to the class of double-natured, or intermediate, types—a class which embraces many artists . . . for example, Leonardo, Michelangelo, Wilde, and Tchaikowsky. We must . . . make clear [however] that the poet himself was never fully aware of his inversion; although, towards the last few years of his troubled life, there are indications that the repressed impulses were breaking through the barriers. . . . He rightly attributed his constant melancholy to this cause [repression of homosexuality], as his self-analysis in *Prince Athenase* shows.[5]

Barnefield is referring to these lines from *Prince Athenase:*

For all who knew and loved him then perceived
That there was drawn an adamantine veil
Between his heart and mind—both unrelieved
Wrought in his brain and bosom separate strife.[6]

Barnefield's ideas concerning Shelley's repressed homosexuality may be controversial, but he is on the mark in linking *Prince Athenase* to same-sex love. In the poem, Shelley speaks of his love for Dr. Lind, the tutor of his youth:

    Dost thou remember yet
When the curved moon, then lingering in the west,
Paused in yon waves her mighty horns to wet,
How in those beams we walked, half resting on the sea?

· · · · · · · · · · · · ·

Then Plato's words of light in thee and me
Lingered like moonlight in the moonless east,

· · · · · · · · · · · · ·

And Agathon and Diotima seemed
From death and dark forgetfulness released.[7]

Shelley refers here to the *Symposium* of Plato, in which same-sex love is a central topic of conversation. He refers specifically to the gender-variant, homoerotically inclined playwright Agathon, who speaks of the beauty of Eros, and to the priestess Diotima, who praises the pedagogical and spiritual dimensions of homoerotic relationships.

Diotima's speech is most acclaimed—and most heavily criticized by feminists—for its exaltation of the productive or creative aspect of male-male relationships. "By intimate association with beauty embodied in his friend," she relates, the lover "succeeds in bringing to birth the children he has long desired to have." These "progeny," Diotima explains, are not "human children," but "immortal" offspring, namely "wisdom and virtue."[8]

Shelley has been described as having a "delicate" complexion, "almost feminine, of the purest red and white," as having a "shrill," effeminate voice, and as walking in a "mincing" manner. Early homosexual rights activist Edward Carpenter believed that Shelley might have cultivated an androgynous or gender-variant ("intermediate") persona, believing the androgyne might "one day become the inspiration of a new world-order."[9] Nathaniel Brown, in *Sexuality and Feminism in*

Shelley, echoes Carpenter in saying that Shelley "achieved a condition of androgynization so complete that sexual differentiation or distinction could only be experienced as seriously frustrating, an unwelcome limitation of human possibility."[10]

Carpenter linked Shelley's gender-variant appearance and behavior to his alleged psychic abilities, explaining that "this double evolution is often accompanied by a considerable development of higher powers, more or less occult. . . . Certainly this development was marked in the case of Shelley [who] was to some degree mediumistic."[11]

From early childhood, Shelley was considered different from others because of his apparent psychic ability and his fascination with the occult. As a youth, the poet "was fascinated by moonlight and candlelight, and fire very soon entered into his rituals as a storyteller, ghost-raiser and alchemist." By 1808 he was attempting to "raise the devil," literally. A professor stumbled upon him while doing so and saw the youth engulfed in a "circle of blue spirit flame." Shelley's friend T. J. Hogg wrote of the young poet:

> He was passionately attached to the study of . . . the occult sciences. . . .
> His pocket money was spent in the purchase of books . . . on magic and
> 'witchcraft. . . . He consulted his books, how to raise a ghost.[12]

Except for two and a half weeks in January 1812 during which Shelley claimed to have given up "romance" for "reason" in an apparent attempt to placate his father-in-law William Godwin, the poet's interest in the magical arts never waned. In his final years he became especially interested in mesmerism, reincarnation, and astral projection.[13]

Inspired by his interest in magic and by the statue of the *Sleeping Hermaphrodite* in the Palazzo Borghese in Rome, Shelley, in *The Witch of Atlas,* describes the magical creation of a winged Hermaphrodite by a Witch, who is in fact a manifestation of the Great Goddess. Because the Hermaphrodite of the poem, like the one of the Palazzo Borghese, is sleeping, commentators Harold Bloom and Camille Paglia have taken the liberty of describing the figure as an "automaton," presumably in an attempt to denigrate the figure's gender variance. In doing so, they misinterpret Shelley's poem and fail to respect his reverence of this figure. Literary historian and biographer Nathaniel Brown, on the other hand, has grasped Shelley's meaning behind the somnambulism of the Hermaphrodite. The Hermaphrodite is sleeping because he-she represents the future, which is only just now being magically awakened by the Witch-Goddess.[14] Shelley tells us:

> Then by strange art she kneaded fire and snow
>   Together, tempering the repugnant mass
> With liquid love—all things together grow
>   Through which the harmony of love can pass:
> And a fair Shape out of her hands did flow,
>   A living Image, which did far surpass
> In beauty that bright shape of vital stone
> Which drew the heart out of Pygmalion.

A sexless thing it was, and in its growth
  It seemed to have developed no defect
Of either sex, yet all the grace of both;
  In gentleness and strength its limbs were decked;
The bosom lightly swelled with its full youth,
  The countenance was such as might select
Some artist that his skill should never die,
  Imaging forth such perfect purity.
From its smooth shoulders hung two rapid wings,
  Fit to have borne it to the seventh sphere,
Tipped with the speed of liquid lightnings,
  Dyed in the ardors of the atmosphere.[15]

COMRADES IN NATURE: HENRY DAVID THOREAU AND WALT WHITMAN

In the United States in the midnineteenth century, the subjects of our present work were taken up by Henry David Thoreau and Walt Whitman, both deeply influenced by American Transcendentalism.

Thoreau is best known for his retreat to the woods, described in *Walden* and elsewhere, and for his radical political beliefs as expressed in *Civil Disobedience*. Much of his writing, however, concerns his belief in the power of friendship, which he sees as blending the physical and the spiritual.

As is the case with Shelley, we possess no definitive proof that Thoreau was homosexually inclined. It is clear, however, that like Shelley he cared for men deeply and that, also like Shelley, he was physically attracted to males. We also know that he admired androgyny or gender variance. Further, we know that Thoreau had a deep respect for the religions of antiquity, which he associated with his reverence for nature.[16]

Passages from his journals reveal his thoughts concerning gender variance, same-sex relationships, and the sacred. In January, 1840, he spoke of a dream he had of founding a "community" of passionate male friends or lovers, writing, "Constantly, as through a remote skylight, I have seen glimpses of a serene friendship-land—and know the better why brooks murmur and violets grow." In this community, he imagined living "henceforth with some gentle soul such a life [as] may be conceived, double for variety, single for harmony,—two, only that we might admire at our oneness,—one, because indivisible. Such community to be a pledge of holy living."

Thoreau believed that the affinity he felt for those he considered comrades was a human expression of the "friendliness of nature," embodied by the "goddess Ceres who presides over every sowing and harvest."

On other occasions, this loving goddess took on the appearance of Diana. In this manifestation, both the goddess's and his own gender variance were celebrated. He wrote: "My dear, my dewy sister, let thy rain descend on me. . . . I am as much thy sister as thy brother. Thou art as much my brother as my sister. . . . O my sister! O Diana, thy tracks are on the eastern hills. . . . I, the hunter, saw them in the morning dew."

Of his passionate attraction to men, he wrote, "All men and women woo me. There is a fragrance in their breath. . . . I love men with the same distinction that I love woman—as if my friend were of some third sex."

For Thoreau, the love of other men was both a private and a sacred matter. "Friendship," he wrote, "is by necessity a profound secret which can never be revealed. . . . There is no need that a man should confess his love of nature—and no more his love of man. . . . That person is transfigured is God in the human form—henceforth—The lover asks no return but that his beloved will religiously accept and wear and not disgrace this apotheosis."[17]

So much has been written about Walt Whitman that it is difficult to know what may still not be commonly known. In recent years, a number of studies have focused—most often, separately—on the homoerotic and shamanic character of his work; for this reason, I shall limit myself to a few remarks.

Whitman celebrated the body and found it indivisible from spirit. In "Song of Myself," he wrote:

Divine am I inside and out, and I make holy whatever I touch or am
    touch'd from,
The scent of these arm-pits is aroma finer than prayer,
This head more than churches, bibles, and all the creeds.

. . . .

If I worship one thing more than another it shall be the spread of my
    own body.[18]

Whitman's spiritual vision was rooted not only in the body and nature but more specifically in the power to transform oneself into or to radically identify with another person, plant, animal, or other entity, a process recalling shamanic transformation—including gender metamorphosis as well as animal and vegetal transformation—and priestly embodiment of the divine. "I am the man," he tells us,

. . . . I suffer'd, I was there.
The disdain and calmness of martyrs,
The mother of old, condemn'd for a witch, burnt with dry wood, her
    children gazing on,
The hounded slave that flags in the race, leans by the fence, blowing,
    cover'd with sweat,
The twinges that sting like needles his legs and neck, the murderous
    buckshot and the bullets,
All these I feel or am.

. . . .

We are Nature. . . .
We become plants, trunks, foliage, roots, bark,

We are bedded in the ground, we are rocks,
We are oaks. . . .
. . . . we are two among the wild herds. . . .
We are two fishes swimming in the sea together,

.   .   .   .

We are snow, rain, cold, darkness. . . .[19]

In the late nineteenth and early twentieth centuries, Whitman's vision came to be called "cosmic consciousness," a term coined or at least popularized by the Canadian psychiatrist Richard Bucke. In *Cosmic Consciousness*, published in 1901, Bucke wrote, "The prime characteristic of cosmic consciousness is . . . a consciousness of the cosmos. . . . Along with [this] there occurs an intellectual enlightenment or illumination which would place the individual on a new plane of existence—would make him a member of a new species."[20]

For Bucke, Whitman was "the best, most perfect, example the world has so far had of the Cosmic Sense." Bucke believed that Whitman had attained this state of consciousness in June 1853 and that this experience had led to the writing of *Leaves of Grass*.[21]

For Whitman, nature was a sanctuary in which to celebrate the love of men for each other. Byrne S. Fone, a literary theorist interested in gay studies, describes this sanctuary in terms of a homoerotic Arcadia. Explaining that the "homosexual imagination finds a special value" in the dream of Arcadia, Fone suggests that for gay men, Arcadia represents a sanctuary "where it is safe to be gay" and a place where same-sex love can be celebrated with myths and rites asserting that same-sex eroticism "is a divinely sanctioned means to an understanding of the good and the beautiful." Of the rituals undertaken in this homoerotic paradise, he writes, "These rites are transformational and involve the union of lovers, the loving and sexual fraternity of men, and the washing away of societal guilt."[22]

"In paths untrodden, / In the growth by margins of pond-waters," Whitman "celebrate[s] the need of comrades" by singing songs "of manly attachment" and by distributing, in a ritualistic manner, tokens of homoerotic intimacy: lilacs, branches of pine, moss, laurel leaves, sage. Foremost of these is the phallic calamus: "And this, O this shall henceforth be the token of comrades, this calamus-root shall, / Interchange it youths, with each other! let none render it back!"[23] Of this ritual, Fone writes, "Memory and desire flood in as he offers the calamus to his troop of young men in a sacred ceremony [by which all are joined] in wedlock. . . . The vow is eternal fidelity not only to one another but to the homosexual life itself, for the calamus is the symbol of that life."[24]

While nature offered the poet a sanctuary in which to express his love of comrades, Whitman, who refused to be "outed" during his lifetime, dreamed of an American city of the future in which nothing would be "greater . . . than the quality of robust love." This was to be the "new city of Friends," a city "invincible to the attacks of the whole rest of the earth," ruled by "the love of comrades / By the manly love of comrades."[25] Whitman's dream ultimately embraced the entire continent; "Come," he beckons us,

. . . . I will make the continent indissoluble,
I will make the most splendid race the sun ever shone upon,
I will make divine magnetic lands,
    With the love of comrades,
    With the life-long love of comrades.[26]

One wonders if Whitman imagined what an enormous role his work would play in the creation of the early homosexual rights movement, the later homophile and gay liberation movements, and the Gay-Spiritual movement(s). Whitman's role in the creation of these movements is forecast in a letter written by John Addington Symonds to Havelock Ellis on May 6, 1890: "In one word, does Whitman imagine that there is lurking in manly love the stuff of a new spiritual energy, the benefit of which would prove of benefit to society?"[27]

Within two years of this letter, Whitman's vision of comradeship had been nicknamed "the new religion." According to William James, by 1902 many persons had come to

regard Walt Whitman as the restorer of the eternal natural religion. He has infected them with his own love of comrades, with his own gladness that he and they exist. Societies are actually formed for his cult; a periodical organ [*The Conservator*] exists for its propagation . . . hymns are written by others in his peculiar prosody; and he is even explicitly compared with the founder of the Christian religion.[28]

ROUGH MAGIC: ARTHUR RIMBAUD AND PAUL VERLAINE

It was a work of "rough magic" undertaken by the sorcerer Bretagne that delivered the young poet and vagabond Arthur Rimbaud into the arms of the Symbolist poet Paul Verlaine.

Rimbaud, born on October 20, 1854, ran away from home at sixteen following a violent argument with his mother. At Paris, he was introduced to Verlaine, ten years his senior. The two became lovers. Their relationship was a passionate one, filled with quarrels, love letters, obscene poems, and even a shooting. By twenty, Rimbaud had left Verlaine and poetry forever. He died at 37, with the name of Djami, an Abyssinian youth, on his lips. Verlaine searched for Rimbaud in the faces of the young men he met. The one whose face most closely resembled Rimbaud's, Lucien Letinois, became Verlaine's lover, only to die of typhoid at 23. Devastated, Verlaine turned to promiscuity and Catholicism. His last best friend was an aging female prostitute.

If Rimbaud believed in anything, it was that poet and sorcerer are one. As a youth, he spent many hours in the library reading treatises on ritual magic, witchcraft, and the Kaballah, including Jules Michelet's *La sorcière* and Eliphas Levi's *Les Clefs des Grands Mystères*. He was also enchanted with Baudelaire's poems, perceiving them as satanic verses. As a devotee of Bretagne, he witnessed the prac-

tice of the magical arts and was apparently instructed in telepathy and astral projection. Rimbaud was also no stranger to opium.[29]

Rimbaud's earliest poems already reflect his identification with the magician or
priest of antiquity. His "Sun and Flesh," a hymn to Greco-Roman paganism, opens
with a hymn to the sun. Perceiving the earth as the goddess, he beseeches her,

> O Venus, o goddess!
> I yearn for the days of antiquity's youth,
> Of lascivious satyrs, of beastly fauns . . .
>
> . . . .
>
> I yearn for the days when the sap of the world
> The water of the river, the rose blood of green trees,
> Flowed in the veins of Pan, sustaining the universe;
> When the sun palpitated, green, under his goatish feet. . . .[30]

Rimbaud sees the modern individual as a soulless robot and believes that the
spirit of paganism has the power to restore our humanity, our passion. Rimbaud's
reverence focuses on the Goddess in her various guises and on her male consort,
who resembles both Pan and an androgynous youth. In "Antique," he writes,

> Graceful son of Pan . . . your cloven hooves glisten. Your chest resembles a
> cithara, and jingling bells ring in your blonde arms. Your heart beats in
> your belly, where a double sex lies sleeping.[31]

He believes that men will be healed only when they have returned to the Goddess and have reincorporated into their psyches the male figures of Pan and the
androgyne, when they have thrown off the chains of Christianity:

> I yearn for the days of great Cybele
> When they spoke of her riding, gigantically beautiful,
> In a bronze chariot, through splendid cities,
> Her breasts spilling into the vastness . . .
>
> . . . .
>
> Oh, if man would still suck at your tit
> Great Mother of the gods and mortals, Cybele!
> If he had not forsaken immortal Astarte . . .
>
> . . . .
>
> I believe in you, I believe in you, divine mother,
> Sea-born Aphrodite! Oh, the way is bitter;
> Since that other God has nailed us to his cross.
> Flesh, marble, flower, Venus, it is in you that I believe![32]

In "Tale" and also in "Genie," Rimbaud invokes the spirit of homoerotic passion. The first poem tells of a Prince who destroys everything around him, including his wives, in order to be able to see the truth, to know satisfaction in a way he
has never known it before, to confront his deepest desires. One evening, when he is
out riding, a Genie appears. Rimbaud describes the Genie as a figure of "ineffable
beauty, even unspeakable." Rimbaud writes, "His countenance and his carriage

spoke of the promise of a complex and multiple love."[33] In "Genie," this figure is more vividly painted:

> He is the charm of vanishing places and the superhuman delight of stops along the way. . . . He is affection and the future, the strength and love that we, in the face of rage and spiritual malaise, see passing by in the tempestuous heavens and in the flags of ecstasy. . . . We have all known the terror of his yielding, and he of ours; Oh, sensuality and well-being, vital spirit of our mental powers, self-love together with passion for him, he who will love us for all of his infinite life . . . [34]

Upon their encounter, the Prince and the Genie merge into a single being: "The Prince was the Genie. / The Genie was the Prince." This being is then annihilated, becoming one with the cosmos.[35]

Nick Osmond, a literary theorist and translator of Rimbaud's work, describes this tale as a reflection of Rimbaud's love for Verlaine, which he perceived as both erotic and mystical. Osmond writes, "The meeting with the Genie represents the sexual revolution which Rimbaud hoped to enact through his relationship with Paul Verlaine, unbearable in its intensity, unspeakable . . . in the sense that it constitutes an almost religious mystery. . . ."[36]

In his illuminating essay "Visions of Violence: Rimbaud and Verlaine," Paul Schmidt describes the relationship of the two poets as one in which the roles of abandoned children were acted out, in which a "disordering of the senses" was cultivated. This disordering, which triggered an almost constant altered state of consciousness, was accomplished in part via drugs and same-sex eroticism, echoing the practices of gender-variant shamans and priests. Schmidt stresses the disordering potential of homosexuality:

> It was the disordered life that Verlaine entered with Rimbaud, and its great disorder was homosexuality. . . .
> To be homosexual, even bisexual, is to be constantly aware of one's life in a way that heterosexuals are not forced to be. It is to be aware of another possibility, another dimension. . . . Homosexuality is a permanent extension of . . . liminality. . . . It is an alienation from the order of society, and it provides, as all alienations do, a view of that order from outside, from the other side. But being permanent, it is more—it is a refusal of that order. . . . It [homosexuality] is [thus] able to constitute itself as an exemplary and natural state of exaltation. It is thus one with the states of trance, of contact with the extraordinary. From this point of view, homosexuality may well be seen . . . as . . . a state of permanent quest for vision. . . . It can be a source of instantaneous illumination.[37]

More specifically, Schmidt suggests that sex magic, especially of a sadomasochistic character, may have been undertaken by Rimbaud and Verlaine as a means of achieving an altered state of consciousness. In their relationship, it would seem that Verlaine often played the role of "bride" or "slave," recalling the hierodule of antiquity, while Rimbaud acted as "the Infernal Bridegroom." Certain lines of

Rimbaud's suggest, however, that occasionally these roles may have been reversed or inverted. In "Adieu," for instance, he speaks of "the thousand loves who have crucified me," an image used by Rimbaud's circle to indicate passive homosexuality, while in "Nuit de L'Enfer," he cries, "Satan, you joker, you yearn to liquidate me with your charms. A stab of your pitchfork, a drop of fire!"[38] Schmidt writes,

> Part of this method was, I think, frankly magical. Rimbaud's readings in nineteenth-century mystic writing have been documented. . . . We know that Rimbaud read Michelet's *La sorcière.*. . . Consider the acts and words of sex as incantation: we perform certain acts . . . in an attempt to transform ourselves: to partake of another being, another world. This is magic, by definition. Rimbaud and Verlaine certainly practiced it, together. And there seems no question that sadomasochistic sex, with its rituals, its cult objects, its litanies, is intended as magic. A black mass is magic, but its intention is the same as a white mass: to unite the participants in a mystical union, a mystical body, forever, world without end.[39]

SYMBOLISTS, AESTHETES, DECADENTS: OSCAR WILDE AND OTHERS

Rimbaud and Verlaine are both considered Symbolist poets. Symbolism was a major movement of the mid- to late nineteenth century, originating in Romanticism, related to Aestheticism and Art Nouveau, and giving birth to the Decadent movement during the *fin de siècle,* the final years of the nineteenth century. While Symbolists and other groups mentioned differed in key respects, they shared in common the desire to express their distaste for contemporary bourgeois existence and their "longing for another sphere of being—aesthetic, ideal, and even supernatural."[40]

Symbolists would have agreed with W. B. Yeats that the chief aim of art lies in its capacity to capture, "in complex colours and forms, a part of the Divine Essence" in order to transform consciousness and to guide humanity toward spiritual enlightenment. Its purpose, in other words, is to work magic, the same purpose as "those symbolic talismans which medieval magicians made." The world of the Symbolists was peopled by "religious and visionary people, monks and nuns, and medicine-men and opium-eaters," as well as those suffering from *ennui,* or "world-weariness."[41] These were persons drawn to pre-Christian religions, Eastern spiritual traditions, Western occult philosophies, visions experienced during altered states of consciousness, lesbianism, homoeroticism, sadomasochism, autumn, twilight, the apocalypse, and the androgyne.[42]

The mystic Josephin Péladan wrote of the androgyne,

> Eros intangible, Uranian, for the coarse men of moralistic epochs you are only an infamous sin; they call you "Sodom." . . . It is the need of hypocritical centuries to attack Beauty. . . . Protect your monstrous mask from profanity! Praise to you![43]

Aesthetes used these same subjects and motifs, although, like many Decadents, they stressed the ornamental or decorative aspect of the work of art. They held what has been characterized as an antinaturalist attitude, emphasizing an opposition between nature and art and preferring the latter over the former. Literary critic Elaine Showalter writes in *Sexual Anarchy*, "The decadent aesthetic rejected all that was natural and biological in favor of the inner life of art, artifice, sensation, and imagination."[44] This is a half-truth; Showalter's brand of heterosexist feminism apparently prevents her from seeing the "natural and biological" in forms of eroticism other than heterosexual coitus; she has missed the esoteric meaning of Wilde's dictum, "Love is a sacrament that should be taken kneeling."[45] Even Wilde, wearer of the green carnation—descendant of the calamus, cousin of the red poppy, ancestor of the red tie, lavender butterfly, and pink triangle—the Aesthete of Aesthetes writes,

> I am conscious . . . that behind all this [artistic] beauty . . . there is
> some spirit hidden of which the painted forms and shapes are but modes
> of manifestation, and it is with this spirit that I desire to become in
> harmony. . . . The Mystical in Art, the Mystical in Life, the Mystical in
> Nature—this is what I am looking for. . . .
> I have a strange longing for the great simple primeval things, such as
> the sea, to me no less of a mother than the Earth. . . .
> . . . We have forgotten that water can cleanse, and fire purify, and that
> the Earth is mother to us all. . . . I feel sure that in elemental forces there is
> purification, and I want to go back to them and live in their presence. . . .
> . . . Nature . . . will hang the night with stars so that I may walk abroad
> in the darkness without stumbling. . . . She will cleanse me in great waters,
> and with bitter herbs make me whole.[46]

Like other poets of the *fin de siècle*, Wilde associated reverence for nature with Greco-Roman paganism. He mourned the passing of paganism, struggled with Christianity, and awaited the rebirth of the old religion. In "Santa Decca," he laments,

> The Gods are dead: no longer do we bring
> To grey-eyed Pallas crowns of olive-leaves!
> Demeter's child no more hath tithe of sheaves,
> And in the noon, the careless shepherds sing,
> For Pan is dead, and all the wantoning
> By sweet secret glade and devious haunt is o'er:
> Young Hylas seeks the water-springs no more;
> Great Pan is dead, and Mary's son is King.[47]

In less cynical moments, however, Wilde imagines that the spirit of paganism lives still. In "The Grave of Shelley," he speaks of the earth as the "great mother of eternal sleep," in "Lotus Leaves" of the "Queen of the gardens of the sky," in "Ravenna" of "Queen Dian . . . / White-limbed and terrible," and in "Panthea" of "Queen Juno" walking

. . . through some dewy mead,
   Her grand white feet flecked with the saffron dust
Of wind-stirred lilies, while young Ganymede
   Leaps in the hot and amber-foaming mist,
His curls all tossed, as when the eagle bare
The frightened boy from Ida through the blue Ionian air.[48]

In "The Garden of Eros," Wilde envisions himself as a "votary" of the old religion; more specifically, he describes himself as a gender-variant, castrated priest, a *gallus* of the "Spirit of Beauty," who is at once both Goddess and androgynous youth. He writes,

Spirit of Beauty! tarry still awhile,
   They are not dead, thine ancient votaries,
Some few there are to whom thy radiant smile
   Is better than a thousand victories. . . .
   . . . tarry still, there are a few
Who for thy sake would give their manlihood
   And consecrate their being, I at least
Have done so, made thy lips my daily food,
   And in thy temples found a goodlier feast
Than this starved age can give me. . . .[49]

If in this poem Wilde alludes to the *galli* and Cybele, in *De Profundis* he honors Marsyas, apostle of Cybele, satyr, musician, lover of males, defeated by Apollo, flayed. For Wilde, Marsyas becomes a many-layered symbol of all these components, as well as an archetypal condensation of the Aesthetic-Symbolist-Decadent style:

When Marsyas was "torn from the scabbard of his limbs"—*della vagina della membra sue,* to use one of Dante's most terrible Tacitean phrases—
he had no more song, the Greek said. Apollo had been victor. The lyre
had vanquished the reed. But perhaps the Greeks were mistaken. I hear
in much modern art the cry of Marsyas. It is bitter in Baudelaire, sweet
and plaintive in Lamartine, mystic in Verlaine. It is in the deferred resolu-
tions of Chopin's music. It is in the discontent that haunts Burne-Jones's
women.[50]

In *Ripe Was the Drowsy Hour,* literary historian J. E. Chamberlin discusses Wilde's fascination with Marsyas:

The cry of Marsyas was a cry of almost comic despair. . . . His skin . . .
was said to dance with joy at the sound of a flute. The most effective
nineteenth-century generalization of the predicament of Marsyas was
the figure of Pierrot, and Wilde's version of his own dilemma as he fought
against madness in the company of his fellow prisoners was that "we are
the zanies of sorrow. We are clowns whose hearts are broken. . . ."

But . . . Marsyas was [also] associated with the worship of . . . Cybele [and] often was [identified with] Pan. . . . Wilde recognized in Pan[-Marsyas] an emblem of rich potential [of] the opposition between Pagan and Christian values. . . .[51]

Indeed, in the figure of Marsyas, as in the figure of the gender-variant priest—not to mention those of Christ, Salomé, and the full moon—Wilde, who would die after being imprisoned and acquiring venereal disease, recognized himself.[52]

UNFORTUNATELY, we cannot possibly consider here all those Aesthetes, Symbolists, and Decadents in whose lives and works the sacred, homoeroticism, and gender variance intermingled; thus we shall mention only a few, all of whom merit further study.

There was the gothic writer and eccentric Count Eric Stenbock, who fell in love with Charles Fowler, "the consumptive son of an Oxford clergyman." Stenbock's pets included lizards and toads. He smoked opium, performed rites to Eros before an altar "tricked out with oriental shawls, peacock feathers, lamps, and rosaries," and composed love poems and tales of horror. Occult scholar Francis King relates that "Stenbock made a genuine attempt to understand his own homosexuality in terms of traditional occultism, eventually coming to view his condition as an aspect of vampirism and lycanthropy."[53]

In one of his tales, based on his love for Fowler, Stenbock assumes the persona of the aristocratic vampire Vardalek, who, on falling in love with Gabriel (Fowler), drains him of life energy without performing any action so coarse as drawing blood. Their final embrace, King suggests, reflects "Charles Fowler's final consumptive hemorrhage."[54]

We have already spoken of the association of the werewolf with homoeroticism. In the late twentieth century, such writers as Anne Rice (in *The Vampire Lestat* and other novels) and Whitley Strieber (in *The Hunger*) have explored the association of vampirism with same-sex eroticism, Strieber's probable source the lesbian vampires of Baudelaire's *Les Fleurs du Mal*. In recent years, the association of vampirism with homoeroticism has unfortunately been linked to HIV or AIDS, with tabloids announcing, "Wary Vampires Pull in Their Fangs!"[55]

And there was Nicolas Kalmakoff, a Symbolist painter born in Italy to an Italian mother and a Russian father in 1873. Spending most of his life in Italy, Russia, and France, Kalmakoff moved in various circles, including those of Rasputin and Diaghilev. According to one writer, he "frequented circles where mysticism and sexual orgy went hand in hand." Kalmakoff became extremely disillusioned when in 1908 a production of Wilde's *Salomé* for which he had designed the sets and costumes was canceled because "the decorative theme was the female pudenda." He spent his last years in Paris, where he allegedly "assisted at Black Masses," helping out with costumes and decorations.[56]

Not all homoerotically inclined or gender-variant artists of this period, however, led such sinister lives, although none was without suffering. Of the gemlike paintings of Gustave Moreau, painter of Salomé and Orpheus, inspired by the occult writings of Eliphas Levi, Philippe Jullian writes, "All of Moreau's work cries with a secret which the official painter did his best to conceal."[57]

Certainly Lord Alfred Douglas's life was marred by his betrayal of Wilde, brought about at least partly by Douglas's internalized homophobia. It was Douglas who spoke of homosexuality as "the love that dared not speak its name." Like Rimbaud's Genie, the spirit of homoeroticism is given form in Douglas's "Two Loves." As opposed to the spirit of heterosexual love, who might be described as a *fin de siècle* Ken doll, the spirit of homosexual love has large, sad eyes, pale cheeks, and lips red as poppies. His head is "wreathed with moon-flowers," and he wears a purple robe embellished with a golden, fire-breathing serpent. In another poem, "In Praise of Shame," the same figure appears as a creation of a goddess figure, "Our lady of strange dreams," recalling Shelley's Witch. She, much like the Witch of Atlas, creates Shame, the spirit of homoerotic love, by way of alchemy; she pours "live fire" from an urn, the flames assuming the form of the spirit. The poet, waking from this dream, sings, "Of all sweet passions Shame is loveliest."[58]

Another figure in whom gender variance, same-sex eroticism, and the sacred merged was the Jewish, mystical, pre-Raphaelite artist and writer Simeon Solomon, who wrote this brief autobiography:

> As an infant he . . . developed a tendency toward designing. He had a horrid temper. . . . He illustrated the Bible before he was sixteen.
>
> He was hated by all of his family before he was eighteen. He was eighteen at the time he was sent to Paris. His behaviour there was so disgraceful that his family—the Nathans, Solomons, Moses, Cohens, etc., et hoc genus homo—would have nothing to do with him. He returned to London to pursue his disgraceful course of Art. . . . His "Vision of Love Revealed in Sleep" is too well known. After the publication of this his family repudiated him forever. . . .[59]

Born in London on October 9, 1840, Solomon was the youngest son of Meyer Solomon, a respected Jewish painter of nineteenth-century London. Simeon's brother Abraham and his sister Rebecca were both artists as well. As a young man, Solomon became friends with Burne-Jones, Dante Gabriel Rossetti, Walter Pater, Swinburne, and others of the Pre-Raphaelite circle. Parties given by this circle allowed Solomon to express himself in wild drag; on one occasion, Solomon and Swinburne allegedly "chased each other naked down the staircase" at Rossetti's, much to the latter's dismay. Swinburne is to be credited with introducing Solomon to sadomasochism and to *Leaves of Grass*. In later life, Solomon and Swinburne would become enemies after Solomon, in a state of dire poverty, sold intimate letters that Swinburne had written to him.

In 1868, Solomon and Oscar Browning, an Eton schoolmaster, became lovers; this was to be the happiest period of Solomon's life. In 1871, having achieved some notoriety as a painter and illustrator, Solomon published his erotic-spiritual prose poem, *A Vision of Love Revealed in Sleep*, which was praised by John Addington Symonds but condemned by many others.

Two years later, on February 11, 1872, Solomon was caught in a public urinal having sex with a man named George Roberts. The two were arrested and convicted. After a time in prison, Solomon may or may not have entered an asylum. Following his arrest, his friends deserted him.

One story has it that Solomon took a room in the house of an art dealer who would lock him in his room for long periods of time, passing food and drink under the door in exchange for a sketch or painting. Another relates that Solomon became a pavement artist and sold matches and shoelaces. Beyond these stories, it is certain that he spent the last years of his life as an inmate of the St. Giles Workhouse in London, where he died of heart failure on August 14, 1905. While the rampant homophobia of his day clearly had much to do with Solomon's demise, it is evident that anti-Semitism and alcoholism, from which his sister also suffered, played a role in his destruction.

Throughout his life, Solomon tried to blend elements of Judaism, Catholicism, Greco-Roman paganism, and Western mysticism in his works. For Solomon, it was the archetypal figure of the androgyne in whom these elements merged. For Solomon, moreover, the androgyne became not only a symbol of spiritual totality but also one of gender and sexual identity. Figures of the androgynous male, representing gender variance and homoerotic love, abound in Solomon's paintings, being portrayed in *Amoris Sacramentum* (1868), *Dawn* (1870), *Love Dreaming by the Sea* (1871), *An Angel* (1887), *Love at the Waters of Oblivion* (1891), and many other works. The Goddess with her son or consort is also a favorite theme of Solomon's, depicted in *Night and Her Child Sleep* (1875) and elsewhere. Works especially revealing the intermingling of gender variance, same-sex eroticism, and sacred experience include: *David Playing to King Saul* (1859), in which David, having long, flowing hair and wearing only jewelry, recalls the image of the *qadesh* of Athirat as he entertains Saul; *The Bride, The Bridegroom and Sad Love* (1865), which depicts a nude heterosexual couple and a winged androgynous youth, showing the right hand of the "heterosexual" male grasping the genitals of "Sad," that is, homoerotic, Love, while the woman, in ecstasy, remains ignorant of this action; *Spartan Boys About to Be Scourged at the Altar of Diana* (1865), in which mothers lead their adolescent sons to the altar, where a bearded priest holding a figurine of the Goddess greets them, while behind him stands a statue of the Goddess against which two effeminate priests or devotees lean; *Heliogabalus, High Priest of the Sun* (1866), showing the gender-variant, homoerotically inclined ruler leaning languidly against an altar (reproduced on cover).[60]

In *A Vision of Love Revealed in Sleep*, which might be described as a vision quest in search of love, Solomon writes,

> A weakness fell upon me, but my Soul supported me; we looked forward,
> and saw one approaching clothed with a soft light; he moved towards us,
> gently lifted by the spirit from the ground. . . . Ever and again his feet,
> wherefrom sprang glowing wings, touched the earth and caused it to bring
> forth flowers; his head was bound with a fillet of violet . . . he carried a
> mystic veil of saffron . . . and his shining body was half girt with fawn-

skin. . . . I went forward until I set myself in front of him who bore the saffron veil; the waves of Love that move about him laved my face, they refreshed me. . . .[61]

SYMPATHY FOR THE DEVIL: ALEISTER CROWLEY

Aleister Crowley was born near Stratford-on-Avon on October 12, 1875, a fitting birthplace for one who would someday emerge as a living fusion of Prospero, Ariel, and Caliban. As a young man, Crowley, a bisexual—or perhaps more appropriately, a pansexual—engaged in homoerotic activities with many partners, one of the most notorious being Herbert Charles Jerome Pollitt, a.k.a. Diane de Rougy. Also as a young man, Crowley began to practice ritual magic. He became deeply involved with the occult order of the Golden Dawn, only to be refused initiation into the grade of Adeptus Minor because, as Francis King explains, "the London adepts had heard that Crowley was a practicing homosexual and decided that, in the words of Yeats, a mystical society was not a moral reformatory."[62]

In 1908 Crowley met a man who would remain his lover until 1914, Victor Neuburg. During 1908, both men are believed to have read Edward Carpenter's *The Intermediate Sex,* inspiring them to explore the relationship of homosexuality to the magical arts. In 1909, Crowley determined to initiate Neuburg into magic. He locked Neuburg in a room, fed him little, instructed him in ritual making, and flagellated him periodically. It would appear that during this initiatory period, their homoerotic relationship was firmly established.[63]

Neuburg envisioned Crowley as an androgyne, naming him "sweet wizard," "the most obscene god" (that is, Pan), and "queen." In his poem "The Romance of Olivia Vane," Neuburg wrote, "O thou who hast sucked my soul, lord of my nights and days, / My body, pure and whole, is merged within the ways, / That lead to thee, my queen."[64]

In December 1909, near Bou Saada in Algeria, on a quest to gain entrance to the magical levels of consciousness Crowley referred to as "aethyrs" or "aires," the two men engaged in a rite of homoerotic sex magic in the hope of thereby achieving the "Fourteenth Aethyr." In the middle of a circle of stones on a mountaintop, on a stone altar, Crowley was anally penetrated by Neuburg, who allegedly became possessed by Pan.

In this rite, elements of both gender and animal transformation may be observed, with Neuburg metamorphosing into the goat-footed god and Crowley taking on an androgynous or possibly feminine persona, echoing the celebrated statue of Pan seducing the Hermaphrodite. Moreover, the shamanic experience of death followed by rebirth is present here.

At 9:50 P.M., Crowley was visited by an "Angel" and by the "Masters of the Temple," or the spirits of the world's greatest magicians.[65]

Four years later, Crowley and Neuburg undertook the so-called Paris Workings. Beginning on December 31, 1913, they determined to summon Jupiter (Zeus), Mercury (Hermes), and Pan in order to be provided with material abundance and magical wisdom, especially of an erotic nature. They chose this date to commemo-rate the six hundredth anniversary of the martyrdom of Jacques de Molay, founder of the Knights Templar. During the three-and-a-half weeks that followed, they would engage in sex-magical rites many times.

During the First Working, King relates, Crowley whipped Neuburg "on the buttocks, cutting a cross over his heart and binding a chain round his forehead." This was followed by the act of anal intercourse. At this time, Crowley and Neuburg chanted, "*Jungitur in vati vates, rex inclyte rhabdou / Hermes tu venia, verba nefanda ferens;* Magician is joined with magician; Hermes King of the Rod, appear, bringing the unspeakable word."

During the Thirteenth Working, Crowley and Neuburg were swept to a previ-ous incarnation in which Crowley had been a hierodulic priestess named Aia and Neuburg had been "her" male companion Mardocles. Crowley and Neuburg ap-parently believed that one was incarnated seven times as one gender, then seven times as the other, in alternating cycles. At the beginnings or endings of seven-lifetime cycles, homosexuality or lesbianism often occurred.

As a result of the Paris Workings, Neuburg deserted Crowley, apparently unable to handle the erotic-magical power that dominated their relationship. Neuburg married, and Crowley cursed him. Years after the relationship with Crowley had ended, a friend of Neuburg's, seeing him sitting on a pedestal in the garden, re-marked, "Great Gods, does Vicky [Victor] look like Pan, or a goblin, or what?" The poet Ethel Archer said of Neuburg, "He was absolutely fay! . . . He was a lep-rechaun! No, not a leprechaun . . . Puck! . . . It was quite unearthly. . . . He wasn't human!"[66]

For his part, Crowley gleaned much from the Paris Workings. He became con-vinced that all forms of eroticism should be accepted and that all could be em-ployed in magical rites. He began to instruct male practitioners to worship the phallus and to practice ritual, including mutual, masturbation. Semen resulting from these rites was often offered to the Goddess, represented by the altar or a tal-isman.

Crowley also came to believe that the power of heterosexuality lay in reproduc-tion, whereas the power of homosexuality lay in the shamanic experiences of transformation and death/rebirth. Related to this, he viewed heterosexual rela-tions as extending outward (as to children) and homosexual relations as creating a circuit or loop of magical energy or power. Crowley continued to experiment with homosexual magic, as he did with heterosexual magic, for the remainder of his life.

A mural on a wall of the Abbey of Thelema at Cefalu in Sicily, Crowley's noto-rious mecca, depicted a scene that characterizes Crowley's approach: a man is being anally penetrated by "the Great God Pan while his [own] semen . . . [sprin-kles] over the accepting body of the Scarlet Woman."[67]

While one hesitates to judge Crowley, it seems unfortunate that he allowed his addictions to overpower him and eventually lost emotional control and physical health. He died of heart failure and bronchitis, triggered by massive doses of heroin, on December 1, 1947. His funeral, a pagan (or neopagan) service held at the Brighton Crematorium, included a reading of his "Hymn to Pan." Perhaps no single work better expresses Crowley's experience of the sacred; in it we read,

. . . . Pan! Io Pan!
I am thy mate, I am thy man,
Goat of thy flock, I am gold, I am god.
Flesh to thy bone, flower to thy rod.[68]

A FALLING STAR: ALASTAIR

Alastair, whose name evokes a falling star, has been nicknamed "the illustrator of decadence." Born around 1887 and of mysterious origins, Alastair, as a youth, learned to speak French, German, and English fluently, to play piano, and to perform mime shows. As a young man, he studied philosophy at the University of Marburgh, where he met Boris Pasternak, the author of *Doctor Zhivago,* and Felix Noeggerath, the latter becoming his lover for several years.

Alastair has been described as resembling both Pierrot and Nosferatu. The contemporary art historian and biographer Victor Arwas writes of him, "Alastair frequently wore . . . makeup. [He was known for his] malicious high-pitched speaking voice, the glitter of his eyes, the studied gesture." In the 1890s, Alastair began producing illustrations in a style influenced by Aubrey Beardsley, his favorite subjects being Salomé, Cleopatra, and androgynous or effeminate youths, including American dandies. His illustrations for Wilde's poem "The Sphinx" are considered among his finest works. In the early 1900s he performed erotic-mystical dances for the circle of the Italian Decadent novelist Gabriele d'Annunzio. Arwas writes of this period, "Alastair, who had by now accumulated a vast wardrobe of exotic costumes . . . needed little encouragement to dress and perform, creating curious ritualized scenes which appeared to conjure up the supernatural."

In 1914 Alastair met André Germain, a writer who was fascinated with the poetry of the lesbian writer René Vivien. Alastair and Germain would share a long-lasting, tempestuous relationship. Nine years later, Alastair met the ritual magician and esoteric artist Austin Osman Spare, who was to wield a great influence upon his life and work. Also in the early 1920s, Alastair became friends with the homosexual or bisexual occultist Ludwig Derleth, a member of the circle of Stefan George, a homosexual German Decadent poet whose love for a youth named Maximin had inspired a cult upon the untimely death of the youth. Also during this period, Alastair became friends with the eccentrics Harry and Caresse Crosby, and a bit later with cellist Pablo Casals, whom he sometimes accompanied on the piano.[69] Art historian Philippe Jullian describes the world of Alastair as one of "Black Masses in transvestite clubs."[70]

In the 1940s, Alastair began to withdraw more and more from the outside world; however, he did continue to receive visitors in the evenings who would bring him bunches of "roses, lilies, chrysanthemums." He reemerged briefly in the

1960s, when his work again became fashionable. He died in 1969. His lover André Germain wrote of him:

> He travelled throughout Europe with a huge number of trunks containing the most magnificent clothes, but had no roof of his own. An air of splendour and decay hung around him. . . . Moving with a kind of effort hieratic costumes resembling chasubles [mantles worn by priests], he executed, as though hypnotised, slow pantomimes which . . . transposed sacerdotal wails and recreated the splendours of an exiled court. . . . He gave one the impression of emerging from a fairy-tale, but a rather 1890s fairy-tale, in which there was some Villiers de l'Isle-Adam as well as some Aubrey Beardsley, some perfected liturgies, and a degree of witchcraft.[71]

MANY LIVING IN the nineteenth and early twentieth centuries, extremely disillusioned with the Judeo-Christian tradition, sought sustenance in pre-Christian and non-Western paths. In their search for traditions allowing for the greater expression of diversity, they recovered the ancient association of homoeroticism, gender variance, and the sacred. As in the period spanning the Middle Ages through the eighteenth century, our domain was often expressed in sublimated, artistic forms. Some artists, like Whitman, linked our domain to nature and to democracy or utopian socialism. Others, like Wilde, linked it to the lost "paradise" of Greco-Roman antiquity. Still others, like Aleister Crowley, were not content to submerge the domain in artistic expression, but rather sought to reclaim in all its grandeur the figure of the sexually variant, androgynous priest. Together, these men and others paved the way for the emergence of the Gay Spiritual movement in the later twentieth century.

PART FOUR

Crossroads

❧

CROSSROADS

*I*T HAS BEEN over a decade since I lay in bed with hepatitis. I remember my friend Gloria having me call a priestess of the Yoruba religion who told me of a bath I might take to ease my pain. Having had no luck with doctors, I felt I had nothing to lose. The bath was a simple one, basil and mint and coconut milk or "two cans of evaporated milk." I was to focus on a white candle and to ask "Mama" to heal me as I scooped up the water, milk, and herbs and poured the mixture over my head. Being a skeptic, I suppose I will never know whether the bath worked or whether I would have gotten well in a week without it. It did, however, lead me to explore the Yoruba religion, and to one of the most powerful, beautiful, and compassionate spiritual teachers I have met.

Since our meeting, my lover and I have continued to observe the rites she shared with us. Each autumn, we dip a pumpkin in honey, adorn it with gold ribbon and five gold bells, and offer it to the *orishá* of fresh water, the arts, and love, Oshún. We have done so now for fourteen years. This October, in the midst of a rainstorm, when we cast the pumpkin into a rushing river, I remembered the warmth of her embrace, her blessing of the love that David and I share.

In those days, as now, the Bay Area of California was, in the priestess's terms, a "psychic seaport." At times we felt like dilettantes, guests at a buffet or wine-tasting party. And yet, we were carried forth by a belief that by weaving together various traditions, we might enrich our experience of the sacred dimension of life. Women, gay people, persons of color, and others were coming together in rituals reflecting the patchwork quilt, the rainbow that is the New World. We were beginning to allow ourselves to drop the various barriers—racism, misogyny, homophobia, antispiritual academic attitudes, and others—that had kept us from experiencing the richness of spiritual traditions. We spoke of a time of great difficulty when we would be called upon to be healers and transformers of consciousness.

It is Halloween night. In a valley among the San Gabriel Mountains, we have joined hands around a pond in a great circle. In the center of the pond is a pentagram of fire. We invoke the Goddess, the Horned One, and the spirits of this place, asking them to be with us this night. Three cloaked figures smear our lips with the water of life, our foreheads with the ashes of death, our breasts with the balm of rejuvenation. We wind our way to a tent where two guards stand. One holds a candle, the other a mirror. Before entering, we must look into the mirror. "See the face of death," they tell us, "it is your face." Inside, huddled together, we invoke the names of ancestors and of loved ones who have died as dancers mime death by illness, old age, catastrophe, and suicide. Some begin to weep.

After a time, a bagpiper begins to pipe. Gradually we are led from the tent to a great bonfire. Here there are drums and bells and harps, and the mood slowly changes from one of grief to one of joy. The rebirth that follows death. "Corn and grain, corn and grain," we sing, "what must die shall live again. Hoof and horn, hoof and horn, what must die shall be reborn. We all come from the Goddess, and to Her we shall return, like a drop of rain, flowing to the ocean." The blossom from the bone.[1]

I have bathed in basil, mint, and coconut milk and have cleaned my body with eggs and red and white carnations. I have dipped the eggs in honey and placed them in a bag with the flowers, peppermint candy, and pennies. I have left the bag at the crossroads as an offering to Elleggúa. May he open the road.

The Epoch of the goddess Xochiquetzal, known as the "Exaltation of the Rose," Aztec, Conquest period.

Exaltation of the Flowers

One of my favorite paintings speaks to the ancient association of gender variance, homoeroticism, and spiritual practice in contemporary Mexico. It is a work by the artist Nahum B. Zenil titled *Gracias Virgencita de Guadalupe*. In the painting, two twinlike male lovers lie in bed gazing at the Virgin, who floats above them. While Zenil's work is very innovative, the reflection of our domain in Latin America may be traced to antiquity.[1] In this chapter, we will focus on its manifestation in precolonial Mesoamerica, especially among the Aztecs and, to a lesser extent, the Toltecs, Huastecs, and Mayas.

GENDER VARIANCE AND HOMOEROTICISM IN ANCIENT MESOAMERICA

At the time of the Spanish Conquest, a majority of Mesoamericans did not sanction same-sex eroticism, nor did they approve of gender variance, except in that instance when an otherwise masculine priest donned feminine garments during—and only during—the course of a ritual. Among the Chichimecs and later the Aztecs, punishment for same-sex eroticism was especially harsh; according to the sixteenth-century Aztec historian Fernando de Alva Ixlilxóchitl, "To the one acting as a female, they removed his entrails from the bottom, he was tied down to a log, and the boys from the town covered him with ash, until he was buried; and then they put a lot of wood and burnt him. The one acting as a male was covered with ash, tied down to a log until he died."[2]

People, both male and female, who dressed in garments traditionally worn by the opposite sex were punished in a similar manner, as were women engaging in same-sex eroticism.[3]

At some as yet undetermined point in the development of Mesoamerican culture, both gender variance and same-sex eroticism generally came to be regarded as manifestations of illness. Indeed, one of the terms used to refer to a sick man, *cocoxqui*, also came to signify a gender-variant, homoerotically inclined male. This "illness" due to homosexual and gender-variant behavior was "discovered" by way of corn divination. One kernel falling upon another and causing the first to stand upright was all the evidence a diviner needed.[4]

By the time of the arrival of the Spanish conquistadors in Mesoamerica, a number of derogatory terms were used to designate such persons. Several Nahuatl terms underscore the punishment awaiting them: *tlatla*, "he burns"; *tlatlani*, "he deserves the flames"; *chichinoloni*, "he deserves to be cast in the fire."[5]

In spite of the extreme hostility directed toward such men, however, Spanish chroniclers reported that not only was same-sex eroticism widely practiced in Mesoamerica, but also that many men who dressed in women's garments were serving as hierodules. Moreover, they reported that despite homophobic and effemiphobic laws, many individuals believed both gender variance and same-sex eroticism to be divinely sanctioned.[6]

Gender-variant and homoerotically inclined men were known to Mesoamericans by various names, including those given above. Among Aztec or Nahuatl terms, some emphasized gender variance: *xochioa (suchioa)*, translated as "effeminate," also suggesting "flower person"; *ci[h]uao[o]quichtli* and *cihuaciuhqui*, also translated as "effeminate"; *cihuayollo*, "heart of a woman"; *mocihuanenequini*, "he passes himself off as a woman"; *cicihuatlatoa (cioatlatole)*, "he talks like a woman"; *cioanotzale*, "he uses the feminine mode of address." Other Nahuatl terms, including *cuiloni*, *chimouqui*, and *tecuilontiani*, referred to a male taking the receptive role in same-sex eroticism.[7]

The Mayas referred to gender-variant men as *ch'upal ol*, *ch'uplal kunabha*, *ch'uplal winik*, and *k'uruch*. When they wished to refer specifically to the practice of homosexuality, the employed the terms *(ah) top chun*, *(ix) p'en*, *x-ch'upul xib*, and *xibil x-ch'up*. They even apparently had a term for oral literary texts produced by women and gender-variant men: *ch'uplak kan*.[8]

GENDER-VARIANT MALES AND FEMALE HIERODULES

What did it mean to be a gender-variant male in Mesoamerica? To have "the heart of a woman"? To "pass oneself off as a woman"? We may begin to sketch a portrait of the *cihuayollo* male (I have chosen this term arbitrarily, because it is my favorite of those given above) by examining traits associated with female hierodules, with whom they were often grouped and to whom they were often compared.

The *cihuayollo* male probably paid a great deal of attention to his appearance, as suggested by the following terms applied to female hierodules: *motopalquetza,* "she looks at herself in the mirror"; *moyeyecquetza,* "she decks herself out."[9]

An article by Latin Americanist Patricia Anawalt suggests that gender variance probably included cross-dressing or mixed-dressing. Anawalt points out that several figures in the Nahuatl *Borgia Group Codices* are wearing both the *maxtlatl,* a loincloth traditionally worn by males, and the *quechquemitl,* a rounded or triangular chest cape traditionally worn by women. Referring to these figures of both sexes as "androgynous" and "bisexual," Anawalt suggests that they may be associated with the Huastec goddess Tlazolteotl, with the central-eastern Veracruz zone, and with the legendary Tlamantinime, the "wise men of . . . Tamoanchan," paradise of the Toltec-Aztec goddess Xochiquetzal. The descendants of the Tlamantinime, incidentally, were famous for "their skill in painting cotton mantles" and were believed to be "particularly knowledgeable in ritual and divinatory lore."[10]

Like the Aztec female hierodule, the *cihuayollo* male probably painted his face and reddened his teeth with cochineal, a scarlet dye made from the coccus cacti. He may have also painted a black butterfly on his mouth or forehead, a custom of the hierodules of Xochiquetzal and Tlazolteotl. He may have worn his hair in the knotted, "two-horned" style of Xochiquetzal. He probably also rubbed his body with perfumed unguents, *maxpetzcoa,* and further perfumed himself with the smoke of copal incense, *mopopochhuia, miyiemotla.*[11]

He may have also worn a garland of the purplish leaves of a type of coleus (*salvia divinorum*) named *poyomatli (puyomaté)* or *pipiltzintzintli.* Its appellation *pipiltzintzintli* seems especially interesting in our context, as *pipil* designates "child" or "youth" and is related to *pilli,* "prince," while *tzin* is an honorific term and *tzintli* designates the "buttocks."

The probable wearing of *pipiltzintzintli* or *poyomatli* garlands by female hierodules and *cihuayollo* males, some of whom were also hierodules, suggests that they may have engaged in magical practices, especially of an amatory nature. Further, the use of *poyomatli* as a mind-altering or sacred hallucinogen suggests that they may have also engaged in shamanic practices.[12]

Among the Aztecs and perhaps other Mesoamericans as well, both female hierodules and gender-variant males were apparently associated with various other traits including: walking in a seductive, haughty manner, *mocuecueloa;* chewing "gum," *tziccuacua, motzictlatlatza;* and ingesting hallucinogenic mushrooms, *motlapahuitinemi.*[13]

GENDER-VARIANT MALES AND LESBIAN WOMEN

If the *cihuayollo* male, often a hierodule, was perceived as resembling the female hierodule (in Nahuatl, *ahuiani*), he was also viewed as the complement of the gender-variant female who engaged in lesbian eroticism. Such a lesbian, often mistakenly identified as a hermaphrodite, was in Nahuatl referred to as a *patlache.*

Whereas the Nahua gender-variant male has "the heart of a woman," the *patlache* is described as *cihuatl xipine*, "the woman with a penis" (also *tepule, chonehua, mihua*) and *atehua*, "the owner of testicles." Whereas he "talks like a woman," she "talks like a man," *o[o]quichtlatoa*, and uses the masculine mode of address, *o[o]quichnotzale*. Whereas he "walks like a woman," she "walks like a man," *o[o]quichnenemi*. Whereas his lovers are generally if not always male, she "seeks another woman as a companion," *mocihuapotiani*. She has a "friction-loving vulva," *pixtlaxaqualole*, she "likes to rub her vulva on the body of another woman," *tepixuia*, and she "never wants to marry [a man]," *aic monamictiznequi*.[14]

Like the female hierodule and the gender-variant *cihuayollo*, the *patlache* appears to have been associated with the goddesses Xochiquetzal and Tlazolteotl. Of the *patlache*, it is said, "*Quitoca patlahuac utli, in tochin, mazatl iyuhui*, She follows the broad road, the path of the rabbit, of the deer." The rabbit and the deer, respectively, are the sacred animals of Tlazolteotl and Xochiquetzal.[15]

TLAZOLTEOTL AND THE HUASTECS

Gender-variant *cihuayollo* males are also linked to Tlazolteotl by way of several ostensibly pejorative terms including *tlaelchichi*, "dog shit." Tlazolteotl, whose name implies "shit goddess," is the deity of illicit sexuality and destructive magic among the Huastecs and Aztecs. She is often depicted as partially nude, as crowned with a horned or conical headdress, as clutching a serpent, and as riding on a broomstick or a bundle of magical-medical herbs.[16]

Tlazolteotl is described as having the power to split herself into at least four aspects: Tiacapan, Teicu, Tlaco, and Xocutxin. She is associated with cotton, hallucinogenic plants (especially peyote and agave), and with the *voladores*, ritual dancers performing while suspended from a tall pole.[17]

Above all, however, Tlazolteotl is associated with variant sexuality and with the Huastec people, a group linguistically related to the Mayas who lived in northern and eastern Mexico. As a goddess of variant and/or illicit sexuality, she is, as mentioned above, a patron of hierodules and prostitutes. Her spiritual "daughters," their bodies perfumed and mouths painted black, often served as companions to warriors.[18]

By way of her role as mother of the Huastecs, Tlazolteotl became linked to homoeroticism. Even her Aztec devotees living in Tenochtlitlan, site of present-day Mexico City, were referred to as Huastecs, especially when they attended ceremonies wearing only masks, headdresses, and artificial phalli. Beyond wearing enormous phalli, which were sometimes striped, the Huastecs were known to perform head deformation, file and redden their teeth, perforate their nasal septums in order to insert gold ornaments and red arara feathers in them, and dye their hair bright red or yellow.[19]

According to the Anonymous Conquistador, the Huastecs depicted scenes of phallic worship as well as of heterosexual and homosexual coitus in their temples, seeing eroticism as a bridge to the divine. The Anonymous Conquistador also mentions the Huastec use of pulque enemas, which they employed in erotic-visionary rites.[20]

The association of Tlazolteotl with gender variance and homoeroticism is underscored not only by her patronage of gender-variant males and her association with Huastec erotic practices but also by her appellation Tzinteotl, "Goddess of the Anus."[21]

XOCHIQUETZAL AND HER CHILDREN

She [is] the one with the thigh painted on her face.
She has left Tamoanchan, the Place-of-our-origin.[22]

The goddess Xochiquetzal is also associated with gender-variant males. As Precious Flower, she is the goddess of spring, the underworld, and nonprocreative sexuality. She is commonly depicted as wearing a blue tunic woven with flowers, a garland of green feathers and red and yellow flowers, and golden earplugs and pendants. Flowers emerge from her mouth, symbolizing eloquence. A knife also emerges from her mouth, suggesting her ability to cut through chatter and lies. A red serpent, signifying unbridled passion, emerges from her vagina.

Beneath her ocelot throne are marigolds and a skull, symbolic of the Underworld. Marigolds, or *cempoalxochitl* ("twenty flowers"), continue to be offered to Xochiquetzal (albeit in the guise of the Virgin Mary) and to the deceased, whom she protects, on the Día de los Muertos (the Day of the Dead) in Mexico, the United States, and elsewhere. Other symbols sacred to Xochiquetzal are spiders, signifying the art of weaving and the interrelatedness of all life, and thorns, used to pierce the ears and other parts of the body during penance.

The sixteenth-century priest and chronicler of Aztec life Father Durán explains that Xochiquetzal is the patron of weavers, embroiderers, silversmiths, sculptors, and painters. She is also the patron of poets, "word weavers" who utter "flower words." As a patron of poets, Xochiquetzal is also the ruler of those who use lyrical speech or song—in other words, charms—to work magic. Called *xochihua*, the "flower persons" mentioned above, these people are depicted as homosexually or bisexually inclined males who excel in amatory magic. They are also depicted as employing hallucinogenic mushrooms in their ritual practice.[23]

According to Jésus Arango Cano, a scholar of Mesoamerican religions, Xochiquetzal is a patron of hierodules (prostitutes) and hermaphrodites. As already noted, the term *hermaphrodite* usually refers not to a biological hermaphrodite but to a gender-variant individual and/or to an individual engaging in same-sex eroticism.[24]

Depictions of male couples associated with Xochiquetzal, appearing in the *Codex Vaticanus* (Rios 3738) and *Codex Borbonicus* with their legs touching or intertwined and their bodies covered by a single blanket, also indicate her linkage with homosexuality, especially when these images are compared with similar depictions of heterosexual couples.[25]

Astrological texts also indirectly suggest that *cihuayollo* males may have been born on "flower days" sacred to Xochiquetzal.

In the *Florentine Codex* is an illustration depicting two men conversing with each other. The man on the left wears masculine clothing, has short hair, and sits on a stool. The man on the right—we know he is male because of his description in the text as a "pervert," "sodomite," and "effeminate... womanish" male—wears feminine clothing, has the knotted braids of Xochiquetzal, and sits gracefully on the ground. A large red flower, sacred to Xochiquetzal, looms between them, suggesting both poetic speech and amatory magic. This illustration, unfortunately, has a companion. In the picture to the right, the *cihuayollo* male no longer sits on the ground but lies on a pile of burning logs. The illustrations were clearly meant to be a warning to those who would follow the path of the *cihuayollo* male.[26]

Xochiquetzal resides in the celestial paradise of Tamoanchan, also known as Ciutlampa, "the Place of Women." In some myths, she shares Tamoanchan with the god Xochipilli and with the Ciuateteo, a band of ghostly women who visit the earth in the guise of eagles to inflict diseases on those who have failed to make sacrifices. In contemporary Mexico and the southwestern United States, *la lechuza* carries on the work of the Ciuateteo.

Tamoanchan is an Eden of butterflies, hummingbirds, and parrots, where the souls of deceased artists and craftspersons dwell between lifetimes. Male souls among them spend their days singing and dancing for the Goddess. As spirits, they are sometimes depicted as having butterfly wings. The implication is that these male souls are *cihuayollo,* not fitting the traditional masculine image of the warrior or state priest. One wonders if their depiction as having butterfly wings may have been responsible in part for the emergence of the term *mariposa* in contemporary Mexico to designate gender-variant gay men. This association does not seem nearly so farfetched as the commonly held opinion that *mariposa* as a slang term for "gay" or "queen" arises from "Maria."

A kind of ladder reaches from Tamoanchan to the earth. This is the *xochitlicacan,* a flowering tree of thirteen branching levels that blooms eternally. Some believe that the flowery ladder touches the earth in the vicinity of Xochicalco in the state of Morelos. It is to Tamoanchan that the bones "out of which men [and women] are created" are brought when they die; here they are recycled to fashion other human beings who will descend the *xochitlicacan* at the hour of birth.[27]

The festivals of Xochiquetzal included the sacrifice of a young woman called the *ixiptla.* The priest, who may or may not have been gender variant, dressed in the flayed skin of the victim and assumed the persona of the Goddess. Seated under a canopy of flowers, he pretended to weave. A *xochitlicacan* was erected, in which youths dressed as butterflies and birds frolicked. Beneath them, other participants, acting as deities, pretended to shoot them with harmless blowguns. Jugglers and acrobats performed, while still others, scantily clad in Spanish moss, engaged in simulated or actual erotic activity. Latin Americanist Burr C. Brundage writes, "For that brief time the people, in company with their gods and under the presidency of her who was love itself, expressed their joy with flowers, drunkenness, and sexual license."[28]

During the period immediately following the arrival of the Spanish in Mexico, black slaves and freedmen began to play a role in Huastec ritual. By 1553, more than twenty thousand blacks were living in Mexico, many of whom, as *calpixques* appointed by the Spanish, were responsible for overseeing the Huastecs and other indigenous peoples. While the Huastecs resented Spanish rule, they appear to have gotten along with the black *calpixques* and to have shared religious and folk beliefs and practices with them. Black participation in Huastec ritual was especially marked in the dance drama called the *payà*.

The *payà*, dedicated to Teem, an aspect of Xochiquetzal designating her as the sister of Tlazolteotl, derived its name from an amphora "decked with dyed featherwork flowers" designed to represent the Goddess. In the *payà*, both the *teponatzli*, an indigenous drum of Mexico, and African drums may have been employed. The *payà* was performed by both Huastecs and blacks "dressed as women with long false hair." During the course of the rite, one or more of the men would become possessed or embodied by the Goddess. It was recorded that in 1624 the *payà* was led by a black slave, perhaps named Peret after his master, who became possessed and thereby imbued with the power to heal the sick.

The *payà* was associated with the *voladores* and hence with the worship of Tlazolteotl as well as that of Xochiquetzal. Black slaves, freedmen, and *calpixques* often participated in or led the *volador* dance ritual during the early seventeenth century. One of the dancing flyers was customarily dressed in women's clothes; at first a representative of the Goddess, the young man later came to be seen as a representation of La Malinche, the Aztec interpreter for Cortez, and has in the twentieth century been replaced by a female performer.

While it is impossible to say whether all of the men who participated in the *payà* were perceived as gender variant, it is probably safe to say that some must have been. Further, whether or not the *payà* represented an occasion of temporary transvestism or a collective *cihuayollo* manifestation, it served to remind the faithful of the Goddess's association with male gender variance.[29]

XOCHIPILLI, NAXCIT-XUCHITL, AND OTHER DEITIES

Xochipilli, the Aztec Prince of Flowers, is the consort of Xochiquetzal. He is known by various names, including Makuil-Xochitl, Xochiwitl, Chikome-Xochitl, Xocbitun, Piltzintekutli, H Kinxoc, and Balon-Mayel; several of these appellations indicate that his worship spread beyond the Aztecs. With Xochiquetzal, he is sometimes portrayed as the parent of the maize god Cinteotl.

Like Xochiquetzal, Xochipilli is a god of flowers and sensual pleasures. He is the patron of entertainers—dancers, singers, actors, jugglers, gymnasts, and game players (especially of the *nexoxochitlaxiliztli*, the "game of throwing flowers"). He is also the patron of perfumers. He delights in perfumes containing many exotic essences, called *xochitlanamactli*.

Like other deities, Xochipilli brings not only joy but also suffering, especially to those who fail to make sacrifices to him. They are likely to be stricken with venereal disease or hemorrhoids. In Nahuatl, incidentally, hemorrhoids are referred to as *xochiciutzlil,* "the flowers of the anus." Offerings to Xochipilli include toasted corn and butterfly-shaped breads.[30]

Xochipilli was honored with Xochiquetzal at the Xochilhuitl festival as well as at the Tecuilhuitontli. Held in the seventh month of the Aztec year, the Tecuil-huitontli was an unusual festival in that human sacrifice played no part in it. It was, in the words of Father Durán, "an occasion for enjoying the flowers which abounded in that season," and in ancient texts it was represented by "a man ar-ranging [or men exchanging] flowers." It was a time when great banquets were held consisting of dainty and exotic dishes and when flowers, "mantles, breech-cloths, and jewels" were exchanged. Hierodules wearing flower garlands and "elaborately embroidered *huipils*" (sleeveless blouses) danced in the streets, while noblemen reclined on couches, "surrounded by flowers, picking one up and lay-ing it down, [then] taking another and abandoning it."[31]

As the god of dance, Xochipilli was honored with the *cuecuechcuicatl,* the "dance of the itch." This dance was compared by Durán to the Spanish saraband, "with all its wriggling and grimacing and immodest mimicry." It was performed by hierodules and by *cihuayollo* males "dressed as women."[32]

As historian David F. Greenberg states, Xochipilli is "the patron of male homo-sexuality and male prostitution."[33] His patronage of individuals engaging in these behaviors suggests a complex set of associations including the role of entertainer, the love of exotic foods and perfumes, male gender variance, and same-sex eroti-cism.

Xochipilli has been identified with the Mesoamerican deity Naxcit-Xuchitl. This god's name means "Four Foot Flower," suggesting the flowering tree of Ta-moanchan and perhaps thereby linking the deity with both Xochipilli and Xochi-quetzal. Naxcit-Xuchitl appears to be a synthesis of several Mesoamerican deities including Xochipilli, Quetzalcoatl, and Kukulcan, a Yucatec culture hero. Naxcit is regarded as a legendary founder of Chichén Itzá. He is variously claimed to have been of Itzá, Toltec, or Mayan heritage.

Naxcit is among those divine beings considered to have introduced homo-erotic practices to the Mayas. According to the folklorist and ethnologist José Imbelloni, same-sex eroticism, at various times tolerated and punished by the Mayas, became known as the "sin" of Naxcit-Xuchitl, as well as the "sin" of the Bolon-ti-ku, the nine gods of the Mayan Underworld.[34]

The myth of Naxcit-Xuchitl may be related to that of another Mesoamerican deity variously named Cu or Cavil (Kauil). This deity may be the Mayan "God K," depicted as a dwarf or infant from whose forehead a smoking mirror, like that of Tezcatlipoca, emerges. From the mirror, an ax, associated with rain, lightning, and fire sometimes emerges. One of K's legs is the body of a serpent. In his mani-festation as Cavil or Kauil, he is a god of nurturance in general and maize in par-ticular. He is especially associated with magic and divination and the destinies of rulers. His image was held by Mayan rulers in the form of a "mannequin scepter," evoking the *marotte,* the scepter carried by the French medieval *sots,* which, in turn, evokes the shaman's staff. Like Naxcit, this deity, as Cu, was said to have in-troduced the Mayas to homoeroticism.[35]

It was further believed that Cu's/K's sanction of same-sex eroticism had inspired some Mayan nobles to purchase handsome youths to be the lovers of their sons. These relationships at least in legal terms, were considered marriages. If a third party attempted to break up the relationship, or if one of the partners wished to dissolve the relationship, he might be forced to pay a fine.[36]

The myths of Naxcit-Xuchitl and Cu/K may also be linked to a Mesoamerican myth concerning homoerotically inclined giants. This myth has been found in sites as far apart as Cholula, Mexico, and Manta, Ecuador. According to the eighteenth-century chronicler Mariano Veytia, the people of Cholula believed that the giants arrived during the year 3979 of their calendar, which some say corresponds to 107 C.E. These giants were sometimes called the Quinames and were thought to be the ancestors of the Toltecs and the subduers of the Olmecs. Their race is also said to have emerged during the second cosmic age of Aztec myth. Their great strength allowed them to survive the hurricane that brought an end to the Second Sun. They were hunters and gatherers, having voracious appetites for food as well as sex.

The men of Cholula (and elsewhere in other traditions) offered the giants their own daughters, but the Quinames were not interested, preferring male erotic companions. Because they allegedly coerced the men of Cholula into having sex with them, they were destroyed by a fiery conflagration or an earthquake, although this part of the myth may have been purposely Christianized so priests could connect this story to that of Sodom in order to dissuade Mesoamerican males from engaging in same-sex eroticism or relationships.[37]

While our focus has been on gender-variant homosexuality, the myths of Cu and the Quinames suggest that other models of same-sex eroticism and same-sex relationships may have been employed as well by ancient Mesoamericans.

TEZCATLIPOCA AND XOLOTL

I would like to return now to two other male Aztec deities who play a role in the life of Xochiquetzal: Tezcatlipoca and Xolotl.

In certain myths, Xochiquetzal is the spouse of the rain god Tlaloc. She dwells with him in Tlalocan until she is abducted by Xolotl or Tezcatlipoca, who takes her to the Underworld. Later, she reemerges as the goddess of sensual pleasures, patron of the dead, and ruler of the paradise of Tamoanchan.[38]

Xolotl is the Aztec god of Venus as the evening star, an intermediary between the earth and the Underworld, and assistant to Xochiquetzal and Citlalinicue, goddess of the Milky Way, in the creation of recycled human beings.[39]

Xolotl is also sometimes identified with Nanahuatl, who is "covered with running sores" and who both bestows and heals "diseases of the skin." In another aspect, he is the "dark twin" of Quetzalcoatl; as such, he is the god of suicide. In another aspect, he is a handsome, unmarried young man who rules the paradise of Xolotlan, the "Land of Young Men." He is a patron of all those who engage in variant forms of eroticism. The literature suggests that he may have been especially associated with practitioners of sadomasochism.[40]

Tezcatlipoca's name refers to the "smoking" obsidian mirror he carries, a mirror in which the future may be seen. Able to transform himself into a woman, a jaguar, a coyote, and a monkey, he has been compared to the Native American trickster Coyote and to shape-shifting shamans. He is the left-handed god of the crossroads and the night sky, a shadowy sorcerer who holds the power to "steal the sun and plunge all things into night." Like the shaman, he is a skilled healer of life-threatening illnesses. He is alone among the Aztec gods in being cursed by desperate suppliants seeking aid from him.[41]

In one of his aspects, he is *cihuayollo,* wearing women's clothes, engaging in same-sex eroticism, and referred to as a "male whore." As such, he is a typical hierodule in his mocking of others. Of him it is said, "We are your spectacle or show, at which you either jeer or rejoice." The nicknames Yaotl, "Enemy," and Telpochtli, "Youth," also appear to carry homosexual or bisexual meaning.[42]

A lyric love spell, probably the composition of a *xochihua,* or gender variant "flower-man," uses the terms *enemy* and *youth.* Both are epithets of Tezcatlipoca, "enemy" referring to him as the opponent of the god Quetzalcoatl (although not of Xochiquetzal) and "youth" referring to the younger aspect of Tezcatlipoca. The text begins:

At the place of the mirrored summit,
    at the place of meeting,
I call out "woman," I sing for woman.
Here I suffer; I come to suffer.
I take my oldest sister, Xochiquetzal.

The text ends:

Perhaps she is truly a goddess.
Perhaps she is truly powerful.
Perhaps tomorrow, perhaps the day
    after tomorrow,
    I will see her.
Immediately. Now.
Myself, I am the Youth. I am the Enemy.
In truth, I am not the enemy.
I am only *cihuayotl.*[43]

Cihuayotl designates the womb, the "matrix where woman conceives." Some translators have decided that in this text *cihuayotl* is a misspelled word, that the author really meant to say *cihuayoh,* "womanizer." These translators err in assuming this lone word among so many others to be misspelled. Perhaps they have assumed so because, on the surface, the image of Tezcatlipoca as youth and enemy appears to contradict the image of him as *cihuayotl,* "womblike," suggesting *cihuayollo.* The translators do us and Tezcatlipoca a disservice in ignoring the god's transformative powers and contradictory nature. Only Noemí Quezada, in *Amor y Magia Amorosa entre los Aztecas,* has correctly interpreted *cihuayotl* as signifying Tezcatlipoca's feminine or gender-variant aspect.

What is particularly interesting about this spell is that the person undertaking the spell, presumably a male or at least male-identified, is asking to become feminized. He wishes to change gender in order to gain the love of the Goddess or her representative, who might well be a female hierodule or a *cihuayollo* male. This exercise in "gender bending" suggests a highly sophisticated model of erotic behavior which contradicts the sharp legal sanctions against homoeroticism and gender variance established by the Aztecs and other Mesoamerican peoples just prior to the Conquest.[44]

In another series of myths, Tezcatlipoca and Quetzalcoatl, like Set and Horus, are engaged in an eternal struggle. In one of these myths, Tezcatlipoca is determined to force Quetzalcoatl to leave the city of Tollan (or Tula), capital of the Toltecs. His strategy involves serving pulque to Quetzalcoatl or to the latter's high priest, Huemac. Tezcatlipoca then transforms into the Youth and seduces Huemac or Quetzalcoatl. In another myth, Tezcatlipoca and several other male deities transform themselves into beautiful women and seduce Huemac. These and other similar episodes ultimately succeed in forcing Quetzalcoatl to depart from Tollan.[45]

The priests of Tezcatlipoca painted themselves black from head to foot with a mixture containing tobacco, morning glory seeds, and sacred mushrooms; one might say, echoing the contemporary anthropologist and Mesaomerican scholar Peter Furst, that they "psychedelized" their own bodies. They pierced themselves repeatedly with maguey thorns; their hair, which they allowed to grow past their buttocks, was thick and matted with blood. Many, apparently, were the sons of chiefs who served in the temples as hierodulic priests, having sexual intercourse with other priests and devotees in order to commune with Tezcatlipoca. Needless to say, the Catholics were shocked by such practices.[46]

MALE GENDER VARIANCE AND SHAMANIC USE OF HALLUCINOGENS

In Aztec culture, *cihuayollo* males were often grouped with males referred to as *telpuchtlahueliloc*; such a man is defined in the Florentine Codex (c. 1555 C.E. an illustrated text of Aztec life composed by Aztecs under the direction of Fray Bernardino de Sahagún) as a "young male libertine . . . he is a catamite, he is a sodomite [He is] crazy, . . . He goes about dealing with mushrooms."[47]

We have already noted the association of both female and male hierodules and males engaging in anal eroticism with sacred hallucinogens; we will pursue the association here in greater depth.

Aztecs referred to sacred mushrooms as *teonanacatl*, "divine flesh" or the "flesh of the gods." Also known as *xochininacatl*, "flowery flesh," such mushrooms were sacred to Xochipilli. Botanist Richard E. Schultes and chemist Albert Hofmann, the discoverer of the hallucinogen LSD, explain that a celebrated statue of Xochipilli portrays him as being in a state of ecstasy. "His body is engraved with stylized flowers which have been identified as sacred, most of them inebriating, plants." They further note that the "pedestal on which he sits is decorated with a design representing cross-sections of the caps of *Psilocybe aztecorum*."[48]

The sacred mushroom may also be linked to the goddess Xochiquetzal; the knotted braids on either side of the top of her head—the style probably worn by *cihuayollo* males—may represent the *teonanactl*. Moreover, in the Tepanitla fresco of Teotihuacan, which portrays the "afterlife journey of the soul of a drowned man as he makes his way to the playing fields of Paradise," sacred mushrooms are depicted alongside the conches of Xochipilli and the butterflies of Xochiquetzal. Indeed, the flowery tree of Tamoanchan is depicted as a hybrid of mushroom, conch, and flower.[49]

The *telpuchtlahueliloc* male was also said to drink fresh pulque. Pulque, a fermented beverage made from the sap of the maguey or agave, is associated with Mayahuel, the goddess of pulque, and with Xochiquetzal, who is often syncretized with the former. One may recall that the use of pulque has been linked to both anal eroticism and shamanic practices among the Huastecs and may have been used in the worship of Tlazolteotl. Pulque's association with female warriors and with rabbit spirits further indicate its association with Tlazolteotl and Xochiquetzal.[50]

The *telpuchtlahueliloc* male was also said to go "about dealing with *mixitl*." *Mixitl*, also called *tlapatl, toloache, toaloatzin,* and *tolohuaxihuitl*, is the thorn apple or jimson weed. Its various names indicate associations with Tlazolteotl and Xochiquetzal. Moreover, its appellation *toaloatzin* suggests not only the inclined head of Xochipilli but also the inclined heads attributed to hierodules and, by extension to *cihuayollo* males. According to Schultes and Hofmann, *mixitl* or thorn apple "was employed not only to induce visual hallucinations but for a great variety of medicinal uses, especially when applied to the body to relieve rheumatic pains and to reduce swellings."[51]

It is possible that the sexually variant *telpuchtlahueliloc* male may have also used peyote, nicknamed *tlazolcihuapilli*, indicating its association with *Tlazol*teotl, Xochi*pilli*, women (*cihua*) and *cihuayollo* males. Peyote, through its association with the deer, was also sacred to Xochiquetzal.[52]

As mentioned above, *cihuayollo* males are also believed to have used the coleus *salvia divinorum*. As *pipiltzintzintli*, "Youthful Prince of the Buttocks," this hallucinogenic plant was linked to the worship of Xochipilli. In ancient Mesoamerica, a beverage made of *pipiltzintzintli* and other ingredients was believed to hold great healing powers. The plant is said to affect the psyche in much the same way as psilocybin. *Pipiltzintzintli* was also ingested in combination with sacred mushrooms and *ololiuhqui*, morning glory seeds. Further, *pipiltzintzintli* has traditionally been used in amatory magic. In twentieth-century Mexico, as *puyomaté*, it continues to be used for this purpose. It is placed with dolls and candles, which are brought closer together each night during the period the spell is being undertaken. Sometimes simply rubbing the scrapings of the plant's root in one's hands may bring love or good fortune. It is believed that *pipiltzintzintli* or *puyomaté* can work especially powerful magic when it has touched the heart or genital area of the desired one. This has led to the creation of talismans containing the plant, worn at the neck or waist.[53]

What emerges from this brief discussion of the use of hallucinogenic and/or intoxicating substances by *telpuchtlahueliloc* and *cihuayollo* males is a web of associations linking male gender variance and homoeroticism with shamanic practices, with deities including Xochiquetzal, Xochipilli, and Tlazolteotl, and with symbols including the butterfly, the rabbit, and the deer.

THE EPOCH OF THE FLOWERS

The Aztecs believed that Xochiquetzal, with Xochipilli at her side, had governed the earth during that cosmic period known as the Fourth, Black, or Flower Sun. This Age of Xochiquetzal is depicted in the *Codex Vaticanus* (*Rios* 3738),[54] and both its beginning and its end are illustrated. In the painting, Xochiquetzal descends from the heavens. She is wearing a red and yellow garment and is crowned with a large yellow flower. She is clutching red and yellow flowers, which form the ends of two twining garlands. While this text is referred to as "The Exaltation of the Roses," the flowers are probably meant to represent marigolds, other flowers or flowering herbs, or possibly *pipiltzintzintli*.

Beneath Xochiquetzal, two figures dressed in masculine clothing and a third dressed in feminine clothing each hold a banner in one hand and a bouquet of flowers in the other. In the heavens, just above Xochiquetzal, float two flint knives, *tecpatl*, used to ritually wound the phallus. To the right of the Goddess and above one of the figures are thirteen stones, *tetl*, signifying male impotence or sterility. In Aztec culture, both flint knives and stones signify male gender variance.[55]

The Mayan people also spoke of the Age of Flowers, an epoch associated with effeminacy and homosexuality. They called it the Nikte Katun, the "Cosmic Cycle of the Four-Petaled Flower." This epoch was ruled by Naxcit-Xuchitl. Unfortunately, our only descriptions of this age occur in texts hostile to the legendary epoch. An extremely hostile passage from the *Book of Chilam Balam* reads:

The flower *katun* arrives then,
    The day of his seating.
Thirteen
    Are the children of the mat,
Of the [ass]hole suckers [*Ah calam chuuch*],
Of the asshole sinners [*Ah cal pach*].[56]

In spite of this later Mayan perception of the Flower *katun*, ethnologists José Imbelloni and Antonio Requeña, anthropologist Clark Taylor, and others have analyzed the data concerning this epoch from a less hostile position. They have concluded that this was an age in which the goddess Xochiquetzal (or her Mayan counterpart) was revered, in which women held political power or fought as warriors, and in which men became *cihuayollo* or "effeminate," spending their days weaving, painting, singing, dancing the "Dance of the Flowers," and engaging in same-sex eroticism. The Epoch of Flowers was said to have ended when a river of blood flooded the earth; it has been suggested that this refers to a disease of the blood that proved fatal to many people.[57]

One wonders what lies behind the myth of the Age of Flowers. Data concerning the Toltecs and early Aztecs indicate that they were organized matrilineally, with women owning property and working as healers and priestesses. Moreover, "the principle of balanced opposition between the sexes existed," symbolized by the goddess Coatlique, "who contained [within her being] the balanced dualities of male and female, light and dark, life and death." The shift from this type of culture to a more patriarchal, militaristic one appears to have begun shortly before or during the ninth century C.E. and to have culminated in the fifteenth century.[58]

This shift may have escalated when the Aztecs and other dominant Mesoamerican and South American groups decided to replace the shamans of tribal society with a political state religion. Stressing that many shamans were gender-variant males, Greenberg argues that legislation against homosexuality and transvestism on the one hand and repression of shamans on the other may have been intimately linked. Gender-variant persons and those engaging in same-sex eroticism may have been perceived as "potential sources of resistance." Greenberg believes, however, that "the harshness of . . . legislation toward homosexuality involved more than a reaction to indigenous berdaches." He asserts that such laws were ultimately devised to "channel all energies into conquest. . . . Anything that might weaken the military strength of the empire by encouraging licentiousness was to be suppressed."[59]

THE ARRIVAL OF THE CHRISTIANS

With the arrival of the Spanish and other Europeans, the peoples of Mesoamerica were forced to adopt Christianity. In *The Conquest of New Spain*, Bernal Díaz describes how Cortés, on entering the city of Zempoala, converted the temples to Catholic churches by painting over the murals of religious scenes and by setting up statues of Mary and Jesus where those of the gods had been. The priests' black robes were exchanged for white, their long hair was shorn and after being baptized they were instructed to "offer no more sacrifices and no longer worship idols, but believe in our lord God." Soldiers were placed at the sites to ensure that the priests carried out Cortés's orders.[60]

As for male gender variance and homoeroticism, the punishments meted out by the Aztecs and Chichimecs were continued by the Europeans. As Greenberg explains, "The conquistadors came from a country that killed men for homosexuality, and they carried the habit with them to the New World."[61]

One of the most terrifying purges took place in Mexico City between 1656 and 1663. Sociologist Stephen O. Murray and anthropologist Clark Taylor explain that "whereas heretics and Jews were burned in the Alameda, now a park near the center of Mexico City, homosexual sodomites were burned in [the plaza of] San Lázaro." The choice of San Lázaro is an intriguing one, as St. Lazarus, who may have been syncretized with the Aztec deity Nanahuatl, is being invoked in the late twentieth century by Mexicans, Mexican Americans, and others as the patron of individuals with HIV or AIDS. Beginning with a gender-variant transvestite nicknamed Cotita de la Encarnación, the men were all strangled. Then, at eight in the evening, they were set ablaze while several hundred people watched.[62]

After a time, the state assumed the role of torturing and executing persons accused of wearing garments of the opposite sex and engaging in same-sex eroticism, while the church began to view such practices as sins that might be absolved if relinquished. This shift is illustrated by certain *novenas,* here, prayers in pamphlet form, which began to circulate in Mexico in the eighteenth century. One prayer is addressed to St. Boniface, Martyr (680–755 C.E.), and is believed to be "efficacious to obtain from God the separation of those needy who have fallen into the misery of the deadly sin of the dishonourable vice." The prayer is believed to have been authored by Father José Manuel García del Vallé y Arauho, who worked in the mideighteenth century at the Hospital de la Limpia Concepción y Jesús Nazareno in Mexico City, "founded by Cortés for the cure of syphilis." Since that time, St. Boniface has been viewed as "the patron saint of homosexuals in Mexico," occasionally joined by St. Sebastian and St. Lazarus.[63]

SURVIVALS AND TRANSFORMATIONS

Needless to say, neither Christianity nor the state has been able to eradicate either gender variance or same-sex eroticism in the Americas.

In the Yucatán, for instance, both male gender variance and homoeroticism play a role in the ritual humor of Carnaval. Gay men are linked in Carnaval to the sea, being referred to as both *b'usóob,* "divers," and *haib'aóob,* "crabs." Throughout Latin America and the Caribbean, incidentally, gay men are associated with waterfowl and shellfish; in Colombia, Venezuela, Chile, Cuba, and Puerto Rico, they are nicknamed *patos,* "ducks." Victoria Bricker, a Latin Americanist, anthropologist, and linguist, reports that gay men are referred to as "crabs" because of "their effeminate gestures" which "resemble those of crabs moving along the beach." While the term *cangrejo,* "crab," is currently used by both Mexicans and Cubans to refer to gay men, its use may date to ancient Mesoamerica. This is suggested by the proximate Nahuatl terms *tecuicitli,* "crab," and *tecuilonti,* "sodomite."[64]

To return to Carnaval, one scene in a humorous ritual drama involves the discovery of crabs by the character Juan Carnaval, who shares his discovery with the Judge. The Judge understands *crab* to mean shellfish and asks Juan Carnaval whether he found them in the sea. But Juan Carnaval takes *crab* to mean homosexual and "replies that he found them in Hidalgo Park, a park in Mérida frequented by homosexuals." According to Bricker, while the main theme of the fiesta is the Inquisition, "a subordinate humorous theme is sexual deviant behavior, performed by female impersonators."[65]

Similar examples are found in Mayan rituals in southern and central Belize, where the *coati* figure "wears women's clothing, as do some of the dancers in the

Deer Dance." One of the figures participating in the Yaqui or Mayo Deer Dance of Mexico also speaks to the ancient association of male gender variance and shamanism. This male dancer is naked to the waist, wears a woman's shawl and a deer pelt around his hips, and is crowned with a small deer head with antlers.[66]

The *cihuayollo* male of ancient Mesoamerica seems to have survived or to have been reborn in the Zapotec town of Juchitán. Years ago, when Zapotecs were asked about the gender-variant, men-loving men living among them, they replied, "What can we do; he was born that way; he is like God made him. . . . It is a thing of the blood." In Juchitán, where "lewd, stately, and powerful" women embrace each other, drink beer, and "laugh loud and hard," a number of men "put on dresses, do the chores, and carry water." Here in Juchitán, gay men "are accepted. . . . They're allowed in the markets where [heterosexual, traditionally masculine] men can't go." What is more, the gay men of Juchitán sell flowers, a profession evoking images of Xochiquetzal and Xochipilli. The linkage of gender and sexual variance to crabs may have also survived in Juchitán, where gay men wear necklaces of crabshells.[67]

For many Mexican and Mexican American gay men, as well as other Latin American and non-Hispanic gay men, the Virgin Mary, especially as the Virgin of Guadalupe, plays an important role in spiritual life, as she does in the lives of women. These men often dedicate altars in their homes to the Virgin of Guadalupe. She is for them a symbol of compassion and healing in the midst of a hostile and illness-plagued society. Some of the Mexican American gay men to whom I have spoken concerning the Virgin are Catholics who regard her as the Mother of God; others see her as the Christian form of various goddesses of ancient Mesoamerica, including Tonantzin, Coatlique, and Xochiquetzal.

During the past decade, in American cities with large Hispanic or Latino populations, linkages of gender variance, same-sex eroticism, and reverence of the feminine have resonated in celebrations on the Día de los Muertos held in gay bars, art centers, homes, and in the streets in honor of those who have died of HIV- or AIDS-related illnesses. Altars laden with marigolds, sugar skulls, skeleton breads, and photographs are offered to the dead and to the Virgin or the goddess Xochiquetzal. These associations of gender variance, same-sex eroticism, and spiritual practice resonate in Mexican and Mexican American folk rituals thought to relieve the suffering of individuals with HIV or AIDS.

When I was visiting my mother in San Antonio in 1986, I asked an elderly woman, a *curandera,* working in an herb shop, or *hierberia,* what one might do for a loved one suffering from AIDS-related illnesses. While she did not suggest that ritual alone might heal AIDS, she did share with me a ritual believed to ease the suffering of people with AIDS:

> You will need a statue of St. Lazarus, two tiny *muletas* (gold-plated crutches), a *novena* (here, a yellow candle in a tall glass) with a picture of Lazarus on it, and bottle of Lazarus Wash.
>
> When you get home, light the candle in honor of Lazarus and place it in front of the statue. Bathe the statue, the crutches, and if possible, the body of the sick one with the Wash.

You should carry one of the crutches with you and meditate on it. The other one you should place in a flower arrangement given to the patient or, if that isn't possible, in the shrubs of the hospital yard.

Then you must pray to St. Lazarus to heal your loved one.[68]

In a jewel-like, as yet unpublished essay, "Born Under the Sign of the Flower," Chicana lesbian writer Gloria Anzaldúa explores the relationship of lesbian and gay Mexican Americans living at the end of the twentieth century to the gender-variant, homoerotically inclined Mesoamericans of antiquity. Having lost a number of gay male friends to AIDS-related illnesses in recent years, she writes in a passage focusing on HIV/AIDS, "If I were dying of AIDS, what words would I need to see me on my way, what rituals would speed me safely on? We need a Gay Book of the Dead." Inspired by Aztec poetry, she sings to a dying friend of the *mariposa*-inhabited paradise of Xochiquetzal:

On your way   On your way
Your flesh is the darkness of flowers
You will die, yet you will live on.
Tender tassel of corn,
I want to see you thicken with life.

. . . .

you will be born in the house
of Tamoanchan
on your way   on your way
flesh on your way   darkness
Here death is born among flowers
and the dead shall take root in the sky[69]

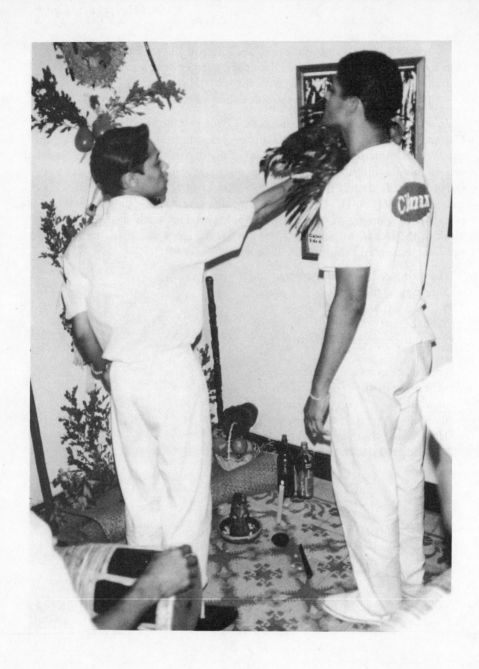

Priest of Santería blesses a gay male practitioner, Havana, 1992.

Chapter
11

Children of the Rainbow

Son of Oxum, Logunedé,
Darling of Oxum, Logunedé, edé, edé
So very beautiful

from "Logunedé," a song by Gilberto Gil[1]

*I*n a conversation in 1981 with our friend Eduardo Mejía, Chicana lesbian-feminist theorist and writer Gloria Anzaldúa asked him if he felt there was any difference between a gay man who follows a spiritual path and one who does not. He responded, "I find the one who does not a very bland person. He goes to work [and runs] around buying things. The spiritual gay man doesn't want to live like that. He's closer to the earth, to nature."[2] ¶ Eduardo's own spiritual tradition was Santería, a branch of the Yoruba religion of West Africa, which is one of the most maligned of all religions, viciously attacked in exploitational and racist films such as *The Believers*. ¶ When Eduardo's mother was pregnant with him, she was visited by the *orishá* (basically translated as "deity") Yemayá, who told her that she, Yemayá, had chosen to become Eduardo's spiritual mother. Because Eduardo's spiritual mother was to be a female rather than a male *orishá*, his mother believed that her son might be or become gay. Eduardo recalled that as a child growing up in Puerto Rico, many practitioners of Santería and Espiritualismo, a related tradition, visited his mother's house. A number of these practitioners were gay men and lesbian women. "All of them picked up on my homosexuality," he remembered, "and when I grew older, and they were certain I was gay, they . . . would encourage me to go into the religion. A lesbian friend said to me, 'You know, we gay people are very intuitive. We have a lot of power. You should go into it.'"[3]

In this chapter, we will explore the relationship of homoeroticism, gender variance, and the sacred to the Yoruba religion, primarily as it is practiced in the Americas.

THE YORUBA RELIGION

The Yoruba religion has its roots in Nigeria. It has been practiced for many centuries, although its exact date of origin is unknown. It is connected to the religion of Dahomey (now Benin), and some scholars have further suggested associations with the ancient religions of Egypt and Phoenicia. The practice of the Yoruba and other African religions in the New World began in the early sixteenth century, with the arrival of the slaves. Many of the twelve million Africans who arrived in the Americas between the early sixteenth and the midnineteenth centuries were of Yoruba ancestry. In Brazil, the Yoruba came to be known as the Nagô; in Cuba, as the Lucumí. While they were forced to outwardly adopt Christianity, many continued to worship their gods, albeit in the guise of Catholic saints, and to hold their ancient celebrations, albeit on the feast days of the saints.

The Yoruba religion is known by various names including [I]sin Orishá, roughly translated as "the way of the *Orishá.*" The religion has many branches. The development of these branches, especially in the Americas, has depended upon which other indigenous religions it has come into contact with as well as upon the degree of influence exerted by Christianity—and, to a lesser extent, Islam—and other spiritual traditions and metaphysical systems, including ritual magic and spiritualism.

In Brazil, the Yoruba religion is generally known as Candomblé. Brazilian branches include: Candomblé proper; Candomblé Caboclo; Macumba; Umbanda; Batuque; and Quimbanda. In Cuba, Puerto Rico, and the United States (especially in New York City, Miami, Oakland, San Francisco, and Los Angeles), the religion is known as Santería, Lucumí, Regla Ocha, or simply as "the religion." Where it has blended with Kongo religion, the tradition of Palo Monté has emerged; this tradition, in turn, is linked to the Secret Society of the Abakúa. The Yoruba religion has also played a role in the development of Vodou(n), the African-based form of Dahomean religion practiced in Haiti, New Orleans, and elsewhere. Likewise, Vodou(n) has influenced the Yoruba religion. This confluence of African-based religions can be seen, for example, in the writings of Luisah Teish, a Lucumí priestess raised in New Orleans and currently living in Oakland.

In the Yoruba religion, which might best be described as a henotheistic religion, there exists a Supreme Being, Olodumaré, from whom all other *orishá* emanate. Practitioners hold that the *orishá,* as well as ancestors, provide spiritual guidance and imbue those who believe with spiritual energy, called *ashé (aché, axé).* Practitioners often experience contact with the *orishá* by way of altered states of consciousness achieved through drumming, chanting, dancing, and other techniques of ecstasy. Devotees learn of the future, and also what the *orishá* require of them, during these states and by consulting the *orishá* through divination. Divinatory tools include palm nuts, cowrie shells, and pieces of coconut. Practitioners believe that offerings and sacrifices must be made to the *orishá* in order to honor and appease them and in order to obtain their blessings.

The Yoruba religion has a hierarchical priesthood. Names referring to priests and priestesses include: *babalawo; babalaô; babalorishá; iyalorishá; pai de santo; mae de santo; santero; santera.* Each person—including nonpractitioners—is believed to be the spiritual "son" or "daughter" of a "father" and "mother" *orishá.* One of these is generally claimed to predominate, to be the "owner of the head." Identity of one's spiritual parents is typically revealed or confirmed in divinatory consultations.[4]

THE PRESENCE OF GENDER-VARIANT, HOMOSEXUAL, AND BISEXUAL PRACTITIONERS

Generally speaking, the Yoruba religion, primarily as practiced in the Americas, has carved out a niche for gender-variant persons and persons engaging in same-sex eroticism. In the religion, more than twenty-five terms, most of African origin, are used to describe such persons. Among those terms used to describe males who are considered gender variant and/or who engage in homoeroticism are:

adê	*akenkén*	*obiniteyo*
adefantô	*asokobo*	*obini-toyo*
adô	*baniyé*	*obodi*
adodi	*ba-yé*	*oko terelago*
adofiró	*diánkune*	*okobo*
afofô	*elenumeyi*	*okunidini*
agbere	*erón kibá*	*wassicúndi*

Of these, three are especially noteworthy: *adofiró* is roughly translated as "the one who has sex out of place"; *adefantô* is translated as "scattering seed from a lofty place"; and *afofo* is defined as "to float in space." Together, these terms suggest a marginal or marginalized person with a rather ethereal character.

Terms for gender-variant and/or bisexual or lesbian women include: *alabua; alakuata; monokó; obinílogun; oremi;* and *panchagayé (panchagárra),* the last term also referring to a prostitute.[5]

In *El Monte,* the classic work on Santería, Lydia Cabrera points out that many practitioners of the Lucumí branch of the religion are homosexually oriented.[6] Seth and Ruth Leacock, in their study of Batuque, a Brazilian branch of the religion, report that almost one-third of all its male practitioners are either homosexual or alleged to be so. They note, "There was often unanimity among our informants . . . that some male mediums lived with other men with whom they had sexual relations."[7] Anthropologists including Ruth Landes, René Ribeiro, and Peter Fry, and writers including Hubert Fichte and João Trevisan have documented the widespread presence of homosexual, bisexual, and gender-variant practitioners in Candomblé.[8]

ORISHÁ AS PATRONS OF HOMOSEXUAL, BISEXUAL, AND GENDER-VARIANT PERSONS

Before proceeding with our discussion of the participation of homosexual (gay, lesbian), bisexual, and gender-variant persons in the religion, I would like to explore a comment made by Brazilian actor and gay activist João Ferreira. According to Ferreira, the *orishá* in general, and certain of them in particular, "defend their sons and daughters against . . . sexual prejudice."[9]

Orishá who are considered patrons of such persons include: Obatalá; Oshún; Yemayá; Olokun; Yewá; Oyá; Inlé; Logunedé; Oshumaré; and Orúnmila. *Orishá* who demonstrate conflicting attitudes toward such persons include Shangó and Ogún. An *orishá* who has recently become associated with HIV/AIDS and thus also with gay and bisexual men is Babaluayé. A specifically Brazilian (and now also North American) *orishá* who is associated with gender-variant, homosexual, and bisexual males is Pomba Gira.

OBATALÁ (OXALÁ, OLOFÍ)

In the Yoruba pantheon, Obatalá is the demiurge, lawgiver, and peacemaker. Obatalá is commonly depicted as an androgynous being having long white hair and dressed in white garments. Obatalá is generally identified with that aspect of the Virgin Mary known as Our Lady of Mercy.

According to one *pataki* or myth, Obatalá is believed to be androgynous. In order to bring about human reproduction, he-she divides him-herself into a male-female pair, Oddudúa and Yemmú. As the original androgyne, he-she is called Oddúaremu or (I)Yekú-(I)Yekú, and is variously syncretized with St. Anne, La Purisima Concepción (Mary of the Immaculate Conception), and la Santisima Trinidad (the Holy Trinity).

It is this aspect or "road" (*camino*) of Obatalá, Oddúaremu, that has been linked by some scholars to both gender variance and homoeroticism. As Oddúaremu, the *orishá* is believed to be an *adodi,* a homosexual male. As such, he is said to have fallen in love with another *adodi*, with whom he dwells in the shade of a cotton plant.[10]

OSHÚN (OCHÚN, OXUM)

Oshún, mentioned in the song "Logunedé" by Gilberto Gil quoted above, is the *orishá* of rivers and lakes, sensuality, and the fine arts. Christianized as Our Lady of Caridad del Cobré, her counterpart in Vodou(n) is Erzulie, patron of prostitutes and gay and gender-variant males. Oshún is also associated with gender-variant and lesbian women in her manifestations as Oshún Yeyé Iponda, Oshún Yeyé Karé, and Oshún Panchagayé (or Panchagárra).[11] Eduardo Mejía shared this with me in a 1986 conversation: "I have heard it said that Oshún is a woman in love with women, a *cachaporra* [*Cachaporra* is Portuguese for "bludgeon" or "cudgel" and is used in Latin American slang for "lesbian" or "dyke."]. There is a story that she and Yemayá love each other."[12] A lesbian daughter of Oshún said this to me: "She has made me aware of all of the realms of sensuality. She finds sensuality in everything. Pansensuality is Oshún's dream."[13]

YEMAYÁ (YEMONJÁ, IEMANJÁ)

Yemayá, identified with Our Lady of Regla, is the *orishá* of the sea and maternal compassion. In one of her aspects, however, she is a sorceress, capable of transforming herself into a man or a mouse. In this aspect, as Yemayá Okutí, she is referred to as an *obiní ologun*, a woman warrior.[14] As Okutí, and as the spouse of the androgynous *orishá* Inlé (see below), she is linked to gender-variant and lesbian women.[15] As Yemayá Olokun, she merges with Olokun, the *orishá* who rules the depths of the sea.

Yemayá's association with homosexuality has not always been—and is not universally—positive. For instance, she is said to have divorced her husband Orúnmila, the god of divination, upon discovering him to be an *adodi*.[16] In our own day, however, her association with homosexuality and male gender variance is generally positive. In *El Monte,* Cabrera relates a story told to her by a Lucumí priest. According to this priest, Yemayá once ventured into the country, or perhaps onto the island, of Laddo. This (is)land was inhabited solely by *adodis*. Yemayá, in spite of this, fell in love with one of the men; the *adodi*, in spite of himself, also fell in love with her. Since that time, she has been viewed as a patron of gay, bisexual, and gender-variant men. In this aspect, she is commonly referred to as Yemayá Oddo, "of the river," indicating her association with Oshún.

In a conversation with a priestess of the religion, she spoke to me of Yemayá's special concern for gay and bisexual men and for persons with HIV/AIDS. "Endless appeals," she said, "should be made to Yemayá. Go to her and speak as a child to its mother. Tell her you did nothing to deserve this [HIV/AIDS] and ask her to wash it away."[17]

OLOKUN

Olokun, mentioned above, is the androgynous ruler of the depths of the sea. He-she is not only androgynous but also a hybrid human-fish (or sea serpent); as such, he-she is linked to both gender and animal transformation. He-she is sometimes depicted as having aquamarine skin and long, flowing, indigo hair. He-she lives in a magnificent palace with his-her intimate companions, mermaids and mermen.

Legend has it that the androgynous Olokun once fell in love with Orisha-Oko, a phallic god of the earth and agriculture. At first Olokun was afraid to tell Orisha-Oko of his-her love. But Oko also loved Olokun. Olokun then became concerned that if their love for each other were made public, they might suffer ridicule. He-she finally confided in Obatalá, who said to Olokun, "Stop worrying. After all, both you and Orisha-Oko are greatly respected by the gods and humankind. What is more, you are the perfect couple, since Oko is the earth and you are the sea."[18]

YEWÁ (YEGGUÁ)

Yewá, identified with Our Lady of Montserrat, is a goddess of death. According to Migene González-Wippler, scholar of Santería, she "feeds on the dead," this feeding referred to as the "dark meal," suggesting a vampiric character.[19] Yewá insists that her priestesses abstain from sexual intercourse with men. This has led to the belief that Yewá is a patron of lesbian women, and certain accounts suggest that lesbian women have numbered among her spiritual daughters.[20] Her relationship to gay, bisexual, and/or gender-variant men has not been established.

OYA (YANSÁ[N], IANSÃ, INHACA)

Oyá, identified with Our Lady of the Candelaria, is a woman warrior, a bringer of tempests, and a guardian of the dead. Anthropologist Roger Bastide has described Oyá as a "queen who vanquishes death," while Macumba priestess Maria-José depicts her as a warrior who dwells "in the sky, armed and helmeted . . . ready to combat injustice."[21] Gary Edwards and John Mason, American theologians of the Yoruba religion, describe her as "the fury of the tempest . . . the sweeping winds of change . . . revolution . . . the destruction of the old society making way for the new."[22]

The anthropologist Ruth Landes, the writer Hubert Fichte, and others have spoken of Oyá as a patron of gender-variant and homoerotically inclined males.

Landes reported in 1940 that a number of male practitioners of Candomblé Caboclo whom she had encountered in Brazil were homosexual and bisexual "votaries of Yansán [Oyá]."[23] Fichte writes, "In Colombia, homosexuals [in the religion] address their prayers to the Afro-American goddess Yansá."[24]

Oyá's association with male gender variance—if not with homosexuality—may be traced to Yorubaland. One exquisitely crafted Yoruba statue depicts Oyá riding on horseback, her skin painted white and her hair dyed indigo. She holds a fan plaque in her right hand and a sacrificial cock, also indigo, in her left. Several figures flank her, among them, a small man who clutches her back and sits on the horse's rump. His hair, according to William Fagg, "is styled in the fashion of a woman," that is to say, his hair has been shaped into the "bell jar" or "beehive" hairdo of the goddess and, like hers, has been dyed indigo. This suggests that the figure may represent a gender-variant male initiate or priest of Oyá.[25]

INLÉ (ERINLÉ)

Inlé, sometimes identified with Ochossí, the *orishá* of hunting, and also with Saint Raphael, is a physician of the Yoruba pantheon. Inlé is also a patron of hunters and fishers as well as, with Orúnmila and Yemayá, an *orishá* of divination.

Once when Inlé was fishing, a beautiful siren or mermaid appeared to him. This figure was Yemayá (or Yemayá-Olokun). Inlé fell in love with the *orishá* at first sight, and the two became lovers. While together, Yemayá taught Inlé the art of divination. When he abandoned her, and she became worried that he might share her secrets with others, she cut out his tongue. Now when Inlé wishes to speak, he must do so through Yemayá.[26]

Inlé is sometimes envisaged as merging with Yemayá. In this androgynous/gynandrous aspect, he-she is known as Inlé Ayayá or as Yemayá Mayéweló (when the feminine "nature" predominates). In this manifestation, Inlé is considered to be the patron of lesbian women, "masculine homosexuals," and gender-variant persons. Cabrera reports that many lesbian women in Regla Ocha "have Inlé for a patron." Cabrera also reports that in prerevolutionary Cuba, there was a society of lesbian daughters of Inlé. For many years, lesbian and gay children of Inlé would gather in Cuba on October 24 to pay homage to the *orishá*. Their festive procession included the lighting of a fish made of straw and filled with firecrackers.[27]

OSANYIN (OS[S]AIN, OSSÃE)

Osanyin, often Christianized as St. Joseph, is the owner of the forest of plants. Because he is a keeper of the knowledge of the medicinal properties of plants, he is portrayed as a powerful healer. Like Tiresias of Greek mythology, this wise healer is depicted as one whose sight and mobility are impaired. His sacred attribute is his *osun*, his staff, which is reminiscent of the shaman's staff, the *sot's marotte*, and the scepter of the Mayan God K. It is made of a twisted branch. In its stylized form the *osun* becomes a rod mounted on a stand, surmounted by a cup to which bells or iron birds are attached and from which a rooster emerges. Through the *osun*, Osanyin protects practitioners against the Sigidi and Ajé, demonic spirits and sorceresses who bring nightmares and sufferings. When a practitioner, typically an herbalist, wishes to use one of the medicines of the forest, he or she must first ask permission from its habitat. Chants or songs concerning the medicinal, restorative, and transformative powers of plants play a special role in the preparation of the *omiero*, a sacred liquid used primarily during initiation ceremonies.[28]

In *The Taste of Blood: Spirit Possession in Brazilian Candomblé*, the postmodern anthropologist Jim Wafer recounts a tale in which Ochossí, the god of hunting, mistakes Osanyin for a woman and consequently rapes him, bringing about Osanyin's death (and perhaps also his rebirth or metamorphosis). Wafer writes,

> The *exus* [demonic spirits] carried this story to the king (Oxalá) [Obatalá] in his castle, but, being tricksters, they inverted the roles. They said that Ossãe [Osanyin] had possessed Oxosse [Ochossí]. Thus there is a Candomblé song in which the king asks Oxosse if he is *odé*, and Oxosse replies that he is as much a man as the king. The punch-line here involves a pun. *Odé* means "hunter," a title conventionally given to Oxosse. . . . But Oxosse hears *adé* . . . used to refer to a man who plays the passive role in relations with other men.[29]

While it is unfortunate that the myth or *pataki* of Osanyin and Ochossí speaks of gender-variant, same-sex eroticism in a veiled and generally negative manner, it does suggest to the practitioner Osanyin's *metá-metá*, or androgynous, character. In his *metá-metá* aspect, representing an *adé* or gender-variant male who engages in homoeroticism, Osanyin appears not as a disabled "leaf-man" but rather as an androgynous figure with female breasts and male genitalia, his male parts covered with leaves.

Wafer suggests that Osanyin, as a *metá-metá orishá* of the forest, is linked in the minds of practitioners to two other *orishá*, Logunedé and Oshumaré. Gender variance and same-sex eroticism, according to Wafer's informants, are especially associated, moreover, with the liminal, or marginal, realm of the forest.[30]

LOGUNEDÉ

Logunedé, identified with St. Michael the Archangel, St. Sebastian, St. Isidro, and St. Expedite, is the son of Inlé or Ochossí and Oshún Yeyé Iponda. As the child of Inlé, patron of lesbian women and "masculine" gay men, and Oshún Yeyé Iponda, a woman warrior, Logunedé is linked to both gender variance and same-sex eroticism. He is believed to spend half of each year as a "male hunter who lives in the forest" and the other half as a "beautiful, vain and honey-tongued nymph who lives in rivers and feeds on fish."

Logunedé's androgynous character is represented in Brazilian branches of the religion in several ways. For instance, he holds the bow and arrow of Inlé-Ochossí and the fan or mirror of Oshún. His colors include indigo, here identified not with Oyá but with Ochossí and masculinity, and yellow-gold, identified with Oshún and femininity. His androgynous nature is also manifested in one of his sacred animals, the seahorse, the male of which carries the developing offspring.[31]

The Brazilian musician Gilberto Gil, allegedly a son of Logunedé, has written a song, partly quoted above, celebrating the *orishá's* androgynous character. In "Gilberto Gil: Praise Singer of the Gods," David Hatfield Sparks writes of this song,

> In this lyric, Gil celebrates the *orixá* as a potent blend of the *astúcia de cacador,* "the artfulness of the hunter," and the *Paciência de pescador,* "the patience of the fisher." As a force depicting both traits simultane-ously, Logunedé becomes a symbol for Gil of androgyny and bisexuality. [Logunedé] is depicted as the beautiful, tender *Mimo de Oxum,* the fondling of his mother, who appears to have come into being primarily to be adored, desired, or embraced. . . . As an openly bisexual musician who seeks to blend the "masculine" and "feminine" elements of his own psyche, it is hardly surprising that Gil has been acknowledged in Candomblé as a *filho* ["son"] *de* Logunedé.[32]

OSHUMARÉ (OXUMARÉ)

Oshumaré is the rainbow-serpent of the Yoruba pantheon, associated with the Vodou(n) deity Damballah Awedo and identified with St. Bartholomew. As a ser-pent, Oshumaré is the ruler of cycles—rain and drought, winter and summer, poverty and wealth. Oshumaré is the god of movement, of action. Occasionally de-picted as a servant of Shangó, Oshumaré's office "consists of taking water from the earth to his [Shangó's] palace in the clouds."[33] As the rainbow, Oshumaré is a bridge linking the various worlds. As St. Bartholomew, Oshumaré is associated with Exú, a sometimes sinister manifestation of Eleggúa, the *orishá* of the crossroads who acts as intercessory between the *orishá* and humankind. In this connection, he is espe-cially invoked by practitioners of Quimbanda, a branch of the religion blending Yoruba and Kongo beliefs and practices and emphasizing sorcery or magic.[34]

As the rainbow, Oshumaré is an androgynous *orishá*, his-her nature repre-sented by the oppositional colors "violet (internal, feminine) and vermilion (ex-ternal, masculine)."[35] As an androgynous deity, Oshumaré, like Logunedé, according to some scholars and practitioners, spends one-half of each year as a hunter and the other as a mermaid or nymph, evoking the above-mentioned *or-ishá,* Inlé, Osanyin, and Logunedé.

Oshumaré is a son of the goddess Nana Burukú, who is thought to be, along with Onilé, one of the eldest female deities of the Yoruba pantheon. He is the brother (or half-brother) of the *orishá* Babaluayé. He is also said to be the *ade* or "crown" of Yemayá. In Umbanda, Oshumaré is an aspect of Oshún; as Oxum Marê, s/he is nicknamed Oxum-of-the-Tides. Anthropologist Esther Pressel notes that in Umbanda, the "bisexual nature of Oxum Marê is emphasized."[36]

As an androgynous deity, Oshumaré is perceived by many worshipers as a patron of gender-variant, homosexual, and bisexual persons. Brazilian priest M. Aparecida explains that when "this saint talks in a man's head, he becomes gay." Thus, in Aparecida's view, to banish a gay person from a Candomblé household, which sometimes happens, is to "kick out the rainbow."[37]

Orúnmila (Ifá)

Orúnmila, identified with St. Francis of Assisi, is the Yoruba god of divination. It is he who controls the Table of Ifá, which reveals "the ultimate destiny of each individual." As mentioned above, Orúnmila is, in one of his manifestations, an *adodi*, a gender-variant male who engages in same-sex eroticism.[38]

Shangó (Changó, Xangô, Hevioso)

Of all the deities of the Yoruba pantheon, Shangó is most often associated with "machismo." As González-Wippler explains, Shangó is an "incorrigible woman-chaser. . . . He is invoked for works of domination, passion."[39]

Some practitioners maintain that Shangó is extremely hostile toward gender-variant, gay, and bisexual males, whom he occasionally punishes with death.[40] I have heard of one gay Cuban "son" of Shangó who is prone to violent outbursts, caused by the god's incessant demanding that his "son" change his ways. The practitioner who told me this believes, however, that Shangó may eventually halt these torments because his love for his "children" outweighs any prejudice he might hold against them.[41] In spite of his macho image, however, Shangó has been linked to homosexuality, bisexuality, and gender variance. In this respect, he is said to have an "effeminate road," in which he dresses and behaves as a sensuous and/or amazonian woman. This includes putting on rouge and braiding his hair in a traditionally feminine style.[42]

Eduardo told me, "Shangó will sometimes appear as a man and sometimes as a woman. Sometimes he will appear on horseback seated in a woman's position. When he comes as a woman, he frequently comes as a lesbian."[43]

Thus it is not surprising that Shangó has blended with the female St. Barbara. Of course, St. Barbara herself is considered gender variant. Reminiscent of Atargatis and Cybele, she is depicted as crowned with a tower and as holding a sword.

What is more, in Nigeria, Shangó, like Oyá, has a gender-variant male servant. His name is Iwèfà; he is a eunuch and, according to Nigerian playwright Duro Ladipo, Shangó's "best praise-singer."[44]

Scholar of religions Benjamin G. Ray tells us that some of Shangó's male devotees emulate the gender-variant aspect of the god by dressing in women's clothes and braiding their hair in feminine style.[45]

Shangó's most important tool is his double ax. This ax often takes the form of a staff crowned by a "woman with a double-edged axe . . . balanced upon her head." Called the *edun ara*, it holds the power to "create or destroy."[46] It is note-worthy that in ancient Crete, the double ax was a sacred attribute of the Minoan goddess, its form evoking that of the butterfly; and that in twentieth-century America and elsewhere, the double ax became a symbol of the lesbian-feminist liberation movement. In agreement with Hubert Fichte, João Ferreira reports that in Brazil, the double ax of Shangó has become "a symbol of the struggle for liber-ation among Black homosexuals."[47]

OGÚN (OGUM)

Ogún, identified with St. George, St. Anthony, and John the Baptist, has been described by priestess Maria-José as a "brave young god . . . full of fire . . . pure of body and spirit." Like Ares or Mars, Ogún is a god of war; like Hephaestus or Vul-can, he is a god of metallurgy. He is a patron of steelworkers, ironworkers, farm-ers, hairstylists, and taxi drivers. It is Ogún who teaches people to combat injustice.[48]

Eduardo told me in 1986, "Ogún doesn't like gays very much. Still, some of his *hijos* [sons] are *bugarones* ["buggers"; here, men who are married to women but who also have male lovers]."[49]

In one of his Brazilian manifestations, however, as Ogum Xoroquê, an aspect in which Ogún merges with Exú, this male-male being is a patron of, surpris-ingly, lesbian women. João Trevisan asserts that when Ogum Xoroquê "falls on the head" of [decides to parent] or possesses a female practitioner, she will be "revealed as gay."[50] Unfortunately, I have not learned as yet whether Ogum Xoroquê is also associated with gay, bisexual, or gender-variant male practi-tioners.

BABALUAYÉ (OBALUAYÉ, OMOLU, SHAPANNA, SOPANNA)

Babaluayé, identified with the Catholic saints Lazarus, Roch, and Sebastian, is in general the *orishá* of life-threatening illnesses, including smallpox, cancer, and HIV/AIDS. Like Osanyin, he is also depicted as a powerful healer.

Thought to have emerged from the swamps, Babaluayé, like Oshumaré, is a son of the goddess Nana Burukú. Tradition has it that he was once very licentious. The *orishá* Olofí (related to Obatalá and sometimes identified with Christ) was offended by his excesses and punished him with venereal disease. Oshún found him in great pain and healed him with her magical honey. She then went to Olofí and cried, "How dare you punish Babaluayé like this when you desire the very same thing!"[51]

Babaluayé is depicted as a man whose skin is covered with lesions. He walks with a cane, and dogs lick his wounds. He wears a cape of purple velvet and burlap.

As mentioned above, Babaluayé is sometimes identified with St. Sebastian. Since the Renaissance, if not before, Sebastian has been linked to both epidemics (or pandemics) and homosexuality. Artists ranging from Il Sodoma to Claude Debussy, Tennessee Williams, Yukio Mishima, and Derek Jarman have depicted Sebastian as the patron saint of men engaging in same-sex eroticism. In Latin America, Sebastian is even now envisaged as a healer of life-threatening illnesses and a patron of gay and bisexual men. In a scene from *The House of the Spirits*, novelist Isabel Allende portrays Sebastian as a certain "church's patron saint [his] body twisted in the most indecent posture, pierced by arrows, and dripping with blood and tears like a suffering homosexual."[52]

Babaluayé, however, is most frequently identified with St. Lazarus. In recent years, Babaluayé/St. Lazarus, like Yemayá/Our Lady of Regla, has become recognized by many practitioners as an *orishá*/saint to be invoked in prayer for those with HIV/AIDS. Describing a Cuban sanatorium in which persons with HIV/AIDS were living fairly comfortably in the mid-1980s, Mark Kurlansky reports in *A Continent of Islands* that by 1986, persons with AIDS were being allowed to make brief pilgrimages to the shrine of St. Lazarus/Babaluayé, where they would pray to be healed.[53]

Eduardo told me, "My mother has told me to pray to Saint Lazarus [concerning HIV/AIDS],"[54] and a priestess of the religion shared with me a ritual, reminiscent of that given to me by the Mexican-American *curandera* (in Chapter 10), meant to ease the suffering associated with AIDS. I will partially recount it here:

> Get an image of St. Lazarus. Make a garment for him out of purple cloth and some old brown burlap. Wipe your body (or that of the person with HIV/AIDS) with the cloth and then drape it around the statue. The statue should be set on a plate, with different kinds of beans surrounding it. Then you should rub any lesions on your (his/her) body with unpeeled purple onions. No more than six onions. Then place the onions in a circle around the plate. Place a seven-day, deep purple candle near the statue and the plate. Remember not to use any water in your ritual, as Babaluayé does not like water. Every day at sunrise and sunset, meditate upon the statue and the candle and pray to Babaluayé, asking him to take your pain upon himself. Those onions should sit there until they absolutely rot. To end the ritual, take the cloak of the statue. Keep the statue, but go to a riverbank and bury the beans and onions. Should one of the onions begin to grow, that's a good sign.[55]

POMBA GIRA

Pomba Gira, as mentioned above, is a Brazilian *orishá*, the spouse or female aspect of Exú, an aspect of Elleggúa. She is primarily associated with sexuality. She dresses in red, wears heavy makeup, strong perfume, and costume jewelry. She haunts crossroads and nightclubs. At the crossroads, she is offered sacrifices of dresses, watches, rings, champagne, beer, cigarettes, goat, chicken, apples, and red roses.[56] While she has a Brazilian rather than a Nigerian origin, her worship has spread to the United States, where she is revered by Cuban Americans, African Americans, and Mexican Americans, as well as Brazilian Americans. I have seen her image in *botanicas*—shops where ritual implements, necklaces, candles, herbs, statues, and other items are sold—in Los Angeles, San Francisco, and New Orleans. I have also seen a statue of her in a corner store on Sunset Boulevard in Los Angeles; around the statue, customers had placed offerings of cigarettes, tiny bottles of wine and perfume, gum, candy, lottery tickets, and coins. In Vodou(n), as practiced in New Orleans, Pomba Gira is identified with Erzulie Flambeau, a goddess who enjoys seducing men so she can then "treat them like dirt."[57] While I am not aware that she has been identified with any Catholic saint, it appears that she has become identified in some circles with Asmodeus, a demonic spirit of European-based ritual magic.[58]

Pomba Gira can be very shocking and cruel, telling "men the truth in the very crudest terms and in a very loud voice," thus revealing in public their "vices and flaws."[59] In the American and other gay subcultures, this action has been a function of drag queens, referred to in the 1970s as "reading someone's beads."

Pomba Gira, however, can be very helpful to those who call on her, especially when devotees wish to attract a lover, patch up a relationship, or wreck another's marriage. When Candomblé priest M. Aparecida "like[s] a man's face," he offers Pomba Gira a bottle of beer, a red rose, a pack of cigarettes, and "a pork chop, cooked in very hot palm oil and Rio flour and lettuce."[60]

According to Aparecida, Pomba Gira is a patron of gender-variant and homosexual men because she is "unisex." By *unisex,* Aparecida seems to refer here to effeminate males and perhaps even more specifically to drag queens, linking their behavior to that of sexually liberated women and prostitutes, and seeing all of these persons as reflecting or embodying the personality of Pomba Gira.[61]

THE ROLE OF DESTINY

Knowledge of the practitioner's spiritual parent(s), as mentioned above, is typically gained through divinatory consultations. Although various configurations of divinatory objects may indicate gender variance, homosexuality, and other such matters, these configurations are not usually discussed in the literature available to the noninitiate.

Hubert Fichte, however, mentions one oracle reached via cowrie shell divination that may indicate homosexuality and perhaps also gender variance. This oracular configuration or *odu* is referred to as *odi* or as "seven cowries up."[62] In the available literature, however, homosexuality and gender variance are not usually listed as possible manifestations of this oracle. Instead, one is cryptically told that if the individual receiving *odi* is male, he may have "problems with his testicles."[63] According to Fichte, some diviners consider *odi* to be a negative configuration. Others, however, simply recognize it as an oracle linked to the expression of gender-variant and homoerotic behavior. *Odi* is especially influenced by Yemayá, in part as the "owner" of the number seven and spouse of the *adodi* (homosexual) Orúnmila, and by Oshún.[64] It is also influenced by the *àbíkú*, the spirits of children "who are born to die." An *àbíkú*, according to anthropologist W. R. Bascom, is a soul that "does not want to remain long on earth, preferring life in heaven or wishing only to travel back and forth between heaven and earth."[65] Bascom points out that the *orishá* Oshumaré is likened to an *àbíkú*: "Rainbow [Oshumaré] returns to heaven the same day he comes to earth, like an *àbíkú*."[66] This piece of information suggests that a complex set of associations may link the *orishá* Yemayá, Oshún, and Oshumaré to: the *àbíkú*; transitoriness; the ability to travel between or among the worlds or to function as an intercessor; a yearning for death or transcendence; gender variance; and homoeroticism.

In addition to the oracle sign of *odi,* many practitioners agree that "a man is destined to be gay if a goddess takes up residence in his body," that is, if a female deity possesses him or chooses to become his spiritual parent.[67] M. Aparecida relates that when it was discovered that he was a "child" of Oxum (Oshún), several priests tried to replace Oshún with Shangó so that Aparecida would not "become a sissy." The goddess, however, had no intention of leaving, nor did Aparecida wish her to do so. Stay she did.[68]

It should be pointed out, however, that not all males considered gender variant or engaging in same-sex eroticism have female *orishá* as primary parents; many, however, do.

GENDER-VARIANT, HOMOSEXUAL, AND BISEXUAL PRACTITIONERS

Many practitioners of the Yoruba religion are considered gender variant, and many also engage in same-sex eroticism, though it is true that some restrictions are placed upon gay male practitioners. They may not, customarily, play the sacred *batá* drums during rituals, although they may play them in non-ritual settings. This appears due to the fact that Shangó is the "owner" of the drums, and the men who play them must reflect his "macho" aspect. Gay men are also restricted from becoming *babalawos,* the highest category of priest in the Yoruba-based traditions—a restriction that also still generally applies to women. Nevertheless, the Yoruba-based religions, in most respects, embrace gay, bisexual, and gender-variant individuals. A gay Cuban santero, Lazaro, told North American traveler Bill Strubbe in 1992, "Because all people are created by God, all are equal and accepted into Yoruba. . . . Some gays quit the Catholic Church because it's homophobic and there is no place for them. Some gays recognize homosexuality in themselves before they come into Santería, while some open to it after they join."[69]

Eduardo told me in 1986 that in Dorado, Puerto Rico, many male practitioners of Santería are either *bugarones,* married men who also have male lovers, and *locas,* "queens." He had earlier informed Anzaldúa that many Puerto Rican and Cuban immigrant practitioners of Santería are gay or bisexual. "In New York," he said to her, "you find a lot of Cuban and Puerto Rican gays who belong to *temp-los*," houses of worship. "They hang out with nothing but lesbians and *locas*. They have a gay *templo*."[70]

Eduardo, as mentioned above, was familiar with the Yoruba religion, and more specifically with Santería and Espiritualismo, from early childhood. As a teenager, he was encouraged to become a practitioner.

At sixteen, he was formally acknowledged as a son of Yemayá. Shortly there-after, he was invited to attend an initiation ceremony for a friend. He described part of the ceremony as follows:

> He was a *hijo* [son] of Shangó. He had invited a lot of guys who were *hijos* of Oshún. [As a child of Yemayá,] I was dressed all in white, my head cov-ered in blue, with blue ribbons around my ankles and wrists, and all my beads.
>
> When I walked in, he said, "This is going to be a good feast!" The sacri-fices were made, the prayers were said, and then it was time to dance with the gods.
>
> We sang a song to Yemayá and one to Liberato, a former slave. Then my friend fell into a trance. He took me on his back. He was dancing with me on his back. He spun me around and around. Everyone made a ring around us. He finally put me down and touched his shoulders to my shoulders.
>
> He liked me very much. I was a *hijo* of Yemayá, and he was a *hijo* of Shangó. Yemayá is one of Shangó's mistresses. He came to me as husband would come to a wife.[71]

The Yoruba religion became for Eduardo a way of life. Each morning, he told me, he would thank Yemayá for all that she had given him. Throughout the day, he would ask himself, "How would Yemayá react in this situation?" During the course of the day, he would repeat the affirmation "All day long the gods protect me, all day long they soothe me." In the evening, he would perform divination not so much to foretell the future as to discover the deep meaning of that day. Be-fore going to bed, he would pray to Yemayá, asking her to "fold her arms about me as I sleep."[72]

In the religion, male practitioners as a whole have tended to be divided—espe-cially in Brazil, where relatively narrow definitions of gender identity and role are found—into camps of *homem,* or "real men," and what might be referred to as non-*homem.* Frequently, heterosexual and bisexual male practitioners have been lumped together as *homem,* while homosexual or gay male practitioners have been categorized as *adé.* It appears that while a heterosexual or bisexual male's *homem* status may be tempered by having a female *orishá* as a primary parent or by being temporarily possessed by a female *orishá,* causing that man to exhibit "feminine" behavior and/or to dress in feminine attire, his *homem* status is not thereby forfeited.

There is disagreement as to whether or not homosexual males can be consid-ered *homem.* Some practitioners and scholars have suggested that if a homosexual male generally conforms to a traditional male role and/or is the son of a male *orishá*, that male may be given *homem* status. Most homosexual male practitioners, however, are categorized as *adé*, whether or not they exhibit traditionally masculine behavior. Thus, the category *adé* is similar to "homosexual" or "gay." *Adé* focuses primarily on sexual object choice; that is, a man is *adé* if he desires what heterosexual women desire, regardless of whether he behaves in a "masculine" or an "effeminate" manner. *Adé*, however, also stresses that this male who desires other males also performs a spiritual function or fulfills a sacred role. Thus *adé* suggests a homosexual spiritual figure who may or may not behave in a gender-variant manner. It would seem, however, that a majority of *adé* practitioners at least occasionally, if not frequently, perform behaviors regarded as gender variant.

The term *bicha* ("bitch") is used by Peter Fry in his article "Male Homosexuality and Spirit Possession in Brazil" to describe male practitioners who engage in same-sex eroticism, frequently assuming the "receptive" role, and who behave in a gender-variant manner. While the term *bicha* is rejected by most of the practitioners with whom I have spoken, it may be useful in distinguishing a subgroup of *adé* practitioners who exhibit "effeminate" behavior and who are frequently, although not always, the children of female *orishá*. Among *adé* practitioners, the *bichas* most closely resemble the *berdaches* of Native American tribes and the gender-variant priests of the goddess of antiquity (such as the *galli* of Cybele).[73]

Among twenty-one practitioners of Candomblé studied by Maria Lina Leão Teixeira (eight women and thirteen men), five of the men were *adé* and one of the women was *monokó* or lesbian. In this case, the males termed *adé* all appear to have been homosexual. Not all, however, could be properly termed *bichas*. Among the *adé* males, ages ranged from twenty-seven to forty-two years old; professions ranged from telephone operator to Navy officer. All but one identified their race as mulatto. Of the five, two were priests, *pais de santo*. Three had female and two had male *orishá* as primary parents. Bene and Inacio were sons of Oxum (Oshún), while Lauro was a son of Iansã (Oyá). Gustavo was a son of Oxossí (Ochossí), while Honorio was a son of Obaluayé (Babaluayé). Tereza, the *monokó* or lesbian practitioner, a fifty-year-old black female, was a daughter of Xangô (Shangó). We have seen that all of these *orishá* are either directly or indirectly associated with same-sex eroticism and/or gender variance.[74]

Like other Yoruba-based traditions, Candomblé may appeal to gender-variant, homosexual/lesbian, and bisexual persons because we discover within it deities who will defend us and whose sacred tales mirror our own. The religion may also hold an appeal because it allows for, indeed often demands, the expression of behavior regarded as gender variant. Temples of the religion may also serve as sanctuaries for those who have been forced out of their homes by intolerant family members. Temples may also serve as meeting places for those seeking community among like-minded individuals.[75]

Anthropologist Jim Wafer describes a gay practitioner of Candomblé named Taís. His portrait of Taís is noteworthy because it speaks to the roles that deities and spirits play in the manifestation of gender-variant behavior. Taís, born in Salvador, was initiated into Candomblé at fourteen. Like many other gay practitioners of Yoruba-based religions, Taís is a "child" of Oyá/Iansã.

In Candomblé, Oyá is served by various *exúas*, or female spirits. Two of these, Sete Saia and Corquisa, often struggle to possess Taís. Both spirits are coquettish and surly, and when Taís is possessed by either, he becomes extremely seductive and rude, participating in a kind of verbal abuse linked to truth-telling, called "reading someone's beads" in the United States and *baixa* in Brazil. In a way, this behavior seems more like that of Pomba Gira than of Oyá. It is noteworthy that the two *exúa* relate differently to Taís's homosexuality. While Sete Saia disapproves of it, calling him a *viado* ("faggot"), Corquisa accepts his way of life. Perhaps this is because Corquisa views herself as more sophisticated than Sete Saia. Wafer writes, "She (Corquisa) too called him *meu viado* ("my faggot"), but said that she adored him."[76]

As mentioned above, Peter Fry has focused on the *bicha* practitioners of Candomblé. *Bichas,* while evoking fear and hostility in some practitioners, tend to be appreciated and respected because they are thought to be "more artistic" than other practitioners, "better equipped to organize and participate in ritual." They are—somewhat stereotypically—believed to be highly accomplished dancers, interior decorators, chefs, and costume designers, all of these professions playing key roles in the creation of a festive rite.[77]

This statement was corroborated by Eduardo, who told me, "A lot of people prefer going to ceremonies that are held by gay *santeros* because there's more space, more sincerity, more teamwork. *Bembés* [ritual feasts] held by gay *santeros* are wild, very Dionysian."[78]

What is more, Fry explains that supernatural power is often attributed to the *bichas* because, in deviating from prescribed gender and sexual roles, they are envisioned as inhabiting quasi-mystical "regions of the cosmos which are defined as outside society."[79] This mystical difference between gender-variant, homosexual practitioners and others is manifested in a ritual that, I am told, takes place in São Paulo. In this rite, "heterosexual men, who represent the sunrise, stand on one side; heterosexual women, who represent the moonrise, stand on the other; and gay people [of both sexes], representing the twilight, stand in the middle."[80] This ritual gives expression to the belief that gender-variant gay persons, in Fry's terminology, *bichas* and their female equivalents, may constitute an alternate gender role.

The *bichas* of Brazil seem remarkably similar to the drag queen practitioners of New York City described by Mejía and Vigo. Eduardo told Anzaldúa, "You visit any Hispanic drag queen's apartment and what do you see—A GRAND ALTAR!" José Vigo echoed, "Yes, that is a tradition. When you visit a drag queen, he will most likely have an altar and will be practicing."[81]

Some priests and practitioners insist that drag has nothing whatsoever to do with the religion—an opinion that is immediately challenged by the wearing of feminine attire by male sons of feminine *orishá*—and that drag queens are more representative of "Western decadence" than of the Yoruba religion. Others feel strongly that drag is intimately linked to spiritual practice. Eduardo said to me, "My friend dresses in drag, in red and white female garments, because Shangó wants him to dress this way." As for Eduardo himself, he explained that he often wore a mixture of blue and white feminine and masculine garments, including "bracelets, a scarf, and a flower in [his] hair because Yemayá [wished] it."[82]

In their conversation with Anzaldúa, José and Eduardo agreed that drag practitioners are considered especially skilled in the divinatory and magical arts. Said José, "In New York, a lot of transvestites read the *caracolés* [cowries]." He continued, "In the Bronx, a lot of them get the reputation of knowing how to work the *obra* [here, magic associated with Santería]."[83]

Eduardo recalled when the brother of a neighbor woman arrived in New York from Puerto Rico:

> He was a teacher that was having a hard time finding a job. The first thing he asked was, "Where's the *templo?*" She [the neighbor] has an uncle who's a drag queen. So he [the teacher] went to this drag queen "aunt" [the uncle] and said, "I need a husband. I need some one to take care of me for awhile."

The "aunt"/uncle, who belonged to "one of those *templos* that are all homosexual and lesbian," performed a *trabajo* ("work," a spell) for his nephew; not long after, the nephew had a new job and a lover.[84]

José noted that, due to their reputation as skilled diviners and powerful magicians, drag practitioners often elicit respect from otherwise homophobic, effemiphobic youths: "Straight boys get the idea that they have to 'watch it' because when they visit the houses of gays, they find in one closet or another an altar. These boys become afraid of their power."[85]

MANY GAY, BISEXUAL, and gender-variant artists of various kinds have been practitioners of or deeply influenced by the Yoruba religion. The Brazilian musician Gilberto Gil has already been mentioned. One also thinks of two other popular Brazilian musicians, Caetano Veloso, a son of Oxossí (Ochossí), and the "genderfuck" performer Ney Matogrosso, a son of Oxumarê (Oshumaré).[86]

One also thinks of the African American musician Blackberri and the Yoruba-British photographer Rotimi Fani-Kayode. Blackberri, who was initiated into the religion in 1984 by a "gay priest and a bisexual priestess," writes, of this experience, "I have sought out my ancient roots and I am proud of my discovery. *Mo fidé fun Orishá Aché.*"[87]

Rotimi Fani-Kayode, frequently compared with Robert Mapplethorpe—whose work, perhaps because he was a white American male and because his work caused an uproar among fundamentalists and reactionary forces within the National Endowment for the Arts, is more widely known—focused in his photography on black, often Yoruba, males, typically nude or in traditional attire.

Rotimi was born in Nigeria and given an "*oriki* or praise-name . . . [meaning] 'Child of Ife.'" His family, film theorist Mark A. Reid tells us, "hails from Ife, the spiritual center of the Yoruba people, and serve as keepers of the shrine of Yoruba deities and priests of Ife." Reid describes Rotimi's work as informed by his identifications with the pan-African and gay movements as well as his profound respect for the Yoruba religion and its myths.[88]

Unfortunately, due to current, Western-influenced homophobic attitudes found among Nigerians, Rotimi decided against exhibiting his work in his homeland, thus adding to a sense of alienation he already felt as a black African educated and living in England. Rotimi, who died in 1989, once said, "If I ever manage to get an exhibition in, say, Lagos, I suspect riots would break out. I would certainly be charged with being a purveyor of corrupt and decadent Western values." He also suspected, however, that Nigerian practitioners of the Yoruba religion dwelling in rural communities might more readily accept his work, recognizing "my smallpox Gods [Babaluayé and perhaps others], my transsexual priests, my images of desirable Black men in a state of sexual frenzy, or the tranquility of communion with the spirit world."[89]

A NUMBER OF writers and practitioners have also spoken of the noticeable presence of gender-variant, homosexual, and bisexual priests and diviners in the Yoruba religion.

In his monumental study of cowrie shell divination, William Bascom describes a diviner, Salako, who was born in Nigeria around 1880. As an infant, Salako was taken to a priest who "confirmed that he belonged to Orishalá [a manifestation of Obatalá]" and that Yemayá was also to play an important role in his life. Salako was initiated in 1895 and by 1926 had become chief diviner of the ruler Oyo. When Bascom met Salako in 1951, when the latter was about seventy, he described him in terms indicating gender variance: he was "slight and delicate of build . . . with his hair plaited like a woman's." In general, Salako was of "a somewhat effeminate appearance."[90]

Where Nigerian priests are concerned, the performance theorist Margaret Thompson Drewal has recently described priests and initiates of Shangó in gender-variant terms. They are often considered the "wives" of the god. This relationship of feminine male priest to masculine male deity is reflected in the priests' hairstyles. One of these hairstyles is the *shuku*, "which refers to the round basket in which the marketwomen carry their wares on their heads"; another is the "Yoruba bridal hairstyle known as *agogô*," resembling that worn by the male priest of Oyá. The relationship between priest and god is thought to be characterized in feminine-masculine terms because the Yoruba, like other peoples we have encountered, think of the state of possession as a receptive, hence traditionally feminine, state (that is, to be possessed or "ridden" by the god is to be penetrated by the god). Drewal also mentions a priest of Oyá from the Ijebu remote area of Nigeria who wears "a women's-style wrapper tied under the arms and Oyá's cowrie vestment over his left shoulder."[91] The gender-variant appearances of Salako and the priests described by Drewal is reflected by the priests and other male practitioners of Candomblé Caboclo, a Brazilian branch of the religion. According to Ruth Landes, who published an article on the practitioners of Caboclo in 1940, the followers of this tradition hold that women possess greater and more immediate access than men to the realm of the *orishá* and other spiritual entities. They also believe, however, that certain men, whom they deem to be "like women," may possess this gift or power. For this reason, many of the original male initiates of Caboclo were homosexuals and bisexuals who exhibited behavior regarded as gender variant. Some were drag queens, some male prostitutes. As it happened, quite a number of these men were sons of Iansã (Oyá). In her study, Landes vividly describes a Caboclo priest, Father João, who wore "straightened hair . . . a symbol of male homosexuals" and "fancy blouses" and who was very open about his homosexuality, "writing love letters to the men of his heart."[92]

Of João and other homosexual and bisexual priests, Landes notes that they are believed to be especially gifted in the divinatory and magical arts, evoking their spiritual descendants, the *bichas* and drag practitioners of New York City. Their "fame as priests," writes Landes, is "overshadowed by their fame as sorcerers." Viewing the Caboclo priests as marginalized persons and perhaps also as religious radicals, Landes says of them, "Least of all do they reflect the masculinity of the patriarchal culture in whose heart they live."[93]

Serge Bramley, a writer on Macumba, another Brazilian branch of the religion, records priestess Maria-José as saying, "Women make better mediums. But there are Fathers of the Gods. . . . They are often homosexual."[94] In Hubert Fichte's words, many Candomblé priests and priestesses "embrace . . . homosexuality."[95] João Trevisan, in his interview with *babalorixá* M. Aparecida, asks, "Tell me something, Mario, do you know many gay priests [of Candomblé]?" to which Aparecida replies, "Most are gay." When Trevisan asks him why he thinks this is so, he responds, "I think it's the way things are."[96]

In *The Taste of Blood*, anthropologist Jim Wafer introduces us to several gay priests of Brazilian Candomblé. Of these, we learn most of Marinalvo. Of Jewish heritage, Marinalvo was from a young age attracted to the Yoruba religion. He and his sister "would sometimes walk down the street dressed as *orixás*." His penchant for transvestism would one day find its way into Bahian Carnaval, and his attraction to Candomblé would lead him to the house, or *terreiro*, of a gay priest, Mané, and ultimately to establish a house of his own. It is noteworthy that Marinalvo, like many other gay practitioners of the Yoruba religion, is a "son" of Oyá/Iansã. He is also quite open about being gay. While Wafer was told that Marinalvo's mother wished he would "go straight," his mother told Wafer that she wasn't so concerned about his homosexuality as she was about his promiscuity, that "she would not mind so much if Marinalvo settled down with one of his nice middle-class boyfriends."[97]

Eduardo assured me that quite a few *santeros* living in Puerto Rico and in New York City are gay or bisexual and are regarded as gender variant,[98] and a priestess of the religion shared this with me: "a lot of priests are gay. [They] become gay if they are initiated into the worship of a goddess. It is believed that the goddess takes up permanent residence in their bodies. . . . In [my tradition], there's a mind-your-own-fucking-business attitude."[99]

In March 1993, I was fortunate to meet a young African-Cuban woman from Havana named Regla. She explained that while gay men still suffer from oppression in Cuba, they are more likely to be protected if they belong to Santería houses. She also informed me that her *padrino*, Eduardo, is gay. "He is Obatalá in his aspect of Oddúaremu." Regla also explained that while in Cuba gay men cannot become *babalawos,* they *may* become *oriatés. Oriatés* like Eduardo are highly respected priests who play key roles in initiation ceremonies and in leading practitioners in Yoruba chants. They are also known as experts at divination by way of cowrie shells.[100]

I have personally encountered, over the past seven years, three gay male priests of the religion, although I am aware, through contacts in the religion, of others. All three follow a tradition closely allied with Lucumí, a Cuban branch of the religion. All have at one time or another lived in the Bay Area of northern California. Two are Cuban-Americans; one is Anglo-American. Two are musicians; one is a writer and an artist. Of the three, none, to my knowledge, was brought up in the religion. Two are children of Yemayá, while the third is a son of Obatalá. Two are "out"; one is not, perhaps because he plays the sacred *batá* drums, usually not played by gay men. One is a gay activist. I have spoken with one of them concerning drag. He feels that drag, other than ritual transvestism during ceremonies, is not an expression of religious sentiment and should be limited "to Halloween"; this attitude runs counter to that of Eddie Mejía, who often dressed in "gender-fuck" drag and claimed that his doing so was an expression of his spiritual beliefs.

Of these persons, I came to know Guillermo González best. I met Guillermo, who was born in Cuba and raised in Venezuela, in September 1986. While studying at the National Autonomous University in Mexico City in 1976 González realized, by way of a series of paranormal experiences, that the Yoruba tradition was to become his own. In 1980, he was told by a priestess in New York City that he was a child of Yemayá and Shangó. In 1985, he was initiated into the religion, which he refers to as (I)sin Orishá. He is now a *babalorishá* of the religion, with the sacred name of Omi Toké, "Water-from-the-Heights." A writer, artist, student of anthropology, and actor, González played the role of a priest of the religion in *Three by Three,* a film directed by Calogero Salvo that depicts the struggles of a gay Cuban refugee. González has also been active in the movement to secure more funding for HIV/AIDS.

González is troubled by what he perceives as divisiveness in the ranks of the gay movement and feels that as a priest of the religion and a Latino male, he may be able to strengthen alliances among various communities. "The gay subculture in the United States needs to open itself up to many more possibilities," he said to me, "than the few that we began to conform to after Stonewall. To reach out to all people. To create ties among all communities. The movement, up to this point, has been mainly white and upper-class oriented. Most of us are neither rich nor white. We must create bridges. If there's one thing I want to get across, it's this: be vulnerable, get close, *love.*"[101]

SAME-SEX RELATIONSHIPS between practitioners are rarely discussed in the literature available to the public. Because practitioners typically belong to "houses" headed by a priest or priestess who assumes the role of "father" or "mother," and practitioners belonging to the same house view their priest/ess as a parent and his/her "children" as their brothers and sisters, exogamy is strongly encouraged. To relate erotically to one's priest/ess would be tantamount to committing incest in the view of some households. Some practitioners tend to have lovers or companions who are also practitioners, while others do not share spiritual traditions with their lovers. Some practitioners suggest that the coming together of the children of particular *orishá* may produce beneficial or disastrous consequences.

Not surprisingly, little has been said of ceremonies blessing same-sex unions. Indeed, one of the few references made to such a union is found in Cabrera's *El Monte;* here, she speaks of a Lucumí priest named Papa Colas, who dressed in drag and was married to another man in prerevolutionary Cuba.[102]

According to Africanist Glenn L. Sitzman, some gay male practitioners of Santería and Espiritualismo are joining in marriage in ceremonies officiated by *santeros/as* and *espiritistas.* In "Wedding in Santería," he describes such a ceremony, which took place in 1989 at Joyuda, a seaside resort about eight miles south of Mayaguez, the "gayest city in Puerto Rico." In this ceremony, two friends of Sitzman, Esteban and José Luis, were joined in marriage. Before proceeding, I should like to mention that this ceremony and Sitzman's article have aroused some controversy among practitioners, with some practitioners (including gay males) questioning the legitimacy of the ceremony and the authority of the writer. I have decided, however, to mention the ceremony as at least a possible model of the form such ceremony might take.[103]

Esteban is a son of Shangó, while José Luis is a son of Oshún. In the ceremony, Esteban took the role of groom, while José Luis took the role of bride, presumably due to their respective *orishá.* While the ceremony was officiated by Doña Anna, an *espiritista, santeros* and *santeras* also played key roles. The clothing worn by the celebrants as well as the decorations were chosen to honor Oshún and Shangó and also Yemayá, because the rite was held at seaside. The vows were traditional, with the exception that the words *man* and *wife* were replaced by *friend.* In place of rings, rosaries were exchanged; while Sitzman does not say so, it is fairly safe to assume that the rosaries depicted Our Lady of Caridad del Cobré/Oshún and St. Barbara/Shangó.[104]

HOSTILITY

Hostility toward gender-variant and sexually variant practitioners of African diasporic religions in the Americas may be traced to the last decade of the sixteenth century, when a black slave or freedman, a cobbler's apprentice named Francisco Manicongo—his last name referring to his tribal group—was denounced by the Inquisition then holding trials in Brazil.[105] Francisco was accused, among other things, of refusing to wear proper masculine attire, instead wearing women's clothes and/or a type of loincloth allegedly associated with gender-variant males engaging in same-sex eroticism. In the *Denunciations of Bahia, 1591–1593,* Francisco is referred to as a *jimbandaa.* According to the *Denunciations,* a *jimbandaa* is a "passive sodomite" in the "language of Angola and the Congo."[106] It appears that *jimbandaa* is a misspelling of *kimbanda,* a Kwanyama-Ambo-Angolan term we have already encountered (in "Ancestors") signifying a female or gender-variant male shaman.[107] Thus, the *Denunciations* suggests that Francisco may not only have been a transvestite and a "passive sodomite" but also a spiritual functionary, occupying an alternate gender role similar to that occupied by the *berdaches* of Native American tribes. It is interesting to note that the Europeans, in a typically reductionist manner, by 1591 had appropriated the term *kimbanda* to mean "passive sodomite." Not only this, but by the midtwentieth century, Brazilians had come to understand *kimbanda*, now usually spelled *Quimbanda*, as a religion blending Kongo and Yoruba beliefs and practices and emphasizing works of *destructive* magic.[108] While it is not clear whether the religion practiced by Francisco Manicongo had yet been influenced by the Yoruba religion, it is certainly possible that some cross-pollination had already occurred. We may also surmise that like-minded practitioners of the Yoruba religion may have suffered fates similar to that of Manicongo at the hands of the Inquisitors.

Almost four hundred years after the denunciation of Francisco Manicongo, Cesar Freire and Alibio Ferreira reported in the Brazilian journal *Gira da Umbanda* that Fernandes Portugal, noted authority on the religion, had publicly attacked the leaders of Candomblé houses for harboring homosexuals, and homosexuals for taking part in Candomblé rites. Portugal, according to this 1976 article, claimed that the elegant dress, exotic foods, and sensuous dancing found in Candomblé encouraged homosexual participation—an odd twist on what the *pai de santo* told Peter Fry.[109]

In the twentieth century, branches of the Yoruba religion influenced by Kongo and various other African traditions, including Palo Monté and the Secret Society of the Abakúa, exclude gay, bisexual, and gender-variant males from the priesthood and often even from membership. One wonders if this might be rooted in the victimization by Europeans and others of the gender-variant, homoerotically inclined practitioners of Kongo and other groups in the past. According to Hubert Fichte, in such traditions, as now practiced in Brazil, if a divinatory consultation should somehow fail to reveal a priest-to-be's homosexual orientation, that priest, if and when this is discovered, will be forced to abdicate his position and will be banished from the community. Further, all objects belonging to or used by him in rituals will be destroyed, as they are believed to be contaminated.[110]

Among some practitioners of the Yoruba religion, personal homophobia and effemiphobia have been strengthened by the appearance of HIV/AIDS. This may be due in part to a fear that the religion as a whole will suffer even greater defamation than it has already due to its accepting or at least tolerating people now considered "members of high-risk groups."[111]

ACTIVISM

In spite of such opposition, gay, bisexual, and gender-variant persons as well as persons with HIV/AIDS who practice the Yoruba religion have sought in recent years to bring together these dimensions of their lives. Groups blending these elements have been established in San Francisco and elsewhere.

Members of Adé Dudu ("Gay Blacks"), a group founded in Salvador, Brazil, in 1981, have asserted that while both Catholicism and Protestantism are antisex in general and antigay in particular, the Yoruba religion, generally speaking, embraces its gender-variant and sexually variant practitioners.

Members explain that in Candomblé, one seldom is condemned for his or her sexual preference (despite the railings of F. Portugal and others). They insist that the "*orixás* do not stifle the sensuality of individuals" because they are themselves *plurissexuais,* "pansexual." Indeed, members of Adé Dudu, with its gay liberationist perspective, speak of Candomblé as fostering a "sexual democracy," which they hope will one day be reflected in the world at large.

Ermeval, a member, writes, "In our religion, these persons are respected as *uma ponte dos Orixás,* a bridge to/of the *orishá.*"[112]

They—we—are, after all, as *babalorixá* M. Aparecida reminds us, the children of the rainbow.

Jean-Baptiste Carhaix, *The Big Sleep*, the Sisters of Perpetual Indulgence,
San Francisco, 1989.

Chapter

12

The Recollection of What Was Scattered

Where there is dismemberment in the beginning there is remembrance at the end. . . . The fulfillment of the cosmic game is the discovery of what was covered and the recollection of what was scattered.

Alan Watts, *The Two Hands of God*[1]

The interrelationship of same-sex desire, gender variance, and spiritual experience or role reaches a climatic point in the late nineteenth and twentieth centuries. ¶ Many factors have contributed to reaching this apex. Among these, two of the most crucial have been disillusionment with the Judeo-Christian tradition and rebellion against totalitarianism. ¶ Disillusionment with the Judeo-Christian tradition has led Westerners to explore non-Western traditions. Both Western and non-Western colonized peoples are reclaiming pre-Judeo-Christian traditions. ¶ Rebellion against totalitarian rule has led to the rise of democratic consciousness, which has encouraged the self-empowerment of many peoples, including the colonized, women, ethnic "minorities," and the homoerotically inclined. The rise of democratic consciousness has also fueled the quest for spiritual traditions embracing a wider humanity, whose deities reflect the rainbow of human (as well as animal, plant, and mineral) variation. In the terms of Wiccan priestess, writer, and political activist Starhawk, we have begun to think in terms of "immanence."[2] The spirit flows within us, and within all life. It is not the private property of Jehovah or the pope.

A third factor playing a crucial role in recent developments is the dramatic rise of self-consciousness or subjectivity, which is often expressed as self-labeling: "I am a Mexican American poet," "I am a lesbian-feminist performance artist," and so on without end. Certainly, people of previous centuries have been self-aware. By the late seventeenth and early eighteenth centuries, readers were aware that Henri III of France and his minions were being compared to Native American *berdaches,* the priests of the goddesses of antiquity, and homoerotically inclined sailors. Nevertheless, the self-consciousness that has allowed us to recognize the multicultural and transhistorical character of our domain, to label its members as "gender-variant spiritual functionaries," and to thereby link the Paleosiberian "soft" shaman to the African *omasenge kimbanda,* the *qadesh* of Athirat, the *megabyzos* of Diana, the *gallus* of Cybele, the Germanic *seiðr* practitioner, the gay *santero,* Qu Yuan, and Rimbaud strikes me as an acutely late nineteenth- and twentieth-century phenomenon.

In the terms of the current debate between social constructionists (the advocates of "nurture") and essentialists (the advocates of a mingling of "nature" and "nurture"), I would say that while our domain and its members have existed since antiquity, it was not until recently that a man like myself could announce, "I am a queer pagan."

In my view, I am engaged in a process of both constructing and deciphering an already existing identity. I am also deconstructing an identity which has been imposed on me by the patriarchal culture in which I live. I strongly believe, however, that like the form of the animal that lies deep within the Native Alaskan's block of wood, so the form of the gender-variant, homoerotically inclined spiritual worker lies deep within many of us, and yearns to be released.

In more personal terms, this type of self-consciousness or subjectivity has inspired the psychological and social process of coming out as a gay, bisexual, or transperson.

Yet another factor influencing our understanding of our domain and having an effect on the Gay Spiritual movement is the emergence of the so-called new science, which includes quantum physics, holographic theory, and chaos theory. This phenomenon and its relation to our domain will be discussed in the Conclusion.

In recent years, Gay Spirituality has come to be rather narrowly defined as a spiritual movement among gay men seeking to link beliefs and practices of the Greeks, Native Americans, Celts, and Christians in order to apply them to contemporary gay experience. While in general I support this project, it is my view that we must reach beyond these cultures to embrace those of Africa, Asia, and elsewhere, as I have attempted in this book. At the same time, of course, we need to be mindful of how we go about borrowing the beliefs and practices of cultures other than our own. I would also suggest that for some persons, Gay Spirituality may not be so much a path of its own as a perspective that allows us to better understand the roles which we have played in the world's spiritual traditions. For still others, Gay Spirituality represents an extremely personal journey that focuses on private symbols, experiences, and reflections as they relate to one's sexuality and gender role as opposed to an emphasis on linking one's personal spirituality to other spiritual systems. For many, Gay Spirituality is not singular, but plural, and suggests a loose cluster of beliefs and practices accepted by contemporary gay men seeking to reclaim or heal a lost or wounded spiritual identity.

SHAMANISM, EXILE, AND COMING OUT

Holger Kalweit, who compares shamanic experiences cross-culturally, explains that they "involve a deautomization of ordinary consciousness." He continues, "A shamanic technique may be anything that disrupts and confuses the normal stream of thoughts, the habitual experience of the emotions."[3] In certain ways, the process of coming out as a gay person resembles the deautomization process undertaken by the shaman.

Like the Paleosiberian or Native American shaman or the Zulu *isangoma,* the individual who is coming out often experiences the disintegration of a former personality and way of life just as another personality or subjectivity, another way of life, is emerging. This metamorphosis is frequently experienced as a descent, dismemberment, or death. Joan Halifax, who examines shamanic narratives, writes, "The often terrifying descent by the shaman initiate into the underworld of suffering and death may be represented by figurative dismemberment." In some cases, the "bones are all that remain of the shaman."[4]

The diaries of the twentieth-century gay American poet Robert Duncan reflect this shamanic process. Duncan, speaking of himself in schizophrenic terms, wrote in 1941, "Robert . . . had made a cross with nails thru his body like wires and he is hung there. I hit him with a shovel cutting his head so that it hangs dangling from the neck. Like a rooster cut by a scythe."[5]

In his discussion of Duncan's life, Eckbert Faas explains that Duncan consciously linked his confrontations with same-sex desire and gender-variant behavior to shamanism. Faas writes, "The surrealist self-portrait from Robert Duncan's diary of January 1941 recalls the dismemberment process undergone by the . . . shaman as described by . . . anthropologists. Robert, in fact, had recently read Edward Westermarck's study of homosexual and transvestite practices in shamanism, and as early as 1939 had proclaimed himself a shaman poet."[6]

Indeed, Duncan went so far as to compare his confrontation with same-sex desire and gender variance to a *bardo,* or mystical, after-death state, described in the *Tibetan Book of the Dead,* which his friend Anaïs Nin had suggested he read.[7]

In a 1991 article in *The Advocate,* Thoth, a young gay neopagan living in Boston, echoed Faas's words concerning Duncan, saying, "Gay people go through an initiation straight people never do when they come out of the closet," an initiation comparable to that of "the shaman being torn to pieces in his initiation rite."[8]

In more external terms, this process has been, and is frequently even now, experienced—as is coming to terms with HIV/AIDS—as a separation from one's "prior social moorings," that is, as exile.[9] Literary theorist and cultural critic Edward Said, in "Reflections on Exile," says that exile is "strangely compelling to think about but terrible to experience."[10] Because those who practice gender variance, same-sex eroticism, and spirituality have frequently been perceived by dominant cultures as perverts or criminals, their experiences of banishment and flight have received less attention than those of people suffering from racism or xenophobia.

Nevertheless, people in whose lives homoeroticism, gender-variant behavior, and spiritual role have converged—as we have seen with the *galli* of Cybele, the *argr-vargr* outlaws of medieval Europe, and others—also know the condition of exile.

In recent centuries, the experiences of "sodomites" and later "inverts" and "homosexuals" have mirrored the earlier experiences of people comprising our domain. Eighteenth-century European sodomites were frequently banished to the Americas, while nineteenth-century inverts struggled to leave England in the aftermath of Oscar Wilde's disastrous trial, which resulted in his imprisonment and death. In the twentieth century, homosexuals have tried to flee, largely unsuccessfully, the totalitarian regimes of Hitler, Stalin, Castro, and others.

Those who have not experienced dispersion have often become the victims of torture or genocide. Thousands perished in Nazi concentration camps and untold numbers in Cuban relocation camps, while in the 1960s and '70s at California's prisons and mental hospitals, including the Atascadero State Hospital and the Vacaville Medical Facility, homosexuals were being subjected to massive shock therapy, lobotomies, and large doses of a potentially toxic experimental drug.[11]

If one is fortunate enough to survive the arduous journey, the exile, exodus, or diaspora, one may experience, as the shaman does, an ascent, reintegration, remembrement, or rebirth. As with the Zulu *isangoma,* it may be experienced as the transformation of the waning moon into the dark, new, and waxing moon, *ukuthwasa.* As Halifax says of the bones of the dismembered shaman, "Like seeds, the bones have the potential for rebirth within them. . . . Bone, like a quartz crystal or seed, is the enduring source from which light and life spring anew."[12]

As mentioned in the Introduction, this rebirth may embrace the psychological, social, political, and spiritual realms. We may discover pride in being gay. We may join gay-sensitive or gay-centered social or political organizations. We may experience political radicalization, becoming gay or queer activists, warriors against patriarchal ideology. We may work to secure a place for ourselves within the faiths in which we have been reared, or we may seek to reclaim or reconstruct spiritual traditions that honor our way of life. In doing so, we open ourselves to other experiences common to shamans and priests.

MANY ARE THE SHAPES OF THINGS DIVINE

The search for supportive and inclusive spiritual traditions, needless to say, is not confined to gay men. Indeed, Terence McKenna refers to this search as the Archaic Revival; in his view, it embraces shamanism, the "rebirth" of the Goddess, and a reawakening of our relationship to Nature and, more specifically, to hallucinogenic plants.[13]

Many who stand on this boundary find non-Western and neopagan spiritual traditions more supportive of their self-definitions. A chief reason is that these traditions tend to be *henotheistic*. While recognizing an ultimate divine source, they suggest that divinity, being protean, may express itself in myriad ways. Thus a deity, as we have seen, may be associated with gender variance and same-sex desire as well as traditional gender roles, no observable gender role, heterosexual desire, or asceticism.

Because in these traditions gender variance is often seen as one reflection of the totality of divinity, people who exhibit gender-variant traits or behavior are often highly valued. Likewise, because same-sex eroticism is often considered an outgrowth or expression of gender variance, those engaging in homoeroticism may also be valued as reflections of divinity and expected to assume sacred roles.

As we reclaim or reconstruct ancient and primal faiths, we reinvest the figures of the elder gods with energy and are, in turn, ourselves invested with energy. Chief among the divinities we seek to reclaim are goddesses, androgynous/gynandrous deities, male deities who do not conform to the figure of the patriarchal father, and elemental spirits such as faeries and elves.

In "The Goddess in Every Man," inspired by the works of archetypal psychologist Jean Shinoda Bolen, Josef Venker expresses his desire to reclaim the Goddess within his own psyche, believing that cultivating his own "femininity" will help to restore him to a "fuller humanity," of which the force of patriarchal ideology has previously deprived him. For Venker, this recovery of the feminine, of the Goddess within, is expressed through working in his garden:

> The garden was perhaps the one place where the men in my family could be in touch with the nurturing and caring sides of themselves. . . . A garden is a very personal expression . . . of the relationship with the Goddess within. . . . Her name is Demeter.[14]

Some of us keep journals in which we give expression to feelings of kinship with female divinities. In a meditation to the *bodhisattva* Guanyin (Kuan Yin), David Sparks writes,

> It has taken a long while to find you, Guanyin
> to match the broken pieces of white jade
> one piece eluding me, that part of me
> that is goddess, Guanyin, Boddhisattva
> . . . .
> Is this the endless mystery of men like me

to become fertile symbols of transformation
to function as men, as women
to attain your compassion
a loving justice transcending all barriers?[15]

Still others, like the Sisters of Perpetual Indulgence, an order of "genderfuck" drag nuns based in San Francisco, invoke the power of female deities in rituals meant to support and protect gay people and others. In their rites, as in those of the Radical Faeries, the Goddess is sometimes invoked in a "camp" or carnivalesque form. Such camp or carnivalesque depictions of the Goddess return us to the world of the *sots,* with their worship of Mère Sotte. These depictions include not only performing artists like Judy Garland, Bette Davis, Tallulah Bankhead, Greta Garbo, and Marlene Dietrich, but also imaginary characters spanning the gamut from Dorothy and Glenda the Good Witch to Disney's Maleficent and Cruella De Vil, all of whom have been occasionally portrayed as contemporary manifestations of the Goddess. Some feminists and others see in such depictions of the Goddess an expression of misogyny. Gay men who honor the Goddess in such forms, however, see themselves as celebrating the powers of humor, wit, "gutsiness," and "bitchiness," which they link to feminine, gender-variant, and gay expressions of rebellion in the face of a patriarchal tyranny. In "Litany for the Women, Take Back the Night," composed by Sister Boom Boom (also known as Jack Fertig), the Sisters chant,

Black Goddess Kali, mother of all,
    creator of all, destroyer of all . . .
Amazon warrior, goddess of wisdom,
    Athena, endow us with might . . .
Themis, goddess of justice and right,
    in your name we call out:
WE TAKE BACK THE NIGHT![16]

Perhaps the most well known lyric among gay men seeking to reclaim Goddess reverence is Charlie Murphy's "Burning Times," which, like the Sisters' chant, weaves together spiritual and political imagery:

Now the Earth is a Witch and the men still burn her
Stripping her down with mining and
    the poisons of their wars
Still to us the Earth is a healer
    a teacher, our mother
The weaver of the web of life
    that keeps us all alive[17]

Gay men participating in neopagan groups also pay homage, as mentioned above, to male deities, including Cernunnos and Pan, as well to more folkloric male figures, including the Green Man and the Wild Man. Some also revere androgynous deities like Diana glas, described by Caradoc ap Cador, a practitioner of Wicca, as a blue-skinned youth with budding breasts and a hard cock. He is the symbol/patron of the exuberant sexuality of spring and the Mystery of Love. He is also addressed as "Our Lord of the Painted Fan." He is the very spirit of androgyny.[18]

Peter Lamborn Wilson is among those who link the androgynous deity to the archetypal Child-Fool. A combination of Peter Pan, the Jungian Puer Aeternus ("Eternal Child"), a *sot,* The Fool of the Tarot, a Punk rocker, and a gang member, the Child-Fool represents "the spirituality of divine disorder."[19]

Finally, some gay men are beginning to honor a specifically "Queer God." Don Engstrom has created a ritual to this deity that is now being performed by Radical Faeries and others; the rite includes this chant by Peter Soderberg:

Faggot God
Fairie God
Purple Hands of Healing
Faggot God
Fairie God
My Love
Come to us
Fight for us
My Love[20]

In "Discovering Queer Archetypes" by Bert Provost, a.k.a. Corona, gay neopagans are encouraged to surrender heterocentric images of the Goddess and the God in favor of more gay-sensitive icons. Provost's is a carnivalesque vision, reminiscent of the *sots* and perhaps also of contemporary punk writing:

I've grown tired of the divine heterosexual couple of contemporary Paganism. While I continue to invoke a variety of spirits, both male and female, the emphasis is on linking them to my queerness. I might invoke the Goddess as the Sacred Bitch, Dyke Sister or Mother of Faggots. Her relationship to male spirits is anything but "traditional." The God I call on has a variety of names. He is the Rising Pillar of Flesh, the Open Hand, Boyfriend, Lover and Gate of Pleasure.[21]

RECLAIMING OUR ANCIENT ROLE

In *Witchcraft and the Gay Counterculture,* Arthur Evans, who founded the fairy circle in San Francisco in the mid-1970s, writes, "We look forward to regaining our ancient historical roles as medicine people, healers, prophets, shamans, and sorcerers."[22]

Similarly, Harry Hay, a cofounder of the Radical Faeries (which constitutes a related but distinct tradition) proclaims,

We have been a SEPARATE PEOPLE . . . drifting together in a parallel existence, not always conscious of each other . . . yet recognizing one another by eyelock when we did meet . . . here and there as outcasts . . .

Spirit-people . . . in service to the Great Mother . . . Shamans . . .
mimes and rhapsodes, poets and playwrights, healers and nurturers . . .
VISIONARIES . . . REBELS.[23]

In "The Moon Singers," the African American gay poet Craig A. Reynolds expresses his feeling of kinship with gender-variant, homoerotically inclined shamans, writing,

The Darbat, Cheyenne, Yoruba and Eskimos,
interpreting the seizures I had as a child,
would have welcomed me as a shaman,
    a wanderer in the wild.
Living with women, I,
hairy-faced like you, would have
    worn their clothes.
One day, I would journey to find
    the familiar who'd name me, help
me to heal . . . [24]

Among those of us who have taken up the role of spiritual functionary are gay Witches or Wiccans. Neopagan Wiccans, generally speaking, revere the Great Goddess (often as Diana) and the horned god (as Cernunnos or Pan); organize themselves into covens; come together at sabbats, especially those held on Halloween, the eve of May, Lughnasadh (August 2), and Imbolc (February 2); and practice the divinatory and magical arts.

Of these, Dr. Leo Louis Martello is perhaps the most well known. A gay rights activist since 1969, he was also among the first spokespersons for Witches' rights, playing a central role in the first "Witch-In" held in Central Park in New York on October 31, 1970. Martello describes Witchcraft as "an underground spring which has occasionally broken through the surface in rivulets and then continued on its way underground, sometimes manifesting as a pond. Now all these rivulets and ponds are merging into a raging river which cannot be dammed up by the Judaeo-Christian tradition."[25]

Concerning the place of gay people in Wicca, he said this in *Witchcraft: The Old Religion,* published in 1973: "Those [Witchcraft] groups who insist on heterosexuality as a requirement for admittance into a coven cannot claim ancient precedence, since so many of the pagan religions had male prostitutes in their temples. And the eunuch priests, most notably of Cybele, would be disqualified."[26]

A decade after Martello published his book, a young gay witch named Michael Thorn, a follower of the neopagan Wiccan tradition founded by Gerald Gardner and, like Martello, a gay activist, described his experiences in Kathexis Anthropos, a gay male coven:

I am usually representative of the Lady [the Goddess] during rituals. . . .
One of the men in the group takes the role of the God during rituals. When we draw down the Goddess she is called down into (or called from within) me. I speak with her voice. . . . It is a very special experience and everyone

should get to partake of it at some time. I suggest to all men and women in the Craft that they not neglect this other part of themselves and experience both the voice of the Goddess and that of the God.[27]

A decade later, Thorn, whom I was fortunate to meet in New York, is still active in the gay-Wiccan circle. He and Martello have been joined in recent years by gay Witches across the United States and in Europe; many of these men have been inspired by *The Spiral Dance* and *Dreaming the Dark,* in which Starhawk acknowledges the positive role played by gay, bisexual, and gender-variant men in Wicca. Several years ago, Greg Johnson and Sparky J. Rabbit cofounded the Sons of the Bitch coven, which hosts the annual Faggot Witch Camp. Closely associated with the gay-Wiccan movement are the queer or lavender pagans, whose ideas are currently being disseminated by the *Lavender Pagan Newsletter,* published in California's Bay Area by Bill Karpen.

I will always treasure the first poem I read by a gay Witch. In 1979, an anonymous poet, perhaps "Forest Flat," wrote in "Witchwork," published in the radical, rural gay journal *RFD:*

Yes, I'm a witch. I've stood before
The Lord of Death and found him not unkind.
I've practiced well the sacred hidden lore;
The words of power and the spells that bind
And loosen, culled from nature's trove,
The herbs that heal. But most of all I
Have danced naked, free and proud
    Beneath the sky,
Unto the Goddess, she who shines above
    and within . . . [28]

And Have My Fortune Told

Gay men are also reclaiming the ancient practices of divination and magic. Among the most well known of these men are the astrologers Jack Fertig (a.k.a. Sister Boom Boom) and the late Gavin Arthur, who wrote *The Circle of Sex* and was the grandson of President Arthur and an intimate companion of Edward Carpenter. A third, the late Herman Slater, was the author of *The Magickal Formulary* and the owner of New York's finest occult shop, Magickal Childe. Unfortunately, however, very few gay-specific texts concerning magic and divination have as yet been published. Nevertheless, since the 1960s, gay men have been self-consciously reinterpreting the ancient systems from a perspective that might now be called Gay Spiritual.

In the early 1970s, for instance, the late gay activist Carl Wittman set out to interpret the Tarot cards in a gay-sensitive way. It occurred to him that the *Fool* might speak to the risky adventure of coming out as a gay person, while the *Magician* might speak to the assumption of the role of gay spiritual worker. The *Empress* might reflect those values that Goddess-revering cultures encouraged both men and women to emulate, while the *Devil,* which he renamed "Pan," might speak to male-male sex-magickal mysteries. Inspired by Wittman's ideas as well as those of the lesbian-feminist writer Sally Gearhart, I created a gay-centered Tarot deck in 1981 for a class project in a Tarot seminar given by Angeles Arrien at the Institute of Integral Studies in San Francisco. In my interpretation, the *Star* became the card of Ganymede, while the *Moon* became that of the dreaming *berdache,* and the *Tower* that of lesbian and gay revolution. Also in the early 1980s, gay scholar John Lauritsen contributed to this gay-sensitive interpretation of the Tarot. For Lauritsen, the *Chariot* represented the model of same-sex love found in Plato's *Phaedrus,* while the *Sun* reflected the search for one's gay soulmate. The *Devil,* in Lauritsen's view, represented the deity Baphomet, allegedly revered by the Knights Templar, while the *Tower* spoke to the torture and execution of the Templars and other heretics during the Inquisition.

In many places where occult supplies are sold, gay-specific products are now beginning to appear. In San Antonio, Texas, for example, at Papa Jim's, I can buy a talisman and a pink powder alleged to attract a gay mate, not to mention a body wash to be used by drag queens desiring lovers. Hopefully, gay-sensitive texts on magic and divination will soon follow.[29]

DIVINE BODY, DIVINE LOVE

Gay, bisexual, and gender-variant men are also seeking to resacralize the body, homoeroticism, and same-sex relationships.

The patriarchal male body is a weapon, a suit of armor, a machine. Like the female body in patriarchal ideology, it is also an object. We seek to reclaim its fluidity, its tenderness, its wholeness, what some have chosen to describe as its femininity, its androgyny.

The French antipsychiatry philosophers Gilles Deleuze and Félix Guattari have discussed this reclaiming the fluid, tender, receptive aspects of the male body in terms of a gender metamorphosis mirroring that experienced by shamans, priests of goddesses, and many others who have embodied our domain. Deleuze and Guattari write in their enigmatic style,

> On the near side [of "becomings"], we encounter becomings-woman. . . .
> (Becoming-woman, more than any other becoming, possesses a special . . .
> power; it is not so much that women are witches, but that sorcery proceeds
> by way of this becoming-woman). . . . [30]

They may have been inspired, incidentally, by Hélène Cixous and Catherine Clément, who tell us, "They, the feminine ones, are coming back from far away, from forever, from 'outside,' from the heaths where witches stay alive."[31] Deleuze and Guattari insist that the experience of gender metamorphosis is crucial to attaining self-realization: "[It] must be said that all becomings begin and pass through becoming-woman. It is the key to all other becomings."[32]

It is ironic that even John Addington Symonds, who tried to excise gender variance and the gender-variant spiritual functionary from the discourse on homosexuality that was emerging at the end of the nineteenth century, confessed to experiencing gender metamorphosis. In a waking dream, for instance, he envisioned himself as a woman loved by the Venetian gondolier Angelo Fusato.[33]

In his diaries, Robert Duncan also speaks of gender metamorphosis, linking it to the experience of coming out:

> I wore paint on my face and eye shadow. . . . I would dress in the dyke end of it . . . but with my hair cut in bangs, and earrings. . . . There is a madness that moves over me. . . . A man will look at me with desire . . . and then I am caught, moving as in a dream, inevitably toward him . . . as [a] woman. . . .[34]

The gay American poet and filmmaker James Broughton has devoted an entire work to this experiencing of what we might also refer to as the *yin-yang* dance of the male body. Like Duncan, Broughton associates this experience with coming out. For Broughton, gender transformation begins when he discovers his nipples. He writes,

> Some years ago I became aware of an intense life in my nipples. Touching them aroused my genitals more immediately than any other self-play act. . . . Now in my male breasts I can directly touch my female heart. . . . I have but to stroke my nipples tenderly and at once she [his own "femininity" or the Goddess within] responds to my caresses. She [then] wakens the He in me. . . .
>
> Always I had wondered why men retain vestigial nipples. Now I no longer question. They are the living doors to the chamber of the Goddess. She is present in every man's breast.[35]

Social constructionists might object to the archetypal associations of woman, witch/Goddess, tenderness, and receptivity voiced in the writings of Broughton and others, branding such associations as essentialist. I suggest that as long as the patriarchal, heterocentric order remains intact, we may expect to see the "feminine" invoked as an alternative to the trope of the patriarchal "masculine," the Goddess/witch invoked as an alternative to the priest, rabbi, minister. It does seem, on the other hand, that some men are beginning to view their so-called feminine side as just another expression of their humanity and not necessarily as a reflection of the behavior of women or of an archetypal feminine.

Men experiencing our feminine, *yin*, or receptive natures carry some of the energy we have hitherto focused on the phallus to our nipples, as Broughton has suggested, as well as to other sites—mouth, anus, the body as a whole. We pay attention to our partners' desire, and to our own, to more fully experience receptivity. We sacralize eroticism with incense, candles, baths of basil, mint, and rose. Eroticism becomes an encounter of Self and Self. We experience what Harry Hay has called "subject-subject consciousness," what Mitch Walker refers to as "double love."[36] In a passage echoing Thoreau, Hay writes, "For all of us, and for each of us, in the dream of Love's ecstasy . . . the god descends—the goddess descends; and for each of us the transcendence of that apotheosis is mirrored in the answering glances of the lover's eyes."[37]

Gay seekers are also reclaiming sex-magickal rites such as may have been undertaken by the Canaanite *qedeshim,* the Germanic practitioners of *seiðr,* and others. They use these rites to celebrate desire and love. In such rites, the partners often represent contrapuntal forces—Sun and Moon, Goddess and God, Beloved and God, Set and Horus, Bull and Stag.[38] Not surprisingly, such rituals nowadays reflect a concern for safe sex.

Speaking to a growing awareness of the "receptive" partner's role in erotic-sacred ritual, these rites may revere deities associated with the anus or anal eroticism, such as Thoth or Tlazolteotl. Among such deities, the Hindu god of fortune and protection, Ganesha, is frequently invoked. In Tantric lore, Ganesha is the ruler of a *chakra* or spiritual center referred to as the *muladhara chakra,* which is located near the anus or perineum of the body. According to Adrian Ravarou, the creator of the "energy flow" dance method, gay lovers may employ the *chakras* of Hindu Tantra not only to attain erotic ecstasy but also to align their hearts and minds so that they are at once finding sexual fulfilment and beginning to weave a potentially long-term relationship.[39]

In terms of long-lasting relationships, gay men are also creating rituals to sacralize these, rites such as were undertaken by "soft" shamans and priests of the Goddess. In many cases, these are unofficial "holy unions" presided over by a neopagan priest or priestess or by a gay or gay-sensitive priest, minister, or rabbi. One of the most publicized of such unions occurred on the evening of July 23, 1978, when James Broughton and Joel Singer, also a filmmaker, celebrated their relationship on a ferryboat in Sausalito, California. The priest chanted,

> These holy mysteries elucidate
> the great enigmas of mankind.
> We are all incarnations of the Androgyne.
> We are all mirrors of the Godbody.
>
> Dearly betrothed, look now upon each other
> as you repeat in unison after me
> the zealous paradoxes of your love. . . .[40]

IN A GOLDEN GOWN

> Fashion is a mysterious goddess, to be obeyed
> rather than to be understood, for its decrees
> transcend human comprehension.
>
> J. C. Flügel[41]

The term "reclaiming" poses a problem when we apply it to the relationship of today's Gay Spiritual seekers to transvestism, cross-dressing, or drag, as there is little evidence to suggest, except perhaps in urbanized societies of the twentieth century, that the alliance between transvestism, male gender variance, homoeroticism, and sacred or aesthetic-sacred expression (and here I include the carnivalesque) has ever been altogether severed. From the "soft" shamans of Siberia to the Goddess-revering priests of Rome to the court of Henri III to the *bicha* practitioners of Candomblé, the relationship of cross-dressing to our domain has repeatedly resurfaced. The central problem with most studies of transvestism or cross-dressing is that their authors employ, perhaps only half consciously, reductionist strategies that are reflected in a singular focus on *ritual* transvestism in non-Western societies and *social* transvestism in the West.

It occurs to me that the practice of transvestism during Carnival (Carnaval, Mardi Gras, and so on), of which we shall say more momentarily, challenges this simplistic dichotomy. Both for Medieval European peasants and contemporary Brazilians (and at least some participants in New Orleans' Mardi Gras), Carnival, to paraphrase Mikhail Bakhtin, represents a homecoming celebration of the pagan gods who have been officially banished by Christianity.[42] It would be extremely difficult in the case of Carnival, and in many other instances as well, to determine whether a particular act of cross-dressing is intended to be interpreted as a ritual or a merely social act. Where Carnival is concerned, transvestism frequently signifies an intermingling of the sacred and mundane realms, as when males who are already transvestites dress as female *orishá* or spirits in Brazilian Carnaval. What I think we may say is that gay men—and perhaps also bisexual and gender-bending heterosexual men—are today *self-consciously* reclaiming the ancient link between cross-dressing and our domain.

In "Spirit in Drag," Hermes Polyandron suggests that in cross-dressing we may recover both our repressed feminine selves and our child selves.[43] I would add that we may also recover a more traditionally masculine self, perhaps bearing resemblance to Pan or the Green Man, which have as well been rejected by patriarchy. Recovering these aspects together often results in a costume that is both divine and human, feminine and masculine, mature and childlike, and sacerdotal and carnivalesque; it may as well suggest a hybridization of human with animal, plant, or other entity.

In the gay cult classic *The Faggots and Their Friends Between Revolutions*, Larry Mitchell celebrates such contemporary manifestations of spiritual cross-dressing:

> The fairies . . . make clothes from the daisies and the buttercups and pansies. . . . They dress according to their latest dreams. . . . The faggots are dressed for play, the queens . . . to live in another world . . . their tatters of tinsel and lace . . . turn them into fantastic creatures.[44]

Mitchell is echoed by Sai, who writes of a 1980 Faerie gathering in Bolinas, California, "Clothes—garments—robes of fantasy—these are our talismans for the journey. . . . I came as Persephone . . . in a flowered, flowing dress and train. Silk Flowers in my hair, golden and green glitter on my face. . . . I smelled of attar of roses. . . . Pan came—decoratively horned . . . and clothed not at all. . . . The Corn King wore green velvet. . . . Nuns of perpetual delight [wore] . . . rhinestones . . . [and] pearls."[45]

Frater Belarion, in "Liber Dionysia: Ritual Uses of Transvestism," employs cross-dressing, as some of those described above have done, in order to invoke into himself a goddess, namely, Aphrodite. He points out that male facial and body hair do *not* pose a problem in this instance of ritual transvestism, since the goddess Aphrodite has a bearded aspect.

Inspired by Aleister Crowley, Belarion suggests that the magician, upon deciding which goddess, or aspect of the Goddess, he wishes to manifest, begin collecting attributes sacred to her and attire appropriate to her. He should then determine a day and time of day sacred to her—in the case of Aphrodite, Friday evening—and at that time should prepare himself by taking a ritual bath and drinking an aphrodisiac tea. He should then invoke the goddess by way of hymns. As Aphrodite is a goddess of eroticism, he may also awaken her by means of auto-erotic stimulation or by taking the receptive role in homoerotic coupling.

Belarion stresses that drag worn for such a rite should be carefully chosen. In this case, while it may be "genderfuck" in character, it should probably not be carnivalesque. Flowing robes, perhaps of pink, red, or aqua, exotic jewelry, and flowers in the hair might be most appropriate. Belarion suggests that the cross-dressing magician should study ancient costume diligently—and should also haunt secondhand shops where Art Nouveau-era attire and accessories may be purchased—before undertaking this rite of "transvestite enthusiasm."[46] Cross-dressing magicians attempting to invoke the Goddess might say with Bianca Garufi, "Let us try to make a mandala of our body, turning it into a temple. . . . We do not remember sufficiently, or often enough, that our body is a *temenos.* . . . How is it possible not to decorate a temple, which shelters a divinity that is truly cherished and respected?"[47]

LAVENDER GREEN

In reclaiming or reconstructing ancient traditions, we often discover, in the course of our journeying, a renewed bond with nature.

Because so many of us have been told and have internalized the notion that we are "unnatural," we often feel alienated from nature. We experience bonding with it as a painful reunion with a parent who once abandoned us.

As an urban gay male whose father left him behind whenever he went on fishing or hunting trips, I will always remember a certain midsummer evening when, standing naked in the middle of an east Texas pine forest bordering a swamp, I wept on realizing that the full moon was gazing down at me.

In "Desert Reflections," Douglas Conwell, director of Earth Walks, writes of the experience of living in the desert,

> Here, like a snake, I must shed all kinds of skins, repeatedly renewing my relationship with the environment.
> When I am at the bottom of some deep chasm, marveling at the naked, raw stuff of land and time, I am drawn through gateways of consciousness. Reflecting, I acknowledge this gift we as gay people have been given—to move between the realms of perception as priests, magicians, shamans and healers.[48]

Twenty years ago, I occasionally attended the gatherings of the Yellow Rose Tribe, an Austin-based group of gay men and their friends, founded by Dennis Paddie, Calvin Doucet, and other local artists. The tribe would meet to celebrate the birthdays of gay luminaries—Whitman, Cocteau, Spicer, and others—as well as to celebrate the solstices and equinoxes. These latter rites were held at sites once deemed sacred by the Coahuiltecas, the Tonkawas, and the Karankawas, such as Enchanted Rock and Padre Island. I should probably mention here that while members of the tribe sought to honor the native peoples of Texas, it was not their intention to appropriate Native American religions. They did, however, participate in the traditional Deer Dance. Legend has it that once, while wearing only skins and antlers and dancing ecstatically in the forest, some of the tribe's members were nearly killed when a group of drunken hunters mistook them—or pretended to mistake them—for deer.

In conversation and in their writings, the Radical Faeries (who, while "refusing to be pinned down," nonetheless tend to be spiritually and politically anarchistic and comunitarian) emphasize this bond with nature, often holding their gatherings in forests, deserts, and mountainous regions. My friend Hyperion describes a Faerie ritual that took place in the Arizona desert in 1979:

> It all began when one . . . faerie decided to go down to the arroyo and play in the mud. Soon others joined him. . . . All emerged from their raiment and started smearing mud on themselves and each other. . . . Body merged with body until we were one mass. . . . One faerie lying on the ground was decorated with leaves and flowers. Then he was lifted to the sky as if he were an emissary bringing earth and sky together.[49]

As a result of sensing this oneness with nature, some of us have become environmental activists. Hyperion, for instance, has begun to promote the concept of xeriscaping, the planting of indigenous species in gardens in order to conserve water. Others, like the Lavender Greens of the Bay Area of California, have founded gay-centered environmentalist organizations.[50]

In *The Archaic Revival*, Terence McKenna identifies nature with the "vegetation Goddess" and links the reverence of this deity to the use of sacred hallucinogens. He writes, "Perhaps this is what the reconnection to the vegetal Goddess through psychedelic plants, the Archaic Revival, actually points toward; that the life of the spirit is the life that gains access to the visionary realms resident in magical plant teachers. This is the truth that shamans have always known and practiced."[51]

Like the *enarees* of ancient Scythia, the *argr-vargr* warrior-outlaws of medieval Europe, and the *cihuayollo-telpuchtlahueliloc* males of Mesoamerica, some of us, in reclaiming ancient and primal traditions, have sought to attain altered or ecstatic states of consciousness by means of magical plants.

In an article in *RFD*, Sean Mariposa describes a peyote ritual, inspired by the Huichols of northern Mexico, undertaken by a circle of gay men. While there were no leaders in the ritual, several men served as facilitators. Representing the four directions, they performed such functions as keeping the central fire lit and soothing fatigued participants with massage and balm. A rattle and staff were passed around the circle, allowing each person, when holding them, to share his thoughts or to lead the others in chanting. Near the climax of the rite, one of the participants suggested that the men suck each others' nipples as a sign of nurturance. Having done so, the men continued chanting, eventually drifting off to sleep as dawn approached. Mariposa wrote of this experience, "The walls move slowly with . . . kaleidoscopic patterns. . . . My own song pours from deep within. . . . Our spirits surge into each other through the web of ritual."[52]

Whenever I consider the association of our domain with sacred hallucinogens the central figure of Jean Genet's *Our Lady of the Flowers,* the drag queen Divine, appears before me. I see her as she searches in the night for the ingredients of a magical brew. Genet writes,

> Words again took on for her [him] magic. . . . Brew . . . is a word from sorcery. . . . As aconite was the only poison he could procure, every night, in a long, stiff-pleated dressing gown, he . . . would gather a bunch of Napel aconite leaves. [The] poison had the double virtue of killing and raising from the dead those it killed. . . . The Borgias, Astrologers, Pornographers . . . would receive him. . . . Beneath the moon [he] became this world of poisoners, pederasts, thieves, warriors, and courtesans . . . possessing and possessed by an epoch. . . . No episode from history or a novel organized the dream mass; only the murmur of a few magic words thickened with darkness . . . "*Datura fatuosa, Datura stramonium,* Belladonna . . . "[53]

THE WORLD OF ART

The Italian filmmaker Franco Zeffirelli has said of the association of homoeroticism, the arts, and spirituality that gay people "are forced to refine certain receptive instruments in the mind and soul. They become much more sensitive, more ready [than others] to talk and to deal with the things of the spirit."[54]

Gay seekers are reclaiming the ancient role of sacred or ritual artist. The gay rights movement has tried to destroy the *myth* of the gay artist. Yet it is abundantly clear that homoerotically and bisexually inclined and gender-variant persons have played a major role in the development of the arts and crafts—and here I include the fashion, perfume, and interior design industries.

We have only to recall the lyrics of the *assinnu* of Inanna, the *semnotatoi* of Hecate, and the *galli* of Cybele to remember that gender-variant and homoerotically inclined individuals and groups have been serving as ritual artists since antiquity. In later epochs, as we have seen, artists including Christopher Marlowe and Jean-Baptiste Lully continued to express the elements of our domain.

With the arrival of the late nineteenth and twentieth centuries came a more self-conscious re-membering of the artist as shaman or priest. André Gide, Vaslav Nijinsky, Mikhail Kuzmin, Nikolai Klyuev, Charles Henri-Ford, Jean Cocteau, Bruce Nugent, Yukio Mishima, Benjamin Britten, Christopher Isherwood, Gore Vidal, Ned Rorem, Parker Tyler, Pier Paolo Pasolini, Allen Ginsberg, William

Burroughs, Harold Norse, Lou Harrison, José Lezama Lima, Reinaldo Arenas, Manuel Puig, Arturo Islas, Maurice Kenny, Blackberri, Aaron Shurin, Efren Ramírez, Emmanuel Ro, Derek Jarman, Rotimi Fani-Kayode, Steven Arnold, Antler, Gavin Dillard, Mark Morris, Michael Clark, Essex Hemphill, Assotto Saint, Marlon Riggs, Francisco X. Alarcón: these are only a few of those whose works seem to acknowledge the sacred role of the artist, blending homoeroticism or gender variance with work of the spirit.

In his introduction to Jean Genet's *Our Lady of the Flowers,* which focuses on the life of a drag queen in prison, Jean-Paul Sartre stresses Genet's self-assumed role of sacred artist, a role inextricably linked to Genet's homosexuality. Explaining that Genet perceived himself as a magician, Sartre writes, "He was forced from the very beginning into the solitude that the mystic and the metaphysician have such difficulty in attaining." Sartre's description of Genet is echoed in a description of the metaphysical poetry of James Merrill by fiction writer and essayist Edmund White: "This sense of sudden metamorphosis and rebirth, of radical transformation of the self, is more available to a gay poet than a straight. . . . Anyone who is gay and conscious must live with an abiding mystery, his or her own inexplicable but unremitting and incorrigible desires; intimacy with this mystery prepares the poet for the greater mysteries."[55]

The Spanish poet and playwright Federico García Lorca, born in 1898, described himself as an "impassioned and silent fellow" who liked "paper dolls" and believed in spirits. He was deeply influenced by the myths and legends of the Spanish gypsies, as he was by the practitioners of the Yoruba religion he encountered in the Americas.[56]

Lorca's play *Blood Wedding* is an example of the subtle way in which many homoerotically inclined artists have explored sexuality and sacred work. In this lyrical romantic tragedy, the Moon, who requires blood in order to grow, is depicted as an androgynous woodcutter. Literary theorist Rupert C. Allen, relating this figure to the gynandrous lunar goddesses of antiquity, explains the character's significance:

> The audience for which he was writing commonly thinks of the moon as the Queen of Darkness; when they see her as a youthful woodcutter, fainting and seeking sustenance, their reaction must be one of surprise: "Why, the Lady is a young man!" . . . "He" is a hermaphrodite, an androgyne . . . almost certainly connected with the ambiguous sexuality of the young. . . . Such was Lorca himself: the seer who, by retaining the androgyny of his childhood, penetrates back beyond the fragmented . . . world of [the] adult. . . . Spiritual androgyny is what Lorca most valued in himself. . . . it was the key to his creativity.[57]

The painter Pavel Tchelitchew, perhaps best known for *Hide and Seek,* also explored our domain in his work. His works are filled with goddesses and androgynous figures; in his final paintings, they become luminescent, as if painted with neon or lasers. We know from his biographer and friend Parker Tyler and from his lover, the poet Charles Henri-Ford, that Tchelitchew, a Russian by birth, was deeply interested in the occult. From the time he was a child, in the early 1900s, Tchelitchew experienced visions of a goddess whom he named the White Lady. In later years, he came to look upon both Gertrude Stein and Edith Sitwell as avatars of the Goddess. Believing in reincarnation, he spent a great deal of time trying to determine who he might have been in former lives. Many of his arguments with Henri-Ford concerned their astrological differences; Ford, he felt, possessed too much Aquarian energy. Tchelitchew became possessed with the notion that water, in some form, would bring about his death. A child of earth, Tchelitchew sought to become less earthy and more a creature of the air. Also a student of Tarot, Tchelitchew saw himself as the card of Strength (which often depicts a woman taming a lion) and Ford as the Wheel of Fortune. Tyler says of him and his work:

> I could not forget that Tchelitchew's imagination was dominated by Astrology. . . . He set great store by the Tarot pack. . . . He was not merely an intuitive cosmic spirit, but a large and devout one. His last style was the transparency of endless night and that still luminosity of the cosmos. . . .
>
> All Tchelitchew's close friends knew that he imagined himself in the occult tradition of the magus, the ancient wise man . . . Hermetic tradition . . . Egypt . . . Orphism, Neo-Platonism . . . Gnosticism and Alchemy. Susceptible to every strain of mysticism . . . Tchelitchew became a painter who portrayed Hermetic eclecticism in a conscious series of real and ideal prisms.[58]

The filmmaker (and author of *Hollywood Babylon*) Kenneth Anger has also given expression to our domain, in *Inauguration of the Pleasure Dome* (1954), *Scorpio Rising* (1966), *Invocation of My Demon Brother* (1969), and other short films. Cast as the changeling prince in Max Reinhardt's elaborate film production of *A Midsummer Night's Dream* in 1934, when he was only four years old, Anger, by the age of seven, had begun making his own experimental films. As a teenager, he read the works of Aleister Crowley, this wielding a profound influence on his work. He came to see film as a potentially magical medium and the camera as a kind of magic wand. He began to pattern his films upon ritual structures, to employ magical symbols in them, and to weave spells into them. The type of ritual on which he focused was that of the invocation of the deity or "Holy Guardian Angel" into the person of the magus or priestess. Of his films, *Inauguration of the Pleasure Dome* most lucidly reflects our domain. In it, an effeminate ritual magician signals the beginning of a bacchanalian rite by swallowing, jewel by jewel, a necklace. The ritual includes Duncan's friend, the diarist Anaïs Nin, as the goddess Astarte, dancing while wearing a bird cage on her head. It ends with the magician metamorphosing into the Hindu deity Shiva and changing his guests "into spirits of pure energy."[59]

The reclamation by artists of the ancient role of gender-variant, often homoerotically (or bisexually) inclined shaman, priest, or even deity is perhaps most clearly seen, however, in the realms of contemporary music and dance.

Some performers have assumed this role temporarily, as if stumbling into the sacred on the way to the stage or dressing room. Some performers have deeply felt their sacred role, while others appear to have assumed it because of market research. I cannot help but wonder which forces might have been at work in such artists as David Bowie, Jobriath, and Frankie Goes to Hollywood.

Some performers who have truly embodied the sacred role have eventually cast it off, perhaps because it proved too demanding to sustain. Like shamans who forsake their sacred callings, the consequences of shirking this role have often been disastrous. I remember a sensitive, gifted musician who left San Francisco to regain anonymity in a small northwestern town, and another who rejected his androgynous persona, shaved his head, burned his records, and joined a totalitarian religious movement.

While their erotic preferences remain controversial, in this light we may also recall the tragedies of Janis Joplin and Jim Morrison. Cultural critic Stoddard Martin says icily of Morrison's last days, "The erstwhile androgyne became fat. . . . His voice became gutsier, boozier. . . . His lyrics [became] decidedly less apocalyptic."[60]

I have wondered if something of this embodiment-rejection of the role of latter-day shaman might not have been at work in the rock artist Elton John's descent into overuse of alcohol and drugs. Philip Norman has suggested this possibility in a *Rolling Stone* interview, "The Rebirth of Elton John." Norman reports that while "never conventionally religious," John "now makes frequent reference to the 'higher power' that AA [Alcoholics Anonymous] encourages."[61]

Another gay rock artist who appears to have undergone and survived the process of disintegration and reintegration is Boy George, who seems, after having assumed a carnivalesque-shamanic role a decade ago, to be resuming it in the 1990s. George credits his recovery and return in part to the influence of Hindu spiritual teachings and practices, specifically those related to Krishna, the blue-skinned god of love, music, and dance. This influence is reflected by his 1991 album, *The Martyr Mantras,* especially in the beautifully rendered "Bow Down Mister (we say *radha syam*)."[62]

One of the gay community's most powerful latter-day shamans was the African American disco diva Sylvester, famous for his "You Make Me Feel Mighty Real." One of the first performers of popular music to risk coming out to the general public, Sylvester's career began in the Palm Lane Church of God and Christ in South Los Angeles. It progressed through involvement with the Cockettes (a group of San Francisco genderfuck drag queen performance artists, some of whom were skilled in the divinatory and magical arts), and culminated in the discos of San Francisco's gay community. Music critic Barry Walters, who has spoken of Sylvester's worship and emulation of Aretha Franklin, writes,

Sylvester assumes a heavenly tone while expressing it with Lady Soul's hell fire ferocity. Through his falsetto, Sylvester became a simmering blues diva wailing gospel mama. . . . Disco was the gospel music of sinners. . . . When Sylvester describes a lover's caress, it's as if he's feeling the mighty surreal touch of God. There are two poles of Sylvester's world—the disco and the church—but unlike Little Richard . . . Sylvester doesn't see the pleasures of the body and the spirit as opposing forces. . . . For Sylvester, God is on the dance floor as He is in Heaven.[63]

Inspired by Sylvester, as well as Patti LaBelle and others, the six-foot-four, blonde-wigged, African-American RuPaul has become the reigning diva of dance music in the early 1990s. Chanting the mantra of fashion models and voguing dancers, "Supermodel (You Better Work)," RuPaul speaks of his genderfuck drag in terms reflecting an awareness of the ancient association of gender variance, homoeroticism, and the sacred:

> Drag is the ultimate in power dressing. When you're in drag . . . you become the God of your imagination, and that's powerful medicine, baby.
>
> I'm definitely a ruling diva when I'm in my Goddess Drag. . . . My masculinity really comes out when I use my Goddess Drag.
>
> With my drag, I encompass both male and female. I become a microcosm of the whole universe, the yin and yang, and people pick up on that and are enthralled by the power.[64]

While their musical styles and performances differ substantially from those of RuPaul, Sylvester, Boy George, Elton John, and others, musicians associated with underground, especially "gothic," music also combine homoeroticism, gender variance, and the sacred and envisage themselves as performing a shamanic or priestly role.

One such group is Coil, whose music has in the early 1990s been labeled "death disco." Contemporary music critic Maria Blount describes Coil's music as rich with "pounding bass rhythms and spiraling dirge melodies," its effect a "hypnotic electronic embrace." They have been inspired by the symbols of ritual magic and the writings of Aleister Crowley, and they make "no secret of their homosexuality," the fusion of sensuality and spirituality being all-important in their music. Indeed, the band's cofounder, Peter Christopherson, explains that part of Coil's admiration for Crowley arises from his having been, in their view, an "advocate for gay rights in a very hostile climate."

Of the transpersonal aim of their music, Christopherson says,

> The music is meant to affect the head, heart and feet simultaneously. . . .
> Originally, music and tribal rhythms were used for ritual purposes—for
> the accumulation of sexual and intellectual energy. We'd like our music to
> affect the listener in that way.

When asked how the presence of HIV/AIDS might have affected their music, Christopherson also speaks as a guide to and transformer of consciousness. He explains that when Coil was recording its early albums, a number of their friends were falling ill and that their lyrics thus "dealt with coming to terms with death and dying." Now, over a decade since the first cases of HIV/AIDS-related illnesses were diagnosed, Christopherson and Coil feel that "constant mourning solves nothing, positive energy does. The spirit is within us to correct any situation."[65]

Mirroring the *fanatici* of Ma, the *baptai* of Kotys, and the *galli* of Cybele, twentieth-century gay, bisexual, and gender-variant persons have reclaimed the transpersonal power of dance.

Rob Dobson, in "Dance Liberation," describes dance as a tool of conscious dismemberment. "What man," he asks, "is readier than a faggot to break the shackles placed upon his body?" But dance allows re-memberment also: "Who more willing to enter forbidden territory? Who more able to explore a traditionally female activity?"

Inspired by Native American reverence for the earth, Dobson writes of dancing in the desert: "when I'm in the Arizona desert I feel close to mystery and power. . . . Often I feel compelled to move in some ritual way, dancing for joy when the rains come, dancing solemn watchful patterns as the desert awakens at dawn. . . .

Dobson relates his experience of dance to shamanic ecstasy:

> Shamans are quite often gay. Almost by definition, that gives them one foot out the door [with which to enter] into other visions, other worlds. Dance is essential as a means of attaining these perceptions. . . . Sometimes [the shaman's] dancing is powerful enough to break up the binding perceptual framework normally used by the shaman's [clients].

Dobson suggests that dancing helps loosen patriarchy's chains, inspires us to reclaim and celebrate our bodies, and opens the door to new worlds. "May we reclaim our bodies from the culture which has tried to possess them for so long," he chants, "May we restore ourselves to beauty."[66]

During the early days of the gay liberation movement, many bars were magically transformed at certain times into temples in which to celebrate our relatedness or *communitas*. In certain places, gay community centers also experienced this metamorphosis. In New York, California, Oregon, Texas, and elsewhere, this awakening sense of radical community was symbolized by circle dances. Lesbian activist and poet Martha Shelley exclaimed, "Everyone in circles!" and Steve Dansky wrote in "Hey man!":

> We have danced the circle dance as a show of community. Our circle dance is the ritual . . . before we enter the struggle. We in our circle dance have felt our sensibilities surge. . . . With acute aggressiveness we have encircled ourselves with protection against our oppressor.[67]

With the emergence of disco, circle dances and the revolutionaries dancing them all but vanished. The essence of their power to foster re-memberment, community, and ecstasy lingered, however, needing only to be called forth once more by Sylvester, Elton John, Boy George, RuPaul, Coil, and workers of magic who have stood with us—Patti LaBelle, Grace Jones, Madonna, and others.

CARNIVALESQUE

Alice Walker, in "All the Bearded Irises of Life," a poignant tribute to the carnivalesque aspect of gay life in San Francisco inspired by the sudden emergence of the HIV crisis, wrote of her experience of being among gay men on Halloween nights in the late 1970s:

> Very often there were parades. On Halloween, for several years, we dressed up as various night creatures and trick-or-treated about the city, taking in

the fabulous costumes, the outrageous hair styles and make-up only gays would have the queerness to make and the imagination to wear. I loved the life that gays gave Halloween, a holiday I learned to enjoy only because of them.[68]

The association of homoeroticism and gender variance with the carnivalesque is an ancient one. While we have already encountered the *sots* of premodern France and the "foolish" sex in which they indulged, the association may be traced to late antiquity, when Christian authorities tried to control or abolish carnivals, which they correctly perceived as celebrations of the exiled gods. "The remains of heathen superstitions of all kinds are forbidden," the Quinisext (or Trullan) Synod found it necessary to declare almost seven hundred years after the "triumph" of Christianity: "The festivals of the Kalendar, the *Bota* (in honor of Pan), the *Brumalia* (in honor of Bacchus), the assemblies on the first of March, public dances of women, clothing of men like women, and inversely, putting on comic, satyric, or tragic masks, the invocation of Bacchus at the winepress, etc. [All] these activities are forbidden."[69]

In our own day, church and state—via parade permits, prescribed zones of activity, and the police—conspire to disrupt such festivities. Despite the element of patriarchal control, however, such celebrations as Carnival, Mardi Gras, and Halloween serve to remind us of the ancient association of gender variance, same-sex desire, the sacred, and the carnivalesque.

In the early 1970s, a group of gay men based in Milwaukee, Wisconsin, naming themselves Les Petites Bonbons, sought to blend gay activism, spiritual experience, aesthetics, and the carnivalesque in their works and lives. "Les Petites Bonbons," they said of themselves,

> are Gay Pansensualists. We acknowledge the gaily erotic nature of all things and we reject the forcible attempt of straight society . . . to define and thereby limit the human experience. . . .
> We are poets and we are painters. We are a Feast of Fools. We are the surprise in your crackerjacks. . . . Les Petites Bonbons is the name of a . . . traveling circus, a musical band of Gay guerillas.[70]

In December 1991, I visited with Leo Martello, mentioned above. Now in his sixties, Martello lives in a Manhattan flat overflowing with old books, ritual paraphernalia, and stuffed animals; indeed, the decor might be described as "magical camp." It is his carnivalesque attitude toward life that is most striking about the elder Martello. While he says that he has generally "given up on people," his sardonic, campy humor keeps him afloat. When he was recently asked if he believed in reincarnation, he replied, "No, I once did, but that was in a former life." In the journal *Fireheart*, he remarks,

> There is a greater Magick. . . . That is . . . the magick of humor, of laughter. . . . The sacredness of silliness. Wouldn't Miss Piggy make a marvelous High Priestess? Or imagine Mae West greeting a visiting [Wiccan] high

priest in that undulating way of hers, asking, "Is that an athame [ritual knife] in your pocket, or are you just glad to see me?"[71]

What is it about Carnival and the carnivalesque that so delights us? Alexander Orloff, a celebrated photographer and essayist, suggests that

> nothing can resist this tidal wave of juggernauting chaos as it turns our ordered world on its head. . . . this is a magical time outside of time in which one and all are changed, everything is reversed, inverted. . . . Through orgiastic excess and folly, through the embrace of the opposite within us, through the baptism of frenzied chaos we are reborn.[72]

Of gay participation in New Orleans's Mardi Gras, Rick Paul explains that while gay and gender-bending men have long participated in the festival, it was in the 1960s that openly gay "krewes" began to emerge. At first, Paul relates, they focused on satirizing the performances of heterosexual krewes. Soon, however, their performances grew to extravagant spectacles reminiscent of those held at the court of Henri III. Frequently, they incorporated mythic and pagan themes. Paul observes, "Like the early court entertainments in France and Italy, these 'gay balls' rely heavily on mythological themes, especially . . . Mediterranean [ones] . . . because of the intuitive resonance with the homoeroticism of the Greeks and with the mystery cults of Egypt and the Fertile Crescent."[73]

Of Carnaval in Brazil, contemporary anthropologist Richard G. Parker explains that it emphasizes the "erotic merging of the [individual] body with other bodies," those bodies together becoming the *povo,* the "people," and transforming into a community in which, for "a few brief moments, hierarch[ies] collapse." Carnaval, Parker continues, "offers a utopian vision . . . of life in a tropical paradise . . . where the struggles, suffering, and sadness of normal human existence have been destroyed. . . . In the *carnaval,* everything is permitted, as it would be in the best of all possible worlds."

Parker, who maintains that "no symbolic form dominates the symbolism of the festival as completely as transvestism," makes it clear that transvestites or drag queens and gay men play a vital role in Carnaval.[74] What Parker neglects to say, however, is that Carnaval celebrates, among other things, the descent of the Yoruba *orishá* to the earth and that many of the celebrants of Carnaval are practitioners of the Yoruba religion. The Yoruba religion recognizes the sacred power of the carnivalesque, one of its chief deities being the trickster Eleggúa.

The carnivalesque, especially in its high camp form, is also an essential ingredient in Radical Faerie rites. Of a festival honoring a carnivalesque goddess, reminiscent of Mère Sotte, and her consort, the Radiant Poodle, the faeries Gloria Mundi and Shastina have written:

> Out of the deep and mysterious twilight of Faerie Dream World, clothed in the ecstasy of multitudinous paper carnations, rose a spectre of Radical Faerie essence . . . the Radiant Poodle. [The] chant "WOOF WOOF ARF ARF" rose from the frenzied participants. . . . The faeries lined up behind

the Goddess [and] Radiant Poodle . . . carrying all manner of colorful banners [and dancing to the] rhythms . . . of the drums.[75]

LEATHER AND THE LEFT-HAND PATH

As gay men are reclaiming the power of the carnivalesque, they are also rediscovering other powers associated with figures embodying our domain. These include powers linked to warriorhood and metamorphosis, such as those known to Germanic warriors. They also include powers sometimes unfortunately referred to as "dark"—a term that I find difficult to disentangle from racist expression as well as from Judeo-Christian concepts of "good" and "evil"—that is, powers of the realm referred to in occult literature as the left-hand path. These are powers known to the Yakut "soft" shamans of Siberia as well as to Rimbaud, Verlaine, Crowley, and others living in the nineteenth and early twentieth centuries.[76]

Although warrior, shamanic, and occult powers sometimes manifest in isolation, they are frequently found in literary works pertaining to homoerotically (or bisexually) inclined and gender-variant men. Genet's *Our Lady of the Flowers,* Bram Stoker's *Dracula,* and the vampire novels of Anne Rice—cult classics in Western gay communities of the late twentieth century—are among the myriad works combining the powers of warriorhood (often psychic rather than physical), metamorphosis, and left-hand magic. The films of Kenneth Anger may also be read in this light.

The relation of these powers to our domain is perhaps most blatantly expressed in the dress of gay men who are known to their communities as "leather queens." While these men often appear to reflect the ultramasculine pole of gay male behavior, the appellation *leather queen* speaks to an awareness of gender variance, which is frequently expressed during rites of lovemaking, when they joyfully take the receptive role in same-sex eroticism. The dress of these men not only depends upon putting on a bovine garment, suggesting in this context animal transformation, but also often includes symbols associated with the occult. These may include rings that pierce the nipples, nose, or penis as well as tattoos with metaphysical significance.

In terms of sexual behavior, the powers are often, although not always, linked to S/M, or sadomasochism (which, needless to say, is also practiced by many non-gay persons). While S/M behavior may include elements of pain, its practitioners insist that it is not hurting another individual that defines S/M, as many in the general populace imagine; rather it consists of rituals and fantasies centering on relationships of power. In terms of gay relationships, these rituals allow each of the partners to experience not only his "butch-ness" and "femme-ness" but also to experience their relation together as warriors in a universe not unlike that described by Carlos Castaneda in his tales of the Yaqui sage Don Juan. For example in "Raw Hide: The Mystery of Power and Leather," Scott Tucker describes the apartment of a San Francisco photographer and artist who is interested in exploring the spiritual dimension of "leather"; he writes,

The first time I met Chester, he showed me portfolios of his photos, and I noticed a home altar with a tarot reading spread before it. In a central spot lay the card called The Hanged Man, showing a man hanging upside down, bound by one heel to a green tree, light shining around his head. In the same room hung a photograph by Chester with the same name; it showed a hooded man in full leather hanging by one heel, chained to a pulley and in a similar posture. In traditional tarot readings, The Hanged Man is a symbol of crucifixion and future resurrection, of wisdom gained through worldly disgrace. No pain, no gain. Sometimes it is interpreted as Lucifer the Lightbringer thrown headlong from heaven. A friend of mine mentioned that in leather tarot readings, The Hanged Man is symbolic of a hanging cock, sexually spent or ready to rise. Lucifer, Christ and cock? The image is heretically rich.[77]

HEALERS AND GUIDES OF THE SOUL

Those who in their lives practice homoeroticism, gender variance, and sacred work—the "soft" shamans, *galli, enarees,* and others—have traditionally served as healers and guides of the soul, counseling and comforting the dying and guiding their spirits from this world to another.

We remember Walt Whitman who, during the Civil War, cared for sick, wounded, and dying soldiers. In his poem "To One Shortly to Die," we see him in the role of psychopomp. "You are to die," he tells his comrade,

> let others tell you what they
>   please, I cannot prevaricate,
> I am exact and merciless, but I love you—
>   there is no escape for you.
> . . . .
> I sit quietly by, I remain faithful,
> I am more than nurse, more than parent or neighbor,
> I absolve you from all except your spiritual bodily,
>   that is eternal . . . [78]

Film historian and critic Leonid Alekseychuk has described the late Armenian-Georgian filmmaker Sergei Paradjanov, well known for his films *Shadows of Forgotten Ancestors* and *The Color of Pomegranates,* in this way: "Like a bewitched and reverent pantheist, for whom everything in existence is full of spirits and universal harmony, Paradjanov worshipped icons and carnival masks . . . folk embroidery . . . smooth skin on a handsome youth."[79]

Due to his homosexual and gender-variant behavior, Paradjanov was sentenced by the Soviets to a number of years in a labor camp in the Ukraine. While there, he painted, designed women's hats, and founded a drag theater, but, more importantly, he, like Whitman or like the *enaree,* his spiritual forebear, served as a healer and psychopomp. He wrote of this experience:

They sent me to severe pathological zones where they expected me to perish. It would have killed a softer man. It's only because I have a clever and cunning character that I managed to survive. . . . I painted a picture of Jesus on the cloth they put over a cadaver. . . .

I became the priest of the zone. I began to close the eyes of corpses and to tie up their jaws. I began healing people, listening to their fates.[80]

Gay neopagans, Wiccans, and Faeries are among those who, in reclaiming the ancient roles of healer and soul guide, have become involved in various healing practices believed to ease the suffering of HIV/AIDS-related illnesses. These practices include established medical care as well as herbal medicine, massage, and visualization.[81] In the words of Tim Cowan, a gay Wiccan, "the gods and goddesses [are] saying to us, 'Hey, wake up. This is your [time to reclaim the] ancient role of healer and death counselor, someone who understands what it means to move between the worlds.'"[82]

We have also begun to create rituals to honor our loved ones who have died of AIDS-related illnesses. A decade ago, very early in the pandemic, a young San Franciscan hanged himself in Golden Gate Park after being told by his doctor that he had AIDS. As the family had control of the body, his friends created a funeral rite for him without having access to his body. They began by purifying his house with water and incense of cedar, sage, and rose and by constructing an altar on which they placed things dear to him as well as his suicide note and a white, seven-day candle. They then gathered in a circle to share memories of him. The rite culminated with visualizing the young man in a joyful mood and bidding him farewell.[83]

I KNOW A PLACE

Why is it that we continue to flock to television sets each year, or occasionally to the Castro Theatre if we're lucky, to view *The Wizard of Oz* one more time? Why do tears appear when Judy Garland or Miss Patti wails "Somewhere Over the Rainbow"?[84]

Exiles, we are continually seeking that glowing neon sign that flashes HOME. Captives of a dream, we are forever waiting for the feather-capped youth to appear at the window, to kidnap us from the suburbs. To harbor us when our families have deserted us. We dream, with Whitman, of a city of comrades, "a city invincible to the attacks of the whole of the rest of the earth, / . . . the new city of Friends."[85]

The poet Jack Spicer became profoundly disillusioned when Whitman's dream failed to become a reality for him. Spicer wrote of the mythical, Whitmanesque land of Calamus,

Calamus cannot exist in the presence of cruelty. . . . Calamus is like Oz. One needs, after one has left it, to find some magic belt to cross its Deadly Desert, some cat to entice one into its mirror. There Walt is, crying like some great sea bird from the Emerald Palace, crying "*Calamus, Calamus.*" And there one is, at the other side of the desert, hearing Walt, but seeing that impossible shadow, those shimmering heat waves across the sky. And one needs no Virgil, but an Alice, a Dorothy, a Washington horse-car conductor, to lead one over that shimmering hell, that cruelty.[86]

This yearning for home may, in terms of our domain, be traced to the beliefs and practices of the Gnostics, who included the Naassenes and others described in our chapter concerning the *galli* of Cybele. Perceiving themselves as "planetary exiles," they sought to regain their "lost homeland," which lay somewhere "beyond Sirius," the Dog Star.

Jacques Lacarrière, who has written an illuminating study on Gnosticism, says of them, "The fundamental difference that separates the Gnostics from their contemporaries is that, for them, their native 'soil' is not the earth, but that lost heaven which they keep vividly alive in their memories. . . . Hence their feeling of having fallen onto our earth like inhabitants from a distant planet, of having strayed into the wrong galaxy, and their longing to regain their true cosmic homeland."[87]

It was only through keeping alive the memory of that other world, through constant vigilance and a program of shamanic deautomization including cultic homoeroticism, that the Gnostics could hope to achieve release and return. Unfortunately for us, although perhaps not for them, the Gnostics vanished. While they appear to have established marginal communities, these were short-lived, probably because they were convinced that only through release from mundane life would they discover true *communitas*. Perhaps they were guided by a belief recently voiced by Edward Said, that "in a secular . . . world, homes are always provisional."[88] This belief also appears to have inspired writer and cultural maverick Hakim Bey to envision "TAZ's," Temporary Autonomous Zones in which bohemians, including radical-spiritual gay men, congregate to experience for a moment in time the "anarchist dream of a free culture."[89]

The Radical Faeries are among those gay seekers who have taken steps to realize the dream of HOME. For almost two decades, Faerie communal households and farms have existed in various parts of the United States, in Oregon, North Carolina, Tennessee, and elsewhere. In Tennessee, the members of Short Mountain Sanctuary—not only faeries but also other gay and bisexual men as well as women and children—have kept bees, raised goats, hosted faerie gatherings, and published the journal *RFD* for a number of years. In 1987, the Faeries, along with the organization Nomenus, purchased land in Oregon on which to establish a sanctuary.

While many of us refuse to surrender the dream of a Never-Never Land, a Calamus, a HOME, we may also look upon communal, rural living as unfeasible. When we discover community, it is often, like Said's, provisional. Our TAZ's are sidewalk cafes, bars, community centers, bookstores, coastal inns, gyms, or theaters showing *The Wizard of Oz*.

Strongly linked to this dream of home, this desire for gay or sexually variant/ gender variant community, is the longing to reclaim ancient alliances. These include those with women, particularly with lesbian and gender-bending women and with contemporary incarnations of "sacred prostitutes" or hierodules. These are women whose spiritual forebears our own befriended in temples of the Goddess millennia ago, as we have observed with the Mesopotamian priests and priestesses of Inanna, the *qadeshim* and *qadeshtu* of the Canaanite Athirat, the priestesses and *galli* of Cybele, and others.

We seek to reclaim, also, alliances with persons of various ethnic groups and economic classes, as we have observed with the devotees of Isis and Atargatis as well as those of the Yoruba *orishá*. In the late twentieth century, such alliances are not easy to build; thanks to the patriarchal order, many of us who lack political, economic, and/or spiritual power have learned to react toward one another, as this order wishes us to do, with mistrust and even rage. Yet gradually the ancient alliances are reemerging. Feminist Witches like Z. Budapest and Starhawk, for instance, are beginning to acknowledge the presence and value of gay men in the neopagan community. Something of these ancient alliances may also be felt in ACT UP and Queer Nation marches and in viewing the AIDS Quilt, sewn in memory of those who have died of AIDS-related illnesses. In my own experience, I have begun to rediscover these alliances at Faerie gatherings, in Wiccan circles, and in the Yoruba-diasporic religion. I remember, for instance, staying up all night at a Faerie gathering in the San Gabriel Mountains sharing ideas with Luna Voidofcourse, a gay Cuban artist and practitioner of Santería, and I remember the strong sense of "home" I felt when my companion David and other gay and lesbian friends danced with a myriad others in honor of Elleggúa and the other *orishá* on a New Year's Day several years ago at the house of the Yoruba-Lucumí priestess Luisah Teish. The reclamation of these alliances remains, however, in its infancy, and the experience of "home" still seems ephemeral.

Perhaps, however, the transitory aspect of these experiences bears its own wisdom. I am reminded of a passage in Hermann Hesse's novella *Demian*. When Sinclair, the intimate friend of the mysterious Max Demian, finally encounters Demian's mother, Frau Eva, a twentieth-century incarnation of the Great Goddess, he thinks he has reached home. Frau Eva, however, tells him, "One never reaches home. . . . But where paths that have affinity for each other intersect the whole world looks like home, for a time."[90]

Hatian-American gay poet Assotto Saint, 1992.

We Are the Same People, Different from Before

I am large,
I contradict myself,
I contain multitudes.

Walt Whitman[1]

The universe is not only queerer than we imagine,
but it is queerer than we can imagine.

J. B. S. Haldane[2]

For millennia, gender-variant and homoerotically inclined men (and perhaps also bisexually inclined males and transpersons) have willfully or otherwise challenged patriarchal and hetero-centric conceptions of gender and sexuality. In doing so, they have represented to others both the terror of the wild and the possibility of a different order of things, an order linked to the arts of healing, divination, and magic, as well as to sacred and fine arts. They have performed sacred and aesthetic-sacred functions, serving those among whom they have lived in beneficial ways, often doing so in an atmosphere of intolerance or oppression. ¶ *Why* they (or we) have done so is, however, a matter of great controversy. ¶ In the Introduction, I spoke briefly of the social constructionist and essentialist perspectives on the identity of homoerotically inclined and, to a lesser extent, gender-variant persons. I also mentioned the work of Will Roscoe and Walter Williams, gay scholars who are trying to move beyond the dualism implicit in this debate and to include spiritual functionaries like the Native American *berdaches* in the discussion.

Others suggest that same-sex eroticism and/or gender variance may have a biological origin. Studies such as those of Simon LeVay, which indicate that one node of the hypothalamus of the brain is roughly similar in women and gay men but three times larger in heterosexual men, and those of UCLA researchers Roger A. Gorski and Laura S. Allen, which indicate that the anterior commissure, a band of fibers connecting the left and right side of the brain that appear to play a role in verbal ability, may be larger in gay men and in women than in heterosexual men, suggest that biological theories merit further investigation. A study published in 1993, led by Dr. Dean Hamer, indicates a link between male homosexuality and a segment of the X chromosome, inherited from the mother, further suggesting that gay men often have maternal uncles.[3] Dr. Laura Allen's interpretations of her findings with Gorski speak to our domain; she observes that "the homosexual individual may have a brain that is organized differently at many different regions. They may not be unique just in terms of their sexual orientation but in the way they perceive the world as a whole. . . . We know so many artists, so many musicians, that are homosexual. . . . Maybe certain anatomical differences in the homosexual brain lend themselves to perceiving the world in a different way that provides many gifts to our culture."[4]

According to sociobiologist E. O. Wilson, homosexuality, present in the animal world among rhesus macaques and other animals, is probably not only "normal in the biological sense" but also a "distinctive beneficent behavior that evolved as an important element of early human organization." He further implies that homosexuality, gender variance, and spiritual role may be biologically linked. Because many persons engaging in same-sex eroticism did not in the earliest periods of humanity reproduce, these persons, Wilson explains, might have been employed as caretakers of their kin, assisting mothers with children as well as assisting the physically disabled, elderly, sick, and dying. He further asserts that such persons might "have taken the roles of seers, shamans, artists, and keepers of tribal knowledge." In his view, "If the relatives . . . were benefited by higher survival and reproduction rates," then genes promoting homosexuality might have proliferated. As evidence in support of this view, Wilson cites the example of the Native American *berdaches*, Amerindian cultures allegedly being "similar to the ones in which human behavior evolved genetically during prehistory."

As caretakers and spiritual workers, persons engaging in same-sex eroticism and possibly perceived as gender variant may have been, according to Wilson and other sociobiologists, carriers of altruism, a trait discovered in the natural world among birds and chimpanzees. Altruism, it is believed, may have inspired the growth of religions. Genes promoting altruism, like those promoting homosexuality and possibly gender variance, may have proliferated because they strengthened the possibility of survival of the group. In this way, Wilson and others suggest that a complex of traits that bears close resemblance to our domain may have existed since the dawn of humanity.[5]

THE LINKING of gender variance, homoeroticism, and sacred work, need not, however, depend upon biology. In this text, we have noticed how this domain of traits reappears in various cultures and historical epochs. From an early date, certain forces may have helped to nourish it. Diffusion, the carrying of a belief, rite, or institution from one place to another, may have helped to spread gender-variant spiritual practices across vast regions of land. Cultural stratification or bricolage, the interpenetration of cultures due to alliances or colonization, may have spread its growth within other regions. In recent years, we have learned that travel was much more extensive in antiquity than previously imagined. We have begun to track vast migration routes from eastern Europe to Britain on the one hand and China on the other, as well as routes from Africa to other parts of the world. It is possible that gender-variant shamanism was carried at an early date from Scythia (or Russia) to other regions in this manner. With the African relief, we have seen how gender-variant, black African priests of Isis may have come into contact with likeminded Roman priests of the Goddess hundreds of years before the birth of Christ. The Gundestrup Cauldron suggests that early encounters may have occurred between spiritual persons of Scythia or Thrace and those of the Celtic and Germanic realms.[6]

MEN CHIEFLY involved in Gay Spirituality have also begun to develop models pertaining to gay identity, models that embrace spiritual or transpersonal experience as well as gender variance.

Not surprisingly, and I would say unfortunately, these models have been scoffed at or ignored by constructionists and others in the gay academic, or queer-theoretical, community. On the other hand, they have been somewhat respectfully received by Jungian and archetypal theorists and therapists. The reason for this may lie in the fact that while constructionist-postmodernists generally shun discussion of the sacred, especially when the possibility of a divinity or archetypal energy, such as the Goddess or "the Feminine," is acknowledged, Jungian and archetypal therapists and writers accept the transpersonal dimension of consciousness and experience as valid, empowering, and transformative.

One such model is that offered by Harry Hay, a longtime gay activist and one of the founders of the Radical Faeries. He writes: "I propose that we Gay Folk, whom Great Nature has been assembling as a Separate People in these last 100,000 years, must now prepare to emerge from the shadows of History *because we are a species-variant with a particular characteristic adaptation-in-consciousness* WHOSE TIME HAS COME!"[7]

Hay perceives gay people as a "folk" who differ in an essential way from the majority of heterosexually inclined persons. In recent years, inspired by Native American and other non-Western conceptions of gender, he has begun referring to gay men as *third gender people* and to lesbian women as *fourth gender people.* Hay suggests that third and fourth gender people differ from others in that they (or we) relate to each other as *subject* to *subject* rather than as *subject* to *object,* such as has traditionally been the case in heterosexual relationships. He explains that *subject-subject consciousness* may be the gift that gay men and lesbian women have to contribute to humanity.[8]

While this model, not surprisingly, has been condemned as essentialist by constructionists, it bears resemblance to certain postmodernist conceptualizations of lesbian identity, such as that offered by feminist theorist Penelope J. Engelbrecht. She suggests that a lesbian metaphysic exists which "inscribes the inter/action of a lesbian Subject and a lesbian Other/self. These designations are inherently and constantly mutual—quite unlike the oppositional polarity of the patriarchal terms [Subject-Object/Other].... These lesbian terms, Subject and Other/self.... are more than interchangeable; they are synonymous."[9]

Another model of gay identity emphasizing the transpersonal dimension of gay experience is that offered by Jungian scholar Mitch Walker. In *Visionary Love: A Spirit Book of Gay Mythology,* Walker coins several neologisms to speak to various spiritual aspects of gay consciousness and expression. For instance, he uses the terms *double love* and *magical twinning* to refer to the transpersonal quality of homoerotic bonding, suggesting another *subject-subject* model; *yan* to refer to the link between same-sex eroticism and gender variance; and *roika* to speak of linking homoeroticism and gender variance to the spiritual functionary.[10]

What constructionists and some postmodernists object to most in such a view of identity is its seemingly rock-solid stability, its lack of fluidity. It's not only academics, however, who object to this view of identity. In recent years we have heard rock star Madonna, performance artist and actress Sandra Bernhard, and a host of others speak out in favor of gender and erotic fluidity and against accepting labels like *gay* and *straight,* which they and others perceive as confining or inadequate. In *Vested Interests: Cross-Dressing and Cultural Anxiety,* cultural theorist Marjorie Garber, using the metaphor of the "third" actor in Greek tragedy (for a long time tragedies depended upon two actors), voices support for gender and erotic fluidity, writing, "The 'third' is that which questions binary thinking and introduces crisis.... But what is crucial here ... is that the 'third term' is not a term. Much less is it a sex ... as signified by a term like 'androgyne' or 'hermaphrodite'.... The 'third' is a mode of articulation, a way of describing a space of possibility."[11]

It seems to me that the core of the mystery of our domain may lie *between* the concept of a relatively constant *third or fourth gender identity* and that of *gender-bending behavior and erotic fluidity.* In my view, these two concepts may coexist simultaneously, albeit in a paradoxical manner, within the psyche. I have been led to this notion by way of a contemporary psychological theory originating in quantum physics.

QUANTUM PHYSICS tells us that "all beings at the subatomic level can be described equally well either as solid particles, like so many minute billiard balls, or as waves, like undulations of the surface of the sea." Indeed, quantum physics insists that "both the wavelike and the particlelike aspects of being must be considered when trying to understand the nature of things."[12]

Physicist-philosopher-therapist Danah Zohar writes, "Quantum 'stuff' is, essentially, *both* wavelike and particlelike, simultaneously." In Zohar's view, when applied to human consciousness, the *self,* one's *identity,* may be described in similar terms. As particles exist, "so do selves," she writes; "the self is not," however, an "eternal, indivisible whole." Indeed, each person expresses a plurality of selves, or *subselves.* She continues, "Both selves and particles are . . . fluid. . . . They flow into and out of existence, now standing alone, now wedding themselves to other selves or particles, now disappearing altogether—teasing us with their dancing forms and shadows."[13] According to Zohar, when we say "I," we are in fact speaking of a relatively intense level of *dialoguing* between our various *subselves.* In general, we might say that while a quantum psychological view acknowledges the concepts of the self and identity, our *particle-ness,* it also acknowledges the fluidity of these, our *waveness.*

While the particlelike aspect of identity might refer to the multicultural, transhistorical persistence of same-sex eroticism, gender variance, sacred role, and their linkage in the "soft" shaman, the *gallus* of Cybele, and so on, the wavelike aspect of identity might refer to differences produced by cultural or historical influences. Further, while the particlelike aspect of identity might speak to the *figure* or *role* of the gender-variant, homoerotically inclined spiritual functionary, the wavelike aspect might refer to the *specific acts* that the sacred person undertakes—as, for instance, the act of sacralized eroticism or that of gender metamorphosis, frequently manifested as cross-dressing or another boundary-dissolving action.

In *Disseminating Whitman,* literary theorist Michael Moon suggests that Walt Whitman's aesthetic emerged from an acute awareness of the wavelike aspect of identity. Moon writes, "Whitman . . . espouses what I am calling 'fluidity.' This is a mode of consciousness poised at the 'washed-out' boundaries of mind and body [as experienced] in drunkenness or in the latter phases of the cycle of sexual arousal. [It is a] boundary-dissolving experience."[14]

While the *third gender* model of identity appears to emphasize the particlelike aspect of identity, the wavelike aspect of identity has not escaped Hay and others in the Gay Spiritual movement. Indeed, while the term "third gender man" suggests a rather solid identity, the term *faerie* or *fairy,* used by these same men, speaks to identity's wavelike character. Hay speaks of *third gender men* "constantly reinventing" themselves "out of the . . . gossamers," that is, out of light, flimsy, delicate, cobweb-like materials,[15] and Walker writes of men embodying *fairy* spirit identity:

Fairies see polarities dancing, changing everywhere, constantly. . . . This
wonderful paradoxical freedom from form . . . enables Fairies to fly. . . .
There is an essence, essence of an eternal, hidden, dark, shining, eerie
secret: the simultaneous and continuous creation and annihilation of
Form. . . . All shapes, forms, are bendings and corners of this flowing-is.
[Fairies] are not static things but riders of lightbeams, weightless dancers
along the edge—indeed are the Dancing itself. . . . They are flow, the
wind . . . [16]

The term *fairy* delights in this paradox of particle-wave or protean essence. It is this sort of paradoxical coexistence that physicists have named the *quantum*.

Quantum physics is not the only contemporary scientific theory that may aid us in better understanding identity in general and the figure of the gender-variant, homoerotically inclined shaman, priest, or artist in particular. Both holographic theory and chaos theory may also help us to more easily grasp the paradoxical nature of identity.

HOLOGRAPHIC THEORY suggests that the existence of figures we might call archetypal, such as those embodying our domain, may originate in an *implicate* or *enfolded* order, a mysterious hologram that is the heart or mind of the universe. When such archetypes manifest in historical epochs and cultures, embodied by men and women, they are said to be reflected in the *explicate* or *unfolded* order of the universe. Thus, we might account for the reiteration of our domain in the lives of men of many times and places. Holographic theory also suggests that the sense of kinship we may feel with "soft" shamans, priests of the Goddess, and others may be rooted in a property of the universe now referred to as *nonlocality*. Basically, nonlocality suggests that everything in the universe is interrelated, and that the barriers we have erected between *locations* such as geographical regions and historical periods may ultimately prove to be illusory. In the view of some scientists, nonlocality may help to explain such phenomena as reincarnation and telepathy. In terms of our own context, it has been suggested to me that by temporarily dismantling or dissolving certain socially constructed barriers, as when experiencing ecstatic states of consciousness, we may come to know *nonlocal* oneness with homoerotically inclined, gender-variant spiritual persons of other cultures and historical epochs.[17]

In his poem "The Sleepers," Whitman seems to forecast holographic identity or consciousness. He writes,

> I go from bedside to bedside, I sleep close with the other sleepers each in
>   turn,
> I dream in my dream all the dreams of the other dreamers,
> And I become the other dreamers.
> . . . .
> I am a dance.[18]

CHAOS THEORY may also hold a key to the mystery of the *third gender/ gender-bending behavior and erotic fluidity paradox*. In common parlance, *chaos* is a derogatory term used to refer to an absence of order. In the Judeo-Christian West, *chaos* more particularly refers to an absence of, or challenge to, the patriarchal order, which is equated with both the natural order of things and divine law. Thus, not surprisingly, the behavior of homoerotically inclined and gender-variant individuals has in the West often been described as chaotic, as "going against the grain," as "unnatural," "disordered," "inverted," or "perverted."

Sociologist Peter Berger explains that in Judeo-Christian societies, individuals who forsake socially accepted sex roles—or the dominant spiritual tradition(s)—may be branded "fools" or "madmen." In the view of a typical patriarchal, hetero-centric, and homophobic society, to come out as a gay, bisexual, gender-variant, or transgenderal person is to risk being "thrust into an outer darkness that sepa-rates one from the 'normal' order of men," in other words, into the realm of chaos.[19]

Berger goes on to say that in such a society's view, one who rejects the hetero-sexual "program" may well be perceived by others as "deny[ing] being itself—the being of the [alleged] universal order of things." In doing so, that person forfeits his/her "own being" in terms of the patriarchal order.[20] Put another way, to reject the heterocentric, patriarchal order is to be rendered invisible, to become one with chaos.

Chaos theorists believe, however, that chaos may be a natural and creative process with its own peculiar kind of order. According to chaos theorists, what we commonly describe as chaotic behavior, including everything from children's scribbles to changes in the weather, may exhibit a higher form of order. This higher order, referred to as *turbulent flow,* is fluid in character and defies tradi-tional notions of order. Chaotic patterns, which constitute a kind of paradox and which are referred to as *strange attractors,* resemble the wings of butterflies.[21] Chaos theorists believe that the brain, and perhaps also the heart, may function "normally—and even optimally—in a chaotic state." They further suggest that chaotic, erratic, or deviant activity, both within the brain and in outward experi-ence, may not only be quite natural but also, at least occasionally, be more benefi-cial than traditionally ordered activity. Indeed, we are told, we may derive therapeutic benefit, artistic inspiration, and perhaps even spiritual wisdom from apparently chaotic activities.[22] If chaos theorists are correct in their assumptions, it is highly possible that individuals might gain transpersonal knowledge from gender-bending and homoerotic experiences, which clearly constitute—at least in terms of patriarchal, heterocentric cultures—chaotic experiences.

As if they were privy to this chaotic-theoretical perspective, many ancient and primal peoples depicted chaos as a deity and associated it with a positive sense of *destruction/fluidity/re-creation* rather than with an utter absence of order. We might say that chaos represents the ultimate expression of wavelike behavior. Not surprisingly, many of the deities linked to chaos, such as the Greek Eris, have been goddesses. As literary theorist N. Katherine Hayles reminds us in *Chaos Bound,* "Chaotic unpredictability and nonlinear thinking [are] aspects of life that have tended to be culturally encoded as feminine" because they have been perceived as opposing the patriarchal order.[23] In terms of our context, deities and semi-divine beings associated with chaos, including the Greek god Eros and the Yoruba *orishá* Oyá, have also often been linked to gender variance or same-sex eroticism.

✂

OF THE SACRED beings associated with our domain and also chaotic behavior (in the terms of chaos theorists), the Greek shaman Tiresias, whose name means "interpreter of signs," is especially exemplary, particularly in his associations with gender metamorphosis, animal transformation, the realms of the living and the dead, and forms of divination depending upon an understanding of chaotic "order."

The story is told that one day, while walking on Mount Cyllene, Tiresias witnessed two serpents coupling. On striking one of them, perhaps out of fear or as a magical gesture, he was transformed into a woman. He, now she, then lived as a woman for seven years until, after the same event repeated itself, he once more became a man. Other storytellers claimed that Tiresias had actually been female at birth and had changed sexes six times afterwards, his experiences including motherhood and warriorhood. According to these storytellers, he ended his life as a wise woman or crone. Also among some of these latter storytellers, it was believed that between Tiresias's phases as men and women, he experienced being a man-woman, or *kinaidos,* and a woman-man, or Amazon.

As a gender-variant male, Tiresias was sometimes depicted as the beloved of Hermes, the god of messages and himself a shaman. Classical scholar Luc Brisson, in describing a portrait of Tiresias on a fifth-century B.C.E. Etruscan mirror, writes: "Tiresias here appears as a young being. His traits, his hair and his garments recall those of a woman. His face and the form of his body present, in effect, no masculine characteristics. . . . His hair [is] very long [and] held by a band. . . . Finally, his garment looks at once like a masculine mantle and a feminine chiton." Tiresias's fluidity, like that of other shamans, extended beyond fluidity of gender role and erotic expression. Like other shamans, he was capable of transforming into animals. He experienced being, among other things, a badger, a mole, a hare, a lizard, a mongoose, a monkey, and a hyena. A number of the animals into which he transformed, not surprisingly, were thought to be either gender-bending or hermaphroditic, especially the hyena and the hare.

Once, during one of his incarnations as a woman or man-woman, depending upon the storyteller, Tiresias was sexually penetrated by the spiderman Arachnos. The latter may himself have been a man-woman, a male-gender variant of the spiderwoman Arachne. At the moment of orgasm, Tiresias changed into a mouse, while Arachnos became a weasel. In my view, suggested by Brisson, this tale may mask a sex-magical encounter, as the animals into which the two transform place them into contact with the goddess Hecate and especially with her knowledge of necromancy.

The animal, however, that looms above all others as a manifestation or attribute of Tiresias is the serpent, a multicultural and multihistorical symbol of the archetypal feminine and of fluidity. Serpents, associated with water, change skins, identities, lives. Not only were they guardians in Greece of sacred, oracular springs, they were also, like butterflies, vehicles of human souls. "It is in the form of a serpent," Brisson tells us, "that the soul leaves the earth, and in this form that it returns."

When it was decided that Tiresias should depart from the earth, he did not die but rather, like the Chinese gender-variant deity Lan Tzai He, was carried to the otherworld, in this case, to Hades. Here, with Eros (as Eros-Amor), he serves Persephone and Hades as a mediator between the realms of the living and the dead.

Finally, as a shaman and prophet, Tiresias was believed to have mastered a great number of divinatory techniques, including two that depend upon the interpretation of chaotic patterns: pyromancy, divination by way of tracking the movements of flames; and libanomancy, divination by tracking the spiralings of incense, the perfume of chaos.

In the figure of Tiresias, we have, it seems to me, a portrait of the paradox of third gender identity/gender-bending behavior and erotic fluidity. Tiresias, like many of those who have embodied our domain, exemplifies chaotic order, holographic consciousness, and the quantum self, the mystery of the particle and the wave.[24]

BEFORE CLOSING, I would like to mention two other theories of identity which may help us to better understand the paradox of third gender identity/gender-bending behavior and erotic fluidity. These are the *Caribbean identity* theory of Antonio Benítez-Rojo and the *border(land) identity* theory of Gloria Anzaldúa. Both theorists, incidentally, are Latino (the former is Cuban-born and the latter Chicana), both are creative writers as well as literary theorists, and both have been profoundly inspired by the postmodernist movement and by contemporary scientific theories.

In *The Repeating Island*, Benítez-Rojo suggests that in the Caribbean, which he views as a kind of book or *text*, certain signs (images, symbols) and behaviors tend to repeat themselves in successive time periods, albeit in a rather chaotic manner and in innovative ways. *Caribbean-ness* is thus a kind of particle that, containing particlelike elements, nevertheless operates as a wave. For Benítez-Rojo—unlike many postmodernists, who have accepted constructionism's antispiritual position—one of the chief particlelike elements of Caribbean identity is the Yoruba religion, or Santería, and its expression in images of the *orishá* as well as in "a kind of ancient and golden powder" that elderly daughters of Oshún dust "between their gnarled legs, a scent of basil and mint"—ingredients of a sacred wash in Santería—"in their dress, [and] a symbolic, ritual wisdom in their gesture and gay chatter."[25] Moreover, particlelike elements include not only the sacred but also other elements that resonate with our domain, including gender variance, ritual artistic expression—as in ecstatic dance—and the carnivalesque. It is in the image and event of Carnival, he explains, that we find the purest and richest manifestation of Caribbean identity. "There is something feminine," he writes, "in this extraordinary fiesta: its flux, its diffuse sensuality . . . its capacity to nourish. . . . Think of the dancing flourishes, the rhythms of the conga . . . *the men dressed and painted as women* [italics mine] . . . the beat of the chaos of the islands."[26]

It is obvious how one might link this description of identity to the gay, bisexual, and gender-variant practitioners of Santería or participants in Carnival. But I think that beyond this, a more general comparison may be made between Benítez-Rojo's Caribbean identity and that of the men embodying our domain. I am especially reminded of the carnivalesque *sots* and the Radical Faeries. In terms of sacred attire and ecstatic dance, I am reminded as well of the "soft" shamans of Siberia and the priests of the goddesses of antiquity. It seems to me that if we imagine those embodying our domain as forming a parade, a great cavalcade— from the shamans and *berdaches* of Siberia and the Americas to the *omasenge kimbanda* of Africa, the shaman-poet Qu Yuan of China, the *assinnu* of Inanna, the *galli* of Cybele, the *sots,* the devilish rakes of the eighteenth century, Rimbaud, Aleister Crowley, and the Radical Faeries—we may sense in the expression of our domain a kind of Caribbean-ness, in which the traits of homoeroticism, gender variance, and spiritual (or sacred-artistic) role, as well as often-repeated subtraits like the carnivalesque, have repeated themselves in a seemingly chaotic way across many cultures and historical epochs, as if by way of the principle of strange attraction. When I spoke with Benítez-Rojo in the spring of 1993 at the University of Texas, he acknowledged this possible resonance between Caribbean-ness and our domain. In his view, Caribbean identity, while concentrated in a particular geographic and historical region, is not limited to that region. To the contrary, it is an *island* that "'repeats' itself, unfolding and bifurcating until it reaches all the seas and lands of the earth."[27]

Like Benítez-Rojo, Anzaldúa describes a kind of identity which embraces both the particle and the wave. While referring to herself in particlelike, seemingly essential(ist) terms—"Chicana *tejana* [Texas] lesbian"—she insists upon the wavelike expression of these terms.[28] She sees these terms not as static but as constantly "shifting" or metamorphosing aspects of identity, conversing and at times even warring with one another. This wavelike aspect of identity, however, does not prevent Anzaldúa from naming as relatively constant, repeated traits of "border-(land)/*frontera*" identity not only mixed or hybrid ethnicity but also the elements of our domain—albeit as related primarily to women—same-sex eroticism, gender variance, and sacred/artistic role. The "border" woman, the "new *mestiza,*" is the "officiating priestess at the crossroads," paying homage to the gods and goddesses of the Aztecs, the spirits of Mexican-American folklore, and the *orishá* of Santería.[29] She tells lesbian women, gay men, and others manifesting gender variant and sexually variant behavior,

> *Cuando vives en la frontera* (When you live in the borderlands)
> .   .   .   .
> you're a . . .
> forerunner of a new race,
> half and half—both woman and man, neither—
> a new gender.
>
> To survive the Borderlands
> you must live *sin fronteras* (without borders)
> be a crossroads.[30]

AS OF THE WRITING of this book, the origins of our domain in general, and of homosexuality and gender variance in particular, remain mysteries. Until these mysteries are solved, however, it seems to me that the ideas of Anzaldúa and other theorists we have discussed can, at the very least, aid us in our search to know more intimately those embodying homoerotic inclination, gender variance, and sacred role.

Like many involved in the Gay Spiritual movement, I have often wondered whether or not the vast majority of gay men, were it not for patriarchal oppression, would gravitate toward the role of spiritual teacher or guide, or whether the gay man and the gender-variant, homoerotically inclined shaman or priest share in common only same-sex desire. Unfortunately, I do not think we will be able to definitively answer this question until we find ourselves living in a world where the prejudices against homosexuality and gender variance have ceased to exist. I would say, however, that the multicultural, transhistorical repetition of our domain indicates that a great many gay men might gravitate toward the spiritual, or at least the artistic, life if their deepest yearnings were allowed to be freely expressed.

More recently, I have wondered as well whether the boundaries between *gay/bisexual/straight/transgenderal* are as solid as they seem. Last spring, I was invited to attend a gathering held by a circle of neopagans in a grove not far from Austin. Shortly after I arrived, I overheard one of the men say that he didn't think homosexuals had any place in their circle, as they didn't understand the importance of heterosexual love and the family in neopaganism; beyond this, homosexual acts were repulsive to him. When the man conversing with him agreed, and no one nearby challenged him, I began to think I must be the only gay person in attendance. Normally, I would have spoken up to him, but not really being a part of the group, I felt it inappropriate to do so. Instead, I did the only thing I could think of; I asked the circle's leader, to whom I felt strangely attracted, what he felt about homosexuality. When he asked me why, I explained that one of the group's members had been making anti-gay remarks. He responded by letting the man know that the circle held no place for homophobia. He then beckoned me into a thicker part of the wood, and explained that he understood my hurt and anger. He was not gay, he told me, but he could empathize as someone who had undergone transsexual surgery. He had been a woman, and was now a man. We embraced. Later, as I stood talking with him and another man, I sensed that the third was drawn to him but could not understand why. I suddenly felt as if I had wandered into one of Shakespeare's cross-dressing comedies. In truth, however, I stood in the presence of a mystery.

When I recall this experience, or when I think of Dil, the hauntingly beautiful transvestite/gay diva of Neil Jordan's film *The Crying Game,* and of the ostensibly heterosexual man who is, in spite of himself, passionately drawn to the former, it strikes me that terms like *hetero-* and *homosexual* may have outlived their usefulness.

It makes me feel somewhat strange to have written a book in which I have focused so intensely on homoeroticism rather than on all forms of erotic activity in relation to the sacred. I feel strongly, however, that it is the homoerotic (and here I refer also to the lesbian) element, and not the heteroerotic, that has been most often suppressed in erotico-sacred literature. Moreover, as a gay man living at the end of the twentieth century, in the midst of a vicious Christian fundamentalist counterrevolution, I feel it is imperative to let others know of the lives and works of homoerotically inclined and gender-variant spiritual workers and spiritually minded artists who have lived in other cultures and periods of history, so that we may draw upon the memory of them for sustenance. I feel it equally imperative that we know the history of the torture and execution of our spiritual ancestors at the hands of patriarchal religious forces, so that we do not uncritically adhere to the patriarchal faiths in which many of us have been reared.

Unlike our spiritual ancestors, the *assinnu, galli, omasenge kimbanda,* and others, our lives are at least seemingly governed by choices, not destinies. We may choose to act upon our same-sex desires or we may submerge them. We may choose to behave freely or conform to the standards of gender role favored by patriarchal ideology. We may choose to sacralize experience, to seek spiritual wisdom, to see ourselves as healers and transformers of consciousness, or we may reject the spiritual dimension of life.

In my view, Gay Spirituality represents, among other things, the reverence of a gay, queer archetypal energy. I would suggest that in our expressions of gender and sexual variance we may be reflecting an essential queerness that is found throughout nature, and in some as yet undeciphered manner, that strange attraction of which chaos theorists speak, and which resembles butterfly or fairy wings, may be responsible for the reiteration of this queerness across many cultures and epochs. In some ways, admittedly, we are "just like everyone else." We yearn for love, we grieve for those we have lost. We have the strength to fight wars and the compassion to struggle for peace. Many of us have raised children. In another sense, however, I believe that we may be, in the depths of our being, queerer than we have ever imagined—as queer as fairies, as queer as spiralings of incense, as queer as the human brain. While he does not speak directly to our domain, I am reminded of something cultural maverick Terence McKenna has said: "To sum up what I've said about religion, it is as though the Father-God notion were being replaced by the alien-partner notion. The alien-partner is like the angelic tetramorph. It is androgynous, hermaphrodite, transhuman."[31]

Indeed, I think we may be as queer as the universe.

*T*HE MOON has hidden behind a cloud. The ashes of the fire lie smoldering. Branches rustle as the dawn approaches. A redbearded man in green tights plays a plaintive tune on a flute made of bone. Another weaves a wreath of wildflowers in remembrance of one he has loved. Slowly, the others rise to bid farewell to the spirits and to greet the sun of spring. A hawk circles overhead. Merry meet, they chant, and merry part, and merry meet again. The circle now is open.

Notes

INTRODUCTION
We Are an Old People,
We Are a New People

1. Sam Gill, *Beyond "The Primitive": The Religions of Nonliterate Peoples* (Englewood Cliffs, NJ: Prentice-Hall, Inc., 1982), 34.
2. Aaron Shurin, "Exorcism of the Straight/Man/Demon," in *The Night Sun: Poems* (San Francisco: Gay Sunshine Press, 1976), 38–39.
3. Assotto Saint, "Heart and Soul," in *The Road Before Us: 100 Gay Black Poets*, ed. Assotto Saint (New York: Galiens Press, 1991), 116–17.
4. For concepts of "domain" and "web of associations," see Sandra T. Barnes, "Introduction: The Many Faces of Ogun," in *Africa's Ogun: Old World and New*, ed. Sandra T. Barnes (Bloomington: Indiana Univ. Press, 1989), 11–16; Carlo Ginzburg, *Ecstasies: Deciphering the Witches' Sabbath*, trans. Raymond Rosenthal (New York: Pantheon Books, Random House, 1991).
5. Sandra T. Barnes, "Introduction," *Africa's Ogun*, 12.
6. Lawrence Mass, "On the Future of Lesbian and Gay Studies: A Dialogue with Will Roscoe," in *Homosexuality as Behavior and Identity: Dialogues of the Sexual Revolution*, ed. Mass (New York: Haworth Press, 1990), 2:241.
7. Walter L. Williams, *The Spirit and the Flesh: Sexual Diversity in American Indian Culture* (Boston: Beacon Press, 1988), 2.
8. Williams, *Spirit and the Flesh*, 252.
9. Diana Fuss, *Essentially Speaking: Feminism, Nature and Difference* (New York and London: Routledge, 1989), ix, also 2, 41, 50.
10. Jennifer Terry, "Theorizing Deviant Historiography," in *differences: A Journal of Feminist Cultural Studies* 3, no. 2 (1991): 58.

11. Walter L. Williams, *The Spirit and the Flesh: Sexual Diversity in American Indian Culture* (Boston: Beacon Press, 1988), 273.
12. Richard D. Mohr, *Gay Ideas: Outing and Other Controversies* (Boston: Beacon Press, 1992), 238.
13. Mohr, *Gay Ideas*, 231–32.
14. Joseph François Lafitau, "Men Who Dress as Women," in *Gay American History*, ed. Jonathan Katz (New York: Thomas Y. Crowell, 1976), 288–89.
15. Edward Carpenter, *Intermediate Types among Primitive Folk: A Study in Social Evolution* (1919; reprint, New York: Arno Press, 1975), 15–16.
16. Carl G. Jung, "The Mother-Son Complex," *The Archetypes and the Collective Unconscious*. Bollingen series 20, second edition. trans. R. F. C. Hull (Princeton: Princeton University Press, 1980), 87.
17. Will Roscoe, "Dreaming the Myth: An Introduction to Mythology for Gay Men," in *Same-Sex Love and the Path to Wholeness*, ed. Robert H. Hopcke, K. L. Carrington, and S. Wirth (Boston: Shambhala, 1993), p. 110–24.
18. Hélène Cixous and Catherine Clément, *The Newly Born Woman*, trans. Betsy Wing (Minneapolis: Univ. of Minnesota Press, 1986), 84.
19. Andrea Juno and V. Vale, "Introduction," *Angry Women: ReSearch #13* (San Francisco: Re/Search Publications, 1991), 4.
20. Sue-Ellen Case, "Tracking the Vampire," *differences: A Journal of Feminist Cultural Studies* 3, no. 2 (1991): 5.
21. For microhistory, see Ginzburg, *Ecstasies*.
22. A chant by an unnamed poet (possibly Forest Flat), appearing in *RFD* no. 22 (Winter 1979): 72, and later augmented by the Faerie Circle of Berkeley, California.

MEDITATION
Bone

1. Father Bartolomé Garcia, *Manual para Administrar los Santos Sacramentos de Penitencia* (1760); W. W. Newcomb, Jr., *The Indians of Texas* (Austin: Univ. of Texas Press, 1961), 51; Thomas H. Guderjan and Carol S. Canty, *The Indian Texans* (San Antonio: Univ. of Texas Institute of Texan Cultures, 1989), 8–9; Peter T. Furst, *Hallucinogens and Culture* (San Francisco: Chandler and Sharp, 1976), 8–9, 166–68; Weston La Barre, *The Peyote Cult* (Hamden, CT: Archon Books, 1975), 105–7; T. N. Campbell, "Coahuiltecans and their Neighbors," *Handbook of North American Indians* vol. 10, ed. Alfonso Ortiz (Washington, DC: Smithsonian Institution, 1983); *Guidelines for a Texas Mission: Instructions for the Missionary of Mission Concepción in San Antonio (ca. 1760)*, trans. and ed. Fr. Benedict Leuteneger (San Antonio, TX: Old Spanish Mission Historical Research Library, 1976), 46–47.

CHAPTER 1
Wearing Our Long Wing Feathers

1. Reclus, quoted in Edward Carpenter, *Intermediate Types among Primitive Folk* (1919; reprint New York: Arno Press, 1975), 19–20.
2. Jamake Highwater, *The Primal Mind: Vision and Reality in Indian America* (New York: Meridian, Penguin, 1982), esp. 1–16; also see: Karl J. Narr, "Paleolithic Religion," in *Encyclopedia of Religion*, ed. Mircea Eliade (New York: Macmillan, 1987), 11:150–(also see 149–159).
3. Narr, "Paleolithic," 159; Riane Eisler, *The Chalice and the Blade: Our History, Our Future* (San Francisco: Harper & Row, 1987), 2–6; Marija Gimbutas, *The Language of the Goddess* (San Francisco: Harper & Row, 1989), 175.
4. Mircea Eliade, *Shamanism: Archaic Techniques of Ecstasy*, trans. Willard R. Trask (Princeton: Princeton Univ. Press, 1964), 5; Anna-Lena Siikala, "Siberian and Inner Asian Shamanism," *Encyclopedia of Religion*, ed. Eliade, 13:208; Michael Harner, *The Way of the Shaman* (San Francisco: Harper & Row, 1980), xiii ff.; Mircea Eliade, "Shamanism: An Overview," *Encyclopedia of Religion*, ed. Eliade, 13:205; Joan Halifax, *Shamanic Voices* (New York: E. P. Dutton, 1979), 3–4; Narr, "Paleolithic," 152–56. For mind-altering substances, see R. Gordon Wasson et al., *Persephone's Quest: Entheogens and the Origins of Religion* (New Haven: Yale Univ. Press, 1986); Terence McKenna, *The Archaic Revival* (San Francisco: Harper Collins Publishers, 1991).
5. Philip Rawson, ed., *Primitive Erotic Art* (New York: G. P. Putnam's Sons, 1973), 47.
6. Alexander Marshack, *The Roots of Civilization: The Cognitive Beginnings of Man's First Art*, *Symbol and Notation* (New York: McGraw-Hill, 1972), 330, also 332, 272, 242.   Also see Elizabeth Fisher, *Woman's Creation: Sexual Evolution and the Shaping of Society* (Garden City, NY: Doubleday, 1979), 148–49, 165; Joseph Campbell, *The Masks of God: Primitive Mythology* (New York: Penguin Books, 1987), 299–354, esp. 321.
7. Marshack, *Roots of Civilization*, 332.
8. Marshack, *Roots of Civilization*, 272, 242.
9. Marshack, *Roots of Civilization*, 242.
10. Marija Gimbutas, *The Prehistory of Eastern Europe: Part I: Mesolithic, Neolithic, and Copper Age Cultures in Russia and the Baltic Area*, American School of Prehistoric Research Bulletin no. 20 (Cambridge, MA: Peabody Museum, 1956), 190–92; Anne Ross, "Celtic and Northern Art," in *Primitive Erotic Art*, ed. Rawson, 81.
11. Narr, "Paleolithic," 150.
12. Köch-Grünberg, cited in Curt Sachs, *World History of the Dance*, trans. Bessie Schonberg (New York: Norton, 1937), 92, also plate 6.
13. Gimbutas, *Language of the Goddess*, 178; 3ff., 43ff.
14. Iole Bovio-Marconi, "Incisioni Rupestri all' Addaura (Palermo)," *Bullettino di paletnologia italiana* 8, no. 5 (1952–1953):5–22, esp. 12; Bovio-Marconi, "Interpretazione dell' arte parietale dell' Addaura," *Bullettino d'arte Ministero della pubblica istruzione* 1, no. 1 (1953):1–8; Bovio-Marconi, "Nuovo graffiti preistorici nelle grotte del Monte Pellegrino," *Bullettino di paletnologia italiana* 64, no. 9 (1954–1955):57–72; Bovio-Marconi, "Sull' esegesi del graffito dell' Addaura (Palermo)," *Quarternaria* 2 (1955):201–8, esp. 208; Bovio-Marconi, "Sui graffiti dell' Addaura (Palermo)," *Revista di antropologia* 40 (1953):55–64; Bovio-Marconi, "Sulle forme schematizzate dei graffiti dell' Addaura (Palermo)," *Actes du IV Congress Internationale du Quarternaria* (1953): 1–7; L. Bernabò Brea, *Sicily: Before the Greeks* (New York: Praeger, 1957), 32–33; G. Chiapella, "Altre considerazioni sugli 'acrobati' dell' Addaura," *Quarternaria* 1 (1954):181–83; Paolo Graziosi, *Paleolithic Art* (New York: McGraw-Hill, 1960), 200–1; Graziosi, "Qualche osservazione sur graffiti rupestri della grotta dell' Addaura presso Palermo," *Bullettino paletnologia italiana* 65 285–96; Margaret Guido, *Sicily: An Archaeological Guide: the Prehistoric and Roman Remains and the Greek Cities* (New York: Praeger, 1967), 61; Luis Pericot-Garcia et al., *Prehistoric and Primitive Art* (New York: Harry N. Abrams, 1967), 79; Ann Sieveking, *The Cave Artists* (New York: Thames and Hudson, 1979), 198; Philip Van Doren Stern, *Prehistoric Europe* (New York: W. W. Norton, 1969), 163.
15. Gimbutas, *Language of the Goddess*, 181, fig. 281.
16. Bovio-Marconi, "Incisioni," 12.
17. Gimbutas, *The Goddesses and Gods of Old*

Europe (Berkeley and Los Angeles: Univ. of California Press, 1982), 135–36.

18. Marshack, *Roots of Civilization,* 272; also see 14.
19. Rawson, *Primitive Erotic Art,* 47, 50; Weston La Barre, *Muelos: A Stone Age Superstition about Sexuality* (New York: Columbia Univ. Press, 1984), 13–14, 31, 34; Narr, "Paleolithic," 153–56; Campbell, *Masks of God,* 321; David F. Greenberg, *The Construction of Homosexuality* (Chicago: Univ. of Chicago Press, 1988), 33–34.
20. Marshack, *Roots of Civilization,* 333.
21. Gilbert H. Herdt, *Guardians of the Flutes: Idioms of Masculinity* (New York: McGraw-Hill, 1981), 1, 114, 234, 319, 320; Douglas L. Oliver, *Oceania: The Native Cultures of Australia and the Pacific Islands* (Honolulu: Univ. of Hawaii Press, 1989), 624–36; John Layard, *Stone Men of Malekula: Vao* (London: Chatto and Windus, 1942), 488–89, 519; Shirley Lindenbaum, "Variations on a Sociosexual Theme in Melanesia," in *Ritualized Homosexuality in Melanesia,* ed. Gilbert H. Herdt (Berkeley and Los Angeles: Univ. of California Press, 1984), 337–61.
22. Greenberg, *Construction,* 25.
23. Layard, *Stone,* 474, 486–87.
24. Herdt, *Guardians,* 239–40, 320; Lindenbaum, "Variations," 343–49; Greenberg, *Construction,* 25–88, esp. 64–65.
25. Joseph Campbell, *The Way of the Animal Powers* (San Francisco: Harper & Row, 1983), 1:175. Also see Vladimir Bogoras, *The Chukchee: Reports of the Jesup North Pacific Expedition* (New York: American Museum of Natural History, 1907); Vladimir Jochelson, *The Koryak: Reports of the Jesup North Pacific Expedition* (New York: American Museum of Natural History, 1905).
26. Ward Houser, "Korea," *Encyclopedia of Homosexuality,* ed. Wayne Dynes (New York: Garland Press, 1990), 1:667.
27. Elliott M. Heiman and Cao Van Lê, "Transsexualism in Vietnam," *Archives of Sexual Behavior* 4, no. 1 (1975):89–95, esp. 91, 93.
28. Walter L. Williams, *The Spirit and the Flesh: Sexual Diversity in American Indian Culture* (Boston: Beacon Press, 1986), 258.
29. Carmen Blacker, *The Catalpa Bow: A Study of Shamanistic Practices in Japan* (London: George Allen and Unwin, 1986), 318, n.6.
30. William P. Lebra, *Okinawan Religion: Belief, Ritual, and Social Structure* (Honolulu: Univ. of Hawaii Press, 1966), 69, 225.
31. Erik Jensen, *The Iban and Their Religion* (Oxford: Clarendon Press, 1974), 143–45; Hans Schärer, *Ngaju Religion: The Conception of God among a South Borneo People* (The Hague: Martinus Nijhoff, 1963), 57; Williams, *Spirit,* 41.
32. Jensen, *Iban,* 145.
33. Joseph Campbell, *Historical Atlas of World Mythology,* vol. 1, *The Way of the Animal Powers: Part 2: Mythologies of the Great Hunt* (New York: Harper & Row, 1988), 173.

34. Ake Hultkrantz, "The Religion of the Goddess in North America," in *The Book of the Goddess: Past and Present,* ed. Carl Olson (New York: Crossroad, 1983), 203; Franz Boas, *The Eskimo of Baffin Land and Hudson Bay* (New York: American Museum of Natural History 1901), 119, 130.
35. Boas, *Eskimo,* 140.
36. Jochelson, *Koryak,* 53, 116; Boas, *Eskimo,* 139–40.
37. Schärer, *Ngaju,* 58–59; Justus van der Kroef, "Transvestism and the Religious Hermaphrodite in Indonesia," *Journal of East Asiatic Studies* no. 3 (1954):257–65, esp. 259.
38. Jensen, *Iban,* 144.
39. Alfred W. Bowers, "Hidatsa Societal and Ceremonial Organization," *Bureau of American Ethnology Bulletin* 194 (1965):167, 256, 260.
40. Carpenter, *Intermediate Types,* 18–20.
41. Jensen, *Iban,* 143.
42. Bowers, "Hidatsa," 167.
43. Alice Fletcher and Francis La Flesche, "The Omaha Tribe," *Bureau of American Ethnology Annual Report* 27 (1905–1906):132–33.
44. James O. Dorsey, "A Study of the Siouan Cults," *BAE Annual Report* 2 (1889–1890):29.
45. Fletcher and La Flesche, "Omaha," 133; Williams, *Spirit,* 28–29; William K. Powers, *Oglala Religion* (Lincoln: Univ. of Nebraska Press, 1977), 58–59; Bowers, "Hidatsa," 326; Jensen, *Iban,* 143.
46. Bowers, "Hidatsa," 166–67, 256–60, 326–27; Schärer, *Ngaju,* 57; Bogoras, *Chukchee,* 450.
47. Jochelson, *Koryak,* 53; Bogoras, *Chukchee,* 450–51.
48. Jochelson, *Koryak,* 53.
49. Jensen, *Iban,* 144; Schärer, *Ngaju,* 133.
50. Jensen, *Iban,* 144.
51. Bowers, "Hidatsa," 166–67.
52. Van der Kroef, "Transvestism," 259; Schärer, *Ngaju,* 56, 58, 156; Eliade, *Shamanism,* 351ff.
53. Bogoras, *Chukchee,* 451.
54. Bogoras, *Chukchee,* 451, 453.
55. Oliver, *Oceania,* 635–36.
56. Bogoras, *Chukchee,* 451.
57. Jochelson, *Koryak,* 53.
58. Bogoras, *Chukchee,* 452–53.
59. Bogoras, *Chukchee,* 454.
60. Bogoras, *Chukchee,* 453.
61. Van der Kroef, "Transvestism," 259; Schärer, *Ngaju,* 137, 156; Carpenter, *Intermediate Types,* 20; Williams, *Spirit,* 35.
62. Jensen, *Iban,* 68, 107, 146.
63. Jochelson, *Koryak,* 53; Bogoras, *Chukchee,* 448–49.
64. Bowers, "Hidatsa," 326–27.
65. Hultkrantz, "Religion of the Goddess," 209; K. Rasmussen, *Intellectual Culture of the Iglulik Eskimos* (Copenhagen: Gyldendalske Boghandel, Nordisk Forlag, 1929), 123ff.
66. Schärer, *Ngaju,* 134.

67. Richard Evans Schultes and Albert Hofmann, *Plants of the Gods* (New York: McGraw-Hill, 1979), 83.

68. Williams, *Spirit*, 83–84.

69. Schärer, *Ngaju*, 56, 59.

CHAPTER 2
Ancestors

1. Michael S. Smith, "African Roots, American Fruits: the Queerness of Afrocentricity," *Outweek*, no. 87 (February 27, 1991): 78.

2. Professor Griff, quoted in *Outweek* (July 11, 1990); see David Bergman, "The African and the pagan in gay Black Literature," in *Sexual Sameness: Textual differences in lesbian and gay writing*, Joseph Bristow, ed. (New York: Routledge, 1992), 159.

3. Alice Walker, *In Search of Our Mothers' Gardens* (New York: Harcourt Brace Jovanovich, 1983), xi–xii, 81("Gifts of Power: The Writings of Rebecca Jackson").

4. Benjamin C. Ray, "African Religions: An Overview," *Encyclopedia of Religion*, ed. Mircea Eliade (New York: Macmillan, 1987), 1:61.

5. See Hermann Baumann, *Das Doppelte Geschlecht: Ethnologische Studien zur Bisexualität in Ritus und Mythos* (Berlin: Deitrich Reimer, 1955); also see Joseph Campbell, *The Way of the Animal Powers: Mythologies of the Great Hunt* 1:142 (Map 33: The Diffusion of Bisexual Mythic Beings and Powers), 1:174 (Map 38: The Ritualistic Permanent Sex Change).

6. Edward E. Evans-Pritchard, *The Azande: History and Political Institutions* (Oxford: Oxford Univ. Press, 1971), 183.

7. Evans-Pritchard, *Azande*, 183.

8. Evans-Pritchard, *Azande*, 199–200.

9. Edward E. Evans-Pritchard, *Witchcraft, Oracles, and Magic Among the Azande* (Oxford: Oxford Univ. Press, 1976), 238.

10. I. Schapera, *The Khoisan Peoples of South Africa: Bushmen and Hottentots* (London: G. Routledge, 1930), 242–43.

11. S. F. Nadel, *The Nuba: An Anthropological Study of the Hill Tribes in Kordofan* (London: Oxford Univ. Press, 1947), 109, 214, 396.

12. Nadel, *Nuba*, 285.

13. J. H. Driberg, *The Lango: A Nilotic Tribe of Uganda* (London: T. Fisher Unwin, 1923), 216–23.

14. Driberg, *Lango*, 210.

15. Driberg, *Lango*, 210.

16. David Tait, "Konkomba Sorcery," in *Magic, Witchcraft, and Curing*, ed. John Middleton (Garden City, NY: Natural History Press, 1967), 164–65 n.

17. John Middleton, "Spirit Possession among the Lugbara," in *Spirit Mediumship and Society in Africa*, ed. John Beattie and John Middleton (London: Routledge and Kegan Paul, 1969), 220, 224.

18. Middleton, "Spirit Possession" 224.

19. David F. Greenberg, *The Construction of Homosexuality* (Chicago: Univ. of Chicago Press, 1988), 60.

20. Rev. Edwin W. Smith and Captain Andrew Murray Dale, *The Ila-Speaking Peoples of Northern Rhodesia* (London: Macmillan, 1920), 2:74.

21. Carlos Estermann, *The Ethnography of Southwestern Angola* (New York: Africana Publishing, 1976), 1:193.

22. Estermann, *Ethnography*, 1:197.

23. Estermann, *Ethnography*, 1:196–97.

24. Estermann, *Ethnography*, 1:196–97.

25. See John T. Schneider, *Dictionary of African Borrowings in Brazilian Portuguese* (Hamburg: Helmut Buske Verlag, 1991), 82–85; João S. Trevisan, *Perverts in Paradise*, trans. Martin Foreman (London: Gay Men's Press, 1986), 55; Gerhard Kubik, *Angolan Traits in Black Music, Games and Dances of Brazil* (Lisbon, Portugal: Centro de Estudos de Antropologia Cultural, 1979), 25; Luiz Mott, "Brazil," *Encyclopedia of Homosexuality*, ed. Wayne Dynes (New York: Garland Press, 1990), 1:162–63.

26. S. G. Lee, "Spirit Possession among the Zulu," in *Spirit Mediumship*, ed. Beattie and Middleton, 134.

27. Harriet Ngubane, *Body and Mind in Zulu Medicine* (New York: Academic Press, 1977), 142.

28. Lee, "Spirit Zulu," 134, 137–38.

29. Lee, "Spirit Zulu," 136, 139.

30. Lee, "Spirit Zulu," 130, 138.

31. Lee, "Spirit Zulu," 140, 143.

32. Lee, "Spirit Zulu," 150–51.

33. Lee, "Spirit Zulu," 135–36, 139.

34. Fremont E. Besmer, *Horses, Musicians, and Gods: The Hausa Cult of Possession-Trance* (Zaria, Nigeria: Ahmadu Bello Univ. Press, 1983), 18–19, 30, 47, 123, 164.

35. Besmer, *Horses*, 18–19, 72–74; on Dan Galadima, see music examples 6, 7, 8.

36. Ron Simmons, "Some thoughts on the challenges facing black gay intellectuals," in *Brother to Brother: New Writings by Black Gay Men*, ed. Essex Hemphill (Boston: Alyson Publications, 1991), 225.

CHAPTER 3
The Fragrance of Orchids

1. Ruan Ji, quoted in Bret Hinsch, *Passions of the Cut Sleeve: The Male Homosexual Tradition in China* (Berkeley and Los Angeles: Univ. of California Press, 1990), 70–71; also see Juan Chi, "Gay Boys," in *New Songs from a Jade Terrace: An Anthology of Early Chinese Love Poetry*, trans. Anne Birrell (New York: Penguin, 1986), 73.

2. Jan J. M. de Groot, *The Religious System of China* (Leiden, 1892–1910), esp. 1:245ff. and

6:1190–91, 1205–14, 1235, 1239, 1248ff.; Wolfram Eberhard, *A Dictionary of Chinese Symbols: Hidden Symbols in Chinese Life and Thought* (New York: Routledge, 1988); David Hawkes, "General Introduction," in *The Songs of the South,* trans. David Hawkes (New York: Penguin Books, 1985); Mircea Eliade, *Shamanism: Archaic Techniques of Ecstasy* (Princeton: Princeton Univ. Press, 1974), 447–61; Philip Rawson and Laszlo Legeza, *Tao: The Chinese Philosophy of Time and Change* (New York: Thames and Hudson, 1984).

3. Hawkes, "General Introduction," *Songs,* 19.

4. Edward T. C. Werner, *A Dictionary of Chinese Mythology* (New York: Julian Press, 1961), 346.

5. Arthur Waley, *The Nine Songs: A Study of Shamanism in Ancient China* (London: George Allen and Unwin, 1955), 53; Chan Ping-leung, "'Ch'u Tzu' and Shamanism in Ancient China" (Ph.D. diss., Ohio State University, 1972), 176–77.

6. Chan, "'Ch'u Tzu,'" 176–77.

7. Marcel Granet, *Festivals and Songs of Ancient China* (London: George Routledge and Sons, 1932), 194–95.

8. David F. Greenberg, *The Construction of Homosexuality* (Chicago: Univ. of Chicago Press, 1988), 161; Hinsch, *Passions of the Cut Sleeve,* 12.

9. Granet, *Festivals,* 194.

10. Hinsch, *Passions,* 36, 44–46, 52–53; Ruan Fang Fu, *Sex in China: Studies in Sexology in Chinese Culture* (New York: Plenum Press, 1991), 107–12.

11. Hinsch, *Passions,* 20, 52–53; Ruan, *Sex in China,* 107–12.

12. Hinsch, *Passions,* 36, 44–46, 52–53, 71.

13. Hinsch, *Passions,* 35, 38–39; also see Herbert Giles, *A Chinese Biographical Dictionary* (Tapei: Literature House, 1964); Louis Frederic, *Encyclopaedia of Asian Civilizations* (Villecresnes: Louis Frederic, 1977); Vern Bullough, *Sexual Variance in Society and History* (Chicago: Univ. of Chicago Press, 1976); Robert Hans van Gulik, *Sexual Life in Ancient China: A Preliminary Survey of Chinese Sex and Society from ca. 1500 B.C. til 1644 A.D.* (Leiden: E. J. Brill, 1961).

14. Hinsch, *Passions,* 35, 42–44, 47–49; also see Giles, *Chinese Biographical Dictionary,* Frederic, *Encyclopaedia,* Bullough, *Sexual Variance,* and Gulik, *Sexual Life.*

15. F. Lieh-Mak, M.D., K. M. O'Hoy, and S. L. Luk, "Lesbianism in the Chinese of Hong Kong," *Archives of Sexual Behavior* 12, no. 1 (1983): 23; Ulrike Jugel, *Politische Funktion und Soziale Stellung der Eunuchen zur späteren Hanzeit (25–200 N.Chr.)* (Wiesbaden: Steiner Verlag, 1976), 114.

16. Hinsch, *Passions,* 12.

17. Wolfram Eberhard, *Local Cultures of South and East China* (Leiden: E. J. Brill, 1968), 306, 46.

18. Hawkes, *Songs,* 81–82nn.

19. Mircea Eliade, *A History of Religious Ideas,* vol. 2, *From Gautama Buddha to the Triumph of Christianity,* trans. Willard R. Trask (Chicago: Univ. of Chicago Press, 1984), 13; Zheng Shifeng et al., *China: All Provinces and Autonomous Regions* (New York: McGraw-Hill, 1980), 191–92; Hawkes, "General Introduction," *Songs,* 18.

20. Chan, "'Ch'u Tzu,'" 164–65; Hawkes, "General Introduction," *Songs,* 19, 42, 45, 46; Eliade, *History of Religious Ideas,* 2:5; Groot, *Religious System of China,* 4:1187; Eliade, *Shamanism,* 454.

21. Eberhard, *Dictionary of Chinese Symbols,* 65.

22. Qu Yuan, "Li Sao," *Songs,* trans. Hawkes, 68–78, ll. 11–12, 73–74, 81–88, 113–14, 123–24, 285–90; Eberhard, *Dictionary of Chinese Symbols,* s.v. "Lotus," "Orchid."

23. Qu Yuan, "Li Sao," *Songs,* trans. Hawkes, ll. 15, 16, 49, 50, 66, 67, 68, 335; Rawson and Legeza, *Tao,* 22–23; Groot, *Religious System of China,* 4:303, 320, 323, 330, 332; Eberhard, *Dictionary of Chinese Symbols,* 63–65, s.v. "Chrysanthemum," "Cinnamon Tree," "Clouds," "Jade," "Magnolia"; Eberhard, *Local Cultures,* 42.

24. Eberhard, *Local Cultures,* 40; Edward H. Schafer, *The Divine Woman: Dragon Ladies and Rain Maidens* (San Francisco: North Point Press, 1980), 9–10.

25. Qu Yuan, "Li Sao," *Songs,* trans. Hawkes, ll. 221–24; Schafer, *Divine Woman,* 68–70.

26. Hawkes, *Songs,* 91nn; Schafer, *Divine Woman,* 38; Patricia Monaghan, *The Book of Goddesses and Heroines* (New York; E. P. Dutton, 1981), 224; Qu Yuan (Ch'u Yuan), *Tian Wen: A Chinese Book of Origins,* trans. Stephen Field (New York: New Directions, 1986), ll. 10, 37–40.

27. Qu Yuan (Ch'u Yuan), *Tian Wen,* trans. Field, ll. 98, p. 113n.

28. Qu Yuan (Ch'u Yuan), *Tian Wen,* trans. Field, ll. 19, 45, p. 109n; Eberhard, *Dictionary of Chinese Symbols,* s.v. "Azalea," "Moon," "Sun"; Eberhard, *Local Cultures,* 85; Hawkes, "General Introduction," 44–45 and "Glossary of Names," 339, *Songs;* Qu Yuan, "Tian Wen," *Songs,* 127, l. 19 and "Li Sao," *Songs,* 73, l. 197.

29. Eberhard, *Dictionary of Chinese Symbols,* 319–20.

30. Schafer, *Divine Woman,* 49, 73, 82; Anonymous (sometimes attributed to Qu Yuan), "The Goddess of the Xiang," *Songs,* 104–7; Hawkes, "Notes" (to "Li Sao"), *Songs,* 87; Eliade, *Shamanism,* 448–49.

31. David Hawkes, "The Quest of the Goddess," *Studies in Chinese Literary Genres,* ed. Cyril Birch (Berkeley and Los Angeles: Univ. of California Press, 1974), 41, 51, 52, 57; Schafer, *Divine Woman,* 51; Eberhard, *Dictionary of Chinese Symbols,* 110–11; Anonymous, "The Goddess of the Xiang," *Songs,* 104–7; Anonymous, "The Lady of the Xiang," *Songs,* 108; Hawkes, "Notes" (to "The Goddess of the Xiang," and "The Lady of the Xiang"), *Songs,* 118–19.

32. Henri Maspero, *Taoism and Chinese Religion*, trans. Frank A. Kierman, Jr. (Amherst: Univ. of Massachusetts Press, 1981), 16.

33. Hawkes, "Quest," 45, 51; Hawkes, "General Introduction," *Songs*, 49.

34. Groot, *Religious System of China*, 4:1192, 1209.

35. Chan, "'Ch'u Tzu,'" 128–29, also 126, 130.

36. Chan, "'Ch'u Tzu,'" 129 and n. 90.

37. Qu Yuan, "Li Sao," *Songs*, ll. 20, 39, 44, 48; Hawkes, "Notes" (to "Li Sao"), *Songs*, 84.

38. Hawkes, "Notes" (to "Li Sao"), *Songs*, 84.

39. *The I Ching, or Book of Changes*, trans. by Richard Wilhelm, rendered into English by Cary F. Baynes, Bollingen Series 19, third ed. (Princeton: Princeton Univ. Press, 1975), 58–59.

40. Eberhard, *Dictionary of Chinese Symbols*, s.v. "Orchid."

41. Qu Yuan, "Li Sao," *Songs*, 68, ll. 19–20 and 69, ll. 56.

42. Eberhard, *Dictionary of Chinese Symbols*, s.v. "Bridge," "Clouds," "Dew," "Dragon," "Horse," "Phoenix," "Rain," "Wind"; Qu Yuan, "Li Sao," *Songs*, 70, l. 65; 73, ll. 183–84, 203–4; 78, ll. 351, 359; Chan, "'Ch'u Tzu,'" 61.

43. Hawkes, "Notes" (to "Li Sao") *Songs*, 82.

44. Qu Yuan, "Li Sao," *Songs*, 68, ll. 20; 69, ll. 39–48; 70, ll. 85–88; 78, ll. 369–72; Anonymous, "Jiu Zhang (Nine Pieces): I: Grieving I Make My Plaint," *Songs*, 156, ll. 9–12; 157, ll. 27–28; Anonymous, "Jiu Zhang: IV: The Outpouring of Sad Thoughts," *Songs*, 167, ll. 13–32; 169, ll. 67–76; Hawkes, "Quest," 54.

45. Hawkes, "General Introduction," *Songs*, 19.

46. Maspero, *Taoism*, 305.

47. Bullough, *Sexual Variance*, 304.

48. Giles, *Chinese Biographical Dictionary*, 119.

49. Giles, *Chinese Biographical Dictionary*, 119–20.

50. Hinsch, *Passions*, 68.

51. Donald Holzman, *La vie et la pensee de Hi K'ang* (Leiden: E. J. Brill, 1957), 25; Giles, *Chinese Biographical Dictionary*, 964–65.

52. Ruan Ji (Juan Chi), "Gay Boys," *New Songs*, trans. Birrell, 73; Anne Birrell, "Notes," *New Songs*, 302, 313–14; Hinsch, *Passions*, 70–71; Eberhard, *Dictionary of Chinese Symbols*, 66, s.v. "Cinnabar," "Jade."

53. Gulik, *Sexual Life*, 346; Giles, *Chinese Biographical Dictionary*, 638; Holzman, *La vie*, 37–38; Hinsch, *Passions*, 68–69.

54. Jugel, *Politische*, xiii, xvi; Bullough, *Sexual Variance*, 306–9.

55. Jugel, *Politische*, 122–24; Bullough, *Sexual Variance*, 306–9.

56. Bullough, *Sexual Variance*, 308.

57. Jugel, *Politische*, 113.

58. Jugel, *Politische*, 113–14.

59. Cornelius Osgood, *Village Life in Old China: A Community Study of Kao Yao, Yunnan* (New York: Ronald Press, 1963), 305–8.

MEDITATION
Earth and Moon

1. Diane Wolkstein and Samuel Noah Kramer, *Inanna: Queen of Heaven and Earth* (New York: Harper & Row, 1983), 8, 16–17, 64; Samuel Noah Kramer and John Maier, *Myths of Enki, the Crafty God* (New York: Oxford Univ. Press, 1989), 118.

CHAPTER 4
Lands of Milk and Honey

1. Quoted in John Gray, *The Canaanites* (New York: Praeger, 1964), 32.

2. On the transition to patriarchy, see Riane Eisler, *The Chalice and the Blade: Our History, Our Future* (San Francisco: Harper & Row, 1987); Gerda Lerner, *The Creation of Patriarchy* (New York: Oxford Univ. Press, 1986); Marija Gimbutas, *The Goddesses and Gods of Old Europe* (Berkeley and Los Angeles: Univ. of California Press, 1982); Marija Gimbutas, *The Language of the Goddess* (San Francisco: Harper & Row, 1989); Marija Gimbutas, "Women and Culture in Goddess-Oriented Old Europe," in *Weaving the Visions: New Patterns in Feminist Spirituality*, ed. Judith Plaskow and Carol P. Christ (San Francisco: Harper & Row, 1989); Nandor Kalicz, *Clay Gods: The Neolithic Period and Copper Age in Hungary*, trans. Barna Balogh (Budapest: Corvina, 1970).

3. See, for example, Warwick Bray and David Trump, *The Penguin Dictionary of Archaeology* (New York: Penguin Books, 1979), esp. "Halaf" and "Ubaid"; Vern Bullough, *Sexual Variance in Society and History* (Chicago: Univ. of Chicago Press, 1976), 51–58; Samuel Noah Kramer, *The Sumerians* (Chicago: Univ. of Chicago Press, 1972); Lerner, *Creation of Patriarchy*, 54–75.

4. Judith Ochshorn, "Ishtar and Her Cult," in *The Book of the Goddess: Past and Present*, ed. Carl Olson (New York: Crossroad, 1983), 16–28; Diane Wolkstein and Samuel Noah Kramer, *Inanna: Queen of Heaven and Earth* (New York: Harper & Row, 1983), esp. 16–17; Paul Friedrich, *The Meaning of Aphrodite* (Chicago: Univ. of Chicago Press, 1978), 13–14; Thorkild Jacobsen, "Mesopotamian Religion: An Overview," *Encyclopedia of Religion*, ed. Mircea Eliade (New York: Macmillan, 1987), 9:459; Michael C. Astour, "Tamar the Hierodule: An Essay in the Method of Vestigial Motifs," *Journal of Biblical Literature* 85 (1966): 188–91; Nancy Qualls-Corbett, *The Sacred Prostitute: Eternal Aspect of the Feminine* (Toronto: Inner City Books, 1988).

5. Ignace J. Gelb et al., *The Assyrian Dictionary of the Oriental Institute of the University of Chicago* (Chicago: Oriental Institute, 1964), esp.

"*assinnu*," "*kurgarru*," "*kulu'u*," and "*inhu*"; Bullough, *Sexual Variance*, 51–58; D. Winton Thomas, "KELEBH 'DOG': Its Origins and Some Usages of It in the Old Testament," *Vetus Testamentum* 10, no. 4 (1960): 426; *Gilgamesh*, trans. John Gardiner and John Maier (New York: Alfred A. Knopf, 1984), 119; Kramer, *Sumerians*, 123, 128; Frederique Apffel Marglin, "Hierodouleia," *Encyclopedia of Religion*, ed. Eliade, 7:311; Gilbert J. P. McEwan, *Priest and Temple in Hellenistic Babylonia* (Wiesbaden: Franz Steiner Verlag, 1981), 14; Helmer Ringgren, *Religions of the Ancient Near East*, trans. John Sturdy (London: S.P.C.K., 1973), 25; Walter Burkert, *Structure and History in Greek Mythology and Ritual* (Berkeley and Los Angeles: Univ. of California Press, 1982), 191 n. 32.

6. Marglin, "Hierodouleia," 311; Daniel Reisman, "Iddin-Daggan's Sacred Marriage Hymn," *Journal of Cuneiform Studies* 25, no. 4 (1973): 185.

7. Edmund I. Gordon, *Sumerian Proverbs: Glimpses of Everyday Life in Ancient Mesopotamia* (New York: Greenwood Publishers, 1968), 13–14, 211, 247–48, 248n. 9, 253, 253–54; and see entries from *Assyrian Dictionary* listed above in n. 5.

8. Alexander Heidel, *The Gilgamesh Epic and Old Testament Parallels* (Chicago: Univ. of Chicago Press, 1963), 126 n. 79.

9. Wolkstein and Kramer, *Inanna*, 64.

10. Bullough, *Sexual Variance*, 57.

11. D. J. Wiseman, *The Alalakh Tablets* (London: British Institute of Archaeology at Ankara, 1953), 25; also see *Assyrian Dictionary*, entries in n. 5 above.

12. See entries from the *Assyrian Dictionary*, n. 5 above.

13. Gordon, *Sumerian Proverbs*, 14, 254–55; also see *Assyrian Dictionary*, n. 5 above.

14. Andre Lemaire, "Mari, the Bible, and the Northwest Semitic World," *Biblical Archaeologist* 47, no. 2 (1984):102; Eva Strommenger, *5000 Years of the Art of Mesopotamia* (New York: Harry N. Abrams, 1964), pl. 21 and p. 93; for comparison see small plates 92, 93, 145, 155, 157, 172, 266, 359.

15. McEwan, *Priest*, 14; Reisman, "Marriage Hymn," 185–87; Wolkstein and Kramer, *Inanna*, 99; also see *Assyrian Dictionary*, entries in n. 5 above.

16. Marglin, "Hierodouleia," 311; Bullough, *Sexual Variance*, 53, 55, 56; Gordon, *Sumerian Proverbs*, 14, 248 and n. 9; Astour, "Tamar," 191 n. 40; *Assyrian Dictionary* entries from n. 5 above.

17. *Gilgamesh*, trans. Gardiner and Maier.

18. See, for example: Lerner, *Creation*, 59, 132–33, 144, 150, 193–94; Starhawk, *Truth or Dare: Encounters with Power, Authority, and Mystery* (San Francisco: Harper & Row, 1987), 49, 53–54;

Merlin Stone, *When God Was a Woman* (New York: Harcourt Brace Jovanovich, 1978), 40, 140–43, 151.

19. Thorkild Jacobsen, *The Treasures of Darkness* (New Haven: Yale Univ. Press, 1976), 218.

20. *Gilgamesh*, trans. Gardiner and Maier, 81–82, 84, 86; *The Epic of Gilgamesh*, trans. and ed. N. K. Sandars (New York: Penguin Books, 1972), 66.

21. Kramer, *Sumerians*, 122; *Gilgamesh*, trans. Gardiner and Maier, 68.

22. *Gilgamesh*, trans. Gardiner and Maier, 68, 91.

23. *Gilgamesh*, trans. Gardiner and Maier, 119.

24. *Gilgamesh*, trans. Gardiner and Maier, 211–13.

25. Wolkstein and Kramer, *Inanna*, 8 ff.

26. Anne Draffkorn Kilmer, "A Note on an Overlooked Word-Play in the Akkadian Gilgamesh," in *Zikir Sumim*, ed. G. Van Driel et al. (Leiden: E. J. Brill, 1982), 128–32; *Gilgamesh*, trans. Gardiner and Maier, 119, 120 n. 19.

27. *Epic of Gilgamesh*, trans. Sandars, 63; Patricia Monaghan, *The Book of Goddesses and Heroines* (New York: E. P. Dutton, 1981), 222.

28. *Gilgamesh*, trans. Gardiner and Maier, 187.

29. James Mellaart, *Earliest Civilizations of the Near East* (New York: McGraw-Hill, 1970), 25, 30, 40, 42; Gray, *Canaanites*, 118.

30. William J. Fulco, "Athirat," *Encyclopedia of Religion*, ed. Mircea Eliade (New York: Macmillan, 1987), 1:491–92; George Hart, *A Dictionary of Egyptian Gods and Goddesses* (Boston: Routledge and Kegan Paul, 1986), 178; Gray, *Canaanites*, 76, 99, 100, 124, 169.

31. A. Caquot, "Western Semitic Lands," in *Larousse World Mythology*, ed. Pierre Grimal (Secaucus, NJ: Chartwell Books, 1973), 89.

32. Johannes C. De Moor, *An Anthology of Religious Texts from Ugarit* (Leiden: E. J. Brill, 1987), 1, 4 n. 17, 121 n. 24, 238–39.

33. De Moor, *Anthology*, 4 n. 17, 121 n. 24; 2 Samuel 23:1; Mircea Eliade, *Death, Afterlife, and Eschatology* (New York: Harper & Row, 1974), 66–70.

34. Samuel Terrien, "The Omphalos Myth and Hebrew Religion," *Vetus Testamentum* 20, no. 3 (1970): 315–38, esp. 326–28; W. F. Albright, "Historical and Mythical Elements in the Story of Joseph," *Journal of Biblical Literature* 37, no. 3–4 (1918): 115–16; Beatrice Brooks, "Fertility Cult Functionaries in the Old Testament," *Journal of Biblical Literature* 60, no. 3 (1941): 250–51; Theodor H. Gaster, *Thespis: Ritual, Myth, and Drama in the Ancient Near East* (Garden City, NY: Doubleday, 1961), 235; Thomas, "KELEBH," 424–26; *Epic of Gilgamesh*, trans. Sandars, 119; Genesis 38:14–15; Deuteronomy 22:5; Leviticus 19:28; Zephaniah 1:8.

35. Gray, *Canaanites*, 77; 1 Kings 14, 15, 18, 22; 2 Kings 10, 14, 21, 23.

36. De Moor, *Anthology*, 120, 121 n. 24; 1 Kings 18:26–28.

37. Michael Grant, *The History of Ancient Israel* (New York: Scribner, 1984), 25; Judith Ochshorn, *The Female Experience and the Nature of the Divine* (Bloomington: Indiana Univ. Press, 1981), 128–29; W. L. Moran, "New Evidence for Mari," *Biblica* 50 (1969): 30 n. 2; Thomas, "KELEBH," 424–26; Terrien, "Omphalos," 326–30; 1 Kings 15:13; Ezekiel 8:7–13, 16:17.

38. John J. McNeill, S.J., *The Church and the Homosexual* (New York: Pocket Books, 1976), 61 etc.; Raphael Patai, *The Hebrew Goddess* (New York: KTAV Publishing House, 1967); John Boswell, *Christianity, Social Tolerance, and Homosexuality* (Chicago: Univ. of Chicago Press, 1980); Stone, *When God*, 148 ff.; Grant, *History of Ancient Israel*, 137; Deuteronomy 7:1, 2, 5; 22:5; 23:17–18; Leviticus 18:22; 20:13; 1 Kings 14:22–24; 15:12, 13:22:46; 2 Kings 10:18–27, 23:7, 14, 16, 20, 24; 2 Chronicles 34:5.

39. Grant, *History of Ancient Israel*, 141.

40. Israel J. Gerber, *Immortal Rebels: Freedom for the Individual in the Bible* (New York: Jonathan David, 1963), 42; Walter Beltz, *God and the Gods: Myths of the Bible*, trans. Peter Heinegg (New York: Penguin Books, 1983), 77–78; Grant, *History of Ancient Israel*, 101; Genesis 9:20–25.

41. Rabbi Dr. H. Freedman, ed., trans., *Midrash Rabbah: Genesis* (London: Soncino Press, 1939), vol. 1, ch.35, sec. 7–8, p. 293; Beltz, *God and the Gods*, 77–78.

42. Philo Judaeus, *Questions and Answers on Genesis: Supplement 1*, trans. Ralph Marcus (Cambridge: Harvard Univ. Press, 1953), 1:172–74.

43. Joseph L. Henderson and Maud Oakes, *The Wisdom of the Serpent: The Myths of Death, Rebirth, and Resurrection* (New York: George Braziller, 1963), 20; Albright, "Historical and Mythological Elements," 115–16; Brooks, "Fertility Cult," 250–51.

44. Henderson and Oakes, *Wisdom*, 20.

45. Thomas Mann, *Young Joseph*, part 2 of *Joseph and His Brothers*, trans. H. T. Lowe-Porter (New York: Alfred A. Knopf, 1939), 105–7.

46. Freedman, *Midrash: Genesis*, vol. 2, sec. 86:2–3, 801–2.

47. Henderson and Oakes, *Wisdom*, 21.

48. Terrien, "Omphalos," 328–29.

49. Grant, *History of Ancient Israel*, 103; McNeill, *Church and the Homosexual*, 54, 57.

50. Walter E. Rast and R. Thomas Schaub, "A Preliminary Report of Excavations at Bab edh-Dhra, 1975," *Annual of American Schools of Oriental Research* 43 (1978): 30 ff.

51. Robert Duncan, "This Place Rumord to Have Been Sodom," *Angels of the Lyre: A Gay Poetry Anthology*, ed. Winston Leyland (San Francisco: Panjandrum and Gay Sunshine, 1975), 53.

CHAPTER 5
Isis Astarte Diana Hecate

1. Empedocles, quoted in Athenaeus, *The Deipnosophists*, trans. Charles B. Gulick (Cambridge: Harvard Univ. Press, 1950), vol. 5, bk. 12, sec. 510, p. 295.

2. David Christie-Murray, *Reincarnation: Ancient Beliefs and Modern Evidence* (London: David and Charles, 1981), 52; Betty Radice, *Who's Who in the Ancient World* (New York: Penguin, 1985), 109–10; Noel I. Garde, *Jonathan to Gide: The Homosexual in History* (New York: Nosbooks, 1969), 27–28; Sir William Smith, *Smaller Classical Dictionary*, ed. E. H. Blakeney and J. Warrington (New York: E. P. Dutton, 1958), 115–16; Lillian Feder, *Crowell's Handbook of Classical Literature* (New York: Harper, 1980), 133–34.

3. Luther H. Martin, *Hellenistic Religions: An Introduction* (New York: Oxford Univ. Press, 1987), 9–10; see also Frederick C. Grant, *Hellenistic Religions: The Age of Syncretism* (New York: Liberal Arts Press, 1953).

4. Martin, *Hellenistic Religions*, 59.

5. Michael Grant, *The World of Rome* (New York: New American Library, 1960), 21.

6. Patricia Monaghan, *The Book of Goddesses and Heroines* (New York: E. P. Dutton, 1981), 155; C. J. Bleeker, "Isis and Hathor, Two Ancient Egyptian Goddesses," in *The Book of the Goddess: Past and Present*, ed. Carl Olson (New York: Crossroad, 1983), 36; James Henry Breasted, *A History of Egypt: From the Earliest Times to the Persian Conquest* (New York: Charles Scribner's Sons, 1937), 570–72, 581; Martin, *Hellenistic Religions*, 72–73.

7. H. te Velde, *Seth, God of Confusion* (Leiden: E. J. Brill, 1977), 36.

8. Merlin Stone, *When God Was a Woman* (New York: Harcourt Brace Jovanovich, 1978), 89–90; Erich Neumann, *The Great Mother* (New York: Pantheon, 1955), 171, 190; H. te Velde, *Seth, God of Confusion* (Leiden: E. J. Brill, 1977), 33, 36, 39, 44–45; John Griffiths, *The Conflict of Horus and Seth* (Liverpool: Liverpool Univ. Press, 1960), esp. 41–46; Joseph Campbell, *The Masks of God: Oriental Mythology* (New York: Penguin Books, 1977), 81; Vern L. Bullough, *Sexual Variance in Society and History* (Chicago: Univ. of Chicago Press, 1980), 63–66; Peter Clayton, *Great Figures of Mythology* (Greenwich, CT: Crescent Books, 1990), 103.

9. Apuleuis, *The Golden Ass*, trans. Jack Lindsay, bk. 11, sec. 8, quoted in *The Ancient Mysteries: A Sourcebook*, ed. Marvin W. Meyer (San Francisco: Harper & Row, 1987), 181.

10. Tertullian, "On the Pallium," *Works*, part 4, ed. Rev. A. Roberts (New York: Christian Literature, 1890), 4:8–9; Ramsay Macmullen, *Paganism in*

the Roman Empire (New Haven: Yale Univ. Press, 1981), 43.

11. Macmullen, *Paganism,* 43.

12. C. Suetonius Tranquillus, *Lives of the Caesars: Libri VII–VIII,* trans. George W. Mooney (London: Longmans, Green, 1930), sec. 12, p. 91 ("Otho"); Aytoun Ellis, *The Essence of Beauty: A History of Perfume and Cosmetics* (London: Secker and Warburg, 1960), 56.

13. *The Syriac Version of the Pseudo-Nonnos Mythological Scholia,* trans. and ed. Sebastian Brock (Cambridge: Cambridge Univ. Press, 1971), 145–46; Ovid, *Fasti,* ed. Sir James Frazer (London: Macmillan, 1929), 3:222; Eusebius Pamphilus, *Ecclesiastical History: The Life of the Blessed Emperor Constantine* (London: Samuel Bagster and Sons, 1845), bk. 4, chap. 25, pp.193–94.

14. Suetonius, *Lives,* sec. 12, p. 91 ("Otho"); Juvenal, *The Sixteen Satires,* trans. and ed. Peter Green (Baltimore: Penguin Books, 1967), 201.

15. *Syriac Version,* ed. Brock, 145–46; Herodotus, *The Histories,* trans. Aubrey de Selincourt (New York: Penguin Books, 1978), bk. 2, sec. 56–63, pp. 152–53.

16. Frank M. Snowden, Jr., *Blacks in Antiquity: Ethiopians in the Greco-Roman Experience* (Cambridge: Harvard Univ. Press, 1971), 189–92; Macmullen, *Paganism,* 21–22.

17. Ovid, *Fasti,* ed. Frazer, 3:222; Eusebius, *Ecclesiastical History,* bk. 4, chap. 25, pp. 193–94.

18. Marija Gimbutas, *The Language of the Goddess* (San Francisco: Harper & Row, 1989), 134; Pliny, *Natural History,* trans. H. Rackham et al. (Cambridge: Harvard Univ. Press, 1952), vol. 9, bk. 35, chap. 46, sec. 165, p. 383; Athenaeus, *Deipnosophists* vol. 5, bk. 12, sec. 525, p. 371, and sec. 540, pp. 445–47.

19. Hesiod, *Theogony,* trans. Dorothea Wender (New York: Penguin, 1986), 36–37, esp. 11. 393–452; Walter Burkert, *Greek Religion,* trans. John Raffan (Cambridge: Harvard Univ. Press, 1985), 171; Charles Picard, *Ephese et Claros: Recherches sur les sanctuaires et les cultes de l'ionie du nord* (Paris: E. de Boccard, 1922), 135 n. 6 and 266 n. 5; J. Hatzfeld, "Inscriptions de Lagina en Carie," *Bulletin des correspondances helleniques* 64, no. 16 (1920): 84; Sarah Iles Johnston, *Hekate Soteira: A Study of Hekate's Role in the Chaldean Oracles and Related Literature* (Atlanta: Scholars Press, 1990), 25; Macmullen, *Paganism,* 48.

20. Jean Shinoda Bolen, *Goddesses in Everywoman* (San Francisco: Harper & Row, 1984), 168.

21. Monaghan, *Book of Goddesses,* 42; Arnobius; *Adversus Gentes (Against the Pagans),* ed. Rev. A. Roberts (Edinburgh: T. and T. Clark, 1861), vol. 19 bk. 5, sec. 25, pp. 249–50; sec. 29, p. 254; sec. 35, p. 259; Arthur Evans, *The God of Ecstasy:*

Sex Roles and the Madness of Dionysos (New York: St. Martin's Press, 1988), 34.

22. Goblet D'Alviella, *The Mysteries of Eleusis* (Wellingborough, Northamptonshire: Aquarian Press, 1981), 17; Karoly Kerenyi, *Eleusis: Archetypal Image of Mother and Daughter,* trans. Ralph Manheim (New York: Bollingen, Pantheon, 1967), 65; Marie Delcourt, *Hermaphrodite* (London: Studio Books, 1961), 13; Arnobius, *Adversus Gentes,* vol. 19, bk. 5, sec. 25, p. 249.

23. Royston Lambert, *Beloved and God: The Story of Hadrian and Antinous* (New York: Viking, 1984), 104–6, 142, 163–65.

24. Picard, *Ephese,* 159; Strabo, *The Geography,* trans. Horace Leonard Jones (Cambridge: Harvard Univ. Press, 1954), vol. 5, bk. 12, sec. 2, 3, pp. 351–53; Franz Cumont, *Oriental Religions in Roman Paganism* (New York: Dover, 1956), 54; Mary Beard and John North, *Pagan Priests: Religion and Power in the Ancient World* (London: Duckworth, 1990), photo of L. Lartius Anthus, priest of Ma; Axel W. Persson, *The Religion of Greece in Prehistoric Times* (Berkeley and Los Angeles: Univ. of California Press, 1942), 146; Cyril Bailey, *Phases in the Religion of Ancient Rome* (Westport, CT: Greenwood Press, 1972), 190; Harry T. Peck, ed., *Harper's Dictionary of Classical Literature and Antiquities* (New York: Harper and Brothers, 1897), S. V. "Comana."

25. Ioan Petru Couliano, and Cicerone Poghirc, "Thracian Religion," *The Encyclopedia of Religion,* ed. Mircea Eliade (New York: Macmillan, 1987), 14:494–96; Alfonso M. di Nola, "Paleobalcanici," *Enciclopedia delle Religioni,* ed. Mario Gozzini (Firenze: Vallecchi, 1972), 4:1372.

26. J. A. MacCullough, "Baptism," *Encyclopaedia of Religion and Ethics,* ed. James Hastings (New York: Charles Scribner's Sons, 1930), 2:374.

27. Hans Licht, *Sexual Life in Ancient Greece* (London: The Abbey Library, 1971), 141, 500; Bernard Sergent, *Homosexuality in Greek Myth,* trans. Arthur Goldhammer (Boston: Beacon Press, 1986), 311 n. 33; Timothy Long, *Barbarians in Greek Comedy* (Carbondale: Southern Illinois Univ. Press, 1986), 34; Jane Ellen Harrison, *Prolegomena to the Study of Greek Religion* (Cambridge: Cambridge Univ. Press, 1908), 417; P. P. [pseud.], *Glossarium Eroticum Linguae Latinae* (Paris: Apud Aug.-Fr. et Pr. Dondey-Dupre, Bibliopolas, 1826), 88 ff.

28. Licht, *Sexual Life,* 500; Harrison, *Prolegomana,* 417; Mircea Eliade, *A History of Religious Ideas,* vol. 2, *From Gautama Buddha to the Triumph of Christianity* (Chicago: Univ. of Chicago Press, 1982), 173.

29. Monaghan, *Book of Goddesses,* 30–31; Robert Graves, *The White Goddess* (New York: Farrar, Straus and Giroux, 1966), 59; Donald Harden,

The Phoenicians (London: Thames and Hudson, 1962), 87ff.; Delcourt, Hermaphrodite, 27; Macrobius, The Saturnalia, trans. and ed. Percival Vaughan Davies (New York: Columbia Univ. Press, 1969), bk. 3, chap. 8, sec. 2–3, p. 214.

30. Hesiod, Theogony, trans. Wender, 29, esp. ll. 178–208, also 152 n. 10; K. J. Dover, Greek Homosexuality (New York: Random House, 1980), 63; Licht, Sexual Life, 123–24; Herodotus, Histories, trans. de Selincourt, bk. 1 sec. 198, p. 120 and bk. 2, sec. 64, p. 154.

31. Licht, Sexual Life, 130.

32. Sir James Frazer, The New Golden Bough, ed. T. H. Gaster (New York: New American Library, 1959), 371–72.

33. Licht, Sexual Life, 203.

34. Dover, Greek Homosexuality, 63.

35. Felix Buffiere, Eros Adolescent (Paris: Les Belles Lettres, 1980), 363 n. 48; Marcel Detienne, The Gardens of Adonis: Spices in Greek Mythology (Hassocks, Sussex: Harvester Press, 1977), 63–68, 108, 122; Eva C. Keuls, The Reign of the Phallus: Sexual Politics in Ancient Athens (New York: Harper & Row, 1985), 23–25.

36. Detienne, Gardens, 65, 101, 104, 105, 109, 118–19, 130; Keuls, Reign, 23–25; Plutarch, Moralia, trans. Edwin L. Minar, F. H. Sandbach, and W. C. Helmbold (Cambridge: Harvard Univ. Press, 1961), "The Dialogue on Love," bk. 9, sec. 756c, p. 349.

37. Olivier Masson and Maurice Sznycer, Recherches sur les Pheniciens a Chypre (Paris: Librairie Droz, 1972), 65–68; D. Winton Thomas, "KELEBH 'DOG': Its Origin and Some Usages of It in the Old Testament," Vetus Testamentum 10, no. 4 (1960): 425.

38. Macrobius, Saturnalia, bk. 3, chap. 8, sec. 2–3, p. 214.

39. Masson and Sznycer, Recherches, 65–68.

40. Eusebius, Ecclesiastical History, 160–61: Nina Jidejian, Byblos Through the Ages (Beirut: Dar El-Machreq Publishers, 1968), 124, 127; Brigitte Soyez, Byblos et la Fête des Adonies (Leiden: E. J. Brill, 1977), 60–67.

41. Colin Thubron, The Hills of Adonis: A Quest in Lebanon (Boston: Little, Brown, 1968), 164.

42. Bailey, Phases, 191; Martin, Hellenistic Religions 82; Lucian, The Goddess of Surrye, in Works, trans. A. M. Harmon (Cambridge: Harvard Univ. Press, 1953), 4:339–411, esp. 357–59.

43. Lucian, Goddess of Surrye, 4:357–59, 377; Lucian, "The Cult of the Syrian Goddess" (excerpt) in Grant, Hellenistic Religions, 116–20; Lewis Bayles Paton, "Atargatis," Encyclopedia of Religion and Ethics, ed. Hastings, 2:166–67; Picard, Ephese, 156, 226–27, 271–72.

44. Cumont, Oriental Religions, 106; Lucian, Goddess of Surrye, 4:377ff.; Paton, "Atargatis," 166–67; Picard, Ephese, 226–27 and n. 6; Grant, World of Rome, 135–37.

45. 2 Maccabees 12:26.

46. Lewis R. Farnell, Greece and Babylon (Edinburgh: T. and T. Clark, 1911), 91; Edward Falkener, Ephesus, and the Temple of Diana (London: Day & Son, 1862), 317–18; Macmullen, Paganism, 35.

47. Callimachus, "To Artemis," Hymns and Epigrams; Lycophron and Aratus, trans. G. R. Mair. (New York: G. P. Putnam's Sons, 1921), 61–83; Persson, Religion of Greece, 112; William Blake Tyrrel, Amazons: A Study in Athenian Mythmaking (Baltimore: Johns Hopkins Univ. Press, 1984), 76–77, 86; Jacques Bonnet, Artemis d'Ephese et la Legende des Sept Dormants (Paris: Librairie Orientaliste Paul Geuthner, 1977), 34–35; William M. Ramsay, Asianic Elements in Greek Civilisation (London: John Murray, 1927), 82; Falkener, Ephesus, 332; John T. Wood, Discoveries at Ephesus (London: Longmans, Green, 1877), appendixes; Strabo, The Geography, trans. Horace L. Jones (Cambridge: Harvard Univ. Press, 1954), vol. 5, bk. 11, chap. 5, sec. 3 and 4, p. 237; Strabo, Geography, trans. Jones (Cambridge: Harvard Univ. Press, 1950), vol. 6, bk. 14, chap. 1, sec. 20–23, pp. 223–29; Picard, Ephese.

48. Falkener, Ephesus, 330.

49. Falkener, Ephesus, 330; also note that H. Lechat, whom Picard follows (Ephese, 180), suggests that the columns of Temple D at Ephesus may represent a procession of megabyzoi. A statuette depicting a megabyzos has also been found at the site of Temple A. Persson further suggests that megabyzoi served Diana at Tiryns and Mycenae and have been depicted on signet rings; ex., ring #24, Persson, Religion of Greece, 146.

50. Athenaeus, Deipnosophists, vol. 5, bk. 12, sec. 525, pp. 369–71; William M. Ramsay, "The Religion of the Hittite Sculptures at Boghaz-Keui," in Luke the Physician and Other Studies in the History of Religion, ed. William M. Ramsey (New York: A. C. Armstrong & Son, 1908), 213; Picard, Ephese, 180–81; Falkener, Ephesus, 144.

51. Falkener, Ephesus, 136–37 and n. 3; Strabo, Geography, vol. 6, bk. 14, chap. 1, sec. 41, p. 253.

52. Falkener, Ephesus, 136; Picard, Ephese, 77–78.

53. Callimachus, "To Artemis," "Epigram LXIV" (a lament at the door of his beloved Conopion), Hymns, 61–83, 181; Asianic Elements, 171–80; Crawford H. Greenwalt, Jr., Ritual Dinners in Early Historic Sardis (Berkeley and Los Angeles: Univ. of California Press, 1978), 45–55.

54. Persson, Religion of Greece, 112, 145, 148; Picard, Ephese, 164–65, 221, 223; Tyrrell, Amazons, 86. For a comparison with twentieth-century Indian eunuch priests of the goddess Bahucharamata, see Serena Nanda, Neither Man Nor Woman: The Hijras of India (Belmont, CA: Wadsworth Publishing, 1990).

55. Picard, Ephese, 40, 52, 129, 157, 556; Falkener, Ephesus, 302–4; Wood, Discoveries, 73.

56. Falkener, *Ephesus,* 144–46.

57. Delcourt, *Hermaphrodite,* 12–13, quoting Hesychius; Persson, *Religion of Greece,* 146–47; *Syriac Version,* ed. Brock, 65; Henri Jeanmaire, *Couroi et Couretes* (New York: Arno Press, 1975), 450–56.

58. *Acts* 19:27 (RSV).

59. Picard, *Ephese,* 171; Wood, *Discoveries,* 12; Falkener, *Ephesus,* 346; John Holland Smith, *The Death of Classical Paganism* (New York: Charles Scribner's Sons, 1976), 175.

60. Smith, *Death of Classical Paganism,* 243.

61. Falkener, *Ephesus,* 346, quoting Chandler.

CHAPTER 6
Sons of Earth

1. Augustine, *City of God,* ed. David Knowles (New York: Penguin Books, 1981), bk. 6, chap. 8, p. 242.

2. Warwick Bray and David Trump, *The Penguin Dictionary of Archaeology* (New York: Penguin Books, 1979), 50, 81.

3. Walter Burkert, *Structure and History in Greek Mythology and Ritual* (Berkeley: Univ. of Calif. Press, 1982), 120.

4. Ovid, *Fasti,* trans. and ed. Sir J. G. Frazer (Cambridge: Harvard Univ. Press, 1959), bk. 4, lines 347–72, p. 215; Martin J. Vermaseren, *Cybele and Attis: The Myth and the Cult* (London: Thames and Hudson, 1977), 127–30; Augustine, *City of God,* ed. Knowles, bk. 7, chap. 24, p. 283; Picard, *Ephese,* 474; Flavius Claudius Julianus Emperor, "Hymn to the Mother of the Gods," *Works,* trans. William Cave Wright (Cambridge: Harvard Univ. Press, 1980), vol. 1, sec. 159A–B, p. 443; sec. 166A–B, pp. 463–65; Pausanius, *Guide to Greece,* trans. Peter Levi (Baltimore: Penguin Books, 1971), vol. 1, bk. 9, sec. 25:3, p. 361.

5. Burkert, *Structure,* 104.

6. Vermaseren, *Cybele,* 129; H. Graillot, *Le culte de Cybèle, mère des dieux* (Paris: Fontemoing et Cie, 1912), 286 ff.

7. Walter Burkert, *Structure,* 120.

8. Charles Picard, *Ephese et Claros: Recherches sur les sanctuaires et les cultes de l'ionie du nord* (Paris: Editions de Boccard, 1922), 223.

9. Picard, *Ephese,* 222; Eva C. Keuls, *The Reign of the Phallus: Sexual Politics in Ancient Athens* (New York: Harper & Row, 1985), 44; Timothy Long, *Barbarians in Greek Comedy* (Carbondale: Southern Illinois Univ. Press, 1986), 29.

10. Long, *Barbarians,* 27.

11. Graillot, *Culte,* 317.

12. Julian, "Hymn," sec. 171A, p. 477.

13. Arnobius, *Adversus Gentes,* ed. Rev. A. Roberts (Edinburgh: T. and T. Clark, 1871), bk. 5, sec. 42, p. 265.

14. Julian, "Hymn," sec. 161D, pp. 451–53; sec. 165B–C, p. 461; sec. 166C–D, p. 465.

15. Arnobius, *Adversus Gentes,* bk. 5, sec. 6, p. 229.

16. Arnobius, *Adversus Gentes,* bk. 5, sec. 6, p. 229.

17. Arnobius, *Adversus Gentes,* bk. 5, sec. 7, pp. 230–31; sec. 13, p. 237.

18. Arnobius, *Adversus Gentes,* bk. 5, sec. 7, pp. 230–31.

19. Julian, "Hymn," 473.

20. Julian, "Hymn," 461, 463, 465, 469, 471, 473, 475, 479; Arnobius, *Adversus Gentes,* bk. 5, sec. 7, pp. 230–31.

21. Giulia S. Gasparro, *Soteriology and Mystic Aspects in the Cult of Cybele and Attis* (Leiden: E. J. Brill, 1985), xvi, 125.

22. Maarten J. Vermaseren, *The Legend of Attis in Greek and Roman Art* (Leiden: E. J. Brill, 1966), 33–34; Friedrich Karl Forberg, *Manual of Classical Erotology* (New York: Grove Press, 1966), 1:125, 1:175.

23. Arnobius, *Adversus Gentes,* bk. 6, sec. 13, pp. 286–87.

24. Sir J. G. Frazer, *The Golden Bough,* 3d ed. (London: Macmillan Press, 1980), 2:288ff.

25. Frazer, *Golden Bough,* 2:289.

26. Gaius Valerius Catullus, *The Poems of Catullus,* ed. William Aiken, (New York: E. P. Dutton, 1950), poem 63 (59 this ed.), p. 134ff.; Frazer, *Golden Bough,* 2:289.

27. Graillot, *Culte,* 298.

28. George W. Elderkin, *Kantharos: Studies in Dionysiac and Kindred Cult* (Princeton: Princeton Univ. Press, 1924), 153.

29. Graillot, *Culte,* 298–99; Clement of Alexandria, *Le Pédagogue,* trans. into French by Claude Mondésert (Paris: Les Editions du Cerf, 1965), bk. 3, chap. 17.4, p. 43; Tertullian, "On the Pallium," *Works,* ed. Rev. A. Roberts (New York: Christian Literature Company, 1890), vol. 4, chap. 4, p. 10.

30. Graillot, *Culte,* 299–300; Augustine, *City of God,* bk. 7, chap. 26, p. 467; Clement of Alexandria, *Pédagogue,* bk. 3, chap. 16. 2–3, pp. 41 and 43; chap. 17.3, p. 43; Apuleius, *The Golden Ass,* trans. W. Aldington (New York: G. P. Putnam's Sons, 1928), 389–91; Athenaeus, *The Deipnosophists,* trans. Charles B. Gulick (Cambridge: Harvard Univ. Press, 1950), bk. 13, sec. 528ff., p. 387; Harold R. Willoughby, *Pagan Regeneration* (Chicago: Univ. of Chicago Press, 1929), 116; Walter Burkert, *Ancient Mystery Cults* (Cambridge: Harvard Univ. Press, 1987), 103.

31. Long, *Barbarians,* 76; Athenaeus, *Deipnosophists,* bk. 12, sec. 526b, p. 373.

32. Long, *Barbarians,* 80, 76, 81.

33. Ovid, *The Art of Love,* trans. Rolfe Humphries (Bloomington: Indiana Univ. Press, 1957), bk. 1, lines 508ff.

34. Dio Chrysostom, *Thirty-third Discourse,* in *Works,* trans. J. W. Cohoon and H. Lamar

Crosby (Cambridge: Harvard Univ. Press, 1940), sec. 63–64, p. 331–33; Clement of Alexandria, *Pédagogue*, bk. 3, chap. 15.3–4, pp. 39–41; sec. 19, p. 47.

35. Quintillian, *Works*, trans. H. E. Butler (Cambridge: Harvard Univ. Press, 1979), vol. 2., bk. 5, sec. 10–12, p. 251.

36. Arnobius, *Adversus Gentes*, bk. 2, sec. 41, pp. 109–110.

37. Aulus Gellius, *The Attic Nights*, trans. John C. Rolfe (Cambridge: Harvard Univ. Press, 1982), bk. 6, chap. 12, pp. 57–59.

38. Dio Chrysostom, *Thirty-third Discourse*, sec. 63–64, pp. 331–33.

39. Clement of Alexandria, *Pédagogue*, bk. 3, chap. 11, sec. 70, p. 139; Firmicus Maternus, *The Error of the Pagan Religions*, trans. Clarence A. Forbes (New York: Newman Press, 1970), chap. 4, pp. 50–51; Juvenal, "Satire II," *The Sixteen Satires*, ed. and trans. Peter Green (New York: Penguin Books, 1979), 75–85; Augustine, *City of God*, bk. 7, chap. 26, p. 286; Dio Chrysostom, *Thirty-third Discourse*, sec. 52, p. 323; Apuleius, *Golden Ass*, p. 387; *Lexicon, Abridged from Liddell and Scott's Greek-English Lexicon* (Oxford: Oxford Univ. Press, 1983), s.v. βαταλοσ, "a lisper."

40. Dio Chrysostom, *Thirty-third Discourse*, sec. 39, p. 309; sec. 54, pp. 323–25; sec. 60, p. 329; Clement of Alexandria, *Pédagogue*, bk. 3, chap. 4, sec. 29.2, p. 67.

41. Graillot, *Culte*, 312ff.; Grant Showerman, *The Great Mother of the Gods* (Chicago: Argonaut, 1969), 80.

42. Gaius Valerius Catullus, *The Poems of Catullus*, ed. William Aiken (New York: E. P. Dutton, 1950), poem 63 (59 this ed.), p. 134ff.

43. Burkert, *Structure*, 119; Ovid, *Fasti*, bk. 4, p. 215.

44. Willoughby, *Pagan Regeneration*, 129; Showerman, *Great Mother*, 17–18.

45. John Ferguson, *An Illustrated Encyclopedia of Mysticism and the Mystery Religions* (New York: Seabury Press, 1977), 27; Axel W. Persson, *The Religion of Greece in Prehistoric Times* (Berkeley and Los Angeles: Univ. of California Press, 1942), 110; Pliny, *Natural History*, trans. H. Rackham (Cambridge: Harvard Univ. Press, 1952), vol. 3, bk. 11, ch. 109, sec. 261, p. 597; Apuleius, *Golden Ass*, 391–93; Günther Zuntz, *Persephone: Three Essays on Religion and Thought in Magna Graecia* (Oxford: Clarendon Press, 1971), 19–20.

46. Pliny, *Natural History*, vol. 9, bk. 35, ch. 46, sec. 165, p. 383.

47. Martin Henig, *Religion in Roman Britain* (New York: St. Martin's Press, 1984), 110–11.

48. Graillot, *Culte*, 297; Vermaseren, *Cybele*, 116–19.

49. Porphyry, quoted in Augustine, *City of God*, bk. 7, chap. 25, pp. 465–67; Graillot, *Culte*, 293.

50. Persson, *Religion of Greece*, 122.

51. Burkert, *Structure*, 120–21.

52. Julian, "Hymn," sec. 174C, p. 487; Carlo Ginzburg, *Ecstasies: Deciphering the Witches' Sabbath* (New York: Random House, 1991), 103, 116 n. 54.

53. Juvenal, "Satire VI," *Satires*, p. 147; E. A. Courtney, *A Commentary on the Satires of Juvenal* (London: Athlone Press, 1980), 327; Athenaeus, *Deipnosophists*, bk. 12, sec. 514, pp. 449–51; Gasparro, *Soteriology*, 16; Graillot, *Culte*, 287ff.; compare to the gender variance of India's *hijras*: Serena Nanda, *Neither Man Nor Woman: The Hijras of India* (Belmont, CA: Wadsworth Publishing, 1990).

54. John Boswell, *Christianity, Social Tolerance, and Homosexuality: Gay People in Western Europe from the Beginning of the Christian Era to the Fourteenth Century* (Chicago: Univ. of Chicago Press, 1980), 52.

55. Julius Firmicus Maternus, *Ancient Astrology: Theory and Practice (Matheseos Libri VIII)*, trans. Jean Rhys Bram (Park Ridge, NJ: Noyes Press, 1975), bk. 6, chap. 30, sec. 3, p. 207; bk. 7, chap. 25, sec. 4, p. 261; bk. 7, chap. 25, sec. 14, p. 263; J. Firmicus Maternus, *Matheseos Libri VIII*, ed. W. Kroll and F. Skutsch (Stuttgart: B. G. Teubner, 1968), same bks., chaps., and secs. as previous entry.

56. Firmicus Maternus, *Ancient Astrology*; Burkert, *Structure*, 120–21.

57. Valerius Maximus, *Dictorum Factorumque Memorabilium, Libri IX* (Elzeviriorum: Amstelodami, 1690), bk. 7, chap. 7, sec. 6; also see bk. 8, chap. 3, sec. 1; Valerius Maximus, *Actions et Paroles Mémorables*, trans. Pierre Constant (Paris: Librairie Garnier Frères, 1935), vol. 2, bk. 7, ch. 7, sec. 6, pp. 168–69; William Smith, *Dictionary of Greek and Roman Mythology* (London: Taylor and Walton, 1846), 2:245.

58. Richard Gordon, "Religion in the Roman Empire: The Civic Compromise and Its Limits," in *Pagan Priests: Religion and Power in the Ancient World*, ed. Mary Beard and John North (London: Duckworth, 1990), 235–40, 248.

59. Cristiano Grottanelli, "Archaic Forms of Rebellion and Their Religious Background," in *Religion, Rebellion, Revolution*, ed. Bruce Lincoln (Houndmills, England: Macmillan, 1985), 22–25.

60. Diodorus Siculus, *Works*, trans. C. H. Oldfather (Cambridge: Harvard Univ. Press, 1979), bk. 2, p. 259.

61. Persson, *Religion of Greece*, 112.

62. William Blake Tyrrell, *Amazons: A Study in Athenian Mythmaking* (Baltimore: Johns Hopkins Univ. Press, 1984), 86.

63. Sextus Empiricus, *Outlines of Pyrrhonism*, trans. Rev. R. G. Bury (Cambridge: Harvard Univ. Press, 1976), bk. 3, sec. 217–18, p. 471.

64. Clement of Alexandria, *Pédagogue*, bk. 3, chap. 3, sec. 21.3, p. 51; Tertullian, quoted in Forberg, *Manual of Classical Erotology* 2:149.

65. Amy Richlin, *The Garden of Priapus: Sexuality and Aggression in Roman Humor* (New Haven: Yale Univ. Press, 1983), 69, also see 66ff.

66. Graillot, *Culte*, 286–87; Firmicus Maternus, *Error*, 152 n. 83.

67. Clement of Alexandria, *Pédagogue*, bk. 3, chap. 4, sec. 29.2, p. 67.

68. Clement of Alexandria, *Pédagogue*, bk. 3, chap. 4, sec. 29.2 and 30.1–3, pp. 67–68.

69. Forberg, *Manual of Classical Erotology* 2:51, quoting Martial, *Epigram* 3.81.

70. Rev. Charles Hefele, *A History of the Councils of the Church* (Edinburgh: T. and T. Clark, 1896), 1:165–66.

71. Graillot, *Culte*, 318.

72. Gaston Vorberg, *Glossarium Eroticum* (Rome: "L'Erma" di Bretschneider, 1965), 164; Juvenal, "Satire IX," *Satires*, ed. Green, 197, 202 n. 8.

73. Burkert, *Structure*, 120.

74. Apuleius, *Golden Ass*, 389.

75. Juvenal, "Satire II," *Satires*, ed. Green, 79–80.

76. Juvenal, "Satire II," *Satires*, ed. Green, 79–80.

77. Juvenal, "Satire II," *Satires*, ed. Green, 79–80.

78. Juvenal, "Satire VIII," *Satires*, ed. Green, 184.

79. Firmicus Maternus, *Error*, 50.

80. Augustine, *City of God*, bk. 6, chap. 8, p. 242.

81. Philostratus, *The Life of Apollonius of Tyana*, trans. F. C. Conybeare (Cambridge: Harvard Univ. Press, 1912), 34.

82. Vermaseren, *Cybele*, 116–17.

83. Philostratus, *Life*, 22.

84. Willoughby, *Pagan Regeneration*, 126–27.

85. Vermaseren, *Cybele*, 116.

86. Vermaseren, *Cybele*, 115; Ovid, *Fasti*, 202 note a; Arnobius, *Adversus Gentes*, bk. 5, sec. 16, pp. 239–40.

87. Vermaseren, *Cybele*, 123.

88. Ovid, *Fasti*, 213.

89. Robert J. Getty, "Galliamb(us)," *Princeton Encyclopedia of Poetry and Poetics*, enlarged edition. ed. Alex Preminger et al. (Princeton: Princeton Univ. Press, 1974), 306; Graillot, *Culte*, 101 n. 2; Quintillian, *Works*, bk. 1, chap. 8, sec. 2, p. 147; bk. 1, chap. 10, sec. 31, p. 175; bk. 9, chap. 4, sec. 142, p. 587.

90. M. J. Vermaseren, and C. C. van Essen, *The Excavations in the Mithraeum of the Church of Santa Prisca in Rome* (Leiden: E. J. Brill, 1965), 188ff.

91. Erucius of Kyzikos, ("I, the priest of Rhea"), trans. Robin Skelton, *The Greek Anthology and Other Ancient Greek Epigrams*, ed. Peter Jay (New York: Oxford Univ. Press, 1973), 186–87.

92. Peter Michael Hamel, *Through Music to the Self* (Boulder: Shambhala, 1978), 81–82.

93. Showerman, *Great Mother*, 18; Graillot, *Culte*, 304.

94. Hamel, *Music*, 81–82.

95. Ovid, *Fasti*, trans. and ed. Sir James G. Frazer (London: Macmillan, 1929), 3:200; Gilbert Rouget, *Music and Trance: A Theory of the Relations between Music and Possession* (Chicago: Univ. of Chicago Press, 1985), 214–18.

96. Johannes Quasten, *Music and Worship in Pagan and Christian Antiquity*, trans. Boniface Ramsey (Washington, DC: National Association of Pastoral Musicians, 1983), 36; Rouget, *Music and Trance*, 223–24, 233.

97. Quasten, *Music and Worship*, 37, 39.

98. *Syriac Version*, ed. Brock, 145–46; Herodotus, *The Histories*, trans. Aubrey de Selincourt (New York: Penguin Books, 1978), bk. 2, sec. 56–63, pp. 152–53; Frank M. Snowden, Jr., *Blacks in Antiquity: Ethiopians in the Greco-Roman Experience* (Cambridge: Harvard Univ. Press, 1971), 189–92; Macmullen, *Paganism*, 21–22; Otto Jahn, "Die Wandegemälde des Columbariums in der Villa Pamfili," in *Abhandlungen der Philosoph.-Philologischen Classe der Königlich Bayerischen Akademie der Wissenschaften* (Munchen: Verlag der Akademie, G. Franz, 1857–1858), 256.

99. Leona Wood and Anthony Shay, "*Danse du Ventre*: A Fresh Appraisal," *Dance Research Journal* 8, no. 2 (1976): 18–30, esp. 19, 23, 25.

100. Lucian, *Saltus (Dance)*, in *Works*, trans. A. M. Harmon (New York: G. P. Putnam's Sons, 1925), vol. 5, sec. 8, p. 221; Athenaeus, *Deipnosophists*, bk. 14, sec. 630, p. 401.

101. Lillian B. Lawler, *The Dance of the Ancient Greek Theatre* (Iowa City: Univ. of Iowa Press, 1964), 108, 113, 120–21; Arnobius, *Adversus Gentes*, bk. 7, sec. 33, p. 344; Clement of Alexandria, *Pédagogue*, bk. 3, chap. 4, sec. 30.1–3, pp. 67–68.

102. Ovid, *Fasti* (ed. Frazer), vol. 3: p.201.

103. Niall Rudd, *Themes in Roman Satire* (Norman: Univ. of Oklahoma Press, 1986); Macrobius, *The Saturnalia*, trans. and ed. Percival Vaughan Davies (New York: Columbia Univ. Press, 1969), bk. 3, chap. 14, p. 232.

104. Peter Marshall Fraser, *Ptolemaic Alexandria* (Oxford: Oxford Univ. Press, 1972), 278.

105. Graillot, *Culte*, 307–8; Walter Burkert, *Greek Religion*, trans. John Raffan (Cambridge: Harvard Univ. Press, 1985), 112; Hans Dieter Betz, ed., *The Greek Magical Papyri in Translation* (Chicago: Univ. of Chicago Press, 1986), 118–19.

106. Iamblichus, *The Mysteries of the Egyptians, Chaldeans, and Assyrians*, trans. Thomas Taylor (London: Bertram Dobell, 1895), 5.

107. Graillot, *Culte*, 306, 309.

108. Graillot, *Culte*, 310.

109. Graillot, *Culte*, 310; Walter Addison Jayne, *The Healing Gods of Ancient Civilizations* (New Hyde Park, NY: University Books, 1962), 486.

110. Graillot, *Culte*, 186, 311–12.

111. Rosemary Ellen Guiley, *The Encyclopedia of Witches and Witchcraft* (New York: Facts on File, 1989), 335–36; Jayne, *Healing Gods*, 486; Pliny, *Natural History*, vol. 8 bk. 28 chap. 27, sec. 106, p. 75; vol 3, bk. 8, ch. 44, sec. 105–6, pp. 77–79; vol.3, bk. 8, ch. 46, p. 79.

112. Vermaseren, *Cybele*, 126–27.
113. Graillot, *Culte*, 311; and see Nanda, *Neither Man Nor Woman*, 30.
114. Graillot, *Culte*, 309.
115. Courtney, *Commentary on the Satires*, 328.
116. Courtney, *Commentary on the Satires*, 328.
117. Lucian, *The Syrian Goddess*, sec. 52–53, as appears in *The Ancient Mysteries: A Sourcebook*, ed. Marvin W. Meyer (San Francisco: Harper & Row, 1987), 139; Franz Cumont, *After Life in Roman Paganism* (New Haven: Yale Univ. Press, 1922), 36.
118. Artemidorus Daldianus, *The Interpretation of Dreams: Oneirocritica*, trans. Robert J. White (Park Ridge, NJ: Noyes Press, 1975), bk. 2, sec. 69, p. 134; Julian, "Hymn," sec. 159A–B, p. 443.
119. Graillot, *Culte*, 317.
120. Clement of Alexandria, *Works*, trans. G. W. Butterworth (New York: G. P. Putnam's Sons, 1919), 51; Clement of Alexandria, *Pédagogue*, bk. 3, chap. 4, sec. 29.2, p. 67; also see Ephesians 5:5, Romans 13:12–13.
121. Augustine, *City of Gods* trans. Knowles, bk. 2, chap. 5, p. 53; bk. 2, chap. 7, p. 55; bk. 2, chap. 4, p. 51; bk. 6, chap. 7, p. 241; bk. 7, chap. 26, p. 286.
122. Ferguson, *Illustrated Encyclopedia of Mysticism*, 240.
123. John Holland Smith, *The Death of Classical Paganism* (New York: Charles Scribner's Sons, 1976), 175; Ferguson, *Illustrated Encyclopedia of Mysticism*, 31.
124. Codex Theodosius 9.7.6, in *Les bûchers de Sodome*, trans. Maurice Lever (Paris: Fayard, 1985), 35; also see *The Theodosian Code and Novels and the Sirmondian Constitutions*, trans. Clyde Pharr (Princeton: Princeton Univ. Press, 1952), xvii, 231–32.
125. J. B. Bury, *History of the Later Roman Empire* (London: Macmillan, 1923), 2:368, 371, 412.
126. Burkert, *Structure*, 105.
127. Graillot, *Culte*, 408–9; Henig, *Religion in Roman Britain*, p. 110; Willoughby, *Pagan Regeneration*, 126.
128. Ferguson, *Illustrated Encyclopedia of Mysticism*, 184–85; Graillot, *Culte*, 404–5.
129. Jacques Lacarrière, *The Gnostics* (New York: E. P. Dutton, 1977), 108, 111.
130. Richard Reitzenstein, *Hellenistic Mystery-Religions: Their Basic Ideas and Significance*, trans. John E. Steely (Pittsburgh: Pickwick Press, 1978), 183–84; F. Legge, *Forerunners and Rivals of Christianity* (London: Cambridge Univ. Press, 1915), 36–82, esp. 57–58; Graillot, *Culte*, 406.
131. Hippolytus, *The Refutation of All Heresies*, trans. Rev. J. H. Macmahon, (Edinburgh: T. and T. Clark, 1870), bk. 5, chap. 1, p. 126 n. 4; bk. 5, chap. 2, pp. 131–32, 135; bk. 5, chap. 3, p. 145; bk. 5, chap. 4, p. 150; Graillot, *Culte*, 406.
132. Hippolytus, *Refutation*, bk. 5, chap. 2, p. 132; bk. 5, chap. 3, p. 140; John 6:53.
133. Laccarière, *Gnostics*, 82–83.
134. Hippolytus, *Refutation*, bk. 5, chap. 4, p. 148.
135. Hippolytus, *Refutation*, bk. 5, chap. 4, pp. 149–50.
136. Epiphanius, *The Panarion*, trans. Frank Williams (Leiden: E. J. Brill, 1987), 77–78; Ferguson, *Illustrated Encyclopedia of Mysticism*, 31.
137. Stephen Gero, "With Walter Bauer on the Tigris," in *Nag Hammadi, Gnosticism, and Early Christianity*, ed. Charles W. Hedrick and Robert Hodgson, Jr. (Peabody, MA: Hendrickson Publishers, 1986), 293–94; Gedaliahu A. Stroumsa, *Another Seed: Studies in Gnostic Mythology* (Leiden: E. J. Brill, 1984), 65; James E. Goehring, "Libertine or Liberated: Women in the So-called Libertine Gnostic Communities," *Images of the Feminine in Gnosticism*, ed. Karen L. King (Philadelphia: Fortress Press, 1988), 343.
138. Goehring, "Libertine," 341; Gero, "With Walter Bauer," 288; Stephen Benko, "The Libertine Gnostic Sect of the Phibionites according to Epiphanius," *Vigiliae Christianae* 21, no. 2 (1967): 116–17.
139. Werner Foerster, ed., *Gnosis: A Selection of Gnostic Texts*, trans. R. McL. Wilson, (Oxford: Oxford Univ. Press, 1972), 323.
140. Goehring, "Libertine," 340; Benko, "Libertine," 110–16.
141. Foerster, ed., *Gnosis*, 323.
142. Gero, "With Walter Bauer," 293 n. 29.
143. Epiphanius, *Panarion*, 13, 1–2, 324–25.
144. Epiphanius, *Panarion*, 13, 1–2, 324–25.
145. Graillot, *Culte*, 407; also see Morton Smith, *The Secret Gospel* (New York: Harper & Row, 1973).
146. Ean Begg, *The Cult of the Black Virgin* (Boston: Arkana, Routledge and Kegan Paul, 1985), 58–59.
147. Begg, *Cult*, 58, 61.
148. Picard, *Ephese*, 404.
149. Vermaseren, *Cybele*, 96.
150. Graillot, *Culte*, 409.

CHAPTER 7
Womanish and Beastly Ways

1. "The Flyting of Loki (*The Lokasenna*)," *The Poetic Edda*, trans. and ed. Lee M. Hollander, (Austin: Univ. of Texas Press, 1962), strophe 24, p. 111.
2. Marija Gimbutas, "Women and Culture in Goddess-Oriented Old Europe," in *Weaving the Visions: New Patterns in Feminist Spirituality*, ed. Judith Plaskow and Carol P. Christ (San Francisco: Harper & Row, 1989), 63.
3. Gimbutas, "Women and Culture," 63.

4. Erna Buffie (with story consultant Starhawk), *The Burning Times,* dir. Donna Read (National Film Board of Canada, 1990).

5. See, for example, Terence McKenna, *The Archaic Revival* (San Francisco: HarperSanFrancisco, 1991).

6. M. Rostovstev, *Iranians and Greeks in South Russia* (Oxford: Clarendon Press, 1922), 105; Herodotus, *The Histories,* trans. Aubrey de Selincourt (New York: Penguin Books, 1978), bk 4, p. 289; British Museum Publications, *Frozen Tombs: The Culture and Art of the Ancient Tribes of Siberia* (London: British Museum, 1978), 287.

7. W. R. Halliday, "A Note on the . . . Feminine Malady of the Skythians," *The Annual of the British School at Athens* no. 17 (1911): 96–97.

8. Halliday, "Note," 97, 100.

9. Marie Delcourt, *Hermaphrodite* (London: Studio Books, 1961), 40.

10. Joanna Hubbs, "The Worship of Mother Earth in Russian Culture," in *Mother Worship: Themes and Variations,* ed. James J. Preston (Chapel Hill: Univ. of North Carolina Press, 1982), 124, 126; Richard G. Klein, *Ice-Age Hunters of the Ukraine* (Chicago: Univ. of Chicago Press, 1973), 85; Halliday, "Note," 95–101; Delcourt, *Hermaphrodite,* 40; Mircea Eliade, *Shamanism: Archaic Techniques of Ecstasy* (Princeton: Princeton Univ. Press, 1964), 394–95; Michael Grant, *The Rise of the Greeks* (New York: Charles Scribner's Sons, 1988), 308; Richard Evans Schultes and Albert Hofmann, *Plants of the Gods: Origins of Hallucinogenic Use* (New York: McGraw-Hill, 1979), 92–93, 95–96.

11. Rostovstev, *Iranians,* 34; Marija Gimbutas, *The Goddesses and Gods of Old Europe* (Berkeley and Los Angeles: Univ. of California Press, 1982), 9; B. Gardanov, "Maeotae," *Great Soviet Encyclopedia: A Translation of the Third Edition* (New York: Macmillan, 1973), 16:44; B. Gardanov, "Adygeians," *Great Soviet Encyclopedia,* 1:116; V. F. Zakharina, "Adygei Autonomous Oblast," *Great Soviet Encyclopedia,* 1:119; Z. I. Iampol'skii, "Caucasian Albania," *Great Soviet Encyclopedia,* 1:594.

12. Hippocrates, *Works* (Cambridge: Harvard Univ. Press, 1972), 1:127–29; Rostovstev, *Iranians,* 105; Aristotle, *Ethica Nicomachea,* trans. W. D. Ross, in *The Basic Works of Aristotle,* ed. Richard McKeon (New York: Random House, 1941), bk. 7, ch. 7, pp. 1048–49; Rev. John Groves, *A Greek and English Dictionary* (Philadelphia: J. B. Lippincott, 1872), 45, 376; Halliday, "Note," 98; Herodotus, *Histories,* bk. 1, p. 84; Meuli, quoted in Eliade, *Shamanism,* 394.

13. Hippocrates, *Works,* 1:127–29; Rostovstev, *Iranians,* 105.

14. Hippocrates, *Works,* 1:127–29; Herodotus, *Histories,* bk. 1, p. 84.

15. Rostovstev, *Iranians,* 104–5; M. Rostovstev, "Le Culte de la Grande Dèese dans la Russie Méridionale," *Revue des Études Grecques* 32 (1921): 477.

16. Herodotus, *Histories,* bk. 4, pp. 292–93.

17. Herodotus, *Histories,* bk. 4, pp. 293, 295.

18. Schultes and Hofmann, *Plants,* 95–96.

19. Schultes and Hofmann, *Plants,* 92–93; Eliade, *Shamanism,* 394–95.

20. Frank Trippett et al., *The First Horsemen* (New York: Time-Life Books, 1974), 9, 15; Herodotus, *Histories,* bk. 4, p. 290; Marija Gimbutas, *Bronze Age Cultures in Central and Eastern Europe* (Paris: Mouton, 1965), 577.

21. Rostovstev, *Iranians,* 34; Herodotus, *Histories,* bk. 4, p. 308; Strabo, *The Geography,* trans. H. C. Hamilton and W. Falconer (London: G. Bell and Sons, 1913), vol. 5, bk. 11, chap. 5, sec. 1–2 pp. 233–37; *Great Soviet Encyclopedia,* s.v. "Sauromatians."

22. Mertury Ale Trekutulye, *These Remote Near Ages* (Keshenev: Ezdatelstvo (Tempul), 1985), 41.

23. Hubbs, "Worship," 126.

24. Herodotus, *Histories,* bk. 1, p. 84.

25. Herodotus, *Histories,* bk. 1, p. 84; bk. 4, p. 295; Grant, *Rise of the Greeks,* 308.

26. Clement of Alexandria, *Works,* trans. G. W. Butterworth (New York: G. P. Putnam's Sons, 1919), ch. 2, p. 48–49.

27. Strabo, *Geography,* vol. 5, bk. 11, ch. 2, sec. 10, p. 199–201.

28. Grant, *Rise of the Greeks,* 308.

29. Joseph Campbell, *The Way of the Animal Powers* (New York: Alfred van der Marck, 1983), 173.

30. Ioan Petru Couliano, "Sexual Rites in Europe," *The Encyclopedia of Religion,* ed. Mircea Eliade (New York: Macmillan, 1987), 13: 187; Joanna Hubbs, *Mother Russia: The Feminine Myth in Russian Culture* (Bloomington: Indiana Univ. Press, 1988), 199–200.

31. Couliano, "Sexual Rites," 187; Hubbs, *Mother Russia,* 199–200.

32. Hubbs, *Mother Russia,* 199–200; Couliano, "Sexual Rites," 187.

33. Nikolai Klyuev, *Poems,* trans. John Glad (Ann Arbor: Ardis, 1977): "The Fourth Rome," 34–35; "A Conversational Melody," 6; preface, ix–xx.

34. Vyacheslav Ivanov, "Incantation," trans. Simon Karlinsky, quoted by Karlinsky, "Russia's Gay Literature and History (11th–20th Centuries)," *Gay Sunshine Journal* 29/30 (1976): 7.

35. Paul Marte Duval, "The Religion and Myths of the Continental Celts of Gaul," in *Mythologies,* ed. Wendy Doniger and Yves Bonnefoy (Chicago: Univ. of Chicago Press, 1991), 1:242–48; John Sharkey, *Celtic Mysteries: The Ancient Religion* (New York: Crossroad, 1981).

36. Nora Chadwick, *The Celts* (Baltimore: Penguin, 1970), 136; Jean Markale, *Women of the Celts* (London: Gordon Cremonesi, 1975), 39; Arthur

Evans, *Witchcraft and the Gay Counterculture* (Boston: Fag Rag Books, 1978), 18–19.

37. Diodorus Siculus, *Works: Library of History*, trans. C. H. Oldfather (Cambridge: Harvard Univ. Press, 1952), vol. 3 bk. 5, chap. 32.7, pp. 183–85; Mary Condren, *The Serpent and the Goddess: Women, Religion, and Power in Celtic Ireland* (San Francisco: Harper & Row, 1989), 89–90; Evans, *Witchcraft*, 19.

38. Timothy Taylor, "The Gundestrup Cauldron," *Scientific American* (March 1992): 84–89; Caradoc ap Cador, "Amazons, Islands of Women, and Homosexual Behavior in Northwest Europe," parts 1, 2, and 3 in *Lavender Pagan Newsletter* 1, nos. 3, 4, 5 (1992); Jean Markale, *Le druidisme: Traditions et dieux des Celtes* (Paris: Payot, 1985); Jean Markale, *Mélusine ou l'androgyne* (Paris: Éditions Retz, 1983); Anne Ross, *Pagan Celtic Britain* (London: Routledge & Kegan Paul, 1967).

39. Anne Ross, "Celtic and Northern Art," in *Primitive Erotic Art*, ed. Philip Rawson (New York: G. P. Putnam's Sons, 1973), 80.

40. Paul Marie Duval, "Cernunnos, the God with the Horns of a Stag," in *Mythologies*, ed. Wendy Doniger and Yves Bonnefoy (Chicago: Univ. of Chicago Press, 1991), 1:268–70; Markale, *Le druidisme*, 142–43.

41. Ross, "Celtic and Northern Art," 84.

42. Evans, *Witchcraft*, 21.

43. Bernard Sergent, *L'homosexualité initiatique dans l'Europe ancienne* (Paris: Payot, 1986), 184–87; Patricia Monaghan, *The Book of Goddesses and Heroines* (New York: E. P. Dutton, 1981), 76, 87.

44. Charles Squire, *Celtic Myth and Legend, Poetry and Romance* (New York: Bell Publishing, 1979), 172; Hamish Henderson, "The Women of the Glen: Some Thoughts on Highland History," in *The Celtic Consciousness*, ed. Robert O'Driscoll (New York: George Braziller, 1982), 257.

45. Henderson, "Women," 257.

46. Markale, *Mélusine*, p. 82.

47. Markale, *Mélusine*, 75–83.

48. Brinley Rees, "Druid and Poet: The Irish *Filidh* and the Welsh *Bardd*," in *Mythologies*, ed. Wendy Doniger and Yves Bonnefoy (Chicago: Univ. of Chicago Press, 1991), 1:250.

49. Eliade, *Shamanism*, 179, 382.

50. Maire Cruise O'Brien, "The Role of the Poet in Gaelic Society," in *The Celtic Consciousness*, ed. Robert O'Driscoll (New York: George Braziller, 1982), 250.

51. See also Caradoc ap Cador, "Amazons."

52. H. R. Ellis Davidson, *Pagan Scandinavia* (New York: Praeger, 1967), 30, 36.

53. Kveldulf Gundarsson, *Teutonic Magic: The Magical and Spiritual Practices of the Germanic Peoples* (St. Paul: Llewellyn, 1990), 148.

54. Gundarsson, *Teutonic Magic*, 238.

55. Gundarsson, *Teutonic Magic*, 238; Davidson, *Pagan Scandinavia*, 30, 117.

56. Gundarsson, *Teutonic Magic*, 239; H. R. Ellis Davidson, *Gods and Myths of Northern Europe* (Baltimore: Penguin Books, 1975), 114–24.

57. See also Kónraðr Trollmaðr, "Freyr: An Ecstatic God from Scandinavia," *Lavender Pagan Newsletter* no. 5 (1992): 1, 6–8.

58. Gundarsson, *Teutonic Magic*, 237.

59. Davidson, *Gods*, 154, 100, 92–110.

60. Davidson, *Gods*, p. 92.

61. See P. V. Denmark Glob, *An Archaeological History from the Stone Age to the Vikings* (Ithaca: Cornell Univ. Press, 1971).

62. Byron J. Nordstrom, *Dictionary of Scandinavian History* (Westport, CT: Greenwood Press, 1986), 8.

63. Davidson, *Gods*, 102, 159, 66, 68, 61–66; Gundarsson, *Teutonic Magic*, 249–50.

64. Gundarsson, *Teutonic Magic*, 226.

65. Davidson, *Gods*, 48–54; Gundarsson, *Teutonic Magic*, 223–26.

66. Gundarsson, *Teutonic Magic*, 149, 226.

67. Gundarsson, *Teutonic Magic*, 149.

68. Gundarsson, *Teutonic Magic*, 229–31.

69. Davidson, *Gods*, 39–40, 42, 176–82; Gundarsson, *Teutonic Magic*, 227.

70. Davidson, *Gods*, 44–45.

71. Brian Froud and Alan Lee, *Faeries* (New York: Harry N. Abrams, 1978); Davidson, *Gods*, 29, 32, 181; Edgar Polomé, "Loki," *The Encyclopedia of Religion*, ed. Mircea Eliade (New York: Macmillan, 1987), 9:17–19.

72. Thorkil Vangaard, *Phallos: A Symbol and Its History in the Male World* (New York: International Universities Press, 1972), 77.

73. Vangaard, *Phallos*, 76.

74. Jaan Puhvel, *Comparative Mythology* (Baltimore: Johns Hopkins Univ. Press, 1987), 207; Sergent, *L'homosexualite initiatique*, 164; Polomé, "Loki," 17–18; Lawrence S. Thompson, *Norse Mythology: The Elder Edda in Prose Translation* (Hamden, CT: Archon Books, 1974), 50; Folke Ström, "Bog Corpses and *Germania* Chapter 12," in *Words and Objects: Towards a Dialogue Between Archaeology and History of Religion*, ed. Gro Steinsland (Oslo: Norwegian Univ. Press, 1986), 226–27.

75. Vangaard, *Phallos*, 77; James A. Chisholm, "Seiðr Excerpts: Part I," *Idunna: A Journal of the Northern Tradition* 3, no. 4 (1992): 1–6; J. Chisolm, "Seiðr Excerpts: Part II," *Idunna* 4, no. 1 (1992): 1–3; "Flying of Loki," trans. and ed. Hollander, strophe 24, p. 111.

76. Folke Ström, *Nið, Ergi, and Old Norse Moral Attitudes*, Dorothea Coke Memorial Lecture in Northern Studies, University College, London, May 10, 1973 (London: Viking Society for Northern Research, 1973), 9–10; Puhvel, *Comparative Mythology*, 209.

77. Ström, *Nið*, 17.
78. Ström, *Nið*, 17; Davidson, *Gods*, 102.
79. Polomé, "Loki," 18.
80. See Vangaard, *Phallos*, and Sergent, *L'homosexualite initiatique*.
81. Davidson, *Gods*, 96, 97, 99; Saxo Grammaticus, *Gesta Danorum: The Nine Books of the Danish History*, trans. Oliver Elton (London: Norreana Society, 1893; reprint, Nendel, Liechtenstein: Kraus Reprint, 1967), 228.
82. Rudolf Poertner, *The Vikings: Rise and Fall of the Norse Sea Kings*, trans. Sophie Wilkins (New York: St. Martin's Press, 1975), 226–27; Davidson, *Gods*, 96–97.
83. Tacitus, *On Britain and Germany* (Harmondsworth, Middlesex: Penguin, 1951), chap. 43, p. 136; Davidson, *Gods*, 169.
84. Davidson, *Gods*, 121.
85. Gundarsson, *Teutonic Magic*, 213, 216; Davidson, *Gods*, 118–19.
86. Ström, *Nið*, 17 and n. 3.
87. Gundarsson, *Teutonic Magic*, 148–49.
88. Gudbrand Vigfusson, ed., *Cleasby's Icelandic-English Dictionary* (Oxford: Clarendon Press, 1874).
89. Ström, *Nið* 8, 19.
90. Ström, *Nið*, 9.
91. Kirsten Hastrup, *Culture and History in Medieval Iceland* (Oxford: Clarendon Press, 1985), 153.
92. Davidson, *Gods*, 118.
93. Gundarsson, *Teutonic Magic*, 128–29, 148–49.
94. Gundarsson, *Teutonic Magic*, 255; Chisholm, "Seiðr Excerpts," pts. I and II.
95. Alfreðr Ingvisson, "Scandinavian Witchcraft," *Idunna* 4, no. 3 (1992): 11; Edred Thorsson, *The Nine Gates of Midgard* (St. Paul: Llewellyn, 1991), 200.
96. Chisholm, "Seiðr Excerpts: Part I, Laxdaela Saga," 4.
97. Puhvel, *Comparative Mythology*, 205, 207; Ström, "Bog," 230, 232.
98. P. V. Glob, *The Bog People: Iron-Age Man Preserved*, trans. Rupert Bruce-Mitford (Ithaca: Cornell Univ. Press, 1969), 147, 191–92.
99. Glob, *Bog*, 116; also see 63, 191–92, plates 38, 39, 56–59.
100. Gundarsson, *Teutonic Magic*, 148–49.
101. Quoted by James D. Steakley, *The Homosexual Emancipation Movement in Germany* (New York: Arno Press, 1975), 118.
102. Puhvel, *Comparative Mythology*, 209–10; Davidson, *Gods*, 170.
103. Snorri Sturleson, *Heimskringla*, ed. Erling Monsen (Cambridge: W. Heffer and Sons, 1932), 68.
104. Sturleson, *Heimskringla*, 68.
105. Snorri Sturleson, *Heimskringla*, ed. Samuel Laing (London: Norroena Society, 1906), 2: 162, 160.

106. Vigfusson, *Cleasby's*; Henry Bradley, ed., *A Middle-English Dictionary* (Oxford: Clarendon Press, 1891); Robert E. Lewis, *Middle English Dictionary* (Ann Arbor: Univ. of Michigan Press, 1986).
107. Diana L. Paxson, "The Holy Hag: In Search of a Crone Goddess in Germanic Religion," *Idunna* 4, no. 3 (1992): 8.
108. Hastrup, *Culture*, 136.
109. Gundarsson, *Teutonic Magic*, 251.
110. Hastrop, *Culture*, 142–44; Gundarsson, *Teutonic Magic*, 251.
111. Gundarsson, *Teutonic Magic*, 252.
112. Sergent, *L'homosexualite initiatique*, 165–67.
113. Sergent, *L'homosexualite initiatique*, 165–67; Gundarsson, *Teutonic Magic*, 252–53; Michael Cheilik, "The Werewolf," in *Mythical and Fabulous Creatures: A Source Book and Research Guide*, ed. Malcolm South (Westport, CT: Greenwood Press, 1987), 269.
114. Cheilik, "Werewolf," 269.
115. Cheilik, "Werewolf," 266–69; Montague Summers, *The Werewolf* (New Hyde Park, NY: University Books, 1966), 66–69; Sabine Baring-Gould, *The Book of Were-Wolves* (New York: Causeway Books, 1973), 48–49; Carlo Ginzburg, *Ecstasies: Deciphering the Witches' Sabbath* (New York: Pantheon, 1991), 158; Sergent, *L'homosexualite initiatique*, 165.
116. Mary R. Gerstein, "Germanic *Warg*: The Outlaw as Werewolf," in *Myth in Indo-European Antiquity*, ed. Gerald James Larson (Berkeley and Los Angeles: Univ. of California Press, 1974), 152.
117. Gerstein, "Germanic *Warg*," 134–35.
118. Vangaard, *Phallos*, 76–77; "First Lay of Helgi," *Poetic Edda*, ed. Hollander, strophe 38–42, pp. 218–19.
119. Gerstein, "Germanic *Warg*," 134–35; Schultes and Hofmann, *Plants*, 39, 68, 69.
120. Gerstein, "Germanic *Warg*," 134–35, 142–43.
121. Margaret Clunies Ross, "Hildr's Ring: A Problem in the *Ragnarsdrápa*, strophes 8–12," *Mediaeval Scandinavia* 6 (1973): 80, 84, 89–92.
122. Hastrup, *Culture*, 136, 142–44.
123. Personal conversation with William Karpen, April 1993.
124. Timothy Taylor, "The Gundestrup Cauldron," *Scientific American* (March 1992): 88.
125. Taylor, "Gundestrup," 84.

CHAPTER 8

Cauldron of Changes

1. Christopher Marlowe, *The Tragical History of Doctor Faustus, The Complete Plays*, ed. J. B. Steane (New York: Penguin Books, 1980), act IV, scene 2, ll. 50–53, p. 310.
2. See Pamela Berger, *The Goddess Obscured* (Boston: Beacon Press, 1985).

3. See William Anderson, *The Green Man: The Archetype of Our Oneness with the Earth* (San Francisco: Harper San Francisco, 1990); Richard Bernheimer, *Wild Men in the Middle Ages* (Cambridge: Harvard Univ. Press, 1952).

4. Nancy Arrowsmith, *A Field Guide to the Little People* (New York: Hill and Wang, 1977), 217; Jean Dufournet, *Adam de la Halle à la Recherche de lui-même* (Paris: Société d'édition d'enseignement supérieur, 1974), 141, 147.

5. Arthur Evans, *Witchcraft and the Gay Counterculture* (Boston: Fag Rag Books, 1978), 71; Jacob Grimm, *Teutonic Mythology,* trans. James S. Stallybrass (London: George Bell and Sons, 1888), 2:478–83 and 4:1424–26; Henry Bradley, ed., *A Middle-English Dictionary* (Ann Arbor: Univ. of Michigan Press, 1986); Gudbrand Vigfusson, ed., *Cleasby's Icelandic-English Dictionary* (Oxford: Clarendon Press, 1874); Willi Apel, *Harvard Dictionary of Music,* 2d ed. (Cambridge: Harvard Univ. Press, 1969), s.v. "Charivari"; John Arnott MacCullough, *The Mythology of All Races,* vol. 2, *Eddic* (Boston: Marshall Jones, 1930), 2:205, 288; Bernheimer, *Wild Men,* 42.

6. Adam de la Halle, *Le Jeu de la Feuillée,* trans. into modern French by Jean Dufournet (Gand: Belgium: Editions Scientifiques E. Story-Scientia, 1977), esp. ll. 377, 418–19, 1093; Adam de la Halle, *Le Jeu de la Feuillée,* trans. into English by Richard Axton and John Stevens, *Medieval French Plays,* ed. Axton and Stevens (New York: Barnes and Noble, 1971), esp. ll. 377, 418–19, 1093; Dufournet, *Adam à la Recherche,* 308–9 and n. 28; Jean Dufournet, *Sur "Le Jeu de la Feuillée": Etudes complémentaires* (Paris: Société d'édition d'enseignement supérieur, 1977), 138, 140; Rosemary Ellen Guiley, *The Encyclopedia of Witches and Witchcraft* (New York: Facts on File, 1989), 341; Randle Cotgrave, *A Dictionarie of the French and English Tongues* (London, 1611; reprint New York: Da Capo Press, 1971).

7. François Rabelais, *The Histories of Gargantua and Pantagrueil,* trans. J. M. Cohen (New York: Penguin, 1981), esp. 55–56; Nicole Belmont, "Mythic Elements in French Folklore," in *Roman and European Mythologies,* ed. Wendy Doniger and Yves Bonnefoy (Chicago: Univ. of Chicago Press, 1992), 245; Nicole Belmont, "Folk Beliefs and Legends about Fairies in France," in *Roman and European Mythologies,* 255.

8. *Renard the Fox,* trans. Patricia Ann Terry (Boston: Northeastern Univ. Press, 1983); Gerald Herman, "The 'Sin Against Nature' and Its Echoes in Medieval French Literature." *Annual Mediaevale* 17 (1976): 78–79; Edward H. Roesner, "Introduction," in *Le Roman de Fauvel,* ed. Les Scrade (Les Remparts, Monaco: Editions de l'Oiseau-Lyre, 1984), iv ff.

9. Marie de France, "Bisclavaret," in *The Lais of Marie de France,* trans. and ed. Robert Hanning and Joan Ferrante (New York: E. P. Dutton,

1978); Marie de France, "The Lay of the Were-Wolf," in *Lays,* trans. Eugene Mason (London: J. M. Dent, 1959); Maureen Duffy, *The Erotic World of Faery* (New York: Avon Books, 1980), 48–49.

10. Herman, "Sin," 75 ff.; Monica McAlpine, "The Pardoner's Homosexuality and How It Matters," *PMLA* 95, no. 1 (1980): 13, also 8–22.

11. Richard of Devizes, *The Chronicle of Richard Devizes, of the Time of King Richard the First* (London: Thomas Nelson and Sons, 1963), 65; Bronislaw Geremek, *The Margins of Society in Late Medieval Paris,* trans. Jean Birrell, foreword by Jean Birrell (New York: Cambridge Univ. Press, 1987) ix, 48, 52–53.

12. Ian Hancock, "Shelta and Polari," in *Language in the British Isles,* ed. Peter Trudgill (New York: Cambridge Univ. Press, 1984), 384, 391–95; Bruce Rodgers, *The Queens' Vernacular* (San Francisco: Straight Arrow Books, 1972), reprinted as *Gay Talk* (New York: Paragon Books, 1979). For those interested in gay studies, this book is invaluable—a lost treasure.

13. Mikhail Bakhtin, *Rabelais and His World,* trans. Helene Iswolsky (Bloomington: Indiana Univ. Press, 1984), 393, also 8, 9, 21, 94, 336, 410, 395; Janet Bord and Colin Bord, *Earth Rites* (London: Granada Press, 1983), 215–18.

14. Anthony S. Mercatante, *The Facts on File Encyclopedia of World Mythology and Legend* (New York: Facts on File, 1988), 426–27, 499; Bernheimer, *Wild Men,* 42–43; Alexander S. Murray, *Manual of Mythology,* ed. William H. Klapp (Philadelphia: Henry Altemus, 1898), 154–55; Marija Gimbutas, *The Language of the Goddess* (San Francisco: Harper & Row, 1989), 195–97.

15. Bernheimer, *Wild Men,* 53, 169; Dufournet, *Sur "Le Jeu,"* 63–65; Bords, *Earth Rites,* 215, 218.

16. Bords, *Earth Rites,* 96, 201, 207, 211, 218; Jacqueline Simpson, *European Mythology* (New York: Peter Bedrick, 1987), 133.

17. Grimm, *Teutonic Mythology,* 1:246–85, esp. 267–82); Simpson, *European Mythology,* 128.

18. Simpson, *European Mythology,* 128.

19. Jeffrey Burton Russell, *Witchcraft in the Middle Ages* (Ithaca: Cornell Univ. Press, 1972), 176; Bernheimer, *Wild Men,* 169.

20. Michael Harrison, *The Roots of Witchcraft* (London: Tandem, 1975), 146; Dufournet, *Sur "Le Jeu,"* 54.

21. Ida Nelson, *La Sottie Sans Souci: Essai d'interprétation homosexuelle* (Paris: Editions Honoré Champion, 1976), 23–25.

22. Garhard Zacharias, *The Satanic Cult,* trans. C. Trollope (London: George Allen and Unwin, 1980), 43.

23. Bords, *Earth Rites,* 218.

24. Carlo Ginzburg, *Ecstasies: Deciphering the Witches' Sabbath* (New York: Pantheon Books, 1991), 189; Simpson, *European Mythology,* 121, 126.

25. Ginzburg, *Ecstasies,* 189; Simpson, *European Mythology,* 122, 126.

26. Simpson, *European Mythology,* 126.

27. Simpson, *European Mythology,* 121; Gail Kligman, *Calus: Symbolic Transformation in Romanian Ritual* (Chicago: Univ. of Chicago Press, 1981), 129–31; entire book is useful.

28. See, for ex., Evans, *Witchcraft;* Judy Grahn, *Another Mother Tongue* (Boston: Beacon Press, 1984). For Murray's theory, see Margaret Murray, *The God of the Witches* (Garden City, NY: Doubleday, 1960).

29. Cotgrave, *Dictionarie;* A. de Ranconet, *Thrèsor de langue francoyse* (1606), 4:829, 831; Pierre Guiraud, *Dictionnaire des étymologies obscures* (Paris: Payot, 1982), 273–74.

30. Russell, *Witchcraft;* Dr. Leo Louis Martello, *Witchcraft: The Old Religion* (Secaucus, NJ: Citadel Press, 1973), and personal conversation with Martello in New York, December 1991.

31. Apel, *Harvard Dictionary of Music,* 531; Edmond Faral, *Les Jongleurs en France au Moyen Age* (Paris: Librairie Honoré Champion, 1910), 27–28.

32. Faral, *Jongleurs,* 64–65, 88–89.

33. Faral, *Jongleurs,* 27.

34. Faral, *Jongleurs,* 27–28; Raleigh Morgan, Jr., "Old French *jogleor* and Kindred Terms: Studies in Medieval Romance Lexicology," *Romance Philology* 7, no. 4 (1954):299, 312.

35. Morgan, "Old French *jogleor*" 299, 304, 312, 315; D. Biggins, "Chaucer's General Prologue," *Notes and Queries* (December 1959), 435 ff.; Paull F. Baum, "Chaucer's Puns," *PMLA* 71, no. 1 (1956): 232ff.; Apel, *Harvard Dictionary of Music,* 101–2, 304–5; Cotgrave, *Dictionarie.*

36. Faral, *Jongleurs,* 28, 103.

37. Lever, *Les bûchers de Sodome* (Paris: Fayard, 1985) 58; Arnaut Daniel, qu. p. 8 in Margarita Egan, ed., *The Vidas of the Troubadours* (New York: Garland Publishing, 1984); John Boswell, *Christianity, Social Tolerance, and Homosexuality* (Chicago: Univ. of Chicago Press, 1980).

38. Lever, *Les bûchers,* 58–59.

39. Faral, *Jongleurs,* 26, 28.

40. See Bieris de Romans, "Na Maria . . . / Lady Maria," in *The Women Troubadours,* ed. and trans. Meg Bogin (New York: W. W. Norton, 1980), 132–33.

41. A. Struebel, "Sotie (ou sottie)," *Dictionnaire des Littératures de langue française,* ed. J.-P. Beaumarchais, Daniel Couty, and Alain Rey (Paris: Bordas, 1987), 4:2354–55; Bakhtin, *Rabelais,* 8.

42. Nelson, *Sottie,* 28.

43. Nelson, *Sottie,* 41, 129, 185ff.

44. Berger, *Goddess Obscured,* 86–87; Nelson, *Sottie,* 153.

45. Nelson, *Sottie,* 153, 156.

46. Nelson, *Sottie,* 44–45.

47. Christine Marchelle-Nizia and Michèle Perret, "Une Utopie Homosexuelle au Quatorzième Siècle: L'Ile Sans Femmes d'Agriano," *Stanford French Review* 14; nos. 1–2 (1990): 232.

48. Stephen Larsen, *The Mythic Imagination* (New York: Bantam Books, 1990), 263.

49. Personal communication with Harry Hay, 1981, 1985, 1989.

50. Alfred L. Rowse, *Homosexuals in History* (New York: Macmillan, 1977), 2; Noel I. Garde, *Jonathan to Gide: The Homosexual in History* (New York: Vantage Press, 1964), 184.

51. Jack Lindsay, *The Normans and Their World* (London: Hurt-Davis, 1974), 412.

52. Rowse, *Homosexuals,* 2; Lindsay, *Normans,* 411–13.

53. Lindsay, *Normans,* 414; Rowse, *Homosexuals,* 2–3; Harrison, *Roots of Witchcraft,* 206–8.

54. Henri Estienne, *Deux Dialogues du Nouveau Langage François, italinizé,* ed. P.-M. Smith (Geneva: Editions Slatkine, 1980), 207; Barbara W. Tuchman, *A Distant Mirror: The Calamitous Fourteenth Century* (New York: Alfred A. Knopf, 1978), 54; Vern L. Bullough, *Sexual Variance in Society and History* (Chicago: Univ. of Chicago Press, 1976), 449; Garde, *Jonathan,* 311; Pierre de L'Estoile, *Memoires-Journaux: Journal de Henri III* (Paris: Librairie des Bibliophiles, 1875–1896). On Mathurine, see Maurice Lever, *Le Sceptre et la Marotte: Histoire des Fous de Cour* (Paris: Fayard, 1983), 243–53.

55. Rowse, *Homosexuals,* 33.

56. L'Éstoile, *Memoires,* 2:113.

57. Jean Hervey, *Le Baiser: Mignons et Courtisanes ou XVIe Siècle* (Paris: Bibliotèque des Curieux, 1924), 39–41; Grillot de Givry, *Witchcraft, Magic, and Alchemy* (1931; reprint, New York: Dover, 1971), 122, 306, 344.

58. Thomas, Artus, *Description de l'Isle des hermaphrodites* (Cologne: Heritiers de H. Demen, 1724), 1–41.

59. Pauline M. Smith, *The Anti-Courtier Trend in Sixteenth Century French Literature* (Geneva: Librairie Droz, 1966), 122; Emire Zolla, *The Androgyne-Reconciliation of Male and Female* (New York: Crossroad, 1981), 48; Jonathan Katz, ed., *Gay American History* (New York: Thomas Y. Crowell, 1976), 613 n. 14, 288–90; Theodore de Bry, *Discovering the New World,* ed. Michael Alexander (New York: Harper & Row, 1976), 132; Hesychius Alexandrini, Lexicon (Geneva: Sumptibus Hermann: Dufftii, Libraria Maukiana, 1867), *badás.*

60. Lever, *Les bûchers,* 47.

61. Michael Goodich, *The Unmentionable Vice: Homosexuality in the Later Medieval Period* (Santa Barbara: Ross-Erikson Publishers, 1979), 31–32; Lever, *Les bûchers,* 43; Henry Charles Lea, *History of the Inquisition of Spain* (New York: Macmillan, 1922), 1:9.

62. Frank Barlow, *William Rufus* (London: Methuen, 1983), 102 ff.

63. Walter Mapes, *De Nugis Curialum (Courtiers' Trifles)*, trans. Frederick Tupper (London: Chatto and Windus, 1924), chap. 24, ll. 9–20.

64. J. T. McNeill and H. M. Gamer, eds., *Medieval Handbooks of Penance* (New York: Octagon Books, 1965), esp. 103, 112–13, 185; Lever, *Les bûchers*, 44, 47.

65. Henry Charles Lea, *History of the Inquisition*, vol. 4, 361–62 and notes.

66. Derrick S. Bailey, *Homosexuality and the Western Christian Tradition* (Hamden, CT: Archon Books, 1975), 139 ff.; Lever, *Les bûchers*, 47.

67. Robert L. Harrison, ed., *Gallic Salt: Eighteen Fabliaux Translated from the Old French* (Berkeley and Los Angeles: Univ. of California Press, 1974), 369; Charles H. Livingston, *Le Jongleur Gautier le Leu: Etude sur les fabliaux* (Cambridge: Harvard Univ. Press, 1951), 95–96; Milan Loos, *Dualist Heresy in the Middle Ages* (Prague: Academia, 1974), 197; and see also Zoe Oldenbourg, *Massacre at Montségur* (New York: Pantheon, 1962); Denis de Rougemont, *Love in the Western World* (New York: Schocken Books, 1990); Jean Markale, *Montségur et l'énigme Cathare* (Paris: Pygmalion, 1986); René Nelli, *La philosophie de catharisme* (Paris: Payot, 1975).

68. Michael Harrison, *The Roots of Witchcraft* (London: Tandem, 1975), 223–25. While this text is grounded in Murrayite theory, its statements concerning the Knights Templar are as valid as any found in texts written by Christian scholars, who tend to whitewash Templar beliefs and practices.

69. Guido Ruggiero, *The Boundaries of Eros: Sex Crime and Sexuality in Renaissance Venice* (Oxford: Oxford Univ. Press, 1985), 112, 121.

70. See Juan de la Cruz (St. John of the Cross), "Noche Oscura / Dark Night," *The Poems*, trans. and ed. Willis Barnstone (New York: New Directions, 1972), 39.

71. Michael Levey, *Early Renaissance* (New York: Penguin Books, 1979), 171.

72. James Robinson Howe, *Marlowe, Tamburlaine, and Magic* (Athens: Ohio Univ. Press, 1976), 157, 36.

73. James M. Saslow, *Ganymede in the Renaissance: Homosexuality in Art and Society* (New Haven: Yale Univ. Press, 1986), 77.

74. Saslow, *Ganymede*, 85, also 77–96; James M. Saslow, "Homosexuality in the Renaissance: Behavior, Identity, and Artistic Expression," in *Hidden from History: Reclaiming the Gay and Lesbian Past*, ed. Martin Bauml Duberman, Martha Vicinus, and George Chauncey, Jr. (New York: New American Library, 1989), 90–105; on Renvoisy, see G. Thibault, "Un recueil de musique imprimé en caractères de civilité," *Bibliothèque d'humanisme et Renaissance* 2 (1935): 302; M. Cauchie, "Note sur Richard de Renvoisy," *La Revue Musicale* 10 nos. 10–11 (1929): 56.

75. Paul H. Kocher, "Marlowe's Atheist Lecture," in *Marlowe: A Collection of Critical Essays*, ed. Clifford Leech (Englewood Cliffs, NJ: Prentice-Hall, 1964), 160–61; Rowse, *Homosexuals*, 30; Garde, *Jonathan*, 331–32.

76. Christopher Marlowe, "Hero and Leander," in *The Penguin Book of Homosexual Verse*, ed. Stephen Coote (Middlesex, England: Penguin Books, 1983), 148–51.

77. Christopher Marlowe, *Edward the Second*, in *The Complete Plays* (New York: Penguin Books, 1980), act I, scene 1, ll. 57–64, pp. 436–37.

78. Claude V. Palisca, *Baroque Music* (Englewood Cliffs, NJ: Prentice Hall, 1968), 160–67; Warren Johansson, "Lully, Jean-Baptiste," *Encyclopedia of Homosexuality*, 1:754–55.

79. *Hell Upon Earth: or The Town in an Uproar* (London: J. Roberts and A. Dodd, 1729), 41–43.

80. Denis Diderot, *Oeuvres complètes*, ed. J. A. Assezat, and M. Tourneux (Paris, 1875–1877), 10:491–93.

81. G. S. Rousseau, "The Pursuit of Homosexuality in the Eighteenth Century: Utterly Confused Category or Rich Repository?" in *'Tis Nature's Fault*, ed. Robert Purks Maccubbin (Cambridge: Cambridge Univ. Press, 1987), 155.

82. Ioan Petru Couliano, "Sexual Rites in Europe," *The Encyclopedia of Religion*, ed. Mircea Eliade (New York: Macmillan, 1987), 13:186; Ronald Fuller, *Hell-Fire Francis* (London: Chatto and Windus, 1939), 24, 27, 28; Rousseau, "Pursuit," 155. See also E. Beresford Chancellor, *The Lives of the Rakes*, vol. 4; *The Hell Fire Club* (London: Philip Alan, 1925).

83. A. D. Harvey, "Prosecutions for Sodomy in England at the Beginning of the Nineteenth Century," *The Historical Journal* 21, no. 4 (1978): 945; Randolph Trumbach, "London's Sodomites: Homosexual Behavior and Western Culture in the Eighteenth Century," *Journal of Society and History* 11, no. 1 (1977): 15–17.

84. Rousseau, "Pursuit," 160, quoting Hans Mayer.

CHAPTER 9

Splendours of an Exiled Court

1. Oscar Wilde, "The Garden of Eros," *Poems and Fairy Tales* (New York: Modern Library, n.d.), ll. 145–49, p. 62.

2. William James, *The Varieties of Religious Experience* (New York: New American Library, 1958), 42, 53–54.

3. Susan Sontag, *Styles of Radical Will* (New York: Farrar, Strauss and Giroux, 1969), 3.

4. Louis Crompton, *Byron and Greek Love: Homophobia in 19th-Century England* (Berkeley and Los Angeles: Univ. of California Press, 1985), 292–93.

5. Carl H. Grabo, *Shelley's Eccentricities* (Albuquerque: Univ. of New Mexico Press, 1950), 56, 64; Edward Carpenter and George Barnefield,

The Psychology of the Poet Shelley (New York: E. P. Dutton, 1925) 57–59, 95–98.

6. Quoted in Grabo, *Shelley's Eccentricities*, 50.

7. Quoted in Grabo, *Shelley's Eccentricities*, 50.

8. Plato, *The Symposium*, trans. Walter Hamilton (New York: Penguin Books, 1986), 208c–209e, pp. 90–91.

9. Grabo, *Shelley's Eccentricities*, 24–25, 52, 57; Carpenter and Barnefield, *Psychology*, 30–35, 57–59.

10. Nathaniel Brown, *Sexuality and Feminism in Shelley* (Cambridge: Harvard Univ. Press, 1979), 225–26.

11. Grabo, *Shelley's Eccentricities*, 54; Carpenter and Barnefield, *Psychology*, 40–41.

12. Richard Holmes, *Shelley: The Pursuit* (London: Weidenfeld and Nicolson, 1974), 3, 24–25.

13. Holmes, *Pursuit*, 103, 626.

14. Holmes, *Pursuit*, 605–6; Harold Bloom, *Shelley's Mythmaking* (Ithaca: Cornell Univ. Press, 1969), 200; Camille Paglia, *Sexual Personae: Art and Decadence from Nefertiti to Emily Dickinson* (New York: Random House, 1991), 367.

15. Percy Bysshe Shelley, "The Witch of Atlas," *The Complete Poetical Works* (Boston: Houghton Mifflin, 1901), from cantos 35–37.

16. See Walter Harding, "Thoreau and Eros," *Thoreau's Psychology: Eight Essays*, ed. Raymond D Gozzi (New York: University Press of America, 1983), 144–59; Walter Harding, "Thoreau's Sexuality," *Journal of Homosexuality* 21, no. 3 (1991): 23–45; Jonathan Katz, ed., "1838–57: Henry David Thoreau," in *Gay American History*, ed. Jonathan Katz (New York: Thomas Y. Crowell, 1976), 481–94.

17. Henry David Thoreau, *Journal*, ed. John C. Broderick and Robert Sattelmeyer (Princeton: Princeton Univ. Press, 1984); H. D. Thoreau, *Journal*, ed. Bradford Torrey and Francis H. Allen (Boston: Houghton Mifflin, 1949); the original publishing date of 1906 is reflected in its somewhat censorial approach.

18. Walt Whitman, "Song of Myself," *Leaves of Grass* (New York: Signet, New American Library, 1980), sec. 24, ll. 28–31, p. 68.

19. Whitman, "Song," sec. 33, ll. 123–28, p. 78 and "We Too, How Long We Were Fool'd," *Leaves of Grass*, ll. 3–17, pp. 109–10.

20. Richard Maurice Bucke, *Cosmic Consciousness* (1901; reprint, (New York: E. P. Dutton, 1969), 3.

21. Bucke, *Cosmic Consciousness*, 225, 227.

22. Byrne R. S. Fone, "This Other Eden: Arcadia and the Homosexual Imagination," *Literary Visions of Homosexuality*, ed. Stuart Kellogg, (New York: Haworth Press, 1983), 13.

23. Walt Whitman, "In Paths Untrodden" and "These I Singing in Spring," *Leaves of Grass*, 112, 116.

24. Fone, "Eden," 29–31.

25. Walt Whitman, "I Dream'd in a Dream" and "For You O Democracy," *Leaves of Grass*, 125, 115.

26. Whitman, "For You O Democracy," 115.

27. John Addington Symonds, *The Letters of John Addington Symonds*, ed. Herbert M. Schueller and Robert L. Peters (Detroit: Wayne State Univ. Press, 1967–1969), 3:458–59.

28. Symonds, *Letters*, 3:533, 675; James, *Varieties*, 81, 321.

29. Paul Schmidt, Introduction to "Fifth Season: The Visionary," by Arthur Rimbaud, *Complete Works*, ed. and trans. Paul Schmidt (New York: Harper & Row, 1976), 117; A. L. Rowse, *Homosexuals in History* (New York: Dorset Press, 1983), 170–76; see also Enid Starkie, *Arthur Rimbaud* (New York: New Directions, 1968).

30. Jean-Arthur Rimbaud, "Soleil et Chair," Oeuvres complètes (Montreal: Valiquette, 1943), ll. 10–12, p. 23. Translated by Randy Conner.

31. Jean-Arthur Rimbaud, "Antique," *Oeuvres complètes*, p. 110. Translated by Randy Conner.

32. Jean-Arthur Rimbaud, "Soleil et Chair," *Oeuvres complètes*, ll.26–29, 38–40, 46–49, p. 24. Translated by Randy Conner.

33. Jean-Arthur Rimbaud, "Conte," *Oeuvres complètes*, p. 134. Translated by Randy Conner.

34. Jean-Arthur Rimbaud, "Genie," *Oeuvres complètes*, p. 158. Translated by Randy Conner.

35. Jean-Arthur Rimbaud, "Conte," *Oeuvres complètes*, p. 135. Translated by Randy Conner.

36. A. Rimbaud, *Illuminations: Coloured Plates*, ed. Nick Osmond (London: Univ. of London, Athlone Press, 1976), 95–96.

37. Paul Schmidt, "Visions of Violence: Rimbaud and Verlaine," in *Homosexualities and French Literature: Cultural Contexts/Critical Texts*, ed. George Stanbolian and Elaine Marks (Ithaca: Cornell Univ. Press, 1979), 234–36.

38. Arthur Rimbaud, "Nuit de L'Enfer," in *Collected Poems*, ed. Oliver Bernard (London: Penguin, 1986), 317. I have, however, used my own translation.

39. Paul Schmidt, "Visions of Violence: Rimbaud and Verlaine," 240.

40. John R. Reed, *Decadent Style* (Athens: Ohio Univ. Press, 1985), 15.

41. William Butler Yeats, "Symbolism in Painting," in *The Symbolist Poem*, ed. Edward Engelberg (New York: E. P. Dutton, 1967), 304–5.

42. Michael Gibson, *The Symbolists* (New York: Harry N. Abrams, 1988), 8, 11, 16; Mario Amaya, "An Introductory Note: The Sacred and Profane in Symbolist Art," in *Symbolists* (an exhibition), ed. Spencer A. Samuels (New York: Spencer A. Samuels, 1970), 4; Philippe Jullian, *The Dreamers of Decadence* (New York: Praeger, 1975).

43. Josephin Péladan, "Hymne à l'Androgyne," *La Plume* 3 (1891), canto 7.

44. Elaine Showalter, *Sexual Anarchy: Gender and Culture at the Fin de Siècle* (New York: Viking Penguin, 1990), 170.

45. Oscar Wilde, *De Profundis and Other Writings* (New York: Penguin, 1987), 175.

46. Wilde, *De Profundis*, 207–8.

47. Oscar Wilde, "Santa Decca," *Poems and Fairy Tales*, ll. 1–8, p. 162.

48. Oscar Wilde, *Poems and Fairy Tales*, "The Grave of Shelley," l. 10, p. 165, "Lotus Leaves," l. 5, p. 224, "Ravenna," l. 49, 146, pp. 34–35, "Panthea," ll. 47, 49, 51, 56, 59, pp. 178–79.

49. Oscar Wilde, "The Garden of Eros," *Poems and Fairy Tales*, ll. 103–13, pp. 60–61.

50. Wilde, *De Profundis*, 182–83.

51. J. E. Chamberlin, *Ripe Was the Drowsy Hour: The Age of Oscar Wilde* (New York: Seabury Press, 1977), 154–55.

52. Wilde, *De Profundis*, 167–68.

53. Francis King, *The Magical World of Aleister Crowley* (New York: Coward, McCann and Geoghegan, 1977), 12–13.

54. King, *Magical World*, 14.

55. Norine Dresser, *American Vampires: Fans, Victims and Practitioners* (New York: W. W. Norton, 1989), 104–5.

56. Samuels, *Symbolists*, 38.

57. Jullian, *Dreamers*, 47, 74.

58. Lord Alfred Douglas, "Two Loves," in *Sexual Heretics: Male Homosexuality in English Literature from 1850 to 1900*, ed. Brian Reade (New York: Coward-McCann, 1971), 361–62; Lord Alfred Douglas, "In Praise of Shame," in *Sexual Heretics*, ed. Reade, 362.

59. Julia Ellsworth Ford, *Simeon Solomon: An Appreciation* (New York: F. F. Sherman, 1908), 24–25.

60. Reade, *Sexual Heretics*, 17; Lionel Lambourne, et al., *Solomon: A Family of Painters* (London: Geffrye Museum and the Birmingham Museum and Art Gallery, 1986); Bernard Falk, *Five Years Dead* (Plymouth: Mayflower Press, 1938); Percy H. Bate, *The English Pre-Raphaelite Painters* (London: George Bell and Sons, 1899), 64–66; William E. Freedman, *Pre-Raphaelitism: A Bibliocritical Study* (Cambridge: Harvard Univ. Press, 1965), 214; A. C. Swinburne, "Simeon Solomon: Notes on His 'Vision of Love' and Other Studies," *The Dark Blue* 1 (March–August 1871): 569–71.

61. Simeon Solomon, *A Vision of Love Revealed in Sleep* (London: F. S. Ellis, 1871): 30–31.

62. King, *Magical World*, 5–6, 28.

63. King, *Magical World*, 43–47.

64. Jean Overton Fuller, *The Magical Dilemma of Victor Neuburg* (London: W. H. Allen, 1965), 133.

65. King, *Magical World*, 55.

66. King, *Magical World*, 83; Fuller, *Magical Dilemma*, 213, 25, 170.

67. King, *Magical World*, 97–112, 130.

68. Aleister Crowley, "Hymn to Pan," *Magick in Theory and Practice* (1929: reprint, New York: Dover Publications, 1976), v–vii.

69. Victor Arwas, *Alastair: Illustrator of Decadence* (London: Thames and Hudson, 1979), 6, 29; Jullian, *Dreamers*, 94.

70. Jullian, *Dreamers*, 94 n. 68.

71. Arwas, *Alastair*, 24, 8–9.

MEDITATION
Crossroads

1. To my knowledge (and forgive me if I err), the chants given here were first recorded by Starhawk in *The Spiral Dance: A Rebirth of the Ancient Religion of the Great Goddess* (San Francisco: Harper & Row, 1979).

CHAPTER 10
Exaltation of the Flowers

1. Pepe y Carlos, "Nahum B. Zenil: La Necesidad de Vivir," *Opus Gay* no. 2 (1987?): 26.

2. Fernando de Alva Ixlilxóchitl, *Obras Historicas*, ed. Edmundo O'Gorman (Mexico City: Universidad Nacional Autónoma de México, 1975), 1:405 and 2:388–89; Friedrich Katz, "The Evolution of Aztec Society," *Past and Present* 13 (1958): 14–25; Francisco Guerra, *The Pre-columbian Mind: A Study into the Aberrant Nature of Sexual Drives* (New York: Seminar Press, 1971), 162; David F. Greenberg, *The Construction of Homosexuality* (Chicago: Univ. of Chicago Press, 1988), 165.

3. Alva Ixlilxóchitl, *Obras*, 1:405, 2:388–89; Katz, "Evolution," 14–25; Guerra, *Pre-columbian Mind*, 162; Greenberg, *Construction*, 165.

4. Alfredo López Austin, *The Human Body and Ideology: Concepts of the Ancient Nahuas*, trans. Thelma and Bernard Ortiz de Montellano (Salt Lake City: Univ. of Utah Press, 1988), 1:305.

5. López Austin, *Human Body*, 2:222–23; 2:265–67; 2:276–80.

6. Greenberg, *Construction*, 164–65.

7. López Austin, *Human Body*, 1:305, 2:222–23, 2:265–67, 2:276–80; Bernardino de Sahagun, *Florentine Codex*, ed. Charles Dibble and Arthur J. O. Anderson, bk 10, chap. 11, pp. 37–38 and illus. 61a and 61b (and see illus. 110 for *patlache*) (Santa Fe: School of American Research, 1970).

8. Alfredo Barrera Vasquez, et al., *Diccionario Maya Cordemex* (Mérida, Yucatán: Ediciones Cordemex, 1980).

9. López Austin, *Human Body*, 2:266–67, 2:277–78.

10. Patricia Anawalt, "Costume Analysis and the Provenance of the Borgia Group Codices," *American Antiquity* 46, no. 4 (1981): 837, 849; Doris Heyden, "The *Quechquemitl* as a Symbol of Power in the Mixtec Codices," *Vicus cuadernos, Arqueología, Antropología, Cultural, Etnología* 1 (1977): 5–24.

11. López Austin, *Human Body,* 2:267–68, 2:278–79.
12. Noemí Quezada, *Amor y Magia Amorosa Entre los Aztecas* (Mexico City: Universidad Nacional Autónoma de México, 1975), 95ff.; Hedwig Schleiffer, ed., *Sacred, Narcotic Plants of the New World Indians* (New York: Hafner, Macmillan, 1973); Sangirardi, Jr., *O indio e as plantas alucinógenas: Tribos das 3 Américas e civilizações pré-colombianas* (Rio de Janeiro: Editorial Alhambra, 1983); Adam Gottlieb, *Legal Highs* (Manhattan Beach, CA.: 20th Century Alchemist, 1987), 42; Mary Jane Superweed, *Herbal Highs* (Philadelphia: Flash Mail Order, Stone Kingdom Syndicate, n.d.), 11.
13. López Austin, *Human Body,* 2:267–68, 2:279–80.
14. López Austin, *Human Body,* 2:267–68, 2:279–80; Sahagun, *Florentine,* bk. 10, chap. 11, pp. 37–38, illus. 61a, b.
15. López Austin, *Human Body,* 2:267–68, 2:279–80; Sahagun, *Florentine,* bk. 10, chap. 11, pp. 37–38, illus. 61a, b.
16. López Austin, *Human Body,* 2:267–68, 2:279–80; Sahagun, *Florentine,* bk. 10, chap. 11, pp. 37–38, illus. 61a, b; C. A. Burland, *The Gods of Mexico* (New York: Capricorn Books, 1968), 101.
17. H. B. Nicholson, "Mesoamerican Religions: Postclassic Cultures," *The Encyclopedia of Religion,* ed. Mircea Eliade (New York: Macmillan, 1987), 9:424; Patricia Monaghan, *The Book of Goddesses and Heroines* (New York: E. P. Dutton, 1981), 288–89; Burland, *Gods,* 101, 122–23, 134–35.
18. Nicholson, "Mesoamerican Religions," 423; Burland, *Gods,* 123.
19. Burr Cartwright Brundage, *The Fifth Sun: Aztec Gods, Aztec World* (Austin: Univ. of Texas Press, 1983), 163; Nicholson, "Mesoamerican Religions," 423; Fray Diego Durán, *Book of the Gods and Rites and the Ancient Calendar,* trans. Fernando Horcasitas and Doris Heyden (Norman: Univ. of Oklahoma Press, 1971), 233 n. 4; Anonymous Conquistador, *Narrative of Some Things of New Spain,* trans. Marshall H. Saville (New York: Cortés Society, 1917).
20. Durán, *Book of the Gods,* 296 n. 5; Peter T. Furst, *Hallucinogens and Culture* (San Francisco: Chandler and Sharp, 1976), 28; Anonymous Conquistador, *Narrative.*
21. Brundage, *Fifth Sun,* 163; Furst, *Hallucinogens,* 28; Nicholson, "Mesoamerican Religions," 423.
22. "Song of the Mother of the Gods," in *Native Mesoamerican Spirituality,* ed. Miguel Léon-Portilla (New York: Paulist Press, 1980), 196–97.
23. Durán, *Book of the Gods,* 239; López Austin, *Human Body,* 2:277.
24. Jésus Arango Cano, *Mitologia en America Precolombina* (Bogotá: Plaza & Janes, 1989), 40.

25. Eduard Seler, ed., *Codex Borgia: Eine alt-mexikanische Bilderschrift* (Berlin, 1904), 77, 81.
26. Sahagun, *Florentine,* bk. 10, chap. 11, pp. 37–38, illus. 61a, b, 110.
27. Brundage, *Fifth Sun,* 46–47.
28. Burr Cartwright Brundage, *The Jade Steps: A Ritual Life of the Aztecs* (Salt Lake City: Univ. of Utah Press, 1985), 34, 63.
29. Robert Stevenson, *Music in Aztec and Inca Territory* (Berkeley and Los Angeles: Univ. of California Press, 1976), 231–33.
30. Quezada, *Amor,* 43.
31. Durán, *Book of the Gods,* 434.
32. Durán, *Book of the Gods,* 295.
33. Greenberg, *Construction,* 165; José Imbelloni, "La Essaltatione delle Rose," *Anales del Instituto de Etnografia Americana* 4 (1943): 161ff., 199.
34. Imbelloni, "Essaltatione," 198; J. Eric S. Thompson, *The Rise and Fall of Maya Civilization* (Norman: Univ. of Oklahoma Press, 1966), 127–28; Miguel Léon-Portilla, "Mesoamerican Religions: Precolumbian Religions," *Encyclopedia of Religion,* ed. Eliade, 9:395.
35. Karen Bassie-Sweet, *From the Mouth of the Dark Cave: Commemorative Sculpture of the Late Classic Maya* (Norman: Univ. of Oklahoma Press, 1991), 27–29.
36. Guerra, *Pre-columbian Mind,* 70, 173.
37. Guerra, *Pre-columbian Mind,* 141, 209–10.
38. Brundage, *Fifth Sun,* 79, 94.
39. Brundage, *Fifth Sun,* 79, 94.
40. Pedro Rafael Gutierrez, *El Horóscopo Indígena* (San José, Costa Rica: Ediciones Lena, 1988), 55.
41. Brundage, *Fifth Sun,* 82, 85; Guerra, *Pre-columbian Mind,* 115.
42. Guerra, *Pre-columbian Mind,* 115; Brundage, *Fifth Sun,* 88; Quezada, *Amor,* 73; López Austin, *Human Body,* 2:266, 277.
43. Quezada, *Amor,* 73; Hernando Ruiz de Alarcón, *Treatise on the Heathen Superstitions,* trans. J. Richard Andrews and Ross Hassig (Norman: Univ. of Oklahoma Press, 1984), 353, also 132–34. I have used a translation by Norma Aguirre and Nora Kelly, Spanish-speaking translators at Austin Community College, Texas.
44. Quezada, *Amor,* 73.
45. Guerra, *Pre-columbian Mind,* 101–2.
46. Bernal Díaz, *The Conquest of New Spain,* trans. J. M. Cohen (Baltimore: Penguin Books, 1963), 124; J. de Acosta, *Natural and Moral History of the Indies* (London: Hakluyt Society, 1880), 2:364–67.
47. López Austin, *Human Body,* 2:276.
48. Richard Evans Schultes, and Albert Hofmann, *Plants of the Gods* (New York: McGraw-Hill, 1979), 151.
49. Schultes and Hofmann, *Plants,* 145, 147.

50. López Austin, *Human Body*, 2:276; Martha Stone, *At the Sign of Midnight: The Concheros Dance Cult of Mexico* (Tucson: Univ. of Arizona Press, 1975), 190.

51. López Austin, *Human Body*, 2:267, 276, 278, 291, 296; Schultes and Hofmann, *Plants*, 78–79, 109–11.

52. Quezada, *Amor*, 87–88.

53. Quezada, *Amor*, 95ff.; Schleiffer, *Sacred Plants;* Sangirardi Jr., *O indio;* Gottlieb, *Legal Highs*, 42; Superweed, *Herbal Highs*, 11.

54. *Il Manoscritto Messicano Vaticano 3738, Detti il Codice Rios: a spese di sua eccellenza il Duca di Loubat* (Rome: Stabilimento Danesi, 1900), unnumbered page titled "Sochiquetzal i esaltatione delle rose."

55. *Il Manoscritto*, same page as above.

56. Munro S. Edmonson, *The Ancient Future of the Itza: The Book of Chilam Balam of Tizimin* (Austin: Univ. of Texas Press, 1982), 68, 188.

57. Imbelloni, "Essaltatione," 192, 198; Thompson, *Rise and Fall,* 127–28; Antonio Requena, "Noticias y Consideraciones Sobre Las Anormalidades de los Aborigenes Americanos: Sodomia," *Acta Venezolana* 1, no. 1 (1945): 46ff.

58. June Nash, "The Aztecs and the Ideology of Male Dominance," *Signs* Vol. 4 no. 2 (Winter 1978): 349; Gloria Anzaldúa, *Borderlands: La Frontera: The New Mestiza* (San Francisco: Spinsters/Aunt Lute, 1987), 31–33.

59. Greenberg, *Construction*, 166–67.

60. Díaz, *Conquest*, 119–24.

61. Greenberg, *Construction*, 168.

62. Stephen O. Murray, and Clark L. Taylor, "Mexico," *The Encyclopedia of Homosexuality*, ed. Wayne Dynes (New York: Garland Press, 1990), 2:803–7, esp. 805–6.

63. Guerra, *Pre-columbian Mind*, 242–43.

64. Hernán Rodríguez Castelo, *Lexico Sexual Ecuatoriano y Latinoamericano* (Quito: Ediciones Libri Mundi, Instituto Otavaleño de Antropología, 1979) 336, 343–47; Victoria R. Bricker, *Ritual Humor in Highland Chiapas* (Austin: Univ. of Texas Press, 1973), 186.

65. Bricker, *Ritual Humor*, 186.

66. Bricker, *Ritual Humor*, 186–87; J. Eric S. Thompson, *Ethnology of the Mayas of Southern and Central British Honduras,* Field Museum of Natural History, Anthropological Series 17, no. 2 (Chicago, 1930), 111–13.

67. Graciela Iturbide, and Elena Poniatowska, *Juchitán de las Mujeres* (Mexico, D.F.: Ediciones Toledo, 1989): G. Iturbide, "Juchitán's Heart," *Mother Jones* (Feb.–March 1990), 39–40.

68. Personal communication with *curandera* in San Antonio, Texas, 1986.

69. Gloria Anzaldúa, "Born Under the Sign of the Flower." Unpublished essay (ca. 1990). Used with permission of the author.

CHAPTER 11

Children of the Rainbow

1. Gilberto Gil, "Logunedé," in *A Linguagem do Candomblé,* ed. Ruy do Carmo Póvoas (Rio de Janeiro: José Olympio, 1989), 123–24.

2. Gloria Anzaldúa, Taped interview with José Vigo and Eduardo Mejía, Cambridge, MA, November 1981.

3. Anzaldúa, Interview.

4. Among the finest works on the Yoruba religion and its various branches are: Lydia Cabrera, *El Monte* (Miami: Colección del Chichereku, Rema Press, 1968); Lydia Cabrera, *Yemayá y Ochún: Kariocha, Iyalorichas y Olorichas* (New York: Colección del Chichereku en el exilio, Eliseo Torres, 1980); Gary Edwards and John Mason, *Black Gods: Orisa Studies in the New World* (Brooklyn: Yoruba Theological Archministry, 1985); Judith Gleason, *Orisha: The Gods of Yorubaland* (New York: Athenaeum, 1971); Judith Gleason, *Oya: In Praise of the Goddess* (Boston: Shambhala, 1987); Migene González-Wippler, *Santería: The Religion* (New York: Harmony Books, 1989); Joseph Murphy, *Santería: An African Religion in America* (Boston: Beacon Press, 1988); John Pemberton, III, William Fagg, and Bryce Holcombe, *Yoruba Sculpture of West Africa* (New York: Knopf, 1982); Luisah Teish, *Jambalaya: The Natural Woman's Book of Personal Charms and Practical Rituals* (San Francisco: Harper & Row, 1985); Robert Farris Thompson, *Flash of the Spirit: African and Afro-American Art and Philosophy* (New York: Random House, 1983).

5. Cabrera, *El Monte*, 58; Lydia Cabrera, *Koeko Iyawo: Apprende Novicia: Pequeño Tratado de Regla Lucumí* (Miami: Colección del Chichereku en el exilio, Ultra Graphics Corporation, 1980), 203, 211; Olga Gudolle Cacciatore, *Dicionario de Cultos Afro-Brasileiros* (Rio de Janeiro: Forense Universitaria, 1977), 36–38.

6. Cabrera, *El Monte*, 56ff.

7. Seth Leacock and Ruth Leacock, *Spirits of the Deep: A Study of an Afro-Brazilian Cult* (New York: Doubleday, 1972), 104.

8. See Ruth Landes, "A Cult Matriarchate and Male Homosexuality," *The Journal of Abnormal and Social Psychology* 35, no. 3 (1940): 386–97; René Ribeiro, "Personality and the Psychological Adjustment of Afro-Brazilian Cult Members," *Journal de la Societé des Americanistes* 58 (1969): 109–20; Peter Fry, "Male Homosexuality and Spirit Possession in Brazil," *The Journal of Homosexuality* 11, nos. 3–4 (1985): 137–53; João Trevisan, *Perverts in Paradise* (London: GMP Publishers, 1986); Hubert Fichte, "La Lame de Rasoir et l'hermaphrodite: notes pur une recherche," *Psychopathologie Africaine* 11, no. 3 (1975): 395–406.

9. Wilson Santos, *A participacão dos homossexuais no movimento negro brasileiro* (Salvador, Bahia: Grupo Ade Dudu, 1984), 48.

10. Cabrera, *Yemayá*, 45; Trevisan, *Perverts*, 172; Lydia Cabrera, *Anago: Vocabulario lucumí* (Miami: Cabrera y Rojas, 1970); de la Soledad, Rosalia and M. J. Sanjuan, *Yorubas en Tierras Cubanas* (Miami: Ediciones Universal, 1988), 217; Natalia Bolivar-Aróstegui, *Los Orishas en Cuba* (Ciudade La Habana: Ediciones Union, 1990), 71, 82–83.

11. Fichte, "La Lame," 402; Cabrera, *Yemayá*, 29, 45–48; personal communication with Guillermo Gonzalez, 1986; communication with E. Mejía, 1986.

12. Communication with E. Mejía, 1986.

13. Pesonal communication with Lea Arrellano, 1986.

14. Cabrera, *Yemayá*, 29, 46.

15. Anzaldúa, Interview.

16. Cabrera, *Yemayá*, 56.

17. Personal communication with Lucumí priestess, 1985 and 1986.

18. Natalia Bolivar-Aróstegui, *Los Orishas*, 147–48, 153; Anzaldúa, Interview.

19. González-Wippler, *Santeria: The Religion*, 64.

20. Cabrera, *El Monte*, 58.

21. Roger Bastide, *The African Religions of Brazil* (Baltimore: Johns Hopkins Univ. Press, 1978), 256; Serge Bramley, *Macumba: The Teachings of Maria-José, Mother of the Gods* (New York: Avon, 1979), 115.

22. Edwards and Mason, *Black Gods*, 71.

23. Landes, "Cult Matriarchate," 395; also see Judy Grahn, *Another Mother Tongue: Gay Words, Gay Worlds* (Boston: Beacon Press, 1984, 122–24; Peter Ackroyd, *Dressing Up: Transvestism and Drag: The History of an Obsession* (New York: Simon and Schuster, 1979), 39, 43.

24. Fichte, "La Lame," 402.

25. Pemberton, Fagg, Holcombe, *Yoruba Sculpture*, 126, plate 37.

26. Oba Ecun, *Orichá: Metodología de la Religion Yoruba* (Miami: Editorial SIBI, 1986), 101.

27. Cabrera, *Yemayá*, 45, 58, 87, 77, 286; also see Pierre Verger, "Yorubá: Mythes et religion, el leurs prolongements afro-americains," *Dictionnaire des mythologies et des religions des societes traditionelles et du monde antique*, ed. Yves Bonnefoy (Paris: Flammarion, 1981), 2:544–53, esp. 552; Hubert Fichte, *Lazarus und die Waschmaschine: Kleine Einfuhrung in die Afroamerikanische Kultur* (Frankfurt am Main: S. Fischer Verlag, 1985), 308.

28. Murphy, *Santería*, 46–47; González-Wippler, *Santería: The Religion*, 54–57; Thompson, *Flash*, 42–51; John Mason, *Four New World Yoruba Rituals* (Brooklyn: Yoruba Theological Archministry, 1985), 42–43.

29. Jim Wafer, *The Taste of Blood: Spirit Possession in Brazilian Candomblé* (Philadelphia: Univ. of Pennsylvania Press, 1991), 85–86.

30. Wafer, *Taste*, 86.

31. Trevisan, *Perverts*, 173; see also Verger, "Yoruba: Mythes," 2:552; Domingo Alzugaray and Catia Alzugaray et al., *Cultos Afro-Brasileiros* (São Paulo: Editora Tres, 1983), 32; Jorge Amado, Carybe, et al., *Iconografia des Deuses Africanos no Candomblé da Bahia* (Bahia: Fundacão Cultural do E. da Bahia, Univers. Federal da Bahia, 1980).

32. David Hatfield Sparks, "Gilberto Gil: Praise Singer of the Gods," *Afro-Hispanic Review* (January 1993): 70–75; also see Antonio Riserio, ed., *Gilberto Gil: Expresso 2222* (São Paulo: Corrupio, 1982).

33. Verger, "Yoruba: Mythes," 2:552.

34. Bramley, *Macumba*, 194–98, esp. 198.

35. Sangirardi Jr., *Deuses da Africa e do Brasil: Candomble & Umbanda* (Rio de Janeiro: Civilizacão Brasileira, 1988), 168.

36. Esther Pressel, "The Clique: Two Children of Mamae Oxum," in *Trance, Healing, and Hallucination: Three Field Studies in Religious Experience*, ed. Felicitas D. Goodman et al. (New York: John Wiley and Sons, 1974), 171ff., esp. 172.

37. Trevisan, *Perverts*, 179.

38. González-Wippler, *Santería: The Religion*, 34; Cabrera, *Yemayá*, 44–45.

39. González-Wippler, *Santería: The Religion*, 40–44.

40. Cabrera, *El Monte*, 56.

41. Personal communication with Regla of Havana, March 1993.

42. Fichte, "La Lame," 402; Mercedes Cros Sandoval, *La Religión Afrocubana* (Madrid: Payor, S.A., Plaza Mayor, 1975), 193.

43. Communication with E. Mejía, 1986.

44. Duro Ladipo, *Oba Ko So (The King Did Not Hang): An Opera*, ed. and trans. R. G. Armstrong et al. (Ibadan: Institute of African Studies, Univ. of Ibadan, 1972), 147 n. 36b.

45. Benjamin C. Ray, *African Religions: Symbol, Ritual, and Community* (Englewood Cliffs, NJ: Prentice-Hall, 1976), 71.

46. González-Wippler, *Santería: The Religion*, 40.

47. Santos, *A participacão*, 48.

48. Bramley, *Macumba*, 113.

49. Communication with E. Mejía, 1986.

50. Trevisan, *Perverts*, 173.

51. Communication with Lucumí priestess, 1985, 1986.

52. Isabel Allende, *The House of the Spirits*, trans. Magda Bogin (New York: Bantam Books, 1986), 2.

53. Mark Kurlansky, *A Continent of Islands: Searching for the Caribbean Destiny* (Reading, MA: Addison-Wesley, 1992), 196.

54. Communication with E. Mejía, 1986.
55. Communication with Lucumí priestess, 1985, 1986.
56. Bramley, *Macumba*, 201, 197.
57. Personal communication with Miriam Chamani, Vodou(n) priestess, New Orleans, March 1993.
58. José Ribeiro, *Pomba-Gira Mirongueira* (Rio de Janeiro: Editora Expiritualista, 1970).
59. Bramley, *Macumba*, 202–3.
60. Trevisan, *Perverts*, 189.
61. Trevisan, *Perverts*, 178–79.
62. Fichte, *Lazarus*, 307–8.
63. Cabrera, *Koeko*, 70.
64. Fichte, *Lazarus*, 308; Julio Braga, *O Jogo de Búzios: Um estudo da adivinhação no candomblé* (São Paulo: Editora Brasiliense, 1988), 188; Cabrera, *Yemayá*, 44–45 on Orunmilá.
65. William R. Bascom, *Sixteen Cowries: Yoruba Divination from Africa to the New World* (Bloomington: Indiana Univ. Press, 1980), 7, 35.
66. Bascom, *Sixteen Cowries*, 52.
67. Communication with Lucumí priestess, 1985, 1986.
68. Trevisan, *Perverts*, 176.
69. Bill Strubbe, "Island of Desire," *Frontiers* 11:23 (March 12, 1993, Los Angeles), 52.
70. Anzaldúa, Interview.
71. Anzaldúa, Interview.
72. Communication with E. Mejía, 1986.
73. Peter Fry, "Male Homosexuality"; Patrícia Birman, "Identidade social e homossexualismo no Candomblé," *Religiãoe e Sociedade* 12, no. 1 (1985): 2–21; Maria Lina Leão Teixera, "Lorogun: Identidades sexuais e peder no candomblé," in *Candomblé Desvendando Identidades: Novos escritos subre a religião dos orixas*, ed. Carlos Eugenio Marcondes de Moura (São Paulo: EMW Editiones, 1987).
74. Leão Teixera, "Lorogun," 36–37.
75. Peter Fry, "Male Homosexuality," 144–46.
76. Jim Wafer, *The Taste of Blood: Spirit Possession in Brazilian Candomblé* (Philadelphia: Univ. of Pennsylvania Press, 1991), 30, 34–37.
77. Peter Fry, "Male Homosexuality," 144–46.
78. Communication with E. Mejía, 1986.
79. Peter Fry, "Male Homosexuality," 144–46.
80. Communication with Lucumí priestess, 1985, 1986.
81. Anzaldúa, Interview.
82. Communication with E. Mejía, 1986.
83. Anzaldúa, Interview.
84. Anzaldúa, Interview.
85. Anzaldúa, Interview.
86. Trevisan, *Perverts*, 116–22.
87. Blackberri, "Searching for My Gay Spiritual Roots," *BLK* 2, no. 6 (June 1990): 9.
88. Mark A. Reid, "The Photography of Rotimi Fani-Kayode," *Wide Angle* 14, no. 2 (April 1992): 41, 39–40.
89. Reid, "Photography," 42.
90. Bascom, *Sixteen Cowries*.
91. Margaret Thompson Drewal, "Trance Among Yoruba Shango Devotees," *African Arts* 20, (1986): 61–62.
92. Landes, "Cult matriarchate," 393–94.
93. Landes, "Cult matriarchate," 395.
94. Bramley, *Macumba*, 129.
95. Fichte, "La Lame," 399.
96. Trevisan, *Perverts*, 187.
97. Wafer, *Taste of Blood*, 110, 113, 138–39.
98. Communication with E. Mejía, 1986.
99. Communication with Lucumí priestess, 1985, 1986.
100. Personal communication with Regla of Havana, March 1993.
101. Guillermo González, quoted in Randolph Conner, "In the Land of Laddo: Gay People and the Yoruba Spiritual Tradition," *The Advocate* 467 (March 3, 1987): 28–31.
102. Cabrera, *El Monte*, 56.
103. Glenn L. Sitzman, "Wedding in Santería," *RFD* 64 (Winter 1990–1991): 30–32.
104. Sitzman, "Wedding," 30–31.
105. Luiz Mott, "Brazil," *Encyclopedia of Homosexuality*, ed. Dynes 1:162–63.
106. Trevisan, *Perverts*, 55.
107. Gerhard Kubick, *Angolan Traits in Black Music, Games and Dances of Brazil* (Lisboa: Junta de Investigacoes Cientificas do Ultramar, 1979).
108. Bramley, *Macumba*, 187ff.; González-Wippler, *Santería: The Religion*, 257.
109. Cesar Freire and Alibio Ferreira, "Denuncia: Estão Acabando Como Candomblé," *Gira da Umbanda* 1, no. 4 (July 1976): 7.
110. Fichte, *Lazarus*, 307–8; Cabrera, *El Monte*, 56.
111. Kurlansky, *Continent*, 189 ff., esp. 193–94.
112. Santos, *A participacão*, 48–49.

CHAPTER 12

The Recollection of What Was Scattered

1. Alan W. Watts, *The Two Hands of God* (Toronto: Collier, 1969), 172.
2. See Starhawk, *The Spiral Dance: A Rebirth of the Ancient Religion of the Great Goddess* (San Francisco: Harper & Row, 1979); Starhawk, *Dreaming the Dark: Magic, Sex and Politics* (Boston: Beacon Press, 1982).
3. Holger Kalweit, *Dreamtime and Inner Space: The World of the Shaman* (Boston: Shambhala, 1988), 226.
4. Joan Halifax, *Shamanic Voices: A Survey of Visionary Narratives* (New York: E. P. Dutton, 1979), 12.
5. Ekbert Faas, *Young Robert Duncan: Portrait of the Poet as Homosexual in Society* (Santa Barbara: Black Sparrow Press, 1983), 95.
6. Faas, *Young Robert Duncan*, 95.

7. Faas, *Young Robert Duncan,* 103.

8. John Yohalem, "Coming Out of the Broom Closet," *The Advocate* no. 589 (Nov. 5, 1991): 72.

9. Kent L. Sandstrom, "Confronting Deadly Disease: The Drama of Identity Construction Among Gay Men with AIDS," *Journal of Contemporary Ethnography* 19, no. 3 (1990): 274.

10. Edward Said, "Reflections on Exile," in *Out There: Marginalization and Contemporary Cultures,* ed. Russell Ferguson, Martha Gever, Trinh T. Minh-ha, and Cornel West (New York: New Museum of Contemporary Art; Cambridge, MA: MIT Press, 1990), 357.

11. See, for example, H. Montgomery Hyde, *The Love That Dared Not Speak Its Name: A Candid History of Homosexuality in Britain* (Boston: Little, Brown, 1970); Don Jackson, "Dachau for Queers," in *The Gay Liberation Book,* ed. Len Richmond and Gary Noguera (San Francisco: Ramparts Press, 1973), 42–48.

12. Halifax, *Shamanic Voices,* 12, 14.

13. Terence McKenna, *The Archaic Revival* (San Francisco: Harper San Francisco, 1991), 219.

14. Josef Venker, "The Goddess in Every Man," *White Crane Newsletter* no. 2 (1989): 1–3.

15. David Hatfield Sparks, unpublished diary entry, 1981.

16. Jack Fertig (a.k.a. Sister Boom Boom), "Litany for the Women, Take Back the Night," Leaflet for San Francisco demonstration, 1981.

17. Charlie Murphy, "Burning Times," 1981, 1992, 1993, Musical Front; *Burning Times* (album), Earth Beat!\Warner Bros. Records.

18. Caradoc ap Cador, "Sharing the Mysteries," *RFD* no. 12 (Summer 1977): 27.

19. Peter Lamborn Wilson, "Runaway Child," in *Choirs of the God: Revisioning Masculinity,* ed. John Matthews (London: Mandala, 1991), 206–14.

20. Don Engstrom, "A Season of Quiet Change," *RFD* no. 53, 14:2 (Winter 1987–88): 31–32; Peter Soderberg, "Faggot God" Chant. *RFD* no. 53, 14:2 (Winter 1987–88), back cover.

21. Bert Provost (a.k.a. Corona), "Discovering Queer Archetypes," *Lavender Pagan Newsletter* 1, no. 2 (1991): 1.

22. Arthur Evans, *Witchcraft and the Gay Counterculture* (Boston: Fag Rag Books, 1978), 154–55.

23. Harry Hay, "A Separate People Whose Time Has Come," Christopher Street West 1983 Gay Pride Festival Souvenir Program (Los Angeles, 1983), 8.

24. Craig A. Reynolds, "The Moon Singers," *The Road Before Us: 100 Gay Black Poets,* ed. Assoto Saint (New York: Galiens Press, 1991), 109.

25. Personal interview with Dr. Leo Louis Martello, New York, December 1991 (although a version may have appeared in print at an earlier date).

26. Dr. Leo Louis Martello, *Witchcraft: The Old Religion* (Secaucus, NJ: Citadel Press, 1975), 101.

27. Michael Thorn, Article in response to Lady Brita and friends, originally appearing in *The Hidden Path* (leaflet), 1983.

28. Anonymous ("Forest Flat"?), "Witchwork," *RFD* no. 22 (1979): 72.

29. Carl Wittman, "In Search of a Gay Tarot," *RFD* no. 2 (Winter 1974–75), 33–37; John Lauritsen, "Uranian Love in the Tarot," *Gay Books Bulletin* no. 5 (Spring 1981), 18–23; also see, Gavin Arthur, *The Circle of Sex,* (New Hyde Park, New York: University Books, Inc., 1966); Herman Slater, *The Magickal Formulary,* (New York: Magickal Childe, Inc., 1981).

30. Gilles Deleuze and Félix Guattari, *A Thousand Plateaus: Capitalism and Schizophrenia,* trans. Brian Massumi (London: Athlone Press, 1988), 248; also see Félix Guattari, *Molecular Revolution: Psychiatry and Politics,* trans. Rosemary Sheed (New York: Penguin Books, 1984).

31. Hélène Cixous and Catherine Clément, *The Newly Born Woman,* trans. Betsy Wing (Minneapolis: Univ. of Minnesota Press, 1986), 69.

32. Deleuze and Guattari, *Thousand Plateaus,* 277.

33. John Addington Symonds, *The Memoirs,* ed. Phyllis Grosskurth, (New York: Random House, 1984), 273.

34. Faas, *Young Robert Duncan,* 101.

35. James Broughton, *The Androgyne Journal* (Seattle: Broken Moon Press, 1991), 3–4.

36. Harry Hay, "A Separate People"; Will Roscoe, "Desert Circle," *RFD* no. 22 (1979): 35; Mitch Walker, *Visionary Love: A Spirit Book of Gay Mythology* (San Francisco: Treeroots Press, 1980), 24.

37. Henry (Harry) Hay, "Western Homophile Keynote Address," *The Ladder* (June/July 1970): 13ff.

38. See, for example, Llee Heflin, *The Island Dialogues* (San Francisco: Level Press, 1973); Alaric naTor, "Great Rite," *RFD* no. 26 (1981): 16; Rev. Paul V. Beyerl, "The Ways of Eros: Homoeroticism and Spiritual Vision," photocopied essay, 1987, based upon a series of columns which first appeared in *The Unicorn* newsletter in 1983.

39. Katon Shual, *Sexual Magick* (Oxford: Mandrake, 1989), 83–84; Adrian Ravarou, personal conversation, April 1993.

40. James Broughton, "Behold the Bridegrooms," in *Ecstasies* (Port Townsend, WA: Syzygy Press, 1983), 109 ff.; also see, Suzanne Sherman, ed., *Lesbian and Gay Marriage: Private Commitments, Public Ceremonies* (Philadelphia: Temple University Press, 1992).

41. J. C. Flügel, quoted by Bianca Garufi, "Fashion Viewed as a Body-Soul Relationship," John Beebe, ed., *Money, Food, Drink, and Fashion and Analytic Training: Depth Dimensions of Physical Existence* (Fellbach-Offingen: Verlag Adolf Bonz GmbH, 1983), 145.

42. Mikhail Bakhtin, *Rabelais and His World*, trans. Helene Iswolsky (Bloomington: Indiana University Press, 1984), 393.

43. Hermes Polyandron, "Spirit in Drag," *RFD* 11:3 (Summer 1985): 26.

44. Larry Mitchell, *The Faggots and Their Friends Between Revolutions* (Ithaca, NY: Calamus Books, 1977), 105.

45. Sai, "Halloween Fairy Gathering at Bolinas," *RFD* 25 (Fall/Winter 1980): 8–9.

46. Frater Belarion, VIII O.T.B. "Liber Dionysia: Ritual Uses of Transvestism," *Ganymede: A Male Spirituality Publication* 1:6 (London, 1987): 30–35.

47. Bianca Garufi, "Fashion," 153–54; for a history of "genderfuck" drag, see, Mark Thompson, "Children of Paradise: A Brief History of Queens," in *Gay Spirit: Myth and Meaning*, ed. Mark Thompson (New York: St. Martin's Press, 1987), 49–68.

48. Douglas Conwell, "Desert Reflections," *White Crane* no. 13 (1992): 18.

49. Hyperion, *Journeys in Fairyland* (Leaflet-letter, 1983).

50. Jim Lovette, "Who the Hell Are the Lavender Greens?" *White Crane* no. 13 (1992): 12.

51. McKenna, *Archaic Revival*, 220.

52. Sean Mariposa, "Peyote Spirit," *RFD* no. 12 (1977): 15–17.

53. Jean Genet, *Our Lady of the Flowers*, trans. Bernard Frechtman (New York: Bantam Books, 1970), 136–37.

54. Edward Guthmann, "Quick Takes from a Passionate Life," *The Advocate* no. 369 (June 9, 1983): 44–46.

55. Edmund White, "The Inverted Type: Homosexuality as a Theme in James Merrill's Prophetic Books," *The Journal of Homosexuality* 8, nos. 3–4 (1983): 51.

56. Paul Binding, *Lorca: The Gay Imagination* (London: Gay Men's Press, 1985), 88–89; Ian Gibson, *Federico García Lorca: A Life* (New York: Pantheon, Random House, 1989), 291.

57. Rupert C. Allen, *Psyche and Symbol in the Theater of Federico García Lorca* (Austin: Univ. of Texas Press, 1974), 198–99.

58. Parker Tyler, *The Divine Comedy of Pavel Tchelitchew* (New York: Fleet Publishing, 1967), 5–6, 17, 40, also see 12, 14, 17–20, 30–44, 113, 244, 453, 463–64, 488.

59. Robert A. Haller, *Kenneth Anger: A Monograph* (New York: Mystic Fire Video, orig. Film in the Cities, 1980); Carel Rowe, *The Baudelairean Cinema: A Trend within the American Avant-Garde* (Ann Arbor: UMI Research Press, 1982), 50–54, 71–86.

60. Stoddard Martin, *Art, Messianism and Crime* (New York: St. Martin's Press, 1986), 154, 160.

61. Philip Norman, "The Rebirth of Elton John," *Rolling Stone* no. 626 (March 19, 1992).

62. Boy George, "Bow Down Mister," *The Martyr Mantras* (Beverly Hills: Virgin Records, 1990–1991).

63. Barry Walters, "He Captured the Ecstasy of Disco: Sylvester Sang of the Soul's Climax," *San Francisco Examiner*, Nov. 20, 1988, E-5.

64. Matthew Gilbert, "What a Drag," *Special Delivery: Supplement to the Austin American-Statesman* (April 14, 1993), 1, 4; David Hershkovits, "RuPaul: World's Biggest Supermodel," *Paper Magazine* (April 1993), 26.

65. Maria Blount, "Coil: Out of Light—Cometh Darkness," *Propaganda* no. 18 (Spring 1992): 22–23; Coil, *Love's Secret Domain* (Chicago: Wax Trax Records, 1991).

66. Rob Dobson, "Dance Liberation," in *Lavender Culture*, ed. Karla Jay and Allen Young (New York: Harcourt Brace Jovanovich, 1979), 176–81.

67. Shelley and Dansky, quoted in Dennis Altman, *Homosexual: Oppression and Liberation* (New York: Discus Books, Hearst Corporation, 1973), 133, 144.

68. Alice Walker, *Living by the Word: Selected Writings 1973–1987* (New York: Harcourt Brace Jovanovich, 1988), 167–68.

69. Rev. Charles Hefele, *A History of the Councils of the Church* (Edinburgh: T. and T. Clark, 1896), 232.

70. Les Petites Bonbons, "Bon Bon Mots," *Gay Sunshine* no. 16 (1973): 12–13.

71. Martello, as quoted in the neopagan journal *Fireheart* no. 5 (1990).

72. Alexander Orloff, *Carnival: Myth and Cult* (Wörgl, Austria: Perlinger, 1981), 15, 89, 94.

73. Rick Paul, "Carnival Gay Balls: Gay Urban Folk Art," *RFD* no. 39, 10:4 (Summer 1984), 46.

74. Richard G. Parker, *Bodies, Pleasures, and Passions: Sexual Culture in Contemporary Brazil* (Boston: Beacon Press, 1991), 144–47.

75. Gloria Mundi, "On the Appearance of the Radiant Poodle," *Nomenews* no. 5 (Aug. 1987): 1–2; Shastina, "Magnificent Collaboration," *Nomenews*, same issue.

76. For the Yakut "soft" shamans, see Jochelson, *Koryak*, 53 and chap. 1 of this book; for Germanic warriors and nineteenth- and twentieth-century occult artists, see chaps. 7 and 9 of this book.

77. Scott Tucker, "Raw Hide: The Mystery and Power of Leather," *The Advocate* (May 12, 1987): 49; also see Mark Thompson, ed., *Leatherfolk* (Boston: Alyson, 1991); Mitch Walker, *Visionary Love: A Spirit Book of Gay Mythology* (San Francisco: Treeroots Press, 1980), 36; Doug Sadownick, "Beyond the Closet: Me and My Shadow," *Magical Blend* issue 29 ("thru January 1991"), 56–62.

78. Walt Whitman, "To One Shortly to Die," *Leaves of Grass* (New York: Signet, New American Library, 1980), ll. 1–8, p. 348.

79. Leonid Alekseychuk, "A Warrior in the Field," *Sight and Sound* 60, no. 1 (1991): 25.

80. Judy Stone, "A Soviet Mad Genius' Output and Odyssey," *San Francisco Chronicle (Datebook)*, March 12, 1989, 25–26, 40.

81. See, for example, Jason Serinus, ed., *Psychoimmunity and the Healing Process* (Berkeley: Celestial Arts, 1986).

82. Yohalem, "Coming Out," 72.

83. Sean McShee, "Dealing With Death," *Cernunnos News* 2, no. 1 (1983): 4.

84. Concerning Oz and gay men, see Robert H. Hopcke, "*The Wizard of Oz:* A Myth of the Archetypal Feminine for Contemporary Gay Men," *Jung, Jungians, and Homosexuality* (Boston: Shambhala, 1989), 136–55.

85. Walt Whitman, "I Dream'd in a Dream," *Leaves of Grass*, ll. 1–2, p. 125.

86. Jack Spicer, "Some Notes on Whitman," *Angels of the Lyre: A Gay Poetry Anthology*, ed. Winston Leyland (San Francisco: Panjandrum Press, 1975), 198–99.

87. Jacques Lacarrière, *The Gnostics* (New York: E. P. Dutton, 1977), 29–30, also 10, 33–34, 72.

88. Said, "Reflections on Exile," 365.

89. Hakim Bey, *T.A.Z.: The Temporary Autonomous Zone, Ontological Anarchy, Poetic Terrorism* (Brooklyn: Autonomedia, 1991), 101.

90. Hermann Hesse, *Demian*, trans. Michael Roloff and Michael Lebeck (New York: Bantam, 1970), 119.

CONCLUSION
We Are the Same People, Different from Before

1. Walt Whitman, "Song of Myself," *Leaves of Grass* (New York: Signet, New American Library, 1958), sec. 51, ll. 6–8, 96.

2. J. B. S. Haldane, quoted in Fred Alan Wolf, *Taking the Quantum Leap: The New Physics for Nonscientists* (San Francisco: Harper & Row, 1981), 100.

3. Chandler Burr, "Homosexuality and Biology," *The Atlantic* 271, no. 3 (March 1993): 47–65; Thomas H. Maugh, II, "New Homosexuality Link Found in Brain," *Los Angeles Times*, August 1, 1992, B-1, 8; Kim Painter, "Is There a Gay Gene?" *USA Today*, July 16–18, 1993, 1–2.

4. *Life and Times: Breaking Science*, featuring Dr. Laura S. Allen. PBS, KCET, Los Angeles. January 14, 1993.

5. Edward O. Wilson, *On Human Nature* (Cambridge: Harvard Univ. Press, 1979), 143–45; E. O. Wilson, *Sociobiology: The New Synthesis* (Cambridge: Harvard Univ. Press, 1976), 311.

6. In a recent debate included in *Transe, Chamanisme, Possession,* Claude Gaignebet has suggested that a web of such associations may have linked the Scythian *enarees* to the cult of the androgynous Saint Sebastian, the legend of Pythagorus, and existing European brotherhoods of archers and rites of May focusing on the song of the cuckoo. See, Claude Gaignebet, "Debats," *Transe, Chamanisme, Possession* (Nice: Editions Serre, 1986), 135.

7. Harry Hay, "A Separate People Whose Time Has Come!" *Christopher Street West Gay Pride Parade Program* (New York, 1983), 9.

8. Harry Hay, "Phrases from the Daisy-Chain Sex-Magicks Workshop," pamphlet (November 1991); Harry Hay, "Neither Boy Nor Girl: Reclaiming Our Ancient Gay Cultural and Spiritual Legitimacy: Third Gender," Pamphlet (November 1992); Harry Hay, "Third Gender Addenda," pamphlet (March 1993).

9. Penelope J. Engelbrecht, "'Lifting Belly Is a Language': The Postmodern Lesbian Subject," *Feminist Studies* 16, no. 1 (1990): 86.

10. Mitch Walker, *Visionary Love: A Spirit Book of Gay Mythology* (San Francisco: Treeroots Press, 1980).

11. Marjorie Garber, *Vested Interests: Cross-Dressing and Cultural Anxiety* (New York: Routledge, 1992), 11.

12. Danah Zohar, *The Quantum Self: Human Nature and Consciousness Defined by the New Physics* (New York: Quill/William Morrow, 1990), 25.

13. Zohar, *Quantum*, 25, 112.

14. Michael Moon, *Disseminating Whitman: Revision and Corporeality in Leaves of Grass* (Cambridge: Harvard Univ. Press, 1991), 59.

15. Harry Hay, "Phrases."

16. Walker, *Visionary Love*, 91–92.

17. Michael Talbot, *The Holographic Universe* (New York: Harper Collins, 1991), 1.

18. Whitman, "The Sleepers," *Leaves of Grass* (New York: Signet, New American Library, 1980), sec. 1, ll. 29–32, p. 331.

19. Peter L. Berger, *The Sacred Canopy: Elements of a Sociological Theory of Religion* (Garden City, NY: Anchor, Doubleday, 1969), 24.

20. Berger, *Sacred Canopy*, 24.

21. John Briggs and F. David Peat, *Turbulent Mirror* (New York: Harper & Row, 1989), 14; Kathleen McAuliffe, "Get Smart: Controlling Chaos," *Omni* 12, no. 5 (1990): 43–47; also see Antonio Benítez-Rojo, *The Repeating Island: The Caribbean and the Postmodern Perspective*, trans. James E. Maraniss (Durham: Duke Univ. Press, 1992), esp. 2–4, 263–271.

22. McAuliffe, "Get Smart," 4, 48, 88, 92.

23. N. Katherine Hayles, *Chaos Bound: Orderly Disorder in Contemporary Literature and Science* (Ithaca: Cornell Univ. Press, 1990), 173.

24. Luc Brisson, *Le Mythe de Tiresias* (Leiden: E. J. Brill, 1976), 124; also see 28–31, 34, 42, 82; and

see Adrian Room, *Room's Classical Dictionary* (Boston: Routledge and Kegan Paul, 1983), 285.

25. Benítez-Rojo, *The Repeating Island,* 10.
26. Benítez-Rojo, *The Repeating Island,* 29.
27. Benítez-Rojo, *The Repeating Island,* 3.
28. Gloria Anzaldúa, *Borderlands: La Frontera: The New Mestiza* (San Francisco: Spinsters/Aunt Lute, 1987), 205.
29. Anzaldúa, *Borderlands,* 80.
30. Anzaldúa, *Borderlands,* 194–95 ("To live in the Borderlands means you," ll. 12, 14–17, 40–42).
31. McKenna, *Archaic Revival,* 73.

Select Bibliography and Suggested Reading

Ackroyd, Peter. *Dressing Up: Transvestism and Drag: The History of an Obsession.* New York: Simon and Schuster, 1979.

Adams, J. N. *The Latin Sexual Vocabulary.* Baltimore: Johns Hopkins Univ. Press, 1982.

Arthur, Gavin. *The Circle of Sex.* New Hyde Park, NY: University Books, Inc., 1966.

Artus, Thomas [pseud.]. *Description de l'Isle des Hermaphrodites.* Cologne: Heritiers de H. Demon, 1724.

Baumann, Hermann. *Das Doppelte Geschlect: Ethnologische Studien zur Bisexualität in Ritus und Mythos.* Berlin: Deitrich Reimer, 1955.

Belarion, Frater, VIII, O. T. B. "Liber Dionysia: Ritual Uses of Transvestism." *Ganymede* (London) 1, no. 6 (1987).

Benko, Stephen. "The Libertine Gnostic Sect of the Phibionites According to Epiphanius." *Vigiliae Christianae* 21, no. 2 (1967).

Bey, Hakim. *T.A.Z.: The Temporary Autonomous Zone, Ontological Anarchy, Poetic Terrorism.* Brooklyn: Autonomedia, 1991.

Binding, Paul. *Lorca: The Gay Imagination.* London: Gay Men's Press, 1985.

Birman, Patricia. "Identidade social e homossexualismo no Candomblé." *Religiãoe e Sociedade* 12, no. 1 (1985).

Boswell, John. *Christianity, Social Tolerance, and Homosexuality.* Chicago: Univ. of Chicago Press, 1980.

Brisson, Luc. *Le Mythe de Tiresias.* Leiden: E. J. Brill, 1976.

Broughton, James. *The Androgyne Journal.* Seattle: Broken Moon Press, 1991.

———. *Ecstasies: Poems 1975–1983.* Port Townsend, WA: Syzygy Press, 1983.

Bullough, Vern L. *Sexual Variance in Society and History.* Chicago: Univ. of Chicago Press, 1976.

Bullough, Vern L., and Bonnie Bullough. *Cross Dressing, Sex, and Gender.* Philadelphia: Univ. of Pennsylvania Press, 1993.

Burr, Chandler. "Homosexuality and Biology." *The Atlantic* 271, no. 3 (March 1993).

Cador, Caradoc ap. "Amazons, Islands of Women, and Homosexual Behavior in Northwest Europe," parts 1, 2, and 3. *Lavender Pagan Newsletter*, nos. 3, 4, 5 (1992).

Alberto Cardín. *Guerreros, Chamanes y Travestis: Indicios de homosexualidad entre los exóticos.* Barcelona: Tusquets Editores, S. A., 1984.

Barcelona: Tusquets Editores, S. A., 1984.

Carpenter, Edward. *Intermediate Types Among Primitive Folk: A Study in Social Evolution* (1919). New York: Arno Press, 1975.

Carrier, J. M. "Homosexual Behavior in Cross-Cultural Perspective." In *Homosexual Behavior: A Modern Reappraisal*, edited by Judd Marmor. New York: Basic Books, Inc., 1980.

Case, Sue-Ellen. "Tracking the Vampire." *differences: A Journal of Feminist Cultural Studies* 3, no. 2 (1991).

Chamberlin, J. E. *Ripe Was the Drowsy Hour: The Age of Oscar Wilde*. New York: Seabury Press, 1977.

Chan, Peng-leung. *"Ch'u Tz'u" and Shamanism in Ancient China*. Ph.D. dissertation, Ohio State Univ., 1972.

Conner, Randolph P. "Buddhism." In *The Encyclopedia of Homosexuality*, edited by Wayne Dynes and S. Donaldson. New York: Garland Press, 1990.

———. "The Feast of Eros." *San Francisco Sentinel* (Feb. 22–March 21, 1980). Reprinted in *Ganymede: A Gay Spiritual Journal* (Fall/Winter 1980).

———. "In the Land of Laddo: Gay People and the Yoruba Spiritual Tradition." *The Advocate*, issue 467 (March 3, 1987).

———. "Wildmen, Faeries, and Beasts: Parts I and II." *Lavender Pagan Newsletter*, no. 6 (1992) and no. 7 (1993).

Cotgrave, Randle. *A Dictionarie of the French and English Tongues (1611, London)*. New York: Da Capo Press, 1971.

Couliano, Ioan. "Sexual Rites in Europe." Vol. 13 in *The Encyclopedia of Religion*, edited by Mircea Eliade. New York: Macmillan, 1987.

Courove, Claude. *Vocabulaire de Homosexualité Masculine*. Paris: Payot, 1985.

Cowan, Tom. *Fire in the Head: Shamanism and the Celtic Spirit*. San Francisco: HarperCollins, 1993.

Crisp, Quentin. *Quentin Crisp's Book of Quotations*. New York: Macmillan Publishing Company, 1989. See especially "Religion," p. 240–54.

Davies, Nigel. *The Rampant God: Eros Throughout the World*. New York: William Morrow, 1984.

Delcourt, Marie. *Hermaphrodite*. London: Studio Books, 1961.

Detienne, Marcel. *The Gardens of Adonis: Spices in Greek Mythology*. Hassocks, Sussex: Harvester Press, 1977.

Domínguez, Ivo, Jr. "'A View From the Bridge:' Gay/Lesbian and Pagan Emergence." *Green Egg* 24, no. 94 (1991).

Downing, Christine. *Myths and Mysteries of Same-Sex Love*. New York: Continuum, 1989.

Duffy, Maureen. *The Erotic World of Faery*. New York: Avon Books, 1980.

Dufournet, Jean. *Adam de la Halle à la Recherche de lui-même*. Paris: Societé d'édition d'enseignement supérieur, 1974.

Dynes, Wayne, and S. Donaldson, eds. *The Encyclopedia of Homosexuality*. New York: Garland Press, 1990.

Eisler, Riane. *The Chalice and the Blade: Our History, Our Future*. San Francisco: Harper & Row, 1987.

Eliade, Mircea. *Shamanism: Archaic Techniques of Ecstasy*. Translated by Willard R. Trask. Princeton: Princeton Univ. Press, 1974.

Elliott, Lin L. "Some Personal Thoughts on Polytheism as a Way of Being." *RFD*, no. 53 (1987–1988).

l'Estoile, Pierre de. *Memoires-Journeaux: Journal de Henri III*. Edited by Mm. G. Brunet, et al. Paris: Librairie des Bibliophiles, 1875–1876.

Evans, Arthur. *The God of Ecstasy: Sex Roles and the Madness of Dionysis*. New York: St. Martin's Press, 1988.

———. *Witchcraft and the Gay Counterculture*. Boston: Fag Rag Books, 1978.

Faas, Ekbert. *Young Robert Duncan: Portrait of the Poet as Homosexual in Society.* Santa Barbara, CA: Black Sparrow Press, 1983.

Fichte, Hubert. "La Lame de Rasoir et l'hermaphrodite: notes pour une recherche." *Psychopathologie Africaine* 11, no. 3 (1975).

———. *Lazarus und die Waschmaschine: Kleine Einführung in die Afroamerikanische Kultur.* Frankfurt am Main: S. Fischer Verlag, 1985.

———. *Xango.* Frankfurt am Main: S. Fischer Verlag, 1976.

Firmicus Maternus, Julius. *Ancient Astrology: Theory and Practice.* Translated by Jean Rhys Bram. Park Ridge, NJ: Noyes Press, 1975.

Fone, Byrne R. S. "This Other Eden: Arcadia and the Homosexual Imagination." In *Literary Visions of Homosexuality,* edited by Stuart Kellogg. New York: Haworth Press, 1983.

Fry, Peter. "Male Homosexuality and Spirit Possession in Brazil." *Journal of Homosexuality* 11, nos. 3–4 (1985).

Fuller, Jean Overton. *The Magical Dilemma of Victor Neuburg.* London: W. H. Allen, 1965.

Fulton, Robert, and Steven W. Anderson. "The Amerindian 'Man-Woman': Gender, Liminality, and Cultural Continuity." *Current Anthropology* 33, no. 5 (Dec. 1992).

Garber, Marjorie. *Vested Interests: Cross-Dressing and Cultural Anxiety.* New York: Routledge, 1992.

Genet, Jean. *Our Lady of the Flowers.* Translated by Bernard Frechtman. Introduction by Jean-Paul Sartre. New York: Bantam Books, 1970.

Gerard, Kent, and Gert Hekma, eds. *The Pursuit of Sodomy: Male Homosexuality in Renaissance and Enlightenment Europe.* New York: Harrington Park Press, 1989.

Gerstein, Mary R. "Germanic *Warg:* The Outlaw as Werewolf." In *Myth in Indo-European Antiquity,* edited by Gerald James Larson. Berkeley: Univ. of California Press, 1974.

Gilgamesh. Translated by John Gardner and John Maier. New York: Alfred A. Knopf, 1984.

Ginzburg, Carlo. *Ecstasies: Deciphering the Witches' Sabbath.* New York: Pantheon/Random House, 1991.

Goodich, Michael. *The Unmentionable Vice: Homosexuality in the Late Medieval Period.* Santa Barbara, CA: Ross-Erikson, 1979.

Grahn, Judy. *Another Mother Tongue: Gay Words, Gay Worlds.* Boston: Beacon Press, 1984.

Graillot, H. *Le culte de Cybèle, mère des dieux.* Paris: Fontemoing et Cie, 1912.

Greenberg, David F. *The Construction of Homosexuality.* Chicago: Univ. of Chicago Press, 1988.

Guerra, Francisco. *The Pre-Columbian Mind: A Study into the Aberrant Nature of Sexual Drives.* New York: Seminar Press, 1971.

Guiraud, Pierre. *Dictionnaire des etymologies obscures.* Paris: Payot, 1982.

Gulik, Robert Hans van. *Sexual Life in Ancient China.* Leiden: E. J. Brill, 1961.

Halliday, W. R. "A Note on the . . . Feminine Malady of the Skythians." *Annual of the British School of Athens,* no. 17 (1911).

Hay, Harry. "Neither Boy Nor Girl: Reclaiming Our Ancient Gay Cultural and Spiritual Legitimacy: Third Gender." *RFD,* no. 74 (1993).

Heflin, Llee. *The Island Dialogues.* San Francisco: Level Press, 1973.

Heiman, Elliott M., and Cao Van Lê. "Transsexualism in Vietnam." *Archives of Sexual Behavior* 4, no. 1 (1975).

Hemphill, Essex, ed. *Brother to Brother: New Writings by Black Gay Men.* Boston: Alyson Publications, 1991.

Herdt, Gilbert H. *Guardians of the Flutes: Idioms of Masculinity.* New York: McGraw-Hill, 1981.

Herman, Gerald. "The 'Sin Against Nature' and its Echoes in Medieval French Literature." *Annual Mediaevale* 17 (1976).

Highwater, Jamake. *Myth and Sexuality.* New York: New American Library/Penguin, 1990.

Hinsch, Bret. *Passions of the Cut Sleeve: The Male Homosexual Tradition in China.* Berkeley: Univ. of California Press, 1990.

Hoffman, Richard J. "Vices, Gods, and Virtues: Cosmology as a Mediating Factor in Attitudes toward Male Homosexuality." *Journal of Homosexuality* 9, nos. 2, 3 (1984).

Holmes, Henry. "Into the Woods: Radical faerie movement combines earthy spirituality with insurgent politics." *BLK* 2, no. 6 (1990).

Hopcke, Robert H. *Jung, Jungians, and Homosexuality.* Boston: Shambhala, 1989.

Hopcke, Robert H., K. L. Carrington, and S. Wirth, eds. *Same-Sex Love and the Path to Wholeness.* Boston: Shambhala, 1993.

Imbelloni, José. "La Essaltatione delle Rose." *Anales del Instituto de Etnografía Americana* 4 (1943).

Ingvisson, Alfredhr. "Scandinavian Witchcraft." *Idunna* 4, no. 3 (1992).

Jensen, Erik. *The Iban and Their Religion.* Oxford: Clarendon Press, 1974.

Jullian, Philippe. *The Dreamers of Decadence.* New York: Praeger, 1975.

Karlinsky, Simon. "Russia's Gay Literature and History (11th–20th Centuries)." *Gay Sunshine Journal* 29/30 (1976).

Keuls, Eva C. *The Reign of the Phallus: Sexual Politics in Ancient Athens.* New York: Harper & Row, 1985.

Kilmer, Anne Draffkorn. "A Note on an Overlooked Word-Play in the Akkadian Gilgamesh." In *Zikir Sumim*, edited by G. Van Driel, et al. Leiden: E. J. Brill, 1982.

King, Francis. *The Magical World of Aleister Crowley.* New York: Coward, McCann, and Geoghegan, 1977.

Klauser, Theodor, et al. *Reallexikon für Antike und Christentum.* Stuttgart: Anton Hiersemann, 1959. See especially Band IV: Dogma II: Empore: "Effeminatus."

Kroef, Justus van der. "Transvestism and the Religious Hermaphrodite in Indonesia." *Journal of East Asiatic Studies* 3, no. 3 (1954).

Lacarrière, Jacques. *The Gnostics.* New York: E. P. Dutton, 1977.

Landes, Ruth. "A Cult Matriarchate and Male Homosexuality." *The Journal of Abnormal and Social Psychology* 35, no. 3 (1940).

Lea, Charles Henry. *A History of the Inquisition of Spain.* New York: Macmillan, 1922. See especially vol. 4.

Lee, Kelly Gabriel. "Are We Not Men?" *Out/Look* 4, no. 4 (1992). This is a review of Robert Bly's *Iron John* and related literature.

Lee, S. G. "Spirit Possession among the Zulu." In *Spirit Mediumship and Society in Africa*, edited by John Beattie and John Middleton. London: Routledge and Kegan Paul, 1969.

LeVay, Simon. *The Sexual Brain.* Cambridge: MIT Press, 1993.

Lever, Maurice. *Les bûchers de Sodome: Histoire des "infâmes."* Paris: Fayard, 1985.

Lindsay, Jack. *The Normans and Their World.* London: Hurt-Davis, 1974.

López Austin, Alfredo. *The Human Body and Ideology: Concepts of the Ancient Nahuas.* Translated by Thelma and Bernard Ortiz de Montellano. Salt Lake City: Univ. of Utah Press, 1988.

McAlpine, Monica. "The Pardoner's Homosexuality and How It Matters." *PMLA* 95, no. 1 (1980).

MacMullen, Ramsay. *Paganism in the Roman Empire.* New Haven, CT: Yale Univ. Press, 1981.

Marchelle-Nizia, Christine, and Michèle Perret. "Une Utopie Homosexuelle au Quatorzième Siècle: L'Ile Sans Femmes d'Agriano." *Stanford French Review* 14, nos. 1–2 (1990).

Marcuse, Herbert. *Eros and Civilization: A Philosophical Inquiry into Freud.* New York: Vintage/Random House, 1962.

Mariposa, Sean. "Peyote Spirit." *RFD*, no. 12 (1977).

Markale, Jean. *Mélusine ou l'androgyne.* Paris: Editions Retz, 1983.

Martello, Leo Louis. *Witchcraft: The Old Religion.* Secaucus, NJ: Citadel Press, 1975.

Martello, Leo Louis. *Witchcraft: The Old Religion.* Secaucus, NJ: Citadel Press, 1975.

Mass, Lawrence. "On the Future of Lesbian and Gay Studies: A Dialogue with Will Roscoe." In *Homosexuality as Behavior and Identity: Dialogues of the Sexual Revolution,* vol. II, edited by Lawrence Mass. New York: Haworth Press, 1990.

———. "Sexual Categories, Sexual Universals: An Interview with John Boswell." *Christopher Street* 151, vol. 13, no. 6 (1990).

Mieli, Mario. *Homosexuality and Liberation: Elements of a Gay Critique.* London: Gay Men's Press, 1980.

Miller, David L. *The New Polytheism: Rebirth of the Gods and Goddesses.* Dallas: Spring Publications, Inc., 1981.

Mitchell, Larry. *The Faggots and Their Friends Between Revolutions.* Ithaca, NY: Calamus Books, 1977.

Mohr, Richard D. *Gay Ideas: Outing and Other Controversies.* Boston: Beacon Press, 1992.

Money, John. *Gay, Straight, and In-Between: The Sexology of Erotic Orientation.* New York: Oxford Univ. Press, 1988.

Moon, Michael. *Disseminating Whitman: Revision and Corporeality in 'Leaves of Grass.'* Cambridge: Harvard Univ. Press, 1991.

Nanda, Serena. *Neither Man Nor Woman: The Hijras of India.* Belmont, CA: Wadsworth Publishing Co., 1990.

Nelson, Ida. *La Sottie Sans Souci: Essai d'interprétation homosexuelle.* Paris: Honoré Champion, 1976.

Nolan, James. "The Third Sex." *Ramparts* (Dec. 1973).

Norton, Rictor. *The Homosexual Literary Tradition: An Interpretation.* New York: Revisionist Press, 1974.

O'Brien, Máire Cruise. "The Role of the Poet in Gaelic Society." In *The Celtic Consciousness,* edited by Robert O'Driscoll. New York: George Braziller, 1982.

O'Flaherty, Wendy Doniger. *Women, Androgynes, and Other Mythical Beasts.* Chicago: Univ. of Chicago Press, 1980.

Ovid. *Fasti.* Translated by Sir James G. Frazer. London: Macmillan and Co., Ltd., 1929.

P. P. [pseud.]. *Glossarium Eroticum Linguae Latinae.* Paris: Apud Aug.-Fr. et Pr. Dondey-Dupré, Bibliopolas, 1826.

Parker, Richard G. *Bodies, Pleasures, and Passions: Sexual Culture in Contemporary Brazil.* Boston: Beacon Press, 1991.

Provost, Bert. "Discovering Queer Archetypes." *Lavender Pagan Newsletter* 1, no. 2 (1992).

Qu Yuan, et al. *The Songs of the South.* Translated and edited by David Hawkes. New York: Penguin, 1985.

Rabbit, Sparky T., Donald Engstrom, and Tess Catalanó. "Meeting the Queer God." *RFD,* no. 55 (1988).

Ratti, Rakesh, ed. *A Lotus of Another Color: An Unfolding of the South Asian Gay and Lesbian Experience.* Boston: Alyson Publications, 1993.

Reade, Brian, ed. *Sexual Heretics: Male Homosexuality in English Literature from 1850 to 1900.* New York: Coward-McCann, Inc., 1971.

Requeña, Antonio. "Noticias y Consideraciones Anormalidades de los Aborigenes Americanos: Sodomia." *Acta Venezolana* 1, no. 1 (1945).

Richlin, Amy. *The Garden of Priapus: Sexuality and Aggression in Roman Humor.* New Haven, CT: Yale Univ. Press, 1983.

Rodgers, Bruce. *Gay Talk.* New York: Paragon/G. P. Putnam's Sons, 1979. Originally published by Straight Arrow Books in 1972 as *The Queen's Vernacular.*

Rosan, Laurence J. "Philosophies of Homophobia and Homophilia." In *The Gay Academic,* edited by Louie Crew. Palm Springs, FL: ETC Publications, 1978.

Roscoe, Will. *Making History.* San Francisco: Vortex Media, 1985.

———. *The Zuni Man-Woman.* Albuquerque: Univ. of New Mexico Press, 1991.

———, with Gay American Indians. *Living the Spirit: A Gay American Indian Anthology.* New York: St. Martin's Press, 1988.

Ross, Margaret Clunies. "Hildr's Ring: A Problem in the *Ragnarsdrápa,* strophes 8–12." *Mediaeval Scandinavia,* no. 6 (1973).

Rousseau, G. S. "The Pursuit of Homosexuality in the Eighteenth Century." In *'Tis Nature's Fault: Unauthorized Sexuality during the Enlightenment,* edited by Robert P. Maccubbin. Cambridge: Cambridge Univ. Press, 1987.

Rowan, John. "The Horned God: Why the Wildman Is Not Enough." *Green Egg* 24, no. 94 (1991).

Rowe, Carel. *The Baudelairean Cinema: A Trend within the American Avant-Garde.* Ann Arbor, MI: UMI Research Press, 1982.

Rowse, Alfred L. *Homosexuals in History.* New York: Macmillan, 1977.

Ruggiero, Guido. *The Boundaries of Eros: Sex Crime and Sexuality in Renaissance Venice.* Oxford: Oxford Univ. Press, 1985.

Sadownick, Doug. "Beyond the Closet: Me and My Shadow." *Magical Blend,* no. 29 (1991).

Saint, Assotto, ed. *The Road Before Us: 100 Gay Black Poets.* New York: Galiens Press, 1991.

Saladin d'Anglure, Bernard. "Penser le 'fémin' chamanique, ou le 'tiers-sexe' des chamanes inuit." *Recherches Amérindiennes au Québec* 18 (1988).

Sandstrom, Kent L. "Confronting Deadly Disease: The Drama of Identity Construction Among Gay Men with AIDS." *Journal of Contemporary Ethnography* 19, no. 3 (1990).

Santos, Wilson. *A participacão dos homossexuais no movimento negro brasileiro.* Salvador, Bahia: Grupo Ade Dudu, 1984.

Saslow, James M. *Ganymede in the Renaissance: Homosexuality in Art and Society.* New Haven, CT: Yale Univ. Press, 1986.

Schaefer-Rodriguez, Claudia. "The Power of Subversive Imagination: Homosexual Utopian Discourse in Contemporary Mexican Literature." *Latin American Literary Review* 17, no. 33 (1989).

Schärer, Hans. *Ngaju Religion: The Conception of God Among a South Borneo People.* The Hague: Martinus Nijhoff, 1963.

Schmidt, Paul. "Visions of Violence: Rimbaud and Verlaine." In *Homosexualities and French Literature: Cultural Contexts/Critical Texts,* edited by George Stambolian and Elaine Marks. Ithaca: Cornell Univ. Press, 1979.

Sergent, Bernard. *L'Homosexualité initiatique dans l'Europe ancienne.* Paris: Payot, 1986.

———. *Homosexuality in Greek Myth.* Translated by Arthur Goldhammer. Boston: Beacon Press, 1986.

Sherman, Suzanne, ed. *Lesbian and Gay Marriage: Private Commitments, Public Ceremonies.* Philadelphia: Temple Univ. Press, 1992.

Shual, Katon. *Sexual Magick.* Oxford: Mandrake, 1989.

Smith, Michael S. "African Roots, American Fruits: The Queerness of Afrocentricity." *Outweek,* no. 87 (Feb. 27, 1991).

Solomon, Simeon. *A Vision of Love Revealed in Sleep.* London: F. S. Ellis, 1871.

Sontag, Susan. "Notes on Camp." In *Against Interpretation and Other Essays.* New York: Dell, 1966.

Sparks, David Hatfield. "Gilberto Gil: Praise Singer of the Gods." *Afro-Hispanic Review* 11, nos. 1–3 (1992).

Stein, Edward, ed. *Forms of Desire: Sexual Orientation and the Social Constructionist Controversy.* New York: Garland Publishing, Inc., 1990.

Stevenson, Ian. "The Southeast Asian Interpretation of Gender Dysphoria: An Illustrative Case Report." *The Journal of Nervous and Mental Disease* 165, no. 3 (1977).

Ström, Folke. *Nidh, Ergi, and Old Norse Moral Attitudes*. Dorothea Coke Memorial Lecture in Northern Studies, University College, London, May 10, 1973. London: Viking Society for Northern Research, 1974.

Symonds, John Addington. *The Memoirs: The Secret Homosexual Life of a Leading Nineteenth-Century Man of Letters*. Edited by Phyllis Grosskurth. New York: Random House, 1984.

Taylor, Timothy. "The Gundestrup Cauldron." *Scientific American* (March 1992).

Teixera, Maria Lina Leão. "Lorogun: Identidades sexuais e poder no candomblé." In *Candomblé Desvendando Identidades: Novos escritos subre a religião dos orixas*, edited by Carlos Eugenio Marcondes de Moura. São Paulo: EMW Editionés, 1987.

Terrien, Samuel. "The Omphalos Myth and Hebrew Religion." *Vetus Testamentum* 20, no. 3 (1970).

Thomas, D. Winton. "KELEBH 'DOG': Its Origin and Some Usages of It in the Old Testament." *Vetus Testamentum* 10, no. 4 (1960).

Thompson, Mark, ed. *Gay Spirit: Myth and Meaning*. New York: St. Martin's Press, 1987.

———, ed. *Leatherfolk*. Boston: Alyson, 1991.

Tor, Alaric na. "Great Rite." *RFD*, no. 26 (1981).

Trevisan, João S. *Perverts in Paradise*. Translated by Martin Foreman. London: Gay Men's Press, 1986.

Trollmadhr, Kónradhr. "Freyr: An Ecstatic God from Scandinavia." *Lavender Pagan Newsletter* 1, no. 5 (1992).

Trumbach, Randolph. "London's Sodomites: Homosexual Behavior and Western Culture in the Eighteenth Century." *Journal of Social History* 11, no. 1 (1977).

Tyler, Parker. *The Divine Comedy of Pavel Tchelitchew*. New York: Fleet Publishing, 1967.

Vangaard, Thorkil. *Phallos: A Symbol and Its History in the Male World*. New York: International Universities Press, 1972.

Velde, H. Te. *Seth, God of Confusion*. Leiden: E. J. Brill, 1977.

Venker, Josef. "The Goddess in Every Man." *White Crane Newsletter* 1, no. 2 (1989).

Vermaseren, Maarten J. *Cybele and Attis: The Myth and the Cult*. London: Thames and Hudson, 1977.

Vorberg, Gaston. *Glossarium Eroticum*. Roma: "L'Erma" di Bretschneider, 1965.

Wafer, Jim. *The Taste of Blood: Spirit Possession in Brazilian Candomblé*. Philadelphia: Univ. of Pennsylvania Press, 1991.

Walker, Mitch. *Men Loving Men*. San Francisco: Gay Sunshine Press, 1977.

———. *Visionary Love: A Spirit Book of Gay Mythology*. San Francisco: Treeroots Press, 1980.

Whitam, Frederick L., and Robin M. Mathy. *Male Homosexuality in Four Societies*. New York: Praeger, 1986.

White, Edmund. "The Inverted Type: Homosexuality as a Theme in James Merrill's Prophetic Books." *Journal of Homosexuality* 8, nos. 3–4 (1983).

Whitman, Walt. *Leaves of Grass*. New York: Signet/New American Library, 1980.

Wilde, Oscar. *De Profundis and Other Writings*. New York: Penguin, 1987.

Williams, Walter L. *The Spirit and the Flesh: Sexual Diversity in American Indian Culture*. Boston: Beacon Press, 1986.

Wilson, Peter Lamborn. "Runaway Child." In *Choirs of the God: Revisioning Masculinity*, edited by John Matthews. London: Mandala/HarperCollins, 1991.

———. *Scandal: Essays in Islamic Heresy*. Brooklyn: Autonomedia, Inc., 1988.

Wittig, Monique. *The Straight Mind and Other Essays*. Boston: Beacon Press, 1992.

Wittman, Carl. "In Search of a Gay Tarot." *RFD*, no. 2 (1974–1975).

Yohalem, John. "Coming Out of the Broom Closet." *The Advocate*, issue 589 (Nov. 5, 1991).

Young, Katherine K. "Goddesses, Feminists, and Scholars." *The Annual Review of Women in World Religions* 1 (1991).

Zimmerman, Andy. "Healing Our Fears of Touching." *The Advocate* (April 26, 1988).
Zissmann, Claude. "Religion antichrétienne, Raison poètique et criticisme." *Rimbaud Vivant*, no. 14 (1978).
Zolla, Elémire. *The Androgyne: Reconciliation of Male and Female.* New York: Crossroad, 1981.

JOURNALS AND NEWSLETTERS

The addresses given below are current as of late 1993; this is only a partial listing of periodicals frequently printing articles pertaining to Gay Spirituality.

Coming Out Pagan
P.O. Box 30811
Bethesda, Maryland 20824-0811

Lavender Pagan Newsletter
P.O. Box 20673
Oakland, California 94620

The Crucible
P.O. Box 951
Stevens Point, Wisconsin 54481-0951

Marilyn Medusa
10093 Shelburn Drive
Cincinnati, Ohio 45140

Enchanté
30 Charlton Street, Box 6F
New York, New York 10014

New Uranian
P.O. Box 42933
Tucson, Arizona 85733

FDR (a Radical Faerie newsletter)
P.O. Box 26807
Los Angeles, California 90026

RFD: A Country Journal for Gay Men Everywhere
P.O. Box 68
Liberty, Tennessee 37095

Hippie Dick
Film at 11
2215-R Market Street, #559
San Francisco, California 94114
(note: contains erotic photography)

White Crane Newsletter
P.O. Box 170152
San Francisco, California 94117-0152

Index

Adonis, 91–93
Africa: homoerotic terms in, 37–38; homo-
eroticism in, 39–40; Isis worship in, 86–87;
spiritual functionaries in, 40–44; spiritual
traditions in, 38–39
AIDS. *See* HIV/AIDS
Alastair, 213–14
Albright, W. F., 79
Alchemy, Chinese, 56, 57, 58–59
Alekseychuk, Leonid, 287
Alexander the Great, 95
Allen, Laura S., 294
Allen, Paula Gunn, 12
Allen, Rupert C., 279
Altered state of consciousness: with dance,
120, 176; with music, 119; with sex, 77,
204–5. *See also* Mind-altering substances
Amazons: and *galli*, 112–13; and Scythians,
142–43. *See also* Lesbians
Anawalt, Patricia, 221
Anaxilas, 96
Anger, Kenneth, 280, 286
Anzaldúa, Gloria, 12, 237, 301, 302
Aparecida, M., 249, 250, 256, 260
Apuleius, Lucius, 86, 115
Aristophanes, 106–7
Aristotle, 119, 139
Arnobius, 102, 106
Arrien, Angeles, 272
Artists, nineteenth-century, 195–214
Arts: *galli* in, 117–21; primal, 21–24; reclaim-
ing domain in, 278–83; under Christianity,
189–91
Artemidorus, 124
Artimpasa, 138–39

Arthur, Gavin, 271
Artus, Thomas, 186
Arwas, Victor, 213
Astarte/Aphrodite, 90–91
Astrology. *See* Divination
Atargatis, 93–94
Athenaeus, 122
Athinat, 75–76
Attis, 102–4
Augustine, 99, 115, 125

Babaluayé, 247–48
Bakhtin, Mikhail, 174, 180
Barnefield, George, 196–97
Barnes, Sandra T., 5
Bascom, W. R., 250, 255
Bastide, Roger, 242
Baum, Paull F., 179
Baumann, Hermann, 38
Belarion, Frater, 275–76
Beltz, Walter, 79
Benítez-Rojo, Antonio, 301–2
Berdaches, 4, 5–6
Berger, Pamela, 170
Berger, Peter, 299
Bible, stories from, 79–81
Biggins, D., 179
Blackberri, 254
Blondel, 179, 180
Bogoras, Vladimir, 31–32, 33
Bolen, Jean Shinoda, 267
Bord, Colin, 175, 176
Bord, Janet, 175, 176
Borges, Jorge Luis, 4
Boswell, John, 188

343

Smith, John Holland, 96
Smith, Michael S., 37
Snowden, Frank, 86, 87
Soderberg, Peter, 269
Sodom, story of, 80–81
Solomon, Simeon, 209–11
Sontag, Susan, 196
Sots, 180–83
Sparks, David Hatfield, 4, 245, 267–68
Spicer, Jack, 288–89
Spiritual functionaries, in Africa, 40–44. *See also* Priests, gender-variant; Shamans
Spiritual traditions: of Africa, 38–39; of China, 48; domain in, 7; Paleolithic/Neolithic, 20–21
Starhawk, 177, 264, 271, 290
Stenbock, Count Eric, 208
Stoker, Bram, 286
Strabo, 142
Strieber, Whitley, 208
Ström, Folke, 156, 157, 159, 160
Struebel, A., 180
Subculture, under Christianity, 173–74
Sylvester, 281
Symonds, John Addington, 202, 272–73
Synesius, 90
Sznycer, Maurice, 92

Taoism, 48; deities of, 49
Taylor, Clark, 231, 232
Taylor, Timothy, 147, 166–67
Tchelitchew, Pavel, 279–80
Teish, Luisah, 238
Teixeira, Maria Lina Leão, 252
Tennyson, 117
Terrien, Samuel, 77, 80
Terry, Patricia, 172
Tertullian, 113
Tezcatlipoca, 228–29
Theodosius, 125
Thoreau, Henry David, 199–200
Thorn, Michael, 270–71
Thubron, Colin, 93
Tiresias, 300–301
Tlazolteotl, 222–23
Transvestism: in carnivalesque rites, 175–76; reclaiming, 274–76
Trevisan, João, 240, 247, 256
Tribal group, 20
Trostchansky, V. F., 33
Tucker, Scott, 286–87
Tyrrell, Walter, 113

Ulrichs, Karl Heinrich, 10

Vale, V., 11
van der Kroef, Justus, 29
Velde, H. te, 85
Veloso, Caetano, 254
Venker, Josef, 267
Verlaine, Paul, 202, 204–5
Visual impairment, of shamans, 28
Voidofcourse, Luna, 290

Wafer, Jim, 244, 252, 256
Waley, Arthur, 49
Walker, Alice, 37, 283–84
Walker, Mitch, 4, 273, 296, 297
Walters, Barry, 281
Watts, Alan, 263
Web of associations. *See* Domain
Werewolf, 172, 208. *See also* Wolfish outlaws
White, Edmund, 279
Whitman, Walt, 4, 200–202, 287, 293, 297, 298
Wilde, Oscar, 195, 206–8
William Rufus, King of England, 183–84
Williams, Walter, 5–6, 8–9, 27, 28, 294
Willoughby, Harold, 116
Wilson, E. O., 294
Wilson, Peter Lamborn, 269
Witches, 177–78; reclaiming tradition of, 269–71
Wittig, Monique, 12
Wittman, Carl, 271–72
Wolfish outlaws, among Germanic peoples, 161–65. *See also* Werewolf
Womanist, 37
Wood, Leona, 120

Xochipilli, 225–26
Xochiquetzal, 223–25
Xolotl, 227

Yeats, W. B., 205
Yellow Rose Tribe, 4, 277
Yemayá, 241–42
Yewá, 242
Yoruba religion, 216, 238–39; activism in, 259–60; deities of, 240–49; divination in, 249–50; hostility toward, 258–59; practitioners of, 239–40, 250–58

Zeffirelli, Franco, 278
Zenil, Nahum B., 219
Zohar, Danah, 297
Zuntz, Günther, 109

Illustration and Text Credits

The author and publisher gratefully acknowledge the permission to use quotations and images from the sources listed below.

Photo Acknowledgments

Cover: Photo courtesy of a private collection.

Introduction: Photo by the author.

Chapter 1: Photo courtesy of the Collections of the American Museum of Natural History; from the Smithsonian Institution Exhibition "Crossroads of Continents: Cultures of Siberia and Alaska."

Chapter 2: Photograph by Dr. S. G. M. Lee, courtesy of his children, by permission of Dr. Susan Young.

Chapter 3: Photo reprinted by permission of Macmillan Publishing Company, from *The Mythology of all Races, Vol. III: Chinese Mythology* by John C. Ferguson, series editor Louis Herbert Gray. Copyright © 1928, 1956 by Macmillan Publishing Company.

Chapter 4: Photo courtesy of Art Resource.

Chapter 5: Photo courtesy of the Phoebe Hearst Museum of Anthropology, University of California, Berkeley.

Chapter 6: Photo courtesy of Art Resource.

Chapter 7: Photo courtesy of the State Hermitage Museum, St. Petersburg, Russia.

Chapter 8: Photo courtesy of the Folger Shakespeare Library.

Chapter 9: Artwork in public domain.

Chapter 10: Photo courtesy of the Biblioteca Apostolica Vaticana.

Chapter 11: Photo courtesy of the photographer, Bill Strubbe.

Chapter 12: Photo courtesy of the photographer, Jean-Baptiste Carhaix.

Conclusion: Photo courtesy of Assotto Saint; photo by Alcindor.

Text Permissions

Note that earlier, substantially different versions of parts of chapters 8 and 11 previously appeared in essay form in *Lavender Pagan Newsletter* and the *Advocate*, respectively. I would like to thank Bill Karpen and Mark Thompson for supporting my work in Gay Spirituality.

Ardis Publishers: excerpt from *Poems* by Nikolai Klyuev, translated by John Glad, Ardis, 1977.

Gloria Anzaldúa and Aunt Lute Books: excerpt from *Borderlands/La Frontera: The New Mestiza*, copyright © 1987 by Gloria Anzaldúa. Reprinted with permission from Aunt Lute Books.

Beacon Press: excerpt from *Gay Ideas: Outing and Other Controversies* by Richard D. Mohr, Beacon Press, 1992; excerpt from *The Spirit and the Flesh: Sexual Diversity in American Indian Culture* by Walter L. Williams, Beacon Press, 1988.

Robert Bertholf, Literary Executor: excerpt from "This Place Rumored to Have Been Sodom," from *The Opening of the Field* by Robert Duncan, New Directions Publishing Corporation. Copyright © 1960 by Robert Duncan.

Black Sparrow Press: excerpt from *Young Robert Duncan: Portrait of the Poet as Homosexual in Society* by Ekbert Faas, Black Sparrow Press, 1983.

Robin Blaser, Literary Executor: excerpt from "Some Notes on Whitman" by Jack Spicer, *Manroot* 6/7 (1972).

Georges Borchardt, Inc.: excerpt from *Gilgamesh*, edited and translated by John Gardner and John Maier, Alfred A. Knopf, 1984.

Charles Boultenhouse, Executor and Oscar Collier Associates: excerpt from *The Divine Comedy of Pavel Tchelitchew*. New York: Fleet Publishing Corporation. Copyright © 1967 by Parker Tyler. By permission of the author's estate.

George Braziller, Inc.: excerpt from *The Two Hands of God* by Alan Watts, Collier, 1969.

E. J. Brill: excerpt from *The Excavations in the Mithraeum of the Church of Santa Prisca in Rome* by M. J. Vermaseren and C. C. van Essen, E. J. Brill, 1965.